MAO'S CHINA AND
THE COLD WAR

MAO'S CHINA AND THE COLD WAR

CHEN JIAN

The University of North Carolina Press

Chapel Hill & London

© 2001
The University of
North Carolina Press
All rights reserved
Manufactured in the
United States of America
Set in Janson and Meta types
by Tseng Information Systems
The paper in this book meets the
guidelines for permanence and
durability of the Committee on
Production Guidelines for Book
Longevity of the Council on
Library Resources.
Library of Congress
Cataloging-in-Publication Data
Chen Jian.
Mao's China and the cold war /
Chen Jian.
    p. cm. — (The new cold war
history)
Includes bibliographical references
and index.
ISBN 0-8078-2617-0 (alk. paper) —
ISBN 0-8078-4932-4 (pbk. : alk. paper)
1. China—Foreign relations—1949-
2. Cold War. I. Title. II. Series.
DS777.8 .C4314   2001
327.51—dc21   00-067240

05 04 03 02 01   5 4 3 2 1

Versions of Chapters 1, 2, 3, 5, and 8 appeared
earlier, in somewhat different form, respectively,
in Chen Jian, "China in 1945: From Anti-Japanese
War to Revolution," in *1945 in Europe and Asia:
Reconsidering the End of World War II and the
Changes of the World Order,* edited by Gerhard
Krebs and Christian Oberländer (Tokyo:
Deutsches Institut für Japanstudien der Philipp-
Franz-von-Siebold-Stiftung, 1997) (reprinted by
permission); Chen Jian, "The Myth of America's
'Lost Chance' in China: A Chinese Perspective in
Light of New Evidence," *Diplomatic History*
(Winter 1997) (reprinted by permission); Chen
Jian and Yang Kuisong, "Chinese Politics and the
Collapse of the Sino-Soviet Alliance," in *Brothers
in Arms: The Rise and Fall of the Sino-Soviet Alliance,
1945–1963,* edited by Odd Arne Westad (Wash-
ington, D.C.: Woodrow Wilson Center Press
and Stanford: Stanford University Press, 1998)
(reprinted by permission); and Chen Jian, "China
and the First Indo-China War, 1950–1954," *China
Quarterly,* no. 133 (March 1993), and Chen Jian,
"China's Involvement in the Vietnam War,
1964–1969," *China Quarterly,* no. 142 (June 1995)
(reprinted by permission of Oxford University
Press).

For my wife, Hong Hong

CONTENTS

MAPS, ILLUSTRATIONS, AND TABLE

ACKNOWLEDGMENTS

The completion of this book would have been impossible without the generous institutional and financial support I have received in the past decade. In particular, I would like to acknowledge a Norwegian Nobel Institute fellowship in 1993, a Dr. Nuala McGann Drescher Leave Program Fellowship from the State University of New York in fall 1994, a summer fellowship and a two-year special research grant from Southern Illinois University in Carbondale in 1996 and 1997–99, and a senior fellowship at the United States Institute of Peace in 1996–97.

John Lewis Gaddis, Michael Schaller, Jonathan Spence, and Odd Arne Westad read the entire manuscript and provided me with critical comments and suggestions. William Turley and David Wilson, my teachers and colleagues at Southern Illinois University, have constantly served as sources of friendship and unfailing support. Jim Hershberg, David Wolff, and Christian Ostermann, who have directed the Cold War International History Project at the Woodrow Wilson International Center for Scholars for the past decade, helped me in many ways—including providing encouragement, offering forums for me to test my ideas, and, together with the staff at the National Security Archive in Washington, D.C., sharing with me newly declassified Cold War documentation. Charles Bailey, David Tamerin, and David Werlich, the three department chairmen with whom I have worked at SUNY-Geneseo and Southern Illinois University, have been most supportive as colleagues and friends. Zhang Shuguang, Michael M. Sheng, and Zhai Qiang, fellow Chinese scholars working on Cold War studies in the United States, as well as Vladislav Zubok, a renowned Russian Cold War scholar who shares a birthday with me, have enhanced my understanding of the Cold War history in many discussions over the years.

I also wish to thank a number of friends, colleagues, and fellow scholars who either have read part of the manuscript during various stages of its making and offered critical comments or have provided support in other valuable ways: William Burr, Warren Cohen, Thomas Christensen, Roger Dingman, John Garver, Leszek Gluchowski, He Di, Michael Hunt, Li Haiwen, Geir Lundestad, Niu Jun, Krzysztof Persak, Shen Zhihua, R. B. Smith, Tao Wenzhao, Marc Trachtenberg, Nancy Berncropf Tucker, Xu Yan, Xue Litai, Yang Kuisong, Marylyn Young, Kathryn Weathersby, and Zhang Baijia. Brian Deason, Hu Shaohua, Li Di, and David Snyder served as my research assistants at Southern Illinois University and the U.S. Institute of Peace and have contributed to the completion of this project.

Earlier versions of several chapters were previously published: Chapter 1 first appeared in Gerhard Krebs and Christian Oberländer, eds., *1945 in Europe and Asia: Reconsidering the End of World War II and the Change of the World Order* (Tokyo and Berlin: Deutsches Institut für Japanstudien, 1997); Chapter 2 in the winter 1997 issue of *Diplomatic History;* Chapter 3 (which I coauthored with Yang Kuisong) in Odd Arne Westad, ed., *Brothers in Arms: The Rise and Fall of the Sino-Soviet Alliance, 1949–1963* (The Woodrow Wilson Center Press and Stanford University Press, 1999); and Chapters 5 and 8 in the March 1993 and June 1995 issues of *The China Quarterly.* They all have been substantially revised and are included in this volume with permission from the original publishers.

Portions of this manuscript have been presented at various lectures, workshops, and conferences at Beijing Capital Normal University; the University of California, Berkeley; the University of California, Santa Barbara; Cambridge University; Colgate University; Columbia University; the University of Connecticut; East China Normal University; Fudan University; Hong Kong University; George Washington University; Guangxi Normal University; the Korean National Defense University; the Institute of Contemporary China in Beijing; the Norwegian Nobel Institute; Oxford University; the University of Southern California; the University of Virginia; the University of Wisconsin, Madison; the Woodrow Wilson Center in Washington, D.C.; Yale University; Yonsei University; and panels at the annual meetings of the Association for Asian Studies, the American Historical Association, Chinese Historians in the United States, and the Society for Historians of American Foreign Relations. I have benefited greatly from the comments these presentations elicited.

The editors at the University of North Carolina Press deserve great credit for their valuable assistance in improving this manuscript and bringing it to publication. In particular I am grateful to Lewis Bateman, David Perry, Alison Waldenberg, and Mary Laur. Mary Caviness did a superb job of copyediting, making this a more accurate and much better book.

I owe a great deal to my father, Chen Liqiang, especially, for his help in collecting Chinese source materials for me over the years. This book is dedicated to my wife, Chen Zhihong, whose love makes my life more meaningful.

ABBREVIATIONS

CCP	Chinese Communist Party
CMAG	Chinese Military Advisory Group
CMC	Central Military Commission of the Chinese Communist Party
CPSU	Communist Party of the Soviet Union
CPV	Chinese People's Volunteers
CPVEF	Chinese People's Volunteer Engineering Force
DRV	Democratic Republic of Vietnam
GMD	Guomindang (Chinese Nationalist Party)
ICP	Indochina Communist Party
JCP	Japanese Communist Party
KPA	Korean People's Army
NATO	North Atlantic Treaty Organization
NEBDA	Northeast Border Defense Army
PANV	People's Army of North Vietnam
PLA	People's Liberation Army
PRC	People's Republic of China
PUWP	Polish United Workers' Party
UN	United Nations
VWP	Vietnamese Workers' Party

MAO'S CHINA AND
THE COLD WAR

INTRODUCTION

The last decade of the twentieth century witnessed sensational developments in the study of the international history of the Cold War—one of the century's most important events. With the collapse of the former Soviet Union and the end of the Cold War, for the first time scholars have been able to study the entire duration of the Cold War from the post–Cold War vantage point. In the meantime, new opportunities to access previously unavailable documents, especially from the Cold War's "other side," have allowed scholars to develop new theses and perspectives supported by multiarchival/multisource research. As a result, a "new" Cold War history—to borrow a term from historian John Lewis Gaddis—came into being.[1]

The study of China's Cold War history has made significant progress since the late 1980s. There was a time when China scholars in the West had to travel to Hong Kong or Taiwan, relying upon contemporary newspapers and Western intelligence information, to study Beijing's policies. Since the mid-1980s, the flowering of the "reform and opening" era in China has resulted in a more flexible political and academic environment compared with Mao's times, leading to a relaxation of the extremely rigid criteria for releasing party documents. Consequently, a large quantity of fresh and meaningful historical materials, including party documents, former leaders' works and memoirs, and oral histories, have been made available to Cold War historians. To be sure, with a Communist regime remaining in Beijing (no matter how quasi it actually is today), China still has a long way to go before "free academic inquiry" becomes a reality, but the contribution of China's documentary opening to the study of the Chinese Cold War experience cannot be underestimated.[2]

Since the early 1990s, I have traveled to China more than a dozen times to do research, conduct interviews, and attend scholarly conferences. This volume is the product of these trips. In writing this book, I have been directed by two primary purposes. The first is to make new inquiries about China's Cold War experience using the new documentation. Indeed, this is an everlasting process. If readers compare the five previously published chapters in this volume with their earlier versions, they will find that all have been substantially revised with the support of insights gained from documentation now available. While each chapter in this volume represents an independent case study, together they form a comprehensive narrative history about China and the Cold War.

My second purpose is to reinterpret a series of fundamental issues crucial to understanding the global Cold War in general and China's Cold War history in particular. My main objectives, concerning three interlocking themes, are to comprehend China's position in the Cold War; to (re)interpret the role ideology played during the period; and to assess Mao's revolution and to analyze Mao's China's patterns of external behavior. I outline these themes below and have tried to integrate them into the narrative of the chapters that follow.

China's Position in the Cold War

The Cold War was characterized by the tension between the two contending superpowers—the United States and the Soviet Union. Yet the position of Mao's China in the Cold War, in many key respects, was not peripheral but central. The observation made by political scientists Andrew J. Nathan and Robert S. Ross certainly makes good sense: "During the Cold War, China was the only major country that stood at the intersection of the two superpower camps, a target of influence and enmity for both."[3]

China's leverage in the Cold War was primarily determined by its enormous size. With the largest population and occupying the third largest territory in the world, China was a factor that neither superpower could ignore. In the late 1940s and early 1950s, when Mao's China entered a strategic alliance with the Soviet Union, the United States immediately felt seriously threatened. Facing offensives by Communist states and revolutionary/radical nationalist forces in East Asia, Washington, with the creation and implementation of the NSC-68, responded with the most extensive peacetime mobilization of national resources in American history.[4] In its efforts to "roll back" the Soviet/Communist threat, the United States became involved in the Korean War and the Vietnam War, overextending itself in a global confrontation with the Soviet/Communist camp. In the late 1960s and early 1970s, the situation reversed completely following China's split with the Soviet Union and rapprochement with the United States. As a result of having to confront the West and China simultaneously, the Soviet Union overextended its strength, which contributed significantly to the final collapse of the Soviet empire in the late 1980s and early 1990s.

China's leverage in the Cold War, though, went far beyond changing the balance of power between the two superpowers. The emergence of Mao's China as a unique revolutionary country in the late 1940s (discussed more extensively below) also altered the orientation of the Cold War by shifting its actual focal point from Europe to East Asia. This shift, as it turned out, would make East Asia *the* main battlefield of the Cold War, while, at the same time, would help the Cold War to remain "cold."

When the Chinese Communist revolution achieved nationwide victory in 1949, the global Cold War was at a crucial juncture. Two important events—the 1948–49 Berlin blockade and the Soviet Union's first successful test of an atomic bomb in August 1949—combined to pose a serious challenge to the two superpowers. If either tried to gain a strategic upper hand against the other—and if a showdown were to occur in Europe, where the dividing line between the two contending camps already had been drawn in a definitive manner—the Cold War could have evolved into a global catastrophe, one that might have involved the use of nuclear weapons. Against this backdrop, Moscow's vision turned to East Asia.[5]

In June–August 1949, on the eve of the victory of the Chinese Communist revolution, the number two leader of the Chinese Communist Party (CCP), Liu Shaoqi, secretly visited Moscow to meet with Joseph Stalin. The two leaders concluded that a "revolutionary situation" now existed in East Asia. In an agreement on "division of labor" between the Chinese and Soviet Communists for waging the world revolution, they decided that while the Soviet Union would remain the center of international proletarian revolution, China's primary duty would be the promotion of the "Eastern revolution."[6]

The implementation of this agreement resulted in China's support for Ho Chi Minh's Viet Minh and, in October 1950, massive intervention in the Korean War, making Mao's China a "front-line soldier" fighting against the U.S. imperialists.[7] Throughout the 1950s and 1960s, East Asia continued to be a main focus of the Cold War. While China was playing a central role in the two Taiwan Strait crises and the Vietnam War—the longest "hot" war during the Cold War period—the strategic attention of the United States, following the assumption that China was a more daring enemy than the Soviet Union, became increasingly fixed on East Asia. Ironically, though, the active role China played in East Asia turned this main Cold War battlefield into a strange "buffer" between Washington and Moscow: with China and East Asia in the middle, it was less likely that the United States and the Soviet Union would become involved in a direct military confrontation. The situation would remain like this until the early 1970s, when détente began to redefine the rules of the U.S.-Soviet confrontation, decisively reducing the possibility of a nuclear showdown between the two superpowers.

In terms of its impact on the essence of the Cold War, China's emergence as a revolutionary country dramatically enhanced the perception of the Cold

War as a battle between "good" and "evil" on both sides, making the conflict more explicitly and extensively framed by ideological perceptions. This was particularly true because, as shall be made clear by a brief comparison of the two Communist countries, Mao's China was more revolutionary in its behavior than the Soviet Union by the late 1940s.

Taking Marxism-Leninism as the guideline for its state policies, Soviet Russia/the Soviet Union had been a revolutionary country from the time of its establishment. While persistently working to establish a socialist society in Russia, the leaders in Moscow made promoting the proletarian world revolution and overthrowing capitalism's global reign the Soviet Union's sacred state mission. However, the situation had changed subtly by the late 1940s. If the dissolution of the Comintern in 1943 symbolized Moscow's retreat from pursuing world proletarian revolution as a state-policy goal, the Soviet-American agreement at Yalta in February 1945 represented the completion of a crucial step in the Soviet Union's "socialization" process. Although Moscow continued to profess its belief in the Marxist-Leninist theory of international class struggle, the Soviet Union was no longer the same kind of revolutionary country it used to be—isolated and excluded from the existing international system; rather, as a main patron of the postwar world order created at Yalta, Stalin's Soviet Union was changing into an insider of the big-power club, assuming the identity of a quasi-revolutionary country and a status quo power at the same time. Consequently, as Vojtech Mastny points out, "despite Stalin's ideological dedication, revolution was for him a means to power rather than a goal in itself."[8]

Mao's China was different. As I will discuss in Chapter 1, the Chinese Communist regime was established by breaking up the Yalta system. When the "new China" was born, Mao and the CCP leadership were determined to break with the legacies of the "old" China, to "make a fresh start" in China's foreign affairs, and to lean to the side of the Soviet-led socialist camp.[9] From its birth date, Mao's China challenged the Western powers in general and the United States in particular by questioning and, consequently, negating the legitimacy of the "norms of international relations," which, as Mao and his comrades viewed them, were of Western origins and inimical to revolutionary China. Thus Mao's China had its own language and theories, its own values and codes of behavior in regard to external policies.[10] The revolutionary features of Chinese foreign policy, combined with the reality that the Cold War's actual emphasis was then shifting from Europe to East Asia, inevitably caused the global Cold War to entail a more ideological form of warfare as a whole.[11]

China's emergence as a revolutionary country also created an important connection between the global Cold War and the decolonization process in non-Western countries, linking the two historical phenomena in ways that would not have been possible without China's input. Different from the Soviet Union, which was established on the ruins of the czarist Russia, China was a country whose modern history was said to have suffered from the aggression and incursion of Western imperialism/colonialism. Throughout the course of the Chinese revolution, the CCP always viewed China's national independence and national liberation as the revolution's key mission. In the late 1940s, Mao introduced his "intermediate zone" theory, claiming that between the United States and the Soviet Union existed a vast "intermediate zone" mainly composed of "oppressed" non-Western countries, including China. Before U.S. imperialists could attack the Soviet Union, according to Mao, they first had to control the intermediate zone, thus making Asia the central arena of the Cold War. When Mao and the CCP seized political power in China, they immediately proclaimed that revolutionary China, as a natural ally of the "oppressed peoples" in the intermediate zone, would hold high the banner of anti-imperialism and anticolonialism, challenging the United States and other Western imperialist/colonial powers. Mao and his comrades regarded this stance as important both for defending the socialist camp and for promoting Communist/radical nationalist revolutions in non-Western countries.[12] Thus Mao's China dramatically enhanced the theme of decolonization in the Communist Cold War discourse that had been overwhelmingly dominated by class-struggle-centered language. As a result, the emerging anti-imperialist/anticolonialist movements in non-Western countries became more tightly connected with the "proletarian world revolution."

By emphasizing the importance of the role played by Mao's China in the Cold War, I do not mean to argue that China's overall position was more important than that of the Soviet Union or the United States. Although China was a major Cold War actor, its capacity and will to influence global issues and international affairs were inevitably compromised by the fact that it was backward in technology and economic development. In addition, its foreign behavior was profoundly restricted by a Chinese ethnocentrism, which was deeply rooted in its history and culture. Therefore, in the Cold War's global framework, China played an important role only in certain dimensions (especially those with close connections to East Asia or in China itself), and it was the Soviet Union and the United States that occupied the indisputable central position. Yet, as John Gaddis points out, "The diversification of power did more to shape the course of the Cold War than did the balancing of power."[13] Indeed, the complexity and singularity of the Cold War were determined by its multipolarity and multidimensionality, which came into being with each and every actor leaving its stamp on them. In this sense, China's position in the Cold War is clearly important.

Ideology Matters

The Cold War was from the beginning a confrontation between two contending ideologies—communism and liberal capitalism. The compositions of the two Cold War camps were defined along ideological lines, and the conflict between them, at its core, represented not only a contest to determine which side was stronger but also, and more importantly, a competition to demonstrate which side was superior. The Cold War did not end as the result of the Soviet empire suffering economic collapse or military defeat at the hands of Western countries; rather, it happened in the wake of the "inner surrender" by the people in the Soviet Union and East European Communist countries to the superiority of liberal capitalism and Western democracy.

However, throughout the Cold War period, a majority of political scientists and diplomatic historians played down ideology as an essential agent in determining the basic orientation of a nation's foreign policy. From "traditionalists/realists" to "postrevisionists," theorists and diplomatic historians differed on many issues, but they had one thing in common: by defining "power" basically in material terms, they did not take the power of ideas seriously.[14] A prevailing assumption among scholars was that although the two contending camps used strong ideological language to attack each other and defend themselves, they did so more to justify already existing policies than to shape decisions yet to be made. Scholars also believe that what mattered was state leaders' concerns over, as well as calculations about, their nation's "vital security interests," rather than their "superficial" ideological commitments.

Within this context, a "China under threat" approach dominated the study of China's Cold War history, until recently. Many scholars assumed that the key to understanding China's external policy lay in a comprehension of Beijing's "security concerns," which, as in any other country, could be defined in terms of its physical safety, its economic development, and its political and societal stability, as well as its perception of external threats.[15]

All of these assumptions are now being challenged. Indeed, one of the most important revelations of the "new" Cold War history is that ideology mattered. To make this assertion more accurate, I will further argue that ideology not only played a decisive role in bringing Communist countries together but also contributed to driving them apart.

During the early phase of the Cold War, a shared belief in Marxist-Leninist ideology served as a central force to unite Communist states and parties in the world. After World War II, when national identity consciousness was stronger than ever before, this force did not produce a monolithic international Communist movement with Moscow as its supreme headquarters; but it did create, and in turn was enhanced by, a profound conviction among Communists all over the world that "history is on our side," thus allowing them to pose a serious challenge to international capitalism, while, at the same time, constructing the moral foundation on which the "socialist camp" was established. It should also be pointed out that, forty years later, the final collapse of this conviction led to the dismantling of the socialist camp and, in the wake of that, the end of the Cold War.

As far as the external policies of Mao's China are concerned, the role played by ideology is evident. The CCP leadership adopted the "lean-to-one-side" approach when it established the People's Republic of China (PRC), which, in a practical political sense, meant allying China with the Soviet Union as well as other socialist countries and confronting the Western "imperialist powers." In October 1950, only one year after the Communists seized power in China, the CCP leadership decided to enter the Korean War. In a series of internal discussions and correspondence, Mao used highly ideological language to argue that if China failed to intervene, the "Eastern revolution" and the world revolution would suffer.[16] Throughout the 1950s and 1960s, Beijing's foreign policy consistently demonstrated a strong ideological color. For example, in October 1956, the CCP leadership urged Moscow to suppress the "reactionary rebellion" in Hungary for the sake of the international Communist movement.[17] In the mid-1960s, Beijing, under the banner of fulfilling China's duties of "proletarian internationalism," provided Vietnamese Communists with substantial support, including the dispatch of 320,000 Chinese engineering and antiaircraft troops to North Vietnam in 1965–69.[18] All of these developments clearly suggest that the role of ideology in Beijing's external policies cannot be overlooked.

In a deeper sense, ideology's impact upon China's Cold War experience is reflected in Mao's "continuous revolution" as his central theme in shaping Chinese foreign policy and security strategy. Mao's revolution never took as its ultimate goal the Communist seizure of power in China; rather, as the chairman repeatedly made clear, his revolution aimed at transforming China's state, population, and society, and simultaneously reasserting China's central position in the world. The domestic and international goals of the revolution were deeply connected. On the one hand, it was precisely by virtue of the revolution's domestic mission that the revolution's international aim became justified; on the other hand, the international aspect of the revolution served as a constant source of domestic mobilization, helping to legitimate the revolution at home and to maintain its momentum. Mao's and his comrades' belief in Marxist-Leninist ideology was always interwoven with their devotion to using ideology as a means to transform China's state, its society, and its international outlook. This belief stood at the core of their conceptual realm, providing legitimacy to the Chinese *Communist* revolution.

It is here we see the complicated interplay between the Mao generation's conversion to Communist ideology and its continuous exposure to the influence of China's age-old history and culture. At a glance, the two experiences are contradictory. As twentieth-century revolutionaries, Mao and his comrades were highly critical of the Chinese past, declaring that their revolution would render a thorough transformation of China's "old" state, society, and culture. But when Mao and his comrades were posing challenges to the Chinese past, the ideology on which they depended as the lodestar and guiding philosophy for the transformation had to be articulated through the discourse, symbols, norms, and identities that had been a part of the Chinese past. Consequently, a profound continuity existed between the Mao generation's revolutionary behavior and the "old" China they meant to destroy. In this regard, a conspicuous example is the impact that the age-old "Central Kingdom" mentality had on Mao and his comrades. Their aspiration for promoting a world proletarian revolution by following the model of China revealed unmistakably how deeply their conceptual realm had been penetrated by that mentality.

The message delivered here is of broad theoretical significance: in a cross-cultural environment, the creation, transmission, and representation of an ideological belief must be subjected to the definition and interpretation of the discourse, symbols, norms, and values that formed a particular actor's historically/culturally bound conceptual lens. The outcome of the process could lead either to convergence of or to divergence between actors with the same ideological belief. Consequently, ideology, like religious faith, could either bring people together or split them apart, and, in certain circumstances, even cause them to engage in deadly confrontations with one another. Indeed, have we not witnessed enough examples of conflicts and wars between different sects within the same religion in world history?

A fundamental flaw of the "old" Cold War history lay in scholars' inability to comprehend this complicated dual function of ideology. As a result of an oversimplified "ideology versus national security interest" dichotomy, a prevailing assumption was that if countries with shared ideological beliefs (such as China and the Soviet Union) were to disagree, then that shared faith must have been overwhelmed by a conflict in national interests. In the study of China's Cold War history, scholars have often used Beijing's split with Moscow and rapprochement with Washington to prove this assumption.

Careful study of the history of Sino-Soviet relations demonstrates that the split was not caused by uncompromising conflicts in national interests but rather by different understandings and interpretations of the same ideology. When serious disagreements began to emerge between Beijing and Moscow in the mid- and late 1950s, China and the Soviet Union had more shared "national interests" than ever: given the hostility of the United States and other Western countries toward the PRC, Beijing's strategic alliance with Moscow served China's national security needs well; the Western economic embargo against China made Sino-Soviet trade relations ever more valuable for Beijing; and China's economic reconstruction benefited greatly from Soviet aid. In turn, China's support significantly enhanced the Soviet Union's position in a global confrontation with the United States. The national interests of China and the Soviet Union were highly compatible at that time, or at least should have greatly outweighed any explicit or implicit conflict that might have existed between them.

But it was exactly at such a moment that conflicts between Beijing and Moscow surfaced. As demonstrated by discussions in Chapter 3, the key to the conflicts lay in Mao's changing perceptions of China's relations with the Soviet Union. After Stalin's death, Mao increasingly perceived the CCP, and himself in particular, as qualified to claim centrality in the international Communist movement. In its criticism of Moscow's "big-power chauvinism" and the Soviet leader Nikita Khrushchev's de-Stalinization effort, Maoist discourse was dominated by metaphors, myths, and symbols crucial to the promotion of Mao's continuous revolution, which also caused Beijing's deepening discord with Moscow. All of these developments served as the prelude to the great Sino-Soviet polemic debate in the 1960s, eventually leading to each of the Communist giants to regard the other as a "traitor" to true Marxism-Leninism. Following the intensifying ideological warfare, the state-to-state relations between China and the Soviet Union deteriorated substantially, causing sharp conflict in their "national security interests." It was the deepening discrepancy over how to define/interpret the same ideology, rather than conflict over national security interests, that should be identified as the primary cause for the Sino-Soviet split.

Ideology matters, yet not without fundamental limits. As indicated by China's Cold War experience, while ideology was central in legitimizing important foreign policy decisions, ideological terms alone could not guarantee "legitimacy." Thus Mao and his comrades *always* tried to present important foreign policy decisions in terms of both ideological *and* other concerns. For example, when Beijing's leaders decided to enter the Korean War, they announced to the Chinese people and the whole world that if they did not participate China's security interests would be seriously jeopardized. In the Taiwan Strait crisis of 1958, Mao argued that shelling Jinmen was necessary to prevent the U.S. imperialists from permanently separating Taiwan from the socialist motherland.[19] In these cases, security concerns were real, but they also helped justify decisions made primarily based on the leadership's ideological commitments.

Ideology's role also withers along with the ideology's declining "inner" support from the people—this was particularly true in the case of communism. As a utopian vision, communism was most beautiful when it was not a political philosophy *in action*. When Communist ideology was put into practice in a favorable historical/social environment—such as in twentieth-century China, where radical revolutions had accumulated tremendous momentum and strength—it ignited popular enthusiasm and support. But when communism repeatedly failed the test of people's lived experience with its inability to turn the utopian vision into reality, popular enthusiasm and support eventually died. In Mao's China, Maoist continuous-revolution programs such as the "Great Leap Forward" and the "Great Proletarian Cultural Revolution" suffered this fate. Consequently, ideology would no longer be able to legitimate Chinese Communist policies—which was in itself a sign that the Chinese Communist regime was losing its legitimacy.

Mao and Foreign Policy Patterns of Mao's China

In any historical study, scholars must pay special attention to the role of personalities, and it is imperative in a study about Mao's China. As revealed in the chapters that follow, Mao was CCP/PRC's single most important policymaker. Behind every crucial decision—such as China's intervention in Korea, its alliance and split with the Soviet Union, its shelling of Jinmen, its support to the Vietnamese Communists, and its rapprochement with the United States—Mao always was the central figure. In order to understand the dynamics and logic of the PRC's revolutionary foreign policy, one must comprehend Mao's concept of continuous revolution. Underlying the concept was Mao's "post-revolution anxiety," a psychological/conceptual force constantly pushing him to persist in a revolutionary agenda for China's domestic and external policies.

As discussed earlier, Mao's revolution aimed to transform China's "old" state and society as well as to destroy the "old" world. Mao never concealed his ambition that his revolution would finally turn China into a land of universal justice and equality and that the Chinese revolution would serve as a model and revive China's central position in the world. China's domestic and external policies thus were deeply interrelated.

When the CCP seized power in 1949, Mao claimed that this event was only "the completion of the first step in the long march of the Chinese revolution," and that carrying out the "revolution after the revolution" was for the CCP a task more complicated and challenging.[20] How to prevent the continuous revolution from losing momentum emerged as one of Mao's major concerns. Around 1956, as the nationwide "socialist transformation" (e.g., nationalizing industry and commerce and collectivizing agriculture) was nearly completed, Mao's concerns changed into worries because he sensed that many of the party's cadres and ordinary members were becoming less interested in deepening the continuous revolution. After the failure of the Great Leap Forward in 1958–60, Mao realized that even among the Communist elite, his revolution was losing crucial "inner support." As Mao approached the last decade of his life, he found that in pursuing the ideals he cherished he had become a "lone monk with a leaky umbrella,"[21] and a majority of the Communist elite were unable — or unwilling — to follow the development of his thinking. A pivotal challenge obsessed Mao constantly: through what means could he transform China and the world? Even with his seemingly unrestricted political power, he often found himself powerless. What he encountered was a paradox sitting deeply in the challenge itself: he had to find the means needed for transforming the "old" world from the very "old" world that was yet to be transformed. Throughout Mao's twenty-seven-year reign in China, he was never able to overcome this profound anxiety.

In order to maintain the momentum of his continuous revolution, Mao needed to find the means to mobilize the masses. It was in the process of searching for such means that he realized that the adoption of a revolutionary foreign policy had great relevance. As indicated in the chapters ahead on Beijing's management of the Korean War, the Taiwan Strait crisis, and the Vietnam War, during the early years of the PRC, a revolutionary foreign policy helped to make Mao's various state and societal transformation programs powerful *unifying* and *national* themes supplanting many local, regional, or factional concerns. When tension between Mao and other members of the Communist elite, as well as between the Communist regime and China's ordinary people, intensified following the failure of the Great Leap Forward, a revolutionary foreign policy further served as an effective—and probably the only available—way through which Mao could enhance both his authority and the legitimacy of his continuous revolution.

The role of revolutionary foreign policy in Mao's continuous revolution must be understood in the context of the Chinese people's "victim mentality" and its connections to the age-old Central Kingdom concept so important in China's history and culture. During modern times, the Chinese people's perception of their nation's position in the world was continuously informed by a conviction that political incursion, economic exploitation, and military aggression by foreign imperialist countries had undermined the historical glory of the Chinese civilization and humiliated the Chinese nation. Consequently, a victim mentality gradually dominated the Chinese conceptualization of its relations with the outside world.

Indeed, this mentality is extraordinary. While it is common for non-Western countries to identify themselves as victims of the Western-dominated worldwide course of modernization, the Chinese perception of their nation being a victimized member of the international community is unique, because it formed such a sharp contrast with the long-lived Central Kingdom concept. The Chinese thus felt that their nation's modern experience was more humiliating and less tolerable than that of any other victimized non-Western country in the world, and they firmly believed that China's victim status would not end until its weaknesses had been turned into strength. So they willingly embraced Mao's revolutionary programs aimed at reviving China's central position in the world.

The central role China's foreign policy played in Mao's revolution drove the ccp leadership to adopt a highly centralized decision-making structure in external affairs. The political institutions of Mao's China were characterized by tight central control; but the control over foreign policymaking certainly was the tightest. As early as August 1944, when the ccp Central Committee issued the first comprehensive inner-party directive on diplomatic affairs, Mao made it clear that party organs and cadres must not take action in diplomatic affairs without Central Committee authorization.[22] On the eve of Communist seizure of power, Mao stressed that "there existed no insignificant matter in diplomatic affairs, and everything should be reported to and decided by the Central Committee."[23] After the prc's establishment, Mao further confirmed that the politburo, the Central Secretariat, and, indeed, Mao himself, controlled the decision-making power. The missions of the Foreign Ministry, headed by Premier Zhou Enlai from 1949 to 1958, were defined as keeping the central leadership well informed of China's external situation and carrying out the central leadership's decisions.[24] Under these circumstances, even Zhou Enlai became more a policy carrier than a policymaker.[25] During the Cultural Revolution years, this highly centralized foreign policy structure became more rigid when Foreign Minister Chen Yi lost virtually all power. For a time even the politburo did not matter, since the real power fell into the hands of the "Cultural Revolution Group," the institutional instrument Mao created to implement the Cultural Revolution.[26]

Because of Mao's perception of the Chinese revolution's sacred mission, which was reinforced by the Chinese victim mentality, he and his comrades were filled with an exceptional sense of insecurity throughout the twenty-seven years he ruled China. In general, it is understandable that, in the divided Cold War world in which peace and stability had been severely threatened by factors such as the emergence of nuclear weapons and the intensifying confrontation between the two superpowers, any country would feel less secure than ever before. Mao's sense of insecurity, however, was special in several respects.

First, the ambitious hope on the part of Mao and the CCP leadership to change China into a central international actor conflicted with China's power status, which was still weak during the Maoist era. As long as Mao and his comrades were determined to chart their own course in the world and to make China a prominent world power, they would continue to feel insecure until China's weakness had been turned into strength.

Second, since Mao and the CCP leadership emphasized the central role the Chinese revolution was to play in promoting the worldwide proletarian revolution, thus making China the primary enemy of world reactionary forces, they logically felt that they faced a very threatening world. The more Mao and his comrades stressed the significance of the Chinese revolution, the less secure they would feel in face of perceived threats from the outside world.

Third, Mao made this insecurity more serious when he highlighted international tension and treated it as a useful tool for domestic mobilization. Through anti-foreign-imperialist propaganda, Mao and his comrades used foreign threats to mobilize the Chinese masses. This propaganda, in turn, would inevitably cause a deepening sense of insecurity on the part of Mao and his comrades.

Hence, in the practical process of policymaking, Beijing broadly defined the threats to China's national security interests. Compared with policymakers in other countries, Beijing's leaders in the Maoist era were under great pressure to take extraordinary steps to defend and promote revolutionary China's security interests. This explains to a large extent why the PRC frequently resorted to violence in dealing with foreign policy crises.[27]

Because of the domestic mobilization function Mao attached to China's external policies, Beijing's use of force during the Maoist period was characterized by three distinctive and consistent patterns. First, Beijing's leaders resorted to force only when the confrontation was in one way or another related to China's territorial integrity and physical security. Even when China's purpose in entering a military confrontation was broader than the simple defense of its border (such as during the Korean War), Beijing's leaders always emphasized that they had exercised the military option because China's physical security was in jeopardy.[28] When China's involvement in a military confrontation resulted in its occupation of foreign territory, such as during the Chinese-Indian border war of 1962, Beijing's leaders ordered a retreat in order to prove that China's war aims were no more than the defense of China's borders.

Second, Beijing's leaders used force *always* for the purpose of domestic mobilization. Mao and his comrades fully understood that the tension created by an international crisis provided them with the best means to call the whole nation to act in accordance with the will and terms of the CCP. This was particularly true when Mao met with difficulty in pushing the party and the nation to carry out his continuous-revolution programs. As shown in Chapter 7, Mao's decision to shell Jinmen in the summer of 1958 was closely related to a nationwide wave of mass mobilization, which made it possible for the Great Leap Forward to reach a high point. On the eve of the Cultural Revolution, as discussed in Chapter 8, China's involvement in the Vietnam War and the extensive mass mobilization that accompanied it created an atmosphere conducive to the rapid radicalization of China's political and social life.

Third, Beijing's leaders used force only when they believed that they were in a position to justify it in a "moral" sense. If they did not morally justify their actions, the mobilization effect they hoped to achieve would be compromised. During the Korean War, the Beijing leadership's public war aims, "Defend our nation! Defend our home!" and "Defeat American arrogance!" were established as central mobilization slogans. During China's involvement in the Vietnam War, Mao compared the relationship between Vietnam and China to that between "lips and teeth," emphasizing that China had an obligation to proletarian internationalism to support the just struggle of the Vietnamese people. "Justice," indeed, became the talisman of China's international military involvement during the Cold War.

China's external behavior during the Maoist era was a contradictory phenomenon. Despite its tendency toward using force, Mao's China was not an expansionist power. It is essential to make a distinction between the pursuit of *centrality* and the pursuit of *dominance* in international affairs in terms of the fundamental goal of Chinese foreign policy. While Mao and his comrades were never shy about using force in pursuing China's foreign policy goals, what they hoped to achieve was not the expansion of China's political and military control of foreign territory or resources—which was, for Mao and his comrades, too inferior an aim—but, rather, the spread of their influence to other "hearts and minds" around the world. Mao fully understood that only when China's superior moral position in the world had been recognized by other peoples would the consolidation of his continuous revolution's momentum at home be assured.

A Brief Note on Sources

The studies in this volume are supported by fresh Chinese sources made available in recent years. They include collections of party documents and leaders' papers, memoirs and diaries by those who were involved in China's Cold War decision making or implementation, scholarly articles and monographs by Chinese researchers and research institutions with less restricted archival access, official and semiofficial publications using classified documents, and oral history interviews.[29] On a limited scale, these studies also have used documents obtained from Beijing's CCP Central Archives and various provincial and regional archives (including Xinjiang, Jilin, Guangxi, Fujian, and Shanghai). While these new sources are valuable in the sense that they have created previously nonexistent research opportunities, it is also clear that they were made available to scholars on a selective basis and, sometimes, by a desire other than to have the truth known. Fully realizing the limitations that restricted access to original historical documentation places on this study, I have tried to treat my sources critically. In particular, I have made every effort to double-check information provided by these sources, and, whenever necessary, in the notes I identify dubious sources or discrepancies in sources.

In the introduction to his acclaimed study on the international history of the Korean War, renowned Cold War historian William Stueck confesses that in completing his book he was dominated by "a feeling of humility over the realization of how little I know about the Korean War, of how much remains to be done by those who will follow me."[30] I am feeling even more humble. Much about Mao's China is yet to be studied. I plan to continue my schol-

CHAPTER 1
THE CHINESE CIVIL WAR
AND THE RISE OF THE
COLD WAR IN EAST ASIA,
1945–1946

*Jiang Jieshi claims that there never exist two suns in the heaven, and
there should never be two masters on the earth. I do not believe him.
I am going to make another sun appear in the heaven for him to see.*
—*Mao Zedong (1946)*

*The diversification of power did more to shape the course of the Cold War
than did the balancing of power.*
—*John Lewis Gaddis*

China's "War of Resistance against Japan" ended in August 1945 when
Japan surrendered unconditionally to the Allies. Peace, however, did not come
to China's war-torn land. Almost immediately after Japan's defeat, in the context of the emerging global confrontation between the United States and the
Soviet Union, the long-accumulated tensions between the Chinese Communist Party (CCP) and the Nationalist Party, or Guomindang (GMD), intensified,
bringing the country to the verge of another civil war. From late 1945 to early
1946, the Communists and Nationalists, with the mediation and intervention
of the United States and the Soviet Union, conducted a series of negotiations
on different levels to solve the problems between them, but they failed to reach
an overall agreement that would allow peace to prevail. By mid-1946, a nationwide civil war finally erupted, which resulted in the victory of the Chinese
Communist revolution in 1949. From an international perspective, the CCP-
GMD confrontation intensified the conflict between the two superpowers, thus
contributing to the escalation and, eventually, crystallization of the Cold War
in East Asia. An examination of China's transition from the anti-Japanese war
to a revolutionary civil war in 1945–46 thus will shed new light on a crucial
juncture in the development of the Chinese revolution, as well as offer fresh
insights into the connections between China's internal development and the
origins of the Cold War. This will be the focus of discussion of this chapter.

CHINA

Zhabarovsk

Zhenbao
Island

Ussuri River

HEILONGJIANG

• Harbin

JILIN

Changchun

Vladivostok

NEI MENGGU
(Inner Mongolia)

Siping

LIAONING

Shenyang

Shanghaiguan KOREA

Beidaihe

Beijing•

hot,

Tianjin

Lüshun
(Port Arthur)

an

HEBEI

JAPAN

Shijiazhuang

Yellow Sea

•Ji'nan

Qingduo

XI

SHANDONG

hengzhou

JIANGSU

ENAN

Hefei Nanjing

.I

Shanghai

uhan

ANHUI

Hangzhou

East China Sea

Lushan

ZHEJIANG

Nanchang

Wenzhou

gsha

JIANQXI Fuzhou

AN

FUJIAN

Taipei

Xiamen

GUANGDONG

Guangzhou

TAIWAN

Hong Kong

South China Sea

AN

The Origins of the CCP-GMD Confrontation

China's movement toward a civil war began in 1945–46, when the profound hostilities between the Communists and the Nationalists that had accumulated during the war years reached a climax. Given the deep historical origins of the tensions between the two parties, indeed, civil war was almost inevitable.

In retrospect, Japan's invasion of China in the 1930s changed decisively the course of China's internal development. From 1927, after the success of the anti-Communist coup in Shanghai led by Jiang Jieshi (Chiang Kai-shek), to 1936, when the Xi'an incident occurred, the GMD and the CCP were engaged in a bloody civil war. The Communists established revolutionary base areas in the countryside (especially in the South) to wage a "land revolution." While making every effort to suppress the Communist rebellion, Jiang's government encountered a series of difficulties from the outset. In particular, Jiang's leadership role within the GMD needed to be consolidated and the anti-Jiang provincial warlords had to be dealt with. But Jiang's biggest dilemma emerged after September 1931, when Japan occupied China's Northeast (Manchuria) and continued to put pressure on the Chinese government through its intrusion into North China. Jiang had to decide who should be treated as his primary enemy—the Japanese or the CCP. Perceiving that "the Japanese were the disease of the skin and the Communists were the threat to the heart," Jiang risked losing his status as China's national leader to focus his efforts on suppressing the CCP and the Red Army.[1] By 1936, this strategy looked promising: under Jiang's military pressure, the CCP gave up its main base area in Jiangxi province in the South, to endure the "Long March" (during which the Chinese Red Army lost 90 percent of its strength), and was restricted to a small, barren area in northern Shaanxi province in northwestern China.[2] However, Jiang underestimated the impact Japan's continuous aggression in China had on Chinese national consciousness and popular mentality. In December 1936, Zhang Xueliang and Yang Fucheng, two of Jiang's generals who opposed his policy of "putting the suppression of the CCP ahead of the resistance against Japan," kidnapped him in Xi'an. Jiang was forced to stop the civil war against the CCP so that the whole nation would be united to cope with the threat from Japan.[3] With the outbreak of the War of Resistance against Japan the next year, the GMD and the CCP formally established an anti-Japanese "united front."

During China's eight years of the war with Japan, Jiang's gains seemed significant. By serving as China's paramount leader at a time of profound national crisis, he effectively consolidated the legitimacy of the rule of his party and himself in China, which, after 1942 and 1943, was further reinforced by American-British recognition of China under his leadership as one of the

"Big Four." In the meantime, however, the foundation of Jiang's government had started to crumble. In fact, in having to focus on dealing with the Japanese invasion, Jiang failed to develop effective plans to cope with the profound social and political problems China had been facing throughout the modern age. Consequently, corruption spread further in Jiang's government and army during the war years, which significantly damaged his reputation as China's indisputable national leader.[4]

The most serious potential challenge to Jiang's government, however, came from the CCP. China's deepening national crisis in the 1930s, and the outbreak of the Sino-Japanese War in 1937, saved the CCP and the Chinese Red Army from imminent final destruction. Holding high the banner of resisting Japan during the war years, the CCP sent its military forces into areas behind the Japanese lines to fight a guerrilla war.[5] Although Mao Zedong, the CCP leader, made it clear to his commanders that, rather than engaging in major battles against the Japanese, they should use most of their energy to maintain and develop their own forces,[6] the simple fact that the Communists were fighting in the enemy's rear had created an image of the CCP as a major contributor to the war against Japan.[7] Throughout the war years, Mao and his fellow CCP leaders were always aware that after the war they would need to compete with the GMD for control of China.

Not surprisingly, relations between the GMD and the CCP quickly deteriorated as the war against Japan continued. Early in 1941, the Communist-led New Fourth Army, while moving its headquarters from south to north of the Yangzi (Yangtze) River, was attacked and wiped out by GMD troops in Wannan (southern Anhui province).[8] The "Wannan incident" (also known as the New Fourth Army incident) immediately caused a serious crisis in the CCP-GMD wartime alliance. In response to the incident, Mao Zedong even asserted that the CCP should begin a direct confrontation with Jiang and prepare to overthrow his government.[9] And Jiang ordered the use of both military and political means to restrict the CCP's movements.[10]

Pressure from the United States and the Soviet Union, however, helped prevent the GMD and the CCP from resuming a civil war at this moment. After the New Fourth Army incident, President Franklin D. Roosevelt sent Lauchlin Currie as his special envoy to China to meet Jiang and other Chinese leaders. Currie expressed Washington's concerns over a renewed civil war between the GMD and the CCP, warning that it would only benefit the Japanese.[11] On 25 January 1941, Georgi M. Dimitrov, the Comintern's secretary-general, sent an urgent telegram to Mao Zedong, warning the CCP leaders that they should not abandon the party's cooperation with the GMD lest they "fall into the trap prepared by the Japanese and the puppets."[12] Consequently, a CCP-GMD show-down was temporarily avoided.

Neither the CCP nor the GMD, though, would trust the other. In the ensuing four years, until the end of the war against Japan in 1945, both parties put preparing for a showdown between them after the war at the top of their agenda. In 1943, Jiang published a pamphlet titled *China's Destiny*, in which he claimed that the Communists would have no position in postwar China.[13] The CCP angrily criticized Jiang's "plot to establish his own dictatorship by destroying the CCP and other progressive forces in China," calling for the Chinese people to struggle resolutely against the emergence of a "fascist China."[14] Both GMD and CCP leaders realized that when the war ended, a life-or-death battle between the two parties was probably inevitable.

The CCP's Diplomatic Initiative in Late 1944 and Early 1945

By the end of 1944 and the beginning of 1945, the balance of strength between the GMD and the CCP had swung further in the latter's favor. The widespread corruption within Jiang's government, the runaway inflation in the Nationalist-controlled areas,[15] and the major military defeats of Nationalist troops in the face of the Japanese Ichi-go campaign[16] combined to weaken significantly Jiang Jieshi's stature as China's wartime national leader. In comparison, the CCP had reached a level of strength and influence unprecedented since its establishment in 1921. By late 1944 and early 1945, the party claimed that it commanded a powerful military force of 900,000 regular troops and 900,000 militiamen, and that party membership had reached over one million.[17] In the meantime, the party had gained valuable administrative experience through the buildup of base areas in central and northern China, and Mao Zedong, through the "Rectification Campaign," had consolidated his control over the party's strategy and policymaking.[18]

Under these circumstances, Mao and his fellow CCP leaders believed that with the continuous development of the party's strength, it would occupy a stronger position to compete for political power in China at the end of the war against Japan. On several occasions, Mao asserted that "this time, we must take over China."[19] To this end, the party adopted a series of new strategies in late 1944. In a political maneuver designed to challenge Jiang's claim to a monopoly of political power in China, the CCP formally introduced the idea of replacing Jiang's one-party dictatorship with a new coalition government including the CCP and other democratic parties.[20] On the military side, the CCP leadership decided to dispatch the party's best units to penetrate into the areas south of the Yangzi River, with the task of creating new base areas in southern China. In several inner-party directives, Mao Zedong made it clear that if the CCP could expand its "liberated zones" from the North to the South, the party would occupy a more favorable position in confronting the GMD after the war.[21] But the CCP adopted the most important initiative in the diplomatic field: perceiving that the United States would play an increasingly important role in China and East Asia, the party leadership decided to pursue a closer relationship with Washington.[22]

Since the early days of the war in the Pacific, the CCP had been pursuing an "international united front" with the United States for two main objectives: first, to "improve China's War of Resistance," and second, to enable the CCP to use the United States to check the power of the Guomindang government.[23] Not until late 1944 and early 1945, however, when policymakers in Washington were actively considering using China as a base for landing operations in Japan, did the CCP find a real opportunity to approach the Americans. CCP leaders realized that by offering the party's assistance to American landing operations, it would not only reduce American suspicion of the Chinese Communists but also allow them to use America's influence to check Jiang's power.[24] The CCP thus made every effort to expose the "darkness" of Jiang's government, while taking every opportunity to convince the Americans that the Chinese Communists were nationalists at the core, and that they favored "democratic reforms" in China.[25] In July 1944, the "Dixie Mission," a group of American military observers, arrived in Yan'an, marking the first direct official contact between the U.S. government and the CCP.[26]

At first, the CCP's new diplomatic strategy appeared to be working well. In June 1944, Roosevelt sent his vice president, Henry Wallace, to visit China to press Jiang toward conducting democratic reforms.[27] In September 1944, a controversy erupted between Jiang and Joseph Stilwell, Jiang's American chief of staff, leading President Roosevelt to request that Jiang turn over "unrestricted command" of China's military forces to Stilwell. Thus a crisis developed in the relationship between Chongqing, Jiang's wartime capital, and Washington.[28]

The CCP's "diplomatic victory," however, was short-lived. Realizing that his controversy with General Stilwell threatened the very foundation of his authority and power, Jiang rebuffed President Roosevelt's request, and, consequently, General Stilwell was recalled in October. In the meantime, in order to prevent the CCP-GMD friction from compromising China's war effort against Japan, President Roosevelt sent Patrick Hurley to China to help mediate the problems between the two parties. In early November, Hurley reached a five-point draft agreement with the CCP leaders in Yan'an that favored the establishment of a coalition government.[29] But when Hurley learned that Jiang firmly rejected the five-point agreement, especially the part concerning the coalition government, he agreed to a three-point plan proposed by Jiang. According to the plan, the CCP would need to earn its legal status by turning over control of its military forces to the GMD government.[30]

CCP leaders were genuinely offended by Hurley's "deceptive abandonment" of the five-point agreement. They rejected the three-point plan and angrily denounced Hurley as untrustworthy.[31] Early in 1945, Mao personally directed a CCP propaganda campaign to criticize Washington's policy toward China. In April 1945, Hurley announced in Washington that the U.S. government fully supported the GMD and would not cooperate with the CCP. In an inner-party directive issued on 7 July 1945, the CCP leadership made it clear that the party would adopt a position of "opposing the mistaken U.S. China policy (a policy of supporting Jiang, opposing the Communists, and guarding against the Soviet Union)" and "challenging those imperialists within the U.S. government (such as Hurley)."[32]

Underlying the CCP's harsh attitude toward the United States was a profound belief that the international situation was turning increasingly in the party's favor. With the Soviet Red Army's rapid advance in Europe early in 1945, Mao and his fellow CCP leaders believed that the Soviet Union would soon become a central actor in East Asian politics. Early in February 1945, Stalin informed Mao of the convening of the Yalta Conference, which convinced the CCP chairman that "the possibility of the Soviet Union's voice in determining important Eastern affairs has increased." Mao thus judged that "under such circumstances, both the United States and Jiang would try to reach political compromises with us."[33] Furthermore, Mao and his comrades believed that the Americans still needed the CCP's help, both logistical and operational, in conducting the counteroffensive against Japan from northern China.[34] As a result, CCP leaders felt that the party was in a position to challenge America's pro-Jiang policy.

In the Vortex of Big-Power Politics

Big-power politics, however, were much more complicated than Mao and his comrades perceived them to be. At the Yalta Conference, Stalin gained Roosevelt's promise that all former Russian rights and privileges lost to Japan during the 1904 Russo-Japanese War, including those in Manchuria, would be restored to the Soviet Union, and, in return, Stalin agreed to enter the war in Asia within two to three months of Germany's defeat. As part of the Yalta compromises, Stalin also promised Roosevelt that he would not support the

CCP in China's internal conflict.[35] Roosevelt informed Jiang of the main contents of the Yalta agreement after the meeting,[36] but Stalin did not brief the CCP leaders on the deal he had made with Roosevelt. For the Russian dictator, the strategic interests of the Soviet Union were more important than those of his Chinese Communist comrades.

Since CCP leaders did not know the details of the Yalta agreement, they continued to base their strategies for preparing for a showdown with the GMD on the assumption that the Soviets' entry into the anti-Japanese war would enhance the party's position in China. On 18 April 1945, two weeks after Moscow announced the abrogation of the Soviet-Japanese Neutrality Treaty, Mao signed an important inner-party directive. The document pointed out that since the date of Soviet entry into the anti-Japanese war was approaching, the international situation in the Far East was undergoing fundamental changes. The main task of the CCP military forces would soon be to cooperate with the military operations of the Soviet Red Army.[37] From 23 April to 11 June 1945, the CCP convened its Seventh Congress in Yan'an. In his speech to the congress, titled "On the Coalition Government," Mao argued that only the Soviet Union's direct entry into the anti-Japanese war would bring about "the final and thorough solution of the Pacific problem." He warned the British and American governments "not to follow a China policy that violated the Chinese people's will." Reviewing the CCP's development in political influence and military strength during the war years, Mao announced that the CCP "had already become the center of the Chinese people's cause of liberation."[38] In his concluding remarks to the congress, Mao further emphasized that the international aid (the Soviet aid) to the Chinese revolution would come, and he even joked that "if it fails to come, I will let you have my head."[39]

At almost the same time that the CCP was holding its Seventh Congress, the GMD was convening its Sixth National Congress from 5 to 21 May in Chongqing. Jiang asserted at the congress that "Japan is our enemy abroad, and the CCP is our enemy at home" and that "our central problem today is how to destroy the CCP."[40] In order to cope with the CCP's increasing military strength and political influence, Jiang planned to convene a national affairs conference and a national assembly to confound the CCP's plans for a coalition government.[41] In the meantime, he ordered GMD forces to strengthen the blockade of the CCP's "liberated areas."[42] Anticipating that the Soviet Union would soon enter the war in the Far East, Jiang made great efforts to reach agreements with Stalin. Early in July, Jiang sent T. V. Soong, his brother-in-law, to Moscow to meet Stalin. Stalin agreed to support Jiang as China's only leader and not to aid the CCP, but he also asked for several vital concessions from the GMD government, including the recognition of the independence of Outer Mongolia and Soviet privileges in Manchuria. Jiang had sincerely hoped to reach an agreement with Stalin, but he now found the price too high. The meeting adjourned in mid-July since Stalin had to attend the Potsdam Conference.[43]

Even at this late stage of the war, neither the CCP nor the GMD foresaw that the war against Japan would end soon. In a telegram dated 15 June 1945, Mao and the CCP Central Committee predicted that "the War of Resistance against Japan will not reach its final stage this year, and dramatic changes are likely the next year."[44] As late as 4 August, the CCP leadership still claimed in an inner-party directive that "our estimate is that the Japanese bandits will be defeated by the winter of 1946." Accordingly, the CCP leaders believed that the party "would have about one year's time to make preparations" for an "inevitable civil war" after Japan's defeat.[45]

Japan's Surrender and Stalin's "Betrayal" of the CCP

On 6 and 9 August, the Americans dropped two atomic bombs on Hiroshima and Nagasaki. On 8 August, the Soviet Red Army entered the war in the East, and on 10 August, Japan first offered to surrender to the Allies. It was apparent that China's war against Japan had come to its conclusion, and the CCP leadership acted immediately to deal with this new situation. On 9 August, one day after the Soviet Union declared war on Japan, Mao Zedong ordered the Communist forces to go all out to "cooperate with the Soviet Red Army" in the final battle to liberate China's lost territory from Japanese occupation.[46] Two days later, Zhu De, commander-in-chief of the CCP's military forces, ordered CCP troops to occupy important cities and transportation links in central and northern China and, particularly, in the Northeast.[47]

In an inner-party directive dated 11 August, Mao emphasized that the end of the war against Japan would most probably be followed by a civil war with the Nationalists. He anticipated that after destroying the Japanese and puppet troops, "the GMD would start an overall offensive against our party and our troops," and that the outcome of the civil war would be determined by the extent to which the CCP had prepared for it. He therefore instructed CCP cadres and military commanders to abandon any illusion of peace between the CCP and the GMD and to "gather our forces in order to prepare for the civil war."[48]

Mao and his fellow CCP leaders believed that the Soviet Union's entry into the war had created favorable conditions for the CCP to fight a renewed civil war. Although they knew that representatives from the GMD and the Soviet Union were conducting negotiations in Moscow, and that the negotiations might lead to a treaty between the GMD and Soviet governments, they tended to believe that "(1) the Soviet Union would not allow the emergence of an American-backed fascist China in the East after the end of the war, and (2) Stalin, as a Marxist, would not sign a treaty with the GMD government that would restrict the development of the Chinese revolution."[49] In ordering the CCP troops to take aggressive actions in northern China and the Northeast, Mao's fundamental estimation was that the Soviet Red Army might not offer direct support to CCP forces but would adopt a cooperative attitude toward the CCP's military maneuvers.[50] Further, Mao and his fellow CCP leaders believed that the Soviet entry into the war would restrict the aggressiveness of U.S. policy toward China, forcing "the United States not to support [Jiang] in China's civil war."[51] Although the CCP chairman, following his longtime revolutionary experience, suggested that the CCP and its forces should never give up "self-reliance" as a guiding principle, he did regard the international situation created by the Soviet entry into the war in the East and support from the Soviet Red Army as two decisive conditions for the party to win a showdown with the GMD.[52]

Jiang fully understood that he could ill afford to lose the competition with the CCP over the lost territory, as he, too, anticipated a civil war would come sooner or later. On 12 August, Jiang used his authority as the leader of China's legal government to order the CCP forces to stay where they were and not to accept the surrender of the Japanese and puppet troops, a directive the CCP rejected angrily.[53] Jiang knew that since most of his troops were still in the remote "Great Rear,"[54] he needed to take extraordinary steps to win the competition with the Communists. He thus authorized T. V. Soong to sign the "Sino-Soviet Treaty of Friendship and Mutual Assistance," in which Jiang acknowledged the independence of Outer Mongolia, the Soviet military occupation of Lüshun (Port Arthur), and Soviet privileges regarding the Chinese Changchun Railroad. In return, the Soviet Union agreed to respect Jiang's position as the leader of China's legal government and acknowledged that Jiang's troops had the right to take over China's lost territory, especially that in the Northeast.[55] On 14 August, the same day that the Sino-Soviet treaty was signed, Jiang telegraphed Mao to invite him to come to Chongqing to "discuss questions related to reestablishing peace in China."[56]

The Jiang-Stalin compromise undermined the optimism that had dominated the CCP leaders' strategic thinking, which was further diminished when the Soviet dictator directly pressured his Chinese Communist comrades to negotiate with Jiang. On 20 and 22 August, respectively, Stalin sent two urgent telegrams to the CCP leaders, advising them that with the surrender of Japan, the CCP should enter discussions with the GMD about the restoration of peace and the reconstruction of the country. "If a civil war were to break out," warned Stalin, "the Chinese nation would face self-destruction."[57]

Stalin's attitude reflected his understanding of how Soviet interests in China would best be served. He not only lacked confidence in the CCP's ability to win a civil war against the GMD, but he also was extremely reluctant to commit the strength of the Soviet Union to supporting his Chinese comrades by risking a direct conflict with the Americans, who were then planning large-scale landing operations in northern China. He had gained much through signing a treaty with the Chinese GMD government and was eager to retain those advancements. However, for Mao and his fellow CCP leaders, Stalin's policy was a cruel betrayal.[58] It had shaken the very foundation of the party's strategy to pursue the Chinese revolution's victory through a head-to-head confrontation with the GMD.[59]

Under these circumstances, the CCP leadership made fundamental adjustments to the party's aggressive strategy vis-à-vis the GMD. On 23 August, the CCP politburo met to discuss the party's response to Stalin's telegrams. Mao made a long speech at the meeting, telling the participants that the Soviet Union had signed a treaty with the GMD government allowing the GMD to take over the Northeast. "Confined by the need to maintain international peace, as well as by the Sino-Soviet treaty," Mao told his comrades, "the Soviet Union is not in a position to act freely to support us . . . because if the Soviet Union were to assist us, the United States would certainly support Jiang, and, as a result, the cause of international peace would suffer and a world war might follow." Mao believed that the CCP had to adjust its strategies in accordance with this situation and "acknowledge that Jiang Jieshi has the legitimate right to accept Japan's surrender" and "to occupy the big cities." The party, Mao suggested, should adopt "peace, democracy, and unity" as the central slogan. Accordingly, Mao believed that he should accept Jiang's invitation to visit Chongqing to discuss how to maintain peace in China. Most of the participants agreed,[60] and on 26 August, the CCP politburo formally authorized Mao to meet with Jiang in Chongqing.[61] In an inner-party circular, the CCP Central Committee made it clear that the main reason for Mao's meeting with Jiang was that "neither the Soviet Union nor the United States favors a civil war in China," and that "the party therefore has to make major concessions" in order to achieve a "new scenario of democracy and peace in China."[62]

On 28 August, Mao Zedong, accompanied by Zhou Enlai and Wang Ruofei, two top CCP leaders, arrived in Chongqing. In the following forty days, Mao and Jiang discussed how to democratize China's politics and nationalize the GMD's and CCP's troops. However, the negotiations proved extremely difficult. The central issue was whether the CCP would be allowed to maintain an independent army. While Jiang insisted that the CCP should place its military forces under the command of the government, Mao was willing only to cut the size of the Communist troops and would do so only on the condition that the GMD would also reduce its forces. The two sides also failed to reach an agreement on how China's government and politics would be "democratized." On 10 October, Jiang and Mao issued a communiqué asserting that they had agreed on convening a political consultative conference as the first step toward constructing peace and democracy in China, but the Jiang-Mao meetings as a whole failed to produce an agreement that would allow peace to prevail.[63]

The lack of concrete results from the negotiations in Chongqing was by no means surprising given that neither the GMD nor the CCP had any confidence in reaching peace through compromise. Indeed, the only reason either party entered the negotiations at all was to demonstrate publicly its own desire for peace. At the same time that Jiang and Mao were meeting in Chongqing, military clashes between GMD and CCP troops escalated in northern and northeastern China. The Americans helped transport large numbers of GMD troops from the "Great Rear" to northern China, and the forces immediately entered into competition with the Communists to recover the "lost territory." In some areas of Shandong, Shanxi, Hebei, and Suiyuan provinces, several major battles took place between GMD and CCP forces. It appeared that the better equipped and more numerous GMD forces generally held the upper hand overall, especially in northern China.

How Manchuria Became the CCP's Revolutionary Base

Under great pressure from the GMD forces, the CCP leaders were determined to adopt a tit-for-tat strategy. However, they had to find the best geographic location to carry out their plans. Their vision quickly focused on the Northeast. As discussed earlier, after Soviet entry into the war, the CCP leadership decided to control the Northeast with the support of the Soviet forces there. Stalin's cautious attitude and the Sino-Soviet treaty made it difficult for the CCP to carry out this decision as originally intended.[64] But the CCP did not give up the plan. Late in August and early in September, the party leadership received several reports from the commanders of CCP military units in the Northeast that the Soviet army was willing to accept the CCP's cooperation.[65] In the meantime, the party also noted that Moscow sharply criticized "China's reactionary forces" for their attempt to drag China backward.[66] The party leadership realized that there was room for maneuver in pursuit of its own objectives in the Northeast within the framework of the Sino-Soviet treaty. On

Soviet Red Army soldiers with Chinese Communist soldiers in Manchuria, August 1945.
Xinhua News Agency.

29 August, in an inner-party directive, the CCP Central Committee stated that while the Soviet Red Army, restricted by the Sino-Soviet treaty, would not offer direct support to the CCP forces in the Northeast, it was also true that the Soviet Union still supported China's "cause of progressive democracy." Therefore, so long as the CCP's actions in the Northeast did not force the Soviets to violate their obligations under the Sino-Soviet treaty, the Soviets would allow the CCP to develop its influence and strength in the Northeast.[67]

In the next three weeks, CCP troops entered the Northeast in large numbers, and they found that the Soviet Red Army's attitude was generally cooperative. On 14 September, Lieutenant Colonel Belunosov, a representative of Marshal Rodion Malinovskii, commander of the Soviet forces in the Far East, arrived at Yan'an. The meetings between him and the top CCP leaders resulted in a series of agreements: While the CCP troops in the Northeast would not enter big cities there, the Soviets would allow them to occupy the countryside and some small and midsize cities. When the Soviet troops had withdrawn from the Northeast, they would not automatically hand over areas under their occupation to the GMD, but would "let the Chinese solve the matter by themselves."[68] Under these circumstances, on 19 September, the CCP leadership formally adopted a grand strategy of "maintaining a defensive posture in the south while waging an offensive in the north" in the confrontation with the GMD.[69]

Jiang Jieshi and the GMD high command also understood the Northeast's strategic importance and decided to send the GMD's best units there. With the help of the Americans, large numbers of GMD troops were transported by air or sea to several Northeast ports. Late in September, U.S. Marines began large-scale landing operations in Tianjin and several other northern ports. Their role, as the CCP perceived it, was essentially to check the movements of CCP troops and to support the actions of the GMD forces.[70]

The cooperative nature of American-GMD military actions in northern China and the Northeast sent a warning signal to Moscow, producing further conflict between American and Soviet policies in East Asia. Almost at the same time that the CCP-GMD conflict over control of the Northeast was escalating, the foreign ministers from the United States, the Soviet Union, Britain, France, and China met in London to discuss important Far Eastern issues, especially the question of military control of Japan. When the Americans made it clear that they would exercise exclusive control of the occupation of Japan, the Soviets immediately decided to harden their policy toward the United States in East Asia and the GMD in China.[71]

The Soviets were now willing to break their obligation under the Sino-Soviet treaty. Beginning in early October their attitude toward the Northeast issue changed further in the CCP's favor. The Soviet Red Army began to create barriers against the GMD troops' movement into the Northeast, claiming that until an overall solution of the Northeast issue had been worked out, they would not allow GMD troops to enter the areas they occupied.[72] In the meantime, the Soviets increased their support for the CCP. On 4 October, the Soviets advised the CCP Northeast Bureau that the Chinese Communists should move as many as 300,000 troops into the Northeast in one month's time, and that the Soviets would provide them with large numbers of weapons.[73] On 19 October, the CCP leadership decided to "go all out to control the entire Northeast."[74]

The new Soviet policy toward the Northeast resulted in a serious crisis between the Soviet Union and the GMD government. When the Soviets refused to observe the Sino-Soviet treaty, the GMD government took dramatic action. It informed the Soviet Union on 15 November that because the GMD's takeover of the Northeast had been hindered by the Soviet forces there, the GMD's Northeast administration headquarters would move out of the Northeast on 17 November.[75] At the same time, Jiang Jieshi telegraphed President

Harry Truman, informing him that as the result of the Soviet Union's violation of the Sino-Soviet treaty in the Northeast, "there has emerged a serious threat to peace and order in East Asia." He asked the United States to offer "active mediation, so that the continuous deterioration of the situation could be avoided."[76] Meanwhile, the GMD accelerated the transportation of troops into the Northeast. Starting on 3 November, the GMD forces began to attack the Communist-controlled Shanhaiguan Pass, a strategically important link between northern China and the Northeast. In the meantime, American naval vessels repeatedly appeared off Soviet-controlled Port Arthur, which the Soviets interpreted as a demonstration of America's military strength.[77] The danger of a nationwide CCP-GMD civil war, as well as a Soviet-American military showdown, increased dramatically.

Under these circumstances, the Soviets found that, in order to avoid a direct confrontation with the GMD government as well as with the United States, they had to make some concessions. On 17 November, Appolon Petrov, the Soviet ambassador to China, informed the GMD government that the Soviet Red Army had not provided CCP troops with any substantial support, and that it was not the purpose of the Soviets to hinder the GMD's takeover of the Northeast.[78] Three days later, the Soviet military command in the Northeast formally requested that CCP troops withdraw from areas along the Chinese Changchun Railroad. The CCP leadership agreed.[79] The Soviet command still allowed CCP troops to control areas 20 kilometers from the Changchun Railroad, however, and Soviet troops continued to deliver military equipment and ammunition to the CCP.[80] With the changing Soviet attitude, the CCP leadership now realized that to control the entire Northeast was too aggressive an objective. Late in November 1945, the CCP again adjusted its Northeast strategy, adopting a policy focusing on occupying the countryside and small and midsize cities.[81]

The Failure of the Marshall Mission and the Outbreak of the Civil War

The escalation of the CCP-GMD confrontation presented a deepening dilemma to the Americans. On the one hand, both for checking the expansion of Soviet influences in East Asia and for maintaining stable order in China, it was necessary for the United States to provide aid to the GMD government (although many Americans disliked Jiang and his regime) and to help promote China's political democratization. On the other hand, America's intervention (especially military intervention) could, in the worst-case scenario, result in its involvement in China's civil war, risking a direct confrontation with the Soviet Union. From October to December 1945, General Albert Weydemeyer, who had replaced Stilwell as commander in chief of U.S. forces in China, repeatedly outlined this dilemma in reports to top policymakers in Washington.[82] After weighing the pros and cons, President Truman made a crucial decision, announcing on 15 December that the United States would continue to support the GMD government but would avoid using American military forces to intervene in China's internal affairs.[83] He also decided to send General George Marshall to China to mediate the conflict between the two Chinese adversaries.[84]

The Marshall mission proved extremely difficult from the outset because of the fundamental differences existing between the CCP and the GMD. In postwar China, the achievement of a peaceful solution to the CCP-GMD conflict would have required both parties to cooperate and share power in a way neither could have accepted. The CCP, as mentioned earlier, had created a powerful military force during the war against Japan. The political influence of the CCP had also grown enormously during and after the war. Compared to the GMD, the CCP appeared full of vitality, and the party thus refused to surrender its hard-won advantages, especially the control over its military forces, for the dubious prospects of a recognized position in the GMD government.[85] Indeed, the first thing that the CCP had noticed about Truman's 15 December 1945 statement was that the United States "had decided not to participate directly in China's civil war on Jiang's side." The CCP leadership decided that they would "take this favorable opportunity to further develop our own strength" in the Northeast while "treating American personnel in China cordially" in order to influence American policy toward China.[86]

Jiang and the GMD were unwilling to compromise with the Communists, believing that any substantial concession to the CCP on the GMD's part would weaken its rule in China. Jiang, a nationalist and an authoritarian ruler, would allow no one, least of all the Communists, to share his political power. Thus Jiang also used Marshall's mediation more as an opportunity to deploy the GMD's military forces for an inevitable military showdown with the Communists than as a preliminary step toward a permanent peace in China.[87]

Marshall sincerely hoped to find a solution acceptable to both sides, and he acted impartially. In the initial stage of his mission, he seemed to have made some progress. The CCP and the GMD agreed to an armistice on 10 January 1946. The same day, representatives from the GMD, the CCP, and other political parties in China convened the Political Consultative Conference to discuss problems concerning the establishment of a coalition government in China. Nevertheless, when Marshall's mediation touched upon the most sensitive problem—the distribution of military and political power in China—he encountered an insurmountable obstacle. Jiang clearly expressed his position that unless the CCP submitted its military forces to the "unified leadership" of his government, he would not allow the Communists to share any of his power. Confident of his own military superiority, Jiang was determined to adopt a policy of force.[88] The CCP, on the other hand, argued that the "democratization" of Jiang's regime should come before the nationalization of China's armed forces. The Communists were ready for a head-to-head confrontation with Jiang.[89] Neither the GMD nor the CCP was willing to make substantial concessions.

Marshall's prospects of success were further weakened by the intensifying confrontation between the United States and the Soviet Union in the world in general and in East Asia and China in particular. In order to reduce Soviet influence in East Asia, early in February 1946, Washington expressed strong opposition to the Soviet-GMD negotiations on economic cooperation in the Northeast.[90] Meanwhile, the United States intentionally publicized the contents of the secret agreements on China between Roosevelt and Stalin at the Yalta Conference, which triggered a tide of anti-Soviet protest among the Chinese people. The Soviets decided to strike back. Late in February, Marshal Malinovskii and other Soviet representatives asserted on several occasions that the Soviet Union would not allow the Americans to control the Northeast.[91] In early March 1946, the Soviet Union suddenly announced that its forces would withdraw from the Northeast. At the same time, the Soviet commanders in the Northeast suggested that the CCP send its troops there to control all large and midsize cities and important transportation lines between Harbin and Shenyang.[92] In other words, the Soviets were now ready to hand the areas in the Northeast under their control to the CCP.

This development greatly encouraged the CCP leaders, who decided immediately that CCP forces "would occupy the areas north of Shenyang as soon as possible."[93] On 24 March, the CCP Central Committee summarized the party's new strategy in a telegram to the party's Northeast Bureau: "Our party's policy is to go all out to control Changchun and Harbin, and the entire Changchun Railroad. We should prevent Jiang's troops from advancing there at any price."[94]

Jiang fully realized that if the Communist forces were allowed to control areas north of Shenyang, the CCP would occupy an extremely favorable position in the forthcoming civil war. He therefore ordered the GMD troops to start a large-scale offensive aimed at occupying Changchun. In early April, a fierce battle began between CCP and GMD troops at Siping, a strategically important small city in southern Manchuria. This battle, as it turned out, became the prelude to an overall CCP-GMD civil war, which finally broke out in June 1946. Although Marshall would not leave China until August, his mission had failed long before the date of his departure.

Conclusion

The period from late 1944 to early 1946 represented a time of grand transition in China's modern history, as well as in the history of East Asian international relations. An outstanding feature of the transition was that during this period the CCP not only survived serious challenges brought about by the complex domestic and international situations at the end of World War II, but also, and more importantly, gathered strength and momentum through both military and diplomatic maneuvers in preparing to wage a revolutionary war that would finally enable the party to seize China. As a result, in the late 1940s, Communist China emerged as a revolutionary power in East Asia, adopting a series of ambitious state and societal transformation programs at home and challenging the Western-dominated international order both in East Asia and in the world. Indeed, as Chinese scholar Niu Jun puts it, this period served as a key juncture in the CCP's "march from Yan'an to the world."[95]

From a larger historical perspective, the CCP's tremendous gains during this transitional period have to be understood in the context of the extreme tensions that had developed in China's state and society during the previous decades. China's modern history, as viewed from a Chinese perspective, is characterized by the humiliation caused by Western incursions. The repeated failure on the part of the Chinese to deal with Western and, after the end of the nineteenth century, Japanese challenges, or indeed to reform China's premodern political, military, and economic institutions, left the Chinese people frustrated and angry. This frustration was further intensified by the unsuccessful outcome of the 1911 revolution, which destroyed an empire but failed to establish a true republic. The desire for rapid and radical changes thus gained tremendous momentum among the Chinese people. In the wake of the Russian Bolshevik revolution, the CCP emerged as the force of radical and revolutionary change in China, embodying defiance of the relatively conservative reign of the GMD, now increasingly perceived by many Chinese, especially radical intellectuals, as a force representing the status quo.

The war against Japan forced the Chinese people to concentrate on "saving China from destructive crises," delaying their efforts to cope with the nation's political, social, and cultural problems. But the momentum for fundamental changes remained. The CCP's dramatic development during the war years can be interpreted in terms of the changing balance of power between the CCP and the GMD — for the first time in the CCP-GMD confrontation the former had possessed the strength to challenge the latter nationwide. However, it is also important to note that on a deeper level, the CCP, as the most radical political force in China, found at the end of the war a highly favorable environment in Chinese society because China's victory "suddenly" released the long-accumulated popular momentum for revolutionary internal changes. For the CCP this was the ideal situation in which to compete for China's political power.

But it would have been more difficult for Mao and his comrades to cope with the tremendous challenges facing the CCP at the end of the war against Japan if Moscow had not provided the party with military and other support (although the support was always short of the CCP's expectations). Indeed, China's gradual movement toward a civil war in 1945–46 occurred in the context of the escalating conflicts between the Soviet Union and the United States. As already argued, the orientation of the CCP's strategies and policies had been strongly influenced by the changes in Soviet and American policies toward East Asia and China. It was because of Stalin's interference that late in August 1945 the CCP leadership made the decision to negotiate with the GMD. Then, however, in September–October 1945 and March 1946, as its confrontation with the United States intensified, Moscow twice changed its policy in the Northeast and became more willing to support the Chinese Communists. The Soviet Red Army's covert and overt support to the Chinese Communist military operations in the Northeast made it feasible for the CCP to confront the GMD nationwide. On the other side, Jiang Jieshi also counted on American support from the beginning, and it was with the assistance of the Americans that the GMD transported large numbers of military forces and equipment to northern and northeastern China. With the escalation of the Cold War, policymakers in Washington found themselves with no other choice but to back Jiang in China's civil war. It is apparent that big-power politics, especially the Soviet-American confrontation, had a profound effect on China's internal development. Therefore, we must regard the conflict between the CCP and the GMD as an integral part of the emerging Cold War in East Asia and in the world; or, as historian Odd Arne Westad puts it, "[T]he civil war in China (1946–1949) originated with the emergence of the Cold War."[96]

Developments in China in 1945–46 were by no means merely negative responses to the international environment or the intensifying Soviet-American confrontation, however. Not only had the policies and strategies of the two superpowers influenced the process and consequences of political change in China, but also, and more relevant from an East Asian perspective, China's political development had influenced and, in a sense, defined the particular shape of the Soviet-American rivalry. Indeed, the most important impact of the intensifying conflict between the CCP and the GMD is that it virtually nullified the Soviet-American Yalta agreement on China and East Asia. While Moscow found in the CCP's struggle against the GMD an instrument to counter American influence in East Asia (especially after the Americans had demonstrated the desire to monopolize the control over Japan), the Americans also used the GMD to counterbalance the impact of the perceived Soviet challenge. During this process, a "CCP-Moscow versus GMD-Washington" alignment along ideological lines—as historian Michael M. Sheng puts it[97]—increasingly became a reality. Consequently, the escalation of the CCP-GMD confrontation exacerbated the conflict between the two superpowers, thus formalizing a Cold War environment in East Asia, as well as in the world.

CHAPTER 2
THE MYTH OF
AMERICA'S LOST
CHANCE IN CHINA

Did there exist any chance in 1949–50 for the Chinese Communist Party and the United States to reach an accommodation or, at least, to avoid a confrontation? Scholars who believe that Washington "lost a chance" to pursue a nonconfrontational relationship with the CCP generally base their argument on two assumptions—that the Chinese Communists earnestly sought U.S. recognition to expedite their country's postwar economic reconstruction, and that the relationship between the CCP and the Soviet Union was vulnerable because of Moscow's failure to offer sufficient support to the Communists during the Chinese civil war. These scholars thus claim that it was Washington's anti-Communist and pro-Guomindang policy that forced the CCP to treat the United States as an enemy.[1] This claim, though ostensibly critical of Washington's management of relations with China, is ironically American-centered on the methodological level, implying that the Chinese Communist policy toward the United States was simply passive reaction to Washington's policy toward China.

This chapter, with insights gained from newly accessible Chinese and, in some places, Russian materials, argues that the CCP's confrontation with the United States reflected the revolutionary essence of the party's perception and management of China's external relations, and that the CCP's alliance with the Soviet Union and confrontation with the United States must be understood in relation to the party's need to enhance the inner dynamics of the Chinese revolution after its nationwide victory. In the environment in which the Chinese Communists and the Americans found themselves in 1948–49, it was next to impossible for the two sides to establish a normal working relationship, let alone for them to reach an accommodation.

"Squeezing the Americans out of the Liberated Zone"

Contrary to the assumptions of the "lost chance" thesis, Chinese materials now available demonstrate that in 1949–50, Mao Zedong and the CCP leadership were unwilling to pursue Western recognition or to establish diplomatic relations with Western countries. This attitude was most clearly demonstrated by the CCP leadership's handling of the Ward case.

In early November 1948, Chinese Communist troops occupied Shenyang (Mukden), the largest city in China's northeast. U.S. consul general Angus Ward, together with his consulate staff, remained in the city after the Communist takeover.[2] In the first two weeks of November, Ward actively pursued establishing official contacts with the new Communist municipal authorities.[3] Local Chinese Communist officials demonstrated some interest in dealing with Ward,[4] but the attitude of the CCP central leadership was intransigent. After a short waiting period, CCP leaders decided to adopt a policy of "squeezing" American and other Western diplomats out of the "liberated zone" in the Northeast, rendering Ward's efforts hopeless. A CCP Central Committee telegram (drafted by Zhou Enlai) to the party's Northeast Bureau on 10 November maintained that because the British, American, and French governments had not recognized Chinese Communist authorities, the CCP in turn would not grant official status to their diplomats either, but would treat them as common foreign residents without diplomatic immunity. The telegram further instructed the Northeast Bureau to take "certain measures" to confine the "freedom of action" of the Western diplomats, so that "they will have to withdraw from Shenyang."[5]

By mid-November, Shenyang's situation had worsened dramatically for Ward and his staff. On 15 November, the Communist Shenyang Municipal Military Control Commission informed "former" British, French, and American consulates in Shenyang that they should hand over their radio transmitters to the commission within thirty-six hours.[6] In reality, this order was particularly targeted at the Americans since the British and French usually relied upon regular Chinese communication services. As it soon turned out, the purpose of this order was to create another excuse for the Communists to force Western diplomats, and the Americans in particular, from the city.[7]

In a few days, when the Americans refused to hand over their radio transmitters, the pressure from the Chinese Communists escalated. On 17 November, Mao Zedong instructed Gao Gang, secretary of the CCP Northeast Bureau, to "act resolutely" to force the British, American, and French diplomats out of Shenyang. The CCP chairman also criticized Zhu Qiwen, the Communist Shenyang mayor, for his unauthorized reception of Ward during the early days after Shenyang's liberation.[8] The next day, Mao authorized the Communists in Shenyang to seize the radio transmitters in the Western consulates and instructed them to isolate the American, British, and French consulates, so that they "would evacuate in the face of difficulties and our purpose of squeezing them out could be reached."[9] On 20 November, when the Americans persistently refused to hand over their radio equipment to Communist authorities, the Communists followed the advice of Soviet representatives in the Northeast and, without advance warning, placed Ward and his staff under house detention.[10] Ward and the other American diplomats were not allowed to leave China until December 1949.[11]

The CCP's challenge to Western presence in Shenyang resulted in part from immediate concerns that Western diplomats might use their radio transmitters to convey military intelligence to the GMD in the ongoing Chinese civil war.[12] The advice from Soviet representatives in Shenyang that the CCP should not permit Western diplomats to remain in the liberated zone also played an important role.[13] Mao, eager to maintain solidarity with Moscow, instructed CCP leaders in the Northeast to inform the Soviets that "in so far as our foreign policy in the Northeast and the whole country is concerned, we will certainly consult with the Soviet Union in order to maintain an identical stand with it."[14]

In a deeper sense, though, the CCP's action against Ward and his staff in Shenyang reflected the party leadership's determination to "make a fresh start" in China's external relations, which required the party to "clean the house before entertaining guests," as well as to "lean to one side" (the side of the Soviet Union).[15] Indeed, these three principles constituted the guidelines of Communist China's early diplomacy. In a telegram to the Northeast Bureau on 23 November 1948, the CCP Central Committee expounded its view that the party would refuse to recognize diplomatic relations between the GMD government and the West.[16] In the Central Committee's "Directive on Diplomatic Affairs," a key CCP foreign policy document issued on 19 January 1949, Mao Zedong declared that "with no exception we will not recognize any of those embassies, legations, and consulates of capitalist countries, as well as the diplomatic establishments and personnel attached to them accredited to the GMD." The directive also made it clear that the CCP would treat American and Soviet diplomats differently since "the foreign policy of the Soviet Union and the other new democratic countries has differed totally from that of the capitalist countries."[17] At the Central Committee's Second Plenary Session in March 1949, the CCP leadership further reached the consensus that the new Chinese Communist regime should neither hastily seek recognition from, nor pursue diplomatic relations with, the United States or other Western countries. "As for the question of the recognition of our country by the imperialist countries," asserted Mao, "we should not be in a hurry to solve it now and need not be in a hurry to solve it even for a fairly long period after nationwide victory."[18] During 1949–50, CCP leaders repeatedly emphasized that the party would go all out to pursue strategic cooperation with the Soviet Union, and that establishing diplomatic relations with the United States or other Western countries was not a priority.[19]

Behind the Huang-Stuart Contacts

After the Chinese Communists occupied Nanjing, the capital of Nationalist China, in late April 1949, John Leighton Stuart, the American ambassador to China, remained in the city. In May and June, Stuart held a series of meetings with Huang Hua, director of the Foreign Affairs Office under the Communist Nanjing Municipal Military Control Commission. They discussed, among other things, conditions under which relations between the CCP and the United States might be established.[20] In the meantime, CCP leaders asserted on several occasions that if Western capitalist countries cut off their connections with the GMD and treated China and the Chinese people as "equals," the CCP would be willing to consider establishing relations with them.[21] Advocates of the "lost chance" thesis have used these exchanges and statements to support their position.

It is true that for a short period in the spring of 1949, Mao and the CCP leadership showed some interest in establishing contacts with the United States. In a telegram to the front-line headquarters of the People's Liberation Army (PLA) on 28 April, Mao mentioned that the Americans were "now contacting us through a third party to inquire into the possibility of establishing diplomatic relations with us." A previously unknown memorandum kept at the Chinese Central Archives indicates that the "third party" was Chen Mingshu, a pro-Communist "democratic figure" who was also a longtime friend of Stuart. On 25 and 26 March, Stuart had two secret meetings with Chen in Shanghai. The American ambassador, according to the memorandum, expressed two major concerns on the part of the United States: "(1) that the CCP might ally with the Soviet Union in a confrontation with the United States . . . , and (2) that the CCP, after unifying China by force, would stop its cooperation with the democratic figures and give up a democratic coalition government." Stuart promised that "if a genuine coalition government committed to peace, independence, democracy and freedom was to be established in China and if the CCP would change its attitude toward the United States by, among other things, stopping the anti-American campaign," the United States would be willing to "maintain friendly relations with the CCP and would provide the new government with assistance in new China's economic recovery and reconstruction."[22]

After receiving Chen Mingshu's report on his meetings with Stuart, Mao and the CCP leadership speculated that the Americans were simply forced to change their position because the old U.S. policy of supporting the GMD had failed. They also asserted that "if the United States (and Great Britain) cut off relations with the GMD, we could consider the question of establishing diplomatic relations with them."[23] As longtime players of the "united front" strategy, Mao and his comrades were determined to stick to their principles, but they would never ignore an opportunity to weaken the threat from enemies and potential enemies.[24] On 30 April, Mao, speaking on behalf of the PLA headquarters, publicly announced that the CCP would be "willing to consider establishing diplomatic relations with foreign countries" if such relations could be placed "on the basis of equality, mutual benefit, mutual respect for sovereignty and territorial integrity and, most importantly, no help being given to the Guomindang reactionaries."[25]

In a telegram dated 10 May 1949, the CCP chairman authorized Huang Hua to contact Stuart, instructing him "to listen more and talk less" in the meeting. In response to the CCP Nanjing Municipal Committee's suggestion of asking "the United States to do more to help the Chinese people" as part of the CCP's conditions to establish relations with the United States, Mao rebutted that this "implied that the U.S. government had done something beneficial for the Chinese people in the past" and that it would "leave the Americans with an impression that the CCP was willing to accept American aid." The chairman particularly ordered Huang Hua to make it clear to Stuart that unless the Americans were willing to sever relations with the GMD regime and to treat China "equally," the Chinese Communists would not consider having relations with the United States.[26]

In retrospect, these two conditions were impossible for the Americans to meet. Cutting off connections with the GMD would require the complete reversal of America's China policy, which had been in place since the end of World War II. And treating the Chinese as "equals" presented the Americans with a profound challenge in a historical-cultural sense. Indeed, reflected in Mao's perception of "equality" was a profound Chinese "victim mentality." When Mao pointed out that Sino-American relations had been dominated by a series of unequal treaties since China's defeat in the Opium War of 1839–42, he revealed a deep-rooted belief that in a moral sense the United States and other Western powers owed the Chinese a heavy historical debt. As the first step toward establishing an equal relationship, he argued, the United States had to end, as well as apologize for, its "unequal" treatment of China. Only when the historical phenomenon of unequal exchanges between China and the West ended would it be possible for the new Chinese Communist regime to establish relations with Western countries. Therefore, Mao's definition of "equality" meant a total negation of America's role in China's modern history and posed a crucial challenge to the existing principles of international relations to which the United States and other Western countries adhered. In Mao's opinion, America's willingness to change its attitude toward China represented a pass-or-fail test for policymakers in Washington; and he simply did not believe that they would pass the test.[27]

Thus, the Huang-Stuart meetings failed to bring the CCP and the United States any closer. Stuart emphasized the legitimacy of American interests in China and tried to convince the Chinese Communists that they had to accept widely recognized international regulations and principles. Huang, on the other hand, stressed that the CCP's two conditions were the prerequisites for any further discussion of establishing relations.[28] Consequently, the more Stuart and Huang Hua negotiated, the wider they found the distance between them and the two political cultures they represented.

Not surprisingly, while the Huang-Stuart contacts were still under way, the CCP dramatically escalated its charges against Ward and his staff. On 19 June 1949, the CCP media alleged that the American consulate in Shenyang had close links with an espionage ring directed by an American "Army Liaison Group." The Xinhua News Agency published a long article about this "espionage case," claiming that "many pieces of captured evidence show clearly that the so-called Consulate General of the United States in Shenyang and the Army Liaison Group are in fact American espionage organizations, whose aim is to utilize Japanese special service as well as Chinese and Mongols in a plot against the Chinese people and the Chinese people's revolutionary cause."[29] On 22 June, Mao instructed the CCP Northeast Bureau not to allow any member of the American consulate in Shenyang to leave the city before the espionage case had been settled.[30] Two days later, the CCP chairman ordered the party's media to use this espionage case to initiate a new wave of anti-American propaganda.[31]

Late in July and early in August, when Stuart, after the failure of his contacts with Huang Hua, returned to the United States and the U.S. State Department published the *China White Paper*, the anti-American propaganda campaign reached its peak. Mao wrote five articles criticizing America's China policy, claiming that, from both historical and current perspectives, the United States was the most dangerous enemy of the Chinese people and the Chinese revolution.[32]

The CCP's "Lean-to-One-Side" Decision

As the CCP's relations with the United States reached an impasse, its dealings with the Soviet Union grew closer. Indeed, new Chinese and Russian evidence reveals that the relationship between the CCP and Moscow in 1949 was much more intimate and substantial than many Western scholars previously realized. While it is true that problems and disagreements (sometimes even serious ones) existed between the Chinese and Soviet Communists, as well as between Mao Zedong and Stalin (as in any partnership), the new evidence clearly points out that cooperation, or the willingness to cooperate, was the dominant aspect of CCP-Soviet relations in 1949.

During China's civil war in 1946–49, the CCP's relations with Moscow were close but not harmonious.[33] When it became clear that the Chinese Communists were going to win the civil war, both the CCP and the Soviet Union felt the need to strengthen their relationship. From late 1947, Mao actively prepared to visit the Soviet Union to "discuss important domestic and international issues" with Stalin.[34] The extensive telegraphic exchanges between Mao and Stalin culminated in two important secret missions in 1949. From 31 January to 7 February, Anastas Mikoyan, a politburo member of the Communist Party of the Soviet Union, visited Xibaipo, the CCP headquarters at that time. Mao and other CCP leaders had extensive discussions with him, introducing to him the CCP's strategies and policies. In particular, Mao explained to Mikoyan the CCP's foreign policy of "making a fresh start" and "cleaning the house before entertaining guests."[35] From late June to mid-August, Liu Shaoqi, the CCP's second in command, visited Moscow. During the visit, Stalin apologized for failing to give sufficient assistance to the CCP during the civil war and promised that the Soviet Union would give the Chinese Communists political support and substantial assistance in military and other areas. Moreover, the Soviets and the Chinese discussed a "division of labor" to promote the world revolution, and they reached a general consensus: the Soviet Union would remain the center of the international proletarian revolution, and promoting revolution in the East would become primarily China's duty. Liu left Moscow in mid-August, accompanied by ninety-six Russian experts who were to assist China's military buildup and economic reconstruction.[36] Mikoyan's mission to China and Liu's visit to Moscow, as the first formal contacts between the CCP leadership and the Soviet Communist leaders in many years, served as two important steps toward cooperation and a new mutual understanding between the CCP and the Soviet Union.[37]

During this period, the CCP frequently exchanged opinions with Moscow on how to evaluate the "American threat" and how to deal with the United

Soviet politburo member Anastas Mikoyan with Mao Zedong in Xibaipo, early February 1949. From left to right, Soviet intelligence officer Doctor Orlov, Mikoyan, Chinese interpreter Shi Zhe, and Mao. Courtesy Shi Zhe personal collection.

States. In November 1948, as discussed previously, the CCP Northeast Bureau accepted Soviet advice to seize the radio transmitters of the American consulate in Shenyang. Early in January 1949, when Jiang Jieshi and the GMD regime started a "peace initiative" to end the civil war, Mao originally intended to rebuff it completely. But Stalin advised Mao and his comrades that the Americans were behind Jiang and that it would better serve the CCP's interests if, instead of simply rebuffing Jiang's proposals, it proposed its own conditions for ending the war through nonmilitary means (Stalin emphasized that the CCP should make these conditions unacceptable to Jiang). After a few exchanges, Mao Zedong "completely agreed with" Stalin's opinions and acted accordingly.[38] In the spring of 1949, Stalin warned the CCP about possible American landing operations in the People's Liberation Army's rear, convincing the CCP leadership to maintain a strategic reserve force in northern coastal China while the PLA's main force was engaged in the campaign of crossing the Yangzi River.[39] During Liu Shaoqi's visit to the Soviet Union in June–August 1949, the CCP presented to Stalin a detailed memorandum, summarizing the party's domestic and, particularly, international policies (including the policy toward the United States).[40]

Particularly revealing are Mao's communications with Stalin on how the CCP should handle Huang Hua's contacts with Stuart. After receiving Chen Mingshu's report about his secret meetings with Stuart in Shanghai, the CCP immediately informed Moscow of the contact.[41] Mao Zedong met with I. V. Kovalev, Stalin's representative to China, on 9 April 1949, asking him to report to Stalin that the CCP was preparing to make minor adjustments in its foreign policy by conducting some "limited contacts" with Western capitalist countries, including the United States. But Mao also promised that the CCP would not formalize these contacts; nor would it legalize the relationship emerging from them. On 19 April, Stalin instructed Kovalev to advise Mao: "(1) We believe that China's democratic government should not refuse to establish formal relations with capitalist countries, including the United States, provided that these countries formally abandon military, economic, and political support to Jiang and the GMD government . . . and (2) We believe that, under some conditions, [the CCP] should not refuse to accept foreign loans or to do business with capitalist countries."[42] During the Huang-Stuart meetings, Mao informed Stalin about the substance of the meetings, emphasizing that "it is unfavorable that the embassies of the United States and other [capitalist] countries remain in Nanjing, and we will be happy to see that the embassies of all capitalist countries get out of China." Stalin, while expressing his gratitude to Mao for informing him about the meetings, advised him that for tactical considerations, "we do not think this is the proper time for the Soviet Union and Democratic China to demonstrate extensively the friendship between them."[43]

One may argue that when Mao informed Stalin of the contacts between the CCP and the United States, he might have been trying to pressure Stalin to strengthen the Soviet Union's support to the CCP. But this interpretation cannot explain the extensive and substantive exchanges between the two Communist leaders concerning CCP-U.S. contacts. Judging from the contents of the Mao-Stalin exchanges, it is more logical to regard them as a means for the two countries to reinforce the foundation of their relationship. From a Chinese perspective, the CCP's "lean-to-one-side" policy was more than lip service.

America's "Lost Chance" in China Is a Myth

There is no doubt that Washington's continuous support of the GMD during China's civil war played an important role in the CCP's adoption of an anti-

American policy. But America's pro-Jiang policy alone does not offer a comprehensive explanation of the origins of the CCP-American crisis. In order to comprehend the CCP's policy toward the United States, we must explore the historical-cultural environment in which it emerged, thus revealing the dynamics and logic underlying it.

The Chinese Communist revolution emerged in a land that was historically known as the Central Kingdom.[44] The Chinese during traditional times viewed China as civilization in toto. In modern times, this worldview had been severely challenged when China had to face the cruel reality that its door was opened by the superior forces of Western powers, and that the very survival of the Chinese nation was at stake. Mao's and his comrades' generation became indignant when they saw the West, including the United States, treat the "old," declining China with arrogance and a strong sense of superiority. They also despised the Chinese governments from the Manchu dynasty to the regimes of the warlords, which had failed to protect China's national integrity and sovereignty. An emotional commitment to national liberation provided the crucial momentum in Mao's and his comrades' choice of a Marxist-Leninist-style revolution.[45] For Mao and his comrades, the final goal of their revolution was not only the total transformation of the old Chinese state and society they saw as corrupt and unjust; they also wanted to change China's weak power status, proving to the world the strength and influence of Chinese culture. In the process, they would redefine the values and rules underlying the international system. In short, they wanted to restore China's *central* position in the international community.

Mao and his comrades never regarded the Communist seizure of power in China in 1949 as the revolution's conclusion. Rather, Mao was very much concerned about how to maintain and enhance the revolution's momentum after its nationwide victory. Indeed, this concern dominated Mao's thinking during the formation of the People's Republic and would be a preoccupation during the latter half of his life.[46] Consequently, Mao's approach toward China's external relations in general and his policy toward the United States in particular became heavily influenced by this primary concern. Throughout 1949–50, the Maoist political discourse challenged the values and codes of behavior attached to "U.S. imperialism," pointing out that they belonged to the "old world," which the CCP was determined to destroy. While defining the "American threat," Mao and his fellow CCP leaders never limited their vision merely to the possibility of direct American military intervention in China; they emphasized long-range American hostility toward the victorious Chinese revolution, especially the U.S. imperialist attempt to isolate the revolution from without and sabotage it from within.⁴⁷ Indeed, when Mao justified the CCP's decision not to pursue relations with the United States, his most consistent and powerful argument was that the decision would deprive the Americans of a means of sabotaging the Chinese revolution.⁴⁸

It is also important to point out that while Washington's hostility toward the Chinese revolution offended Mao and his comrades, the perceived American disdain for China as weak and the Chinese as inferior made them angry. In the anti-American propaganda campaign following the publication of the *China White Paper*, Mao sought to expose the "reactionary" and "vulnerable" nature of U.S. imperialism and to encourage ordinary Chinese people's national self-respect. In other words, Mao used anti-American discourse as a means of mobilizing the masses for his continuous revolution, a practice that would reach its first peak in 1950–53, during the "Great War of Resisting America and Assisting Korea" (the Chinese name for China's participation in the Korean War).⁴⁹

The CCP's adoption of an anti-American policy in 1949–50 had deep roots in both China's history and its modern experiences. Sharp divergences in political ideology (communism versus capitalism) and perceived national interests contributed to the shaping of the Sino-American confrontation; and suspicion and hostility were further crystallized as the result of Washington's continuous support to the GMD and the CCP's handling of events such as the Ward case. But, from a Chinese perspective, the most profound reason underlying the CCP's anti-American policy was Mao's grand plans for transforming China's state, society, and international outlook. Even though it might have been possible for Washington to change the concrete course of its China policy (which was highly unlikely given the policy's complicated background), it would have been impossible for the United States to alter the course and goals of the Chinese revolution, let alone the historical-cultural environment that gave birth to the event. America's "lost chance" in China must therefore be regarded as a myth.

CHAPTER 3
MAO'S CONTINUOUS REVOLUTION
AND THE RISE AND DEMISE OF THE
SINO-SOVIET ALLIANCE, 1949–1963

Fluttering high are the banners of victory,
shaking the earth and mountain is the singing of millions;
Mao Zedong–Stalin,
like the sun(s) shining in the heaven.
— "Song of Sino-Soviet Solidarity"

Never are there two suns in the heaven,
Never should there be two emperors on the earth.
—Age-old Chinese proverb

No other event during the Cold War contributed more to changes in
perceptions of the Communist powers than the rise and demise of the Sino-
Soviet alliance. Emerging in the late 1940s and early 1950s, the "brotherly
solidarity" between the People's Republic of China and the Soviet Union was
claimed to be "unbreakable" and "eternal." But by the latter part of the decade, serious disputes began to develop between Chinese and Soviet leaders,
causing the alliance to crumble and then, in the mid-1960s, to collapse. In the
years that followed, the hostility between the two countries grew so intense
that it led to a bloody border war in 1969.[1] In the 1960s and 1970s, the complete break in the two Communist giants' alliance became a basic element of
international affairs.

What, then, were the causes underlying the rise and demise of the Sino-
Soviet alliance? Scholars may answer this question in many ways. This chapter
adopts a domestic-politics-centered approach. Without ignoring the merits of
other interpretations, especially those emphasizing the role played by China's
security concerns and international ideological commitments, this chapter argues that China's alliance policy toward the Soviet Union was *always* an integral part of Mao Zedong's grand continuous revolution plans designed to
transform China's state, society, and international outlook. While security

concerns and socialist internationalism conditioned the rise and fall of the alliance, it was Mao's efforts to define and redefine the mission and scope of his continuous revolution—which constituted the central theme of Chinese politics during his era (1949 to 1976)—that had shaped Beijing's attitude toward China's alliance with the Soviet Union.

The "Lean-to-One-Side" Approach

On 30 June 1949, Mao Zedong issued his famous "lean-to-one-side" statement. In a long article titled "On People's Democratic Dictatorship," he announced Communist China's special relationship with the Soviet Union. He said that revolutionary China must "unite in a common struggle with those nations of the world that treat us as equal and unite with the peoples of all countries—that is, ally ourselves with the Soviet Union, with the People's Democratic Countries, and with the proletariat and the broad masses of the people in all other countries, and form an international united front. . . . We must lean to one side."[2]

Why did Mao choose these extraordinary terms? The statement was obviously linked to the longtime revolutionary policy of the Chinese Communist Party of attaching itself to the international "progressive forces" led by the Soviet Union. By the late 1940s, CCP leaders clearly perceived the postwar world as divided into two camps, one headed by the Soviet Union and the other by the United States, and regarded their revolution as a part of the Soviet-led international proletarian movement.[3] It is apparent that Mao's statement was consistent with this view of the postwar world structure.

The lean-to-one-side approach also grew out of the CCP's assessment of the serious nature of the threat from Western imperialist countries, especially from the United States, to the completion of the Chinese revolution. As the CCP neared final victory in China's civil war in 1949, Mao and his fellow Chinese Communist leaders became very much concerned about the prospect of direct U.S. intervention in China.[4] Although the American military did not intervene directly during the latter phase of the civil war, the CCP chairman and his comrades, given their belief in the aggressive and evil nature of Western imperialism, continued to view the Western capitalist countries in general and the United States in particular as dangerous enemies.[5] In the eyes of Mao and his comrades, "it was the possibility of military intervention from imperialist countries that made it necessary for China to ally itself with other socialist countries."[6]

Mao's lean-to-one-side decision cannot be viewed in terms of these ideological commitments and security concerns only, though. It also must be understood in the context of his determination to maintain and enhance the inner dynamics of the Chinese Communist revolution at the time of its nationwide victory. The final goal of Mao's Chinese revolution, as the CCP chairman himself repeatedly emphasized, was the transformation of China's "old" state and society and the destruction of the "old" world in which, as Mao and his comrades viewed it, China had been a humiliated member during modern times. Mao never concealed his ambition that his revolution would finally turn China into a land of universal justice and equality, and that, simultaneously, through presenting the experience of the Chinese revolution as a model for other "oppressed nations" in the world, China would reestablish its central position in the international community.[7]

In 1949, when the Chinese Communist revolution approached nationwide victory, Mao and his comrades understood that the new China would have to meet such challenges as establishing and consolidating a new revolutionary regime and reviving China's war-worn economy. But what concerned the CCP chairman the most was how to prevent the revolution from losing its momentum. In his 1949 New Year's message, the CCP chairman called upon his party "to carry the revolution through to the end," by which he meant not only the thorough destruction of the Guomindang regime but also the promotion of the revolution toward its higher, post-takeover stage.[8] Throughout 1949 Mao repeatedly warned against imperialist plots to sabotage the revolution from within either using the "sugar-coated bullet" to shoot down the weak-willed Communists or dividing the revolutionary camp by applying the "doctrine of means" to confuse the distinction between revolution and counterrevolution.[9] He stressed that "after the destruction of the enemies with guns, the enemies without guns are still there, and they are bound to struggle desperately against us." The CCP chairman therefore warned his party: "If we fail to pay enough attention to these problems, if we do not know how to wage the struggle against them and win victory in the struggle, we shall be unable to maintain our political power, we shall be unable to stand on our feet, we shall fail."[10]

It was primarily for the purpose of creating new momentum for the Chinese revolution that the CCP leadership made three fundamental decisions on Communist China's external relations, what Zhou Enlai referred to as "making a fresh start," "cleaning the house before entertaining guests," and "leaning to one side."[11] These three decisions were closely interconnected. While the first two represented CCP leaders' determination not to be influenced by the legacy of "old" China's diplomatic practice, the last one reflected their conviction that an alliance with the Soviet Union would help destroy any remaining illusions among the Chinese people, especially the intellectuals, of the utility of assistance from Western capitalist countries. Because the Soviet Union had been the first socialist country in the world and had established the only example for building a socialist state and society, Mao's continuous revolution had to follow the example of the Soviet experience. In this regard, the argument of Zhang Baijia, a leading Chinese scholar in Chinese diplomatic history, certainly makes good sense: "Contrary to the prevalent view, Mao treated the 'lean-to-one-side' concept as a grand strategy to influence the party's foreign *and* domestic policies. The key question Mao tried to answer by introducing the lean-to-one-side approach was how to define the *general* direction of New China's development." [12]

Not surprisingly, despite the tortuous development of the CCP-Soviet relations during the course of the Chinese revolution, Mao and the CCP leadership made genuine efforts to strengthen their relations with Moscow when the party was winning China's civil war. For example, as discussed in Chapter 2, Anastas Mikoyan made a secret trip to Xibaipo in early 1949 and Liu Shaoqi met with Stalin in Moscow in the summer of 1949. The Chinese Communist efforts to achieve a strategic alliance with the Soviet Union culminated in December 1949–February 1950 when Mao personally visited the Soviet Union. The CCP chairman's experience during the visit, however, was uneasy. During his first meeting with Stalin on 16 December, the Soviet leader asked him what he hoped to achieve from the visit. The CCP chairman, according to his interpreter's recollections, first replied that he wanted to "bring about something that not only looked nice but also tasted delicious"—a reference to his wish to sign a new Sino-Soviet treaty. [13] However, Stalin greatly disappointed Mao by initially emphasizing that it was neither in Moscow's nor in Beijing's interest to abolish the 1945 Sino-Soviet treaty the Soviet Union had signed with the GMD. [14] Mao's visit then hit a deadlock for almost three weeks before the Soviets relented. [15] Chinese premier Zhou Enlai arrived in Moscow on 20 January to negotiate the details of the new alliance treaty, which was signed finally on 14 February 1950. The Chinese, however, had to agree to allow the Soviets to maintain their privileges in China's Northeast and Xinjiang; [16] in exchange, the Soviets agreed to increase military and other material support to China, including providing air-defense installations in coastal areas of the People's Republic. [17]

Mao must have had mixed feelings when he left Moscow to return to China. On the one hand, he had reasons to celebrate the signing of the Sino-Soviet alliance treaty. The alliance would greatly enhance the PRC's security, and, more important, it would expand the CCP's capacity to promote the post-

Joseph Stalin (center) *and Mao Zedong at the celebration rally for Stalin's seventieth birthday, Moscow, 21 December 1949. At the far left is Chinese interpreter Shi Zhe. Courtesy Shi Zhe personal collection.*

victory revolution at home. With the backing of the Soviet Union, Mao and his comrades would occupy a more powerful position to wipe out the political, economic, social, and cultural legacies of the "old" China and carry out "new" China's state-building and societal transformation on the CCP's terms. It was not just rhetoric when the CCP chairman, after returning to Beijing, told his comrades that the Sino-Soviet alliance would help the party cope with both domestic and international threats to the Chinese revolution.[18]

On the other hand, however, Mao could clearly sense that divergences persisted between Stalin and himself. Stalin's raw use of the language of power put off Mao. Mao's wish to discuss revolutionary ideals and the Communists' historical responsibilities came to nothing. The CCP chairman never enjoyed meeting Stalin face to face, and he was extremely sensitive to the way Stalin treated him, the revolutionary leader from the Central Kingdom, as the inferior "younger brother."[19] The Sino-Soviet treaty made the lean-to-one-side approach the cornerstone of China's external relations, yet, because of the way the agreement was designed, the future development of Sino-Soviet relations was bound to be rocky.

The Alliance and China's Korean War Experience

The first major test for the Sino-Soviet alliance came just eight months after it had been established, when, in October 1950, the CCP leadership decided to dispatch Chinese troops to enter the Korean War. From Beijing's perspective, such a test not only allowed Mao and his comrades to define more specifically the alliance's utility for China's national security; it also provided them with a valuable opportunity to achieve a better understanding of how the alliance would serve Mao's revolutionary projects. China's Korean War experience, consequently, would profoundly influence both Mao's concerns about the prospect of the Chinese revolution and the future development of the Sino-Soviet alliance.

The Korean War, as revealed by new Russian and Chinese sources, was, first of all, North Korean leader Kim Il-sung's war, which he initiated on the basis of his judgment (or misjudgment) of the revolutionary situation existing on the Korean peninsula.[20] Stalin initially feared that such a war could result in direct military conflict between the Soviet Union and the United States, and he did not endorse Kim's plans of unifying his country by military means. At the end of January 1950, however, U.S. secretary of state Dean Acheson's statement indicating that Korea would be excluded from America's western Pacific defense perimeter appears to have convinced him that direct U.S. military intervention in the peninsula was unlikely.[21] In the months prior to the outbreak of the Korean War, the Soviet Union provided large amounts of military aid to the Korean Communists, but Stalin never made the commitment to use Soviet military forces in Korea, and he insisted that Kim travel to Beijing to consult with Mao Zedong, so that the Chinese Communists would share responsibility for Kim's war preparations.[22]

Mao and the CCP leadership faced a dilemma on the Korean issue. Mao and his comrades were reluctant to see a war break out in Korea because they worried that that might complicate the situation in East Asia and jeopardize the CCP's effort to liberate Taiwan, which was still occupied by Nationalist forces.[23] Yet, because Mao and his comrades were eager to revive China's central position on the international scene through supporting revolutionary movements in other countries (especially in East Asia), and because profound historical connections existed between the Chinese and North Korean Communists, it would have been inconceivable for Mao to veto Kim's plans to unify his country through a revolutionary war.[24] From 1949 to 1950, in meetings with North Korean leaders (including Kim Il-sung in mid-May 1950), Mao made it clear that the CCP supported the Korean revolution but hoped that the Koreans would not initiate the invasion of the South until the PLA had seized Taiwan.[25] In the meantime, during Mao's 1949–50 visit to the Soviet Union, the CCP chairman shared with Stalin his belief that it was unlikely for the United States to involve itself in a revolutionary civil war in East Asia, thus enhancing Stalin's determination to back Kim's plans to attack the South.[26] Furthermore, from summer 1949 to spring 1950, the Chinese sent 50,000 to 70,000 ethnic Korean PLA soldiers (with weapons) back to Korea.[27] As a result, Mao virtually gave Kim's plan a green light.

The Korean War erupted on 25 June 1950, and U.S. president Harry Truman promptly decided to come to the rescue of Syngman Rhee's South Korean regime and to dispatch the Seventh Fleet to "neutralize" the Taiwan Strait, a decision that turned the Korean War into an international crisis. Chinese leaders quickly decided to postpone the invasion of Taiwan and to focus on dealing with the crisis in Korea.[28] On 13 July the CCP leadership formally established the Northeast Border Defense Army (NEBDA), assigning it with the task of preparing for military intervention in Korea in the event that the war turned against North Korea.[29] On 18 August, after over a quarter million Chinese troops had taken up positions along the Chinese-Korean border, Mao set the end of September as the deadline for these troops to complete preparations for military operations in Korea.[30]

Beijing based its handling of the Korean crisis on the assumption that if China entered the Korean War, the Soviet Union would honor its obligations in accordance with the Sino-Soviet alliance treaty and provide China with all kinds of support, including supplies of ammunition, military equipment, and air cover for Chinese land forces. Early in July, when the Chinese leaders informed Stalin of the decision to establish the NEBDA, Stalin supported the plan and promised that if the Chinese troops were to fight in Korea, the Soviet Union would "try to provide air cover for these units."[31] In the following weeks the Soviets accelerated military deliveries to China, and a Soviet air force division, with 122 MiG-15 fighters, entered China's Northeast to help with air defense there.[32] These developments must have enhanced Beijing's belief that if China entered the Korean War, the Soviets would provide them with substantial military support.

When the course of the war reversed after U.S. troops landed at Inchon on 15 September, however, Stalin's attitude regarding Soviet military assistance changed. He became more determined than ever to avoid a direct military confrontation with the United States. In a telegram to Chinese leaders dated 1 October, Stalin pointed out that the situation in Korea was grave and that without outside support, the Korean Communist regime would collapse. He then asked the Chinese to dispatch their troops to Korea. It is noticeable, however, that he did not mention what support the Soviet Union would offer China, let alone touch on the key question of Soviet air support.[33]

At this moment, serious differences in opinions already existed among top

Chinese leaders on whether or not China should enter the war. Mao favored dispatching troops to Korea, and on 2 October he personally drafted a long telegram to respond to Stalin's request, informing Stalin that the Chinese leadership had decided "to send a portion of our troops, under the name of [Chinese People's] Volunteers, to Korea, assisting the Korean comrades to fight the troops of the United States and its running dog Syngman Rhee." Mao summarized the reasons for this decision, emphasizing that even though China's intervention might cause a war between China and the United States, it was necessary for the sake of the Korean and Eastern revolutions. Mao also made it clear that in order to defeat the American troops in Korea, China needed substantial Soviet military support.[34] He used plain language to ask Stalin to clarify "whether or not the Soviet Union can provide us with assistance in supplying weapons, can dispatch a volunteer air force into Korea, and can deploy large numbers of air force units to assist us in strengthening our air defense in Beijing, Tianjin, Shenyang, Shanghai, and Nanjing if the United States uses its air force to bombard these places."[35]

Mao, however, apparently did not dispatch this telegram, probably because the opinions among top CCP leaders were yet to be unified and he also realized the need to bargain with Stalin on the Soviet air support issue.[36] According to Russian sources, Mao met with Nikolai Rochshin, the Soviet ambassador to China, later on 2 October, informing him that because dispatching Chinese troops to Korea "may entail extremely serious consequences," including "provoking an open conflict between the United States and China," many leaders in Beijing believed that China should "show caution" in entering the Korean War. Mao told Stalin that the Chinese leadership had not decided whether to send troops to Korea.[37]

Over the ensuing two weeks, the Sino-Soviet alliance underwent a major test. Before 7 October (when Stalin informed Kim of Mao's communication), the Soviet leader cabled the Chinese leadership, advising Beijing that for the sake of China's security interests as well as the interests of the world proletarian revolution, it was necessary for China to send troops to Korea. Indeed, Stalin even introduced a thesis that may be called the Communist version of the domino theory, warning Mao and his comrades that Beijing's failure to intervene could result in grave consequences first for China's Northeast, then for all China, and then for the entire world revolution. Ironically, Stalin again failed to mention how the Soviet Union would support China if Chinese troops did enter operations in Korea.[38]

By 7 October, Chinese leaders had already made the decision to enter the war. From 3 to 6 October the CCP leadership held a series of strictly secret

菲里波夫同志：

十月一日来电收到了。兹将我们的意见答复如下：（一）我们决定用志愿军名义派一部分军队至朝鲜境内和美国及其走狗李承晚的军队作战，援助朝鲜同志。我们认为我们应当这样做。因为如果让整个朝鲜被美国人占去，朝鲜革命力量受到根本的失败，则美国侵略者将更为猖獗，于整个东方都是不利的。（二）我们既然决定出动中国军队到朝鲜和美国人作战，第一，就要能解决问题，即要准备在朝鲜境内歼灭和驱逐美国及其他国家的侵略军；第二，既然中国军队在朝鲜境内和美国军队打起来，……

……的时候，是否可以用空军帮助我们防御上述诸地……，另以告复。敬祝健好！

毛泽东
一九五〇年十月二日

meetings to discuss the Korean issue. Although most CCP leaders had opposed, or at least had reservations about, entering the war in Korea, Mao used both his authority and his political insights to secure the support of his colleagues for the decision to go to war.[39] On 8 October Mao Zedong formally issued the order to establish the Chinese People's Volunteers (CPV), with Peng Dehuai as the commander,[40] and informed Kim Il-sung of the decision the same evening.[41]

In order to strengthen China's bargaining position in pursuing Soviet military support, Mao found it necessary to "play tough with" Stalin.[42] On 10–11 October, Zhou Enlai met with Stalin at the latter's villa on the Black Sea. Zhou, according to Shi Zhe, Mao's and Zhou's Russian-language interpreter, did not tell Stalin that China had decided to send troops to Korea but persistently brought the discussion around to Soviet military aid, especially air support, for China. Stalin finally agreed to provide China with substantial military support but explained that it was impossible for the Soviet air force to engage in fighting over Korea until two to two and a half months after Chinese land forces entered operations there.[43]

Stalin's ambiguous attitude forced Mao again to order Chinese troops to halt preparations for entering operations in Korea on 12 October.[44] The next day the CCP politburo met again to discuss China's entry into the Korean War. Pushed by Mao, the politburo confirmed that entering the war was in the fundamental interests of the Chinese revolution as well as the Eastern revolution.[45] Mao then authorized Zhou Enlai, who was still in Moscow, to inform Stalin of the decision. At the same time, Mao instructed Zhou to continue to "consult with" the Soviet leaders, to clarify whether they would ask China to lease or to purchase the military equipment that Stalin agreed to provide, and whether the Soviet air force would enter operations in Korea at all.[46]

On 17 October, the day Zhou returned to Beijing, Mao again ordered the troops on the Chinese-Korean border to halt their movements to give him time to learn from Zhou about Stalin's exact position.[47] The next day, when Mao was convinced that the Soviet Union would provide China with all kinds of military support, including air defense for major Chinese cities and air cover for Chinese troops fighting in Korea in a later stage of the war, he finally ordered Chinese troops to enter the Korean War.[48]

The concerns over China's physical security certainly played an important role in convincing Beijing's leaders to enter the war. Yet factors more complicated than these narrowly defined "security concerns" dominated Mao's conceptual world. When Chinese troops entered the Korean War, Mao meant to pursue a glorious victory over the American-led United Nations (UN) forces.

The triumph, he hoped, would transform the challenge and threat posed by the Korean crisis into added political energy for securing Communist control of China's state and society as well as promote the international prestige and influence of the People's Republic.

These plans explain why, at the same time Mao and his comrades were considering entering the Korean War, the CCP leadership started the "Great Movement to Resist America and Assist Korea," with "beating American arrogance" as its central slogan. The party used every means available to stir the "hatred of the U.S. imperialists" among common Chinese, emphasizing that the United States had long engaged in political and economic aggression against China, that the declining capitalist America was not as powerful as it seemed, and that a confrontation between China and the United States was inevitable.[49] When the Chinese troops were crossing the Yalu River to Korea late in October 1950, a nationwide campaign aimed at suppressing "reactionaries and reactionary activities" emerged in China's cities and countryside.[50] All of these developments must be understood as part of Mao's efforts to mobilize the Chinese population to promote his grand programs for carrying on the Chinese revolution.

Mao's already ambivalent feelings toward Stalin must have been even more uncertain during the first three weeks of October. If Mao intended to use the Korean crisis as a new source of domestic political mobilization, it would follow that he would have welcomed Stalin's constant push for China to enter the war as well as his promise, however late, to provide China with ammunition, military equipment, and eventual air cover. In turn, Mao would be in a prime position to persuade the party leadership to approve his decision to enter the war. But Stalin's behavior of always putting Moscow's own interests ahead of anything else demonstrated to Mao the limits of the Soviet leader's proletarian internationalism. Meanwhile, Mao's decision to rescue the Korean and Eastern revolution at a time of real difficulties inevitably heightened the CCP chairman's sense of moral superiority—he was able to help others out, even if the Soviet "elder brother" could not. As a result, in conceptual and psychological terms, the seed for the future Sino-Soviet split was sown.

During the three years of China's intervention in Korea, the practical aspect of the relationship between Beijing and Moscow intensified. Mao consulted with Stalin on almost all important decisions. In December 1950 and January 1951, when Mao and his comrades were deciding to order Chinese troops to cross the 38th parallel, Beijing maintained daily communication with Moscow and received Stalin's unfailing support.[51] In May–June 1951, when Beijing's leaders were considering shifting their policy emphasis from fighting to negotiation to end the war, they had extensive exchanges of opinions with Stalin and did not make the decision until Moscow fully backed the new strategy.[52] After 1952, when the armistice negotiations at Panmunjom hit a deadlock on the prisoner-of-war issue, Beijing consulted with Moscow and concluded that the Chinese/North Korean side would not compromise on this issue until its political and military position had improved.[53]

As far as the foundation of the Sino-Soviet alliance was concerned, Mao's decision to send Chinese troops to Korea seemed to have boosted Stalin's confidence in his comrades in Beijing as genuine proletarian internationalists. During the war years, the Soviet Union provided China with large amounts of ammunition and military equipment. Units of the Soviet air force, based in Manchuria, began to defend the transportation lines across the Chinese-Korean border as early as November 1950 and entered operations over the northern part of North Korea in January 1951.[54] In the meantime, Stalin became more willing to commit Soviet financial and technological resources to China's economic reconstruction—during the war years, as a consequence, the Soviet Union's share in China's foreign trade increased from 30 percent (in 1950) to 56.3 percent (in 1953).[55] In retrospect, it would have been virtually impossible for China to have fought the Korean War without the strategic alliance with the Soviet Union.

Soviet support also played a crucial role in bolstering Mao's plans for continuing the revolution at home. Indeed, China's involvement in the Korean War stimulated a series of political and social transformations in the country that would have been inconceivable during the early stage of the new republic. In the wake of China's entrance into the war, the Communist regime found itself in a powerful position to penetrate almost every area of Chinese society through intensive mass mobilization under the banner of "Resisting America and Assisting Korea."[56] During the three years of war, three nationwide campaigns swept through China's countryside and cities: the movement to suppress counterrevolutionaries, the land reform movement, and the "Three Antis" and "Five Antis" movements.[57] When the war ended in July 1953, China's society and political landscape had been altered: organized resistance to the new regime had been destroyed; land in the countryside had been redistributed and the landlord class had been eliminated; many of the Communist cadres whom Mao believed had lost the revolutionary momentum had been either "reeducated" or removed from leading positions; and the national bourgeoisie was under the tight control of the Communist state and the "petit-bourgeoise" intellectuals had experienced the first round of Communist reeducation. Consequently, the CCP effectively extended and deepened its organizational control of Chinese society and dramatically promoted its authority and legitimacy in the minds of the Chinese people.

These domestic changes were further facilitated by the fact that during the war, Chinese troops successfully forced the U.S./UN forces to retreat from the Chinese-Korean border to the 38th parallel, a development that allowed Beijing to call its intervention in Korea a great victory. Mao and his comrades believed that they had won a powerful position from which to claim that international society—friends and foes alike—had to accept China as a Great Power.[58] This position, in turn, would allow Mao, as the mastermind of the war decision, to enjoy political power inside China with far fewer checks and balances than before. His view of China's international victory in Korea made him more confident and enthusiastic to undertake a series of new steps to transform China. Mao had good reason to be thankful for the Sino-Soviet alliance during the Korean crisis.

Yet, on another level, the Chinese experience during the Korean War also ground away at some of the cement that kept the Sino-Soviet alliance together. The extreme pragmatism Stalin had demonstrated in his management of the Korean crisis, especially in his failure to commit Soviet air support to China during the key weeks of October 1950, revealed the superficial nature of the Soviet dictator's proletarian internationalism. What really offended Mao and his comrades, however, was the Soviet request that China pay for much of the military support Beijing had received during the war, which added to China's long-term economic challenges.[59] To the Chinese, Stalin's stinginess made the Soviets seem more like arms merchants than genuine Communist internationalists.

Consequently, although China's Korean War experience made Beijing more dependent on Moscow, psychologically Stalin's attitude bolstered Mao's and his fellow Chinese leaders' sense of moral superiority in relation to their Soviet comrades. Stalin's death in March 1953 further hardened this feeling. As will be discussed later, this subtle change in Mao's and his comrades' perception of themselves and their comrades in Moscow would leave a critical stamp upon the fate of the Sino-Soviet alliance.

The Alliance's Golden Years

For a period of several years immediately after Stalin's death, Sino-Soviet cooperation developed smoothly. The Soviets offered the Chinese substantial support to assist the PRC's economic reconstruction, as well as to promote its international status. From 29 September to 12 October 1954, Nikita Khrushchev, the first secretary of the Communist Party of the Soviet Union

(CPSU), led a top-level Soviet delegation to visit China to participate in the PRC's fifth anniversary celebrations. During this visit, the Soviets signed a series of agreements with the Chinese. They agreed to return to China Soviet military bases in Lüshun (Port Arthur), together with its equipment, to give up Soviet shares in four Sino-Soviet joint ventures,[60] and to provide China with loans totaling 520 million rubles. In addition, they offered technological support to China in initiating or upgrading 156 key industrial projects for the PRC's first five-year plan.[61] In April 1955 the Soviet Union and China signed an agreement under which Moscow provided Beijing with nuclear technology, purportedly for peaceful purposes.[62] It appeared that Khrushchev and the new Soviet leadership were willing to establish a more productive and cooperative relationship with their Chinese comrades.[63]

Chinese leaders in Beijing also demonstrated solidarity with Khrushchev and the new Soviet leadership on a number of important domestic and international issues. When the Soviet leaders made the decision to purge Lavrenty Beria, Stalin's chief of the secret police, and when Khrushchev became the CPSU's first secretary, the CCP leadership quickly offered its approval. In the meantime, on pivotal Soviet foreign policy decisions such as the formation of the Warsaw Pact Organization, the establishment of diplomatic relations between the Soviet Union and West Germany, the signing of a peace treaty with Austria, and the improvement of relations with Yugoslavia, Beijing provided Moscow with timely and firm support.[64]

On important international issues, Chinese and Soviet leaders carefully consulted with each other to coordinate their strategies and policies. A revealing example in this regard was Beijing's and Moscow's management of the Geneva Conference of 1954. Before the conference, Zhou Enlai twice visited Moscow to hold a series of meetings with Soviet leaders, which resulted in well-coordinated Sino-Soviet strategies toward the Korean and the Indochina questions that were to be discussed at the conference.[65] At Geneva, the Chinese and the Soviet delegations exchanged opinions and intelligence information on a daily basis. When the Vietnamese Communists hesitated before accepting the temporary division of their country along the 17th parallel, both the Chinese and the Soviets pressured the Vietnamese, convincing them that such a solution was in the interests of both the Vietnamese revolution and the cause of world peace. In this sense it is fair to say that the conference's settlement of the Indochina issue should be attributed to the cooperation between Zhou Enlai and Vyacheslav Molotov.[66] The 1954–55 period shined as a golden age of the Sino-Soviet alliance.

The continuous enhancement of the alliance during this period reflected, to some degree, Moscow's and Beijing's coinciding strategic concerns. From a Soviet perspective, these were the years that Khrushchev and his colleagues slowly began to rid themselves of Stalin's shadow. Khrushchev, who had just emerged as the top Soviet leader and needed time to consolidate his leadership role, certainly understood that the support from China was indispensable to him.[67]

Beijing, on the other hand, also needed Moscow's assistance. The CCP leadership was adjusting China's internal and external policies after the end of the Korean War. Domestically, in 1953–54 the Central Committee was contemplating the introduction of the first five-year plan as well as liberating the Nationalist-controlled Taiwan either by peaceful or, if necessary, by military means.[68] After five years of being excluded from the international community, Beijing's leaders (including Mao at that time) were eager to escape China's isolation.[69] Under these circumstances, especially considering that China's socialist reconstruction had to be modeled after the Soviet example, political, military, and economic support from the Soviet Union became highly valuable. In other words, the specific needs of Mao's continuous revolution at this stage were well served by the Sino-Soviet alliance.

A vague undercurrent of disagreement and distrust, however, lingered between Chinese and Soviet leaders. Even during the heyday of Sino-Soviet solidarity, Mao and his comrades were never comfortable with the junior partner's role they had to play in China's relations with the Soviet Union. As they would explain later, Mao and his comrades felt a deep sense of inequality in their dealings with the Soviets, and particularly with Stalin. Making Beijing a real equal partner with Moscow was the constant aim of Mao and his fellow Beijing leaders.[70] After Stalin's death, as we shall see, Beijing's pursuit of an elusive "equality" would eventually cause friction with the new Soviet leadership.[71]

Related to the Chinese discomfort over "inequality" were the potential tensions between Moscow's dominance in the international Communist movement and Beijing's aspiration for recognition as a central part of the "world revolution." Such international recognition would, among other things, further legitimate Mao's plans for bringing the Chinese revolution to deeper levels. When Stalin was alive, Mao and his comrades had to respect his authority and yield to his reputation; with Stalin gone, Mao became increasingly reluctant to acknowledge the authority of Stalin's much younger and, in Mao's eyes, less sophisticated successor, Nikita Khrushchev.

One outstanding example of the problems existing between Beijing and Moscow during this time can be found in Mao's management of the Gao Gang affair. Gao was a CCP politburo member and the vice chairman of the PRC Central People's Government. Mao and other politburo members believed Gao had been a close friend of Moscow since his days as the CCP leader in the Northeast. Beginning in December 1953, Gao became the target of a series of escalating attacks from the CCP leadership. He was labeled as a "conspirator who intended to split the party" and removed from his position. He was reported to have committed suicide in August 1954.[72]

It is now believed that Gao Gang's purge was the result of a long-standing conflict between him and other top CCP leaders, especially Liu Shaoqi and Zhou Enlai, and probably was not directly related to his presumed close ties with the Soviets. However, the timing of the purge was important and revealing. Although the tensions between Gao Gang and Liu Shaoqi had existed for years, Mao did not decide to take Liu's side to criticize Gao until after Stalin's death. Despite Gao's close relations with the Soviets, the CCP did not keep Moscow abreast of what was happening to him. Gao died two weeks before Mao informed the Soviet leaders officially that Gao had committed "serious crimes in trying to split the party" on 1 September 1954.[73] Ignoring Moscow's "right to know"—if not "right to lead"—in this way would have been inconceivable if Stalin had been alive, or if genuine trust had existed between the Chinese and Soviet leaders.

Accumulated Tension

A turning point came in February 1956, when the CPSU held its Twentieth Congress. Toward the end of the meeting, Khrushchev delivered a lengthy speech criticizing Stalin and his personality cult at a secret session, to which the CCP delegation to the congress had not been invited. The Soviets did provide the Chinese delegation with a copy of Khrushchev's speech afterward,[74] but the fact that they failed to consult Beijing in advance greatly offended Mao and his fellow CCP leaders.[75]

Khrushchev's speech shocked Mao and the CCP leadership. From mid-March to early April 1956, top CCP leaders held a series of meetings to discuss Khrushchev's speech and formulate strategies to deal with the situation it created.[76] At the first of such meetings, convened on the evening of 17 March, Mao set the tone for the discussion, pointing out that Khrushchev's speech not only "exposed the problems" (*jie le gaizi*) in Stalin's Soviet Union but also "made a mess" (*tong le louzi*).[77]

Mao and his comrades believed that Khrushchev's criticism of Stalin's mistakes had shattered the myth that Stalin and the Soviet Union had always been correct and would thus contribute to "correcting Stalin's mistakes as well as the erroneous tendency of treating other parties as inferiors within the international Communist movement."[78] Within this context, Mao detailed the mistakes Stalin had made during the Chinese Communist revolution. He stated that during the early stage of China's War of Resistance against Japan, Stalin supported Mao's chief rival Wang Ming's "rightist" policy of "putting the interests of the united front above the interests of the Communist Party," and that after the end of the War of Resistance, he "forced" the CCP not to fight against the Guomindang's anti-Communist civil war plot. The CCP chairman also recalled that during his visit to the Soviet Union from December 1949 to February 1950, Stalin was reluctant to sign a new alliance treaty with the PRC. Not until after Chinese volunteers entered the Korean War, he observed, did Stalin begin to regard the CCP as a genuine Communist party devoted to true proletarian internationalism.[79]

Despite Stalin's mistakes, Mao emphasized, he should still be regarded as a "great Marxist-Leninist revolutionary leader." He told his comrades that Stalin should be evaluated on his historical merit: "The realization of Communism is an extremely difficult task since there exists no example [for the Communists] to follow. . . . During the process of fulfilling this arduous task, it is impossible that mistakes would not be committed. This is because what we are doing is something that no one has tried in the past. I thus always believe [the Communists would] inevitably commit mistakes. The fact that Stalin has committed many mistakes should not be taken as a surprise. Comrade Khrushchev will commit mistakes. The Soviet Union will commit mistakes. And we will also commit mistakes."[80] Therefore, Mao concluded, in making an overall assessment of Stalin as a historical figure, it was necessary to adopt a "seventy-thirty ratio" methodology—that is, acknowledging that achievements should account for 70 percent of Stalin's career and mistakes for only 30 percent.[81]

As a result of these discussions, Mao and his comrades decided to make public China's view on de-Stalinization, in order to control the confusion prompted by Khrushchev's speech. Considering that the Soviets had not formally published Khrushchev's speech and that de-Stalinization was still a developing process, the CCP leadership decided to promulgate the party's official view through the editorial board of *Renmin ribao* (People's Daily). On 5 April 1956, *Renmin ribao* published a lengthy editorial, titled "On the Historical Experience of Proletarian Dictatorship," arguing that Stalin, in spite of all his "serious mistakes," still needed to be respected as a "great Marxist-Leninist."[82]

Mao and his comrades defended Stalin, first and foremost, for defending the CCP's own experience of building socialism in China. Since the early days of the People's Republic, the experience of Stalin's Soviet Union had served as a model for the CCP's own designs for China's state-building, societal transformation, and economic reconstruction. While it is true that Mao and his comrades never intended to copy completely the "Stalin model," they found in the Soviet experience basic strategies and tactics highly useful for promoting China's "socialist revolution and reconstruction." In particular, they were more than willing to learn from the Soviet practices of establishing a highly centralized economic planning system, controlling the rural population through collectivization movements, putting emphasis on developing heavy industry and defense industry, and entrenching the top party leader's authority over the party and the state. In exploring a Chinese path toward socialist modernization, Mao criticized the "Stalin model" in many respects, but he also found that it offered him valuable grounds on which to establish basic understandings of several fundamental relationships with which he and his party had to deal in China.[83] Therefore, for Mao and his comrades to negate Stalin completely would mean to repudiate Mao's grand enterprise of continuous revolution.

Mao's reluctance to embrace de-Stalinization also reflected China's changing domestic political situation and his perception of it in the mid-1950s. In 1955–56, Mao's great enterprise had reached a pivotal point, creating tension between the CCP chairman and many of his prominent colleagues. On the one hand, the inauguration of the first five-year plan, the successful completion of agricultural cooperativization in the countryside, and the advancement of the socialist transformation of industry and commerce in the cities combined to convince Mao that the continuous revolution should be elevated to a higher stage, one that would accelerate China's economic development and its growth into a socialist and Communist society.[84] On the other hand, however, many members of the CCP leading elite—Zhou Enlai and Chen Yun in particular—believed it essential to maintain balanced economic development and societal transformation, and that "rash advance" (*maojin*) should be opposed.[85] Although this difference in opinion between Mao and his colleagues would not surface fully until late 1956 and 1957, the CCP chairman already had realized by early 1956 that China's Communist elite did not always understand the direction of his train of thought, let alone follow it.[86] As a result, he increasingly felt that one of the best guarantors of his continuous revolution was further consolidation and expansion of his own leadership role.

These developments, in turn, conditioned the Maoist rhetoric on de-Stalinization in two important respects. First, Mao's criticism of the Soviet leader focused on the (re)construction of a grand narrative about his unfailing resistance to Stalin's erroneous interference in the Chinese revolution, creating and enhancing the myth that he himself had been the symbol of eternal correctness. Second, he adopted a unique approach toward the "cult of personality" issue. In his initial response toward de-Stalinization, Mao generally avoided sharp criticism of Stalin's personality cult. With the radicalization of China's political and social life in 1957–58, he would make it clear that he had no intention of opposing personality cults in general and his own personality cult in particular. It is not surprising that Ke Qingshi, a CCP politburo member with close ties to the chairman, would openly argue that "it is all right to worship Chairman Mao to the extent of having a blind faith in him."[87] Mao agreed, saying that he favored distinguishing "correct" from "incorrect" personality cults.[88]

Mao's specific response to de-Stalinization also revealed his new perception of Beijing's more superior position in the international Communist movement in the post-Stalin era. Indeed, now Mao, consciously or unconsciously, behaved with a stronger sense of moral superiority. On 31 March 1956, he gave one of the first of his many long monologues to Pavel Yudin, the Soviet ambassador to China, in which he systematically presented his overall view on criticism of Stalin. Again, the CCP chairman reviewed the history of Stalin's relations with China, emphasizing that the late Soviet leader had committed serious mistakes during all stages of the Chinese revolution; in particular, Mao said, Stalin had failed to treat his Chinese comrades as equals. In a more general discussion about how to evaluate Stalin, though, the chairman argued that "the simple fact that the population of the Socialist Camp had grown from 200 million to 900 million speaks for itself"—that is, overall, "Stalin, without doubt, is a great Marxist, a good and honest revolutionary."[89] One week later, in another long monologue-style conversation with Anastas Mikoyan, the CCP chairman again discussed the "serious mistakes" Stalin committed in regard to the Chinese revolution but argued that in general, "Stalin's achievements surpass his mistakes" and that it was thus necessary to "concretely analyze" and "comprehensively evaluate" the Stalin issue.[90]

Through these talks, Mao meant to deliver several crucial messages. First, he conveyed to Khrushchev and the other Soviet leaders his conception of the proper tone for criticizing Stalin. Despite all of Stalin's "serious mistakes," the chairman advised his Soviet comrades that it was wrong to condemn him completely and that continuing to praise him was in the fundamental interests of both the Soviet Union and the international Communist movement. Second, by criticizing Stalin's wrongdoings toward the Chinese Communist revolution, especially his failure to treat his Chinese comrades as "equals," Mao was reminding Khrushchev and his fellow Soviet leaders that they should not repeat the same mistake and that a new pattern of Sino-Soviet relations, one based on the principle of "equality"—as Mao himself defined the term—should be established between Beijing and Moscow. Third, in a more fundamental sense, Mao revealed his new mentality in handling relations with Moscow—after Stalin's death, Mao already felt that he should have a greater voice on questions concerning not only matters between Beijing and Moscow but also the fate of the entire international Communist movement. When Mao spoke about Stalin's mistakes and achievements, he was asserting that he, not the Soviet leaders, now occupied the morally paramount position to dominate the cause of the world proletarian revolution.

Within this context Mao endeavored during 1956 to make known his views on the Stalin issue to Communist leaders from other parts of the world. On 28 June 1956, in a conversation with Romania's ambassador to China, Mao reiterated that Communists should not be surprised by Stalin's mistakes. "After all," the chairman said, "good things exist in the world together with bad things. This has been so since ancient times, and will continue to be so in the future. This is why we need to, and can, transform the world." [91] In September 1956, in a meeting with a Yugoslav Communist Union delegation attending the CCP's Eighth National Congress, Mao repeated his views about the "serious mistakes" Stalin had committed toward the Chinese revolution, yet he again announced that achievement should be regarded as the main Soviet experience during Stalin's era.[92] On these occasions, indeed, the CCP chairman acted as if he had become the "new emperor" of the international Communist movement.

Consequently, by late 1956, China's relations with the Soviet Union changed significantly. Although in public Mao continued to maintain that Moscow remained the center of the socialist camp, he really believed that it was he who was more qualified to dictate the principles underlying the relations between and among socialist countries. This shift in Mao's view of the relationship between Beijing and Moscow was demonstrated most clearly in Beijing's management of the Polish and Hungarian crises in late 1956.[93]

As Mao and his fellow CCP leaders viewed them, the crises emerging in Poland and Hungary were not of the same nature. While they believed that both crises had resulted from Soviet "big-power chauvinism," they saw the crisis in Poland as basically anti-Soviet and the one in Hungary (after initial uncertainty) as essentially anti-Communist. Therefore, when Beijing learned that Moscow was planning to intervene militarily in Poland on 19–21 October, CCP leaders held several urgent meetings to discuss the situation. They concluded that if the Soviets were to use military force to solve the Polish issue, they would be intervening in Poland's internal affairs.[94] Mao twice summoned Ambassador Yudin to his quarters and requested that he inform Moscow urgently that China would publicly protest if Moscow were to launch any military intervention in Poland.[95]

On 23–31 October a high-ranking CCP delegation headed by Liu Shaoqi and Deng Xiaoping traveled to Moscow to consult with the Soviet leaders about the Polish (and, it turned out, Hungarian) crisis. Largely because of the pressure from the Chinese, reportedly, Khrushchev and his fellow Soviet leaders not only decided not to use force to solve the Polish question but also agreed, on 30 October, to issue the "Declaration on Developing and Enhancing the Friendship and Cooperation between the Soviet Union and other Socialist Countries," in which Moscow promised to follow a pattern of more equal exchanges with other Communist states and parties.[96] Mao and his comrades regarded this as Beijing's victory.

Beijing's attitude toward the Hungarian crisis was very different. Although Mao and his fellow CCP leaders initially believed that the origins of the crisis lay in Moscow's failure to treat the Hungarians as equals, they were alarmed when reports came in that anti-Communist riots began to spread all over Hungary. On 30 October, after receiving Liu's and Deng's report from Moscow that the Soviet leaders were planning to withdraw their troops from Hungary, Mao chaired a meeting of top CCP leaders, which decided to oppose Moscow's abandonment of Hungary to "reactionary forces."[97] Liu, following instructions from Beijing, met with Khrushchev and other Soviet leaders on the same day, informing them that it was the Chinese leaders' belief that Soviet withdrawal would be a betrayal of the Hungarian people and that it would put the Soviet leaders on the stand as "historical criminals." The next day, on their way to the airport, Khrushchev told Liu and other members of the Chinese delegation that the Soviet leadership would use military force to suppress the "reactionary revolt" in Hungary.[98] Four days later the Soviet Red Army began its attack on Budapest.

Beijing's intransigent attitude toward the Hungarian crisis reflected Mao's persistent belief that reactionary elements and class enemies had been one of the main causes of the turmoil. Drawing lessons from the Hungarian crisis, Mao argued that the continuous revolution in China should be further enhanced, especially in the fields of politics and ideology.[99] In the wake of the Hungary crisis, an Anti-Rightist movement swept across China in summer 1957; as a result, over 300,000 Chinese intellectuals were branded as "rightists," a label that would effectively silence them and ruin their careers, and Mao and the CCP established absolute control over China's "public opinion."[100]

Along with the Anti-Rightist movement, Mao initiated an equally important yet less well known (at least in the West) political offensive within the
CCP leadership aimed at those of his comrades who had opposed "rash advance" in handling China's economic development in 1956 and early 1957. The
main target was Premier Zhou Enlai. Beginning in late summer 1957, Mao
claimed that Zhou had been seriously mistaken in emphasizing the utmost importance of achieving balanced development in China's economic reconstruction. The chairman told his comrades that he favored "rash advance," despite
its risks, because it would accelerate China's transformation into a socialist and
Communist society. The chairman distrusted the premier to such an extent
that he even considered removing Zhou and replacing him with Ke Qingshi,
whom the chairman regarded as more faithful to his continuous-revolution
programs.[101] The outcome of the Hungarian incident complicated Chinese
politics at the same time that it pushed Mao's continuous revolution onto a
more radical stage.

The conviction that the Chinese had made a significant contribution toward
the "correct resolution" of the Polish and Hungarian crises also facilitated
Mao's belief in Beijing's more prominent position in the international Communist movement. Beijing's leaders thus felt more justified to adopt a critical attitude toward the seemingly less sophisticated Soviet leadership. On 7–
18 January 1957, Zhou Enlai visited the Soviet Union, Poland, and Hungary.[102]
In his report summarizing the visit, he commented extensively on how the
Soviet leadership lacked sophistication in managing the complicated situations both within the Soviet Union and in Eastern Europe. What this report
epitomized, indeed, was China's new self-image as the most qualified candidate to be the leader in the Communist world.[103] Not surprisingly, when Mao
discussed in several internal speeches in 1957 how the CCP diverged from the
Soviet leaders on de-Stalinization, he charged that Khrushchev and his comrades had abandoned not only "the sword of Stalin" but also, to a large extent,
"the sword of Lenin." The subtext of the statement was that the sword was
already in Mao's hands.[104] In the wake of Khrushchev's de-Stalinization and
the Polish and Hungarian crises, the tension between Beijing and Moscow was
escalating.

Yet, in the public eye, Sino-Soviet relations seemed to be proceeding
smoothly in 1956–57. While the Soviet Union continued to provide China
with extensive economic and military assistance, China openly endorsed the
Soviet Union's leading position in the international Communist movement.
In November 1957 Mao Zedong visited Moscow to attend celebrations for the
fortieth anniversary of the Russian Bolshevik revolution of 1917. At a meeting

Mao Zedong (center) and Soviet leader Nikita Khrushchev at the celebration rally for the fortieth anniversary of the Russian Bolshevik revolution, Moscow, 6 November 1957. Xinhua News Agency.

of leaders of Communist and workers' parties from socialist countries, Mao called upon the whole socialist camp to recognize the Soviet Union's leadership role. On one occasion the CCP chairman used a metaphor to compare himself with Khrushchev, saying that the flower of Khrushchev was more beautiful than the flower of Mao Zedong.[105]

But Mao's high-profiled rhetoric should be read critically. By endorsing the Soviet Union's leading position in the international Communist movement, the CCP chairman virtually had placed himself in the capacity of a judge from a higher court, implying that it was he who now occupied a morally superior position to his comrades in Moscow, and that the legitimacy of Moscow's leadership role lay in his approval.

It was at the Moscow meeting that Mao emphasized that the Communists should not be frightened by the prospect of a nuclear war started by the imperialists but should realize that such a war, although carrying a high price, would bring the imperialist system to its grave.[106] Mao's statement was a deliberate challenge to Khrushchev's emphasis on the necessity and possibility of "peaceful coexistence" with Western imperialist countries, and it inevitably worried Moscow's leaders. Were Khrushchev and his colleagues ready to yield to such Maoist discourse? If not, a storm would be gathering in the relationship between Moscow and Beijing.

From Tension to Crisis

The year 1958 was pivotal in the history of the People's Republic as it witnessed one of the most radical episodes of Mao's continuous revolution: the Great Leap Forward. In January 1958 Mao chaired two meetings attended by central and provincial party leaders in Hangzhou and Nanning. At both meetings the chairman continued his criticism of Zhou Enlai's opposition to "rash advance" in previous years, labeling it "a mistake concerning principles, which has damaged the revolutionary vigor of 600 million [Chinese] people." He further warned Zhou that he was "only fifty meters" from becoming a rightist.[107] Facing Mao's repeated criticism, Zhou Enlai acknowledged at the Nanning conference that "as far as the mistake of 'opposing rash advance' is concerned, I should take the main responsibility." [108]

On 31 January, Mao summarized the discussions in an important document titled "Sixty Articles on Work Methods"; in it he attempted to be as explicit as the political situation allowed in defining the mission of his continuous revolution:

> Our revolutions come one after another. The seizure of political power in the whole country in 1949 was soon followed by the antifeudal land reform. As soon as the land reform was completed, the agricultural cooperativization followed. Then the socialist transformation of privately owned industry, commerce, and handicraft occurred. . . . The socialist revolution in the field of the ownership of means of production will be completed by 1958, and will be followed by the socialist revolution on the political and ideological fronts. . . . [We are] now preparing to make a revolution in the technological field, so that [we may] overtake Britain in fifteen or more years.[109]

This text was one of the foundation statements Mao made at an important juncture of his continuous revolution. Through a typical Mao-style review of history, the chairman revealed his deep-rooted postrevolution anxiety; that is, if he failed to push the revolution forward constantly, the revolution would die. By conceptualizing what needed to be done in order to bring his revolution to a higher stage, he defined the mission of the Great Leap Forward, which, in a few short months, was to sweep across China, dramatically radicalizing the country's domestic and external policies.

Dominated by a profound revolutionary fever, Mao chaired another Central Committee working conference in Chengdu, from 8 to 26 March, and further escalated his criticism of "opposing rash advance." The chairman claimed that "rash advance is a Marxist way and 'opposing rash advance' is an anti-

Marxist way." He announced that "we shall continue to commit to rash advance in the future." On 19 and 25 March, Zhou Enlai, on the verge of a total political defeat, made a more comprehensive self-criticism.[110] In addition to dealing with his mistakes on domestic issues, Zhou devoted a large portion of his self-criticism to his "conservative and rightist tendency" in handling the PRC's foreign relations. He admitted that the Foreign Ministry's work under his direction had neglected the necessary struggle in dealing with nationalist countries, had maintained a kind of wishful thinking concerning imperialism (especially toward Japan and the United States), and had failed to conduct necessary criticism of the revisionist policies of other socialist countries. He particularly mentioned that while it was reasonable to learn from the experience of the Soviet Union, it was a mistake to copy it completely.[111]

Zhou's self-criticism clearly showed that profound connections existed between the domestic and international aspects of Chinese politics in the late 1950s. Following Mao's ideas, the CCP leadership at the Chengdu conference decided to revise boldly China's economic development plans, so that China "would catch the right opportunity to surpass Britain in a period even shorter than fifteen years." [112] When the Great Leap Forward was implemented, not surprisingly, Beijing's external policy became dramatically radicalized.

It was against this backdrop that the tensions between China and the Soviet Union became a political problem in China. In November 1957, during the visit of China's defense minister, Peng Dehuai, to the Soviet Union, the two sides reached an agreement that they would cooperate closely on developing naval and air forces in East Asia.[113] In a letter dated 18 April 1958, Soviet defense minister Rodion Malinovskii proposed to Peng that, in order to communicate with the Soviet Union's submarines in the Pacific area, the Soviet high command and the Chinese Ministry of Defense cooperate over a four-year period in constructing a long-wave radio transmission center and a long-wave radio receiving station specially designed for long-distance communication. The Soviet Union would cover 70 percent of the construction costs.[114] Mao immediately considered these plans a threat to China's sovereignty and integrity. He decided that China would accept the proposal only on the condition that China would pay all the expenses and would retain exclusive ownership of the station. Following Mao's instructions, Peng responded to Malinovskii on 12 June, proposing that the two governments sign a formal agreement along these lines.[115]

On 11 July, the Soviet Union provided a draft agreement for the construction of the radio stations. Without a proper understanding of the nature of Beijing's request for exclusive ownership, the Soviets still insisted that the stations be jointly constructed and managed by China and the Soviet Union.[116] Beijing responded with several suggestions for revision: China would take the responsibility for constructing the stations and they would belong to China; China would purchase from the Soviet Union the equipment it was unable to produce and would invite Soviet experts to help construct the station; and after the station's completion, it would be solely owned by China but jointly used by China and the Soviet Union.[117]

Before the radio station issue was settled, a second dispute in the military field emerged, this one concerning the establishment of a joint Soviet-Chinese submarine flotilla. In late 1957, Soviet military and naval advisers in China had indicated to the Chinese that they should purchase new naval equipment from the Soviet Union.[118] On 28 June 1958, Zhou Enlai wrote to Khrushchev requesting that the Soviet Union provide technological assistance for China's naval buildup, especially the designs for new-type submarines.[119] On 21 July, Ambassador Yudin called on Mao Zedong. Speaking on behalf of Khrushchev, Yudin proposed that China and the Soviet Union establish a joint submarine flotilla. Yudin explained that unlike the geography of China, with its long coastal lines and good natural harbors, the Soviet Union's made it difficult for the Soviet navy to take full advantage of the new submarines. Mao was offended by the proposal. "First, we should make clear the guiding principle," he told the ambassador, asking, "[Do you mean that] we should create [the fleet] with your assistance? Or [do you mean] that we should jointly create [the fleet], otherwise you will not offer any assistance?" Mao emphasized that he was not interested in creating a Sino-Soviet "military cooperative."[120]

The next day Mao summoned Yudin to his quarters for a lengthy and very emotional conversation. Once again, the CCP chairman surveyed the history of the relations between the CCP and the Soviet Union, charging that the Soviets had always treated their Chinese comrades from a posture of "big-power chauvinism." He then stressed that behind the Soviet proposals for establishing long-wave radio stations and a joint submarine flotilla was Moscow's attempt to control China. The chairman said angrily, "[Y]ou may accuse me of being a nationalist or another Tito, but my counterargument is that you have extended Russian nationalism to China's coast." As was the case during many of Mao's meetings with Yudin, the chairman presented a near monologue and the Soviet ambassador had few opportunities to respond. If an observer did not know the nature of the two officials' relationship, Yudin could have been the head of a "barbarian" tribute mission who was receiving the teachings of the Chinese "son of heaven." As the conversation approached its end, Mao told

Yudin to "report all my comments to Comrade Khrushchev," emphasizing that "you must tell him exactly what I have said without any polishing." [121]

Alarmed by Yudin's report, Khrushchev visited Beijing from 31 July to 3 August, meeting four times with Mao and other Chinese leaders. At the first meeting, Khrushchev explained to Mao that the Soviets had no intention of controlling China. On the radio station issue he emphasized that it was the "personal opinion" of Malinovskii, rather than the decision of the Central Committee of the CPSU, to construct "jointly" the long-wave station. He agreed that the Soviet Union would provide financial and technical support for establishing the station but would let the Chinese own it. On the joint fleet issue, Khrushchev explained that Yudin might not have accurately conveyed the message from Moscow, stressing that the Soviets were more than willing to treat their Chinese comrades as equals. Mao Zedong, however, would not easily accept Khrushchev's explanations, claiming that "big-power chauvinism" did exist in the Soviet attitude toward China, and that the two issues were just the two most recent examples.[122] On 3 August, after four days of intensive meetings, Malinovskii and Peng, representing the Soviet and Chinese governments, signed an agreement on the construction of long-wave stations and the dispatch of Soviet experts to China.[123] Yet the psychological rift between the Chinese and Soviet leaders, and especially between Mao and Khrushchev, persisted and intensified.[124] Mao would later recall that "the overturning of [our relations with] the Soviet Union occurred in 1958; that was because they wanted to control China militarily." [125]

Mao's harsh reaction to these two issues reflected his increasing sensitivity regarding China's sovereignty and equal status in relation to the Soviet Union. Underlying this sensitivity, though, was a strong and unique "victim mentality" that characterized Chinese revolutionary nationalism during modern times. This mentality had been informed by the conviction that the political, economic, and military aggression of foreign imperialist countries had undermined China's historical glory and humiliated the Chinese nation. Consequently, it was natural for the Chinese Communists, in their efforts to end China's humiliating modern experiences, to suspect the behavior of *any* foreign country as being driven by ulterior, or even evil, intentions. Although the Soviet Union was a Communist country, when Mao claimed that Khrushchev and his Kremlin colleagues intended to control China, he apparently equated them with the leaders of Western imperialism.

That Mao's suspicion and distrust of Soviet "chauvinist intentions" toward China came to a head in the summer of 1958, rather than earlier or later, should

Mao Zedong greets Nikita Khrushchev at the Beijing airport, 31 July 1958.
Xinhua News Agency.

be understood in the context of the chairman's criticism of "opposing rash advance" within the CCP leadership. Reading the transcripts of Mao's talks with Yudin and Khrushchev, one gets an impression that they were quite similar to many of the chairman's inner-party speeches throughout late 1957 and 1958. In both circumstances, Mao believed that he had absolute command of the truth; and, in these monologues, the chairman became accustomed to teaching others in critical, often passionate, terms. Indeed, since Mao was turning his own revolutionary emotion into the dynamics for the Great Leap Forward, it is not surprising that he adopted the same challenge-oriented stance in dealing with his Soviet comrades.

When Khrushchev arrived in China at the end of July 1958, the leaders in Beijing already had decided to begin large-scale shelling of the Nationalist-controlled Jinmen (Quemoy) islands off the coast of Fujian province.[126] In determining the timing of the shelling, the chairman hoped not only to confront international imperialism and call attention to the issue of Taiwan being part of the People's Republic, but also to help stimulate the rising tide of the Great Leap. The shelling would be accompanied by an anti–Jiang Jieshi and anti-U.S. propaganda campaign—with "we must liberate Taiwan" as its central slogan. Mao, however, did not have an established plan to invade Taiwan or to involve China in a direct military confrontation with the United States.[127] What he needed was a sustained and controllable conflict, one that would enhance popular support for his radical transformation of China's polity, economy, and society. As the chairman pointed out at the peak of the Taiwan Strait crisis, "[B]esides its disadvantageous side, a tense [international] situation could mobilize the population, could particularly mobilize the backward people, could mobilize the people in the middle, and could therefore promote the Great Leap Forward in economic construction."[128]

Mao did not inform Khrushchev of his tactical plans during their meeting in Beijing.[129] When the PLA began an intensive artillery bombardment of the islands on 23 August, the Soviet leaders were at a loss to interpret China's aims. In the following six weeks, several hundred thousand artillery shells exploded on Jinmen and in the waters around it. The Eisenhower administration, in accordance with its obligations under a 1954 American-Taiwan defense treaty, reinforced U.S. naval units in East Asia and used U.S. naval vessels to help the Nationalists protect Jinmen's supply lines.

The Soviet leaders, fearing that Beijing's actions might cause grave consequences, sent Foreign Minister Andrei Gromyko on a secret visit to Beijing in early September to inquire about China's reasons for shelling Jinmen. At this time the Chinese leaders said that the shelling was designed to attract the world's attention to the Taiwan question and to divert American strength from other parts of the world (especially the Middle East), but not as a step leading to the invasion of Taiwan, let alone to provoke a direct confrontation with the United States.[130] Only after receiving these explanations from Beijing did the Soviet government issue a statement on 8 September to show its solidarity with the Chinese.[131] Nonetheless, the fissure between Beijing and Moscow widened.[132]

On the domestic front, the Great Leap Forward was progressing rapidly. In the fall and winter of 1958, tens of thousands of people's communes appeared in China's countryside and cities, which, with their free supply system, were supposed to form the basic units of an emerging Communist society. In the meantime, hundreds of millions of ordinary Chinese were mobilized to produce steel from small backyard furnaces in order to double the nation's steel production in one year's time.[133] Khrushchev and his colleagues were confused by what was occurring in China. Thousands of Soviet advisers there issued warnings about the possible negative economic consequences of the Great Leap, but the Soviet media avoided making any public reference to the Chinese plans. During a meeting with U.S. senator Hubert Humphrey, according to Western sources, Khrushchev even dismissed the people's communes as "reactionary." [134] The Soviets' reaction offended Mao deeply, intensifying his belief that the Soviet leaders, and Khrushchev in particular, lacked political wisdom and revolutionary vigor.[135]

Further Deepening of the Crisis

In early 1959, a number of events combined to further stress the relations between Moscow and Beijing. First, the negative effects of the Great Leap Forward began to be felt in the Chinese economy. Beginning in the spring of 1959, the rural population increasingly resisted the slogan of a "continuous leap forward," and, in urban areas, China's industrial production began to decrease.[136] What made the situation more complicated for Beijing was that in March, an anti-Chinese and anti-Communist rebellion erupted in Tibet. Although the rebellion itself was quickly suppressed, it caused new tensions between China and India, who, since the early 1950s, had maintained friendly relations. International pressure on Beijing mounted.[137]

Although Mao Zedong's continuous revolution was facing its most serious challenge since the establishment of the People's Republic, Khrushchev and the other Soviet leaders were willing to add to Beijing's misfortune. On 20 June the Soviets informed the Chinese that because of the Soviet-American negotiations at Geneva to ban nuclear weapon tests, it was difficult for Moscow to provide China with assistance on nuclear technology. If the Western countries learned that the Soviet Union had agreed to share its nuclear secrets with China, the Soviet leaders explained, "it is possible that the efforts by socialist countries to strive for peace and the relaxation of international tensions would be jeopardized." The Soviets thus told the Chinese that they would no longer honor some of their obligations that had been set up in the agreement they signed with the Chinese on 15 October 1957, and would not provide Beijing with atomic bomb prototypes and technical data for producing the bomb.[138] Mao regarded this turn of events as an indication of Moscow's attempt to put pressure on the CCP and especially on himself to change the course of Chinese policy,[139] which further contributed to the distrust and tension between Beijing and Moscow.

The escalating crisis in the Sino-Soviet alliance coincided with the growing tensions within the CCP leadership in the wake of the Great Leap. In July 1959, top CCP leaders gathered at Lushan to discuss the consequences of the Great Leap Forward and strategies to deal with them.[140] Peng Dehuai, who had just returned from a formal visit to the Soviet Union and Eastern European countries, wrote to Mao on 14 July to propose that the party leadership "overcome petit bourgeoisie enthusiasm" and carefully evaluate the "losses and achievements" of the Great Leap.[141] The chairman, sensing that Peng's letter might pose a serious threat to both his continuous revolution programs and his position as China's indisputable leader, responded fiercely. He claimed that Peng had long been a careerist and that his "total negation" of the Great Leap aimed to overturn the party's general plan for socialist reconstruction and to overthrow the party's top leadership. Using his authority and power, the chairman converted the Lushan conference into a denunciation of Peng's "antiparty plot." Peng, in turn, lost his position as China's defense minister.[142] In terms of its historical significance, the Lushan conference represented Mao's crucial first step toward initiating the disastrous "Great Proletarian Cultural Revolution," of which the "Soviet revisionism and social imperialism" would become a major target.

It is notable that when Peng Dehuai became the main target of criticism and denunciation during and after this conference, many CCP leaders connected the defense minister's letter to his visit to the Soviet Union and his meetings with Khrushchev. Those who supported Mao asked repeatedly whether Peng's "intentional attack" against Mao and the party had an "international background," that is, the support of the Soviets. Although Peng categorically denied any such connections, Mao and other party leaders, including Liu Shaoqi—who himself would later be labeled "China's Khrushchev"—persistently claimed that at Lushan, Peng acted as a "Soviet agent."[143]

The contention between China and the Soviet Union was made public for the first time in August 1959, when a border conflict occurred between China and India. In spite of China having maintained friendly relations with India throughout the 1950s, New Delhi's acceptance of the Tibetan Dalai Lama's exile government in the spring of 1959 caused severe discord between the two countries, making the tensions that had accumulated along the Sino-Indian borders more difficult to control.[144] On 9 September the Soviet media issued a statement expressing "regret" at the conflict between India and China. To Mao and his comrades, this statement, which failed to express that the Soviets stood clearly on Beijing's side, indicated that Moscow "had virtually adopted a policy to support India's position."[145]

On 30 September 1959, Khrushchev, after extensive conversations with President Dwight Eisenhower in the United States, arrived in Beijing to participate in celebrations of the People's Republic's tenth anniversary. The same evening he made a forty-minute speech at the state banquet held by Chinese leaders at the newly completed Great Hall of the People. Without paying any attention to the mood of his Chinese hosts, Khrushchev emphasized the "Camp David" spirit, which, according to him, would contribute to the relaxation of tensions between East and West.[146] In Mao's eyes this was a real offense—how could the Soviet leader bring such a topic to an occasion that was supposed to be devoted to celebrating the victory of the Chinese revolution? When Khrushchev mentioned that "it is unwise to use military means to test the stability of the capitalist system," Mao believed that the Soviet leader meant to insult him and revolutionary China.[147]

It was within this framework that Khrushchev and other members of the Soviet delegation had an important meeting with Mao and other Chinese leaders on 2 October.[148] This meeting was supposed to offer an opportunity for Chinese and Soviet leaders to find ways to remedy the divergence between them, but it quickly degenerated into vitriolic debate. At the beginning of the meeting, Khrushchev delivered a message from President Eisenhower to the Chinese leaders, requesting that China release five American "prisoners of war," including two American pilots, who had been detained by the Chinese. While Zhou Enlai argued that these Americans were not POWs, Mao Zedong categorically denied the request, telling Khrushchev that these Americans would be eventually released but certainly not immediately after the Soviet leader's visit.[149]

The meeting then turned to the Taiwan issue. Khrushchev criticized the Chinese for having adopted a policy of adventurism in handling the Taiwan crisis in 1958 and was particularly upset with Beijing's failure to inform Moscow of its intentions in shelling Jinmen. To show Mao and his fellow Chinese leaders that it was necessary to make compromises with the enemy, Khrushchev lectured about history, citing as an example Lenin's establishment of the Far Eastern Republic as a buffer between Soviet Russia and Japan. He proposed that Moscow and Beijing consult with each òther on the Taiwan issue in the future. The Chinese leaders angrily rebutted Khrushchev's criticism, claiming that not using force in Taiwan had been an American position and that Khrushchev wanted to acquiesce in Washington's plot to create "two Chinas."[150]

Khrushchev then shifted the conversation to Beijing's policy toward India and Tibet. He declared that Beijing was wrong in trying to solve their disputes with New Delhi by military means. He also challenged the sovereignty claim of the People's Republic over certain areas along the unsettled Chinese-Indian border, calling Beijing unwise to be competing with India over "a few square kilometers of barren land." Concerning Tibet, Khrushchev ridiculed the Chinese for "having committed the mistake of allowing the Dalai Lama to escape to India." In response, Zhou Enlai ridiculed Khrushchev for his "inability to tell right from wrong." Marshal Chen Yi, China's foreign minister, angrily reproached Khrushchev, saying that while it was necessary for socialist countries to unite with nationalist countries, it was a mistake for the former to yield to the latter's wrongdoings. Chen singled out in particular the Soviets' statement of 9 September that indicated their belief that the Chinese-Indian border conflict was "a huge mistake." While Khrushchev told the Chinese that he would never accept the Chinese claim that the Soviets had sided with India, Mao announced that the Chinese would never accept the Soviet stand on India and Tibet either.[151]

At this point the meeting deteriorated into complete disorder as leaders of both sides attacked their alliance partners. On one occasion Khrushchev complained, "Mao Zedong sternly criticized our party face-to-face with Comrade Yudin last year, and we tolerated it, but we will not tolerate [it] now." The meeting ended in discord.[152]

During his stay in Beijing, according to several Chinese sources, Khrushchev also advised Mao that the CCP's criticism of Peng Dehuai was groundless, and he urged Mao to restore Peng to his former position. This advice, as can be imagined, did Peng no good. Instead, Mao was further convinced that Peng's "antiparty plot" was instigated by the Soviets. In an inner-party speech two months later, Mao identified Peng's action at Lushan as "a coup attempt supported by [his Soviet] friends."[153] The CCP Central Committee formally declared that Peng's antiparty activities were related to a foreign "plot" to overthrow the party leadership headed by Mao Zedong.[154]

Khrushchev left China on 4 October 1959. On his way back to Moscow, he stopped at Vladivostok and made a public speech there on 6 October. He talked about his recent visits to the United States and China, and praised the "brotherly solidarity" between Moscow and Beijing as a cornerstone for world peace. It was difficult at the time for a general audience to detect that serious discord had developed between Chinese and Soviet leaders.[155] Mao and his comrades in Beijing, however, carefully read the message contained in the speech, and found that Khrushchev had claimed that "it was unwise to behave like a bellicose cock and to long for war." The Chinese leaders believed that Khrushchev was preparing to go public in his criticism of them.[156] Mao now saw little chance to avoid a serious confrontation with the "revisionist traitors" in Moscow.

Breakdown

As the 1960s began, the chasm between Beijing and Moscow deepened. The prospect of future amicable Sino-Soviet relations was further damaged by Khrushchev's belief that putting more pressure on the Chinese would enable him to take advantage of the potential differences between Mao and his comrades, forcing Mao to change his domestic and international policies. With no understanding of Mao's confrontational, challenge-oriented character,[157] Khrushchev recalled all Soviet experts from China and drastically reduced material and military aid to Beijing in July 1960, just as China was being deeply affected by the disastrous aftermath of the Great Leap Forward.[158]

Moscow's decision to recall the Soviet experts hindered Beijing's ability to deal with the extraordinary difficulties brought on by the Great Leap. Still, Khrushchev's order was not necessarily unwelcome from Mao's perspective. The disastrous consequences of the Great Leap Forward had shaken the myth of Mao's infallibility, weakening for the first time the chairman's leadership of the party and state. Beginning in 1960 the CCP leadership—with Mao having relegated himself to the "second line"—adopted a series of moderate and flexible domestic policies designed for economic recovery and social stability. Mao could clearly sense that both his grand revolutionary enterprise and his own indisputable position as the party's paramount leader were at stake.

Thus Mao used the recall of Soviet experts as a convenient excuse to make the Soviets the scapegoat for the Great Leap Forward's disastrous consequences. The chairman also found in the conflict with the Soviets a long-term weapon he badly needed to enhance the much-weakened momentum of his continuous revolution. In the early 1960s Mao repeatedly used the conflict with Moscow to claim that his struggle for true Communism was also a struggle for China's national integrity. And as far as Chinese politics was concerned, the growing confrontation with Moscow made it more difficult for those of Mao's comrades who disagreed with some of the chairman's radical ideas to challenge him.[159]

There is a striking similarity between the new patterns that emerged in China's domestic politics and in its external relations in the early and mid-1960s. On the one hand, Mao, especially after 1962, repeatedly argued that in order to avert a Soviet-style "capitalist restoration," it was necessary for the Chinese party and people "never to forget class struggle," pushing the whole country toward another high wave of continuous revolution. On the other hand, Mao personally initiated the great polemic debate between the Chinese and Soviet parties, claiming that the Soviet party and state had fallen into the "revisionist" abyss and that it had become the duty of the Chinese party and the Chinese people to hold high the banner of true socialism and communism.[160]

Mao's wrecking of the Sino-Soviet relationship did not happen without challenge from other members of the CCP leadership. Beginning in February 1962 Wang Jiaxiang, head of the CCP's International Liaison Department, submitted to the party's top leadership several reports on China's international polices. He argued that the strategic goal of China's foreign policy should be the maintenance of world peace, so that it would be able to focus on socialist construction at home. He particularly emphasized that "it is necessary [for China] to carry out a foreign policy aimed at easing international tension, and not exacerbating" it.[161]

Wang's views seemed to have received the consent (if not active support) of several party leaders, including Liu Shaoqi and Deng Xiaoping. Mao, understandably, was upset. The CCP chairman characterized Wang's ideas as an attempt to be conciliatory toward imperialists, revisionists, and international reactionaries, and to reduce support to those countries and peoples fighting against the imperialists. Mao stressed that this policy of "three reconciliations and one reduction" came at a time when some leading CCP members (as it turned out, he had Liu and Deng in mind) had been frightened by the international reactionaries and were inclined to adopt a "prorevisionist" policy line at home. He emphasized that his policy, by contrast, was to fight against the imperialists, revisionists, and reactionaries in all countries and, at the same time, to promote revolutionary developments at home and abroad.[162] Those of Mao's colleagues who may have had doubts about the chairman's ideas yielded to his argument without a fight.

With the continuous radicalization of China's political and social life, the relationship between Beijing and Moscow rapidly worsened. By 1963–64, when the great Sino-Soviet polemic debate escalated in highly emotional and confrontational language, the alliance between Beijing and Moscow had virtually died. On several occasions, Mao even mentioned that China now had to consider the Soviet Union, which represented an increasingly serious threat to China's northern borders, as a potential enemy.[163] Even Khrushchev's fall from power in October 1964 could not reverse the trend of deteriorating relations. In November 1964, Beijing sent a delegation headed by Zhou Enlai to Moscow to discuss with the new Soviet leadership the prospect of stopping the Sino-Soviet polemic debates and improving Sino-Soviet relations. Zhou's visit, however, completely failed in reaching these goals, especially after Soviet defense minister Malinovskii reportedly asked the Chinese to take action to overthrow Mao Zedong as the CCP's top leader.[164]

In 1965–66, the rhetoric centering on preventing a Soviet-style "capitalist restoration" from happening in China played an essential role in legitimizing Mao's efforts to bring the whole Chinese party, state, and population into the orbit of the "Great Proletarian Cultural Revolution." When the Cultural Revolution officially began in summer 1966, the CCP chairman linked his widespread domestic purges to the "antirevisionist" and "anti–social imperialist" struggles on the international scene, labeling Liu Shaoqi, the major target of his purge during the Cultural Revolution, "China's Khrushchev." Consequently, until the last days of his life, Mao made the rhetoric of antirevisionism (and, after the Sino-Soviet border clashes in 1969, anti–social imperialism) central to mobilizing the Chinese people to sustain his continuous revolution. The Soviet Union, accordingly, became China's worst enemy throughout the 1970s. Not until the mid- and late 1980s, when Mao's continuous revolution had long been abandoned in China and Deng Xiaoping's "reform and opening" policies had dominated Chinese politics, would Beijing and Moscow move toward normal state relations.

CHAPTER 4
CHINA'S STRATEGIES
TO END THE KOREAN WAR,
1950–1953

Resist America! Assist Korea!

Defend our nation! Defend our home!

Beat American Arrogance!

—*Chinese slogans during the Korean War*

When China entered the Korean War in October 1950, Mao Zedong and the Beijing leadership intended to win a glorious victory by driving the Americans out of Korea.[1] Nine months later the cruel reality of the battlefield forced the Beijing leadership to adjust this goal. On 10 July 1951, negotiations to end the Korean conflict began at Kaeson. Although neither Chinese nor American combat forces subsequently demonstrated an ability to overwhelm the other side and, in reality, the military lines between the two sides never changed significantly, fighting would not end until July 1953.

Military conflict, as Karl von Clausewitz puts it, is the continuation of politics by other means. In this sense, how the Korean War ended is as important as how it began. However, because of the political sensitivity involved in the origins of the Korean War, scholars, as well as the general public, have devoted much of their attention to the war's beginning rather than to its end. Scholars who do realize the importance of the war's conclusion have long encountered another obstacle: the lack of reliable sources for exploring the Communist side of the story. While plausible studies about U.S./UN strategies to end the war do exist,[2] our knowledge of the Chinese Communists' handling of negotiations leading to an armistice remains in short supply.[3]

This chapter offers a critical review of the changing Chinese Communist strategies to end the Korean War. It first analyzes the implications of the Korean crisis for Beijing and the perceptions pertinent to and the goals pursued in Beijing's management of the war. It then presents a discussion of

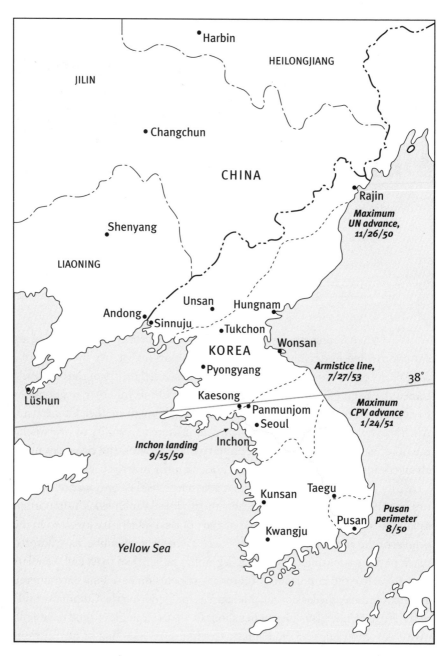

KOREA AND CHINA'S NORTHEAST

how Beijing's aims in Korea changed during the process of its intervention and, accordingly, how the strategies designed to serve these aims had to be adjusted and readjusted. The central assumption is that three related factors shaped Beijing's perceptions and management of the changing course of the Korean crisis: the Chinese Communist leaders' overall domestic and international concerns, the Communist versus the U.S.'s/UN's strategies to end the war, and Beijing's perceptions of its needs and those of Moscow and Pyongyang in Korea.

Implications of the Korean Crisis in Beijing's Eyes

The eruption of the Korean War on 25 June 1950 did not take Beijing's leaders by surprise, but Washington's decision to intervene not only in Korea but also in Taiwan did.[4] The Korean crisis presented to Beijing a series of challenges as well as opportunities. On the one hand, the Korean crisis threatened Beijing's key interests in several ways: it presented potential threats to China's physical security, especially the safety of China's industrial bases in the Northeast; it called into question the correctness of Beijing's overall perception that East Asia represented "the weak link of the chain of international imperialism," an opinion CCP leaders had held since 1946–47; it changed the scenario of the CCP-Nationalist confrontation across the Taiwan Strait, forcing Beijing's leaders to postpone and, finally, to call off the military campaign to "liberate Taiwan";[5] it darkened the prospects for an ongoing East Asian revolution, which, in Beijing's view, should follow the model of the Chinese revolution; and, last but not least, it created tremendous internal pressures on Mao and the CCP leadership as the rulers of the newly established People's Republic of China.[6]

On the other hand, the Korean crisis offered the CCP leadership potential opportunities. In evaluating how the Korean crisis might influence China, Mao and his fellow CCP leaders could clearly sense that by firmly and successfully confronting the "U.S. imperialist aggression" in Korea and Taiwan, they would be able to translate the tremendous pressure from without into dynamics that would help enhance the Chinese people's revolutionary momentum while legitimizing the CCP's authority as China's new ruler. This would help establish the foundation for Mao's grand plans to transform China's old state and society into a new socialist country.[7] And, although the Korean crisis challenged the international structure in the Asian-Pacific region, one of the main objectives of Communist China's foreign policy was to pound at the Western-dominated existing international order, and Beijing's leaders realized that a North Korean victory (preferably, with China's support) could help establish a new order in East Asia. From Beijing's perspective, even an expansion of the conflict in Korea, certainly not desirable, might not be intolerable.[8] The relationship between the CCP and the North Korean Communists had been complex. Kim Il-sung, while endeavoring to maintain cooperation with his Chinese comrades, was vigilant against Chinese influence.[9] To Mao and the CCP leadership, expanding warfare in Korea would inevitably menace China's national security interests, but, at the same time, it could offer the Chinese Communists a possible opportunity to expand the influence of the Chinese revolution into an area at the top of the CCP's Asian revolutionary agenda.[10] From the beginning, Mao and the CCP leadership viewed the Korean War with mixed feelings: failure to eject the Americans from Korea would create insecurity for China; success in defeating the Americans, especially with China's help, would advance revolutionary China's domestic mobilization and international reputation and influence.

Setting the Stage for Entering the War

By early July, Beijing's leaders had decided to postpone the plans for a Taiwan campaign to focus on Korea.[11] Preparing for a "worst-case scenario," Beijing created the Northeast Border Defense Army in mid-July, and, by early August, more than 260,000 Chinese troops had taken position along the Chinese-Korean border.[12] On 18 August, after a series of deliberations and adjustments, Mao Zedong established the end of September as the deadline for NEBDA to complete preparations for commencing operations in Korea.[13] On the home front, the Beijing leadership started the "Great Movement to Resist America and Assist Korea," with "beating American arrogance" as its central slogan.[14] Beijing's leaders used every means available to stir the "hatred of the U.S. imperialists" among common Chinese. They particularly emphasized that the United States had long engaged in political and economic aggressions against China, that the declining capitalist America was not as powerful as it seemed to be, and that a confrontation between China and the United States was inevitable.[15] At the same time, the Beijing leadership decided to promote a nationwide campaign aimed at suppressing "reactionaries and reactionary activities." The campaign would reach its climax a few months later, shortly before the Chinese troops were entering the Korean War.[16] All of these developments indicate that the Beijing leadership's management of the Korean crisis was comprehensive by nature. In the eyes of Mao and his fellow CCP leaders, Communist China's security interests would be best served by guaranteeing the safety of the Chinese-Korean border, enhancing the CCP's authority and credibility at home, and promoting the new China's prestige on the international scene. Beijing's leaders were determined to achieve all of these goals.

Within this context, on 12 July, Zhou Enlai personally drafted five conditions for a "peaceful settlement" of the Korean crisis: that all foreign troops withdraw from Korea; that U.S. military forces withdraw from the Taiwan Strait; that the Korean issue be solved by the Korean people themselves; that Beijing take over China's seat in the UN and Taipei be expelled; and that an international conference be called to discuss the signing of a peace treaty with Japan.[17] Beijing would announce these conditions on several occasions in the following two months.

The introduction of these conditions revealed a fundamental tendency in Beijing's perception of the Korean crisis: since, in Beijing's view, the crisis was much broader than the Korean conflict itself, its settlement should include such issues as the Taiwan question and the PRC's seat at the UN.[18] However, until the Inchon landing, the central Communist actors in Korea were Pyongyang and, to a lesser extent, Moscow. Kim Il-sung, as a Korean nationalist, was unwilling to allow Chinese interference as long as he believed the situation was under control.[19] Stalin, on the other hand, assigned top priority to avoiding a direct confrontation with the United States and thus maintained a "wait-and-see" approach. Under these circumstances, Beijing's conditions to end the war served as a means to justify its comprehensive military preparation and political mobilization rather than as a specific strategy designed to settle the war.

After Inchon: Defining China's War Aims and Making the Decision on Intervention

The successful American landing at Inchon on 15 September 1950 changed the entire course of the Korean War. With the gradual collapse of the North Korean resistance and the northward march of UN forces, Mao and his comrades had to decide whether or not China should enter the Korean War.

Beijing made the decision to send troops to Korea in the first three weeks of October.[20] The process leading to the decision was complex. Top Chinese leaders were under intense pressure because of cruel domestic and international conditions, and the party leadership was divided on the necessity of entering the fighting.[21] Further, although Stalin pushed the Chinese to enter the war "to give our Korean comrades an opportunity to organize combat reserves under the cover of your troops," he failed to clarify what military support Moscow would give Beijing if the Chinese did send troops to Korea.[22]

Under these circumstances, members of the CCP Central Secretariat met on 2 October to discuss the Korean crisis and made the preliminary decision to send Chinese troops to Korea.[23] Mao then personally drafted a telegram to Stalin to inform the Soviet leader that Beijing had decided "to send a portion of our troops" to Korea and to request major Soviet air support.[24] However, because top CCP leaders were yet to reach a consensus on intervention and Mao hoped to strengthen China's bargaining position in getting Soviet air support, he probably did not dispatch this telegram.[25] Instead, he met with Soviet ambassador N. V. Rochshin, asking him to inform Stalin that, since many leaders in Beijing believed that China should "show caution" in entering the war, the CCP leadership had not made the decision to send troops to Korea.[26]

But Mao's heart was with intervention. Although the majority of the party leaders hesitated to endorse sending troops to Korea when the politburo met to discuss the matter, Mao used both his political wisdom and authority to push his colleagues to support the war decision.[27] On 8 October, he issued the formal order to enter the war.[28] But he had to postpone the deadline for Chinese troops to enter Korea twice, respectively on 12 and 17 October,[29] when Stalin indicated that "it will take at least two to two and a half months for the Soviet air force to be ready to support the Chinese Volunteers' operations in Korea."[30] As historian Michael Hunt argues, "any effort to pin down the exact motive behind Mao's decision to intervene must enter a mind as complicated as the crisis it wrestled with."[31]

Yet how Mao came to decide to enter the war is clear. From the very beginning, Mao was inclined to enter the war, and he played a central role at every crucial juncture in formulating Beijing's war decision. At the 2 October Central Secretariat meeting, Mao made it clear that China had to enter the war, and he urged top CCP leaders to make the preliminary decision.[32] At the politburo meetings that followed, Mao applied both his authority and political wisdom to secure top party leaders' support for the war decision.[33] Finally, when Moscow reneged on supplying Soviet air support in Korea, Mao convinced his comrades that sending troops to Korea was China's only option.[34]

Mao justified his decision by reemphasizing that it was in China's fundamental interests to pursue a victory over the United States in Korea. In his correspondences with Stalin and his speeches to the CCP leadership, the chairman stated that the Chinese troops should enter the war to "resolve the Korean problem," that is, to "eliminate the invaders from the United States and from other countries, and [thus] drive them out [of Korea]." He linked the "settlement of the Korean problem" with China and the "whole East," emphasizing that China's entry into the war would strengthen the CCP's control of China's state and society and serve to promote an Eastern revolution following the Chinese model.[35]

However, Mao's ambition of winning a glorious victory over the United States was from the beginning bound by the means at his disposal, especially in light of Stalin's failure to commit Soviet air forces to cover China's war operations in Korea.[36] Nevertheless, the CCP leadership, under Mao's pressure, relented, and Chinese troops were to take the defensive during their first six months on the Korean battlefield.[37] On 19 October, a quarter million Chinese troops began entering Korea.

Refusing to Negotiate: The Pursuit of a Total Victory

The UN forces' rapid march toward the Chinese-Korean border in the weeks of late October and November 1950 placed more pressure on the Chinese while offering them new opportunities. With Mao's approval, Peng Dehuai, the commander in chief of the Chinese People's Volunteers in Korea, adopted a strategy of inducing the enemy to march forward and then eliminating them by superior forces striking from their rear and on their flanks. On 25 October, the CPV initiated its first campaign in Korea in the Unsan area, forcing UN troops to retreat to the Chongchun River from areas close to the Yalu.[38]

Chinese appearance on the Korean battlefield should have sent a strong warning to UN forces, but General Douglas MacArthur did not pay heed to it. In mid-November, he initiated a new "end the war" offensive. Peng ordered all Chinese units to retreat for about thirty kilometers, to occupy favorable positions, and to wait for the best opportunity to eliminate the enemy.[39] In late November, advancing UN forces entered areas where Chinese troops had laid their trap. Starting on 25 November, Chinese troops began a vigorous counteroffensive. By mid-December, the Chinese and North Korean troops had regained control of nearly all North Korean territory.

The Chinese military victory in Korea put Beijing's leaders in a favorable position to conclude the war through negotiations, if they so desired. On 5 December, thirteen non-Western countries headed by India handed a peace proposal to Beijing. They suggested that the Chinese stop their offensive at the 38th parallel and that, on the basis of a cease-fire, a meeting of the big powers with interests in Korea would be convened to discuss the final solution of the crisis.[40] Nine days later, the UN passed the thirteen-nation resolution and established a three-person group to seek a "basis on which a satisfactory ceasefire in Korea could be arranged."[41] In order to persuade Beijing that a cease-fire was in its interests, the Indians repeatedly promised the Chinese that the thirteen-country proposal did not originate in the West, and that in exchange for Beijing's acceptance of a cease-fire, other Chinese interests would be taken into account.[42]

Beijing's leaders, however, were unwilling to accept anything short of a total victory, and for this they gained Moscow's full support.[43] On 8 December, Chen Jiakang, a high-ranking Chinese foreign ministry official, asked the Indians why the thirteen countries had failed to propose a cease-fire when the U.S./UN forces crossed the 38th parallel, and why they called for a cease-fire at a time when the Chinese/North Korean forces were advancing. Three days later, in a meeting with K. M. Panikkar, Indian ambassador to China, Zhou Enlai emphasized that since the 38th parallel had been crossed by the Americans, there was no need for the Chinese to respect it.[44]

Chinese field commanders, and especially Peng Dehuai, had reservations about Chinese troops' continued offensive operations. They understood that the Chinese troops, although having achieved initial success against the UN forces, were vulnerable as the result of a weak logistical system and lack of air support. Peng therefore believed that the Chinese should discontinue the advance until reinforcements arrived from China.[45]

However, Mao, in light of the glorious achievements of the first two Chinese campaigns in Korea, believed that the original goal of "eliminating the enemy troops and forcing the Americans out of Korea" should be maintained. The CCP chairman pointed out on 4 December that the Chinese victory in the first two campaigns had tipped the balance in Beijing's favor. Under Chinese pressure, the chairman speculated, the Americans might ask for a cease-fire. And if they did, he would demand that they promise to withdraw from Korea and, as the first step toward a cease-fire, that U.S. forces retreat to areas south of the 38th parallel.[46] He refused to consider any proposal about ending the Korean conflict through negotiation before the Chinese won a more decisive victory over the enemy, arguing that "it will be most unfavorable in political terms if [our forces] reach the 38th parallel and stop north of it."[47] On 21 December, he ordered Peng "to fight another campaign" and "to cross the 38th parallel."[48] The next day, Zhou Enlai formally rejected the thirteen-nation cease-fire resolution, condemning it as a U.S. plot to gain time for resuming the military offensive in Korea.[49]

On the last day of 1950, Chinese troops began a third offensive campaign, and UN forces continued to retreat. Seoul fell to Chinese and North Korean troops on 4 January 1951. By 8 January, advance Chinese/North Korean units had reached the 37th parallel. Peng reported to Beijing that the third Chinese offensive campaign in Korea was victorious.[50]

On 11 January, the UN's three-person cease-fire group suggested five principles for resolving the Korean conflict, among which the most important were an immediate cease-fire in Korea, the gradual withdrawal of foreign troops from Korea, and a meeting of the four powers (the Soviet Union, the United States, Britain, and China) to settle outstanding Far East problems, and at which both the Taiwan issue and the PRC's representation in the UN would be discussed.[51]

In retrospect, this resolution might have offered Beijing a golden opportunity to end the war. Although the Chinese/North Korean gains in the third campaign were impressive, their offensive potentials had been almost exhausted as a result of their overextended supply lines, lack of air support, and heavy casualties. Worrying that further advance by Chinese/North Korean forces would expose their flanks to the enemy's attacks, Peng ordered them to stop offensive operations and focus on consolidating their gains.[52] An immediate cease-fire would have allowed the Communists to hold their place and would have offered them a valuable break to rebuild their offensive momentum in the event that the cease-fire failed.[53]

From the United States' perspective, the Communist acceptance of this resolution certainly would have placed Washington in a diplomatic dilemma. As Secretary of State Dean Acheson stated later, Washington faced a difficult choice: supporting the thirteen-country resolution could result in "the loss of the Koreans and the fury of Congress and the press"; failing to support it could lead to "the loss of our majority and support in the United Nations." Acheson confessed that the decision to support the proposal was largely based on the hope that China would reject it.[54]

Beijing indeed decided to reject this proposal. On 17 January, Zhou Enlai, arguing that the resolution was "designed to give the American troops breathing space" in Korea, introduced Beijing's own terms for negotiations. He called for a seven-power meeting to be held in China, for the PRC to seize immediately China's seat in the UN, and for the withdrawal of all foreign troops from Korea and Taiwan.[55] These terms made ending the war through negotiations impossible for the moment.

Underlying Beijing's inflexible attitude were several crucial assumptions. First of all, Mao believed that the Chinese/North Korean troops still held the upper hand on the battlefield. Although Peng and other Chinese field commanders in Korea found it difficult for their troops to advance farther south, Mao had a different view. Basing his observations of the Korean conflict on his experience in China's civil war, the CCP chairman believed that the Chinese troops, by outnumbering the enemy forces and maintaining higher morale,

Chinese People's Volunteers commander Peng Dehuai (left) and North Korean Communist leader Kim Il-sung at CPV headquarters, 1951. Xinhua News Agency.

could expand their gains. In a telegram to Peng on 14 January, Mao wrote of the two possibilities he foresaw in the future movement of U.S./UN forces in Korea: "(1) Under pressures from the great Chinese-Korean forces, [the enemy] may retreat from South Korea after a symbolic resistance. . . . (2) The enemy may resist stubbornly in Taegu and Pusan but will finally retreat from Korea after we have exhausted their potential."[56]

The need to maintain solidarity with the North Koreans served as another reason for Beijing's inflexibility. The North Korean leaders, including Kim Il-sung and Pak Hon-yong, hoped to unify all of Korea and were not convinced by Peng's argument that the Chinese/North Korean forces were unable to continue the offensive.[57] They complained about Peng to both Stalin and Mao.[58] On 10 and 11 January, Peng Dehuai, "following Kim Il-sung's suggestion," met with Kim Il-sung and Pak Hon-yong. Although Peng repeatedly emphasized the extreme difficulties Chinese troops in Korea had been facing at that time, he could not persuade his North Korean comrades. Pak Hon-yong, whose main power base had been in South Korea, angrily argued that the Chinese/North Korean forces should continue to march southward.[59]

Top Chinese leaders in Beijing, realizing the necessity of coordinating Beijing's position with North Korea's, sent two telegrams to Kim Il-sung on 14 January to clarify Beijing's official stand and to explain Chinese military strategy in Korea. In a highly publicized memo, sent in the name of the Chinese government, Beijing emphasized that an immediate cease-fire was unacceptable for the Communist side. Only when the U.S./UN side had agreed to such important conditions as withdrawing all foreign troops from Korea, settling the Taiwan question, and addressing other important Far Eastern issues would Beijing agree to negotiate.[60] In another telegram sent to Kim Il-sung via Peng Dehuai, the CCP chairman pointed out that the Chinese forces "must be well prepared" before they could be put into another offensive campaign, otherwise they would "recommit the mistakes the Korean troops had committed in June–September 1950."[61] The North Koreans now had to yield to the Chinese position, and they gave their consent when Kim Il-sung met with Peng Dehuai on 16–18 January.[62] The next day, Mao instructed the CPV commanders in Korea to demonstrate "a whole-hearted respect" for the North Korean people, government, party, and, particularly, "the Korean people's leader, Comrade Kim Il-sung."[63] On 17 January, Zhou Enlai rejected the three-person group's ceasefire proposal.

In a deeper sense, Mao's pursuit of a total victory in Korea must be understood in the context of his desire to use the victory to push forward the political mobilization of the Chinese people on the CCP's terms. China's entry into the Korean War, as Mao had expected, triggered a new wave of patriotism and revolutionary nationalism among the Chinese people. The propaganda related to "The Great Movement to Resist America and Assist Korea" quickly went beyond the original focus of "safeguarding our homes and defending our motherland," entering a new stage in which the emphasis was the Communist leadership's contribution to the creation of a powerful and prestigious "new China." Mao and his fellow Beijing leaders clearly felt that continuous Communist victories on the Korean battlefield would broaden and deepen this movement. On 2 February, the CCP Central Committee issued "Instructions on Promoting the Movement to Resist America and Assist Korea among All Walks in the Country." The document called upon the whole party and the entire country to echo the CPV's victories in Korea by bringing the "Great Patriotic Movement to Resist America and Assist Korea" to deeper levels. It particularly emphasized that the movement should be directed to "raise the contempt and hatred of the U.S. imperialists" while "encouraging [Chinese people's] national self-confidence and self-respect." Beijing's leaders hoped that by allowing this movement to penetrate into every cell of Chinese society it would result in the Chinese people's innermost acceptance of "the leadership of Chairman Mao, the People's Government, and the Chinese Communist Party."[64] Two weeks later, an enlarged CCP politburo meeting reemphasized Mao's view of the importance of making the "Great Movement to Resist America and Assist Korea" a nationwide endeavor, so that everyone in China would be "reeducated" through their participation.[65] Beijing clearly did not welcome a cease-fire at this moment.

However, the Chinese/North Korean forces lacked the capacity to turn Beijing's ambition into reality. To the surprise of the Chinese commanders in Korea, a U.S./UN counteroffensive began on 25 January. Peng Dehuai's troops were short of ammunition and food, and the commander thus proposed to Mao on 27 January that they retreat. He also asked if "the Chinese and Korean side would favor a cease-fire by a certain deadline and [whether] the Chinese People's Volunteers and Korean People's Army (KPA) could offer to retreat 15–30 kilometers" in order to "deepen the contradictions within the imperialist camp."[66] Mao, not ready to give up the illusion of a total victory, ordered Peng the next day to answer the American offensive with a Chinese counteroffensive (which would be the fourth Chinese offensive campaign in Korea). He even believed that the CPV/KPA forces had the strength to reach the 37th or even the 36th parallels.[67] Peng, again, had to obey Mao's order.

But the Chinese counteroffensive, as Peng had predicted, was quickly repulsed by U.S./UN troops, presenting Chinese forces with greater difficulties.[68] On 21 February, Peng returned to Beijing to report to Mao in person the real situation on the battlefield. Peng believed that the Chinese/North Korean forces should take up defensive positions, that new troops should be sent to Korea to replace those units that had suffered heavy casualties, and that preparations should begin for a counteroffensive in the spring.[69] In light of Peng's report, Mao's ideas on Chinese strategy in Korea began to change subtly. He now acknowledged that the war would be prolonged and that the best strategy was to rotate Chinese troops in Korea so that they could take turns fighting the UN forces. Still, however, Mao believed that the Chinese could push the UN forces out of Korea by annihilating American reinforcements continuously.[70]

After two months of readjustment and preparations, the Chinese/North Korean high command gathered twelve armies to launch an offensive in late April, hoping to destroy the bulk of UN forces and to establish clear Communist superiority on the battlefield. In a 19 April order to mobilize the troops for this campaign, Chinese field commanders in Korea pointed out that "this is the campaign that will determine the fate and length of the Korean War."[71] Without proper air cover[72] and reliable logistical supply, however, the offensive failed. In the last stage of the campaign, several Chinese units that had penetrated too deeply into the UN-controlled areas were surrounded by counterattacking U.S./UN forces. The Chinese 180th Division was almost totally lost.[73]

Coming to the Negotiation Table

The Communist defeat in the fifth campaign forced Mao and the other Chinese leaders to reconsider their aims on the Korean battlefield. Realizing that a huge gap existed between the capacity of Chinese troops in Korea and the ambitious aims that Beijing had assigned to them, Mao became willing to conclude the war short of a total Chinese/North Korean victory.[74] In late May 1951, Beijing's military planners, following Mao's instructions, conducted an overall review of China's strategies in Korea. Nie Rongzhen, China's acting chief of staff, summarized the consequences of this review process in his memoirs: "After the Fifth Campaign, the Central Committee met to consider what steps we should take next. The opinion of the majority is that our forces should stop at the 38th parallel, continue fighting during the armistice talks, and strive to settle the war through negotiations. I, too, agreed with this opinion. In my view, by driving the enemy out of northern Korea, we had achieved our political objective. Stopping at the 38th parallel, which meant a return to the prewar status, would be easily accepted by all sides involved."[75] Furthermore, in reassessing the probable impact that an armistice would have on China's domestic situation and international status, Mao and his fellow Beijing leaders concluded that the success of the Chinese troops in pushing the U.S./UN forces back from the Yalu River to areas close to the 38th parallel had sufficiently put them in a position to claim that China had *already* achieved a great victory.[76] Under these circumstances, the CCP leadership decided at the end of May that China would adopt a new strategy, one with a keynote of "fighting while negotiating," and China's operational aims would now be redefined as pursuing an armistice by restoring the prewar status in Korea.[77]

Kim Il-sung, however, hoped to maintain the Communist offensive. In a letter to Peng Dehuai on 30 May, Kim emphasized that "certainly we may predict that the Korean problem cannot be solved in peaceful ways, and that the war will not end at the 38th parallel. In view of this, my opinion is that we should prolong our military offensive, and should continue to attack the enemy."[78] In order to coordinate the strategy between the Chinese and North Koreans, the Chinese leaders invited Kim Il-sung to visit Beijing in early June.[79] Chinese and Russian sources now available do not offer detailed coverage of the discussions between Mao and Kim, but evidence indicates that because Kim was unwilling to accept China's new position, it was difficult for the two parties to reach a consensus. Kim argued that the Chinese/North Korean forces still held a superior position on the battlefield and that it would be better if they put the negotiation option on hold until more enemy forces were annihilated. Mao, however, emphasized that if the negotiations would include conditions such as the gradual withdrawal of foreign troops from Korea and the settlement of the Korean question, the Chinese/North Korean side had no reason not to come to the negotiation table.[80] Since the Chinese troops were the main combat force in Korea and Kim himself had no strength to fight the UN forces independently, he had to yield to the new Chinese strategy.[81] Consequently, Mao and Kim agreed that they would start formal negotiations with the Americans to stop the war at the 38th parallel, and that, at the very least, Chinese/North Korean forces would not start another strategic offensive in the coming two months.[82]

In mid-June, Mao and the CCP leadership were ready to implement the new strategy of "preparing for a prolonged war while striving to end the war through peace negotiations."[83] In a telegram to Gao Gang and Kim Il-sung dated 13 June, Mao Zedong pointed out that because the Chinese and North Korean forces must maintain "a defensive position in the next two months," it would be better to "wait for the enemy to make an appeal [for negotiation]." He also hoped that "the Soviet government would make an inquiry to the American government about an armistice." In terms of the conditions for the armistice, the Chinese would be willing to accept the restoration of the border at the 38th parallel and the creation of a neutral zone between North and South Korea. The PRC's entrance into the UN, Mao made clear, would not be a condition for armistice. On Taiwan, Mao believed that "the question should be raised in order to bargain with them," but "if America firmly insists that the question of Taiwan be resolved separately, then we will make a corresponding concession."[84]

Probably because Kim Il-sung was not completely persuaded by Beijing's argument,[85] on 10 June Gao Gang, representing Beijing, and Kim Il-sung, representing the North Koreans, traveled to Moscow to consult with Stalin, whom they met on 13 June. According to the memoirs of Shi Zhe, the Chinese interpreter attending the meeting, the discussions focused on three crucial questions: (1) What was the real situation on the battlefield? (2) By comparing the strength of the two sides, did the Chinese/North Korean forces still hold an upper hand? (3) Was the enemy planning a counteroffensive? And, if it was, were the Chinese/North Korean troops in a position to repulse it? In presenting their opinions to Stalin, Gao Gang and Kim Il-sung must have misused such terms as "armistice," "reconciliation," "cease-fire," "truce," and "peace agreement" because Stalin asked them to define these terms clearly, so that he would know where the discussions would lead. Gao Gang and Kim Il-sung finally agreed that what the Chinese and North Koreans wanted to pursue was an *armistice* on the basis of a *cease-fire*. Consequently, with Stalin's endorsement, the Chinese and North Koreans reached a consensus that they would now work for an armistice through negotiations, and that their bottom line would be the restoration of Korea's prewar status.[86] On 13 June, Stalin informed Mao Zedong that he, Gao Gang, and Kim Il-sung had reached the conclusion that "an armistice is now advantageous."[87]

On 23 June, Jacob Malik, Soviet representative to the UN, formally called for "a cease-fire and an armistice providing for the mutual withdrawal of forces from the 38th parallel," and he mentioned nothing about the withdrawal of foreign troops from Korea, China's seat in the UN, or the Taiwan question.[88] Beijing immediately endorsed the Soviet initiative.[89] The U.S./UN side responded positively to the Communist call for negotiation, and on 24 June, Trygve Lie, UN secretary general, stated that he hoped the armistice negotiations would start at the earliest possible time. The next day, President Truman announced that the United States was willing to participate in negotiations leading to an armistice in Korea.[90] By early July, the two sides had agreed that negotiations would start on 10 July at Kaesong.

Defining China's Negotiation Strategies

Negotiating with the Americans was a new challenge for Beijing's leaders. From 1944 to 1946, the Chinese Communists had been engaged in a series of contacts with the Americans during the CCP-Nationalist talks for averting the civil war, but that experience did not involve direct negotiations between the CCP and the United States.[91] To guarantee Beijing's direct control of the negotiation process, top CCP leaders acted immediately to organize China's negotiation team. Generals Deng Hua and Xie Fang of the CPV and General Nam Il of the KPA would lead the Chinese/North Korean negotiators; but a behind-the-scenes "negotiation direction group" was formed to guarantee that the negotiations "follow[ed] correct strategies and tactics." Li Kenong, vice foreign minister and the CCP's longtime military intelligence head, and Qiao Guanhua, head of the Foreign Ministry's International Information Bureau who had had extensive experiences in dealing with the Americans in the 1940s, were assigned to lead the group.[92] Before Li and Qiao left Beijing, Mao had a long conversation with them, emphasizing that they should treat the coming negotiations as a "political battle" and should always follow the policy lines formulated in Beijing. Mao also instructed them to maintain daily telegraphic communications with Beijing's top leaders.[93] This group arrived at Kim Il-sung's headquarters early on 6 July, and the North Koreans agreed that the negotiations would be directed by this group, with Li as the "team head" and Qiao as the "director."[94]

Beijing's other main concern was how to justify to the Chinese people the new strategy of ending the war. On 3 July, the CCP Central Committee issued "Instructions on the Propaganda Affairs Concerning the Peace Negotiations in Korea." The CCP leadership stated that "we have always favored settling the Korean problem through peaceful means, and that peace has been the very purpose of the CPV's participation in the anti-aggression war in Korea." The document then pointed out that the "War of Resisting America and Assisting Korea" had succeeded in the past eight months not only in "defending the security of the Democratic People's Republic of Korea and PRC," but also in "forcing the Americans to give up their original plans of aggression and to acknowledge the Chinese people's strength." It was the Americans, the CCP leadership emphasized, who solicited negotiation and an armistice. Whether or not the negotiation would lead to peace, the CCP leadership alleged, the political initiative was already firmly in Beijing's control.[95]

Beijing's leaders believed that an armistice agreement could be reached in a short period (perhaps in weeks). In a telegram to Peng Dehuai and Gao Gang (and conveyed to Kim Il-sung) on 2 July, Mao predicted that "it would take ten to fourteen days to prepare and to conduct the negotiations with the representatives from the other side." He ordered Gao Gang to "make the maximum effort" to transport the Chinese "reinforcements, weapons, and ammunition into North Korea within ten days . . . , in order to prepare for a situation in which no personnel and matériel transportation would be allowed." He also instructed Chinese negotiators to "think about what could occur after the signing of an agreement on cessation of military operations and [to] be prepared for everything that needs to be done."[96] The Chinese negotiators in Korea, including Li Kenong and Qiao Guanhua, brought only summer clothing with them since they all assumed that the negotiation would end long before Korea's bitter winter set in.[97]

Underlying Beijing's assumption that the negotiation process would be brief was the belief that the Chinese/North Korean forces still held a superior position on the battlefield. Although the Chinese setbacks in the fifth campaign had convinced both Beijing's leaders and the Chinese field commanders that it was impossible for China to achieve a total military victory in Korea, they believed that the conflict of the past eight months would have taught the Americans that a UN victory was equally impossible.[98] Furthermore, Beijing's leaders assumed that their conditions for an armistice—the restoration of the prewar status, that is, the forces of both sides returning to the 38th parallel—would be acceptable to (if not necessarily welcomed by) the Americans. Among other things, Beijing's leaders believed that it was the Americans who first proposed such a solution, and that the solution would allow each side to claim that it had not been defeated in the war.[99] The most difficult spots in the negotiation, in Beijing's view, would not be over reaching an armistice, but on issues such as the withdrawal of all foreign troops from Korea, the settlement of the Taiwan question, and China's seat at the UN. Since Beijing's leaders were now willing to resolve these tough issues after the armistice was reached, they expected that the negotiations leading to an armistice would not last long.[100]

However, as they had been taught by China's civil war, Beijing's leaders would leave other options open. They understood that only when they were backed by a strong military position on the battlefield would they be able to pursue the best terms at the negotiation table. Because it was still possible that the negotiations would be prolonged, they must remain powerful militarily. When the date and place for negotiations had been decided, the Beijing leadership and CPV commanders in Korea began planning a sixth campaign. On 2 July, Peng Dehuai ordered all CPV and KPA units to "maintain high vigilance" against the enemy, who, in Peng's view, might conduct a sudden offensive under the cover of negotiation. He emphasized that "peace would not be achieved without going through onerous struggles." [101] The same evening, Mao ordered Chinese troops in Korea to get ready to launch an offensive and to punish the enemy at any time.[102] In turn, the staff at CPV headquarters began to formulate plans for a sixth Chinese offensive campaign in Korea. Chinese commanders planned to gather thirteen CPV and four KPA armies, with the assistance of twenty-two Soviet and Chinese air brigades, to annihilate two UN divisions and drive UN forces on the eastern front back to areas south of the 38th parallel. On 8 July, CPV headquarters ordered the start of preparations for the campaign (also known as the September campaign).[103]

The negotiations at Kaesong quickly encountered a series of obstacles. In the first two weeks, the two sides were unable to reach an agreement on the negotiation agenda. While the Chinese/North Korean negotiators argued that, in addition to a cease-fire, the withdrawal of "all foreign troops" should be an integral part of an armistice, the U.S./UN representatives insisted that only the military issues related to ending the conflict in Korea should be discussed. Not until 26 July did the two sides approve a five-part agenda for continuous negotiations. They agreed to (1) adopt an agenda; (2) fix a military demarcation line; (3) make concrete arrangements for an armistice in Korea; (4) make arrangements related to prisoners of war; and (5) make recommendations on related issues to governments of both sides.[104]

The next stage of negotiations was even more tortuous. After 26 July, the two parties began to focus their discussions on the second item on the agenda, the fixation of the demarcation line. The Chinese/North Korean side, follow-ing the agreement reached between Beijing, Pyongyang, and Moscow, pro-posed that the demarcation line be on the 38th parallel. The U.S./UN side, how-ever, countered with a line running basically between Pyongyang and Wonsan, about twenty to thirty (in some places forty) kilometers north of the exist-ing front line between the Communist and UN forces, demanding more than 13,000 square kilometers of territory still under Communist control.[105] Admi-ral Charles Turner Joy, the chief U.S./UN negotiator, argued that since the UN forces controlled the airspace over all Korean territory and the sea around the Korean Peninsula, they should be awarded additional territory on the ground in an armistice agreement.[106] The Americans used arguments like this to bar-gain for a solution to end the war that was most advantageous to them, but Beijing's leaders viewed them as evidence of Washington's lack of interest in reaching an armistice.[107]

The slow progress of the negotiations caused differences of opinion to emerge among CPV commanders and Chinese negotiators. Peng Dehuai be-lieved that there was little hope for the negotiations to move forward unless the Chinese/North Korean forces could put new military pressure on the Ameri-cans. He cabled Mao on 24 July, stating that it was doubtful that the Ameri-cans would be willing to reach an armistice at this moment. He believed that in order to pursue an armistice, the Communist forces needed to win "sev-eral victorious battles, and advance to areas south of the 38th parallel." And then, Peng suggested, "we may return to the 38th parallel and conduct nego-tiations [with the enemy], so that all foreign troops will gradually withdraw from Korea on a mutually balanced basis." Peng proposed that the Communist forces complete preparations for a counteroffensive by mid-August, and that, if the enemy had failed to start an offensive by then, they conduct the offensive in September.[108] Two days later, Mao approved Peng's plans. The CCP chair-man emphasized that "it is absolutely necessary that our troops actively pre-pare for starting the offensive in September."[109] On 1 August, Mao approved the dispatch of the Twentieth Army Corps, a force composed of over 100,000 soldiers, to Korea to reinforce Chinese troops there. He also instructed the CPV to stockpile sufficient ammunition for the September campaign.[110]

Washington's aggressive attitude toward fixing the demarcation lines fur-ther convinced Peng and his comrades that a "reasonable settlement" of the Korean conflict would not be reached unless the Chinese could teach the Americans "another lesson" on the battlefield.[111] On 8 August, Peng Dehuai cabled Mao, reporting that the CPV had started the mobilization for the sixth campaign, and that this campaign aimed to annihilate the American Third

Division and the South Korean Second Division, thus pushing the front line back to areas south of the 38th parallel.[112] On 17 August, the CPV headquarters issued the primary order to start the sixth campaign.[113]

Deng Hua, the CPV's vice commander, and several other top CPV officers, however, concluded that the Chinese intention of using military strength to enhance their position at the negotiation table had encountered an equally determined American response. Policymakers in Washington seemed willing to risk, in a worst-case scenario, the breakdown of the negotiation process to ensure that an armistice would be reached on their terms.[114] In mid-August, before the CPV's sixth campaign began, the U.S./UN ground forces started an offensive. Meanwhile, the American air force intensified its bombardment of the Communist supply network. The Communist lines were slowly pushed northward. Deng Hua sent a telegram to Peng Dehuai on 18 August, emphasizing the dramatic danger involved in the CPV's sixth offensive campaign. He pointed out that the U.S./UN forces had established a highly consolidated defensive system and that a Chinese/North Korean offensive campaign might result in another major failure, which would place the Chinese/North Korean side in a much less favorable position both on the battlefield and at the negotiation table. Deng believed that it would be better for the Communist forces to maintain a defensive position, force the enemy to take the offensive, and then repulse the enemy.[115]

Deng's view was widely shared by Chinese negotiators at Kaesong. In mid-August, members of the Chinese negotiation team, including Li Kenong, Qiao Guanhua, and Xie Fang, held a series of discussions about the prospects of and problems facing the negotiations. They all agreed that "considering the other side's consistent attitude from the beginning of the negotiations and the overall situation outside of the negotiations," the Americans would likely be unwilling to yield to the Chinese/North Korean proposal of setting up the armistice line along the 38th parallel. They also concluded that the Americans' bottom line would be an on-site armistice plus some minor adjustments and that if the Chinese/North Korean side stuck to the 38th parallel solution, the negotiations would fail. On 12 August, they proposed that Beijing adopt a new stand based on an on-site cease-fire.[116]

Beijing's leaders had to reconsider how best to define China's strategies to end the war. As early as 10 August, Mao instructed Zhou Enlai and Nie Rongzhen to review the CPV's plans for the sixth campaign, focusing on the feasibility of the campaign's goals as set by Chinese commanders.[117] On 18 August, the day after the CPV issued the mobilization order for the sixth campaign, top Beijing leaders met to further contemplate all factors related to the campaign.[118] On 19 August, the Central Military Commission of the CCP (CMC) sent a long telegram to Chinese commanders in Korea, instructing them to reconsider campaign plans. The telegram began with an analysis of the situation in Korea and Washington's intentions to cope with it. The CMC believed that the American objection to setting up the 38th parallel as the demarcation line was based more on political considerations than on military ones: on the one hand, sustained tension in Korea would help maintain the unity between the United States and its allies; on the other, Washington did not want to solve the Korean problem before the signing of a peace treaty with Japan. Therefore, the CMC predicted that, although it was unlikely for Washington to break off negotiations completely or to expand the war to China (since this would cause serious problems between Washington, London, and Paris), it was possible that the armistice negotiations would be drawn out. In line with these observations and speculations, the CMC instructed the CPV commanders to reconsider the necessity of waging a sixth campaign. The CMC particularly emphasized that unless Chinese commanders in Korea were certain that the sixth campaign would lead to the destruction of two enemy divisions and that it would not result in another Chinese/North Korean military setback, the campaign should be called off.[119]

While the Chinese were examining their strategies to end the war, a series of potentially explosive incidents occurred at Kaesong. On 4 August, a group of armed Chinese soldiers "mistakenly" entered the site where the armistice talks were conducted, and two weeks later, on 19 August, a Chinese platoon leader was shot in the neutral zone at Kaesong. Three days later, the Chinese/North Korean side alleged that the conference site had been bombed by a UN plane.[120] On 23 August, the day after the last incident, top leaders in Beijing instructed the Chinese negotiators to respond to this American violation with a "firm strike, even if that meant that the negotiations would be prolonged or broken."[121] The Chinese/North Korean side immediately suspended the negotiations.[122]

The Chinese walkout at this moment did not mean that Beijing was no longer interested in ending the war through negotiations;[123] nor was it simply a gesture designed to strengthen Beijing's bargaining power. Beijing's leaders wanted an opportunity to reassess their position on the battlefield, as well as at the negotiation table, so that they could clarify and, if necessary, redefine China's negotiation strategies in light of the first forty days of the armistice talks.[124] In addition, since Western powers were to meet in San Francisco early in September to sign a unilateral peace treaty with Japan, excluding China and the Soviet Union, Beijing's leaders wanted to see what Washington would do in Korea after that.[125]

In the ensuing two months, top leaders in Beijing and CPV commanders and Chinese negotiators in Korea focused their review of China's negotiation strategies on three key questions: (1) What caused the seemingly unyielding American attitude at the negotiation table? (2) What were the best terms that the Chinese/North Korean side could obtain through negotiations and what should be their bottom line? (3) Given the need to maintain Beijing's bottom line and the means available to do so, what were the best strategies for the Chinese/North Korean side to adopt?

During this review process, Beijing's leaders realized that their initial ideas about how to conduct the negotiations had been too simplistic and too optimistic. Among other things, they could clearly sense that underlying the American arrogance at the negotiation table was a strong sense of U.S./UN superiority on the battlefield, and that unless they could let the Americans "cool their heels," it would be next to impossible for the negotiations to be settled under the Chinese terms.[126] Furthermore, Beijing's seven-week contact with the Americans made it apparent that the outcome of the negotiations for both sides involved a question of "face." If the Americans were allowed to win an upper hand in this "serious political struggle," Beijing's leaders believed, the Chinese Communist authority at home and its reputation and influence abroad, two main concerns behind China's intervention in Korea, would suffer.[127] Beijing's leaders concluded that they could not afford to lose this battle of wills.

However, both top Beijing leaders and CPV commanders had by now realized that weak points did exist in the Chinese/North Korean positions on the battlefield. Even with the long-planned Chinese air force's entry into the war in September 1951, the U.S./UN side still maintained solid control of Korea's airspace. Logistical vulnerability thus continued to hamper the CPV's combat capacity. In addition, there was always the possibility that UN forces, with control of the sea, would carry out amphibious landing operations in the rear of the Chinese/North Korean line, which would doom any Chinese/North Korean offensive to failure. Considering these factors, Beijing's leaders and CPV commanders agreed that it would not be in their interests to try to put more pressure on the Americans by expanding war operations.[128] In late October 1951, they finally decided to call off the sixth campaign.

As a result of this comprehensive review, a series of more clearly defined Chinese negotiation strategies came into shape. Even though "preparing for a prolonged war while striving to end the war through peace negotiations" remained the keynote of Chinese strategies, the Chinese/North Korean forces would give up using large-scale offensive operations to force the enemy to come to China's terms. The Chinese now adopted a strategy of aggressive defense on the battlefield, with the hope that the prospect of increasing casualties in an endless war would eventually force U.S./UN forces to meet Beijing's minimum demands at the negotiation table. In other words, Beijing's leaders believed that as long as the Chinese troops were not defeated in Korea, they would be in a position to claim a victory.[129] The Chinese were now ready to return to the negotiation table. On 25 October, armistice talks were resumed at Panmunjom.

Although they talked about the possibility of "prolonged negotiations," top Beijing leaders still looked forward to a relatively quick ending of the war. On 14 November 1951, Mao Zedong sent a lengthy telegram to Stalin in which he discussed China's negotiation strategies. The CCP chairman postulated that as the talks resumed, the United States faced increasing domestic and international pressures to reach an armistice in Korea, improving the chance for peace. Beijing's leaders thus believed that China's new strategy of accepting a demarcation line based on the actual line of contact between the two sides had swept away the main barriers on that issue. They also maintained that adding countries such as Sweden to the list of neutral countries that would be supervising the armistice could resolve that issue, and that the prisoners-of-war issue could be resolved by a mutual agreement to return all POWs after the armistice. Mao and the CCP leadership thus concluded that it was possible to achieve an armistice before the end of the year. Nevertheless, Mao's telegram stated that Chinese negotiators should not demonstrate excessive eagerness to reach an armistice and should prepare for the war to continue for another six months or one year. The fundamental Chinese approach, the telegram emphasized, should be that "it is fine if peace can be reached, but it will not worry us if the war is prolonged."[130]

The Chinese negotiation direction group discussed Mao's instructions on 20 November. The majority of the group believed that if an agreement could be reached on the demarcation lines, there was a good opportunity to conclude an armistice by the end of the year; and since the enemy had demonstrated no ability to break Chinese defensive lines, there was no reason that an agreement on the demarcation lines would not be reached in the near future. Only Qiao Guanhua suggested that the POW issue might cause trouble.[131]

For a while, Chinese optimism seemed to be well-founded. Two days after their meeting, an agreement on the demarcation lines was reached. On 27 November, negotiators agreed to accept the actual line of contact between the two sides.[132] An armistice now seemed near.

Deadlock: The POW Issue

Optimism about an early end to the war, however, proved to be short-lived. When the two sides established a demarcation line on the map, a condition was attached to it: the line would be held only if other issues outstanding at the armistice talks were settled within thirty days. This time limit proved too brief to resolve the remaining issues. The discussions on item three of the agreed-upon negotiations agenda (making concrete arrangements for an armistice in Korea) began on 27 November. By the 27 December deadline, only marginal progress had been achieved. The two sides would not settle this item until early May of 1952. To speed up the negotiation process, discussions about item five (making recommendations on related issues to governments of both sides) began on 31 January 1952. On 19 February, the two sides finally agreed that within ninety days after the signing of the armistice agreement, a political conference would be convened to discuss the withdrawal of all foreign forces from Korea and the general issues regarding a peaceful settlement of the Korean problem.[133] It was soon clear, however, that the real obstacle lay in item four, the POW issue. The negotiations for solving this issue began on 11 December 1951, and they continued for seventeen long months.

The Chinese had not anticipated that the POW issue would create a deadlock in the armistice talks. In the initial stage of China's entry into the war, guided by the People's Liberation Army's experience during the Chinese civil war, Chinese commanders, with Mao's approval, ordered the release of several groups of U.S./UN prisoners on the battlefield with the hope that this would help demolish the enemy troops' morale.[134] Not anticipating that the POW issue could become so important, Mao even put the power of determining when and how many enemy POWs should be released into the hands of Chinese field commanders, allowing them to make decisions without reporting to Beijing in advance.[135]

Indeed, after the armistice talks were under way, Mao and the Beijing leadership did not take the POW issue too seriously. In several telegrams to CPV commanders and Chinese negotiators in July 1951, Mao treated the POW issue lightly, believing that after other "important issues" had been resolved, it would be quickly decided that all POWs would be exchanged.[136] As late as 14 November 1951, when analyzing Washington's negotiation strategies, Mao continued to believe that the Chinese/North Korean desire to exchange all POWs after the armistice would be acceptable to the Americans.[137] Although some Chinese negotiators, such as Qiao Guanhua, suspected that the settlement of the POW issue could be complicated, Beijing's leaders and Chinese negotiators generally treated it as one of secondary importance.[138]

The first major conflict regarding prisoners of war occurred in mid-December 1951, when each side challenged the numbers of POWs under the other side's custody: the Americans found that only 25 percent of America's missing in action were contained on the Communist list, and the Chinese/North Korean negotiators wanted to know why the UN command had removed 44,000 names from its previous list of Communist POWs.[139] When little progress was made in clarifying these problems, the Chinese and North Koreans became increasingly suspicious, claiming that the U.S./UN side was attempting to retain large numbers of Communist POWs.[140] This suspicion was finally confirmed on 2 January 1952, when the U.S./UN side formally proposed that the repatriation of POWs be carried out on a voluntary basis and that those refusing to return home would be released on the condition that they would not bear arms in the Korean conflict again.[141]

The Americans justified their stand on the POW issue by arguing that this was a problem concerning basic human rights.[142] In actuality, policymakers in Washington realized that, from a political point of view, if large numbers of Communist POWs chose to remain in the "free world," the U.S./UN side would occupy an extremely favorable position to launch an anti-Communist propaganda offensive. American military planners believed that returning all Communist POWs, who outnumbered the U.S./UN prisoners by almost ten to one, would certainly infuse new blood into the Communist regime and was thus unacceptable. In terms of its impact on America's bargaining power at the negotiation table, the fact that the U.S./UN side had more POWs under its custody than the Communists was a chip no one could ignore. Finally, the Syngman Rhee government's tough attitude toward this issue limited the flexibility of U.S./UN negotiators.[143] Within this context, the Americans firmly adhered to the position of nonforcible repatriation after its introduction in early January 1952. On 28 April, the U.S./UN negotiators introduced a "final" package proposal, the key part of which was that the POWs would not be repatriated forcibly and that only 70,000 Chinese/North Korean prisoners, instead of the earlier agreed-upon number of 116,000, would be returned.[144]

In the face of this unpredicted complexity, top Beijing leaders and Chinese negotiators focused their attention on the political aspect of the POW issue. In early May 1952, in a series of discussions on the essence of the U.S./UN package proposal of 28 April, members of the Chinese negotiation direction group concluded that the Americans aimed to achieve a politically superior position. In addition, Li Kenong pointed out that the Truman administration might not want to end the war at this moment for two reasons: first, in a presidential election year, Truman was concerned that a soft appearance might jeopardize the Democratic Party's electoral position; second, in order to increase military expenditures in the 1953 budget, the Korean War had to be continued.[145]

When the POW question was put before top Beijing leaders, they further emphasized that the matter was in essence "a serious political struggle" and thus decided to fight the war for another year if necessary.[146] On 12 July 1952, the U.S./UN negotiators proposed to increase the total number of Chinese/ North Korean POW returnees from 70,000 to 83,000. In two telegrams to Beijing dated 13 and 14 July, Li Kenong and the other Chinese negotiators suggested that this proposal be accepted as the basis for solving the POW issue, since 83,000 was not far below the 90,000 bottom-line figure that the Chinese negotiators had proposed.[147] But Mao Zedong immediately rebutted the suggestion and sternly criticized Li and his comrades for being politically naive. He stressed that the key question was not how many Chinese/North Korean POWs would be repatriated but which side, through the arrangement, would occupy a politically and militarily favorable position. If the Chinese accepted this U.S./UN proposal, the chairman warned, it would mean that they had yielded to the enemy's terms under political and military pressures.[148] Following Mao's instructions, the Chinese and North Korean negotiators rejected the proposal on 18 July.

Against this background, Beijing's leaders reexamined China's strategies to end the war in summer 1952. They were determined to give up any illusion of a quick end to the war and to carry out tit-for-tat struggles with the Americans both in the political sphere and on the battlefield. Not until the Chinese/North Korean side had improved both its military and political positions, Mao made it clear, would Beijing consider compromising on the POW issue.[149]

It is within this context that Beijing initiated a propaganda campaign condemning Washington's alleged "dirty biological warfare" in North Korea and in China's Northeast. According to Chinese sources, as early as 28 January 1952, the CPV reported signs of possible American use of "biological weapons" in North Korea.[150] After careful deliberations and consultations, Beijing and Pyongyang decided to make the story public. On 22 February 1952, Pak Hon-yong, North Korea's foreign minister, issued a formal statement to condemn "the U.S. imperialist crime of conducting biological warfare against the Korean people." Two days later, Zhou Enlai issued a similar statement.[151]

Then the Chinese and North Korean Communists started a "condemning America" campaign to criticize this alleged crime and called for international investigation.[152]

In retrospect, what really happened in Korea in the winter of 1951–52 must be regarded as one of the most mysterious aspects of the Korean War history: in my investigations into Beijing's archival sources, I found enough evidence to show that in early 1952 both CPV commanders and Beijing's leaders *truly believed* that the Americans had used biological weapons against the Chinese and North Koreans. On 18 February, for example, Nie Rongzhen sent to Mao and Zhou a report pointing out that the Americans had been engaged in biological warfare in Korea.[153] The next day, Mao read the report and instructed Zhou Enlai to "pay attention to this matter and take due measures to deal with it."[154] However, no convincing evidence has ever been produced on the American side to confirm the Chinese version of this story or to explain what really happened.[155]

In any case, the Beijing leadership did find in the "American biological warfare" issue an effective weapon to counter Washington's use of the POW issue to gain a politically superior position.[156] When discussions about item four stalemated, Beijing made every effort to turn the condemnation of "American biological warfare" into a nationwide and even a worldwide campaign. From late March to early September, Beijing and Pyongyang invited three "international groups of investigation" to North Korea and China's Northeast to "gather evidence of U.S. use of biological weapons in the war."[157] Starting in May 1952, Beijing released "confessions" made by twenty-five captured American pilots who allegedly had been engaged in "biological warfare" against China and North Korea.[158] This "condemning America" campaign would reach its peak in late 1952 and early 1953.

In the meantime, Beijing made real efforts to strengthen the Communists' military position on the Korean battlefield. In August and September 1952, Zhou Enlai led a Chinese delegation to visit the Soviet Union to discuss, among other things, the acceleration of Soviet military aid to China.[159] Beijing also hastened the rotation of Chinese troops in Korea. The Twenty-third, Twenty-fourth, and Forty-sixth Armies entered Korea in fall 1952, and the First, Sixteenth, Twenty-first, and Fifty-fourth Armies entered Korea in January 1953. By early 1953, the total number of Chinese troops in Korea reached 1.35 million (including logistics units), the highest level during China's intervention in Korea.[160] In addition, extraordinary efforts were made to guarantee the Chinese/North Korean forces' logistical supply. During Zhou's visit to the Soviet Union, Stalin agreed to send five additional Soviet antiaircraft regiments to Korea.[161] In late 1952 and early 1953, Beijing dispatched six divisions of railway engineering troops to Korea to construct new railways and maintain existing ones. The CPV's Logistics Department stockpiled more than 120,000 tons of ammunition and more than 248,000 tons of grain in the winter and spring of 1952–53.[162] Beijing's leaders also paid special attention to establishing a consolidated defensive system on Korea's east and west coasts to prevent possible U.S./UN landing operations in the Chinese/North Korean forces' rear. In November and December 1952, how to prepare for possible enemy landing operations became the single most important issue on the CPV's agenda. Mao believed that "if we could defeat this American attempt, the enemy would have nowhere to go, and his defeat will be certain."[163]

Underlying China's rigid attitude toward the solution of the POW issue was a belief that the Chinese occupied a better position to fight a protracted war than did the United States. In a report to the Chinese People's Political Consultative Conference on 4 August 1952, Mao Zedong emphasized that the United States had three fundamental weaknesses in fighting a prolonged war in Korea: First, the continuation of the war would cost more American lives, and the American population was much smaller than that of the Chinese. Second, a drawn-out war placed a severe financial burden on Washington. Third, America's strategic emphasis was in Europe, and an extended war in Korea would continue to disturb America's global strategic status.[164] On 17 October, Mao and Zhou sent a series of instructions to CPV commanders, stressing that the United States would encounter growing difficulties if it continued the war in Korea. They reasoned that the Americans were accustomed to letting other people fight for their interests, but they had been directly involved in the Korean War from the beginning. Furthermore, the continuation of the war would keep American military forces bogged down in Korea, and under such circumstances, Beijing's leaders asked, how could the United States afford a prolonged war in Korea?[165]

There is no evidence to show that the Beijing leadership, while formulating this tough strategy, paid any significant attention to whether or not the Americans would use nuclear weapons in Korea. Although military planners in Beijing probably considered the possibility that the Americans would use nuclear weapons for tactical targets in Korea, Mao and the other Chinese leaders firmly believed that the outcome of the Korean conflict would be determined by ground operations.[166] Not surprising at all, then, when Mao and the other CCP leaders analyzed the means Washington might use to put pressure on the Communists, they did not even bother to mention the atomic bomb.

China's rigid strategies, combined with America's unyielding attitude, led the negotiations at Panmunjom to a deadlock. After May 1952, when both sides announced a stalemate over the POW issue, talks at Panmunjom were frequently interrupted for weeks. On 8 October 1952, after the Communist side rejected the U.S./UN delegation's "final offer" on the POW question, the U.S./UN negotiators announced an indefinite recess of the negotiations.[167] The conclusion of the war seemed remote.

Breaking the Deadlock

Many researchers of the history of the Korean War have noted that a dramatic change in the Chinese/North Korean position came after Stalin's death in March 1953.[168] On 27 March, the Communists agreed to the U.S./UN suggestion that sick and wounded prisoners be exchanged first. Three days later, Zhou Enlai proposed that the POWs who were unwilling to be repatriated be transferred to a neutral state "so as to ensure a just solution to the question of their repatriation."[169] This statement reopened the door to an armistice, and discussions on resolving the POW issue resumed in late April. Some scholars, such as historian Kathryn Weathersby, have powerfully argued that Stalin's death played an important, if not decisive, role in the softening of the Communist attitude toward the POW issue, and that a logical argument following this speculation is that the tough Chinese approach over the POW issue reflected Stalin's unwillingness to end the Korean War.[170]

New Chinese and Russian sources provide these arguments with some support. According to Chinese sources, when Zhou Enlai attended Stalin's funeral and then visited the Soviet Union from 7 to 24 March, he held extensive discussions with the new Soviet leaders. On the evening of 21 March, Zhou had a long meeting with almost all the members of the new Soviet leadership, including Georgy Malenkov, Nikita Khrushchev, Lavrenty Beria, Vyacheslav Molotov, and Nikolay Bulganin, to discuss the best possible solution of the Korean War. The result of these discussions was a consensus that "the Chinese and North Korean side was now in a position to conclude the war on the basis of reasonable compromises with the enemy."[171] Recently released Russian sources also confirm that, while Zhou was in Moscow for Stalin's funeral, the Chinese and the Soviets worked out a common stand to "speed up the negotiations and the conclusion of an armistice" in Korea.[172]

However, it is implausible to attribute completely the changing Chinese attitude over the POW issue to Stalin's death. Chinese sources now available demonstrate that a more conciliatory approach on Beijing's part had its own logic that can only be understood in a broader and more complex framework. Beijing's tough attitude toward the POW issue was designed not to close the door to an armistice but to achieve favorable political and military positions before the Chinese returned to the negotiation table.[173] This position was certainly compatible with Beijing's overall management of the Korean crisis, which from the beginning centered around the crisis' domestic and international political implications. Therefore, Beijing's unyielding stand on the POW issue should be regarded more as a response to the Americans' use of the issue to put Beijing on the defensive than as an unwilling gesture made under Stalin's pressure.

No evidence in the Chinese and Russian sources now available indicates that serious differences existed between Beijing and Moscow regarding how the war should be ended in late 1952 and early 1953. When, in mid-August 1952, Zhou Enlai led a Chinese delegation to visit the Soviet Union, Stalin met with him at the Kremlin. Zhou briefed Stalin on China's domestic situation, international status, and recent developments in battlefield operations in Korea. He told Stalin that China would be willing to end the war based on acceptable conditions but would not yield to the unreasonable American terms. In Mao's view, he informed Stalin, if the Communists could demonstrate more patience than the Americans, the enemy would sooner or later make additional concessions. Zhou particularly emphasized that it was Mao's belief that a firm Communist stand in the armistice negotiations might prolong the war in Korea but would not trigger a third world war. Rather, in Mao's opinion, the conflict in Korea had exposed the weakness of the United States and delayed the coming of another world war. However, Zhou mentioned that the Chinese were having difficulties continuing war operations under the current conditions, especially since the Americans' artillery pieces outnumbered those of the Communist forces nine to one.[174]

The focus of the discussion then turned to the Chinese/North Korean bottom line in negotiations with the United States, and how the bottom line would be maintained. Stalin offered detailed advice about negotiation strategies. He suggested that the Chinese/North Korean side take three steps in dealing with the Americans on the prisoner issue. First, if the enemy insisted on holding 30 percent of Chinese/North Korean prisoners, Beijing and Pyongyang could suggest holding about 13 percent of enemy's prisoners in exchange. The purpose would be to force the Americans to change their attitude. Second, if the first design failed to work, the Chinese/North Korean side could propose a cease-fire to be followed by an exchange of prisoners. Third, if the second proposal was unacceptable to the Americans, the Communists could recommend that prisoners who did not want to be returned be held temporarily by a neutral third country, and then, after the POWs' intentions were determined, they would either be released or returned. In addition, Stalin agreed to send five Soviet antiaircraft artillery regiments to Korea in order to strengthen the Chinese/North Korean position at the negotiation table. However, he warned the Chinese not to use their air force near the 38th parallel. He believed that, if the Chinese/North Korean side could be patient in negotiations while maintaining a powerful position on the battlefield, the Americans, who were not in a position to engage in a prolonged war in Korea, would sooner or later yield to one of the three alternatives.[175]

To further coordinate the Communist strategies in dealing with the fighting and negotiations in Korea, at Zhou's suggestion, Stalin agreed to receive a high-ranking CPV and North Korean delegation in Moscow.[176] On 1 September 1952, Peng Dehuai, Kim Il-sung, and Pak Hon-Yong arrived in Moscow to join Zhou and Stalin in the discussions.[177] Stalin met with them three days later. The central issue was Soviet military support to the Chinese and North Koreans, and Stalin promised that the Soviet Union would strengthen the Chinese/North Korean air-defense system.[178] In another discussion between Stalin and Zhou on 19 September, which Mao instructed Zhou to arrange, the Chinese and the Soviets reached a consensus that the Chinese/North Korean side would not make concessions to the Americans until its political and military status had been further improved.[179]

Beijing alone was responsible for its unyielding attitude over the POW issue, and that is most clearly demonstrated in two important documents. On 16 December 1952, in a telegram drafted by Zhou Enlai and signed by Mao Zedong, the leaders expressed that "the armistice negotiations had encountered a deadlock" and that "operations in Korea could be intensified in a given period in the future (say, a year)." The basis for this assessment was the belief that "the losses of American troops in Korea had not reached the extent that would force them to stop the fighting." Furthermore, Mao and Zhou were willing to wait to see what would happen after Eisenhower had assumed the presidency. They perceived that the only card the Americans had to play was to "conduct landing operations on both coasts to the rear of our troops," arguing that a key test would probably come in the spring of 1953. The implication was that Chinese policy could change after that time because the military situation in Korea would by then certainly have turned in their favor.[180]

On 19 February 1953, Qiao Guanhua, following Zhou Enlai's instructions, sent a report to Beijing summarizing the Chinese negotiation team's analysis of the situation in Korea and the Chinese strategy at the moment. The report observed that there existed little possibility that the United States would initiate major military offensives on the Korean battlefield, and that the Eisenhower administration's new policy of "releasing Jiang" in the Taiwan Strait was designed to place more pressure on China rather than to allow Jiang to attempt amphibious operations against the Chinese mainland. (In other words, the Chinese negotiators believed that the Chinese/North Korean forces had achieved a relatively favorable position on the Korean battlefield.) But since the United States had referred the Korean problem again to the United Nations, and since the American military had not given up the illusion that UN forces could achieve further military superiority on the battlefield, it was unlikely that the Americans would soon return to Panmunjom. If China proposed an unconditional reopening of negotiations under these circumstances, the report speculated, the Americans might take it as an indication of Chinese weakness. The report therefore suggested that China should do nothing and wait for the Americans to take the next initiative.[181] Mao and Zhou agreed with this analysis, and Mao even predicted that the Americans most likely would appeal to the Soviets to make the first move.[182]

In this context, China's shifting attitude toward the POW issue in late March 1953 appears much more logical and less dramatic than it would seem otherwise. Stalin's death might have contributed to this reversal, but it was more an outgrowth of Beijing's existing policies based on Chinese leaders' assessment of the changing situation than a reflection of altering Soviet directives.

In the spring and summer of 1953, both the Chinese and the Americans were more willing than ever to accept an armistice. After the armistice talks resumed on 26 April, the negotiations progressed more smoothly than before. Although neither side had ever given up military preparations for another possible breakdown in the talks, the two sides resolved the POW question and reached an agreement regarding voluntary repatriation on 8 June.[183] Late in the evening, Zhou Enlai personally called Li Kenong, conveying his congratulations to all members of the Chinese negotiation team at Panmunjom.[184] By 15 June, the military staffs of the two sides had worked out what was supposed to be the final demarcation line. After twenty-three months of difficult negotiations, peace seemed just around the corner. At 6:00 P.M. the same day, Peng Dehuai, in the name of the commander of the joint Chinese-Korean headquarters, ordered all Chinese and North Korean units to cease offensive operations after 16 June.[185]

The situation suddenly changed on the early morning of 18 June, when President Syngman Rhee released more than 25,000 anti-Communist North Korean prisoners held by South Korean forces.[186] That afternoon, top Beijing leaders Mao Zedong, Zhou Enlai, and Zhu De discussed the situation. In a telegram to the CPV and Chinese negotiators the next day, Mao said that he believed it unlikely that the United States would support Rhee's attempt to delay a final agreement because this would put Washington under "tremendous pressures" at home and abroad. It was more likely, observed the chairman, that the Americans would force Rhee to accept an armistice. Mao now believed that the Chinese strategy should focus on "taking advantage of the contradictions between the Americans and the South Koreans." [187]

At this moment, Peng Dehuai was on his way from Beijing to the Korean front to sign the armistice agreement. Believing that Rhee's behavior offered the Communist forces an opportunity to pursue a victorious campaign before the war finally concluded, he cabled Mao on 20 June, suggesting that the armistice be postponed until the end of the month and that in order "to deepen the contradictions among the enemies, we give Syngman Rhee's puppet forces another strike by annihilating 15,000 puppet troops." [188] Mao approved Peng's suggestions the next day,[189] and although Kim Il-sung had reservations about launching an offensive at this last stage of the war, Peng issued the operation order.[190]

On 13 July, after three weeks of preparations, Chinese forces began an offensive campaign designed to punish the South Koreans, mauling Rhee's Capital Division and the Third Division before the South Korean troops were able to hold their ground. The CPV/KPA forces stopped the offensive on 20 July.[191] Seven days later, the armistice was finally signed, and the three-year-long Korean War was over.

Conclusion

In order to understand the logic of China's shifting strategies during the Korean War, one must first comprehend Beijing's evolving aims during the war. Beijing's leaders, and Mao Zedong in particular, decided to enter the Korean War in October 1950 to protect China's physical security and, more importantly, to pursue a glorious victory over the American-led UN forces. Underlying this approach was the CCP leadership's desire—and Mao's desire in particular—to use the challenge and the threat brought about by the Korean crisis to cement Communist control of China's state and society, as well as to promote Communist China's international prestige and influence. China's strategies to end the war were therefore comprehensive and assertive.

The Chinese experience in Korea from October 1950 to May 1951, however, made it clear to Beijing's leaders that China's capacity to wage war did not equal its ambitious aims. It thus became necessary for Beijing's leaders to make fundamental adjustments to China's war objectives, as well as its strategies to end the war. After reassessing China's gains and losses in Korea and

consulting with Moscow and Pyongyang, Beijing's leaders changed their definition of "China's victory in Korea" by arguing that Communist China was
already victorious since Chinese troops had pushed the U.S./UN force back
to the 38th parallel. The Chinese negotiators came to the negotiation table in
July 1951, believing that an armistice would soon follow.

The negotiation process turned out to be much more complicated than Beijing's leaders had expected. Not a single issue on the negotiation agenda could
be resolved easily and, to the surprise of Beijing's leaders, the POW issue became the obstacle that produced a deadlock. Beijing's leaders found that the
struggles at the negotiation table, especially those concerning the POW issue,
were related to the essence of China's intervention in Korea, and they were determined not to lose this "serious political struggle." As a result, they adopted
a tit-for-tat approach in handling the negotiations and in planning military
operations on the battlefield. Consequently, this approach combined with an
equally rigid American policy to make military conflicts in Korea drag on for
another two years.

Beijing's changing policies toward concluding the military conflict in Korea
had been shaped by many concerns, including how to accurately assess America's intentions and capabilities, how to coordinate with Pyongyang and Moscow in formulating diplomatic policies and military strategies, and how to
evaluate China's comprehensive political and military gains and losses in a particular armistice agreement. But, most of all, Beijing's strategy toward ending
the war was determined by the rationale behind the transformation of China's
state and society and the promotion of its international prestige and influence.
When the war ended, Mao and his fellow Beijing leaders could claim that they
had been successful in reaching both their domestic and their international
aims—although the price had been heavy.[192] This success, in turn, would encourage Mao and his fellow Beijing leaders to treat Communist China's foreign policy as an integral part of China's continuous revolution. Communist
China had further secured its status as a revolutionary power.

CHAPTER 5
CHINA AND THE
FIRST INDOCHINA WAR,
1950–1954

Despite its obvious significance, China's involvement in the First Indochina War has long been an under-researched and inadequately understood
subject in Cold War studies. Until recently, because Chinese and Vietnamese
sources were inaccessible, the many plausible English-language publications
on the First Indochina War either completely ignore, or give only marginal
attention to, China's connection to it. King Chen's *Vietnam and China, 1938–
1954*, using contemporary newspapers and radio broadcasts, offers the most detailed and generally reliable treatment of the Chinese–Viet Minh relationship,
but even this study is restricted by its sources and fails to provide a comprehensive picture of the strategic cooperation between the Chinese and Vietnamese
Communists. Consequently, the study leaves a crucial lacuna in judging the extent and nature of their relations.[1] This chapter uses recently released Chinese
sources to shed new light on China's role in the First Indochina War.

Early Contacts between the Chinese and Vietnamese Communists

The Chinese Communist Party and the Vietnamese Communists had a history of close associations. Early in the 1920s, Ho Chi Minh, who could speak
fluent Chinese and often visited China, and many other Vietnamese Communists established contacts with their Chinese comrades in Europe.[2] In 1924,
Ho was dispatched by the Comintern to China to assist Mikhail Borodin, the
Soviet agent working for Sun Yatsen and the Guomindang government in
Guangzhou.[3] In the late 1930s and early 1940s, Ho, while conducting revolutionary activities in China, became a member of the CCP-led Eighth Route
Army and stayed in the CCP's Red capital Yan'an for several weeks.[4] After the
end of the Second World War, Ho's Indochina Communist Party (ICP; after
1951, the Vietnamese Workers' Party, or VWP)[5] led a national uprising and
established the Democratic Republic of Vietnam (DRV) with Ho as president.
When the French returned to reestablish their control, Ho and his fellow

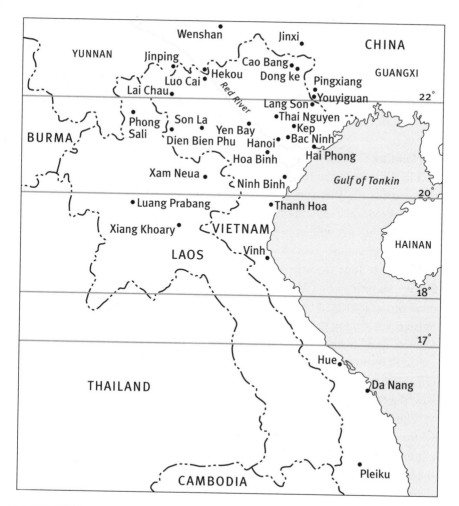

INDOCHINA

Communists moved to mountainous areas to fight for independence. The First Indochina War began.

When the DRV was established, the CCP decided to send many of its Vietnamese members back to their own country to promote the Vietnamese revolution. After the outbreak of the First Indochina War, the Chinese Communist guerrilla forces in Chinese-Vietnamese border areas occasionally assisted the Viet Minh's military operations.[6] The CCP's Hong Kong Bureau Branch, following the party Central Committee's orders, provided intermittent financial support for Ho and the Viet Minh.[7] However, having its own revolution as top priority, the CCP was unable to provide direct and substantial support to the Viet Minh before the end of 1949. Because of technical difficulties, no reliable telegraphic communications existed between the Chinese and Vietnamese Communist leaderships during this period.[8] Consequently, the Vietnamese Communists had to fight a war against the French basically by themselves from 1946 to late 1949.

Planning China's Support to the Viet Minh

The Chinese Communist victory in 1949 changed the international environment for the Vietnamese revolution. For the purpose of promoting the PRC's international reputation and enhancing its southern border security, the CCP leadership was willing to play an outstanding role in supporting the cause of their Communist comrades in Vietnam.

From late June to early August 1949, the CCP's second in command, Liu Shaoqi, secretly visited Moscow and held a series of meetings with Stalin and other Soviet leaders. A main part of the discussions covered how to promote an Asian revolution in general and the Vietnamese revolution in particular. The Chinese and Soviet leaders reached a general consensus that it was primarily the CCP's responsibility to provide support to the Vietnamese revolutionaries.[9] On 24 December, during a meeting between Mao Zedong and Stalin in Moscow, the two leaders confirmed this arrangement.[10]

The Vietnamese Communists were also eager to receive support from their Chinese comrades. In August 1949, when the victorious Chinese People's Liberation Army, in chasing the remnants of the GMD forces, was about to reach the Chinese-Vietnamese border area, Ho Chi Minh wrote a letter to Mao Zedong, describing the situation in Vietnam and asking for Chinese aid in any and all forms. Ly Ban and Nguyen Duc Thuy, two ICP envoys with close personal ties to the CCP, delivered the letter to Beijing in October.[11] On 24 December 1949, Liu Shaoqi chaired a CCP politburo meeting to discuss China's support to Vietnam, which concluded with the decision to invite a high-ranking Vietnamese delegation to Beijing to "discuss all important issues." In order to learn more about the situation in Vietnam and to establish direct contacts with the Vietnamese Communists, the CCP leaders also decided to send Luo Guibo, a PLA commander who, as a guerrilla leader during the anti-Japanese war, had extensive experience in dealing with complicated situations, to Vietnam as the CCP's general representative.[12] On 25 and 28 December, Liu Shaoqi twice telegraphed Ho to inform him of these decisions, particularly mentioning that the PRC would dispatch a high-ranking adviser to Vietnam and was ready to grant diplomatic recognition to the DRV.[13] Early in January 1950, Hoang Van Hoan, an ICP Central Committee member with close ties to China, arrived in Beijing to establish direct contact with the CCP.[14] On 18 January, the PRC formally recognized and established diplomatic relations with the DRV.[15]

Early in January, when Liu Shaoqi met with Luo Guibo to assign him to work in Vietnam, he made it clear that Luo's appointment was approved by Mao and the CCP Central Committee. Luo's task in Vietnam was to establish communications between the two parties as well as to provide the CCP leadership with firsthand materials for formulating plans to assist the Vietnamese Communists. Liu stressed to Luo that "it is the duty of those countries that have achieved the victory of their own revolution to support peoples who are still conducting the just struggle for liberation" and that "it is our international obligation to support the anti-French struggle of the Vietnamese people."[16]

While Luo was on his way to Vietnam, Ho Chi Minh, after walking for seventeen days on foot, secretly arrived at China's Guangxi border around 20 January 1950.[17] When Ho arrived in Beijing on 30 January, Liu Shaoqi received him the same evening and reported his visit to Mao Zedong, who was then in Moscow. Liu emphasized in his telegram to Mao that it was necessary for the CCP to "satisfy all of Ho's requests," to which Mao agreed completely.[18] The CCP Central Committee immediately established an ad hoc commission composed of Zhu De, vice chairman of the Central People's Government and commander in chief of the People's Liberation Army, Nie Rongzhen, acting general chief of staff of the PLA, and Li Weihan, director of the United Front Department of the CCP Central Committee, to discuss with Ho his mission in China.[19] Ho made it clear that he came to obtain a substantial Chinese commitment to support the Vietnamese Communists.[20] He also wished to meet Stalin and Mao in Moscow and obtain Soviet and Chinese military, political, and economic assistance. Through arrangements by the CCP and the CPSU, Ho left Beijing by train on the evening of 3 February and arrived in Moscow one week later.[21]

Ho's secret trip to Moscow brought him mixed results. Although the Soviet Union decided to recognize Ho's government, Stalin, in the wake of the 1948–49 Berlin crisis, had concerns in Europe and was unfamiliar with, and to a certain extent even suspicious of, Ho's intentions. He was therefore reluctant to commit the strength of the Soviet Union directly to the Vietnamese Communists and turned Ho to the Chinese.[22] To Ho's great satisfaction, Mao and Zhou, first in Moscow and then in Beijing (to which Ho returned with Mao and Zhou on 3 March), promised that the CCP would do its best "to offer all the military assistance Vietnam needed in its struggle against France." When Ho returned to Vietnam he was certain that he could now rely on China's support.[23]

The CCP's attitude toward Vietnam was first and foremost the natural result of the Chinese Communists' belief that it was Beijing's mission to promote an Asian revolution following the Chinese model. Mao and other CCP leaders had consistently seen the Chinese Communist revolution as part of a world proletarian revolutionary movement initiated by the Russian Bolsheviks. As it progressed, however, and differed from the Russian revolution by concentrating on largely rural instead of urban areas, Mao and the CCP leadership had second thoughts about the nature and significance of their revolution. During 1948–49, they began to talk in terms of a much broader anti-imperialist Asian and world revolution. First, their model of revolution transcended China and offered an example of universal significance to other peoples struggling for national liberation. Second, the victory of the Chinese revolution represented the beginning of a new high tide of revolutionary movements of oppressed peoples in Asia and in the world. Consequently, they believed it their duty to assist Communist revolutionaries and national liberation movements in other countries in order to promote an Asia-wide or even worldwide revolution.[24]

The CCP's policy of supporting the Vietnamese Communists was also consistent with Mao's "lean-to-one-side" approach, one of the cornerstones of the CCP's domestic and international policies in the early years of the PRC. As discussed earlier, during Liu Shaoqi's secret visit to the Soviet Union in late June–early August 1949, Stalin strongly encouraged the Chinese to take a larger role in promoting revolutionary movements in East Asia. When Mao visited Moscow, the Chinese and the Soviets further divided the sphere of responsibility between them, leaving the support of Communist revolutionaries in Vietnam as China's duty. The CCP's commitment to Ho's struggle in Vietnam was apparently compatible with this basic strategic arrangement between Beijing and Moscow.

CCP leaders also believed that standing by their Vietnamese comrades would serve their goal of safeguarding China's national security interests. Interestingly, Mao, though a Marxist-Leninist revolutionary, demonstrated an approach similar to many traditional Chinese rulers: the safety of the Central Kingdom could not be properly maintained if its neighboring areas fell into the hands of hostile "barbarian" forces. In 1949–50, while considering potential threats to China's national safety, Mao and the CCP leadership were particularly concerned with the prospect of a possible military confrontation with imperialist countries and their acolytes in the Korean Peninsula, Indochina, and the Taiwan Strait. Convinced that events in these areas were closely interrelated, they viewed supporting the Vietnamese Communists as an effective means of strengthening their position against the threat to China from the United States.[25] This view was supported by the fact that some Chinese Nationalist units who were still loyal to Jiang Jieshi had fled to the Chinese-Vietnamese border area, making it a source of insecurity for the newly established Chinese Communist regime.[26] After the outbreak of the Korean War, although Mao and the CCP leadership placed the emphasis of their strategy regarding the United States on Korea, they continued to view the Vietnamese Communist struggle against the French as part of the overall anti-imperialist struggle in the Far East.[27] Thus, from Beijing's perspective, providing support to the Vietnamese Communists became an integral part of enhancing the PRC's vital security interests.

The Establishment of the Chinese Military Advisory Group

When the decision to support the Vietnamese Communists was made, the CCP moved forward immediately. On 13 March 1950, Liu Shaoqi telegraphed Luo Guibo, who had arrived in the Viet Minh's Viet Bac (northern Vietnam) base four days earlier, instructing him to start his work in two stages. First, he was to deal with the most urgent problems, including providing the CCP Central Committee with a clear idea about the way in which Chinese military, economic, and financial aid should be given to the Vietnamese and how that aid could reach Vietnam. Second, Luo was instructed to carefully investigate the overall military situation in Vietnam so that he could offer the CCP Central Committee suggestions about how to prepare a long-term strategy for beating the French colonialists.[28]

In April 1950, the ICP Central Committee formally forwarded to Beijing a series of requests for support, including dispatch of Chinese military advisers, China taking the responsibility for training Viet Minh troops, and China's delivery of large amounts of ammunition and military equipment.[29] The CCP leadership responded immediately. On 17 April, the Central Military Commission of the CCP ordered each of the PLA's Second, Third, and Fourth Field Armies to provide advisers at battalion, regiment, and division levels for a Vietnamese division. The Third Field Army organized the headquarters of the Chinese Military Advisory Group (CMAG), and the Fourth Field Army set up a military school for the Vietnamese.[30] On 26 April, the CMC instructed the PLA Northwestern, Southwestern, Eastern, and South Central Headquarters to offer another thirteen cadres over battalion level to join the CMAG to work with the Vietnamese Communists at the top commanding positions.[31] The military advisers gathered in Beijing during May and received indoctrination courses on the CCP's international policy. They also met top CCP leaders to receive instructions. General Wei Guoqing, political commissar of the Tenth Army Corps of the Third Field Army, was placed in charge of the preparation work.[32]

On 25 June 1950, before the Chinese advisers' training was completed, the Korean War broke out. As the war quickly changed into an international crisis, with Washington announcing that it would rescue South Korea and dispatch the Seventh Fleet into the Taiwan Strait, Beijing's leaders were convinced of an overall American plot of aggression in the Far East, against China, Korea, and Vietnam.[33] Accordingly, Mao and the CCP leadership decided to push forward their support to the Viet Minh.[34]

On 27 June, two days after the outbreak of the Korean War, Mao Zedong, Liu Shaoqi, Zhu De, and other top CCP leaders received the Chinese military advisers who were preparing to work in Vietnam. Stressing that supporting the Vietnamese Communists was the "glorious internationalist duty" of the Chinese revolutionaries, Mao assigned the advisers two major tasks: to help the Vietnamese organize and establish a formal army, and to assist them in planning and conducting major operations to defeat the French colonialists. Liu Shaoqi explained the reasons for the decision to support the Viet Minh. He emphasized that Vietnam was an important area and that sending Chinese military advisers there would have worldwide significance. If the Chinese failed to support the Vietnamese revolutionaries and allowed the enemy to stay, Liu stated, this would cause more difficulties for the Chinese.[35]

Late in July, the CMAG, composed of seventy-nine experienced PLA officers, was formally established, with General Wei Guoqing as the head, associated with Generals Mei Jiasheng and Deng Yifan, both army-level commanders from the Third Field Army. To maintain secrecy, they were known publicly as the "Working Group in Southern China." Members of the group finally arrived in Vietnam in early August and began to serve with the Vietnamese Communist forces.[36]

Chen Geng and the Border Campaign

As early as May 1950, the CCP leadership had decided to send Chen Geng— one of the most talented high-ranking commanders in the PLA, a member of the CCP Central Committee, and commander of the PLA's Twentieth Army Corps—to Vietnam to help organize a major military campaign along the

Vietnamese-Chinese border, so that the Viet Minh would be directly backed by the PRC.[37] Ho had suggested that Chen Geng be put in this position during his visit to China in early 1950 (Ho had known Chen Geng since the 1920s), and his idea was received with much enthusiasm by the CCP leadership.[38] On 18 June, Liu Shaoqi sent a telegram to Chen Geng, outlining his main tasks in Vietnam:

> In addition to discussing and resolving some specific issues with the Vietnamese comrades, your primary task is to work out a generally practical plan based on Vietnam's conditions (including military establishments, politics, economy, topography, and transportation) and on the limits of our assistance (including, in particular, the conditions for shipping supplies). We will use this plan as a guide to implement various aid programs, including making a priority list of materials to be shipped, training cadres, training and rectifying troops, expanding recruits, organizing logistical work, and conducting battles. The plan should be practical, and it should be approved by the Vietnamese party Central Committee.[39]

Chen traveled to the Viet Bac bases in mid-July. After a series of meetings with Ho Chi Minh, Vo Nguyen Giap, and other Viet Minh leaders, he suggested that in carrying out the Vietnamese-Chinese Border campaign the Viet Minh should "concentrate [its] forces and destroy the enemy troops by separating them," a principle that had proved effective for the Chinese Communists during China's civil war. Ho and the Vietnamese accepted Chen's plan.[40] On 22 July 1950, Chen reported by telegraph to the CCP Central Committee that he had reached a consensus with the Vietnamese leaders concerning the general strategy of the forthcoming Border campaign. They would first annihilate some automotive units of the enemy in mobile operations and destroy a few small enemy strongholds. This would allow the Vietnamese to gain experience, stimulate and consolidate the momentum of their soldiers, and win the initiative on the battlefield, so that they would be ready for large-scale operations. Then they would start an offensive against Cao Bang, a small town on the Vietnamese-Chinese border, by adopting a strategy of "besieging the enemy to annihilate its relief force": instead of attacking the town directly, they would surround it and sweep out the enemy's strongholds in the peripheral areas one by one, while attracting and destroying the enemy's reinforcements from Lang Son, and then seize Cao Bang. Chen believed that this strategy would guarantee the occupation of Cao Bang, "thus thoroughly changing the balance of power between the enemy and us in northeastern and northern Vietnam."[41] The CMC approved Chen's plan in a telegram on 26 July, instructing Chen "not to begin the campaign by directly attacking Cao Bang, but by attacking some of the enemy's small strongholds and then eliminating the enemy's reinforcements."[42] To guarantee that Vietnamese units would fully follow Chen's strategy, Chinese military advisers, with Ho's approval, were assigned to the various battalion, regiment, and division headquarters of Vietnamese troops.[43]

In order to strengthen the Viet Minh's combat capacity in the Border campaign, the Chinese also provided assistance with military equipment and other war materials. As early as the end of March 1950, Luo Guibo asked the CCP Central Committee for military equipment, ammunition, and communication equipment for 16,000 soldiers, to be used in military operations aimed at Cao Bang and Lao Cai.[44] From April to September 1950 the Chinese delivered to the Viet Minh more than 14,000 guns, 1,700 machine guns, about 150 pieces of different types of cannons, 2,800 tons of grain, and large amounts of ammunition, medicine, uniforms, and communication equipment.[45] In the meantime, the Viet Minh sent its troops to China's Yunnan province for training and reorganization by PLA officers.[46]

The Border campaign started on 16 September. After forty-eight hours of fierce fighting, Viet Minh troops seized Dong Khe, a strategically important spot on Route Colonial Four, which linked Cao Bang with Vietnam's interior.[47] The French Command was surprised and dispatched a mobile army corps to Dong Khe while sending five battalions to attack Thai Nguyen, the location of the Viet Minh center. Chen judged that their real purpose was to rescue their isolated units in Cao Bang. So, instead of withdrawing troops from the Dong Khe–Cao Bang area to defend the Viet Minh center, he increased the pressure on Cao Bang. On 3 October, as he had predicted, French troops retreated from the Dong Khe–Cao Bang area and moved south, to fall into his trap in the nearby mountains. In Beijing, Mao Zedong paid close attention to the battles in the Vietnamese-Chinese border area. In response to Chen's report about the situation there, Mao dispatched a lengthy telegram on 6 October to give Chen clear instructions on how the final stage of the campaign should be fought:

> It is correct for you to plan to first concentrate your main forces to eliminate the enemy troops southwest of Dong Khe whom we have now surrounded, and then, according to the situation, surround and annihilate the enemy troops escaping south from Cao Bang. If the enemy troops southwest of Dong Khe can be annihilated in a few days, the enemies from Cao Bang can be held, and the enemy reinforcements in Lang Son and other places will

not dare to come out, or we can use part of our troops to stop the enemy's reinforcements, defeat the enemies both in Cao Bang and in Dong Khe, and thus win two victories. So, you have to annihilate the enemy troops southwest of Dong Khe swiftly, resolutely, and thoroughly; your determination should not waver even in the face of heavy casualties (and you must anticipate that some cadres will start to waver). Meanwhile, you have to hold the enemies escaping from Cao Bang and make due preparations for the enemy reinforcements from Lang Son and other places. If you can properly solve these three problems, victory will be yours.[48]

Chen shared Mao's instructions with Ho and other Vietnamese Communist leaders. They, in turn, ordered the Viet Minh troops to begin the final assault on 6 October. By 13 October, seven battalions of French troops, about 3,000 men, were defeated, and the French were forced to give up the blockade line along the Vietnamese-Chinese border, which they had held for years.[49] Chen Geng left Vietnam in early November 1950 to take new commanding responsibility in Korea.[50]

Setbacks in 1951

The Viet Minh's victory in the Border campaign changed the balance of power on the Indochina battlefield. With the vast territory of the PRC backing them, Ho Chi Minh and the Vietnamese Communists were now in an unbeatable position. Encouraged by their new victory, Vo Nguyen Giap, commander of Viet Minh forces, and other Viet Minh military leaders, together with members of the CMAG, planned to lead the war to the Tonkin Delta area. They hoped that a series of victories against the weak links of the French defensive system on the Delta would create the conditions for a total Viet Minh victory in Indochina.[51] Beijing's leaders and the ICP Central Committee endorsed the plan.[52]

In the wake of the Border campaign, at almost the same time that the Viet Minh's new offensive was planned, major changes were being made to the French strategy in Indochina. General Jean de Lattre de Tassigny was appointed by the French government as high commissioner and commander in chief in Indochina. Immediately after his arrival in Saigon, he started a program to strengthen the French defensive system in the Delta area. By integrating into his defensive planning every means available, including the French air force, which was now using new American techniques, he ordered French soldiers to dig in to the last in defense of the Delta.[53] The Viet Minh's new offensive plan was now faced with a difficult French general.

From late December 1950 to June 1951, Viet Minh troops initiated three major offensive campaigns, respectively, in the Vinh Yen area, about twenty miles north of Hanoi (the Tran Huong Dao campaign), the Mao Khe area next to Hai Phong (the Hong Hoa Tham campaign), and the Ninh Binh area (the Quang Trung campaign). The Viet Minh high command used its best units, including the "iron division" (the 308th Division), in these operations, hoping that this "general counteroffensive" would bring the Vietnamese Communists closer to a final victory. In the face of firm French defense supported by superior artillery fire, however, Viet Minh forces suffered heavy casualties without making any significant strategic gains. General Giap had to give up plans for head-on attacks against fortified positions in the Red River delta area by mid-1951,[54] and the Viet Minh high command and the Chinese advisers working in Vietnam had to reconsider their whole strategy. Chinese advisers were now convinced that it was premature for Viet Minh forces to wage a "general counteroffensive" aimed at seizing the Delta area, and that they must instead shift the direction of their operations.[55]

Meanwhile, the French hoped to expand their victory. While continuing to consolidate their control over the Delta area, French troops began a counteroffensive against Hoa Binh, the key point in the Viet Minh's north-south line of communication. If the French were allowed to control this area, they would, among other things, occupy a favorable position to establish a corridor from Hai Phong through Hanoi and Hoa Binh to Son La, thus totally cutting off the connection between Viet Minh forces in the north and the south.[56]

Facing this urgent situation, Giap asked advice from Luo Guibo and Deng Yifan (Wei Guoqing and Mei Jiasheng were then taking sick leave in China).[57] After asking for instructions of the CMC in Beijing, Deng suggested that the Viet Minh's forces cope with the French attack with medium- or small-scale mobile wars. Luo further proposed that Viet Minh troops not only focus on defending the Hoa Binh area, which they could not afford to lose, but also dispatch some units into the rear of the French-occupied zones to conduct guerrilla operations aimed at harassing the enemy and restoring guerrilla bases.[58] The Vietnamese Communist leadership carefully studied these suggestions and decided in late November to start an all-out effort aimed at repulsing the French offensive. They would deploy four divisions to defend the Hoa Binh area and send the 316th and 320th Divisions into areas behind the enemy's lines.[59] The Viet Minh's counteroffensive began in early December 1951. After three months of struggle, General Giap and his troops successfully turned away the French offensive, maintained their position in Hoa Binh, and strengthened their overall strategic status.

The Northwest Campaign

The Viet Minh's setbacks in 1951 convinced their Chinese military advisers of the necessity of leading the war into the enemy's rear by breaking up the weak link in the enemy's defensive system. Luo Guibo, who was then also in charge of the CMAG during General Wei Guoqing's sick leave,[60] recommended that the Viet Minh consider bringing the war to Vietnam's northwestern region adjacent to Laos, so that the overall military situation in Indochina could be turned to the Viet Minh's favor.[61]

Early in 1952, after several months investigating the situation on the battlefield, the CMAG sent two reports, "A Study of the Conditions between the Enemy and Us in Northern Vietnam and Our Tasks and Policy Lines in the Future" and "Tasks and Policy Lines for 1952," to the Vietnamese, proposing to start a new campaign—the Northwest campaign. Chinese advisers believed that this effort would further consolidate the Viet Minh's liberation zone in northwestern Vietnam and form the basis for a general strategic counteroffensive in the future.[62] On 16 February 1952, the CMAG proposed to the Viet Minh high command that for 1952 they focus on guerrilla tactics and small-scale mobile wars so that their main formations could go through political and military training in preparation for combat in the Northwest.[63] The same day, Luo Guibo stated in a report to the CMC that in the first half of 1952 Viet Minh troops would focus on reorganization and training; in the second half of 1952 they would try to eliminate enemies in Son La, Lai Chau, and Nghia Lo, all in northwestern Vietnam, and consolidate their control of these areas; and then in 1953, they would establish bases in northwestern Vietnam from which to initiate operations in upper Laos.[64] This plan was quickly approved by Chinese leaders in Beijing. Liu Shaoqi commented that "it is very important to liberate Laos."[65] The Vietnamese Communists also gave their approval. On 18 March, the Viet Minh high command decided to include the organization of the Northwest campaign as one of its three major tasks of 1952 (the other two being conducting political rectification of Viet Minh troops and leading guerrilla operations into the rear of the enemy). In April 1952, the VWP politburo formally decided to initiate the Northwest campaign, and Chinese military advisers were authorized by Ho himself to command it.[66]

On 14 April, Luo sent a telegram to Beijing, reporting on the CMAG's initial plan for the Northwest campaign. Offensive operations in the northwestern provinces would begin in mid-September. Viet Minh troops would first attack Nghia Lo, the northwestern province closest to the Viet Minh's Viet Bac bases, and then march toward Son La. After the liberation of most of the Northwest region in 1952, Viet Minh troops would attack Lai Chau in 1953. Beijing's leaders approved Luo's plan in a telegram to him on 19 April. Anticipating fierce fighting in seizing Nghia Lo, they stressed the importance of making proper preparations before the start of the campaign.[67]

Luo and Mei Jiasheng, then deputy head of the CMAG, further analyzed the military situation in the Northwest and sent a telegram to Beijing on 11 July, suggesting that the Northwest campaign be conducted in two stages. In the first, the Viet Minh would use two divisions to seize Nghia Lo and at the same time annihilate the enemy's paratroopers, if they were used as reinforcements. In the second stage, three regiments would be dispatched to enter Son La, while the other three regiments, together with another two regiments in Phu Tho, would march toward Lai Chau. Viet Minh troops, Luo and Mei believed, would thus be able to occupy Vietnam's entire northwestern territory by the end of 1952. Responding to the requests of the Vietnamese, they also asked Beijing to send Chinese troops in Yunnan province to take part in the attack on Lai Chau.[68]

On 22 July, the CCP Central Committee replied that it was impossible for China to send troops directly into the fighting in Vietnam, and that this had long been an established principle. Chinese troops, however, could be deployed along the Chinese-Vietnamese border, in the Hekou and Jinping areas in Yunnan province. The telegram also instructed Chinese military advisers to adopt the strategies of "concentrating our own forces" and "the easiest first and the most difficult last" by seizing Nghia Lo province before considering occupying the entire Northwest. Beijing's leaders reminded the Chinese advisers that Viet Minh troops lacked the experience of offensive operations and asked the CMAG and the Viet Minh high command not to pursue a total victory in the Northwest by the end of 1952 but to prepare for a protracted war.[69] In early September, the VWP politburo decided to conduct the Northwest campaign following these suggestions.[70]

In late September, Ho Chi Minh secretly visited Beijing, where he and the CCP leaders reached a consensus on the overall strategy for the next stage: the Viet Minh's forces would first direct their main attention to the Northwest (including northwestern Vietnam and upper Laos), then march southward from upper Laos to push for the Red River delta. Meanwhile, in terms of the concrete plan of the campaign, following the suggestions of CCP leaders, and Mao Zedong's and Peng Dehuai's in particular, Chinese and Vietnamese military planners decided to concentrate on Nghia Lo. After seizing Nghia Lo, Viet Minh troops would not attack Son La immediately but focus on establishing revolutionary bases around Nghia Lo and constructing a highway linking Nghia Lo with Yen Bay. General Giap may have had different opinions about the narrowing down of the campaign goals, but the Chinese emphasized the importance of winning a steady victory, and Giap finally yielded.[71] Wei Guoqing, after almost a year's sick leave, returned to his post in mid-October to participate in commanding the campaign.

The Northwest campaign began on 14 October 1952. The Viet Minh high command concentrated eight regiments in attacking French strongholds in Nghia Lo. In ten days, they annihilated most enemy bases and, after a short period of readjustment, continued to attack the French in Son La and Lai Chau. By early December 1952, Nghia Lo, Son La, southern Lai Chau, and western Yen Bay, all in northwestern Vietnam, had been liberated by Vietnamese Communists.[72]

After the victory, the VWP Central Committee, having consulted with the CCP leadership several times, decided in February 1953 to move farther to the west by organizing the Xam Neua campaign in upper Laos. The purpose would be to connect the "liberation zone" in northwestern Vietnam with Communist occupied areas in northern Laos, thus placing greater pressure on the French.[73] On 23 March 1953, Wei Guoqing and Mei Jiasheng led some members of the CMAG to Laos to organize the campaign, which began in late March and lasted until early May. According to Chinese statistics, the Viet Minh's troops annihilated three battalions and eleven companies, seizing control of the entire Xam Neua province and part of Xiang Khoary and Phong Sali provinces.[74] The Viet Minh's bases in northwestern Vietnam were now linked with these areas in upper Laos, further enhancing the Communists' military position.

The Path toward Dien Bien Phu

By the summer of 1953, the confrontation between Vietnamese Communists and the French on the Indochina battlefield had changed dramatically: the Viet Minh's gains in the past two years put the Vietnamese Communists in a position to pursue other victories aimed at establishing an overriding superiority in the war. Meanwhile, the end of the Korean conflict in July 1953 meant that the Chinese were able to give more attention to their southern neighbor. It was within this framework that the VWP leadership and the CMAG began to formulate military plans for the fall and winter of 1953 and spring of 1954.

The French were also making changes. In the face of a series of setbacks under the pressure of Viet Minh offensives in northwestern Vietnam and upper Laos, in May 1953 General Henri Navarre replaced General Raoul Salan (who had succeeded General Lattre de Tassigny in 1952) as the commander of French forces in Indochina. Supported by the United States, Navarre adopted a new three-year strategy aimed at winning back the advantage on the battlefield. He divided Indochina into northern and southern theaters along the 18th parallel and planned to eliminate Viet Minh guerrillas in southern and south central Vietnam by spring 1954, and then, by spring 1955, to concentrate the main formation of French forces to fight a decisive battle with the Communist forces in the Red River delta.[75] To carry out this plan, the French began to send additional troops to Indochina. The United States, released from its heavy burden in Korea and worried about the serious consequences of a French loss in Indochina, dramatically increased its military and financial support to France (by an additional $400 million) in order to check "Communist expansion" in another key part of East Asia.[76]

Facing this potentially disastrous scenario, the vwp Central Committee asked the ccp Central Committee on 13 August 1953 "to help offer opinions" concerning "the understanding of the current situation as well as strategies for operations in the future." [77] The vwp politburo, following Giap's initiative, decided on 22 August to transfer the focus of Viet Minh's future operations from the mountainous northwestern area to the Red River delta. The former area would remain on the Viet Minh's operation agenda but no longer as a priority. Luo Guibo attended the meeting of the vwp politburo and reported this strategic change to Beijing.[78]

The ccp leadership immediately discussed Luo's report and sent two urgent messages to Luo and the vwp Central Committee on 27 and 29 August, opposing the change of strategic emphasis and insisting that the original plan of focusing on the northwestern battlefield be continued. In the 29 August telegram the ccp Central Committee stated:

> We should first annihilate enemies in the Lai Chau area, liberating northern and central Laos, and then extend the battlefield gradually toward southern Laos and Cambodia, thus putting pressure on Saigon. By adopting this strategy, we will be able to limit the human and financial resources of the enemy and separate the enemy's troops, leaving the enemy in a disadvantageous position. . . . The realization of this strategic plan will surely contribute to the final defeat of the colonial rule of French imperialists in Vietnam, Laos, and Cambodia. Of course, we need to overcome a variety of difficulties and prepare for a prolonged war.[79]

The vwp politburo again met in September to discuss the message from Beijing. Ho favored the opinions provided by the Chinese, and the vwp politburo, after much debate, decided that the strategic emphasis of the Viet Minh's operations would be kept in the northwestern area.[80] On 10 October, the ccp Central Committee informed the vwp Central Committee that Wei Guoqing had been appointed as the general military adviser and Luo Guibo the general political adviser, representing the CCP in all military and political decision making in the future.[81] Wei came back to Beijing to report personally on the situation in Indochina to the CCP Central Committee. Mao received him and emphasized again that the Viet Minh should continue to treat the northwestern area as the emphasis of its military operations.[82]

In late October and early November 1953, Wei and the Viet Minh high command worked out the operation plans for winter 1953 and spring 1954. According to this plan, Vietnamese Communist forces would continue to focus on operations in Lai Chau, and would try to seize the entire Lai Chau province in January 1954; then, they would attack various French strongholds in upper and central Laos. At the same time, Viet Minh troops would also march from the mountainous areas in central Vietnam toward Laos, making lower Laos the target of attacks from two directions. The VWP politburo approved this plan on 3 November 1953.[83] Beginning in the middle of that month, five regiments of Viet Minh forces headed toward Lai Chau.

When General Navarre received intelligence reports about the Viet Minh troops' new movement, he, following the spirit of his original plan, decided on 20 November to drop six parachute battalions to Dien Bien Phu, a strategically important village located in Vietnam's northwestern mountains. If the French troops controlled Dien Bien Phu, Navarre believed, they would be able to prevent the Communists from occupying the entire northwestern region and attacking upper Laos. Dien Bien Phu would also form a "launching point" for offensives to destroy Viet Minh forces. The French quickly reinforced their troops at Dien Bien Phu, constructed airstrips, and started building defensive works, making this little-known village a real fortification. Dien Bien Phu was quickly changed into the focus of the whole Indochina battlefield.

On his way from Viet Bac to the northwestern area, Wei Guoqing learned that French paratroopers had landed at Dien Bien Phu. After consulting other Chinese advisers, Wei suggested to Beijing's leaders that the Viet Minh start a major campaign to surround French forces in Dien Bien Phu while still sticking to the original plan of attacking Lai Chau.[84] Beijing approved Wei's plan and instructed him to convey these ideas to the Viet Minh high command. Beijing's leaders particularly stressed that in addition to its military and political importance, a victory by the Viet Minh at Dien Bien Phu could have enormous impact on the development of the international situation.[85]

Beijing's emphasis on the international significance of the Dien Bien Phu campaign should be understood in the context of the Communists' new general strategy that took shape in late 1953 and early 1954. With the end of the Korean War, the Communist world launched a "peace offensive" in late 1953. On 26 September, the Soviet Union proposed in a note to the French, British, and American governments that a five-power conference (including China) should be convened to discuss ways of easing international tensions. On 8 October, Zhou Enlai issued a statement supporting the Soviet proposal and followed with another two months later, on 9 January 1954, asserting that international tensions in Asia needed to be resolved through direct consultations by the big powers.[86] The Berlin four-power conference at the end of January finally endorsed the Soviet-initiated plan to convene an international conference at Geneva to discuss the restoration of peace in Korea and Indochina.[87] A victory at Dien Bien Phu would greatly enhance the Communist position at the forthcoming conference.

The Viet Minh high command responded favorably to the CMAG's Dien Bien Phu campaign proposal. The VWP Central Committee decided on 6 December to start the campaign, and a front-line headquarters, with General Giap as the commander in chief and Wei Guoqing as the top Chinese military adviser, was established.[88] The same day, Ho Chi Minh called on the whole Vietnamese party, people, and army "to use every effort to ensure the success of the campaign."[89] Thousands of peasants had been mobilized to build roads and carry artillery pieces and ammunition over impassable mountains. From mid-December Viet Minh troops gradually positioned themselves in the areas around Dien Bien Phu to encircle the French forces. In response, General Navarre sent more troops. By the end of 1953, sixteen battalions of French troops were deployed at Dien Bien Phu.

The Chinese advisers nevertheless firmly believed that the Viet Minh's campaign efforts in Dien Bien Phu should continue, and they received full support from top leaders in Beijing. On 24 January 1954, the CMC gave Wei Guoqing instructions on the strategy for the Dien Bien Phu siege: "While attacking Dien Bien Phu, you should avoid making assaults of equal strength from all directions; rather, you need to adopt the strategy of separating and encircling the enemy, and annihilate them bit by bit."[90] Through a series of discussions with Chinese advisers, the Viet Minh high command decided to accept and adopt the strategies as proposed by the CCP leaders in Beijing.

In order to enhance the Viet Minh's offensive strength, Beijing's leaders ordered the acceleration of China's military delivery and other support to the Viet Minh. To cut off Dien Bien Phu from French airborne support, China sent back to Vietnam four Vietnamese antiaircraft battalions that had been receiving training in China.[91] During the months of the Dien Bien Phu campaign, more than 200 trucks, over 10,000 barrels of oil, over 100 cannons,

3,000 pieces of various types of guns, around 2,400,000 gun bullets, over 60,000 artillery shells, and about 1,700 tons of grain were rushed to Viet Minh troops.[92]

By March 1954, Vietnamese Communist troops had surrounded Dien Bien Phu for three months. The Geneva Conference on Korea and Indochina was scheduled for April, so Zhou Enlai instructed Chinese advisers in Vietnam: "In order to achieve a victory in the diplomatic field, you may need to consider whether you will be able to follow our experiences on the eve of the Korean armistice and win several battles in Vietnam."[93] Chinese military advisers consulted with the Viet Minh high command, which decided to start the offensive in Dien Bien Phu in mid-March.

On 13 March Communist forces began to attack French positions in the northern part of Dien Bien Phu. By 17 March, they had overrun three strongholds there and temporarily knocked out two French airstrips. The French, suddenly realizing that "the stronghold of Dien Bien Phu was a deadly trap,"[94] rushed another three battalions into the area. In the meantime, France's chief of staff, General Paul Ely, who was visiting Washington, asked for a more active American involvement in Indochina.[95] But the Communist offensive went ahead. On 30 March Communist forces attacked the central part of Dien Bien Phu, where the French frontal command was located. When their advance was slowed by strong French defensive barriers, Beijing's leaders, after receiving reports from Chinese advisers in Vietnam, summoned several engineering experts from the Chinese volunteers in Korea to teach the Vietnamese how to dig trenches and underground tunnels.[96]

Mao Zedong was eager for the Viet Minh to win an overriding victory in Dien Bien Phu, and thus to lay the foundation for a future victory in northern Vietnam. In a letter dated 3 April 1954 to Peng Dehuai, vice chairman of the CMC in charge of its daily affairs and former commander in chief of Chinese forces in Korea, Mao stated that the Vietnamese needed to form four additional artillery regiments and two new engineering regiments, which should complete training in six months. If the Chinese did not have enough cannons to equip these new Vietnamese units, Mao suggested, they could transfer the equipment from their own units to the Vietnamese. Also, Mao continued, the Chinese should supply the Vietnamese with instructors and advisers selected from among the Chinese troops who had fought in Korea, including some division and army-level officers. The best training site for these units would be in Vietnam, but somewhere in the Guangxi province would also be acceptable. Six months was a short time to execute this plan, Mao acknowledged, so he asked Peng, along with the General Staff and Artillery Command of the PLA, to contact the Viet Minh immediately to seek an agreement. Mao believed that with these new artillery units, together with another artillery division already under the command of the Viet Minh, and by amassing five infantry divisions, the Vietnamese would be able to launch direct attacks against Hanoi and Hai Phong. Mao asked Peng immediately to start preparing a sufficient supply of artillery shells and engineering equipment for these units while offering more antiaircraft guns to the Viet Minh. Concerning the current fighting in Dien Bien Phu, Mao stressed: "Dien Bien Phu should be conquered resolutely, and, if things go smoothly and success is certain, the final attack [against Dien Bien Phu] should begin ahead of schedule." In addition, Mao mentioned that the Viet Minh, after their victory in Dien Bien Phu, should quickly mobilize 5,000–8,000 new soldiers to supplement their forces and prepare to attack Hanoi no later than early 1955.[97]

When the Viet Minh's assaults at Dien Bien Phu encountered tough French resistance, the CMC telegraphed Wei Guoqing twice on 9 April, promising him that a sufficient supply of artillery ammunition would be guaranteed to the Vietnamese so that they could use as many artillery shells as they wanted. The CMC also instructed Wei to adopt the following strategies in attacking Dien Bien Phu: cut off the enemy's front by attacking in the middle; destroy the enemy's underground defenses one section at a time by using concentrated artillery fire; consolidate your position immediately after seizing even a small portion of ground, thus continuously tightening the encirclement of the enemy; use snipers widely to restrict the enemy's activities; and use political propaganda against the enemy.[98] In addition, on 17 April, Mao Zedong instructed PLA deputy chiefs of staff Huang Kecheng and Su Yu, "Considering the possibility that a cease-fire might be reached in Vietnam, the training of the new [Vietnamese] artillery divisions should not be conducted in China, and artillery pieces should be transported to Vietnam at the earliest possible time."[99]

By late April, under the fierce offensive of the Communist forces, French troops in Dien Bien Phu were confined to a small area of less than two square kilometers, with half their airstrips occupied by the Communists. At this stage the United States threatened to interfere. In a speech to the Overseas Press Club of America on 29 March, John Foster Dulles, the American secretary of state, issued a powerful warning that the United States would tolerate no Communist gain in Indochina and called for a "united action" on the part of Western countries to stop it.[100] One week later, President Dwight Eisenhower invoked the "falling domino" theory to express the necessity of a joint military operation against Communist expansion in Indochina.[101] Policymakers in

Washington even considered the possibility of using tactical nuclear weapons to stop a Communist victory in Dien Bien Phu.[102]

Without the support of either U.S. Congress or the Allies, the Americans probably were not ready to intervene in the Indochina War in 1954. The threat of direct intervention was primarily used for diplomatic reasons during the Dien Bien Phu crisis and at the Geneva Conference.[103] As will be seen, this tactic eventually worked, though in a complicated way. But it did not save the remaining French resistance in Dien Bien Phu. Chinese advisers in Vietnam insisted on continuing the campaign efforts. Wei Guiqing believed that the American warning was just an empty threat to make the Vietnamese Communists give up the current offensive. Since the Vietnamese had achieved a superior position in the battlefield, Wei stressed, they should not yield to the American threat and lose this opportunity.[104] The VWP politburo, after carefully weighing the arguments, decided on 19 April to commence the final offensive in early May.[105] To facilitate the move, the Chinese transferred a large amount of military equipment and ammunition to the Vietnamese. Two Chinese-trained Vietnamese battalions, equipped with 75 mm recoilless guns and six-barrel rocket launchers, arrived at Dien Bien Phu on the eve of the final assault. Beijing's leaders emphasized to the Chinese advisers in Vietnam: "To eliminate the enemy totally and to win the final victory in the campaign, you should use overwhelming artillery fire. Do not save artillery shells. We will supply and deliver sufficient shells to you." [106]

To guarantee the final victory in the campaign, top CCP leaders carefully considered every possible contingency that might endanger a total Viet Minh victory. On 28 April, Mao Zedong instructed Peng Dehuai and Huang Kecheng to guard against the possibility of a French paratrooper landing at the rear of the Vietnamese, which would cut off their supply line. Mao emphasized that this should be taken as the "most possible danger," which, if it occurred, could force the Vietnamese to give up the campaign. Mao instructed Peng and Huang to "ask the Vietnamese to deploy immediately more troops in proper areas" so that the French parachute landing could be prevented.[107] On 30 April, the CMC, following Mao's instruction, directed Wei Guoqing to consult with the Vietnamese to take preemptive measures against such an attack. On 3 May, General Su Yu, then the Chinese chief of staff, again contacted General Wei, reiterating the importance of preventing a French airborne landing.[108]

The final offensive of the Communist forces at Dien Bien Phu began on the evening of 5 May. The newly arrived Chinese rocket launchers played an important role by destroying the French defenses in minutes. By the afternoon of 7 May, French troops had neither the ability nor the will to fight and announced surrender. The Dien Bien Phu campaign ended with a glorious victory for the Vietnamese Communists.

The Geneva Conference of 1954

As has happened on many other occasions in history, the First Indochina War was fought on the battlefield but concluded at the negotiation table. On 8 May, the day after the end of the Dien Bien Phu campaign, the Geneva Conference, which had started on 26 April, began its discussion of the Indochina problem. It was at this moment of victory, ironically, that sharp divergences emerged between the Vietnamese and Chinese Communists. Evidence shows that the CCP leaders' view of Indochina was strongly influenced by Washington's warning of direct American intervention there. This development, in turn, caused the Chinese Communists and their Vietnamese comrades to disagree.

In retrospect, the close relationship between the Chinese Communists and their Vietnamese comrades offers no support to the theory of a monolithic international Communist movement. Even at the height of cooperation between the Chinese and Vietnamese Communists, there were signs of contradictions and, in some cases, conflicts between them. Chinese advisers complained that the quality of Viet Minh troops was too poor to realize some of their strategic designs. General Chen Geng mentioned in his diary that General Giap and some other Vietnamese Communists lacked "Bolshevik-style self-criticism" and were unhappy with the Chinese criticism of their "shortcomings." On one occasion, Chen even described Giap as "slippery and not very upright and honest" in his relationship with his Chinese comrades.[109] The Vietnamese, on the other hand, were not satisfied with some of the Chinese advisers' suggestions, especially those concerning land reforms and political indoctrination following China's experiences. The Vietnamese discontent was shown most explicitly in the 1979 official review of Vietnamese-Chinese relations, where, in recalling history, the Chinese were called "traitors" even during the First Indochina War.[110] Seeing signs of Chinese-Vietnamese friction, the CCP leadership stressed in several telegrams to Chinese advisers in Vietnam that they should avoid "imposing their own opinions on Vietnamese comrades."[111] Indeed, the Chinese did not feel comfortable dealing with the Vietnamese, a people who had struggled against Chinese control for centuries and who had so vigorous a nationalist tendency.

With victory in sight, the disagreements between the Chinese and the Vietnamese surfaced, focusing on the final settlement of the Indochina problem. While the Vietnamese hoped for a solution that would leave clear Communist

The Chinese delegation attending the Geneva conference of 1954. At the center table (from right to left) are Zhang Wentian, Wang Bingnan, Shi Zhe, and Zhou Enlai. Photo courtesy Shi Zhe personal collection.

domination not only in Vietnam but also in Laos and Cambodia, the Chinese, supported by the Soviet Union, were eager to reach a compromise, if necessary, by temporarily dividing Vietnam into two zones.[112]

Beijing's attitude toward the Geneva Conference reflected several of its leaders' basic considerations at the moment. First of all, with the end of the Korean War, Beijing's leaders sensed the need to devote more of the nation's resources to domestic issues. In 1953 and 1954, they were contemplating the introduction of the first five-year plan, as well as the liberation of Nationalist-controlled Taiwan, either in peaceful ways, or if necessary, by military means. After five years of sharp confrontation with the United States and the West, many leaders in Beijing perceived that China needed a stable outside environment. They thus did not want to see the continued escalation of the conflict in Indochina. Second, with insights gained from their Korean War experience, Beijing's leaders saw in the wake of the Dien Bien Phu siege the possibility of direct American military intervention. They approached this problem with a "worst-case assumption": they would try everything possible, including pursuing a compromise at Geneva, to prevent American intervention; only if the Americans directly entered the war in Indochina would they consider sending troops to stop American forces from approaching China's borders while maintaining the momentum of the Vietnamese revolution.[113] Third, Beijing's leaders also believed that a reconciliatory Chinese approach at the Geneva Conference would help strengthen Beijing's new claim to peaceful coexistence as the foundation of the PRC's international policy and create opportunities for "breaking up the American blockade and embargo" against the PRC.[114]

Beijing's considerations were consistent with a central concern of the leaders in Moscow, who, after Stalin's death, also needed to focus on domestic issues and avoid a confrontation with the West in Asia. In the first three weeks of April, Zhou Enlai visited the Soviet Union two times to discuss the Chinese-Soviet strategy at the Geneva Conference. According to the recollections of Shi Zhe, who was Zhou's interpreter during these visits, the Chinese and the Soviets agreed to cooperate with each other at the forthcoming conference. Zhou's views seemed to have been greatly influenced by those of Vyacheslav Molotov. In his meeting with Zhou, Molotov stressed that it was possible for the Geneva Conference to solve one or two problems, but the imperialist countries would certainly look out for their own interests. So the Communist camp should adopt a realistic strategy that would be compatible with this situation. Since this was the first time the Chinese had attended an important international conference, Zhou made it clear that they would try their best to cooperate with the Soviets.[115] These discussions resulted in a consensus: although the imperialist countries, and the United States in particular, would try to sabotage the conference, if the Communist side adopted a realistic strategy, then it was still possible that a peaceful solution of the Indochina problem could be worked out.[116]

The Vietnamese Communist leaders, according to Chinese sources, originally posed no apparent opposition to Beijing's view. From late March to April 1954, Ho Chi Minh, the DRV's president, and Pham Van Dong, the DRV's premier and foreign minister, led a Vietnamese delegation to visit Beijing, which then, accompanied by Zhou Enlai, visited Moscow. In discussions with the delegation, Mao Zedong, Liu Shaoqi, and Zhou Enlai spoke about in particular China's experience gained from the negotiations to end the Korean War, emphasizing that it was necessary to maintain "realistic expectations" for the Geneva Conference. According to Chinese sources, the Vietnamese leaders agreed.[117]

Nevertheless, the victory at Dien Bien Phu made the Vietnamese believe that they were in a position to squeeze more concessions from their adversaries at the conference table. Pham Van Dong, head of the DRV delegation, announced at the conference that the Indochina problem would be settled if, first, the Viet Minh were to establish virtual control of most parts of Vietnam (through an on-the-spot truce, followed by a national plebiscite, which they knew they would win), and, second, if it were to pursue positions for Communist forces in Laos and Cambodia (by treating the settlement of the Laos and Cambodian problems as part of a general settlement of the Indochina problem).[118]

Behind the scenes of the Geneva Conference, Dong's unyielding approach caused subtle tensions in the relations between the Chinese and the Soviets, on the one side, and the Vietnamese Communists, on the other. In several discussions among the Chinese, Soviet, and Vietnamese delegations, Zhou Enlai pointed out that Dong's attitude reflected how the inexperienced Vietnamese had been out of touch with reality. In justifying his willingness to accept the solution of temporarily dividing Vietnam into two areas, with the north belonging to the Communists and the south to the French and pro-French Vietnamese, and to wait for a national plebiscite, Zhou emphasized that this would allow the Viet Minh to control the entire north and gain back the south after the vote. On the Laos and Cambodia problems, Zhou favored a separate solution, which, he believed, would simplify the whole issue and make the total settlement of the Indochina problem possible.[119] Zhou's stand was fully backed by Mao and the other CCP leaders in Beijing. In order not to jeopardize the prospect of reaching an agreement at Geneva, on 20 June Mao instructed the CMAG not to expand military operations in Vietnam throughout July.[120] However, Dong was not ready to accept the Chinese arguments.

American policymakers believed the United States had important strategic interests in Southeast Asia and did not want to see the Geneva Conference reach a compromise. Dulles, the head of the American delegation, followed a line of blocking any Communist initiative at the conference. He truly believed that an inconclusive result was better than any agreement that would provide the Communists with even minimal gains.[121] Dulles's uncompromising stand was matched by Dong's, leading the conference to a deadlock by mid-June.

At this moment a major political change occurred in France: the French parliament, reflecting the public's impatience with the immobility at Geneva, ousted Prime Minister Joseph Laniel and replaced him with Pierre Mendès-France, who, as a longtime leading critic of the war in Indochina, promised that if he did not lead the negotiation to a successful conclusion by 20 July, he would resign. Zhou seized the opportunity to push negotiations at Geneva forward. On 15 June, the Chinese, Soviet, and Vietnamese delegations held a crucial meeting. Zhou pointed out that the key to the deadlock of the conference lay in the Vietnamese refusal to admit the existence of their forces in Laos and Cambodia. He warned that this attitude would render the negotiations on Indochina fruitless, and that the Vietnamese Communists would also lose an opportunity to achieve a peaceful solution of the Vietnam problem. Zhou proposed that the Communist camp adopt a new line in favor of withdrawal of all foreign forces from Laos and Cambodia, including those of the Viet Minh. The Soviets strongly supported Zhou's proposal, and the Vietnamese, under heavy pressure from the Chinese and the Soviets, finally yielded.[122] On 16 and 17 June, Zhou communicated the change of Communist attitude toward Laos and Cambodia to the French and the British.[123] In late June, in order to prepare for further discussions on the Indochina problem, the foreign ministers agreed to adjourn for three weeks.

From 3 to 5 July in Liuzhou, a city located in Guangxi province close to the Chinese-Vietnamese border, Ho Chi Minh, accompanied by Vo Nguyen Giap and Hoang Van Hoan, visited China and met Zhou Enlai to coordinate their strategies.[124] Zhou particularly emphasized the danger involved in a possible direct American intervention in Indochina, arguing that it would greatly complicate the situation there and undermine the Viet Minh's achievements. He thus convinced Ho that it was in the interests of the Vietnamese Communists to reach an agreement with the French at Geneva. The two sides reached a consensus on strategies for the next phase of the conference: on the Vietnam problem, they would favor dividing the country temporarily along the 16th parallel, but since Route Colonial Nine, the only line of transport linking Laos to the seaport, was located north of the 16th parallel, they would be willing to accept some slight adjustment of this resolution; on the Laos problem, they would try to establish Xam Neua and Phong Sali, two provinces adjacent to China, as the concentration zone for pro-Communist Laos forces; on the Cambodia problem, they would allow a political settlement that would probably lead to the establishment of a non-Communist government there.[125]

When Ho returned to Vietnam, the vwp Central Committee issued an instruction on 5 July (known as the "5 July Document") that reflected the agreements Ho had reached with Zhou at Liuzhou.[126] In mid-July, the vwp Central Committee held its sixth meeting. Ho endorsed the new strategy of solving the Indochina problem through a cease-fire based on temporarily dividing Vietnam into two areas, which would supposedly lead to the unification of the whole country after the withdrawal of French forces and through a nationwide plebiscite. It is notable that Ho criticized the "leftist tendency" among party members who ignored the danger of American intervention and paid no attention to the importance of struggles at international conferences.[127] Ho's comments, and especially his stress on the danger of American intervention, clearly reflected Zhou's influence.

In Beijing, the CCP politburo held an enlarged meeting on 7 July to hear Zhou Enlai's report on the Geneva Conference and the Liuzhou meeting. Zhou reported that the Chinese delegation had adopted a policy line of uniting with France, Britain, southeast Asian countries, and the three Indochina countries—that is, uniting with all international forces that could be united, in order to isolate the United States and to contain and break up the U.S. imperialist plan of expanding America's hegemony in the world. The central part of this policy line, emphasized Zhou, lay in achieving a peaceful settlement of the Indochina problem. Zhou believed that, judging from the progress that had been made at the Geneva Conference thus far, the settlement could be reached. Mao praised and approved Zhou's report.[128]

The foreign ministers' meeting at Geneva resumed on 12 July. Zhou found that Pham Van Dong was still reluctant to accept the new negotiation line. In an overnight meeting with Dong to try to persuade him of the necessity of reaching a compromise, Zhou used America's intervention in the Korean War as an example to emphasize the tremendous danger involved in direct American military intervention in Indochina. Zhou promised, "[W]ith the final withdrawal of the French, all of Vietnam will be yours." Dong finally yielded—probably to Zhou's logic, if not to Zhou's pressure.[129]

Zhou dominated the final stage of the Geneva Conference. Mendès-France insisted that the 17th parallel be the final line of his concession, and that if it was not acceptable, he would have to resign. Zhou made the decision to change the Communist demand from the 16th parallel to the 17th to meet the French prime minister's stand, and he persuaded the Soviets and the Vietnamese in particular to accept this change.[130] The Geneva Conference reached a settlement on the Indochina problem in the early morning of 21 July, before Mendès-France's deadline officially expired.[131]

The real winner at the conference was Zhou. He left Geneva with nearly everything he could have anticipated. The creation of a Communist-ruled North Vietnam would serve as a buffer zone between Communist China and the capitalist world in Southeast Asia (and in this respect, the difference between the 16th and the 17th parallels did not matter to China). The opening of new dialogue between China and Western powers such as France and Great Britain would help break the PRC's isolated status in the world; and, much more important, the crucial role China played at the conference implied that for the first time in modern history (since the 1839–42 Opium War) China had been accepted by the international society—friends and foes alike—as a real world power.

The Geneva agreement of 1954 ended the First Indochina War, but the con-

CHAPTER 6
BEIJING AND THE
POLISH AND HUNGARIAN
CRISES OF 1956

There is fire in Poland, and there is fire in Hungary. Since the fire is there, it will blaze up sooner or later. Which is better, to let the fire blaze, or not to let it? Fire cannot be wrapped up in paper. Now the fires have blazed up; that's just fine, as many reactionaries in Hungary have been exposed. The Hungarian incident has educated the Hungarian people and at the same time some Soviet comrades as well as us Chinese comrades.
—Mao Zedong

In retrospect, the Polish and Hungarian crises of 1956 stand together as a landmark in the development of the Cold War history. These two important events not only revealed the long-existing tensions within the Soviet bloc, especially between the Soviet Union and Poland and the Soviet Union and Hungary; they also triggered a series of more general confrontations within the Communist world, eventually leading to the decline of international communism as a twentieth-century phenomenon.

The international nature of the Polish and Hungarian crises is clearly indicated in their connections with Beijing. The crises erupted at a time when serious disagreements had begun to surface between the Chinese and Soviet leadership in the wake of Stalin's death and the Soviet leader Nikita Khrushchev's de-Stalinization effort.[1] Beijing's response to the crises epitomized Mao Zedong's perception of Beijing's and Moscow's changing positions in the world proletarian revolution, revealing his intention to adopt a more aggressive agenda on promoting China's "socialist revolution and reconstruction." Consequently, while both the peaceful settlement of the Polish crisis and the tragic result of the Hungarian revolution reflected the CCP's increasing influence in the international Communist movement, Beijing's experience during these two events enhanced Mao's determination to bring China's continuous revolution to a more radical phase. As a result, disastrous events such as the Anti-Rightist movement and the Great Leap Forward in 1957–58 took place, which created conditions for deeper splits to develop between Beijing and Moscow. This chapter uses Chinese source materials made available in recent years, reinforced by Russian, Polish, and Hungarian documents, to discuss Beijing's involvement in the Polish and Hungarian crises of 1956.

The Polish Crisis

In October 1956, months of accumulated tensions and a workers' uprising in Poznan resulted in the election of a new politburo of the Polish United Workers' Party (PUWP) excluding pro-Soviet, Stalinist leaders. The new PUWP leadership headed by Wladyslaw Gomulka also planned to remove Marshal Konstantin Rokossovskii, a Russian who had held the position as Poland's defense minister since 1949. In order to put pressure on the Polish leadership and to control the situation in Warsaw, a high-ranking Soviet delegation headed by Khrushchev rushed to Warsaw on 19 October.[2]

From the beginning, Mao and his fellow CCP leaders watched the crisis emerging in Poland alertly. In accordance with their understanding of the function of the "people's democratic dictatorship," they did not regard mass revolt as a legitimate way to solve the problems existing between the Communist state and a Communist-controlled society.[3] But, comparing the situation in Poland to their own past experience of having to behave as Moscow's junior partner, Mao and his comrades believed that the origins of Poland's crisis lay in Moscow's "big-power chauvinist" policy toward Eastern European countries.[4]

On 19 October, Pavel Yudin, Soviet ambassador to China, made an urgent appointment with Liu Shaoqi to deliver to the CCP Central Committee an important message from the CPSU Central Committee. Yudin told Liu that some PUWP leaders were planning to transform the party's politburo, which meant that there existed the danger that Poland might leave the socialist camp and join the Western bloc. Because of the serious situation in Poland, the Soviet leadership had decided to send a high-ranking delegation composed of Khrushchev, Vyacheslav Molotov, Anastas Mikoyan, and Lazar Kaganovich to visit Warsaw.[5] In the meantime, through other channels, including foreign news reports and reports from the Chinese embassy in Warsaw, CCP leaders learned that Moscow was planning to use military means to solve the Polish problem.[6]

On the afternoon of 20 October, Mao called an urgent enlarged meeting of the CCP Politburo Standing Committee[7] at his residence at Zhongnanhai (the location of the CCP central headquarters) to discuss the Polish crisis. According to the recollections of Wu Lengxi, director of the Xinhua News Agency and one of Mao's secretaries, Mao did not even wait to get dressed and chaired the meeting in his pajamas. He first told the CCP leaders that he had called the meeting because the CPSU Central Committee had dispatched an urgent telegram to the CCP Central Committee, in which the Soviets emphasized that anti-Soviet elements in Poland had been rampant and had demanded the withdrawal of Soviet troops from Poland. The Soviets believed that, in accordance with the Warsaw Pact, they had the right to station troops in Poland. Mao observed that although Moscow had not made the final decision to intervene militarily, it seemed that the Soviet leaders intended to do so. Wu Lengxi quoted foreign news reports to brief participants of the meeting that Polish troops and security forces had begun to mobilize, that workers in Warsaw had been armed, and that the Soviets had anchored their warships outside the Polish port Gdansk, and had even mobilized their troops on the western borders of the Soviet Union and in East Germany. At this moment, Mao commented: "When the son fails to obey, the rude father picks up a stick to beat him. When a socialist power uses military forces to intervene in the internal affairs of a neighboring socialist country, this is not only a violation of the basic principles of international relations; this is also a violation of the principles governing the relations between socialist countries. This is serious big-power chauvinism, which should not be allowed in any circumstances."[8]

Top CCP leaders quickly reached a consensus that the CCP must firmly oppose Moscow's military intervention in Poland, and must do everything possible to stop it. Mao proposed that a warning should be sent to the Soviets immediately, making it clear that if they were to use force in Poland, the CCP would be the first to protest it. Participants at the meeting unanimously approved the chairman's proposal.[9]

After the meeting, Mao summoned Yudin to his quarters. He asked the Soviet ambassador to inform Moscow that the CCP politburo had just met to discuss the Polish crisis, and that it was the CCP leadership's unanimous conclusion that the Soviet Union's intervention in Poland's internal affairs would be a serious violation of the principles of proletarian internationalism. Mao told Yudin that if the Soviets intervened militarily, the Chinese party and government would be vehement in its protest against it. Mao asked Yudin to convey this message "word for word" to Khrushchev. The Soviet ambassador, according to Wu Lengxi, who was present at the meeting, was sweating while listening to Mao and left Mao's quarters saying nothing but "yes, yes!" According to Chinese sources, he reported Mao's message to Moscow by telephone immediately after the meeting.[10]

Top CCP leaders' discussions at the 20 October meeting reveal two basic tendencies that would consistently dominate Beijing's handling of the Polish crisis and, later, the Hungarian crisis. First, in exploring the origins of the crises, Beijing's leaders placed great emphasis upon the impact of Moscow's "big-power chauvinism," believing that things would not have gone so wrong if the Soviets had not treated their junior partners in Eastern Europe with a mistaken "father-son" mentality. Thus, in Beijing's view, Moscow's behavior bore considerable responsibility for causing the crises. Second, in contemplating strategies to deal with the crises, Beijing's leaders did not restrict their vision to the situation at hand. Indeed, they believed that in order to solve the crises, and to prevent similar crises from occurring in other parts of the Communist world, the international Communist movement had to be restructured to allow equality to prevail in relations between fraternal parties. But since the concept "equality" would be defined in Beijing's terms, the logical consequence of this restructuring was self-evident: Moscow would be removed from the center of the world proletarian revolution, and Beijing, by virtue of its moral superiority, would climb to that central position.

As the Polish crisis worsened, the CPSU Central Committee sent another urgent telegram to the CCP Committee on 21 October. The Soviet leaders informed the Chinese that a top Soviet delegation had met with PUWP leaders, but the situation in Warsaw deteriorated continuously. Moscow regarded this as a matter of utmost importance, since the unrest, among other things, could trigger great chaos in other Eastern European countries. Soviet leaders thus hoped that the CCP could send a high-ranking delegation, best headed by either Liu Shaoqi or Zhou Enlai, to Moscow to discuss how to deal with the crisis. The telegram also mentioned that leaders from other socialist countries in Eastern Europe would join the discussion.[11]

After receiving the second telegram from Moscow, Mao summoned another enlarged Politburo Standing Committee meeting on the evening of 22 October.[12] The chairman told his colleagues that Beijing's opposition to Soviet intervention in Poland had caused repercussions in Moscow, and the Soviet leaders now invited two top CCP leaders to visit Moscow to "exchange opinions" with them. He asked the participants he had gathered to discuss and decide how Beijing should respond to Moscow's invitation. After analyzing the reports Beijing had received "through various sources" about the situation in Poland,[13] CCP leaders attending the meeting all agreed that although the situation in Warsaw was complicated, it looked "unlikely that Poland [would] immediately leave the socialist camp or join the Western bloc." Therefore, they believed, it was still possible, even necessary, to recognize the current Polish leadership and to cooperate with it "on the basis of equality." Liu Shaoqi and Zhou Enlai also mentioned that the Soviets had not already used force in Poland for two reasons: first, they had encountered firm resistance from the Polish leaders, and, second, Khrushchev should have learned of the CCP's opposition to Soviet intervention in Poland after he returned to Moscow from Warsaw, making him and other Soviet leaders feel that they had no other choice but to consult with the CCP. Both Liu and Zhou believed that Beijing should send a top delegation to Moscow, to which Mao and other CCP leaders agreed. Touching upon the delegation's tasks in Moscow, Mao emphasized that the Chinese should not be directly involved in discussions between the Soviets and the Poles but should talk to each party separately, playing the role as a mediator between them. The meeting lasted until the early morning hours of 23 October.[14]

Twenty minutes after the meeting ended, Mao, accompanied by Liu Shaoqi, Zhou Enlai, Chen Yun, and Deng Xiaoping, met with Yudin at Zhongnanhai. The chairman now was ready to present to the Soviets Beijing's comprehensive evaluation of the Polish crisis and the Chinese plan to deal with it. He told the Soviet ambassador that Beijing had its own sources of information about what had been happening in Poland. Although it was true that reactionary elements were among the participants of the Polish incident, the overwhelming majority were ordinary workers and other common people. It seemed to him, said Mao, that the Polish comrades did not plan to leave the socialist camp but only wanted to reorganize the party's politburo. Then Mao commented that the Soviets had two options: they could either adopt a "soft" attitude or take a "hard" policy toward the Polish incident. Whereas taking a hard policy would mean dispatching troops to Poland to suppress the people there, the adoption of a soft attitude would involve providing advice to the Polish comrades. But if the Poles refused to follow the advice, the Soviets might need to make further concessions to them, such as acknowledging the new Polish leadership headed by Gomulka. In economic affairs, Mao continued, the Soviet Union should continue to provide assistance to Poland and cooperate with the Polish comrades on the basis of equality. By doing so, Mao claimed, Poland could be convinced to stay in the socialist camp.[15]

The chairman then turned to the Stalin issue. He stressed that although it was necessary to criticize Stalin's mistakes, the CCP disagreed with the Soviet leaders on how it should be done. The correct way, according to the chairman, was to criticize Stalin's mistakes only after his overall reputation had been properly protected. Following the tone he had established months before, Mao again stated that in evaluating Stalin's historical position, a "seventy to thirty ratio," or even an "eighty to twenty ratio," methodology should be used, acknowledging that Stalin's merits far surpassed his offenses. "Stalin is a sword," concluded the chairman. "It can be used to fight the imperialists and various other enemies. . . . If this sword is put aside completely, if it is damaged, or if it is abandoned, the enemies will use this sword to try to kill us. Consequently, we would be lifting a rock only to drop it on our own feet." [16]

After the Soviet ambassador had left, at about 3:00 in the morning of 23 October, Mao Zedong, Liu Shaoqi, Zhou Enlai, and Deng Xiaoping met to finalize the composition of the CCP delegation and the agenda it was to follow in its meeting with Khrushchev and other Soviet leaders in Moscow. They decided that the delegation would be headed by Liu Shaoqi and Deng Xiaoping, and it would include Wang Jiaxiang, a member of the Central Committee and Central Secretariat and former Chinese ambassador to the Soviet Union, Hu Qiaomu, Mao Zedong's political secretary and a member of the CCP Central Committee in charge of the party's propaganda affairs, and Shi Zhe, the longtime (since 1941) Russian-language interpreter for CCP leaders.[17] They also decided that Liu and Deng would not attend the meetings between Soviet and Polish leaders, but would meet the leaders of the two parties separately. The delegation's main task was defined as mediating the problems between the Soviet and Polish comrades by, on the one hand, criticizing the Soviet party's "big-power chauvinism" and, on the other hand, advising the Polish comrades to consider the overall interests of the socialist camp.[18] A few hours later, the Chinese delegation left Beijing for Moscow by air.[19]

Liu Shaoqi and Deng Xiaoping in Moscow

The CCP delegation arrived in Moscow late on the afternoon of 23 October (Moscow time).[20] According to Shi Zhe, Khrushchev personally welcomed the delegation at the Moscow airport. On their way to the guest house, Khrushchev talked to Liu Shaoqi nonstop, and his conversation, in Shi Zhe's words, "was full of complaints and had no order at all." While interpreting for Khrushchev, Shi Zhe felt that the Soviet leader was "extremely nervous." He also noticed that Liu Shaoqi sensed Khrushchev's extreme uneasiness but recalled that Liu did not make any substantial comments.[21]

When the Chinese arrived at the guest house, a meeting with Khrushchev began immediately.[22] The Soviet leader again dominated the conversation and touched upon a number of issues. In addition to explaining to the Chinese that the new Soviet leadership had made great efforts to deal with various complications left over by Stalin (such as the ongoing ethnicity problem in the Soviet Union and the problem of how to treat the cadres who had been purged during Stalin's times), Khrushchev particularly emphasized that Moscow had reformed its policies toward the socialist countries in Eastern Europe after Stalin's death, especially after the party's Twentieth Congress. Regarding the developments in Poland, Khrushchev provided a detailed description of the CPSU delegation's visit to Warsaw. He mentioned that initially the Soviets did have strong suspicion about the motives of the new PUWP leadership headed by Gomulka, fearing that the Polish meant to abandon the socialist camp. But, the Soviet leader confessed, after meeting Gomulka and his comrades in Warsaw, he found that despite all kinds of differences in opinion between Moscow and the new Polish leadership, his suspicion was groundless. Therefore, Khrushchev emphasized, Moscow was ready to acknowledge the new Polish leadership, and was willing to establish a cooperative relationship with it. Furthermore, since distrust and tension remained between Moscow and Warsaw, he hoped that the Chinese comrades, who had had a better image among the Poles, would provide "friendly advice" to Warsaw to persuade the Polish comrades to maintain solidarity with the Soviets. "This will be beneficial to the Soviet Union," Khrushchev stressed, "as well as beneficial to the whole socialist camp." Liu Shaoqi and Deng Xiaoping, who felt that Khrushchev's statement was generally compatible with the principles set up by the CCP leadership in managing the Polish issue, promised to the Soviet leader that he had Beijing's full support.[23]

While the meeting was under way, Khrushchev received a phone call from Erno Gero, the first secretary of the Hungarian Workers' Party. Gero told Khrushchev that since he had been preoccupied with domestic affairs, he was unable to come to Moscow to attend the meeting of leaders of socialist countries. Then Khrushchev received two phone calls from Marshal Georgy Zhukov, in which the Soviet defense minister reported that a mass riot, targeting mainly party and government offices, had broken out in Budapest, and that the Hungarian military had requested the Soviet Red Army stationed outside of Budapest to intervene. Both Khrushchev and Liu, according to Shi Zhe, were surprised by Zhukov's reports, since Gero mentioned nothing about the mass riot in his earlier phone call. Khrushchev commented that if the Hungarian government indeed wanted the Soviet Red Army to intervene, the decision must be made by the CPSU presidium.[24]

As the end of the meeting approached, Liu Shaoqi followed the CCP delegation's prepared agenda to turn the conversation to the Stalin issue, stressing that Stalin, together with Lenin, was a "sword" highly valuable to international communism and thus should be appreciated and carefully protected. Khrushchev, however, carelessly responded that if Stalin had been a sword, it was now completely useless and, therefore, should be abandoned. Before the discussion could go any further, Khrushchev left in a hurry, saying that he needed to contact other presidium members to discuss the situation in Hungary.[25]

The next day, 24 October, the CPSU presidium held a plenary session at the Kremlin, to which Liu Shaoqi and Deng Xiaoping were invited.[26] After a brief discussion of the situation in Poland, the main part of the meeting focused on the emerging crisis in Hungary. Khrushchev, who chaired the meeting, said that the Soviet Red Army had already entered Budapest and that social order there had gradually returned to normal. Emphasizing that the Red Army's intervention had been welcomed by the workers in Budapest, he hoped the Chinese comrades would understand that the situation in Hungary was different from that in Poland: the latter reflected problems existing within the Communist Party, while the former demonstrated an anti-Communist and counterrevolutionary tendency. Several other presidium members, including Molotov, Bulganin, and Malenkov, rose to support Khrushchev's view.[27]

Liu delivered a long speech at the meeting, which, together with the time spent on interpretation provided by Shi Zhe, lasted more than two hours. In accordance with Mao Zedong's opinions, Liu pointed out that the new PUWP leadership headed by Gomulka was still a Communist leadership, and that Poland should continue to be regarded as a socialist country. He emphasized that the divergence between Warsaw and Moscow was a matter of right and wrong, not a conflict between revolution and counterrevolution. Therefore, the problems with Poland should be solved through comrade-style criticism and self-criticism by both the Soviet and the Polish sides. Moscow would have been absolutely mistaken, Liu stressed, if it had decided to use military means to settle the crisis. He expressed Beijing's support of the Soviet leadership's decision to solve the Polish crisis through direct discussion with the new Polish leaders.[28]

Liu then analyzed the origins of the tensions emerging between the Soviet Union and Poland, Hungary, and other Eastern European countries. He argued that the tensions originated in Moscow's "big-power chauvinism," particularly emphasizing that during Stalin's later years, the CPSU often imposed its will on other fraternal parties, forcing them to obey Moscow's command. If they failed to obey, Moscow would suppress them. On several occasions, the Soviet Union intervened in other countries without cause, which made them feel that their sovereignty was violated.[29] Liu believed that the emerging nationalist mood in Poland and Hungary was closely connected to the negative impact of Stalin's "big-power chauvinism," which had yet to be eliminated. Consequently, the relations between socialist countries were far from normal, a situation that turned out to be one of the most important causes of the Polish and Hungarian crises. Liu, however, also made it clear that, in any circumstance, Beijing would continue to regard Moscow as the center of the international Communist movement. "Comrade Togliatti[30] introduced a 'multi-centrality' thesis," stated Liu, "but we told him that we must oppose that thesis. The center can only be the Soviet Union."[31]

Liu's carefully prepared speech expressed Beijing's concerns over some of the "big issues" facing the international Communist movement. Most important of all, Liu made it very clear that unless Moscow was to abandon completely its "big-power chauvinism" in dealing with other fraternal parties and states, crises similar to the ones taking place in Poland and Hungary would develop elsewhere. Although Liu stated that Moscow would remain the sole center of the socialist camp, the subtext was that Moscow's centrality was now being defined in Beijing's terms. Therefore, Liu's long speech must be read as a Chinese declaration of Beijing's virtual centrality in international communism.[32]

On 26 October, the CPSU presidium held another meeting, and members of the Chinese delegation were again invited to attend. Liu and his comrades had hoped that this meeting would be devoted to correcting Moscow's "big-power chauvinism," and, consequently, they had spent the whole day of 25 October preparing for the discussion.[33] However, when the meeting began, it again focused on specific "small" problems related to Poland and Hungary; the "big-power chauvinism" issue did not come up. At one point, when Khrushchev mentioned that it seemed Gomulka was determined to remove Rokossovskii, Liu commented that it would be better for Gomulka to retain Rokossovskii and take no revenge on those who had purged him. Khrushchev, believing that Gomulka should hear this directly from the Chinese, proposed that Liu and the Chinese delegation visit Warsaw after completing their activities in Moscow. Liu, emphasizing that he needed to get Beijing's authorization as well as Warsaw's invitation, did not give an affirmative response to Khrushchev's proposal.[34]

Substantial discussion on the "big issues," especially the ones concerning the general principles governing the international Communist movement, did not begin until the evening of 29 October, when Khrushchev, Molotov, and Bulganin met with Liu Shaoqi and Deng Xiaoping at the guest house. The Soviet leaders mentioned that both the Polish and Hungarian leaders had requested the Soviet Red Army to withdraw from their countries. Khrushchev emphasized that if the Red Army completely withdrew from these two countries, and if other Eastern European countries also requested that the Red Army leave, the Warsaw Pact would collapse, which would only benefit the imperialist countries.[35]

In response, Liu Shaoqi conveyed to the Soviet leaders "a fundamental suggestion" from Mao Zedong: The Soviet Union should adopt a thoroughly new policy toward Eastern European countries. Moscow should let them handle their own political and economic affairs and not interfere with their internal matters. In addition, Moscow should respect not only Poland's and Hungary's but also Bulgaria's and Romania's desires for independence and should follow the principles of "pancha shila" in handling state-to-state relations with them.[36] In military affairs, Liu continued, Moscow should take the initiative to consult with Eastern European countries about how the Warsaw Pact should function, or about whether the Warsaw Pact should even exist. According to Liu, the Soviets had three options: they could maintain the Warsaw Pact completely, maintain the Warsaw Pact but withdraw Soviet troops from Eastern European countries and send them back when a war with the imperialist countries broke out, or maintain the Warsaw Pact but withdraw Soviet troops permanently. Liu explained to the Soviet leaders that Mao wanted these ideas introduced to the Soviet leaders, so that a better way would be found to consolidate the socialist camp, to strengthen the relations between the Soviet Union and Eastern European countries, to enhance the Warsaw Pact, and to help the Soviet comrades achieve the support of the masses in Eastern European countries. It was, Liu emphasized, an indication of the Chinese goodwill toward, as well as solidarity with, the comrades in Moscow.[37]

Khrushchev seemed willing to follow the Chinese advice. Although he explained that the Soviet Union had never interfered with other countries' internal affairs, and that "big-power chauvinism" was a phenomenon that might have existed during Stalin's period but had been eliminated completely after Stalin's death, he expressed his "sincere thanks" to and general acceptance of Mao's suggestions. He agreed that Eastern European countries should have the right to make their own political, economic, and military decisions.[38] When the meeting adjourned at 2:00 A.M. on 30 October, the two sides reached an agreement that a general statement concerning the basic principles governing relationships between socialist countries should be prepared and issued immediately.[39]

Although several top Soviet leaders had reservations about whether or not the language of pancha shila should be used in directing relations between socialist countries, the CPSU presidium approved the document at a meeting on 30 October.[40] The same day, the Soviet government formally issued the

"Declaration on Developing and Enhancing the Friendship and Cooperation between the Soviet Union and other Socialist Countries," in which Moscow promised to follow a pattern of more equal exchanges with other Communist states and parties. Two days later, the Chinese government issued a statement to support the Soviet declaration, praising it as a document with "great significance" that will "enhance the solidarity between socialist countries."[41]

The Decision to Suppress the "Reactionary Riots" in Hungary

When the Chinese delegation was in Moscow, the situation in Hungary changed dramatically. The uprisings in Budapest, which began on 23 October, gradually paralyzed the Communist regime there, pushing it to the verge of collapse. This development alarmed both the Chinese delegation in Moscow and Mao and the other CCP leaders in Beijing.

As discussed earlier, when the Hungarian crisis erupted, Beijing's leaders regarded it as another problem caused by Moscow's failure to treat the Hungarians as equals. Liu Shaoqi and Deng Xiaoping, in meetings with top Soviet leaders in Moscow, argued that it was time for Moscow to adopt a more equal approach toward the comrades in Budapest, which, they believed, would contribute to the settlement of the Hungarian crisis. They originally had strong reservations about Moscow sending tanks into Budapest to suppress the uprising there.[42]

But the situation in Hungarian deteriorated rapidly, quickly exceeding the expectations of the Chinese leaders. Around 29 and 30 October, Mao Zedong in Beijing received a series of reports, the most important of which were from Hu Jibang, *Renmin ribao's* chief correspondent in Budapest, which stated that "reactionary forces, with the support of international imperialists, were doing everything possible to overthrow the Hungarian [Communist] government."[43] These reports led Mao and his fellow CCP leaders to reconsider the nature of the Hungarian crisis. They now speculated that behind the Hungarian crisis lay a well-coordinated plot directed by the international imperialists and that, if the turmoil was not stopped, a "reactionary restoration" would occur in Hungary. Consequently, they began to believe that indeed "the Hungarian crisis was different from the Polish crisis in nature—while the latter is anti-Soviet, the former is anti-Communist."[44]

The view that the events in Hungary were "counterrevolutionary" in nature was further reinforced by reports from the Chinese delegation in Moscow. With the situation in Hungary worsening on a daily basis, the Soviet leaders had been under great pressure to determine whether or not to keep the Red Army there, especially after the new Hungarian prime minister, Imre Nagy, formally requested that the Red Army leave. Between 27 and 31 October their attitude fluctuated.[45] At the meeting with the Chinese delegation on the evening of 29 October, Khrushchev told Liu Shaoqi and Deng Xiaoping that Moscow planned to withdraw Soviet troops from Hungary. Liu and Deng immediately reported this new development to Beijing.[46] The next morning, the Chinese delegation received a copy of a report on the situation in Hungary by Anastas Mikoyan, who, together with Mikhail Suslov, had been in Hungary since the crisis broke out. The report pointed out that after Nagy assumed the position as prime minister, the situation in Budapest deteriorated continuously. When Soviet troops, following the request of Nagy's government, withdrew from Budapest on 29 October, the Hungarian party was quickly paralyzed. Indeed, the reactionary forces were taking control of Budapest and other parts of Hungary, and many party members and members of the security forces were being persecuted, or even brutally murdered. Mikoyan proposed in the report that Moscow carefully reconsider its policy toward the Hungarian crisis.[47]

Members of the Chinese delegation spent the whole day of 30 October discussing Mikoyan's report. They carefully weighed the pros and cons of two basic options. The first option was to advise Moscow to continue withdrawing the Red Army from Hungary. But if the Red Army were to withdraw, the Chinese predicted that Hungary would be taken over by pro-imperialist reactionary forces. The second option was to encourage Moscow not only to retain the Red Army in Hungary but also to use it by joining forces with the remaining revolutionary elements there and suppressing the reactionary riots. While the second option seemed to be the right one to choose, Liu Shaoqi and Deng Xiaoping also saw its obvious contradiction with what the Chinese delegation had just pushed Moscow to do: refrain from using military forces to intervene in the internal affairs of a fraternal country. Liu Shaoqi decided to ask for Beijing's instruction.[48]

In Beijing, the CCP leadership held a series of politburo enlarged meetings from 29 to 31 October to discuss the worsening situation in Hungary.[49] Basing their judgment on the reports from Budapest and Moscow, top CCP leaders finally reached the conclusion that the Hungarian crisis had changed from being anti-Soviet in nature to anti-Communist as the result of the escalating riots in Budapest, that there existed the danger of a "reactionary restoration" in Hungary, and that behind the deteriorating crisis was a huge "international imperialist plot." The CCP leadership thus decided to send an urgent telegram to the Chinese delegation in Moscow, instructing Liu Shaoqi and Deng Xiaoping to meet the Soviet leaders immediately and, in the name of the CCP Central Committee, express firm opposition to Soviet troops' withdrawal from Hungary.[50] But Mao also emphasized that although the Soviet Red Army certainly should intervene, it was better to wait to take decisive action until after the reactionary elements had further exposed themselves.[51]

Liu Shaoqi and Deng Xiaoping, following Beijing's instruction, brought the Chinese opinions to the CPSU presidium's plenary session on the evening of 30 October. At the meeting, Liu Shaoqi made it clear that Beijing believed it a mistake for the Soviets to withdraw their troops from Hungary. He pointed out that this would be a betrayal of the Hungarian people and that the Soviet leaders would be looked back upon as "historical criminals."[52] Deng Xiaoping made three proposals: First, the Soviet army should remain in Hungary and should not "abandon the revolutionary ground and allow the enemy to occupy it." Second, "everything should be done to support the loyal members of the Hungarian party, help them to control the political power, so that they will unite party members, revolutionary elements, and activists around them, forming a stronghold to support the party." Third, the Soviet and Hungarian parties should "control the military and the police, using them to hold the ground, protect the government, and maintain order, making sure that the party organs and the government will not be sabotaged." Deng stressed that it was important for the Soviet troops to "play a model role, demonstrating true internationalism."[53] However, according to Liu's later report, the Soviet leaders did not accept Deng's suggestion because they believed that they had to withdraw Soviet troops from Hungary.[54]

The situation took a complete turn the next day as the Chinese delegation was preparing to leave Moscow. Late that afternoon, the delegation received a phone call from the Kremlin that asked the Chinese to arrive at the airport one hour earlier than originally scheduled.[55] When the Chinese arrived at the airport, they found that all the members of the Soviet presidium were there to say farewell to them. Khrushchev immediately informed Liu that the Soviet presidium, after meeting for the whole day, had reached the decision to use military force to suppress the "reactionary revolt" in Budapest and to "help the Hungarian party and people to defend socialism in Hungary."[56] Before the Chinese boarded the airplane, according to Liu's later report, the Soviet leaders expressed their "sincere thanks" for the assistance from the Chinese party, first on the Polish issue, and then on the Hungarian issue.[57] Three days later, on 4 November, the Soviet Red Army's offensive against the "reactionary forces" in Budapest began. These latest developments made CCP leaders in Beijing firmly believe that they had played a central role in Moscow's decision to "suppress the reactionary elements in Hungary."[58]

Lessons Beijing Learned from the Polish and Hungarian Crises

Liu Shaoqi and Deng Xiaoping returned to Beijing late on the evening of 1 November. They immediately gave a brief report to Mao and several other top CCP leaders (Zhou Enlai, Chen Yun, and Peng Zhen) about the meetings they held with Soviet leaders in Moscow.[59] The Chinese delegation's experience in Moscow, which indicated the CCP's increasing influence within the international Communist movement, excited Mao and other CCP leaders. Indeed, according to Wu Lengxi, CCP leaders were "elated and in buoyant spirits."[60] Liu, in analyzing the causes of the Polish and Hungarian crises, again emphasized that it was the Soviet leaders' deep-rooted "big-power chauvinism" that had resulted in serious discontent from other parties, especially those in Eastern Europe, where nationalism had deep historical roots.[61] Deng Xiaoping used vivid language to describe how the Polish comrades complained emotionally to the Chinese about their suffering at the hands of the Soviets, just like "[China's] poor peasants and farm laborers denounced the landlords during the land reforms." Deng also pointed out that although the Soviet leaders had begun to realize that big-power politics was no longer working in dealing with other socialist countries, they had yet "to change their old course of action and make a new start." Deng believed it necessary for the Chinese party to play an important role in mediating relations between the Soviet and Eastern European parties.[62]

From 2 November to mid-December, the CCP leadership held a series of meetings, including the Central Committee's Second Plenary Session (held from 10 to 15 November), to discuss important domestic and international issues. How to summarize and learn from the lessons of "Hungary's reactionary riots" became a central theme of these meetings.[63]

The CCP leaders again confirmed the understanding that what happened in Hungary late in October was a "reactionary incident," which bore serious danger of "capitalist restoration" in a socialist country. They believed that the incident certainly had a profound international background, "representing the most serious attack of the international imperialist forces against the socialist camp since the Korean War."[64] On one occasion, Zhou Enlai mentioned that the Western countries had been using the Hungarian crisis to stir up anti-Soviet and anti-Communist sentiment, causing Communist Party members in many countries to vacillate in their loyalty to, or even to betray, the party. He emphasized that the CCP should be a vanguard in repulsing this tide of international reactionaryism.[65]

Mao Zedong pointed to "the existence of class struggle as an unavoidable reality" in socialist countries, regarding it as a deep-rooted cause underlying the crisis. In the chairman's view, "The fundamental problem with some Eastern European countries is that they have not done a good job of waging class struggle and have left so many reactionaries at large; nor have they trained their proletarians in class struggle to help them learn how to draw a clear distinction between the people and the enemy, between right and wrong, and between materialism and idealism. And now they have to reap what they have sown; they have brought the fire upon their own heads."[66]

Both Mao Zedong and Liu Shaoqi argued that the discontent that had long existed among Hungary's people, and workers and students in particular, was the foundation for the Hungarian crisis and that domestic and international reactionary forces took advantage of it. In the chairman's view, if the Hungarian party leadership had been more resolute and experienced, the mass riots might not have occurred in the first place. But because the Hungarian party and its leadership were weak, reactionary forces at home and abroad were able to manipulate the situation in Hungary, sending the mass riots out of control.[67] These perceptions would play an important role in the continuous radicalization of Chinese politics and social life in the late 1950s and 1960s.

The CCP leaders also believed that a vulnerable, confusing, and inconsistent attitude on the part of the Soviet leaders (and Khrushchev in particular) contributed to the Hungarian crisis' escalation. Their general criticism of the Soviet leadership focused on three areas. First, Moscow's "big-power chauvinism," especially during the Stalin era, created tension between the Soviet Union and Eastern European countries. Second, Khrushchev's de-Stalinization caused widespread confusion among Communist Party members throughout Eastern Europe. Third, the Soviet leaders were not sophisticated enough to have a correct understanding of the crises when they erupted in Poland and Hungary. As a result, while they planned, mistakenly, to intervene in Poland, they considered, equally mistakenly, withdrawing from Hungary. Consequently, the situation in Hungary went out of control.[68]

On the basis of these discussions, the CCP leadership decided to publish on 29 December 1956 a lengthy article, titled "Another Discussion of the Historical Lessons of the Proletarian Dictatorship," in *Renmin ribao*, expressing the party leadership's general views on the Hungarian crisis and its relation to Khrushchev's de-Stalinization.[69] When the article was being drafted, Mao had specific instructions regarding its contents: First, the article should define the Hungarian crisis as a reactionary incident but should not touch upon small details. Second, the article should confirm that, in general, the CPSU's Twentieth Congress had its positive side (including its criticism of Stalin's mistakes) but should make it clear that it was incorrect to negate Stalin completely. Third,

Zhou Enlai (second from left) *talking to Hungarian Communist leader János Kádár* (far right), *January 1957. Xinhua News Agency.*

the article should point out the importance of making distinctions between two kinds of contradictions existing within socialist countries—those between the enemy and the people, and those among the people. Fourth, the article should regard the direction of the Soviet Union's socialist revolution and reconstruction as positive and correct in general but should also point out that the Soviet leaders had committed many mistakes. Fifth, the article should use explicit language to confirm that Stalin, regardless of all the mistakes he had committed, remained a great Marxist-Leninist revolutionary leader. "Khrushchev abandoned Stalin," Mao emphasized, "and the others [the imperialists and the revisionists] used it [the abandonment] to attack him, causing him to be besieged from all directions." Thus, Mao concluded, Stalin's banner should never be forsaken.[70]

Conclusion

The Polish and Hungarian crises had a profound impact on the orientation of China's domestic and international policies, as well as on the future development of the international Communist movement. As far as China's domestic situation was concerned, Beijing's attitude toward the Hungarian crisis reflected Mao's persistent belief that "class struggle continued to exist in a socialist country." The crisis, in turn, further strengthened Mao's determination to promote China's continuous revolution, especially in the fields of politics and ideology.[71] In early 1957, in the wake of the Polish and Hungarian crises, Mao initiated the Hundred Flowers Campaign to encourage China's intellectuals to help the CCP to "correct its mistakes." But when some intellectuals did voice their criticism of the party, an Anti-Rightist movement began to sweep across China, branding over 300,000 intellectuals (the overwhelming majority of whom never said anything against the party) as "rightists," a label that would effectively silence them and ruin their careers.[72] When opposition to and/or suspicion of Mao's "revolutionary offensives" emerged, either within or without the CCP, Mao and his close followers would invoke the "lessons of the Hungarian reactionary incident" to justify Mao's policies, claiming that if the Chinese did not heed these lessons, China would face the "danger of a Hungarian incident." Mao made it clear that one purpose of the CCP's Hundred Flowers Campaign was to "induce" the bad elements to come out into the open so that they would be "divided and isolated" in many "small Hungaries," and could then be eliminated.[73] In retrospect, the outcome of the Polish and Hungarian crises complicated Chinese politics and social life while pushing Mao's continuous revolution to ever more radical stages.

The crises in Poland and Hungary also enhanced Mao's and the CCP leadership's consciousness of China's centrality in the world proletarian revolution. The Beijing leadership's perception of China's great contributions to the settlement of the Polish and Hungarian crises strengthened the belief that the CCP should occupy a more prominent position in the international Communist movement, as well as justified its critical attitude toward the seemingly less sophisticated Soviet leadership. In Liu Shaoqi's summary of Beijing's management of the Polish and Hungarian crises, which he delivered to the party Central Committee's Second Plenary Session on 10 November 1956, he spent much time exposing Moscow's inability to handle complicated international issues.[74] After Zhou Enlai returned from a trip to the Soviet Union, Poland, and Hungary in January 1957, he presented a comprehensive report summarizing the visit. In it he made extensive comments on the Soviet leadership's lack of sophistication in managing the complex and potentially explosive situations both within the Soviet Union and in Eastern Europe. He particularly emphasized that the CCP leadership's understanding of important international issues had been more farsighted than that of the Soviet leaders.[75] In several internal speeches, Mao Zedong discussed the CCP's disagreements with the Soviet leaders, emphasizing that Khrushchev and his comrades had abandoned not only "the banner of Stalin" but also, to a large extent, "the banner of Lenin." Thus it became the duty of the CCP to play a central role in "holding high the banner" of true Marxism-Leninism.[76]

All of these developments, as an indication of a deep rift between Beijing and Moscow, produced a profound and long-lasting effect on the development of the international Communist movement and, at the same time, the orientation of the Cold War. For decades, especially after the end of the Second World War, Communists all over the world had shared a strong sense that "history is on our side." This belief allowed the international Communist movement constantly to gain strength and momentum while creating a consciousness of unity among Communist parties and states. The Polish and Hungarian crises of 1956, and the ways in which Beijing and Moscow dealt with them, exposed the profound contradictions between communism as a set of utopian ideals and as a practical human experience. For the first time in twentieth-century history, Communists throughout the world began to lose confidence in the ideals in which they once had believed. As a result, Communist states increasingly felt the need to use state power to control the minds and behavior of both party members and ordinary citizens. The Cold War was from the beginning a battle over which system—communism or liberal capitalism—was superior and which would prevail. International communism was now losing this battle.

*We must not fear the ghost. The more we fear the ghost, the more it
will present a deadly threat to us, and then it will invade our house and
swallow us. Since we do not fear the ghost, we decide to shell Jinmen.*
—*Mao Zedong (1958)*

*Besides its disadvantageous side, a tense [international] situation can
mobilize the population, can particularly mobilize the backward people,
can mobilize the people in the middle, and can therefore promote the
Great Leap Forward in economic construction.*
—*Mao Zedong (1958)*

At 5:30 P.M. on 23 August 1958, the People's Liberation Army units
in Fujian province suddenly began an intensive artillery barrage of the GMD-
controlled Jinmen islands.[1] In the first minute, some 2,600 rounds were fired.
When the shelling ended around 6:55 P.M., the PLA shore batteries had poured
more than 30,000 shells on Jinmen. About 600 GMD officers and soldiers were
reportedly killed, among whom were three deputy commanders of the GMD's
Jinmen garrison.[2]

In the ensuing six weeks, the PLA's artillery bombardment continued, and
several hundred thousand artillery shells exploded on the Jinmen islands and in
the waters around them. By early September, a massive PLA invasion of Jinmen
and other GMD-controlled offshore islands seemed imminent. In response to
the rapidly escalating crisis in the Taiwan Strait, the Eisenhower administration reinforced the strength of the Seventh Fleet in East Asia and ordered U.S.
naval vessels to help the GMD protect Jinmen's supply lines.[3] The leaders of the
Soviet Union were also alarmed. Fearing that Beijing's provocation might get
out of control and cause a general confrontation involving the use of nuclear
weapons between the Communist and capitalist blocs, they sent Foreign Minister Andrei Gromyko to Beijing early in September to inquire about Chinese

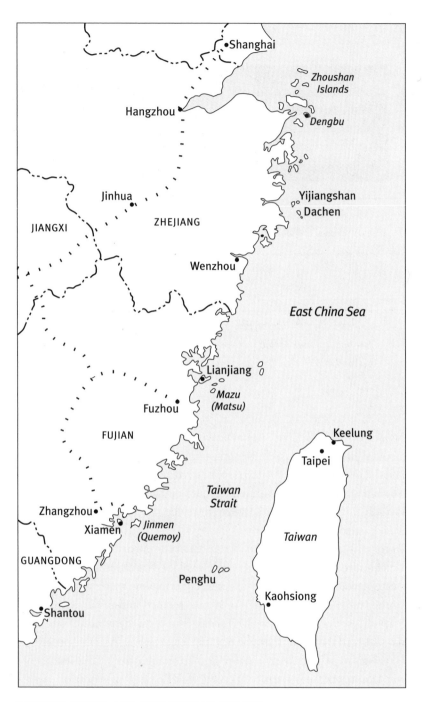

EASTERN CHINA AND THE TAIWAN STRAIT

leaders' intentions.[4] Early in October, however, the situation changed abruptly. On 6 October, Beijing issued a "Message to the Compatriots in Taiwan" in the name of Defense Minister Peng Dehuai, calling for a peaceful solution to the Taiwan issue so that all Chinese might unite in opposition to the "American plot" to divide China permanently.[5] From that day on, the PLA dramatically relaxed its siege of Jinmen. Consequently, the 1958 Taiwan Strait crisis ended without provoking a major confrontation between the Communist and capitalist camps.

Why and how did Beijing's leaders decide to shell Jinmen in August 1958? How did Beijing's leaders—and Mao Zedong in particular—manage the crisis? What factors caused Beijing's leaders to end the crisis as abruptly as they initiated it?[6] With the support of insights gained from Chinese sources recently made available, this chapter will first review the evolution of Beijing's Taiwan policy from 1949 to 1958; it will then discuss the domestic and international situations facing Beijing prior to the crisis, emphasizing the impact of the revolutionary atmosphere prevailing in China in 1958; it will examine how Beijing's leaders handled the crisis, and how and why Beijing's perceptions and policies changed during the course of the crisis; and it will conclude with some general discussion about what we may learn from the Taiwan Strait crisis of 1958.

Beijing's Taiwan Policy, 1949–1958

Since 1949, when the Nationalist regime was defeated by the CCP in the civil war and fled to Taiwan, the CCP and the GMD had been engaged in a continuous confrontation across the Taiwan Strait, making this area one of the main "hot spots" of the Cold War. The development of Beijing's Taiwan policy from 1949 to 1958 can be divided into four distinctive phases.

The First Phase: Preparing to "Liberate Taiwan," Fall 1949–Summer 1950

During this period, when the PLA was cleansing the GMD remnants on the Chinese mainland, the CCP leadership actively prepared for conducting a major amphibious campaign to "liberate Taiwan," so that mainland China and Taiwan could be unified under a new Chinese Communist regime.

The CCP leadership began planning for an attack on Taiwan in mid-June 1949. On 14 June, Mao Zedong sent a telegram to PLA commanders in East China, urging them to "pay attention to seizing Taiwan immediately."[7] A week later, Mao dispatched another telegram to top PLA commanders in coastal provinces, again stressing the utmost importance of quickly settling the Taiwan issue and ordering them to "complete all preparations during summer and autumn [of 1949] and occupy Taiwan in the coming winter."[8] Contemplating the means needed for seizing Taiwan, Mao paid special attention to getting assistance from Communist operatives in the GMD and air and naval support from the Soviet Union.[9] During Liu Shaoqi's secret visit to Moscow from late June to early August, the CCP's second in command endeavored to persuade Stalin to commit the strength of the Soviet Union behind the PLA's Taiwan campaign. The Soviet leader, however, agreed only to help the CCP establish its own air force and navy.[10] Consequently, the CCP leadership had to extend the deadline for completing the Taiwan campaign preparations to summer 1950.[11]

In October and November 1949, the CCP's Taiwan campaign preparations suffered a big setback when the PLA experienced two significant defeats in attempting to occupy Jinmen and Dengbu (a small island off Zhejiang province).[12] These defeats shocked both PLA commanders in East China and CCP leaders in Beijing, forcing them to reconsider the feasibility of conducting operations against Taiwan in the summer of 1950. After a series of deliberations and readjustments, by early summer 1950, CCP military planners again postponed an attack on Taiwan to summer 1951.[13]

The Second Phase: Korea, Not Taiwan, Becomes the Focus, June 1950–July 1953

The outbreak of the Korean War on 25 June 1950, as well as President Harry Truman's subsequent announcement that the Seventh Fleet would enter the Taiwan Strait to neutralize this area, completely changed the strategic scenario in East Asia. Around the same time, the GMD's secret services successfully unearthed a deep-rooted CCP underground spy network in Taiwan, shattering Beijing's hope for collaboration with elements within the GMD during a Taiwan campaign.[14] These two events combined to force Beijing's leaders to postpone further the plan to attack Taiwan, and Beijing's Taiwan policy entered the second phase.

On 30 June, five days after the eruption of the war in Korea, Zhou Enlai ordered Xiao Jinguang, the Chinese navy commander, to postpone preparations for invading Taiwan.[15] In mid-July, PLA commanders in East China received additional orders from Beijing to postpone the Taiwan campaign, so that China's military emphasis would be placed on "resisting America and assisting Korea."[16] On 11 August, the CMC followed General Chen Yi's suggestion to delay the Taiwan campaign until 1952 and postpone the attack on Jinmen until after April 1951.[17] After Chinese troops entered the Korean War in October 1950, the CCP leadership formally called off the plan to invade Taiwan.[18]

During the three years of China's intervention in Korea, Beijing maintained a defensive posture in relation to the GMD across the Taiwan Strait. While the PLA made no effort to attack the GMD-controlled offshore islands, the Nationalists occasionally invaded the Communist-controlled coastal areas.[19] In the meantime, the GMD leader Jiang Jieshi conducted a series of reforms in Taiwan, including a comprehensive land reform program, thus effectively enhancing the GMD regime's foundation there.[20] Consequently, the CCP-GMD confrontation across the Taiwan Strait, as the extension of the Chinese civil war, was prolonged.

The Third Phase: The First Taiwan Strait Crisis, 1954–1955

With the end of the Korean War in July 1953, CCP leaders found it necessary and possible to turn their attention back to the Taiwan issue. Because of specific domestic and international considerations, Mao decided to "highlight" the Taiwan issue, which led to the eruption of the first Taiwan Strait crisis.

In December 1953, Chen Yi, then commander and political commissar of the PLA's East China Military Region, proposed to Mao to concentrate five armies in Fujian to prepare for attacking Jinmen. He also suggested constructing several new airfields in East China and two major railway lines into Fujian.[21] Mao initially approved all of Chen Yi's proposals but then quickly changed his mind. The chairman believed that before attacking the GMD-controlled islands off the Fujian coast, the PLA should first invade and liberate several islands still occupied by GMD troops, especially Dachen and Yijiangshan, off the coast of Zhejiang province.[22] In December 1953, the PLA's East China Military Region formally established a joint headquarters for naval, air, and land operations in the Zhejiang area.[23] In January 1954, the CMC approved the operational plan involving the use of the PLA's three services in the Zhejiang campaign.[24] Throughout the first half of 1954, Beijing prepared for the campaign.

Mao, as well as Beijing's top military planners, decided to liberate the islands off Zhejiang province before attacking Jinmen for two tactical reasons. First, the Zhejiang area was close to Shanghai, China's main industrial center, and the mouth of the Yangzi River. Since 1949, the GMD had continuously used the islands off Zhejiang as bases to harass the mainland's coastal region, threatening the security of Shanghai and neighboring areas, as well as blocking the maritime transportation route south of the Yangzi River. Seizing these islands would greatly enhance the PRC's coastal security in the Shanghai-Zhejiang region.[25] Second, Fujian was one of China's most backward regions and had no railway or modern airport at that time, making it difficult for the PLA to organize large-scale amphibious landing operations there. In comparison, the GMD had greatly strengthened Jinmen's defensive system since 1949–50, transforming the island into an enhanced fortress. Beijing's leaders thus believed that until the PLA could improve logistic capacity and receive proper air support in Fujian, the plan to invade Jinmen should be put on hold.[26]

When the PLA's East China Military Region was actively preparing for the Zhejiang campaign, Mao suddenly changed the emphasis of Beijing's Taiwan strategy again. In a telegram to Zhou Enlai on 23 July 1954, Mao sternly criticized the premier, who had just attended the Geneva conference and was then visiting several socialist countries in Eastern Europe. The chairman claimed: "After the end of the Korean War, we failed to highlight the task [the liberation of Taiwan] to the people in the whole country in a timely manner (we are about six months behind). We failed to take necessary measures and make effective efforts in military affairs, on the diplomatic front, and also in our propaganda to serve this task. If we do not highlight this task now, and if we do not work for it [in the future], we are committing a serious political mistake."[27]

Following Mao's instruction to "highlight the Taiwan issue," the Chinese media immediately initiated a propaganda campaign with "We must liberate Taiwan" as the central slogan.[28] In the meantime, the PLA high command revised the original campaign plan: in addition to conducting landing operations against the islands off Zhejiang province, the PLA's shore batteries in Fujian were to prepare to shell Jinmen.[29]

This latest decision made some sense from a military perspective. As a military strategist, Mao certainly understood that by shelling Jinmen before conducting landing operations from Zhejiang, the PLA would distract the attention of the GMD high command, thus better guaranteeing the success of the Zhejiang campaign. Indeed, this is exactly how Beijing's official history interpreted the change of plans.[30]

But the military interpretation alone does not satisfactorily reveal the main reasons underlying the decision to shell Jinmen.[31] Mao and the CCP leadership also intended to use the shelling to "highlight" the Taiwan question, stressing that it was an internal Chinese issue. A CCP Central Committee telegram to Zhou Enlai dated 27 July 1954 pointed out: "After the armistices in Korea and Indochina, the Americans will not be willing to accept their failure at the Geneva conference, and will inevitably carry out policies designed to create international tension, to seize more spheres of influence from the British and the French, to expand military bases and prepare for fighting a war, and to remain hostile toward our country." In particular, the telegram stressed, Washington had been "discussing signing a treaty of mutual defense with Jiang Jieshi," which made it necessary for Beijing to continue "the war against Jiang's bandit clique in Taiwan" by introducing "the slogan of liberating Taiwan."[32] Therefore, Mao and the Beijing leadership decided to order the PLA to shell Jinmen to expose Washington's plot of "interfering with China's internal affairs."[33]

The decision to shell Jinmen must also be understood in the context of Mao's aspiration for creating new momentum for his continuous revolution. The end of the Korean War allowed Mao and his comrades to devote China's resources to the "socialist revolution and reconstruction" at home. From the chairman's perspective, 1954–55 represented a crucial transitional period for the CCP to build the foundation for a socialist society in China. In search of means to mobilize the party and the ordinary Chinese citizens for this new stage of the Chinese revolution, Mao, informed by his Korean War experience, again sensed the need to emphasize the existence of outside threats (be it from Jiang's GMD or from the United States). In justifying Beijing's new Taiwan strategy, Mao and the CCP leadership stressed in an internal correspondence: "The introduction of the task [the liberation of Taiwan] is not just for the purpose of undermining the American-Jiang plot to sign a military treaty; rather, and more important, by highlighting the task we mean to raise the political consciousness and political alertness of the people of the whole country; we mean to stir up our people's revolutionary enthusiasm, thus promoting our nation's socialist reconstruction."[34]

This emphasis upon using the Taiwan issue to promote domestic mobilization, however, contradicted from the beginning the "peaceful coexistence" foreign policy line Zhou Enlai was endeavoring to promote around the same period.[35] It also caused great confusion in terms of Beijing's goals for the new strategy (that is, deterring American interference in China's internal affairs and driving a wedge between Taipei and Washington). When the PLA's shore batteries fiercely bombarded Jinmen on 3 and 22 September,[36] and especially after the PLA increased pressure on the GMD-controlled Dachen and Yijiang-shan islands off Zhejiang, Washington and Taipei accelerated negotiations toward signing a defense treaty.[37] On 2 December 1954, the treaty was formally signed, with Washington officially committing to using military force to defend Taiwan in the case of a Communist invasion.[38] The treaty, though, did not include explicit U.S. commitment to defending the GMD-controlled off-shore islands. When the PLA finally conducted a full-scale landing operation in Dachen and Yijiangshan in January 1955, Washington, except for helping GMD troops to withdraw from these islands, did not intervene.[39] When the PLA occupied all GMD-controlled islands off Zhejiang province in February 1955 and, two months later, Zhou Enlai announced in Bandung, Indonesia, that Beijing was willing to negotiate with Washington to "reduce the tension in the Far East," the first Taiwan Strait crisis ended.[40]

The Fourth Phase: The Peace Initiative, Mid-1955–1957

The consequences of the 1954–55 Taiwan Strait crisis presented to Beijing's leaders a paradoxical challenge. On the one hand, the crisis caused the international community to pay attention to the Taiwan issue (although not exactly in the way Beijing's leaders had wanted), and the PLA's liberation of offshore islands in Zhejiang significantly improved the PRC's coastal security north of Fujian province. Therefore, Mao and his comrades felt justified in telling the Chinese people that Beijing's handling of the crisis was a great success.[41] On the other hand, the American-Taiwan defense treaty made it more difficult for the PLA to "liberate Taiwan" and, as a result, the separation between the mainland and Taiwan became further formalized. In order to deal with this challenge, the CCP leadership began to reexamine its Taiwan policy in 1955, which resulted in a shift toward a possible peaceful settlement of the Taiwan issue through negotiations with the GMD.

Zhou Enlai was one of the main architects of the new peace initiative, and at this moment Mao supported him.[42] In July 1955, Zhou stated at the Second Session of the People's Congress that "there are two ways for the Chinese people to liberate Taiwan, one military way and one peaceful way. If possible, the Chinese people are willing to liberate Taiwan through the peaceful way."[43] On 30 January 1956, Zhou announced the CCP's new policy toward Jiang Jieshi and the GMD at a plenary session of the Chinese People's Consultative Conference. While reiterating that the CCP was prepared to use military means to liberate Taiwan whenever necessary, the Chinese premier also made it clear that Beijing was now willing to consider "solving the Taiwan issue" in peaceful ways. He also welcomed GMD members living in Taiwan to come back to visit the mainland, claiming that "anyone who is willing to contribute to the unification of the motherland" would be pardoned for "whatever wrongdoing" they might have committed in the past.[44] After a series of probes, Zhou Enlai announced publicly on 28 June 1956 that Beijing was "willing to discuss with the Taiwan authorities about the concrete steps toward, as well as conditions for, a peaceful liberation of Taiwan." He invited the Taiwan authorities to "dispatch representatives to Beijing, or to another proper location, to begin such discussion with us."[45] This statement represented a radical departure from Beijing's militant policy during the first Taiwan Strait crisis less than two years earlier.

Beijing continued to carry out its new moderate policy toward Taiwan throughout late 1956 and 1957. In addition to openly announcing the CCP's willingness to negotiate with the GMD, Beijing's leaders also explored contacting Jiang and other GMD leaders in Taipei through secret channels. One such channel was through a Hong Kong–based freelance journalist named Cao Ju-ren, who had extensive connections with GMD leaders. In a meeting with Cao on 7 October 1956, Zhou outlined Beijing's conditions for a peaceful settlement of the Taiwan issue: After Taiwan's "return to the motherland," the island would continue to be governed by the GMD, and a "proper position" would be arranged for Jiang Jieshi in the central government. Zhou also emphasized that Beijing had stopped anti-Jiang propaganda in order to create an atmosphere for negotiating with the GMD.[46] From 1956 to 1958, Cao frequently traveled to Beijing to serve as a messenger between top CCP and GMD leaders. On one occasion, Zhou claimed that in carrying out the moderate policy toward Taiwan, "we are sincere and patient, we can wait."[47]

Beijing's peace initiative toward Taiwan in 1955–57 was a natural outgrowth of the CCP's longtime tradition of pursuing a "united front" with the GMD whenever the party leadership deemed it necessary.[48] When the GMD regime in Taiwan signed the treaty of mutual defense with the United States, Mao and his comrades not only realized that liberating Taiwan by military means had become next to impossible but also were aware of the urgent need to do everything possible to prevent Taiwan from being "colonized" by a hostile imperialist foreign power.[49] In addition, two important international and domestic pursuits supported China's Taiwan policy. First, during this same period, Beijing was seeking to improve the PRC's international status through the introduction of the principles of pancha shila and the "Bandung spirit," and the peace initiative toward Taiwan became an important component of this endeavor.[50] Second, in September 1956, CCP's Eighth National Congress adopted a policy that emphasized economic reconstruction rather than class struggle in following China's path toward a socialist society, and the Taiwan initiative was compatible with this policy.[51] Not surprising at all, with dramatic changes in these two pursuits in 1958, Beijing would return to a highly militant policy toward Taiwan, resulting in the second Taiwan Strait crisis.

1958: The Year of Mao's Revolutionary Outburst

Beijing's return to a more militant strategy toward Taiwan began around late 1957 and early 1958. On 18 December 1957, Mao Zedong instructed Peng Dehuai, China's defense minister, to "consider the question of moving our air force into Fujian in 1958."[52] In mid-January, the headquarters of Fujian Military Region formulated plans for PLA air units to enter Fujian by early summer

1958.[53] On 31 January 1958, Peng reported at a CMC meeting that a main railway line leading to Xiamen had been completed (which was key to the PLA's large-scale military operations aimed at Jinmen), that numerous PLA artillery units had been deployed in Fujian, and that the PLA air force would finish all preparations for occupying the newly constructed airfields in Fujian in July or August. Early in March, Mao approved Peng's plans.[54] In April, the headquarters of the Fujian Military Region followed the CMC's instruction to work out a detailed contingency plan to shell Jinmen and formally submitted it to Beijing for approval on 27 April.[55] Behind these changes was Mao himself. When top CCP leaders met in Chengdu in March, Mao announced that he had not been personally involved in military decision making since the Korean War and that "this year I will come back to do some military [commanding] work."[56] All of these developments, as it soon turned out, would became the prelude to Mao's decision to shell Jinmen in summer 1958.

Why did Beijing harden its policy toward Taiwan in 1958? In exploring the causes, some scholars have referred to CCP leaders' frustration with Taipei's lack of positive response to their peace initiative in the previous two years. The more militant policy, these scholars argue, was designed to pressure the GMD to take the CCP's peace initiative more seriously.[57] Other scholars have focused their attention on Beijing's deepening confrontation with Washington. They point out that by late 1957 and early 1958, while the Chinese-American ambassadorial talks in Warsaw (which began in 1955) had hit a deadlock, Beijing's leaders became alarmed by Washington's increasingly complicated military involvement in Taiwan following the signing of the U.S.-Taiwan mutual defense treaty. Consequently, Mao and his comrades found it necessary to "do something substantial" to probe Washington's real intention toward Taiwan, as well as to determine to what extent Washington was willing to commit to Taiwan's defense.[58]

These interpretations make good sense as far as they go. But they do not take into consideration the profound connections between Beijing's changing policy toward Taiwan and the broader domestic and international environment in which Beijing's leaders formulated the policy. In order to understand the dynamics underlying Beijing's decision to shell Jinmen in summer 1958, the decision must be placed into the context of the emerging Great Leap Forward, one of the most important episodes in the development of Mao's continuous revolution. Indeed, as revealed by recently released Chinese evidence, the CCP leadership's handling of the Taiwan issue in 1958 was from the beginning shaped by the revolutionary zeal prevailing in Chinese political and social life during this unique moment in China's modern history.

Mao's revolutionary outburst began early in 1958, with the Chinese chairman using every opportunity to argue that the "revolutionary enthusiasm" of the masses was required to push China's "socialist revolution and reconstruction" to a higher level.[59] In the chairman's vision, the successful completion of the "socialist transformation" of China's industry, commerce, and agriculture in 1956 had already prepared conditions for Chinese society to enter a new stage in the Marxist order of socioeconomic development. By turning the Hundred Flowers Campaign into an Anti-Rightist movement in 1957, the chairman clearly revealed his determination to create a new wave of mass mobilization by manipulating China's "public opinion." At a series of conferences attended by top party leaders early in 1958, Mao fiercely criticized the mistakes of "opposing rash advance" committed by Zhou Enlai and others in 1956–57.[60] In the meantime, he repeatedly outlined the blueprint for building a Communist society in China, calling upon the whole party and the whole country to "do away with all fetishes and superstitions, and [to] defy laws both human and divine."[61] Consequently, in summer 1958, Mao and the CCP leadership, formally announcing that "the realization of a Communist society in China is not far away," unleashed the Great Leap Forward throughout China's cities and countryside.

While China's political landscape was being rapidly transformed by this Maoist revolutionary discourse, Beijing's security concerns and foreign policies were also undergoing profound changes. In March, yielding to Mao's insistent pressure, Zhou Enlai criticized his handling of Chinese foreign policy in the 1954–58 period at the Chengdu conference. The premier admitted that in dealing with nationalist countries he had put too much emphasis on unity with them to the extent of neglecting the "necessary struggle" against the reactionary elements in these countries, and that he should have taken a more aggressive approach to struggle against capitalist/imperialist countries like Japan and the United States.[62] Zhou then resigned from his post as China's foreign minister. When Marshal Chen Yi took over the Foreign Ministry, his first move was to follow Mao's instructions to convene a series of rectification meetings at the ministry aimed at "clearing up" the "rightist tendency" among members of the Chinese diplomatic service.[63]

Against this background, in the spring and summer of 1958, Beijing initiated a series of diplomatic "offensives." As discussed in Chapter 3, when the Soviet leaders proposed to form a joint submarine flotilla with China and to establish a long-wave radio station on Chinese territory, Mao immediately characterized these proposals as indications of Moscow's "big-power chauvinism," throwing the leaders in the Kremlin on the defensive.[64] Early in May, after two right-wing Japanese youth destroyed the PRC's flag at a Chinese exhibition in Nagasaki, Beijing's leaders quickly characterized this incident as a "serious imperialist plot" designed to attack the dignity and reputation of the People's Republic. In protest, Beijing decided to cancel all of China's trade and cultural exchanges with Japan, which led to further erosion of Beijing's already highly strained relations with Tokyo.[65] It was within the context of these "offensives" that Mao made the decision to shell Jinmen.

What should be emphasized is that the rapid radicalization of China's domestic and foreign policies reflected Mao's unique perception of the serious threats facing the People's Republic. Ironically, although Mao had repeatedly announced since late 1957 that "the East Wind has overwhelmed the West Wind" and that "while the enemy is becoming weaker everyday, we are getting stronger all the time,"[66] his sense of insecurity seems to have increased dramatically. On several occasions, the chairman fretted: "It is destined that our socialist revolution and reconstruction will not be smooth sailing. We should be prepared to deal with many serious threats facing us both internationally and domestically. As far as the international and domestic situations are concerned, although it is certain both are good in a general sense, it is also certain that many serious challenges are waiting for us. We must be prepared to deal with them."[67]

It is apparent that Mao's concerns for China's security were not limited to the country's physical safety but were broader and more complicated. In order to fully comprehend the implications of Maoist rhetoric concerning China's security status, we must understand Mao's profound "postrevolution anxiety." According to Mao, the final goal of his revolution was the transformation of China's old state and society and the reassertion of China's central position in world affairs. For Mao, the Communist seizure of power in China represented the completion of only the first step in the "Long March" of the Chinese revolution. Since the PRC's establishment, Mao repeatedly warned his comrades that if the revolution was not constantly pushed forward, it would lose its momentum. Therefore, in Mao's vision, the threats to revolutionary China did not just come from without—such as from the imperialist/reactionary forces hostile to the People's Republic—but also from within, especially from the chronic decline of the revolutionary vigor on the part of party cadres and ordinary party members. For the chairman, how continuously to mobilize the party and the masses thus became a central issue in dealing with the threats that revolutionary China would have to face.[68] In 1958, when Mao was leading the whole party and the whole nation to begin the Great Leap Forward, he found that the tension emerging in the Taiwan Strait provided him with much needed means to legitimize the unprecedented mass mobilization in China:

> Besides its disadvantageous side, a tense [international] situation can mobilize the population, can particularly mobilize the backward people, can mobilize the people in the middle, and can therefore promote the Great Leap Forward in economic construction. . . . Lenin once introduced this point in his discussions about war. Lenin said that a war could motivate people's spiritual condition, making it tense. Although there is no war right now, a tense situation caused by the current military confrontation can also bring about every positive factor.[69]

Mao's statement is telling because it reveals that Beijing's decision to shell Jinmen was made not only to punish the GMD's lack of interest in the CCP's peace initiative or to probe Washington's intention in East Asia but also, and more importantly, to promote the extraordinary revolutionary outburst in China in 1958. The shelling served as a crucial means for Mao to mobilize the Chinese people to devote their innermost support to the Great Leap Forward. In retrospect, given the revolutionary atmosphere prevailing in Chinese society in 1958, it would have been inconceivable for Mao not to make Taiwan an outstanding security issue.

The Decision to Shell Jinmen

Although Mao had actively considered "taking major military actions" in the Taiwan Strait since early 1958,[70] not until July did he decide to conduct large-scale shelling of the Jinmen islands. What triggered the decision, interestingly, was the crisis emerging in the Middle East following American and British intervention in Lebanon and Jordan.

On 14 July, a group of young nationalist officers led by Abdel Karim Kassim staged a coup in Iraq, which resulted in the establishment of a new regime friendly to the socialist bloc. In response, U.S. marines landed on Lebanon and British paratroopers landed in Jordan the next day. Beijing angrily protested the U.S.-British intervention. While millions of ordinary Chinese held protest demonstrations and rallies in Beijing, Shanghai, and other major cities, the PRC government announced that it firmly opposed Washington's and London's imperialist behavior in the Middle East and supported the newly born Republic of Iraq.[71]

Beijing's protest was not confined to mere words. On 17 July, without consulting other top leaders in Beijing, Mao asked Peng Dehuai to convey the following order to the PLA's General Staff: In response to the crisis situation in the Middle East, the air force should move into Fujian as soon as possible, the Fujian shore batteries should be prepared to shell Jinmen and blockade Jinmen's supply lines, and the General Staff should work out plans for conducting these operations immediately.[72]

The next evening, Mao chaired a meeting attended by Beijing's top military planners to discuss how to carry out the shelling operation.[73] He told the participants that the U.S.-British intervention in Lebanon and Jordan had made the Middle East the focus of an international confrontation between progressive and reactionary forces. China's aid to the Arab people, claimed the chairman, should not be restricted to moral support but must be given "through taking practical actions." He announced that he had decided to use the PLA's shore batteries to shell GMD troops in Jinmen and Mazu. "The first wave," he instructed, "will include the firing of 100,000 to 200,000 shells, and will be followed by 1,000 shells every day for two to three months." The chairman said that he intended to make Jiang Jieshi the main target and, at the same time, try to gauge the strength of the Americans. He also reasoned that since Jinmen and Mazu were Chinese territories, and the shelling was a matter of China's internal affairs, the Americans could not use it as an excuse to strike back.[74]

Late on the evening of 18 July, Peng Dehuai called a CMC meeting to work out more detailed plans to carry out Mao's order. It was decided that PLA's air force, unless hindered by bad weather, should move into the airfields in Fujian by 27 July to cover the shelling operation. In addition, more artillery units would be transferred to Fujian immediately to join the shore batteries already stationed there. The shelling would focus on Jinmen's harbor and GMD supply vessels, so that the islands' supply lines would be cut off. In making plans for the air force, Peng and his colleagues showed caution. They believed that the air force should restrict its operations to the airspace over the mainland and should never enter operations over open sea. The meeting participants also decided that the shelling of Jinmen would begin in one week, on 25 July.[75]

The Chinese military machine was promptly put into motion after the meeting. At 11:00 P.M. on 18 July, the PLA General Staff relayed the CMC's order by security telephone to General Ye Fei, political commissar of the Fujian Military Region who, according to Mao's order, would assume the frontal commanding duty for the shelling operation. Ye immediately met with his staff to discuss how to implement the order. They decided to concentrate, by the evening of 24 July, thirty artillery battalions in the Xiamen area directed against Jinmen and another four artillery battalions in the Lianjiang area directed against Mazu.[76] In the meantime, the air force decided that their air units would move into several Fujian and nearby eastern Guangdong airfields in two groups on 24 and 27 July, and that additional antiaircraft artillery units and radar units would be dispatched to Fujian.[77] On 20 July, the naval headquarters ordered the units under its command to complete all preparations for operations in Fujian.[78]

In the next several days, the railways and highways leading to the Fujian coast became jammed by large numbers of PLA artillery and other supporting units being transferred to the front. Despite the difficulties created by a severe typhoon on 21 July, Ye Fei was able to report to Mao and the CMC on 23 July that thirty-three artillery battalions had taken position on the Fujian coast, that about 50,000 artillery shells had been distributed among front units, with another 100,000 shells on their way, and that all other preparations would be completed by 24 July. Ye also summarized the Fujian Military Region's operation plans: "(1) We plan to use our artillery forces to conduct abrupt and fierce shelling of the enemy in Jinmen and Mazu simultaneously. (2) In terms of the targets of our artillery strike in Jinmen, we will concentrate on attacking the enemy's docks, artillery grounds, and important warehouses. (3) We will then be prepared to enter operations in the air and, at the same time, will use our shore batteries to blockade the enemy's ports and airfields, striking continuously the enemy's artillery forces and other reinforcements."[79] Although no landing operation was mentioned in these well-calculated plans, it is logical to conclude that the PLA would try to take over Jinmen and Mazu after significantly weakening the enemy's defense capacity and cutting off its supply lines.

As PLA units nearly completed their preparations on the Fujian front, top CCP leaders in Beijing postponed the deadline for the shelling operation twice. On 24 July, after learning that Taipei had dispatched two more divisions to Jinmen as reinforcements, Peng Dehuai proposed to Mao to change the deadline from 25 to 27 July, and Mao approved.[80] On the morning of 27 July, when Ye Fei and his staff were waiting for the final order from Beijing to commence the shelling, Mao decided to postpone the operation again. In a letter to Peng Dehuai and Huang Kecheng (a copy of which was simultaneously cabled to Ye Fei), the chairman stated:

I could not sleep and have thought about the question again. It seems more appropriate to hold the shelling on Jinmen for several more days. While holding our operations, we will observe the development of the situation. . . . We will wait until the other side launches a provocative attack and then respond with our counterattack. The solution of the problem in the Middle East will take time. Since we have time, why should we be in a big hurry? We will hold our attack plan for the moment, but one day we will implement it. If the other side invades Zhangzhou, Shantou, Fuzhou, and Hangzhou, that is the best scenario. . . . It is extremely beneficial to have politics in a commanding position and to make a decision only after repeated deliberations. . . . Even if the other side attacks us, we still can wait for a few days to make clear calculations and then start our counterattack. . . . We must persist in the principle of fighting no battle we are not sure of winning.[81]

Why did Mao decide to put the shelling of Jinmen on hold at the last minute? One possible explanation was that the chairman was not certain if the PLA artillery units on the Fujian front had indeed reached full readiness, and that he knew that his air force would need more time to occupy the airfields in Fujian.[82] As a longtime advocate of "never fighting a battle without being fully prepared," the chairman must have felt it necessary to give the PLA more time to complete all preparations. The chairman also must have realized that the shelling would inevitably escalate the tension between China and the United States, and although he repeatedly claimed that he would never be scared by the American "paper tiger," he would like to calculate possible American reactions more carefully.[83] Furthermore, given the emphasis he had placed upon the political impact of the shelling, it is possible that Mao hoped that the PLA's military concentration in the coastal area might trigger a GMD preemptive military attack on the mainland (most likely by air bombardment), which would provide additional justification for the PLA to shell Jinmen and thus greatly enhance the shelling's mobilization effect upon ordinary Chinese people.

In addition, Mao may have decided to postpone the shelling because Soviet leader Nikita Khrushchev was scheduled to visit Beijing in a few days to deal with a potential crisis recently emerging between Beijing and Moscow. In summer 1958 Moscow proposed to Beijing to establish a joint Soviet-Chinese submarine flotilla and a jointly owned long-wave radio station on the Chinese coast, which Beijing opposed immediately. On 22 July 1958, five days before Mao decided to postpone the shelling of Jinmen, he had a highly emotional talk with Pavel Yudin, Soviet ambassador to China, during which he criticized Moscow's proposals as evidence of Soviet leaders' "big-power chauvinism," as well as their desire to control China.[84] Khrushchev, after receiving Yudin's report, quickly decided to travel to Beijing to meet Mao. Although we have no way of knowing exactly how this turn of events might have influenced Mao's consideration of the Taiwan issue, one thing is certain: the Chinese chairman did not want to let the Soviet leader have any impact on his decision making on Taiwan. When Khrushchev was in Beijing from 31 July to 3 August, he had four substantial meetings with Mao and other Chinese leaders, but Mao never informed Khrushchev that the PLA was planning to shell Jinmen.[85] From the beginning, for Mao, the shelling was a challenge not just to Taipei and Washington but to Moscow's domination of the international Communist movement as well.

Militarily speaking, Mao's decision to postpone the shelling did give the PLA more time to complete pre-operation preparations. From 27 July to 13 August, several PLA air regiments successfully moved into airfields in Fujian and eastern Guangdong, thus establishing effective air coverage for the artillery and ground units that had taken position in Fujian.[86] In the meantime, PLA field commanders in Fujian gained more time to establish better communications and logistical support for their troops.[87] From Mao's perspective, though, prolonging the preparations gave him more opportunity to contemplate the shelling's possible consequences, especially Washington's likely reaction. Indeed, as we shall see, how to avoid a direct confrontation with the Americans became a main concern for Mao when he made the final decision to shell Jinmen.

Mao's decision to postpone the shelling operation, however, also confused some of his own commanders. By mid-August, since they had not received further orders from Mao, top PLA commanders began to believe that the chairman meant to call off the shelling operation or postpone it indefinitely. On 13 August, Peng Dehuai instructed the Operation Department under the General Staff that if the American/GMD side did not initiate any military activity in the next few days, the shelling operation in Fujian should be called off and the PLA units there should return to "normal status." On 19 August, the General Staff formally notified the Fujian Military Region that the "combat readiness" status on the Fujian front had been lifted.[88]

At this point, though, Mao was actually ready to execute the shelling plan. Beginning on 17 August, the CCP leadership convened an enlarged politburo conference at Beidaihe, a summer sea resort for top CCP leaders, to discuss how to propel the Great Leap Forward into its most radical phase: the communization of China's rural population and the militarization of the entire Chinese workforce (that is, the commencement of the nationwide "everyone a soldier" campaign). Although the Jinmen issue originally was not on the meeting's agenda, on the first day of the conference, Mao suddenly announced that he had decided to shell Jinmen.[89] Mao then offered one of the most outspoken statements he had given during the 1958 Taiwan Strait crisis to justify his decision, emphasizing that, as far as its mobilization effect is concerned, international tension was not a bad thing at all:

> In our propaganda, we say that we oppose tension and strive for détente, as if détente is to our advantage [and] tension is to their [the West's] advantage. [But] can we or can't we look at [the situation] the other way around: is tension to our comparative advantage [and] to the West's disadvantage? Tension is to the West's advantage only in that they can increase military production, and it is to our advantage in that it will mobilize all [our] positive forces. . . . Tension can [help] gain membership for Communist parties in different countries. [It] can [help] us increase steel as well as grain [production]. . . . To have an enemy in front of us, to have tension, is to our advantage.[90]

No statement could be more revealing about Mao's intentions. Following this singular logic, Mao acted to create an enemy. Early on the morning of 18 August, he personally wrote a letter to Peng Dehuai, telling the defense minister to "prepare to shell Jinmen now, dealing with Jiang [Jieshi] directly and the Americans indirectly." The chairman also asked Peng to "call the air force headquarters' attention to the possibility that the Taiwan side might counterattack us by dispatching large numbers of aircraft (dozens, or even one hundred planes) to try to take back air control over Jinmen and Mazu." "[I]f this happens," he instructed Peng, "we should prepare to use large numbers of our air units to defeat them immediately." Demonstrating his willingness to maintain a balance between strategic aggressiveness and tactical cautiousness, the chairman advised the defense minister that "in chasing them, our planes should not cross the space line over Jinmen and Mazu."[91] After being put on hold for more than three weeks, the shelling operation was again activated.

Two days later, Mao further defined the operation's scope and objective. He reduced the operation's size from what he had planned one month before, deciding that intensive shelling would be conducted only toward the Jinmen islands, but not Mazu. He also made it clear that the shelling's main goal was to isolate the GMD troops on Jinmen, cutting them off from supplies. He also clarified that he intended to take over Jinmen, although not necessarily through a landing operation. "After a period of shelling," the chairman pointed out, "the other side might withdraw its troops from Jinmen and Mazu, or might continue to struggle in spite of huge difficulties. Then, whether or not we will conduct landing operations will be determined by the specific situation at that time. We should take one step and watch to take the next step."[92]

Mao's main concern was how the United States would respond to the shelling. In a general sense, Mao did not believe that Washington would intervene militarily for the sake of Jinmen and other GMD-controlled offshore islands; nor did he anticipate that the shelling on Jinmen would result in a general war between China and the United States.[93] But as an experienced military strategist, he had been accustomed to "striving for the best while preparing for the worst," and he thus needed to have contingency plans in hand. Consequently, before he gave his orders, Mao talked to his field commanders in person. Late on 20 August, the General Staff telephoned Ye Fei, who had been waiting for Mao's final order since late July, instructing him to fly immediately to Beidaihe to meet with Mao.[94] Ye arrived at Mao's quarters on the afternoon of 21 August, and the meeting was also attended by Marshals Peng Dehuai and Lin Biao. After Ye reported to Mao in detail the situation on the Fujian front, the chairman abruptly asked: "You use so many cannons in the shelling, is it possible that some Americans would be killed?" Ye, knowing that there were American advisers in Jinmen, replied that it was possible. Mao also asked: "Is it possible that you might avoid hitting the Americans?" Ye said that it was impossible. Mao did not ask another question before peremptorily adjourning the meeting. The next day Mao again summoned Ye to his quarters and told him that even though the shelling might result in the deaths of Americans, it should go on. And in order to assure that the central leadership, and Mao in particular, would directly control the shelling the chairman ordered Ye to stay in Beidaihe to command the operations by telephone.[95]

The fact that Mao made the final decision in mid- and late August to begin the shelling is highly revealing. By that time, the tension in the Middle East had already been greatly reduced—since early August, Washington and London had recognized the new nationalist government in Iraq, and they both had begun to withdraw their troops from Lebanon and Jordan. As a result, Mao's main original reason to shell Jinmen—"to support the people in the Middle East"—was no longer a valid justification for the decision. The logical interpretation, as will be discussed below, can only be that he was driven by domestic political considerations.

On the morning of 23 August, all PLA units in Fujian entered a "first-class alert of operation readiness." At the PLA's frontline headquarters in Xiamen, General Zhang Yixiang, the vice commander of the Fujian Military Region who had been assigned the frontal commanding duty during Ye Fei's absence, maintained constant telephone communication with Ye in Beidaihe. After almost a whole day's waiting, at around 5:20 P.M., Zhang received the order from Mao via Ye that the shelling should start at 5:30 P.M. Ten minutes later, a large-scale barrage of the Jinmen islands began.[96]

The Shelling and the Crisis

The PLA's intensive bombardment of Jinmen on 23 August touched off a major international crisis. Although the Eisenhower administration was not caught entirely off guard by the shelling since for weeks American officials had observed Beijing's massive military buildup in Fujian and had formulated various contingency plans, policymakers in Washington were not certain about Beijing's intentions.[97] Fearing that the shelling could be a prelude to a major invasion of the GMD-controlled offshore islands or even Taiwan itself, President Eisenhower ordered U.S. forces in East Asia to enter "readiness alert" for war operations. To enhance American naval strength in the Taiwan Strait, he ordered two aircraft carrier groups (recently deployed in the Middle East during the crisis over Iraq and Lebanon) to sail to East Asia. In the meantime, Washington expedited the shipment of all kinds of military equipment and ammunition, including the deadly Sidewinder air-to-air missile, to Taiwan.[98] Indeed, as historian Gordon H. Chang points out: "Within days the United States had assembled off the Chinese coast the most powerful armada the world had ever seen."[99]

These developments did not come as a surprise to Mao, since one of his main purposes was to stir up international tension on his own terms. On the evening of 23 August, Mao called a Politburo Standing Committee meeting at Beidaihe and delivered a long and comprehensive speech, divulging his understanding of the international impact of the shelling. According to Wu Lengxi, who attended the meeting as director of the Xinhua News Agency and one of Mao's political secretaries, the chairman was in very high spirits. He first explained why he chose 23 August for the barrage. The chairman pointed out that just three days earlier the UN Assembly had passed a resolution requesting that American and British troops withdraw from Lebanon and Jordan, a request that, in his view, made "American occupation of Taiwan look even more unjust than before," thus making the timing perfect for beginning shelling on Jinmen. In elaborating what he saw as the purpose of the shelling operation, the chairman stressed: "Our demand is that American armed forces withdraw from Taiwan, and Jiang's troops withdraw from Jinmen and Mazu. If they do not do so, we will attack. Taiwan is too far away to be bombed, so we shell Jinmen and Mazu. This will surely produce a shock wave in the world. Not only will the Americans be shocked but the Asians and the Europeans will be shocked too. The people in the Arab world will be delighted, and the vast masses in Asia and Africa will take our side."[100]

As he did on so many other occasions in the summer of 1958, the chairman again explained how international tension could be beneficial to China's continuous revolution. He told Wu Lengxi that the Chinese media should continue to propagandize that China opposed the international tension created by the imperialists and was in favor of relaxing international tension. However, stressed the chairman, his real belief was that "all bad things have two sides." While "international tension is certainly a bad thing, there is a good side of it: it will bring about the awakening of many people, and will make them determined to fight against the imperialists." [101]

During the course of his long talk, the chairman stated that the bombardment of Jinmen was also meant to "teach the Americans a lesson." "The Americans have bullied us for many years," claimed the chairman, "so now that we have a chance, why not give them a hard time?" He emphasized that "the Americans started a fire in the Middle East, and we are now starting a fire in the Far East." In his opinion, "we did not put the Americans in the wrong; they did it by themselves—they have stationed several thousand troops on Taiwan, plus two air force bases there." Beijing should observe how the international community, and especially the Americans, respond to the shelling operation, the chairman continued, and "then we will decide on our next move." [102]

Fighting continued in the Taiwan Strait area on 24 August. In addition to inflicting another day of the fierce artillery bombardment (about 10,000 rounds were fired), the PLA navy dispatched six torpedo boats to attack several GMD supply ships off the Jinmen port. It was reported that one GMD ship, *Zhonghai*, was severely damaged, and another one, *Taisheng*, was sunk. [103] In retaliation, the GMD used forty-eight F-86 fighters to attack the PLA air force the next afternoon, leading to a major air battle over the Fujian coast. The outcome of the battle has become a myth since each side claimed that it had won a victory. [104]

As the conflict in the Taiwan Strait escalated, Mao called another Politburo Standing Committee meeting on the afternoon of 25 August, specifically devoted to the discussion of Washington's reaction and Beijing's next move. [105] Again the chairman dominated the meeting. Beginning his talk by joking that "now we are taking our summer vacation here at Beidaihe, but we have made the Americans extremely nervous," the chairman told the participants that, according to his observations, Washington was worried that the PLA not only would land on Jinmen and Mazu but also would attack Taiwan itself. "In reality," commented the chairman, "although we have fired dozens of thousands of rounds on Jinmen, we only mean to probe [the Americans' intention]. We will not say if we are, or if we are not, going to land on Jinmen. We will be doubly cautious and will act in accordance with the situation." The chairman further clarified that he was taking such a cautious attitude not because there were 95,000 GMD troops stationed on Jinmen islands but because he needed to assess the attitude of the American government. "Washington has signed a treaty of mutual defense with Taiwan, but it does not clearly spell out whether or not the U.S. defense perimeter includes Jinmen and Mazu." Thus, Mao continued, "we need to see if the Americans want to carry these islands on their backs." In the chairman's opinion, the best way to deal with the Americans at the moment was to keep them guessing. Thus Mao directed the Chinese media not to link U.S. actions in the Middle East directly with the PLA's bombardment of Jinmen for the moment, but rather to criticize Washington's "imperialist behavior" in broad terms, including its "occupation of China's Taiwan." "We should build up our strength and store up our energy, that is, draw the bow but not discharge the arrow," concluded the chairman.[106]

In response to Mao's vague instructions, the planners at Beijing's General Staff headquarters spent the whole evening of 25 August working out what specific strategy the PLA's three services in Fujian should take in the next few days. On 26 August, Peng Dehuai, with Mao's approval, summarized the planners' conclusions in a telegram to Vice Commander Zhang Yixiang: The artillery forces should do everything possible to isolate the Jinmen islands, cutting off communications between Big Jinmen and Small Jinmen and between the Jinmen islands and Taiwan, while destroying airstrips at the Jinmen airport; the navy should strengthen attacks on the GMD's small and middle-size vessels; and the air force should guarantee the defense of the mainland's airspace by repulsing any air attack the GMD might launch against targets on the mainland, and in no circumstance should the air force engage in fighting outside the mainland's airspace.[107] It is apparent that Beijing's military strategy now concentrated on strangling the Jinmen islands rather than landing on them directly, with eventually seizing Jinmen, Mazu, and other GMD-controlled offshore islands as the operation's objective.

In an international crisis, the big picture sometimes can be changed by a small incident. On 24 and 27 August, the PLA's Fujian frontline radio station, without Beijing's authorization, announced that "our army's landing operation is imminent" and called on the GMD troops to surrender and "join the great cause of liberating Taiwan."[108] Policymakers in Washington, as well as the Western media, immediately took this provocative message as evidence that Beijing was about to launch an amphibious landing operation against Jinmen. The same day, for the first time since the crisis began, the U.S. State Department publicly announced that the GMD-controlled offshore islands such as Jinmen and Mazu were vital to the defense of Taiwan itself.[109]

Beijing's leaders were alarmed by Washington's statement since it revealed that, with any mistake, the shelling of Jinmen could turn from a CCP-GMD conflict into a direct Chinese-American military showdown. This prospect was unacceptable to Mao. No matter how provocative the chairman had been toward the United States in internal speeches and open propaganda, what he really wanted was, to borrow a phrase from the political scientist Thomas Christensen, "a conflict short of war." [110] After learning of the contents of the Fujian radio station's broadcast from *Cankao ziliao* (an internally circulated journal by the Xinhua News Agency that published translations of Western news reports on a daily basis), Mao "lost [his] temper." He sternly criticized this "serious mistake," reemphasizing that no one should comment on issues related to the Taiwan Strait crisis without Beijing's approval.[111]

In the face of a greater American military threat in the Taiwan Strait, Mao needed to adjust Beijing's strategies. He wanted to continue the military pressure on GMD troops in Jinmen, but his attention increasingly turned to using other measures to contain the danger in direct American intervention. One was announcing the limits of the PRC's territorial water.

Right after the shelling of Jinmen began, Mao had instructed the Foreign Ministry and the General Staff to study how best to define the boundaries of China's territorial water. At the end of August, Mao decided that the time for a decision had come.[112] On 1 and 2 September, Mao chaired a two-day Politburo Standing Committee meeting, which was also attended by several international law experts from the Foreign Ministry, to discuss the issue. Although the experts believed that the limits should be set up at three nautical miles from the coastline, Mao and other top CCP leaders, for political and strategic considerations, decided that the limits should be established at twelve miles.[113]

On 4 September, Beijing formally established the PRC's territorial waters at twelve nautical miles and declared that no foreign military aircraft or naval vessels would be allowed to cross the boundary without Beijing's permission.[114] In Zhou Enlai's words, this declaration was made at this particular moment to "prevent American military vessels from coming close to the Jinmen islands, which were situated well within the twelve-mile zone of China's territorial water." [115] In the meantime, in order to observe Washington's responses, Mao ordered the PLA to stop shelling GMD targets for three days.[116]

The "Noose Strategy"

Beijing's leaders did not have to wait long for Washington's response. The same day that Beijing announced the extent of its territorial water, U.S. secretary of state John Foster Dulles, after meeting with President Eisenhower, issued a statement on the Taiwan Strait crisis. He emphasized that "[t]he

United States is bound by treaty to help defend Taiwan (Formosa) from armed attack" and that "we have recognized that the securing and protecting of Quemoy [Jinmen] and Matsu [Mazu] have increasingly become related to the defense of Taiwan." In the same statement, Dulles also indicated that Washington was willing to resume the ambassadorial talks with Beijing in order to reach an agreement on "mutual and reciprocal renunciation of force" in the Taiwan Strait.[117] Dulles's statement, along with Washington's subsequent announcement that the Seventh Fleet would begin escorting GMD supply vessels to Jinmen, brought the Taiwan Strait crisis to a crucial juncture. Now Beijing's leaders had to face the tough reality that if the shelling on Jinmen went out of control, a direct military confrontation with the United States could follow. Within this framework, Mao introduced his "noose strategy."

When Dulles's statement reached Beijing, Mao was chairing a Politburo Standing Committee meeting to discuss the new situation in the Taiwan Strait, focusing on analyzing Washington's intentions. Mao emphasized that it seemed to him that the Americans were afraid of fighting a war, and it was unlikely that they would engage in a major war for Jinmen. Zhou Enlai pointed out that the current world situation was different from that of the Korean War period, and none of the U.S. allies—such as Britain, Japan, and the Philippines—would support American military action in the Taiwan Strait. Therefore, claimed Zhou, the U.S. government would be unwilling to use military means to end the crisis. The meeting participants concluded that although the Americans certainly would help the GMD defend Taiwan, it was doubtful that they would help defend Jinmen and Mazu as well.[118]

Participants of the meeting believed that the shelling of Jinmen had already successfully probed Washington's intentions toward Taiwan and the offshore islands, as well as mobilized the people in the world. Regarding Beijing's future strategy, Mao pointed out that now was the time to turn Jinmen into a "noose" for Washington by not landing on Jinmen but putting more pressure on the Americans. When American ships entered China's newly established territorial water, the chairman asserted, they should first be warned to leave, and, then, if they refused to leave, "due measures should be taken." The chairman was also prepared to return to the ambassadorial talks in Warsaw, thus "employing the diplomatic means to coordinate the fighting on the Fujian front"; at the same time, he stressed, Beijing should further mobilize the people in the whole country through a big propaganda campaign centered on condemning America's "interference with China's internal affairs." [119]

On 5 and 8 September, Mao made two speeches at the Fifteenth Meeting of the Supreme State Council, in which he explained in particular what he meant by using a "noose strategy" to deal with the Americans. The chairman repeatedly stressed that international tension was more a "good thing" than a "bad thing" because it would help mobilize the people both in China and in the world, that Washington feared Beijing more than Beijing feared Washington, and that, in the final analysis, "the East Wind has overwhelmed the West Wind." Within this context, the chairman claimed that Jinmen and Taiwan, like many other places in the world where the United States had military bases, were "nooses" for the United States:

> At present, America has committed itself to an "all-round responsibility" policy along our coast. It seems to me that the Americans will only feel comfortable if they take complete responsibility for Jinmen and Mazu, or even for such small islands as Dadan, Erdan, and Dongding [small islands within the Jinmen archipelago]. America has fallen into our noose. Thereby, America's neck is hanging in China's iron noose. Although Taiwan is [for America] another noose, it is a bit farther from [the mainland]. America is now moving its head closer to us, since it wants to take responsibility for Jinmen and other islands. Someday we will kick America, and it cannot run away, because it is tied up by our noose.[120]

Despite Mao's provocative language, his "noose strategy" did not represent any significant escalation of Beijing's belligerence toward Washington. Behind Mao's radical rhetoric and metaphorical language lurked cunning and careful calculations. He understood that the American military presence in the Taiwan Strait made it impossible for Beijing to "liberate Taiwan" through military means and that it would be necessary to deal with the Americans at the negotiation table. But, to prevent the negotiations from jeopardizing the mobilization effect he hoped to achieve through the shelling of Jinmen, he figured that a dramatic propaganda campaign, with a provocative concept as its central symbol, had to be introduced. In other words, the primary designated audience of the "noose strategy" was not the Americans but China's ordinary people. Not surprising at all, when millions of Chinese were told that Jinmen and Mazu had become "nooses" for the Americans and were holding anti-American demonstrations and rallies throughout China, Mao was turning his attention to the diplomatic front and preparing to negotiate with the Americans.

"Dancing" with Moscow, Negotiating with Washington

On 6 September, Zhou Enlai issued a formal response to Dulles's statement of two days earlier. The Chinese premier sternly condemned Washington's "policy of aggression" in the Taiwan Strait and "continuous intervention in China's internal affairs." He reiterated that it was within China's sovereignty for Beijing to use military means to deal with the GMD's "sabotage and harassment activities." But Zhou also stated that Beijing would make a distinction between the "international dispute between China and the United States in the Taiwan Strait" and the "internal matter of the Chinese people's efforts to liberate Taiwan," and thus was willing to "sit down at the negotiation table with the Americans to discuss how to relax and eliminate the tension in the Taiwan Strait." [121]

The timing of Zhou's statement was probably related to a secret visit to Beijing by the Soviet foreign minister Andrei Gromyko. Since the beginning of the shelling on Jinmen, Beijing had kept Moscow in the dark about the plans for the operation. Dulles's 4 September statement and the prospect of a Sino-American clash in the Taiwan Strait alarmed the leaders in Moscow. On 5 September, Khrushchev personally telephoned Beijing's leaders, informing them that he intended to dispatch Gromyko to China. [122] The next day, Zhou Enlai met with N. G. Sudarikov, a counselor at the Soviet embassy in China. The Soviet diplomat informed Zhou that Khrushchev was planning to send a message to Eisenhower regarding the Taiwan Strait crisis, and the major goal of Gromyko's visit was to inform Beijing's leaders of the message and to "exchange opinions on this matter." Zhou, for the first time since the outbreak of the Taiwan Strait crisis, explained to the Soviets Beijing's aims in conducting the shelling. Zhou emphasized that by shelling Jinmen, Beijing meant to have the Americans "get stuck" in Taiwan, "just as they have 'gotten stuck' in the Middle East and Near East." The shelling, according to Zhou, would also cause "more acute contradictions" between Jiang Jieshi and Dulles, as well as "prove to the Americans that the People's Republic of China is strong and bold enough and is not afraid of America." The shelling's domestic aim, Zhou continued, was "to raise the combat spirit of our people and their readiness for war, to enhance their feeling of not being afraid of war and their hatred toward American imperialism and its aggressive, insolent foreign policy." [123] Zhou stated that the shelling of Jinmen and Mazu would not be followed by a landing operation on the GMD-controlled offshore islands, let alone on Taiwan. In particular, Zhou promised that Beijing would take full responsibility for its own behavior and would not "drag the Soviet Union into the water" if "big trouble" resulted from the shelling. [124]

Gromyko arrived in Beijing on the morning of 6 September and met with Zhou Enlai at 2 P.M. the same day. At the beginning of the meeting, Zhou gave Gromyko a copy of the statement he had issued that day, and the Soviet foreign minister presented to Zhou a draft letter Khrushchev was preparing to send to Eisenhower. With Gromyko's prodding, Zhou again explained Beijing's aims and plans regarding Taiwan, basically repeating what he had told Sudarikov the day before. Gromyko stated that "the CC CPSU is in full support of the stand and measures taken by the Chinese comrades." He also mentioned that Zhou's statement and Khrushchev's letter to Eisenhower represented "two important actions that are highly compatible and mutually supplementary on the diplomatic front." [125] At 6:30 P.M. Gromyko met with Mao. He again expressed Moscow's support for the "stand, policies, and measures" Beijing had taken during the Taiwan Strait crisis. In addition, he emphasized that Khrushchev's letter to Eisenhower would send a "serious warning" to the Americans, which should make the Americans calm down, "as if they had taken a cold bath." [126] Mao found that "ninety percent" of Khrushchev's message to Eisenhower was "correct" and only "a few points may need to be further discussed." [127] With Beijing's consent, Khrushchev sent the letter to Eisenhower on 7 September, warning Washington that an attack on China "is an attack on the Soviet Union" and that Moscow would "do everything" to defend both countries.[128]

Behind this open demonstration of solidarity between Beijing and Moscow, the Sino-Soviet schism that had emerged after Khrushchev's de-Stalinization widened. According to Soviet documentary records and Gromyko's recollections, how to deal with Washington's nuclear threat was an important topic the Soviet foreign minister discussed with both Zhou and Mao. Zhou told Gromyko: "Inflicting blows on the offshore islands, the PRC has taken into consideration the possibility of the outbreak in this region of a local war between the United States and the PRC, and it is now ready to take all the hard blows, including atomic bombs and the destruction of its cities." The Chinese premier advised the Soviet foreign minister that the Soviet Union should not take part in the Sino-American war "even if the Americans used tactical nuclear weapons." Only if Washington resorted to using "larger nuclear weapons" and risked broadening the war "should the Soviet Union respond with a nuclear counterstrike." [129] In his memoirs, Gromyko recorded a similar conversation with Mao. The Chinese chairman, according to Gromyko, stated that if the Americans were to invade the Chinese mainland or to use nuclear weapons, the Chinese forces would retreat, drawing American ground forces into China's interior. The chairman proposed that during the initial stage of the war, the Soviets should do nothing but watch. Only after the American forces had entered China's interior should Moscow use "all means at its disposal" (which Gromyko understood as Soviet nuclear weapons) to destroy them.[130]

Although China's official account of the conversation angrily rebutted Gromyko's story after it was first published in 1988, claiming it to be a "serious distortion of the historical truth,"[131] I believe that both Mao and Zhou had made these statements concerning the danger of a nuclear war since both remarks were consistent with Mao's own philosophy and view on this issue. Since the mid-1950s, Mao had repeatedly expressed his unique views on the destructive effects of nuclear weapons, claiming that "even if the American atom bombs were so powerful that, when all dropped on China, they would make a hole right through the earth, or even blow it up, that would hardly mean anything to the universe as a whole, although it might be a major event for the solar system."[132] For Mao, the discussion concerned not a strategic matter but rather a philosophical issue. With a profound belief that "history is on our side," Mao, especially in the 1950s and 1960s, often adopted a very special definition of space and time in discussions of important policy and strategic issues, referring to the universe (or "all under the heaven"—*Tianxia* in Chinese) and "ten thousand years" as the basic scale in measuring the grand mission of his revolution. Within this context, Mao would often describe nuclear weapons as nothing but a "paper tiger." Mao's unconventional attitude toward nuclear weapons had already scared many of his Communist comrades in other parts of the world (especially at the summit of Communist leaders in Moscow in November 1957); this time, he alarmed his comrades from Moscow.[133]

Despite Mao's belligerent rhetoric, Beijing acted cautiously toward American participation in the GMD's supply convoys to Jinmen. During the early days of the shelling, Beijing issued a strict order to PLA units on the Fujian front that they should not take any action toward the Americans without Beijing's authorization.[134] On 7 September—when, for the first time since the outbreak of the crisis, American ships were involved in escorting GMD supply vessels to Jinmen—the PRC Foreign Ministry issued a "serious warning" to Washington, but the PLA's shore batteries maintained complete silence.[135] Actually, Beijing's leaders were carefully considering how to respond to this new development, taking into account all possible contingencies. They finally reached a decision close to midnight and sent the following order to the Fujian Frontal Headquarters:

(1) Our artillery units on the Xiamen front should conduct another punitive barrage on important GMD military targets at Jinmen. The strike should be both accurate and fierce. The scale of the barrage should be larger than that of 23 August with a plan to fire about 300,000 rounds.

(2) Concerning American military ships' action of escorting Jiang's vessels

and invading our territorial water, the spokesman of our Foreign Ministry has already issued a warning. If the American ships come again, we will issue another warning. After these two warnings, if the American ships continue to invade our territorial water to escort Jiang's ships, we will concentrate the strength of our artillery force and navy to bombard Jiang's vessels stationed in the Liaolowan beach [of the Big Jinmen]. However, no strike should be aimed at American ships.[136]

The order puzzled the PLA's front commanders since they could not figure out how their units, in a long-distance artillery bombardment of the mixed American-GMD convoy, might manage to hit only GMD vessels. Ye Fei, who had returned from Beidaihe to resume the command post in Fujian late in August, personally called Mao seeking clarification. When he asked if he should order the firing in the event that American and GMD ships were mixed together, Mao said, "Yes." He then asked if he could strike both American and GMD ships. Mao replied: "No, only strike the GMD but not the Americans." He also asked if he could retaliate if the Americans opened fire first. Again, Mao said, "No." The chairman also instructed Ye to report the position, composition, and direction of the mixed GMD-American convoy at least once every hour and not to open fire until he received the final order from Beijing.[137] When another joint GMD-American convoy approached Jinmen the next day, Ye strictly followed Mao's orders. When he ordered firing, to his surprise, he found he only needed to deal with the GMD because all American ships were staying at least three miles offshore to avoid exchanges with the PLA's shore batteries.[138]

Mao's insistence that the PLA avoid hitting American ships reflected not only his caution in dealing with Washington in a military situation but also the emergence of a new focus in Beijing's management of the Taiwan crisis: while the seizure of Jinmen and other offshore islands remained one of Mao's key goals, his main attention had moved from the military conflict in Jinmen to the Sino-American ambassadorial talks in Warsaw, which, after being suspended for more than nine months, would soon resume.

The Sino-American ambassadorial talks first opened in Geneva in August 1955, serving as the only channel of communication between Beijing and Washington. In December 1957, the meetings were suspended when the American negotiator, Ambassador U. Alexis Johnson, was reassigned to Thailand and the Chinese refused to accept his replacement, Edwin Martin, because he was not an ambassador.[139] On 30 June, the Chinese Foreign Ministry issued a statement, demanding that Washington appoint an ambassadorial negotiator in fifteen days; if Washington did not comply, Beijing would regard the talks as being terminated by the American side.[140] Washington, though missing the fifteen-day deadline to name a new negotiator, announced on 28 July that the U.S. ambassador to Poland, Jacob Beam, had been appointed as the American representative to the talks, which would be moved to Warsaw.

As soon as the shelling on Jinmen began, Mao started formulating Beijing's strategy for the ambassadorial talks. Late in August, he recalled Ambassador Wang Bingnan, the chief Chinese negotiator at the bilateral talks. Two days after Wang arrived in Beijing, he attended a politburo meeting to brief top party leaders on the progress of the ambassadorial talks from 1955 to 1957. At this meeting and then during a private talk with Wang, Mao demonstrated a keen interest in knowing if Washington could be persuaded to force the GMD to withdraw from the offshore islands through the ambassadorial talks.[141] Before Wang left for Warsaw on 10 September, he received a five-point draft proposal and a signed letter from Zhou Enlai. In addition to reiterating that Taiwan and the offshore islands were Chinese territory and that the Taiwan issue belonged to China's internal affairs, the proposal included two new points. First, in order to "remove the immediate threat" Jinmen and Mazu posed to Xiamen and Fuzhou, Beijing proposed that if "GMD troops are willing to withdraw from the islands on their own initiative, the PRC government will not pursue them." Second, after the PRC government had recovered Jinmen, Mazu, and other offshore islands, it would "strive to liberate Taiwan and Penghu by peaceful means and [would], in a certain period, avoid using force to liberate Taiwan and Penghu."[142] These two points represented a major concession on Beijing's part because, if Washington accepted them, Beijing would be obliged to give up use of force as a means to liberate Taiwan. Zhou Enlai's letter provided detailed instructions on the tactics Wang should follow:

> Here are the main points of your presentation (draft). At the first meeting, if the Americans are eager to present their opinions, you may let them speak first. . . . If the Americans present their proposal first and if there are some parts in it that are worth our consideration, you should not hurriedly present our proposal but should comment on the ridiculous parts in the American proposal and wait to give a comprehensive response to the other parts at the next meeting. If the American side does not present anything concrete and is eager to learn about our opinion, you may use the points drafted here and present the proposal we have prepared.[143]

The new Chinese stand demonstrated that Mao was now willing to bring the Taiwan Strait crisis to an end through negotiating with the Americans. Mao triggered the crisis himself in the first place, so he could have ended it easily—for example, just by ordering the PLA to lift the siege of Jinmen—if he had wanted to do so. But Mao needed the crisis to end in a way that would allow him to claim a great victory. This was particularly important for Mao since the shelling of Jinmen was central to promoting his Great Leap Forward. He also knew that profound differences in opinion existed between Taipei and Washington, so he believed it possible to "persuade" the Americans to force the GMD to withdraw from Jinmen and other offshore islands.[144]

At the same time that Beijing was preparing to resume the ambassadorial talks with Washington, Zhou Enlai began to explore the possibility of reestablishing contacts with Jiang and the GMD in Taiwan. On 8 and 10 September, the premier twice met with Cao Juren, who had served as a messenger between Beijing and Taipei since 1956. Zhou asked Cao to tell the GMD leaders that they had three options in Jinmen: first, they could "live and die together with the islands"; second, they could "withdraw the whole force back to Taiwan"; and third, they could "be forced by the Americans to withdraw." Zhou commented that the second option should be the best for Jiang, since the GMD troops on the offshore islands accounted for almost one-third of Jiang's whole military strength, and "by withdrawing them back to Taiwan, Jiang will have more capital to bargain with the Americans." Zhou also asked Cao to inquire of the GMD leaders: "If the Americans can openly negotiate with us, why cannot the CCP and the GMD also begin another round of open negotiations?"[145]

Wang Bingnan returned to Warsaw on 11 September, and, in two days, he and Beam had agreed that the ambassadorial talks would reopen on 15 September at the Swiss embassy. At that moment, however, Mao changed his mind again about how to proceed with the talks. By then the chairman had left Beijing for an inspection tour in the South. On 13 September he wrote a two-part letter to Zhou Enlai and Huang Kecheng from Wuchang. In the first part of the letter, the chairman ordered the PLA artillery units in Fujian, in addition to bombarding GMD ships "entering the Liaolowan harbor to unload supplies," to also begin "sporadic shelling (by firing 200 to 300 rounds a day)" on Jinmen's military targets, in order to make "the enemy panicky and restless day and night." In the second part of the letter, the chairman dictated a new negotiation strategy at Warsaw: "As far as the Warsaw talks are concerned, in the next three to four days, or one week, [we] should not lay out all of our cards on the table at once but should first test [the attitudes of the Americans]." He also predicted that it was "unlikely that the other side would lay out all of their cards at once, and they will try to test us as well."[146]

Mao's letter reflected his calculations at both tactical and strategic levels. In a tactical sense, the chairman, himself a longtime player of all kinds of power games, fully understood that unless his representative was able to speak from a position of strength at the negotiation table, the Americans would not easily make concessions. Therefore, the shelling of Jinmen needed to be continued in ways new and disturbing to the enemy. In a strategic sense, the last thing Mao wanted to do was to create the impression that Beijing had significantly softened its stand on Taiwan. To do so, from Mao's perspective, would be extremely harmful to the revolutionary reputation Mao had persistently strived to create for the PRC abroad, and, especially, to the huge political mobilization effect Mao had managed to initiate through the shelling campaign at home.

Although Zhou Enlai informed Mao in a note dated 13 September that, after receiving Mao's letter, he had instructed Wang Bingnan to "go around with the Americans to force them to lay out all of their cards first," [147] Wang, for whatever reason, failed to act in accordance with Mao's new instructions. When the ambassadorial talks reopened on 15 September, Beam, the American negotiator, argued for an immediate cease-fire in the Taiwan Strait before any other issue could be discussed. Wang asked for a ten-minute recess and then presented Beijing's five-point proposal. Beam immediately countered that the Americans could not "entertain" the proposal because it "would mean surrender of territory" belonging to an American ally.[148] The next day, Dulles publicly announced that immediate cease-fire was the first step toward resolving the Taiwan Strait crisis.

Mao flew into a rage when he received the reports about Wang's performance. In the chairman's view, Wang exposed what was supposed to be Beijing's bottom line on the first day of the negotiations, thus making the Americans think that Beijing was vulnerable. The chairman commented: "Wang Bingnan is worse than a pig; even a pig knows to how turn around when it hits the wall, and Wang Bingnan does not know how to turn around after he hits the wall." [149] He intended to fire Wang immediately. Only after Zhou Enlai "took the responsibility" for Wang's mistakes and pointed out that firing Wang would cause more confusion did Mao decide to keep him in Warsaw.[150]

But this episode had already completely changed Mao's view of and, as a result, strategies toward the ambassadorial talks. Instead of regarding the talks as a chance to bring about acceptable solutions to the crisis in the Taiwan Strait, Mao now firmly believed that he had no other choice but to treat the talks as a forum to expose the "reactionary" and "aggressive" nature of America's imperialist policy in East Asia. Following Mao's instructions, Zhou called a series of meetings at the Foreign Ministry to consider new diplomatic alternatives. The participants concluded that Beijing "should adopt a policy line of positive offensive" toward the Americans at the forthcoming meetings.[151]

Chinese-American ambassadorial talks at Warsaw, 15 September 1958.
Xinhua News Agency.

"If the American side fails to respond to our proposal directly and continues to argue for an immediate cease-fire," reported Zhou in a letter to Mao on 17 September, "we should immediately present another proposal, demanding that the Americans withdraw all of their armed forces from Taiwan, Penghu, and the Taiwan Strait, stop all provocative military actions in China's territorial space and water, and cease interference in China's internal affairs, thus relaxing the tension existing in the Taiwan Strait."[152]

Mao probably was not totally satisfied with Zhou's response because the next day, after having met with several other top party leaders, the premier presented a more comprehensive plan "for struggling against the United States":

> In order to counter America's cease-fire request, we should expand our activities in all respects to demand that U.S. armed forces stop all provocations and withdraw from Taiwan and the Taiwan Strait. Concrete measures are as follows: (1) Prepare a statement by the foreign minister to rebut Dulles's UN speech. (2) After the issuance of the statement, mobilize newspapers, various parties, and people's organizations all over the country to echo it. (3) Convey our strategies to Soviet chargé d'affaires and Liu Xiao

[Chinese ambassador to the Soviet Union], letting them convey [our plans] to Khrushchev and Gromyko, so that the Soviet Union and other fraternal countries will cooperate with us.[153]

Zhou's new plans delighted Mao. The chairman immediately wrote to the premier, praising these plans as "very good indeed" since they "will allow us to gain the initiative." The chairman also instructed Zhou to "take due action immediately"; in particular, he asked Zhou to convey these plans both to Wang Bingnan in Warsaw and to Ye Fei in Fujian, "making sure that they understand that the keys to our new policy and new tactics are to hold the initiative, to keep the offensive, and to remain reasonable." The chairman commented at the end of the letter: "Sweeping down irresistibly from a commanding height, and advancing like a knife cutting through a piece of bamboo—this is what our diplomatic struggle needs to be." [154] With the implementation of Mao's instructions, the possibility of ending the crisis through the ambassadorial talks in Warsaw virtually disappeared.[155]

"Leaving Jinmen in Jiang's Hands"

In late September, when the crisis was entering its second month, the tension in the Taiwan Strait looked as bad as—if not worse than—it did at any point in the previous four weeks. On 22 September, when Wang and Beam met for the third time in Warsaw, the Chinese ambassador was primed for a counteroffensive. He called the proposal Beam presented on 18 September, which emphasized immediate cease-fire as the first step toward relaxing tension in the Taiwan Strait, "absurd and absolutely unacceptable." Abandoning his own offer from one week earlier, Wang presented a new three-point proposal, which established U.S. withdrawal of all its armed forces as the precondition to ease the tension in the Taiwan Strait area. The Swiss embassy was turned into a battlefield of sharp accusations and denunciations, with Wang and Beam rebutting every point the other side was making and charging the other side for causing the crisis in Taiwan and in East Asia.[156]

At the same time that Wang was "taking the offensive" in Warsaw, Zhou Enlai was making every effort to mobilize international support. On 18 September, Zhou met with S. F. Antonov, Soviet chargé d'affaires in Beijing, to brief him on recent developments in the Taiwan Strait crisis. Zhou told him that after the first meeting of the Sino-American ambassadorial talks in Warsaw, Beijing firmly believed that "the central issue is that the United States should withdraw all of its armed forces from Taiwan and the Taiwan Strait area, and that only after the withdrawal of U.S. armed forces will the tension in this area be eliminated." Zhou also told Antonov that if Washington continued to request an immediate cease-fire in the Taiwan Strait, Beijing would demand the withdrawal of all U.S. forces first. In the meantime, Beijing would "mobilize the entire Chinese media to demand that the U.S. armed forces withdraw from the Taiwan Strait area," and the PLA would "continue to concentrate on conducting punitive shelling of Jiang's troops on Jinmen and Mazu." Zhou asked Antonov to convey these points to the Soviet government as well as to the Soviet representative to the UN.[157] In the following days, Zhou met with Indian, Burmese, and Ceylonese ambassadors to China, as well as a governmental delegation from Cambodia, denouncing Washington's "cease-fire plot" at Warsaw and asking the representatives of these "friendly countries" to prevent Dulles from "playing with the same cease-fire plot" at the UN.[158] On 20 September, Chinese foreign minister Chen Yi issued a statement to rebut Dulles's speech of four days earlier, claiming that "the six hundred million Chinese people are determined to unite together to resist the U.S. aggressors and to maintain the sovereignty and territorial integrity of the great socialist motherland."[159]

Despite the highly provocative language used in open propaganda, Beijing's leaders did not want to escalate the military conflict in the Taiwan Strait. What Mao desired from these "offensives" was to win back the "initiative" in a diplomatic confrontation with the United States rather than to trigger a military showdown. When commanders at the Fujian Frontal Headquarters received the instruction from Beijing to "win back the initiative," they immediately worked out a new plan to escalate military operations aimed at Jinmen so as to "coordinate with the diplomatic struggle in Warsaw." According to the plan, in addition to continuing artillery shelling, the PLA's air force would begin bombing Jinmen to "increase pressure on GMD troops there," and, then, ground shelling and air bombardment would be coordinated to pursue "bigger and more comprehensive results."[160] When the plan was submitted to Beijing for approval, Zhou found it inappropriate. In a letter to Mao dated 22 September, the premier pointed out:

> Under the current situation, it is appropriate for the guidelines for operations in Jinmen to remain "shelling but not landing" and "cutting off [the enemy's supplies] but not letting [the enemy] die," so as to make the enemy panicky day and night without being able to take any rest. It is indeed not easy to coordinate a joint operation of the navy, air force, and ground artillery force, and there is the possibility that American ships and planes could be hit. It is even more inappropriate for our air force to bomb Jinmen, as

this will provide Jiang's air force with an excuse to bomb the mainland. At present, the U.S. is controlling Jiang's air force, not allowing it to bombard the mainland, and one main reason for this is that they are not certain how our air force will retaliate: by bombing Jinmen or Taiwan? Since the Americans are unable to predict the direction of our air force's operations, it is beneficial to us not to trigger Jiang's air force to bomb the mainland. If Jiang's air force bombs the mainland and we are only able to bomb Jinmen (but not Taiwan), we are showing our weaknesses.[161]

Mao approved Zhou's letter as soon as he read it. The chairman commented that the premier's opinions about operations in Jinmen were "all correct, as they will allow us to occupy an unbeatable position while at the same time completely holding the initiative."[162] In accordance with Mao's and Zhou's instructions, the PLA shore batteries in Fujian continued sporadic daily shelling of the Jinmen islands, striking the GMD's supply convoys, while the PLA's air force and navy occasionally attacked the GMD's transport planes and ships in the Jinmen area (but always avoided the Americans).[163] Consequently, the actual combat intensity in the Jinmen area had reduced significantly by the end of September.

Within this context, Beijing's leaders again considered how to bring the crisis to an end. In a meeting with Soviet chargé d'affaires Antonov on 27 September, Zhou discussed three future scenarios for the Taiwan Strait crisis. The first scenario was that "when the conditions become mature, the United States will be ready to make concessions. . . . If the United States guarantees the withdrawal of Jiang's troops [from Jinmen], we may agree to hold fighting for a period to allow Jiang's troops to withdraw." The second and third scenarios were that "the current confrontation will continue as both sides will stick to their positions," or that "the United States will voluntarily put its neck into the noose" by directly involving itself in the military conflict. In Zhou's opinion, the second scenario was the most possible.[164]

However, at the end of September, when signs indicated that Washington might be willing to end the crisis along the lines of the first scenario, Beijing's whole approach toward seizing Jinmen, a key goal of the shelling campaign, changed completely. On 30 September, Dulles made extensive comments on the Taiwan Strait crisis at a news conference. In response to a question concerning whether it would be feasible for the GMD troops to withdraw from the offshore islands, the secretary of state asserted, "[I]t all depends upon the circumstances under which they would be withdrawn. . . . If there were a cease-fire in the area which seemed to be reasonably dependable, I think it would be foolish to keep these large forces on these islands."[165]

Dulles's message immediately caught Beijing's attention. By that time, Mao had returned to Beijing from his inspection tour of southern China. On 3 and 4 October, the CCP Politburo Standing Committee met to discuss Beijing's overall strategy toward the Taiwan Strait crisis. Zhou reported to his colleagues that, in his opinion, Dulles intended to "use the current opportunity to create two Chinas." What Dulles wanted, according to the premier, was for Beijing to commit to a nonmilitary policy in dealing with the Taiwan issue, and Washington in turn would pressure Taiwan to give up the plan to "recover the mainland." In Zhou's view, Dulles's unspoken goal was to "trade Jinmen and Mazu for Taiwan and Penghu," thus formalizing the separation between Taiwan and the Chinese mainland. Zhou particularly emphasized that this was exactly what the Americans had tried to do at the ambassadorial talks in Warsaw, and that "the American negotiators spoke even more undisguisedly at the talks than had been suggested in Dulles's speech." Reacting to Zhou's introduction, Liu Shaoqi and Deng Xiaoping pointed out that both China and the United States had been probing the other's real intentions, and, by now, both sides had gained some idea about the other side's bottom line. They also argued that both China and the United States had acted cautiously during the crisis to avoid a direct military confrontation. Now, in their views, "the shelling had mobilized the Chinese masses, had mobilized world opinion, had played the role of supporting the Arab people, and had created dramatic pressure on American rulers." In short, they believed that it was time to bring the crisis to an end.[166]

At this point, Mao asked a crucial question: "How about leaving Jinmen and Mazu in Jiang Jieshi's hands?" The chairman, who obviously had carefully considered this issue, presented his reasoning: "The advantage [of doing so] is that since both islands are very close to the mainland, we may maintain contacts with the GMD through them. Whenever necessary, we may shell them. Whenever we are in need of tension, we may tighten this noose, and whenever we want to relax the tension, we may loosen the noose. We will let them hang there, neither dead nor alive, using them as a means to deal with the Americans." The chairman also argued that even if Jiang were allowed to continue to occupy Jinmen and Mazu, he could not "stop the socialist construction in the mainland"; nor would his troops at Jinmen and Mazu alone be capable of constituting a serious security threat to Fujian province. In comparison, argued the chairman, if Jiang lost Jinmen and Mazu or if his troops were forced by the Americans to withdraw from them, "we will lose a card to deal with the Americans and Jiang, thus leading to the emergence of a de facto 'two Chinas' situation."

At Mao's urging, the politburo agreed to adopt this new policy of "leaving Jinmen in Jiang's hand," so that the offshore islands might be "turned into a burden for the Americans." Mao then pointed out that, to justify the new policy domestically and internationally, it was necessary to begin a huge propaganda campaign. Indeed, how to present Beijing's new strategy to end the crisis became an important issue for Mao. The chairman knew very well that if he failed to present his case powerfully, the very reasons for the entire shelling operation, as well as Beijing's initiation and management of the crisis, would be called into serious question. Mao proposed that Beijing's propaganda emphasize that the Taiwan issue was a matter of China's internal affairs, that the shelling of Jinmen was the continuation of the Chinese civil war and thus should not be meddled in by any foreign power or international organization, that the presence of American troops in Taiwan was a violation of China's sovereignty and territorial integrity, and that after the Americans left, the Taiwan issue could be solved through direct negotiation between the CCP and the GMD. At the end of the meeting, Mao instructed the Chinese media, and *Renmin ribao* in particular, to "hold the fire" for a few days in order to "prepare and replenish munitions," and then "ten thousand cannons will boom with one order." [167]

As soon as Mao had made up his mind, he moved to change his will into action. What he put together was an extraordinary drama, one that would combine in one act unexpected military maneuver, well-calculated diplomatic feints, and, most important of all, an unconventional propaganda effort. On 5 October, Mao wrote a letter to Peng Dehuai and Huang Kecheng in which he laid out his operational plans: "Our batteries should not fire a single shell on 6 and 7 October, even if there are American airplanes and ships escorting [the GMD]. If the enemy bombards us, our forces should not return fire. [We should] cease our activities, lie low, and wait and watch for two days. Then, we will know what to do." The chairman stressed to Peng and Huang not to "issue any public statement during these two days because we need to wait and see clearly how the situation will develop." [168]

At the same time that Mao was shuffling military deployments, Zhou was busy with diplomatic activities. He first met with Indonesia's ambassador to China. The premier told him that he had learned that eight countries, with Indonesia as one of the main initiators, had been preparing to issue a statement concerning the Taiwan Strait crisis. Zhou advised the Indonesian ambassador that the statement should acknowledge that Taiwan was part of Chinese territory, that the crisis was the result of America's policy of aggression in the Taiwan area, and that Washington had no right to intervene in Jinmen and Mazu.[169] Zhou then met with the Soviet chargé d'affaires. After informing Antonov that Beijing had decided that "it is better to leave Jinmen and Mazu in Jiang's hands," the premier gave a detailed explanation about why Beijing had reached this decision. In particular, said the premier, the new policy would turn Jinmen and Mazu into a huge burden for Washington; "whenever we wanted tension, we will strike at them, and whenever we want relaxation, we will loosen [the noose] there." Thus the new policy would play the role of "educating the people of the world, and primarily the Chinese people," while deepening the already profound contradictions between Taipei and Washington. The premier asked that Moscow give the policy its full support.[170]

Early on the morning of 6 October, Beijing stopped all regular radio broadcasts to deliver a "Message to the Compatriots in Taiwan" in the name of Defense Minister Peng Dehuai. Written in powerful and shrewd yet elegant language, this document actually was Mao's creation. The chairman originally did not plan to issue a statement because he wanted to observe how Taipei and Washington would respond to the PLA's holding of fire on Jinmen. But he quickly changed his mind and decided to draft a message himself.[171] "We are all Chinese and reconciliation is the best course for us to take," the message asserted. The shelling of Jinmen was designed to punish the "rampant actions" of Taiwan's leaders and to highlight that "Taiwan was part of Chinese territory, not part of American territory" and that "there exists only one China, not two Chinas." "The U.S. imperialists are the common enemy for all of us," the message continued, and, beginning on 6 October, on the condition of "no American escorts," the PLA would suspend shelling on Jinmen for seven days so as to allow supplies to be "freely delivered" to the islands.[172]

After seven days, on 13 October, Peng Dehuai announced that the shelling would be put on hold for another two weeks.[173] Yet Mao still wanted to show that Beijing was in full control of the situation. Therefore, taking Dulles's forthcoming official visit to Taiwan as an excuse, Mao ordered the PLA's shore batteries to conduct a one-hour barrage of Jinmen on 20 October. Mao instructed that the shelling should be announced in both Chinese and English in order to achieve the biggest propaganda effect.[174] On 25 October, Peng Dehuai issued "Another Message to the Compatriots in Taiwan" (again drafted by Mao), announcing that, from that day on, the PLA would shell the Jinmen islands only on odd days, leaving even days for GMD troops to receive supplies and take rests.[175] After more than two months, the PLA stopped regular and intensive shelling on Jinmen, and the Taiwan Strait crisis of 1958 finally came to an end.

Conclusion

Given the fact that the use of nuclear weapons had been widely considered and discussed during the course of the Taiwan Strait crisis of 1958, the event must be regarded as one of the most dangerous international crises in Cold War history. Yet, from a conventional "threat reaction" perspective— even by taking into account the usually extraordinary sense of insecurity prevailing during the Cold War era—this crisis should not have occurred in the first place. Despite frequent military clashes between Taiwan and the mainland since 1949, neither the GMD nor the United States presented a serious and immediate threat to the PRC in 1958. Indeed, since the first Taiwan Strait crisis in 1954–55, the tension in the strait had been declining continuously, with Taipei dramatically reducing its hostile military activities aimed at the mainland (partly because it was bound by the 1954 U.S.-Taiwan treaty of mutual defense) and with Beijing offering peace overtures to the GMD. When the crisis erupted in the summer of 1958, Mao and his comrades saw little challenge from the United States and its allies (including the GMD regime in Taiwan) to the PRC's physical safety; and they did not believe that the United States was either willing or ready to involve itself in a major military confrontation with the PRC in East Asia.[176] Thus, narrowly defined "security concerns," which emphasize only "hard" and physical threats, cannot be the main reason that Beijing initiated the crisis.

As indicated in this study, Mao decided to bring China into the crisis primarily for the purpose of creating an extraordinary environment in which the full potential of the Great Leap Forward—a crucial episode in the development of Mao's grand enterprise of continuous revolution—would be thoroughly realized. No other world leader had ever used such straightforward and enthusiastic language as did Mao in 1958 to discuss the huge advantage involved in using international tension to initiate domestic mobilization. Mao certainly was obsessed by a tremendous sense of insecurity, but his fear in no way resembled any of the conventional "threat perceptions" that prevailed during the Cold War period; first and foremost, Mao's obsession was the product of his unique "postrevolution anxiety." What worried the chairman most was that if he failed to find new and effective means to enhance the inner dynamics of his continuous revolution, the revolution would lose its momentum and, as a result, would eventually wither. For Mao, this was a threat of a fatal nature, and he was determined to do anything possible to prevent it from happening. In 1958, in the context of the emerging Great Leap, Mao's determination was easily transformed into his decision to initiate a crisis in the Taiwan Strait by ordering the PLA to shell the Jinmen islands. In a sense, the Great Leap was for Mao a great drama, one that was designed to mobilize and enhance the revolutionary enthusiasm of China's ordinary people. The shelling and the crisis played a role similar to the drumbeats in a Beijing opera—without them the drama would completely lose its rhythm, dramaticism, and theatricality, and thus would lose the very elements for which it is performed in the first place.

The special way in which Mao used international tension to promote domestic mobilization reflected the chairman's reading of a key factor shaping popular Chinese perceptions of China's relations with the outside world, that is, the Chinese people's profound victim mentality. Throughout modern times, the Chinese consistently believed that the political, economic, and military aggression by foreign imperialist countries had humiliated China and the Chinese people. As a result, a victim mentality—one that had been reinforced by China's age-old Central Kingdom concept—emerged to dominate the Chinese view of China's position in the world. Consequently, almost every time that China encountered an international crisis (no matter how the crisis began), the deep-rooted Chinese victim mentality would readily provide the Chinese leaders with a theme to encourage nationwide mobilization—provided that the leaders were able to present the Chinese as a victimized party or as endeavoring to resist China being continuously victimized in the international community. In the 1958 crisis, Mao consistently justified his shelling decision by emphasizing that Jinmen and Mazu, together with Taiwan and Penghu, were Chinese territories that had been "lost" during modern times as the result of imperialist aggression (first by the Japanese and then by the Americans) against a weak China. In doing so, Mao effectively appealed to the Chinese people's victim mentality, thus making the decision to shell Jinmen almost unchallengeable from a Chinese perspective.

Mao also used the crisis to challenge the postwar international order dominated by the United States and the Soviet Union. That Mao acted to put the United States on the defensive by constantly probing Washington's intentions and strategic bottom lines was evident in terms of both his rhetoric and diplomatic and military strategies. What should be emphasized is that underlying his behavior was also a profound desire to push the United States to recognize that his China was a qualified challenger to America's regional and global hegemony, thus making China a central actor in international politics. This is why, despite the fact that China is so far away from the Middle East and had so few practical interests there, Mao still found it necessary for Beijing to respond to the American-British intervention in Lebanon and Jordan in dramatic ways.

Equally revealing is Mao's attitude toward Moscow before and during the crisis. Although the Soviet Union was China's most important ally in the 1950s, Mao intentionally kept the Soviet leaders in the dark about the timing, course, and purpose of his actions against Taiwan. Particularly troublesome was Mao's consistent expression of contempt for the danger involved in the possibility that the crisis might lead to a nuclear catastrophe. The chairman certainly did not believe that the crisis would lead to such a dire situation—indeed, it was exactly because he did not believe so that he ordered the shelling. However, he enjoyed repeatedly bringing the topic—in his highly dialectic and philosophical manner—to the attention of the Soviet leaders. What Mao wanted was to challenge the moral courage and ideological values of the Soviet leaders, thus making them appear morally inferior. Consequently revolutionary China's centrality in the international Communist movement and in the world—since communism represented the future of the human race—would naturally be established and recognized.

For China 1958 turned out to be a year of great disaster. Following the failure of the Great Leap Forward, it is estimated that between 20 and 30 million Chinese people died in a three-year-long nationwide famine. The effects of the Taiwan Strait crisis were for China no less serious. In the wake of the crisis, the conflict between China and the United States intensified, the distrust between Beijing and Moscow deepened continuously, and the hostility between the mainland and Taiwan, especially in a psychological sense, increased dramatically. However, from Mao's perspective, his initiation and management of the crisis remained a successful case of promoting domestic mobilization by provoking international tension. The experience set a decisive precedent in Mao's handling of China's domestic and external policies in the 1960s, especially when he was leading China toward another crucial episode in his continuous revolution—the Great Proletarian Cultural Revolution. That, as is well known today, was a path toward another great disaster.

CHAPTER 8
CHINA'S INVOLVEMENT
IN THE VIETNAM WAR,
1964–1969

The Vietnam War was an international conflict. Not only was the United States engaged in large-scale military operations in a land far away from its own, but the two major Communist powers, China and the Soviet Union, were also deeply involved. Scholars have long assumed that Beijing played an important role in supporting Hanoi's efforts to fight the United States. Because of the lack of access to Chinese source materials, however, it has been difficult for scholars to illustrate and define the motives, decision-making processes, magnitude, and consequences of China's involvement in the Vietnam War.

This chapter, as the continuation of the examination in Chapter 5 of China's connections with the First Indochina War, aims to shed some new light on China's involvement in the Vietnam War. It covers the five crucial years from 1964 to 1969, with emphasis on an analysis of the failure of an alliance that was once claimed to be "between brotherly comrades."

Background: Chinese–North Vietnamese Relations, 1954–1962

The 1954 Geneva agreement on Indochina concluded the First Indochina War but failed to end military conflicts in Southeast Asia. When it became clear that a peaceful reunification through the plebiscite scheduled for 1956 would be indefinitely blocked by Washington and the Ngo Dinh Diem government in Saigon, the Vietnamese Communist leadership decided in 1959–60 to resume "armed resistance" in the South.[1] Policymakers in Washington, perceiving that the battles in South Vietnam and other parts of Southeast Asia (especially in Laos) represented a crucial contest against further Communist expansion, continuously increased America's military involvement there.[2] Consequently, the Second Indochina War intensified.

Beijing was a main participant, as well as a beneficiary, of the Geneva agreement of 1954. China's policy toward the settlement of the First Indochina War reflected its strategic considerations at that time, which included a desire to focus on domestic problems after the end of the Korean War, the need to take precautions against possible American military intervention in the Indochina area, thus preventing another direct Sino-American confrontation, and the need to forge a new international image to correspond with its new claims of peaceful coexistence.[3]

Because of these considerations, the Beijing leadership neither hindered nor encouraged Hanoi's efforts to "liberate" the South by military means until 1962. After the Geneva agreement was signed, the leaders in Beijing seemed more willing than their comrades in Hanoi to accept that Vietnam would be indefinitely divided. In several exchanges between top Beijing and Hanoi leaders in 1955–56, the Chinese advised that the most urgent task facing the Vietnamese Communists was how to consolidate the revolutionary achievements in the North.[4] In December 1955, Beijing's Defense and Foreign Ministries decided to recall the Chinese Military Advisory Group, which had been in Vietnam since July 1950. Peng Dehuai, China's defense minister, informed his Vietnamese counterpart, Vo Nguyen Giap, of this decision on 24 December 1955, and all members of the group returned to China by mid-March 1956.[5] In the summer of 1958 the VWP politburo formally asked Beijing's advice about the strategies for the "southern revolution." In a written response, the Beijing leadership emphasized that "the most fundamental, most important, and most urgent task" facing the Vietnamese was "how to promote socialist revolution and reconstruction in the North." "[R]evolutionary transformation in the South," according to Beijing, "was impossible at the current stage." Beijing therefore suggested that Hanoi adopt in the South a strategy of "not exposing our own forces for a long period, accumulating our own strength, establishing connections with the masses, and waiting for the right opportunities."[6] The nationwide famine following the failure of the Great Leap Forward forced the Beijing leadership to focus on domestic issues. During his meetings with Ho Chi Minh and Pham Van Dong, the DRV's prime minister, in Hanoi in May 1960, Zhou Enlai advised the Vietnamese that they adopt a flexible approach in the South by combining political and military struggles. He emphasized that even when military struggle seemed inevitable, political struggle was still necessary.[7] All of these developments indicate that Beijing's leaders were not enthusiastic about their Vietnamese comrades initiating military action in the South in 1959–60 and that the Vietnamese themselves made the decision "to resume the resistance."[8]

However, Beijing took no active steps to oppose a revolution in South Vietnam. The relationship between the PRC and the DRV was very close in the late 1950s and early 1960s, and the leaders from Beijing and Hanoi frequently visited each other and coordinated their domestic and foreign policies.[9] This close connection, as well as Beijing's revolutionary ideology, precluded the Chinese from hindering the Vietnamese cause of revolution and reunification. During this period, Beijing also implemented a propaganda campaign emphasizing that China was a natural ally of the oppressed peoples of the world in their struggles for national liberation. It would be inconceivable, in such a circumstance, for Beijing to impede the Vietnamese revolution. In addition, from a strategic point of view, since Sino-American relations experienced several crises during this period, especially in the Taiwan Strait in 1958, the Chinese leaders would not ignore the fact that intensifying revolutionary insurgence in South Vietnam might overextend America's commitment, thus improving China's position in its conflict with the United States in East Asia.[10]

Under these circumstances and in response to Hanoi's requests, China offered substantial military aid to Vietnam before 1963. According to one highly reliable Chinese source, during the 1956–63 period, China's military aid to Vietnam totaled 320 million yuan. China's arms shipments to Vietnam included 270,000 guns, over 10,000 pieces of artillery, 200 million bullets of different types, 2.02 million artillery shells, 15,000 wire transmitters, 5,000 radio transmitters, over 1,000 trucks, 15 planes, 28 naval vessels, and 1.18 million military uniforms.[11] Beijing's leaders used this material support rather than their direct military presence to show to their comrades in Hanoi their solidarity.

Beijing's Increasing Support to Hanoi, 1963–1964

Beijing's policy toward Vietnam began to take a radical turn in late 1962 and early 1963. In the summer of 1962, a DRV delegation led by Ho Chi Minh and Nguyen Chi Thanh visited Beijing. The Vietnamese summarized the situation in South Vietnam, emphasizing the possibility that with the escalation of military conflicts in the South, the United States might use air and/or land forces to attack the North.[12] The Chinese leaders were very much alarmed by this assessment. In a meeting with the DRV defense minister, General Vo Nguyen Giap, on 5 October, Mao Zedong emphasized that "in the past several years, we did not think much about whether or not the imperialists might attack us, and now we must carefully think about it."[13] Accordingly, Beijing offered to equip an additional 230 Vietnamese battalions.[14]

Beijing made general security commitments to Hanoi throughout 1963. In March, a Chinese military delegation headed by Luo Ruiqing, PLA chief of staff, visited Hanoi. Luo told Vietnamese leaders that if the Americans were to attack North Vietnam, China would come to its defense. The two sides also discussed how they should coordinate their operations in the event that

America invaded North Vietnam.[15] In May, Liu Shaoqi visited Vietnam, and in his meetings with Ho Chi Minh and other DRV leaders, he promised that if the war expanded as the result of their efforts to liberate the South, they could "definitely count on China as the strategic rear."[16] In September, the leaders of four Communist parties (Zhou Enlai from China, Ho Chi Minh, Le Duan, and Nguyen Chi Thanh from Vietnam, Kaysone Phomvihane from Laos, and D. N. Aidit from Indonesia) held an meeting in Chonghua, China's Guangdong province. In a keynote speech, Zhou Enlai pointed out that Southeast Asia had been the focus of a confrontation between international revolutionary and reactionary forces. He encouraged Communist parties in this region to promote an anti-imperialist, antifeudal, and "anti–comprador capitalist" revolution by mobilizing the masses and conducting armed struggles in the countryside. He also emphasized that China would serve as the great rear of the "revolution in Southeast Asia" and would try its best to support the anti-imperialist struggles by the people in Southeast Asian countries.[17]

Beijing's leaders certainly were willing to turn these promises into actions. In October, Kaysone Phomvihane, head of the Laotian People's Revolutionary Party (the Communist Party), secretly visited Beijing. He requested China's support for the Communist forces in Laos for their military struggles and base-area buildup. Zhou Enlai agreed to the request. As the first step, a Chinese work team, headed by General Duan Suquan, entered Laos early the next year "to investigate the situation there, as well as to prepare conditions for large-scale Chinese assistance."[18] At the end of 1963, after the Johnson administration demonstrated its intention to expand American military involvement in Vietnam, military planners in Beijing suggested that the Vietnamese strengthen their defensive system in the Tonkin Delta area. Hanoi asked the Chinese to help complete the construction of new defense works there, to which the Chinese General Staff agreed.[19]

Beijing extended its security commitments to Hanoi in 1964. In June, Van Tien Dung, North Vietnam's chief of staff and the person in charge of military operations in the South, led a delegation to Beijing. Mao told the delegation that China and Vietnam should unite more closely in the struggle against the common enemy. Referring to the crucial question of how China would respond if the war expanded to North Vietnam, Mao told the Vietnamese: "If the United States risks taking the war to North Vietnam, Chinese troops should cross the border [to enter the war]. It is better for our troops to be [called] volunteers. We may claim that they are organized by the people, and that the [PRC] government has no control over them. You may also organize your own volunteers and dispatch them to the South, and you may claim that they have been organized by the people without the knowledge of President Ho." In analyzing the prospect of American intervention, the CCP chairman advised his Vietnamese comrades: "[T]he more you fear the Americans, the more they will bully you. . . . You should not fear, you should fight. . . . In my opinion, the less you fear [the Americans], the less they will dare to bully you." Liu Shaoqi, who was also present at the meeting, reiterated the chairman's message: "The less you fear them, the more they respect you. If China does not fear them, and if the Vietnamese people do not fear them, they will have to consider again and again before taking any action. . . . When they do something about Vietnam, they will have to think of China."[20]

One month later, in a conversation with Tran Tu Binh, Hanoi's ambassador to Beijing, Mao again used powerful language to promise to Hanoi that if the war expanded to North Vietnam, China would intervene: "We must be prepared. Both North Vietnam and China must be prepared. If they [the Americans] start bombing or landing operations [against North Vietnam], we will fight them. . . . If the United States attacks North Vietnam, that is not just your problem. They will have to remember that we Chinese also have legs. The Americans can dispatch their troops. Cannot we Chinese also dispatch our troops? From our country to your country, we take one step and we are already there."[21]

Believing that the war in Indochina was facing a crucial juncture, on 5–8 July 1964, Chinese, Vietnamese, and Laotian Communist leaders held a planning meeting in Hanoi to discuss how to evaluate the situation and to coordinate their strategies.[22] In assessing the possible development of the war in Indochina, the three delegations agreed that the United States would continue to expand the war in Vietnam by sending more land forces to the South and, possibly, using air forces to attack important targets in the North. Zhou Enlai promised that China would increase its military and economic aid to Vietnam, help train Vietnamese pilots, and, if the Americans were to attack the North, provide support "by all possible and necessary means." The Chinese premier emphasized that "if the United States takes one step, China will respond with one step; if the United States dispatches its troops [to attack the DRV], China will also dispatch its troops."[23] These words, together with Mao's promises to Van Tien Dung and Tran Tu Binh, indicate that Beijing's leaders were now more willing than before to commit China's resources to supporting their comrades in Indochina, and especially in North Vietnam, if the war expanded further.

There were profound domestic and international reasons behind Beijing's adoption of a more aggressive strategy toward the escalating conflicts in

Southeast Asia. First, Beijing's more enthusiastic attitude toward Hanoi has to be understood in the context of the rapid radicalization of China's political and social life in the 1960s. Since the early days of the PRC, Mao had never concealed his ambition to transform China into a land of universal equality and justice under the banner of socialism and communism. In the late 1950s, Mao's grand revolutionary plans led to the Great Leap Forward, which turned out to be a nationwide catastrophe. For the first time in Communist China's history, the myth of Mao's "eternal correctness" was called into question. Starting in 1960, with Mao's retreat to the "second line," the Beijing leadership adopted more moderate and flexible domestic policies designed for economic recovery and social stability (such as allowing the peasants to maintain small plots of land for their families). Mao, however, gave up neither his revolutionary plans nor his position as China's paramount leader. When China's economy began to recover in 1962, Mao called the whole party "never to forget class struggle" at the Central Committee's Tenth Plenary Session.[24] In early 1963, a "Socialist Education" movement began to sweep across China's cities and countryside, which would finally lead to the Great Proletarian Cultural Revolution.[25]

Mao, informed by his previous experience, fully realized that creating the impression that China was facing serious external threats would help strengthen the dynamics of revolutionary mobilization at home, as well as legitimize his authority and controlling position in China's political life.[26] On a series of occasions from late 1962 to 1964, Mao repeatedly emphasized that China was facing an international environment full of crises, arguing that international reactionary forces were preparing to wage a war against China and it was therefore necessary for China to prepare politically and militarily for this coming challenge.[27]

In the meantime, Mao used the party's international strategy in general and its Vietnam policy in particular to win the upper hand in a potential contest with other party leaders who, in his view, had demonstrated a "revisionist" tendency on both domestic and international issues. Wang Jiaxiang, head of the CCP's International Liaison Department, was the first target of his criticism. In the spring and early summer of 1962, Wang submitted to the party's top leadership a series of reports on international affairs in which he argued that China should not allow itself to be involved in another Korean-style confrontation with the United States in Vietnam.[28] Mao quickly characterized Wang's ideas as an attempt to conciliate imperialists, revisionists, and international reactionaries and to reduce support to those countries and peoples fighting against imperialists. He stressed that the policy of "three conciliations and one reduction" came at the time when some leading CCP members had been frightened by the international reactionaries and therefore were in-clined to adopt a "pro-revisionist" policy line at home. He emphasized that his policy, by contrast, was to fight against the imperialists, revisionists, and reactionaries in all countries and, at the same time, to increase support to anti-imperialist forces in other countries.[29] Mao would later use these accusations to challenge and overwhelm his other more prominent "revisionist" colleagues in the party's central leadership, especially Liu Shaoqi and Deng Xiaoping. It is not surprising, then, that with the reconsolidation of Mao's leadership role, there emerged a more radical Chinese policy toward Vietnam.

Beijing's new attitude toward the escalating Vietnam conflict was also closely related to the deteriorating relationship between China and the Soviet Union. The honeymoon between Beijing and Moscow in the 1950s ended quickly after the Twentieth Congress of the CPSU in 1956. The divergences were political, economic, ideological, and psychological. Mao strongly dis-agreed with Khrushchev's de-Stalinization, viewing it as evidence of "capital-ist restoration" in the Soviet Union. Khrushchev's decision to withdraw Soviet experts from China, to cut Soviet assistance, to take a pro–New Delhi attitude during the Chinese-Indian border conflict in 1962, and not to share nuclear se-crets with China further damaged the relationship.[30] In 1962 and 1963, the split between the two Communist giants was publicized, with Beijing and Mos-cow openly criticizing each other's lack of loyalty to Marxism-Leninism. As far as this rift's immediate impact on China's policy toward Vietnam is con-cerned, two points should be stressed. First, in order to guarantee that Hanoi would stand on Beijing's side, it became more important than ever for Bei-jing's leaders to give resolute backing to their Vietnamese comrades. Second, since Beijing was escalating its propaganda criticizing Moscow's failure to give sufficient support to revolutionary national liberation movements, Beijing's leaders must have realized that they would be seen as hypocritical if they them-selves failed to offer support. In the context of the rapidly deteriorating rela-tionship between China and the Soviet Union, Vietnam had become a litmus test for "true communism."

Beijing's new attitude toward Vietnam also grew out of its understanding of the central role China was to play in promoting revolutionary movements in Asia, Africa, and Latin America. Ever since the victory of the Chinese revo-lution in 1949, the CCP leadership had believed that China's experience had established a model for the struggles of other oppressed peoples, and that the significance of the Chinese revolution went far beyond China's boundaries.[31] But in the 1950s and early 1960s, Beijing's interpretation was still subordi-nate to the "two-camps" theory, which contended that the center of the world revolution remained in Moscow. With the emergence of Sino-Soviet split in the early 1960s, the Chinese changed their attitude, alleging that the center of the world revolution had moved from Moscow to Beijing. Applying China's experience of "encircling the cities by first liberating the countryside" to the entire world, Beijing viewed Asia, Africa, and Latin America as the "world's countryside." China, by virtue of its revolutionary past, was entitled to play a leading role in promoting revolutionary struggles in the "world cities."[32] Beijing's new policy toward Vietnam was certainly compatible with this line of thinking.

It is apparent that underlying Beijing's more radical policy toward Vietnam were the ambitious Maoist revolutionary programs of transforming China and the world. While the intensifying crisis situation in Vietnam in the early and mid-1960s posed an increasing threat to China's security interests, Mao's primary concern lay in the interplay between the changing situation in Vietnam and his grand plans of promoting China's continuous revolution. The vision of Beijing's Vietnam policy was never restricted to Vietnam itself. The policy seemed to have complicated aims: Mao and his comrades certainly hoped that the Vietnamese revolutionaries would eventually defeat the U.S. imperialists and their "lackeys," and it was thus necessary for Beijing to support their struggles, but it would be against Mao's interests if such support indeed led to a direct Chinese-American confrontation, which would thus sabotage his efforts to bring about the Cultural Revolution at home. American expansion of warfare in Vietnam would threaten China's security in general, but the war's expansion on a limited scale could provide Mao with much-needed stimulus to mobilize the Chinese population. Beijing's belligerent statements about war in Vietnam were certainly aimed at both Hanoi and Washington, but they were also aimed at the ordinary people in China.

After the Gulf of Tonkin Incident

Early in August 1964, Vietnamese torpedo boats purportedly twice attacked American naval vessels in the Gulf of Tonkin area. The Johnson administration immediately ordered retaliation with air bombardment of selected North Vietnamese targets.[33] As Chinese and Vietnamese leaders had been predicting for months, the war in Vietnam had reached a crucial turning point.

Beijing responded promptly to the incident. On 5 August, Zhou Enlai and Luo Ruiqing cabled Ho Chi Minh, Pham Van Dong, and Van Tien Dung, advising them to "investigate and clarify the situation, discuss and formulate proper strategies and policies, and be ready to take action." Without going into details, they proposed closer military collaboration between Beijing and Hanoi to meet the American threat.[34] The same day, as a precautionary measure, the Central Military Commission and the General Staff in Beijing ordered the military regions in Kunming and Guangzhou (the two regions adjacent to Vietnam) and the air force and naval units stationed in southern and southwestern China to enter a state of combat readiness, advising them to "pay close attention to the movement of American forces, and be ready to cope with any possible sudden attack."[35]

In order to coordinate Chinese and Vietnamese strategies, Le Duan, VWP first secretary, secretly visited Beijing in mid-August. On 13 August at Beidaihe, he had a two-hour meeting with Mao Zedong, at which the two leaders exchanged intelligence information on the Gulf of Tonkin incident. Le Duan confirmed to Mao that the incident of 2 August was the result of a decision made by the Vietnamese commander at the site, and Mao told Le Duan that, according to Beijing's intelligence sources, the incident of 4 August was "not an intentional attack by the Americans" but was caused by "mistaken judgment" as the result of wrong information. While discussing the prospect of the war's expansion into North Vietnam, Mao pointed out: "It seems that the Americans do not want to fight a war, you do not want to fight a war, and we do not necessarily want to fight a war. Since none of the three sides wants to fight a war, the war will not happen." When a member of Le Duan's delegation mentioned that "the enemy is now making outcries to attack North Vietnam," Mao responded: "If the United States attacks the North, they will have to remember that the Chinese also have legs, and legs are used for walking." But the Chinese chairman also advised the Vietnamese that, no matter how unlikely, in case the Americans did send "several hundred thousand" troops to invade North Vietnam, the Vietnamese should give up some land in the coastal area and should fight a protracted war against the aggressors in the interior. "As long as the green mountains are there," commented the chairman, "you need not worry about firewood supplies." Le Duan told Mao that "the support from China is indispensable, it is indeed related to the fate of our motherland, and the Soviet revisionists only want to use us as a bargaining chip."[36]

While Mao was meeting Le Duan at the scenic Beidaihe, the Chinese air force was busy moving a large number of air and antiaircraft units into the Chinese-Vietnamese border area. On 12 August, the air force's Seventh Army headquarters was moved from Guangdong to Nanning, so that it would be able to take charge of possible operations in Guangxi and in areas adjacent to the Tonkin Gulf.[37] Four air divisions and one antiaircraft artillery division were moved into areas adjacent to Vietnam and were ordered to maintain combat readiness. In the following months, two new airfields were constructed in

Guangxi to serve the needs of these units. Beijing also designated eight other air force divisions in nearby regions as second-line units.[38]

Allen Whiting, relying on American intelligence information, argues that Beijing's transfer of new air units to the border area and the construction of new airfields there were carefully designed to deter further American expansion of war in the South and bombardment in the North.[39] This interpretation certainly deserves credit. As quoted above, Mao told Le Duan on 13 August that it was unlikely that the Americans would expand the war to North Vietnam.[40] In the same conversation, the Chinese chairman also mentioned that Beijing had transferred several air divisions and antiaircraft artillery divisions to Yunnan and Guangxi provinces and planned to construct new airfields in the Chinese-Vietnamese border area. It is interesting to note that the chairman then emphasized that "we will not make this a secret but will make this open."[41] A logical deduction from Mao's words is that, as Whiting has argued, Beijing intended to use these actions to deter the Americans.

Beijing's leaders also used these actions to assure their comrades in Hanoi of their backing, to allow themselves the time to work out the specifics of China's strategy toward the Vietnam War in light of Beijing's domestic and international needs, and to turn the tensions caused by an external crisis into a new driving force for a profound domestic mobilization.

Not surprisingly, then, Mao immediately used the escalation of the Vietnam War in August 1964 to revolutionize further China's political and social life, bringing about a "Resist America and Assist Vietnam Movement" throughout China. On 5 August, the Chinese government announced that "America's aggression against the DRV was also aggression against China, and that China would never fail to come to the aid of the Vietnamese."[42] Following the CCP Central Committee's instructions, according to the statistics of the Xinhua News Agency, over 20 million Chinese took part in rallies and demonstrations all over China on 7–11 August, protesting against "the U.S. imperialist aggression against Vietnam," as well as showing "solidarity with the Vietnamese people."[43] Through many such rallies and other similar activities in the next two years, the concept of "resisting America and assisting Vietnam" would penetrate into every part of Chinese society, making it a dominant national theme that Mao would use to mobilize the Chinese population along his "revolutionary lines."[44]

Several of Mao's internal speeches further revealed his mind-set. In mid-August 1964, the CCP Central Secretariat met to discuss the international situation and China's responses. In his addresses on 17 and 20 August Mao emphasized that the imperialists were planning to start a new war of aggression against China, and it was therefore necessary for China to fundamentally re-structure its economic framework. Mao paid particular attention to the fact that, since most industry was then located in coastal areas, China was eco-nomically vulnerable to sudden attacks. To safeguard the industrial bases, Mao believed it necessary to move a large number of factories to the interior of the country and to establish the Third Front (*san xian*, that is, the industrial bases located in the interior). Meanwhile, in order to cope with the situation in Indochina, Mao called for rapid completion of three new railway lines—the Chengdu-Kunming line, the Sichuan-Guizhou line, and the Yunnan-Guizhou line, all of which would provide better connections between China's interior and the Chinese-Vietnamese border area. All of China's economic planning, Mao emphasized, should now be oriented toward China's national defense, to prepare for a coming war with the imperialists.[45]

The escalation of the Vietnam War in late 1964 thus triggered a profound transformation of the entire structure of China's national economy.[46] Follow-ing Mao's ideas, the CCP Central Committee discussed the need to establish a "Headquarters for National Economy and National Defense," with Mao Ze-dong and Liu Shaoqi as its co-commanders.[47] By early 1965, a large portion of the coastal industry had begun to move into the inner areas, and the em-phasis of China's economic development changed from agriculture and light industry to heavy industry, particularly in the sectors related to the military build-up.[48] A large portion of China's population (especially in coastal areas) were affected by these changes, which, as Mao had intended, created a broad-reaching and intense revolutionary popular mentality in Chinese society and politics.

Defining China's Aid to Vietnam, Late 1964–Early 1965

In a strategic sense, the security commitments Beijing had previously of-fered Hanoi had been given in general terms. Thus in late 1964 and early 1965, Beijing's leaders needed to define the specifics of China's support to Vietnam in light of both how Mao perceived the country's domestic and international needs and the changing situation in Vietnam.

At first, as indicated by the conversations between Mao and the visiting Vietnamese delegations, Beijing's leaders seemed to believe that the "reso-lute struggles on the part of the Vietnamese people" would effectively prevent Washington from dramatically escalating the war in Vietnam.[49] Therefore, the Johnson administration's decisions in February and March 1965 to launch a sustained bombing campaign against North Vietnam (Operation Rolling Thunder) and deploy a growing number of ground forces in South Vietnam came as an unpleasant surprise to Beijing's leaders. Mao and his comrades were forced to reconsider the implications of American actions in Vietnam and, accordingly, formulate Chinese strategies to deal with the worsening crisis. While doing so, Beijing's leaders were influenced by the lessons of the Korean War, as well as the assumption that the Americans would also learn from their experience in Korea.

In March and April 1965, top Beijing leaders held a series of discussions about the situation in Vietnam, putting special emphasis on whether Washington would further expand the war by bringing the ground war to North Vietnam and air/ground war to China. A speech made by Deng Xiaoping at a politburo meeting of 12 April, which was also attended by Liu Shaoqi and Zhou Enlai, revealed some of Beijing's basic considerations:

> It seems that the [American] bombardment will continue. The U.S. imperialists' first step was fighting a special war. According to the Vietnamese comrades, the [American] special war has reached a new stage. Our view is that the special war has failed and the war will be expanded. The American air bombardment has penetrated into the airspace only twelve kilometers south of Hanoi, and, if the bombardment continues, it is inevitable that even Hanoi, Hai Phong, and Thai Nguyen will become the targets. . . . [I]t is even possible for them, under the excuse of chasing after Vietnamese planes, to invade our airspace. . . . If this is allowed to continue, they will come to Yunnan and Guangxi. Then the war will expand to part of China, and then, to all of China.[50]

Deng Xiaoping also identified four possible ways the war could develop: "First, the war [could] be fought in South Vietnam; second, the war [could] be fought both in South and North Vietnam, and [could] be linked to the war in Laos; third, the war [could] be fought in our provinces neighboring Vietnam; or, fourth, the U.S. imperialists [could] fight a larger regional war with us, even including Korea."[51] In order to avert the worst-case scenario, Beijing's leaders decided to adopt three basic principles in formulating China's strategy. First, if the Americans went beyond the bombing of the North and used land forces to invade North Vietnam, China would have to send military forces. Second, China would give clear warnings to the Americans so that they would not feel free to expand military operations into the North, let alone to bring the war to China. Third, China would avoid a direct military face-off with the United States as long as possible; but it would not shrink from a confrontation.[52]

Guided by these principles, Beijing sent out a series of warning signals to Washington in spring 1965. On 25 March, the *Renmin ribao* (People's Daily) announced in an editorial that China was to offer "the heroic Vietnamese people any necessary material support, including the supply of weapons and all kinds of military materials" and that, if necessary, China was also ready "to send its personnel to fight together with the Vietnamese people to annihilate the American aggressors."[53] Four days later, Zhou Enlai made the same announcement at a mass rally in Tirana, the capital of Albania, where Zhou was making a formal visit.[54]

Beijing's most serious effort to warn Washington occurred on 2 April, when Zhou Enlai, visiting Karachi, Pakistan, asked President Mohammad Ayub Khan to convey several points to Washington: "(1) China would not take the initiative to provoke a war against the United States; (2) China means what it says, and China will honor whatever international obligations it has undertaken; and (3) China is prepared."[55] Since Ayub Khan's visit to Washington was later abruptly postponed by the Johnson administration,[56] Beijing tried other channels to make sure that the same message (but with a more clearly defined fourth point) would get to Washington. On 28 May, in a meeting with Indonesian first prime minister Subandrio, Zhou Enlai issued a four-point statement: "(1) China will not take the initiative to provoke a war against the United States; (2) China will honor what it has said; (3) China is prepared; and (4) If the United States bombs China, that means bringing the war to China. The war has no boundary. This means two things: First, you cannot say that only an air war on your part is allowed and the land war on my part is not allowed. Second, not only may you invade our territory, we may also fight a war abroad."[57] Three days later, Chinese foreign minister Chen Yi met with British chargé d'affaires Donald Charles Hopson, formally asking him to deliver the same four-point message to Washington: "(1) China will not provoke war with [the] United States; (2) What China says counts; (3) China is prepared; and (4) If [the] United States bombs China that would mean war and there would be no limits to the war." Chen Yi emphasized that Zhou Enlai had asked Ayub Khan to convey these messages to Washington but that since the Pakistani president's visit was canceled, "perhaps this message had not gotten through," so "he would be grateful if the British government would pass it on."[58]

It is apparent that Beijing's warning messages were carefully crafted. The explicit language of these messages left no doubt about what Beijing would do if Washington failed to listen to them. Particularly noteworthy is the addition of the fourth point in later messages, especially in the ones Chen Yi asked the British to convey to Washington, which Beijing's leaders believed certainly would not fail to reach top American policymakers. By making sure that Washington would under no circumstances misunderstand the meaning of these messages, Beijing's leaders hoped to prevent the war's expansion into North Vietnam and, in particular, into China.[59]

While sending out these warnings, Beijing's leaders were also preparing for a worst-case scenario. The same day, following the decision reached at the 12 April politburo meeting, the CCP Central Committee issued "Instructions for Strengthening the Preparations for Future Wars," a set of directives that ultimately was relayed to every part of Chinese society and became one of the most important guiding documents in China's political and social life for the rest of the 1960s. The document pointed out that the U.S. imperialists were escalating their military aggression in Vietnam and directly invading the DRV's airspace. This move represented a serious threat to China's safety. In light of the situation, the Central Committee emphasized, it was necessary for China to further its preparations for a war with the United States, and it therefore called on the party, the military, and the whole nation to be prepared both mentally and physically for the worst possibility. Supporting the Vietnamese people's struggle to resist the United States and save their country, the document concluded, was to become the top priority in China's political and social life.[60] This document served the dual purpose of mobilizing China's military and economic potential to deal with the possible worsening of the Vietnam War and of radicalizing China's polity and society by inspiring a revolutionary atmosphere at home.[61]

In the meantime, Beijing and Hanoi were discussing the specifics of their cooperation in the escalating war. In early April 1965, a Vietnamese delegation led by Le Duan and Vo Nguyen Giap secretly visited Beijing.[62] On 8 April, Liu Shaoqi, on behalf of the CCP Central Committee, met Duan and Giap. Duan, according to Chinese records, told his hosts at the beginning of the meeting that the Vietnamese "always believed that China was Vietnam's most reliable friend" and that "the aid from China to Vietnam was the most in quantity, as well as the best in quality." Liu thanked Duan and told him that "it was the consistent policy of the Chinese party that China would do its best to provide whatever was needed by the Vietnamese." Duan then stated that the Vietnamese hoped China would send volunteer pilots, volunteer troops, and other volunteers—such as engineering units for constructing railways, roads, and bridges—to North Vietnam. He emphasized that the dispatch of these forces would allow Hanoi to send its own troops to the South. Duan further expressed the hope that the support from China would achieve four main goals: restrict American bombardment to areas south of either the 20th or the 19th parallel; defend Hanoi and areas north of it from American air bombardment;

defend North Vietnam's main transportation lines; and raise the morale of the Vietnamese people. Following Mao's instructions, Liu agreed to most of Duan's requests. He told Duan that the CCP had made the decision that "it is our policy that we will do our best to support you. We will offer whatever you are in need of and we are in a position to offer." Liu also stressed that "if you do not invite us, we will not come; and if you invite one unit of our troops, we will send that unit to you. The initiative will be yours completely." [63]

In spite of these promises, there are clues that divergences existed between the two sides. First, although Duan asked for the dispatch of Chinese air force units (in the form of volunteer pilots) to Vietnam, the Chinese were reluctant to do this, at least at this stage.[64] Second, Duan invited the Chinese to play a role in defending Vietnam's transportation system and important targets in areas up to the 19th parallel, whereas the Chinese, as it turned out, would in most circumstances not let their antiaircraft troops go beyond the 21st parallel. Third, Duan requested China's assistance in constructing, maintaining, and defending both railways and roads in Vietnam, but, for whatever reason, the subsequent discussion between him and Liu involved only railways.

With the need to clarify further the scope and nature of China's support, Ho Chi Minh secretly visited China in May and June 1965. On 16 May, he met Mao Zedong in Changsha, the capital city of Mao's home province, Hunan. Ho expressed his gratitude for China's support and his satisfaction with the achievements of Le Duan's visit a month earlier. Then he clarified that the Vietnamese were determined "to take the main burden of the war by themselves." What the Vietnamese needed, Ho stated, was China's material and military support so that Hanoi could send its own people to fight in the South. Mao was ready to provide such assistance, and he promised Ho that China would offer "whatever support was needed by the Vietnamese." Ho then asked Mao to commit China's resources to building twelve new roads for Vietnam. Mao gave his consent immediately.[65]

To follow up on Ho's trip to China, Van Tien Dung visited Beijing in early June 1965. His meetings with Luo Ruiqing finalized the guiding principles and concrete details of China's support to Vietnam under different scenarios. If the war remained in its current status, that is, if the United States remained directly involved in military operations in the South while using only air force to bombard the North, the Vietnamese would fight the war by themselves and China would provide military and material support in ways that the Vietnamese had chosen. If the Americans used their naval and air forces to support a South Vietnamese invasion of the North, China would send its air and naval forces to support North Vietnam operations. If American land forces were directly involved in invading the North, China would use its land forces as strategic reserves for the Vietnamese and carry on operations whenever necessary. Dung and Luo also had detailed discussions about the actual form China's military involvement would take depending on the situation. If the Chinese air force was to enter the war, the first option would be to use Chinese volunteer pilots and Vietnamese planes in operations; the second option would be to station Chinese pilots and planes on Vietnamese airfields and enter operations there; and the third would be to adopt the "Andong model," [66] that is, when engaging in military operations, Chinese pilots and planes would take off from and return to bases in China. If Chinese land forces were to be used in operations in Vietnam, they would basically serve as a reserve force; but if necessary, Chinese troops would participate in fighting. Luo emphasized that the Chinese would enter operations in any of these forms according to the circumstances.[67]

Beginning in late May, in order to coordinate China's military and material support to Vietnam, Zhou Enlai chaired a series of meetings attended by governmental and military officials, who decided to establish two authorities in Beijing to take charge of making and implementing the Vietnam policy. The first body was a seven-person committee called the Leading Group on Vietnamese Affairs. Its initial members were Li Xiannian, a politburo member and vice premier in charge of economic and financial affairs; Bo Yibo, a politburo member and vice premier in charge of economic planning; Luo Ruiqing, chief of staff; Liu Xiao, deputy foreign minister; Yang Chengwu, deputy chief of staff; Li Qiang, minister of foreign trade; and Li Tianyou, another deputy chief of staff. Luo Ruiqing, until his purge in December 1965,[68] was the head of the group.[69] Its main tasks were to carry out the central leadership's grand strategy, to make decisions and suggestions on matters associated with Vietnam, and to examine and determine if any new support to Vietnam was necessary.

The second authority was called the Group in Charge of Supporting Vietnam under the Central Committee and the State Council. This group was composed of leading members from the Ministries of Foreign Affairs, Railway, Transport, Postal Service, Material Supply, and Foreign Trade; the Commissions of Economic Affairs, State Economic Planning, and Foreign Economic Affairs; and the PLA's General Political Department, General Logistics Department, General Staff, and different arms and branches. Yang Chengwu was appointed in charge of the group, with Li Tianyou his deputy. Its main tasks were to coordinate and implement the decisions made by the party and the State Council (through the Leading Group on Vietnamese Affairs) as they concerned support for Vietnam.[70]

The Chinese-Vietnamese cooperation during the Vietnam War demonstrated some notable features from the very beginning. First, unlike during the First Indochina War, in which Chinese military and political advisers were directly involved in the Viet Minh's decision making and Beijing was well aware of their every important move, the Vietnamese Communists did not let the Chinese interfere in decision making. If necessary, they would consult with or provide information to Beijing, but decision making was now completely in Hanoi's hands. Communist North Vietnam was a much more mature, independent, and self-confident international actor than the Viet Minh had been during the First Indochina War. Second, Beijing and Hanoi appeared to have reached a fundamental agreement in the spring and summer of 1965 that the Vietnamese would fight the war with their own forces; China's main role would be to guarantee logistical support and to defend the North, so that the Vietnamese could send as many of their own troops to the South as possible. Third, although top Chinese and Vietnamese leaders did consider the possibility of large-scale direct Chinese military involvement in Vietnam, the consensus seems to have been that unless the American land forces directly invaded the North, Chinese land forces would not be used in operations in Vietnam.

China's Aid to North Vietnam, 1965–1969

From 1965 to 1969, China's aid to Vietnam took three main forms: the dispatch of Chinese engineering troops for the construction and maintenance of defense works, airfields, roads, and railways in North Vietnam; the use of Chinese antiaircraft artillery troops for the defense of important strategic areas and targets in the northern part of North Vietnam; and the supply of large amounts of military equipment and other military and civilian materials.

The Dispatch of Chinese Engineering Troops
In his visit to China in April 1965, Le Duan made it clear that in order to strengthen Vietnam's war potential it was essential to improve and expand the railway system in the North and to keep the system working under the American air attack. He asked the Chinese for assistance both in constructing new railways and in maintaining and defending the railway system.[71] On 17 April 1965, when Le Duan's delegation was in Moscow, the North Vietnamese General Staff cabled the Chinese General Staff, requesting that Chinese engineering troops be sent to the offshore islands in the Tonkin Gulf area to take responsibility for constructing the defense system there.[72] The Chinese General Staff, following the order of the CMC, decided on the next day to establish the Chinese People's Volunteer Engineering Force (CPVEF), which was composed

of some of China's best engineering units[73] and would carry out the tasks of building and rebuilding railways, building defense works, and constructing airfields in Vietnam.[74] On 21 and 22 April, respectively, Luo Ruiqing and Yang Chengwu met with Vo Nguyen Giap, confirming that Chinese engineering troops would soon be sent to Vietnam.[75]

After a series of discussions, on 27 April 1965, the Chinese and Vietnamese governments signed an agreement that provided that China would help Vietnam construct new railways and supply Vietnam with transportation equipment. According to this and a series of supplementary agreements thereafter, China was to offer assistance on a total of 100 projects. Among the most important were rebuilding the Hanoi-Youyiguan Railway and Hanoi–Thai Nguyen Railway, which involved transforming the original meter-gauge rail to one of standard gauge, and adding dozens of new stations, bridges, and tunnels; building a new standard-gauge railway between Kep and Thai Nguyen to serve as a circuitous supplementary line for both the Hanoi–Thai Nguyen and Hanoi-Youyiguan lines; constructing a series of bridges, ferries, temporary railway lines, and small circuitous lines in the northern part of North Vietnam; and reinforcing eleven important railway bridges to make sure they could better withstand air attacks and natural flooding.[76]

During Ho Chi Minh's meeting with Mao Zedong in Changsha on 16 May 1965, Ho asked Mao to commit China's strength to the construction of twelve roads in North Vietnam, to which Mao agreed.[77] Following Mao's instructions, the PLA General Staff quickly worked out a preliminary plan to send around 100,000 Chinese engineering troops to Vietnam for road construction. On 25 May, Zhou Enlai chaired a meeting to discuss the plan. He told the participants that since the Americans were expanding the war in Vietnam, they would naturally increase their efforts to cut off the North's support to the revolutionary forces in the South. It was therefore necessary for Hanoi to send more of its own people to reinforce the transportation corridors in lower Laos. For this reason, it was also necessary for China to take over the primary responsibility of consolidating and expanding the road capacities in North Vietnam, and in the northern part in particular. Yang Chengwu then reported to the meeting that the PLA General Staff had two different plans for dispatching troops to Vietnam. The first one, Ho Chi Minh's suggestion, would involve the construction of all twelve roads at the same time, which would require more than 100,000 engineering troops. The second plan involved concentrating first on the construction of five to seven of the most needed roads, which would require an initial dispatch of around 80,000 troops. Yang recommended the second plan, which Zhou also favored. The meeting concluded with the decision that the two plans would be presented to the Vietnamese simultaneously, but the Chinese would make it clear that they favored the second.[78]

A Vietnamese governmental delegation for transportation affairs visited Beijing in late May and insisted on their original plan. The Chinese quickly yielded. On 30 May, the Chinese and Vietnamese delegations signed a formal agreement stipulating that China would send its engineering troops to build and rebuild twelve roads in North Vietnam and to link them to China's road system. During construction, China would also be responsible for defending its engineering units against American air attack.[79]

Following these agreements, the CMC and PLA General Staff issued a series of orders to mobilize Chinese troops in May and June 1965.[80] Beginning in early June 1965, seven divisions of CPVEF units entered Vietnam during different periods.

The first division of the CPVEF was composed of six regiments of China's best railway corps (another two would join after August 1968), one railway prospecting team, and around a dozen antiaircraft artillery battalions. At its peak, the total strength of the division reached 32,700. It began arriving in Vietnam on 23 June 1965, and most of its units stayed until late 1969. According to Chinese statistics, when the last unit left Vietnam in June 1970, the division had completed 117 kilometers of new railway lines, rebuilt 362 kilometers of old lines, built 39 new rail bridges and 14 tunnels, and established 20 new railway stations.[81]

The second division of the CPVEF consisted of three engineering regiments, one hydrology brigade, one maritime transportation brigade, one communication engineering brigade, one truck transportation regiment, and a few antiaircraft artillery units, with a total strength of over 12,000 men. It entered Vietnam on 6 June 1965 and was the first group of Chinese engineering troops to assume responsibilities there. Its main tasks were to construct permanent defense works and establish communication systems on fifteen offshore islands and eight coastal spots in the Tonkin Gulf area. The division was also called on to fight together with North Vietnamese troops in the event that the Americans invaded the North.[82]

The CPVEF's third division was mainly comprised of Chinese air force engineering troops. Its main task was to build in Yen Bay a large air base, which would allow the use of jet planes, and an underground plane shelter. The Vietnamese originally requested this project in January 1965, and in May, the advance team of the third division arrived in Yen Bay to make surveys. The main force of the division entered Vietnam in November 1965. The air base was completed in May 1969, and the underground plane shelter in October of the same year; then the division quickly left Vietnam.[83]

The fourth, fifth, and sixth divisions of the CPVEF were all comprised of road construction engineering troops under the command of the independent "Road Construction Headquarters under the CPVEF" and totaled over 80,000 soldiers. The five engineering regiments of the fourth division, who were from the Guangzhou Military Region, were given the task of rebuilding the main road linking Pingxiang and Jinxi, both in China's Guangxi province, to Cao Bang, Thai Nguyen, and Hanoi. The main task of the five regiments of the fifth division, who were from the Shenyang Military Region, was to construct a new road from Lao Cai, a town bordering China's Yunnan province, to Yen Bay, and to link it with the road to Hanoi. The six regiments of the sixth division were from the Kunming Military Region and the Railway Corps and were responsible for the construction of a new road from Wenshan in Yunnan to link the road constructed by the fifth division. They were also assigned to construct a new road along the Vietnamese-Chinese border so that all the main north- and southbound highways would be connected. All these divisions, which had their own antiaircraft artillery units, entered Vietnam in October–November 1965 and returned to China by October 1968.[84] The statistics offered by an official Chinese military source show that they built or rebuilt seven roads with a total length of 1,206 kilometers, 395 bridges with a total length of 6,854 meters, and 4,441 road culverts with a total length of 46,938 meters. In addition, a total of 30.5 million cubic meters of earth and stone were involved in completing these projects.[85]

The CPVEF's seventh division, which was slated to replace the second division and entered Vietnam in December 1966, was composed of three construction and engineering regiments and several antiaircraft artillery battalions and had over 16,000 soldiers. The division's main tasks were to construct permanent underground defense works in the Red River delta area and build underground plane shelters for Hanoi airport. The division completed these tasks and left Vietnam in November 1969.[86]

In addition to these engineering troops, in accordance with a July 1965 agreement between Beijing and Hanoi, China sent a communication engineering brigade to Vietnam in October of the same year. The brigade was mainly engaged in the repair and construction of the communication system in the Lai Chau–Son La–Dien Bien Phu area. Before the brigade returned to China in July 1966, according to Chinese sources, it had erected a total of 894 kilometers of telephone lines and constructed four carrier telephone stations.[87]

Beijing's dispatch of Chinese engineering troops to Vietnam occurred mainly between late 1965 and late 1968. These troops were assigned the tasks of constructing defense works, roads, and railways in the northern part of North Vietnam. Most of their projects were located in areas north of Hanoi, and none of them was south of the 20th parallel. The majority of the troops left Vietnam before the end of 1969, and by July 1970 all of them had returned to China.

The Use of Chinese Antiaircraft Artillery Troops

During Le Duan's visit to China in April 1965 and Ho Chi Minh's meeting with Mao Zedong on 16 May 1965, the Vietnamese requested that China send antiaircraft artillery troops to Vietnam. In Van Tien Dung's meetings with Luo Ruiqing in early June 1965, Dung specifically requested that China send two antiaircraft artillery divisions to defend Hanoi and the areas north of Hanoi in the event that the American air force struck there. Luo agreed.[88]

On 24 July 1965, the Vietnamese General Staff telegraphed the Chinese General Staff, formally requesting that China send "the two antiaircraft artillery divisions that have long completed their preparations for operations in Vietnam. The earlier the better. If possible, they may enter Vietnam on 1 August." The next day, the Chinese General Staff cabled the Vietnamese General Staff, saying that China would send two antiaircraft artillery divisions and one regiment to Vietnam immediately, and that these units would take the responsibility of defending the Bac Ninh–Lang Son section of the Hanoi-Youyiguan Railway and the Yen Bay–Lao Cai section of the Hanoi–Lao Cai Railway, two main railways linking China and North Vietnam. On 1 August 1965, the Sixty-first and Sixty-third Divisions of the Chinese antiaircraft artillery forces entered Vietnam from Yunnan and Guangxi respectively.[89]

The Sixty-first Division arrived in Yen Bay on 5 August. Four days later, it was put into action against American F-4 fighter-bombers for the first time. Using 37 mm and 85 mm antiaircraft guns, they shot down one F-4, which, according to Chinese records, was the first American plane to be downed by Chinese antiaircraft units. The troops of the Sixty-third Division entered the Kep area and engaged in their first battle with the Americans on 23 August. Reportedly, they shot down one American plane and damaged another.[90]

From early August 1965 to March 1969, a total of sixteen divisions (sixty-three regiments) of Chinese antiaircraft artillery units, with a total strength of over 150,000 men, engaged in operations in Vietnam. These units, which entered Vietnam in eight separate stages, were mainly from the artillery forces, the air force, the navy, and, in some cases, the Kunming and Guangzhou Military Regions. Following their experience during the Korean War, the Chinese military leadership adopted a rotation strategy for these troops—usually a unit would stay in Vietnam for around six months and then be replaced by another. These units were deployed to defend strategically important targets, such as critical railway bridges on the Hanoi-Youyiguan and Hanoi–Lao Cai lines, and to provide cover for the Chinese engineering troops. There is no evidence that any of these units were engaged in operations south of Hanoi or in the defense of the Ho Chi Minh Trail. The last unit of Chinese antiaircraft artillery forces left Vietnam in mid-March 1969. Chinese records claim that these troops had fought a total of 2,154 battles and were responsible for shooting down 1,707 American planes and damaging another 1,608.[91]

It is interesting to note that the Chinese air force was never directly engaged in operations over Vietnamese territory even though Chinese antiaircraft artillery troops were sent there. Nevertheless, there is evidence that this arrangement had been discussed by Chinese and Vietnamese leaders in the spring and summer of 1965. Was this noninvolvement a product of Hanoi's reluctance to allow the Chinese air force access to Vietnamese airspace or a reflection of Beijing's desire to restrict China's military involvement in Vietnam? Or were there more complicated or hidden factors at work? Unfortunately, Chinese source materials now available provide no definite answer to these questions.

We now know, though, that Beijing's policy toward American planes invading Chinese airspace underwent a major change in early 1965. Before the end of 1964, the guideline for Chinese policy toward invading American planes was to avoid direct confrontation. A CMC order dated 25 June 1963, for example, made it clear that when an American military vessel or plane entered Chinese territorial water or airspace, the Chinese commanding officer should pay more attention to the political, rather than the military, consequences of his reaction. The officer should therefore be cautious in taking actions, even at the expense of losing military opportunities, in order to avoid putting China in a politically and diplomatically disadvantageous position. The CMC reiterated its previous instructions as late as January 1965, when Chinese air forces on the Chinese-Vietnamese border area entered combat readiness in response to the Gulf of Tonkin incident. In addition, an order dated 11 January 1965 emphasized that Chinese air units in southern China should be restrained when American military planes entered China's airspace and that they should take off to monitor the movement of the American planes but not to attack them.[92]

The situation changed in early April 1965. On 8 and 9 April, two groups of American fighters invaded the airspace over China's Hainan Island. Following the CMC's instructions, four Chinese planes took off to monitor the Americans, and the Americans reportedly opened fire on the Chinese. On 9 April, Deputy Chief of Staff Yang Chengwu reported the two incidents to Zhou Enlai and Mao Zedong, suggesting that the Chinese air force should "give a firm strike" to American planes invading China's airspace. That afternoon Mao ordered the air force and the navy to send their best units to southern China and the South China Sea, to unify their command system, and to strike the Americans firmly if they invaded China's air.[93] On 17 April, the CMC issued a new order formally implementing Mao's instructions.[94] From this time to November 1968, according to Chinese statistics, the Chinese air force engaged in 155 operations against American planes invading China's airspace, shooting down twelve American fighters and other planes (unmanned reconnaissance planes not included).[95] Although the exact motive behind this change of Chinese attitude is not clear, the effect of the new policy seems evident. By responding unhesitatingly to incursions into Chinese airspace, Beijing sent a clear warning signal to the Americans while demonstrating to their comrades in Hanoi their resolve in dealing with the American threat.

Military and Other Material Support to Vietnam

When Chinese troops entered Vietnam, China's military and other support to Vietnam increased dramatically. Mao issued explicit instructions that supporting Vietnam should be given top priority. On 25 May and 2 June 1965, Mao stressed that China's economic structure should be further transformed in order to "prepare for coming wars."[96] Late in July, in the context of the escalating military conflicts in Vietnam, China's State Planning Council decided to make the strengthening of national defense and "preparing for an early and major war with the imperialists" the central task of China's third five-year plan. The council decided also that the Chengdu-Kunming Railway, which was designed to improve travel between China and Vietnam, should be completed by the end of 1969.[97]

One Chinese source reveals the contents of an agreement signed on 11 June 1967 by Liao Kaifen, deputy director of the Logistical Department of the Kunming Military Region, and his Vietnamese counterpart, the deputy head of the logistical bureau of the People's Army of North Vietnam's (PANV's) Northwestern Military Region, in which China offered material support to Vietnamese troops stationed in upper Laos in 1967. The total number of Vietnamese troops there, as claimed by the Vietnamese side, was 1,870. In addition to weapons and other military equipment, China pledged to equip the Vietnamese forces right down to the level of supplies for personal hygiene: 5,500 sets of uniforms, 5,500 pairs of shoes, 550 tons of rice (0.8 kilogram per per-

TABLE I. CHINA'S MILITARY AID TO VIETNAM, 1964–1975

	1964	1965	1966	1967	1968	1969	1970	1971	1972	1973	1974	1975
Guns	80,500	220,767	141,531	146,600	219,899	139,900	101,800	143,100	189,000	233,600	164,500	141,800
Artillery pieces	1,205	4,439	3,362	3,984	7,087	3,906	2,212	7,898	9,238	9,912	6,406	4,880
Bullets (thousands)	25,240	114,010	178,120	147,000	247,920	119,170	29,010	57,190	40,000	40,000	30,000	20,060
Artillery shells (thousands)	335	1,800	1,066	1,363	2,082	1,357	397	1,899	2,210	2,210	1,390	965
Radio transmitters	426	2,779	1,568	2,464	1,854	2,210	950	2,464	4,370	4,335	5,148	2,240
Telephones	2,941	9,502	2,235	2,289	3,313	3,453	1,600	4,424	5,905	6,447	4,633	2,150
Tanks	16	–	–	26	18	–	–	80	220	120	80	–
Ships	–	7	14	25	–	–	–	24	71	5	6	–
Aircraft	18	2	–	70	–	–	–	4	14	36	–	20
Vehicles	25	114	96	435	454	162	–	4,011	8,758	1,210	506	–
Uniforms (thousand sets)	–	–	400	800	1,000	1,200	1,200	1,200	1,400	1,400	1,400	–

Source: Li Ke and Hao Shengzhang, *Wenhua dageming zhong de jiefangjun*, 416.

son daily), fifty-five tons of pork (2.4 kilograms per person monthly), twenty tons of salt, twenty tons of fish, twenty tons of sesame and peanuts, twenty tons of white sugar, 6.5 tons of soy sauce, 8,000 toothbrushes, 11,000 tubes of toothpaste, 24,000 bars of regular soap, 10,600 bars of scented soap, and 74,000 cases of cigarettes. Altogether, this agreement covered 687 items, including such things as Ping-Pong balls, volleyballs, pens, mouth organs, and sewing needles.[98]

China's supply of weapons and other military equipment to Vietnam sharply increased in 1965. Compared with 1964, the supply of guns nearly doubled, from 80,500 to 220,767; gun bullets increased almost five times, from 25.2 million to 114 million; pieces of different types of artillery increased over three times, from 1,205 to 4,439; and artillery shells increased nearly six times, from 335,000 to 1.8 million. The amount of China's military supplies fluctuated between 1965 and 1968, although the total value of material supplies remained at roughly the same level. But then in 1969–70, a sharp drop occurred, at the same time that all Chinese troops were pulled back. Not until 1972 would there be another significant increase in military supplies delivered to Vietnam from China, but for reasons very different from those behind China's support from 1965 to 1969.[99]

From 1965 through 1969, China's aid to Vietnam was substantial. Over 320,000 Chinese engineering and antiaircraft artillery forces (the peak year was 1967, when 170,000 Chinese troops were present in Vietnam) were directly engaged in the construction, maintenance, and defense of North Vietnam's transportation system and strategically important targets, especially in areas north of the 21st parallel.[100] Such support allowed Hanoi to use its own manpower for more essential tasks, such as participating in battles in the South and maintaining the transport and communication lines between the North and the South. Moreover, Beijing's support, as both Allen Whiting and John Garver point out, played a role in deterring further American expansion of war into the North.[101] It is therefore fair to say that, although Beijing's support may have been short of Hanoi's expectations, if it had not been provided, the course, and even the outcome, of the Vietnam War might have been different.

The Widening Gap between Beijing and Hanoi, 1966–1969

Any analysis of China's involvement in the Vietnam War must ultimately address a single, crucial question: why did Beijing and Hanoi enter the war as close allies—"brotherly comrades" in the oft-repeated words of Ho Chi Minh—yet become bitter adversaries a few short years after the war's conclusion?

In retrospect, the foundation of the cooperation between Beijing and Hanoi in the 1960s was tenuous because their respective policies were driven by distinct priorities. Whereas how to unify their country by winning the war was for the Vietnamese the overriding aim, China's Vietnam strategy, as discussed earlier, involved complicated factors such as Mao's desire to use the Vietnam conflict to promote China's continuous revolution. Not surprisingly, when large numbers of Chinese engineering and antiaircraft artillery troops entered Vietnam in late 1965, problems between the two countries began to develop. As the Vietnam War went on, differences of opinion turned into friction, and sometimes confrontation. The rift between the Communist neighbors continued to deepen until Beijing, offended by Hanoi's decision to begin negotiations with the United States in Paris, recalled all of its troops from Vietnam.

The first sign of disharmony appeared over disagreements regarding the role that the Chinese troops were to play in Vietnam and the proper relationship between Chinese troops and local Vietnamese. When Chinese troops entered Vietnam, they were exhorted to "use every opportunity to serve the Vietnamese people." The underlying assumption was that not only was China providing military support, it also had a political mission. It was therefore important for Chinese soldiers to play the role of model while in Vietnam, thus advancing China's image as the great promoter of proletarian internationalism. Such efforts, however, were often thwarted by Vietnamese authorities. The Chinese units found that the services they intended to provide to local Vietnamese people, especially those offered by Chinese medical teams, were intentionally blocked by Vietnamese officials.[102] Several such incidents were reported to Mao in late August 1965, only two months after the first Chinese units had entered Vietnam. Mao instructed Chinese troops in Vietnam "not to be too enthusiastic [in offering service to the Vietnamese]."[103]

As it turns out, however, such a precaution did little to improve the situation. The feeling of solidarity between Beijing and Hanoi waned quickly. This subtle change in attitude is illustrated by the personal experiences of the commanding officers of the CPVEF's Second Division. In June 1965, when the division entered Vietnam, the commanding officers were invited to Hanoi, where they were warmly received by Ho Chi Minh, Pham Van Dong, and Vo Nguyen Giap. But the division representatives reported that the atmosphere in Hanoi when they left in October 1966 had cooled significantly. They felt that "something was wrong in the Chinese-Vietnamese relationship."[104]

The deteriorating relationship between Beijing and Moscow, together with the beginning of the Cultural Revolution in China, triggered more tension and conflict between Beijing and Hanoi. Until the mid-1960s, Beijing assumed that the VWP was on China's side in the struggle against the "Soviet revisionists."[105] But Hanoi and Moscow established closer ties as the Vietnam War progressed. After Khrushchev was ousted by his colleagues in October 1964, Moscow began to provide Hanoi with substantial support and called on socialist countries to adopt a unified stand in supporting Vietnam.[106] On 11 February 1965, the Soviet prime minister, Alekei N. Kosygin, stopped in Beijing on his way back from Vietnam to meet Mao Zedong and Zhou Enlai. He suggested that China and the Soviet Union stop the polemic between them so that they would take joint steps to support the struggle of the Vietnamese people. Mao refused Kosygin's suggestion, asserting that his debates with the Soviets would last for another 9,000 years.[107] Since the Kosygin visit, Hanoi had become silent in its criticism of "revisionism."[108]

Mao's linking of the polemic against Moscow to the inner-party struggle taking place in China at the time further complicated the situation. In February and March 1966, a high-ranking Japanese Communist Party delegation headed by Miyamoto Kenji, the JCP's general secretary, visited China and North Vietnam in an attempt to promote an "anti-imperialist international united front" including both China and the Soviet Union. Learning that Hanoi had demonstrated great interest in this idea, CCP delegation, headed by Liu Shaoqi and Deng Xiaoping, managed to work out an agreement with Miyamoto, according to which China would eventually join this "international united front." However, Mao, who had not attended the meeting but had been kept abreast of its progress, intervened suddenly at the very last moment, claiming that neither Liu Shaoqi nor Deng Xiaoping had been authorized to speak for the CCP. He insisted that the Soviet Union had become the most dangerous enemy of the peoples of the world and called for the establishment of an "anti-imperialist and antirevisionist international united front."[109] Mao would later relate this event to his earlier criticism of Wang Jiaxiang, charging that both Liu and Deng had become China's "revisionists." With Mao's criticism of Liu's and Deng's handling of the Miyamoto mission came the first indication to the outside world that a profound division had emerged among top CCP leaders. As it soon turned out, both Liu and Deng would become the main targets of the Cultural Revolution.

The failure of the Miyamoto mission further distanced Hanoi from Beijing. Beijing's leaders, while feeling increasingly uneasy about Hanoi's lack of interest in keeping a distance from Moscow, noted with surprise that the Vietnamese media began to use China's invasions of Vietnam in the past to spur patriotism among ordinary Vietnamese people. Convinced that the Vietnamese were in fact inclined toward Moscow, Beijing's leaders were genuinely offended.[110]

Among Chinese sources now available, two accounts indicate that sharp differences had emerged in 1966 between Beijing and Hanoi as the result of Hanoi's improving relations with Moscow. The first details China's reaction to Hanoi's gestures of friendship toward Moscow. In March 1966, Le Duan led a VWP delegation to attend the CPSU's Twenty-third Congress. During his visit, he reportedly described the Soviet Union as his "second motherland." When Beijing's leaders learned of this, they were "angrily shocked." A few months later, the Vietnamese requested that the CPVEF's Second Division stay longer in Vietnam after it had completed its original assignments, but the Chinese turned down the request and the Second Division returned to China in July 1966. One Chinese source points out that this move was designed to demonstrate Beijing's anger toward Le Duan's praise of the Soviets in Moscow.[111]

The second account more directly reveals Chinese resentment of Hanoi giving any priority to the Soviets. In early 1966, a Chinese cargo ship, *Hongqi* (Red Flag), was assigned to carry materials in aid to Vietnam. As the ship approached the Hai Phong port it was stopped so that a Soviet cargo ship, which arrived later than the Chinese, could enter the port first. As the result of this delay, *Hongqi* was exposed to an American air raid and was severely damaged. When Le Duan visited China in April, Zhou Enlai insisted that Duan explain why Vietnam had given the Soviet cargo ship an unfair priority. Duan, according to Chinese sources, was greatly embarrassed. He was made to promise that the Vietnamese would not allow the same thing to happen again, as well as repeatedly praise the importance of the Chinese support, before Zhou would turn to other topics.[112]

The rift between Beijing and Hanoi deepened as North Vietnam received more support from Moscow. In addition, Beijing would not agree to cooperate with the Soviets in establishing a united transport system, as suggested by Moscow, to handle Soviet materials going through Chinese territory.[113] China did help deliver Soviet materials to Vietnam, but only on the condition that the operation would be placed under Beijing's direct control and would be interpreted as a favor from Beijing to Hanoi.[114] The Vietnamese obviously did not appreciate such an attitude. By 1968, it became evident to the Chinese that Hanoi was growing closer to Moscow than to Beijing. When a series of conflicts occurred between Chinese troops and Soviet military personnel in Vietnam, the Vietnamese authorities took the Soviets' side, alleging that the Chinese "had impinged upon Vietnam's sovereignty."[115]

Hanoi's deep involvement in other parts of Indochina, and especially in Laos, was another reason for suspicion and friction between the Chinese and the Vietnamese. Historically the relationship between Communists in Vietnam, Laos, and Cambodia had been very close (they once belonged to the same Indochina Communist Party). This was not a problem for the Chinese during the First Indochina War. But the situation became quite different during the second war. After a Chinese working team arrived in Laos in early 1965, the members reported to Beijing that the Vietnamese virtually controlled the Laotian People's Revolutionary Party and viewed the presence of the Chinese team as a threat to Hanoi's interests there.[116] In addition, in September 1968, apparently under pressure from Hanoi, Kaysone Phomvihane suggested that Li Wenzheng, the head of the Chinese team at that time, take a vacation back in China. Beijing interpreted this suggestion as an indication that the Chinese team's presence was no longer appreciated, and they ordered the withdrawal of the team.[117]

The changing situation in China in 1968–69, as well as China's changing relationship with the two superpowers, made the Beijing leadership feel less obligated to continue the same level of support to Vietnam. As discussed before, when Mao decided to commit a large portion of China's military and other material resources to backing the Vietnamese Communists in 1964 and 1965, he was preparing to start the Cultural Revolution, which began to sweep across China in the summer and fall of 1966. But by 1968 and 1969, China's domestic situation and Mao's needs had changed. The ongoing Cultural Revolution destroyed Mao's perceived opponents within the party leadership, but, at the same time, it brought Chinese society, as well as the Communist state and party apparatus, to the verge of total collapse. As a sign of the fading status of Mao's continuous revolution, the chairman began to call the country back to order in 1968–69.[118] In the meantime, the relationship between Beijing and Moscow deteriorated, leading eventually to a border clash between the two countries in March 1969. The perception that the "Soviet social-imperialists" were China's most dangerous enemies gradually came to dominate Beijing's strategic thinking. Starting in early 1969, Beijing's top leaders, and Mao and Zhou in particular, began to reconsider the role the United States could play in China's security.[119] These changing domestic and international conditions significantly altered the underlying assumptions of Beijing's policy toward the Vietnam War, making a radical approach to the conflict obsolete.

Consequently, all the accumulated tensions between Beijing and Hanoi culminated with one crucial question: Should Hanoi engage in negotiations with the United States for a possible peaceful solution of the war? From the very moment Hanoi demonstrated a vague interest in negotiating with the Americans Beijing expressed a strong objection.[120] In several conversations with Vietnamese leaders in late 1967 and early 1968, Beijing's top leaders advised Hanoi to stick to the policy of military struggle.[121] When Pham Van Dong visited Beijing in April 1968, for example, Mao and other Chinese leaders repeatedly emphasized to him that "what could not be achieved on the battlefield would not be achieved at the negotiation table."[122] But Beijing now found that its influence over Hanoi's decision making had become so limited that Hanoi would go its own way. Zhou Enlai commented during a talk with a Vietnamese delegation headed by Xuan Thuy in early May 1968 that Hanoi's agreement on starting negotiations with the Americans was "too fast and too hurried."[123] Not surprisingly, Beijing maintained a displeased silence during the initial exchanges between Hanoi and Washington throughout 1968. The distrust, or even disgust, between Beijing and Hanoi was most explicitly revealed in a 17 October 1968 meeting between Chen Yi and Le Duc Tho, Hanoi's chief negotiator with the Americans in Paris. The Chinese and Vietnamese leaders accused each other of making basic errors in handling the issues of negotiating with the Americans:

> *Chen Yi:* Since last April, when you agreed to the United States' partial cessation of bombing and held peace talks with the Americans, you have lost the initiative in the negotiations to them. Now, you accept quadripartite negotiation. You [have] lost to them once more. . . .
>
> *Le Duc Tho:* On this matter, we will wait and see. And the reality will give us the answer. We have gained experience over the past fifteen years. Let reality judge.
>
> *Chen Yi:* We signed the Geneva accord in 1954 when the United States did not agree to do so. We withdrew our armed forces from the South to the North, thus letting the people in the South be killed. We at that time made a mistake in which we [Chinese] shared a part.
>
> *Le Duc Tho:* Because we listened to your advice.
>
> *Chen Yi:* You just mentioned that at the Geneva conference, you made a mistake because you followed our advice. But this time, you will make another mistake if you do not take our words into account.[124]

This exchange reads like a replay of the heated debate between Chen Yi—with Mao sitting beside him—and Khrushchev on 2 October 1959, when both Chinese and Soviet leaders blamed each other for allegedly committing fundamental mistakes in assessing the international situation and formulating policies and strategies. That meeting, as it turned out, became a landmark event

Chinese party and government delegation visiting Hanoi, March 1971. From left to right in front row: Nguyen Duy Trinh, Vo Nguyen Giap, Ye Jianying, Pham Van Dong, Zhou Enlai, Le Duan, Qiu Huizuo, Le Thanh Nghi, Hoang Van Hoan. Xinhua News Agency.

symbolizing the existence of an unbridgeable chasm between Beijing and Moscow.[125] In the Chen-Tho conversation quoted above, one can sense the extreme tension in their language, although the meeting minutes do not specifically describe the emotions of the two leaders. At about the same time, Chinese engineering troops and antiaircraft artillery units began to leave Vietnam.

The Failure of an "Alliance between Brotherly Comrades"

By late 1969, except for a small number of Chinese engineering units engaged in the final stages of construction projects that had lasted for years, all Chinese engineering and antiaircraft artillery troops had left Vietnam. In July 1970, the last Chinese units returned to China.[126] China's military and material support to Vietnam continued, but the quantity began to drop in 1969 and 1970 after it peaked in 1968. In Beijing's and Hanoi's open propaganda, the assertion that China and Vietnam were "brotherly comrades" could still be heard from time to time, but the enthusiasm disappeared.

Before the Paris Peace Accords concluded in January 1973, there was another wave of Chinese support for Hanoi. In May 1972, Beijing honored Hanoi's request for more military aid when the Nixon administration started another round of bombardment of key North Vietnamese targets and mined the Hai Phong harbor.[127] But this episode was short-lived. Chinese-Vietnamese relations again cooled down after the signing of the Paris Peace Agreement, and the two countries immediately fell into a series of disputes after the Vietnamese Communists won their country's unification in 1975. Four years later, when Vietnamese troops invaded Cambodia, Beijing responded by using its military forces to attack Vietnam "to teach Hanoi a lesson." It turned out that after committing much of China's resources to supporting the Vietnamese Communists, Beijing had created a new enemy, and a comprehensive confrontation characterized the relationship between Beijing and Hanoi throughout the 1980s. In this sense, the Vietnam War was also a "lost war" for Beijing.

What were the causes? One may argue that the Chinese-Vietnamese relations had been under the heavy shadow of the past conflicts between the two countries. One may point out that from a geopolitical perspective there existed potential conflict between Beijing's and Hanoi's interests in Southeast Asia. One may also refer to the escalating Sino-Soviet confrontation, which made the maintenance of the solidarity between Beijing and Hanoi extremely difficult. One may even find the "brotherly comradeship" itself a source of contention: if Beijing and Hanoi had not been so close, they would have had fewer opportunities to experience the differences between them; too intimate a tie created more opportunities for conflict.

However, a more fundamental reason can be found in the logic of China's foreign policy and security strategy. As argued in this chapter, China's foreign policy was always an integral part of Mao's continuous revolution, which aimed to promote the revolutionary transformation of China's "old" state and society and to pursue new China's central (but not dominant) position in the international community. Beijing's support of Hanoi had a critical connection to Mao's desire to use the tensions caused by the crisis in Vietnam to stimulate the mass mobilization that was essential for the Cultural Revolution and to establish revolutionary China's influence and reputation in Southeast Asia and other parts of the world. When Beijing tried to carry out a Vietnam policy designed with these goals in mind, it immediately encountered paradox. On the one hand, in order to create the momentum for the ongoing continuous revolution, as well as to establish Beijing as a model of international anti-imperialist struggles, the Beijing leadership stressed the danger of a war with the United States and its determination to fight against it. It asserted repeatedly that China would support Vietnam by any means, "even if it meant making heavy national sacrifices." On the other hand, however, Beijing's actual policy choices were limited: at a time when the Cultural Revolution could throw China into nationwide turmoil, it was simply impossible for Mao and his comrades to allow China to enter a direct confrontation with the United

States (unless American land forces invaded North Vietnam or China), and Mao's idealism had to yield to that reality. From a Vietnamese perspective, though, there was a huge gap between Beijing's words and deeds (in spite of China's enormous military and material support), and the gap widened with the development of the Vietnam War.

From a historical-cultural perspective, Beijing's seemingly revolutionary and idealistic policy toward Vietnam ironically had been penetrated by an age-old Chinese ethnocentrism and universalism. While Beijing's leaders, and Mao in particular, emphasized repeatedly that the Vietnamese should be treated as "equals," the statement itself revealed the Chinese revolutionaries' strong sense of superiority and that they believed that they had occupied a position from which to dictate the values and codes of behavior that would dominate their relations with their neighbors. In the realm of the Chinese-Vietnamese relations, although Beijing had never pursued political and economic control in Vietnam (which was for the Chinese too inferior an aim) and its huge military and material aid was seldom accompanied by formal conditions, Beijing asked for something bigger, that is, the Vietnamese recognition of China's morally superior position. In other words, what Beijing intended to create was a modern version of the relationship between the Central Kingdom and its subordinate neighbors. This practice effectively reminded the Vietnamese of their problematic past with the Chinese. When Beijing reduced its support to Hanoi in the wake of China's changing domestic and international situations, Vietnam's suspicion of China developed into aversion. And when Vietnam's unification made it possible for the regime in Hanoi to confront China's influences, the aversion turned into hostility. The Chinese, on the other hand, found it necessary to "punish" their former comrades in order to defend their heavily wounded sense of superiority. The result was the final collapse of the "alliance between brotherly comrades."

CHAPTER 9
THE SINO-AMERICAN
RAPPROCHEMENT, 1969–1972

He said he was not a complicated man, but really very simple. He was, he said, only a lone monk walking the world with a leaky umbrella.
—*Edgar Snow after interviewing Mao Zedong (18 December 1970)*

Early in 1969, it seemed that the conflict between the People's Republic of China and the United States had reached the worst in two decades. When the newly elected U.S. president Richard Nixon delivered his inaugural address on 20 January, Beijing's propaganda machine immediately fiercely attacked the "jittery chieftain of U.S. imperialism." *Renmin ribao* (People's Daily) and *Hongqi* (The Red Flag), the Chinese Communist Party's mouthpieces, jointly published an editorial essay characterizing Nixon's address as nothing but "a confession in an impasse," which demonstrated that "the U.S. imperialists . . . are beset with profound crises both at home and abroad."[1] Indeed, the wording of the essay appeared quite similar to the anti-American rhetoric prevailing in the Chinese media during the Great Proletarian Cultural Revolution. There appeared nothing new or unusual in it. Yet this was not one of the many ordinary anti-American propaganda pieces that the Chinese media churned out during the Cultural Revolution years. What made it unique was that it was published alongside Nixon's address in its entirety. More interestingly, major newspapers all over China, although following the general practice during the Cultural Revolution of reprinting the commentator's essay, also reprinted Nixon's address. This was unprecedented in the history of the People's Republic.

Not until the late 1980s did we learn through newly released Chinese documents that it was Mao Zedong who personally ordered the publication of Nixon's address.[2] The likely reason behind the chairman's order was a point the U.S. president made in his speech: the United States was willing to develop relations with *all* countries in the world.[3] The Chinese chairman, who had been paying attention both to the U.S. presidential election and to Nixon as a presidential candidate, immediately caught the subtext of Nixon's statement.[4] Perhaps he ordered the publication of the U.S. president's address to reveal that he had noticed Nixon's message.[5]

This was the beginning of a dramatic process that would lead to Nixon's visit to China in February 1972, during which the U.S. president met face-to-face with the Chinese chairman in Beijing. Toward the end of the "week that changed the world" Nixon and Chinese premier Zhou Enlai signed the historic Shanghai communiqué symbolizing the end of an era of intense conflict between China and the United States that had lasted for over two decades.

The conventional interpretation of Beijing's rapprochement with the United States emphasizes the role strategic/geopolitical considerations played. Scholars favoring this interpretation usually argue that when the Soviet Union had emerged as the most serious threat to the PRC's security interests, especially to China's border safety in the north and northeast, it was impossible for Beijing's leader to maintain simultaneously the same level of discord with the United States. By achieving a rapprochement with Washington, Beijing's leaders drastically improved China's strategic position vis-à-vis the Soviet threat, thus serving China's security interests.[6]

Indeed, Beijing's rapprochement with Washington yielded considerable improvements in China's strategic position, as well as its international status. The simple fact that the PRC, after being excluded from the United Nations for over two decades, gained its position at the UN in October 1971 proves the enormous strategic value of the Sino-American rapprochement to Beijing. This chapter, however, argues that the geopolitics-centered interpretation alone does not fully reveal the complicated reasons behind Mao's decision to improve relations with the United States. In order to achieve a better understanding of the issue, this chapter places the Sino-American rapprochement in the context of the fading status of Mao's continuous revolution. It is important to note that the Sino-American rapprochement came at a time when the Cultural Revolution and the more general enterprise of Mao's continuous revolution had been declining. This chapter argues that a profound connection existed between these two phenomena and that the interpretation emphasizing the strategic/geopolitical element will make better sense if its link to the end of Mao's continuous revolution is properly comprehended.

China in 1968–1969: Deteriorating Security, Fading Revolution
Undoubtedly China in 1968–69 was facing a rapidly worsening security situation. The contention between China and the United States, which began at the very moment of the PRC's establishment, seemed more intense than

ever before. In response to the escalation of the Vietnam War and increasing American military involvement in it, Beijing dispatched large numbers of engineering and antiaircraft artillery forces to North Vietnam while providing the Vietnamese Communists with substantial military and other support.[7] Beijing and Washington thus were in danger of repeating their Korean War experience—when they were both dragged into a direct military confrontation. Such security threats from China's southern borders were made worse with the sustained military standoff between the CCP and the GMD across the Taiwan Strait, as well as by Japan's and South Korea's hostile attitudes toward the PRC. Consequently, Beijing perceived that, from Bohai Bay to the Gulf of Tonkin, all of China's coastal borders were under siege.[8]

The security situation along China's long western border with India was no better. Since the Chinese-Indian border war of 1962, Beijing and New Delhi each regarded the other as a dangerous enemy. Although India, in the wake of its humiliating defeat in the 1962 clash, was not in a position to threaten Chinese border safety militarily, it was more than capable of damaging Beijing's reputation as a self-proclaimed "peace-loving country" among Third World nations. It was also likely to pin down Beijing's valuable resources and strategic attention in China's remote western areas.[9]

The worst threat to China's border security existed in the north, from a former ally—the Soviet Union. Since the late 1950s, significant differences between Chinese and Soviet leaders had begun to develop in the wake of the Soviet leader Khrushchev's de-Stalinization campaign. Starting in the early 1960s, along with the escalation of the great Sino-Soviet polemic debate, the disputes between Beijing and Moscow quickly spread from the ideological field to state-to-state relations.[10] The hostility between the two Communist giants flared into hatred when the Cultural Revolution swept across China, with Beijing and Moscow each regarding the other as a "traitor" to true communism. Since 1965, both countries had continuously increased their military deployments along their shared borders. By 1968–69, each side had amassed several hundred thousand troops along the border areas that, only less than a decade ago, had been boasted as a region characterized by "peace and eternal safety."[11]

China's already extremely tense security situation dramatically worsened in March 1969, when two bloody conflicts erupted between Chinese and Soviet border garrison forces on Zhenbao Island (Damansky Island in Russian), located near the Chinese bank of the Ussuri River. This incident immediately brought China and the Soviet Union to the brink of a general war, and, reportedly, the Soviet leaders even considered conducting a preemptive nuclear strike against their former Communist ally.[12]

Chinese soldiers patrolling at Zhenbao Island, March 1969. Xinhua News Agency.

Given the dramatic deterioration of China's security situation in 1968–69, it is not surprising that Beijing's leaders had to improve their nation's security environment by making major changes in China's foreign policy and security strategy. The scholars who have argued that the Sino-American rapprochement represented a calculated effort by Beijing to counter the grave Soviet threat have the support of strong historical evidence. However, although this interpretation makes good sense in explaining why in 1968–69 it was *necessary* for Beijing to make major changes in Chinese foreign policy and security strategy, it does not explain how and why it became *possible* for Beijing's leaders to achieve such changes in the late 1960s and early 1970s.

Historically, how to deal with the United States was for Beijing not just a foreign policy issue but rather an issue concerning the very essence of the Chinese revolution. From the moment that the "new China" came into being, Beijing's leaders regarded the United States as China's primary enemy. They consistently declared that a fundamental aim of the Chinese revolution was to destroy the "old" world order dominated by the U.S. imperialists. Through endless propaganda campaigns and constant indoctrination efforts, Beijing had portrayed the United States as the "bastion of all reactionary forces in the world," as responsible for sinking China into the abyss of national humiliation in modern times, and as keeping China divided after the "liberation" of the Chinese mainland by supporting the GMD in Taiwan after 1949. For almost two decades, the United States had been thoroughly demonized in the Chinese popular image. As a result, the theme of "struggling against U.S. imperialism" had occupied a central position in Mao's efforts to legitimize his continuous revolution and was frequently invoked by the CCP to mobilize hundreds of millions of ordinary Chinese to participate in Mao's revolutionary movements—most recently, the Cultural Revolution.[13] Beijing's pursuit of fundamental changes in Chinese policy toward the United States therefore was fraught with political hazards, not least of which was possible detriment to the legitimacy of the Chinese Communist revolution. It seemed that unless Beijing's leaders were willing to make basic compromises in their commitments to the anti-imperialist Communist ideology, it would be impossible for them to pursue a rapprochement with the United States.

In explaining why Beijing was able to achieve such comprises, scholars favoring the geopolitics-centered interpretation have argued that for policymakers in *any* country, ultimately, ideological beliefs do not matter if they are in conflict with vital "national security interests." In the case of Mao's China, these scholars believe that despite Mao and his comrades' strong commitment to Marxist-Leninist ideology, they were willing to sacrifice this ideological faith if it was in conflict with China's "national security interests." Therefore, according to these scholars, ideological beliefs as essential agents in foreign policymaking are only of secondary importance compared to geopolitics and security concerns.[14]

These arguments, however, have ignored two important factors. First, Beijing's leaders were pursuing a rapprochement with the United States within the context of radically redefining their concept of imperialism by identifying the Soviet Union as a "social-imperialist country" and arguing that Moscow had replaced Washington as the "bastion of reactionary forces in the world." Second, in terms of the relations between ideology and security concerns the Sino-American rapprochement was less a case in which ideological beliefs yielded to the security interests than one in which ideology, as an essential element shaping foreign policy decisions, experienced subtle structural changes as the result of the fading status of Mao's continuous revolution.

In Leninist vocabulary, "imperialism" represented the "highest stage" in the development of capitalism. Therefore, an imperialist country had to be capitalist in the first place; thus, few would ever call the Soviet Union "capitalist" given its overwhelmingly socialist/Communist-dominated economic and political structures. However, in the wake of the great Sino-Soviet polemic debate, Beijing claimed that capitalism had been "restored" in the Soviet Union with the emerging dominance of a new "privileged bureaucratic capitalist class."[15] During the height of the Cultural Revolution, and especially after the Soviet invasion of Czechoslovakia in August 1968, Beijing charged that the Soviet Union had become a "social-imperialist country." Consequently, both in the Chinese Communist definition of the "main contradiction" in the world and in Chinese propaganda, "Soviet social-imperialism" gradually replaced "U.S. imperialism" to become the primary and most dangerous enemy of the world proletarian revolution.[16] Within this new theoretical framework, U.S. imperialism remained China's enemy but no longer the primary one.

Such basic changes in Beijing's definition of "imperialism" did not take place simply as a justification of Chinese efforts to counter the escalating Soviet threat to China's security interests, they were determined by the essence of the Cultural Revolution. Indeed, according to Mao, the fundamental reason that he initiated the Cultural Revolution was to prevent a Soviet-style "capitalist restoration" from taking place in China.[17] Beijing thus would have to identify the Soviet Union as an imperialist/capitalist country. In addition, excluding the Soviet Union completely from the revolutionary camp would help guarantee China's central position in the world proletarian revolution.

All of these changes had provided the much needed ideological space for Beijing to justify a rapprochement with the United States. In Maoist political philosophy, which had been heavily influenced by the traditional Chinese political culture emphasizing the necessity of "borrowing the strength of the barbarians to check the barbarians," it was always legitimate to pursue a "united front" with a less dangerous enemy in order to focus on the contest against the primary enemy.[18] Since Beijing identified the "social-imperialist" Soviet Union as the most dangerous among all imperialist countries in the world, a rapprochement with the imperialist United States, an enemy now less dangerous in comparison, became feasible and justifiable for Beijing's leaders even in ideological terms.

In a deeper sense, Beijing was also able to pursue a rapprochement with Washington because, for the first time in the PRC's history, Mao's continuous revolution was losing momentum due to the chairman's *own* reasons. A belated socialization phenomenon finally was taking its bite to reduce the vigor of Mao's revolution.

From a historical perspective, the Cultural Revolution represented the climax of Mao's efforts to transform China's "old" state and society through extensive mass mobilization. Mao initiated the Cultural Revolution for two purposes. First, he hoped that it would allow him to discover new means to promote the transformation of China's party, state, and society in accordance with his ideals—that China should be transformed into a land of prosperity and universal justice and equality. Second, he desired to use it to enhance his much weakened authority and reputation in the wake of the disastrous Great Leap Forward. In the chairman's mind, his strengthened leadership role would best guarantee the success of his revolution.[19]

By carrying out the Cultural Revolution, Mao easily achieved the second goal, making his power and authority absolute. But he failed to get any closer to achieving his first goal. Although the power of the mass movement released by the Cultural Revolution destroyed both Mao's opponents and the "old" party-state control system, it was unable to create the new form of state power Mao desired so much for building a new society in China.[20] Despite all of this, however, Mao was ready to halt the revolution in 1968–69.

In summer 1968, Mao dispatched the "Workers' Mao Zedong Thought Propaganda Team" to various universities in Beijing to reestablish the order that had been undermined by the "revolutionary masses." At the Qinghua University, the Red Guards, who were once Mao's main instrument for initiating and carrying out the Cultural Revolution, responded by opening fire on the team. It was at this point that Mao decided it was time to dismantle the Red Guards movement, thus leading his continuous revolution to a crucial turning point.[21] For almost two decades, "mobilizing the masses" had been the key for Mao to maintain and enhance the momentum of his revolution; but now the chairman openly stood in opposition to the masses in an upside-down effort to reestablish the Communist state's control over society. It was against this background that, with the chairman's repeated pushes, the notion of China being "the center of the world revolution," which had been prevailing since the beginning of the Cultural Revolution, began to disappear in Maoist discourse.[22] In the meantime, Mao completely stopped talking about the role "tension" could play in stirring up revolutionary spirit and creating a revolutionary environment. Instead, he frequently emphasized the importance of "consolidating" the achievements of the Cultural Revolution—which, in reality, meant no more than strengthening his own authority and political power.[23] These were critical signs that Mao's China as a revolutionary state, after being an uncompromising challenger to the "old world" (and attempting to transform China's "old" state and society) for two decades, was now beginning to demonstrate a willingness to live with the yet-to-be-transformed "old" world order. In other words, a "socialization" process—to borrow a critical concept from David Armstrong—had been eroding the Maoist revolution.[24] It was within this context that, when the security threat from the Soviet Union escalated dramatically in 1969, Mao began to consider adopting a new policy toward the United States.

The First Probe: Reports by the Marshals

Since the 1950s, Mao's main source for information about the outside world had been *Cakao ziliao*, an internally circulated journal edited by the Xinhua News Agency.[25] Late in 1967, he noticed an article written by Richard Nixon, in which the former U.S. vice president claimed: "Taking the long view, we simply cannot afford to leave China forever outside the family of nations, there to nurture its fantasies, cherish its hates and threaten its neighbors. There is no place on this small planet for a billion of its potentially most able people to live in angry isolation."[26] Reportedly, Mao not only read the article himself but also recommended it to Zhou Enlai, commenting that if Nixon was to become the next president, U.S. policy toward China might possibly change.[27] Yet this was a time that both the Cultural Revolution and American intervention in Vietnam were peaking. For the moment, neither Beijing nor Washington did anything to reduce the hostility between them.[28]

The first sign of change appeared in November 1968, when the United States proposed to resume the stagnant Sino-American ambassadorial talks in Warsaw. China responded positively and with "unprecedented speed."[29] Then, in January 1969, Mao ordered the publication of Nixon's inaugural address. One month later, however, because Washington provided asylum to Liao Heshu, a Chinese chargé d'affaires in the Netherlands who defected to the West in February 1969, Beijing canceled the ambassadorial talks that had been scheduled to resume on 20 February.[30]

Although we cannot know exactly what Mao was thinking when he showed some interest in dealing with the United States, one thing is certain: the chairman now was turning more of his attention to international issues, trying to understand the orientation of Moscow's and Washington's global strategies in the wake of the Soviet invasion of Czechoslovakia in August 1968. Late in 1968 and early in 1969, in a series of conversations with foreign visitors to China, the chairman revealed his deep concern about the expansionist nature of Soviet foreign policy. Indeed, he tried hard to comprehend the significance of Soviet behavior, wondering aloud if the Soviet invasion should be interpreted as the prelude to a more general war. In the chairman's view, now "all under the heaven is in great chaos."[31]

It was against this background that Mao asked four veteran military commanders, Marshals Chen Yi, Ye Jianying, Xu Xiangqian, and Nie Rongzhen, all of whom had been excluded from the decision-making inner circle during the Cultural Revolution and were then "conducting investigation and study" at four factories in Beijing, to "pay attention to" international affairs. In late February, Zhou Enlai, following Mao's instructions, told Chen Yi and the other three marshals to meet "once a week" to discuss "important international issues" in order to provide the party Central Committee with their opinions.[32] The four marshals began to meet on 1 March, and, by late March, they had held four meetings. The first meeting was a general discussion. The next three were held after the Sino-Soviet border clash at Zhenbao Island, so the discussion focused on assessing the implications of the clash and analyzing Soviet strategy toward China. On 18 March, the marshals finished their first report, "An Analysis of War Situation in the World"; eleven days later, they had completed their second report, "The Zhenbao Island as a Tree in the Forest of the Whole World." In both reports, the marshals cast doubt on the notion that the Soviet Union was ready to wage a major war against China since this would "require the mobilization of at least three million troops." They also pointed out that the focus of the American-Soviet global dispute was "the competition over oil resources in the Middle East" and that before the situation there had been resolved, the Soviet Union could not easily turn its main strategic attention to China. Their main policy suggestions focused on upgrading the troops' training level, strengthening the militia forces, and further developing China's national defense industry. Nowhere in the reports did the marshals refer to the sensitive question of adjusting Chinese policy toward the United States.[33]

We do not know whether Mao had read the two reports. At the CCP's Ninth National Congress held from 1 to 24 April, the party leadership, while emphasizing the danger of a major war with "social-imperialists" and "imperialists," continued harsh attacks on the United States. In the main political report delivered by Lin Biao, then China's second in command and Mao's designated successor, there was nothing to indicate that Beijing had changed its attitude toward the United States.[34]

Lin's report, however, was prepared for a public audience. When Mao wanted a more sophisticated understanding of the changing world situation, he again turned to the four marshals. Right after the conclusion of the Ninth Congress, Mao instructed the marshals to resume regular meetings to "study the international situation."[35] The marshals were reluctant to accept the mission since the party congress had already defined China's foreign policies. If they simply repeated the official statement, the "study" would be meaningless;

but if they presented something new, they risked being charged with "challenging" the party's established policy. In order to dispel the marshals' doubts, Zhou Enlai told them in mid-May that Mao assigned them this task because the international situation was "too complicated" to fit the Ninth Congress's conclusions. Zhou also asked the marshals not to be "restricted by any established framework" in their thinking and to try to help Mao to "gain command of the new tendency in the strategic development" in the world. Zhou stressed that Mao decided to assign them the task because they were marshals and had much experience and superb strategic visions.[36] The premier also appointed Xiong Xianghui and Yao Guang, two experienced high-ranking diplomats, to assist the marshals in conducting discussions and drafting reports.[37]

The marshals began to meet on 7 June 1969. On 11 July they submitted a comprehensive report, "A Preliminary Evaluation of the War Situation," to Mao and the Central Committee. They argued that the United States and the Soviet Union were "two 'brands' of representatives of the international bourgeoisie class." While taking China as their enemy, they took "each other as the enemy" too. For them, "the real threat is the one existing between themselves." Since both the United States and the Soviet Union were facing many difficulties at home and abroad, and since the focus of the strategic confrontation between them existed in Europe, stressed the marshals, "it is unlikely that U.S. imperialists and Soviet revisionists will launch a large-scale war against China, either jointly or separately."[38] Because the marshals focused their attention on whether China was facing a serious war threat, they did not further probe into the question of adjusting Chinese foreign policy.

After the marshals adjourned on 11 July, several signs indicated that subtle changes were taking place in Washington's attitude toward China. On 21 July, the U.S. State Department announced that it was relaxing restrictions on American citizens traveling to China; five days later, Prince Norodom Sihanouk, Cambodia's chief of state, conveyed a letter by Senator Mike Mansfield to Zhou Enlai, in which the veteran American politician expressed the desire to visit China to seek solutions to the "twenty-year confrontation" between the two countries. Moscow also proposed a meeting between top Chinese and Soviet leaders around the same time.[39]

To better understand these new developments, the marshals resumed their discussions on 29 July. In addition to contemplating the possibility of "intentionally utilizing the contradictions between the United States and the Soviet Union," they believed that not only should border negotiations with the Soviet Union be held in order to strengthen "our position in the struggle against

Zhou Enlai (right) *and Aleksei Kosygin at the Beijing airport, 11 September 1969.*
Xinhua News Agency.

America" but other policy options should also be considered. However, they did not believe that the time was right to accept Mansfield's request to visit China and proposed to "let him wait for a while."[40]

Before the marshals could put these opinions into writing, another major border clash, one larger than the two clashes at Zhenbao Island in March, occurred between Chinese and Soviet garrisons in Xinjiang on 13 August, in which an entire Chinese brigade was eliminated.[41] Beijing reacted immediately to this incident, and to other signs indicating that Moscow probably was preparing to start a major war against China. On 28 August, the CCP Central Committee ordered Chinese provinces and regions bordering the Soviet Union and Outer Mongolia to enter a status of general mobilization.[42] The marshals, meanwhile, still believed it unlikely for the Soviet Union to wage a large-scale war against China, but, at the same time, they emphasized the need for Beijing to be prepared for a worst-case scenario. Within this context, Chen Yi and Ye Jianying mentioned that in order for China to be ready for a major confrontation with the Soviet Union, "the card of the United States" should be played. In another written report, "Our Views about the Current Situation," completed on 17 September, they pointed out that although Moscow indeed was intending to "wage a war against China" and had made "war deployments," the Soviet leaders were unable "to reach a final decision because of political considerations." They proposed that in addition to waging "a tit-for-tat struggle against both the United States and the Soviet Union," China should use "negotiation as a means to struggle against them," and then perhaps the Sino-American ambassadorial talks should be resumed "when the timing is proper."[43] After submitting the report, Chen Yi confided some of his "unconventional thoughts" to Zhou Enlai, proposing that in addition to resuming the ambassadorial talks in Warsaw, China should "take the initiative in proposing to hold Sino-American talks at the ministerial or even higher levels, so that basic and related problems in Sino-American relations can be solved."[44]

We do not know exactly how Mao responded to these reports. Yet the fact that the chairman, through Zhou Enlai, encouraged the marshals to present ideas that were not necessarily consistent with the general foreign policy line set up by the party's Ninth Congress is revealing enough. Apparently, what the chairman wanted to get was exactly such "unconventional thoughts." According to Mao's doctor, Li Zhisui, the chairman said in August 1969: "Think about this. We have the Soviet Union to the north and the west, India to the south, and Japan to the east. If all our enemies were to unite, attacking us from the north, south, east, and west, what do you think we should do? . . . Think again. Beyond Japan is the United States. Didn't our ancestors counsel negotiating with faraway countries while fighting with those that are near?"[45]

With these "unconventional thoughts" in mind, apparently the chairman was determined to explore the possibility of opening relations with the United States. Now the main question facing him was: through what channel could Beijing establish communication with the Americans? Not just by coincidence, Nixon was eager to find the answer to the same question.

Opening Moves

In fall 1969, there existed no channel of communication between China and the United States. The last meeting of the Sino-American ambassadorial talks was held in Warsaw in January 1968, which since had been indefinitely suspended. Therefore, when President Nixon intended to let the Chinese know of his "readiness to open communication with Peking [Beijing],"[46] he had to travel a circuitous path. During an around-the-world trip beginning in late July 1969, the U.S. president talked to Pakistani president Mohammad Yahya Khan and Romanian leader Nicolae Ceauşescu, both of whom had good relations with Beijing, asking them to convey to the Chinese leaders his belief that "Asia could not 'move forward' if a nation as large as China remained isolated."[47] When Zhou Enlai received the message from Yahya Khan via Zhang Tong, Chinese ambassador to Pakistan, he commented in a report to Mao on 16 November 1969: "The direction of movement of Nixon and [Henry] Kissinger is noteworthy."[48] But Beijing made no immediate response to the message.

Washington took the first substantial move toward reopening channels of communication with Beijing on 3 December 1969, when the American ambassador to Poland, Walter Stoessel, following Nixon's instructions, approached a Chinese diplomat at a Yugoslavian fashion exhibition in Warsaw. The diplomat, caught off guard, quickly fled from the exhibition site. However, Stoessel was able to catch the Chinese interpreter, telling him in "broken Polish" that he had an important message for the Chinese embassy.[49]

This time Beijing's response was swift. After receiving the Chinese embassy's report on the American ambassador's "unusual behavior," Zhou Enlai immediately reported it to Mao, commenting that "the opportunity now is coming; we now have a brick in our hands to knock the door [of the Americans]."[50] The premier acted at once to let the Americans know of Beijing's interest in reopening communication with Washington.

In mid-October, the U.S. consulate in Hong Kong had inquired with Guangdong provincial authorities about the conditions of two Americans who had been held in China since mid-February, when their yacht had strayed into China's territorial water off Guangdong. Early in November, the Chinese Foreign Ministry, regarding the American inquiry as an "intentional probe designed to see how China would respond," proposed that the two Americans be released "at a suitable time," and that the American embassy in Warsaw be informed of the release. The proposal had sat on Zhou's desk for almost one month until 4 December, when the premier decided to approve the Foreign Ministry's proposal. Two days later, after Mao approved Zhou's decision, the two Americans were freed.[51]

In the meantime, the Chinese embassy in Warsaw followed Beijing's instructions to inform the American embassy by telephone that Lei Yang, Chinese chargé d'affaires, was willing to meet Ambassador Stoessel. On 11 December 1969, Lei and Stoessel held an "informal meeting" at the Chinese embassy, at which the American ambassador, in addition to proposing a resumption of the ambassadorial talks, asked the Chinese to "pay attention to a series of positive measures the American side has taken in recent months."[52] The next day, after receiving Lei's three reports detailing the discussions, Zhou, while proposing to Mao to "hold off" resuming formal talks with the Americans "for a while" so as to "watch reactions from various sides," immediately met with K. M. Kaiser, the Pakistani ambassador to China. Through him, he asked Yahya Khan to inform Washington that "if President Nixon intends to resume contacts with China," he should first try to use the "official channel of communication in Warsaw."[53] One week later, Zhou's message was delivered by Agha Hilaly, Pakistani ambassador to the United States, in Washington.[54]

On 8 January, Lei and Stoessel held another informal meeting at the American embassy in Warsaw. The two sides agreed to resume the ambassadorial talks on 20 January, which would be held in turn at the Chinese and American embassies.[55] When the Sino-American ambassadorial talks formally resumed on 20 January at the Chinese embassy, Stoessel expressed Washington's intention to improve relations with China, stating that, in order to have a "more thorough discussion" on "any question" related to Sino-American relations, Washington was willing to dispatch an envoy to Beijing or accept one from the Chinese government in Washington. Lei Yang, already having received detailed instructions from Beijing concerning how to deal with different scenarios, replied that if Washington was interested in "holding meetings at higher levels or through other channels," the Americans might present more specific proposals "for discussion in future ambassadorial talks."[56]

The second formal meeting between Lei and Stoessel was scheduled to be held at the American embassy on 20 February 1970. Top leaders in Beijing carefully prepared for it. On 12 February, Zhou Enlai chaired a politburo meeting to draft instructions and prepare speech notes for Lei Yang. The politburo decided that Lei should inform the American side that "if the U.S. government is willing to dispatch a minister-level official or a special envoy representing the president to visit Beijing to explore further solutions to the fundamental questions in Sino-American relations, the Chinese government will receive him." The decision was approved by Mao on the same day.[57] When Lei met with Stoessel on 20 February, he highlighted the Taiwan issue, emphasizing that Taiwan was part of Chinese territory and that "withdrawal of all U.S. armed forces from the Taiwan Strait area" and the "solution of the Taiwan issue" were the preconditions for "fundamentally improving Sino-American relations." The Chinese chargé d'affaires, though, also mentioned that China was willing to "consider and discuss whatever ideas and suggestions" the American side would present to "reduce tensions between China and the United States and fundamentally improve the relations between them in accordance with the five principles of peaceful coexistence." In particular, he informed the American ambassador that the Chinese government "will be willing to receive" a high-ranking American representative in Beijing.[58]

This meeting turned out to be the last one of the decade-long Sino-American ambassadorial talks. After the meeting, President Nixon, eager to bring contact with Beijing to a higher and more substantial level, conveyed (again through Yahya Khan) the following message to Beijing: "We prepare to open a direct channel of communication from the White House to Beijing. If Beijing agrees [to establish such a channel], its existence will not be known by anyone outside the White House, and we guarantee that [we have] the complete freedom to make decisions." Zhou Enlai received the message on 21 March and commented: "Nixon intends to adopt the method of the [American-Vietnamese] negotiation in Paris and let Kissinger make the contact."[59]

But Nixon's message arrived at a bad time. Just a few days before, Prince Norodom Sihanouk, while on an annual vacation abroad, was removed by the National Assembly as Cambodia's chief of state, and the pro-American general Lon Nol became the head of the new government. Sihanouk went to Beijing and established an exile resistance government. In the meantime, the Khmer Rouge, now a Sihanouk ally, dramatically increased military activities in Cambodia with the cooperation of North Vietnamese troops. These new developments in Indochina complicated Washington's and Beijing's efforts to move forward with communications. On 24 March, in a report to Mao and Lin Biao, Zhou Enlai proposed to postpone the next Sino-American ambassadorial meeting until after mid-April; Mao approved.[60] In April, because Taiwan's vice premier Jiang Jingguo (Jiang Jieshi's son) was to visit the United States, the State Department found it "unwise to schedule talks with Peking [Beijing] in Warsaw within two weeks before or ten days after the trip," and thus the meeting date again was postponed to 20 May.[61]

Early in May, Nixon ordered American troops in South Vietnam to conduct a large-scale cross-border operation aimed at destroying Vietnamese Communist bases inside Cambodia. On 16 May, Zhou Enlai chaired a politburo meeting to discuss the situation in Indochina. The participants decided that the Sino-American ambassadorial meeting scheduled for 20 May in Warsaw should be postponed, that a statement would be issued in Mao's name to support the anti-American imperialist struggle throughout the world, and that anti-American protests and rallies would be held in major Chinese cities.[62] On 18 May, Beijing announced the postponement of the Sino-American talks in Warsaw. Two days later, when a million Chinese held a protest rally at Tiananmen Square, Mao issued a statement written in tough anti-American language, calling for "the people of the world to unite and defeat the U.S. aggressors and all their running dogs."[63]

Despite Beijing's renewed anti-American propaganda, the Nixon administration decided not to give up its effort to open channels of communication with China. In analyzing Mao's statement for Nixon, Kissinger found that "in substance . . . it is remarkably bland. . . . [I]t makes no threats, offers no commitments, is not personally abusive toward you [Nixon], and avoids positions on contentious bilateral issues." [64] On 15 June, Vernon Walters, military attaché at the American embassy in Paris, followed Washington's instructions to approach Fang Wen, the Chinese military attaché there, asking the Chinese to open another "confidential channel of communication" since the "Warsaw forum was too public and too formalistic." [65] But Beijing was not ready to come back to the table at the moment. On 16 June, at a politburo meeting chaired by Zhou Enlai, CCP leaders decided that, "given the current international situation," the ambassadorial talks in Warsaw "will be postponed further" and that only the Chinese liaison personnel would continue to maintain contacts with the Americans.[66] But Beijing did not want to allow the process toward opening relations with Washington to lose momentum completely. On 10 July, Beijing released Bishop James Walsh, an American citizen who had been imprisoned in China since 1958 on espionage charges.[67]

Beijing slowed the pace of opening communications with Washington in summer of 1970 not just because Nixon had ordered the invasion of Cambodia. A potential storm was brewing between two of China's most powerful men, Mao Zedong and Lin Biao, which forced the chairman to turn his main attention to domestic, and especially inner-party, affairs. After the party's Ninth Congress in April 1969 Lin's relations with the chairman turned sour, and they deteriorated rapidly during the summer of 1970. In designing China's new state structure reflecting "the achievements of the Cultural Revolution," Lin, as Mao's designated successor and China's second in command, argued that Mao should reclaim the position as chairman of the state, which, in Mao's eyes, reflected Lin's own ambition to occupy the position himself.[68] The struggle between Mao and Lin escalated significantly in the summer of 1970, leading to a de facto showdown between Mao and several of Lin's main supporters at a party Central Committee plenary session held from 23 August to 6 September at Lushan, the mountain summer resort for top party leaders. At one point, it seemed that Lin and his followers gained the support of most Central Committee members and that only after Mao personally addressed the plenary session did he control the situation.[69] This major power struggle at the Lushan conference occupied much of Mao's time and energy, making it difficult for him to take new steps in pursuing contacts with the Americans. Consequently, the process of opening relations with the United States was again deferred.

The Role of Edgar Snow

Mao began to refocus his attention on the Americans after he had temporarily stalled what he called "a serious struggle within the Central Committee" at the Lushan conference.[70] Like Nixon, Mao was not happy with the "formalistic" nature of the Warsaw channel. In contrast to the U.S. president, though, the Chinese chairman probably was ambivalent about entering direct secret contacts with Washington by receiving a high-level American envoy in Beijing. Because of some complicated concerns—to be discussed below—Mao, though willing to establish secret connections with Washington, did not want to follow the pace set by and communicate under terms defined by Washington.

In October and November 1970, Beijing received more overtures from Washington through Pakistan and Romania indicating that Nixon remained willing to dispatch a high-ranking representative to China.[71] Beijing's leaders decided to respond positively to these messages. On 14 November, Zhou Enlai told President Yahya Khan, who was in China for a state visit, that "if the American side indeed has the intention to solve the Taiwan issue," Beijing would welcome the U.S. president's "representative to Beijing for discussions." The premier also emphasized that this was the first time Beijing's response "has come from a Head, through a Head, to a Head."[72] One week later, in a meeting with Romanian vice premier Gheorghe Radulescu, Zhou asked China's "friends in Bucharest" to convey to Washington that the Chinese government would welcome Nixon's representative, or even Nixon himself, to Beijing to discuss "solving the Taiwan issue" and improving Sino-American relations.[73] Interestingly, Zhou also advised the Pakistanis and Romanians to hold the message for a while before delivering it to Washington. As a result, the Pakistanis did not convey the message to Washington until 9 December, and the Romanians, even later, not until 11 January 1971. Kissinger reported in his memoirs that he had found such delay puzzling.[74] The likely reason for the delay was that Mao, for the purpose of legitimizing the coming changes in Sino-American relations, was planning to make an initiative in his own way, and his vision had fallen on the American writer Edgar Snow.

Snow had been a friend of Mao and the Chinese Communists since the mid-1930s, when he visited the Chinese Communist base areas in northern Shaanxi province and interviewed Mao and many other CCP leaders. His highly acclaimed book, *Red Star over China*, published in 1938, helped create a positive image of the Chinese Communist revolution both within and outside China. After the PRC's establishment, Snow visited China in 1960 and 1965 and continued to write about the "great achievements" of Mao's "long revolution."[75]

Mao Zedong and Edgar Snow (far left) *looking down at Tiananmen, 1 October 1970. Between Mao and Snow is Chinese interpreter Ji Chaozhu. Xinhua News Agency.*

During the Cultural Revolution years, Snow attempted several times to revisit China, but he was unable to get a Chinese visa. The situation suddenly changed in August 1970. Snow, then living in Switzerland, received several urgent calls from Huang Zhen, the Chinese ambassador to France who was also one of the American writer's old friends. When Snow arrived at the Chinese embassy in Paris, he was urged by Huang to reapply for visiting China. The Chinese ambassador, in response to the American writer's complaint that Beijing had ignored him in previous years, told him that the invitation "comes from the top," promising that "he will be treated as a distinguished guest by Chairman Mao himself."[76]

On 1 October 1970, when Snow and his wife were invited to review the annual National Day celebration parade at the top of the Gate of Heavenly Peace, they were escorted by Zhou Enlai to meet Mao and stand by the chairman's side. A picture of Snow and Mao together was later printed on the front page of major Chinese newspapers.[77] Mao was sending a message, which he intended not only for the Americans but also for people all over China. Kissinger mentioned in his memoirs that Washington completely ignored this signal because the Chinese "overestimated our subtlety."[78] But, from Mao's perspective, it was more crucial for the Chinese people to notice it. For over two decades, the United States had been thoroughly demonized in the minds of Chinese people by the CCP's widespread anti-American propaganda campaigns and indoctrination efforts. Now, since the chairman was planning to pursue a new relationship with the United States, he would need to create a new American image in the Chinese people's minds. A subtle signal such as this one would serve to gradually prepare the Chinese people psychologically for big changes in Sino-American relations.[79]

Mao obviously did not invite Snow to Beijing merely to take a publishable photo, however. He also planned to use Snow in pursuit of larger goals. After several delays, the chairman received Snow on 18 December for a lengthy interview.[80] As far as the prospect of Sino-American relations was concerned, Mao's most noteworthy statement during the interview was that he was willing to receive Nixon in Beijing. The chairman told Snow that Beijing was considering allowing Americans of all political persuasions—Left, Right, and Center—to come to China. He particularly emphasized that he would like to welcome Nixon in Beijing because the U.S. president was the person with whom he could "discuss and solve the problems between China and the United States." The chairman made it clear that he "would be happy to meet Nixon, either as president or as a tourist."[81] After the interview, Snow received a copy of the interview transcribed by the Chinese interpreter Tang Wensheng (Nancy Tang) but was advised not to publish it "at the moment." Snow did not publish the interview "with the use of direct quotation" until April 1971.[82] According to Nixon, however, Washington "learned of Mao's statement [on welcoming Nixon to Beijing] within days after he made it."[83]

Kissinger regarded Mao's talks with Snow as another signal to Washington and speculated that the main reason that Beijing provided Snow with a verbatim transcript of the interview without permitting him to publish it right away was because the Chinese leaders wanted to heighten the signal's authenticity when it reached Washington.[84] In actuality, Mao's calculations were again related to his domestic concerns.[85] The chairman's five-hour interview with Snow covered a wide range of issues. In addition to Sino-American relations, he particularly focused on the Cultural Revolution. As the chairman had done on many other occasions, he argued compellingly that the Cultural Revolution was absolutely necessary because it exposed the "bad elements" by creating chaos "all under the heaven." But he also mentioned that he did not favor two tendencies prevailing during the Cultural Revolution: one was "not telling the truth," and the other was "the maltreatment of captives" in an "all-round civil war." This rare confession from the chairman on the fading status of the Cultural Revolution was also linked to his ongoing political struggle with Lin Biao. Implicitly targeting his designated "heir and successor" and the "Cultural Revolution star," the chairman claimed that it was too much and ridiculous for him to be called the "Great Teacher, Great Leader, Great Supreme Commander, and Great Helmsman" and that "one day every title will be eliminated except for the title 'Teacher.' "[86] Throughout the interview, Mao jumped freely between domestic and international topics, implying that improving relations with the United States would have to be closely interwoven with major changes in China's political and social life.[87] Indeed, when Mao was being interviewed by Snow, both the Americans and the Chinese people must have been his designated audience. Ironically, it appears that although he consciously defended the Cultural Revolution as much as he could, on a subconscious level he was virtually saying farewell to this most radical phase of his continuous revolution.

The transcript of Mao's interview with Snow was another masterpiece from the chairman designed to influence the minds of the Chinese masses. The content of this message, though, was different from that of any of the chairman's previous ones in that, rather than trying to encourage the people to enter a revolutionary movement, it attempted to convince them of the need to end an existing one. The chairman knew that such messages had to be delivered to the party and the nation in calculated ways. Indeed, Snow was the chairman's carefully picked agent—by having a well-known American sympathizer of the Chinese Communist revolution deliver the message, the chairman, as he had done so many times in his long political career, was staging an unconventional political drama, one that he hoped would justify the rapprochement with the Americans and convince the Chinese masses that his revolution was still alive. As does any drama, this one needed a climactic episode to produce its maximum effect. This episode was something Mao much needed but could not plan well in advance, although he must have believed that it would emerge during the course of events. Indeed, in a few months, that dramatic event took place, and it was what would be recorded in history as the "Ping-Pong diplomacy."

The Ping-Pong Diplomacy

In the first several months of 1971, the exchanges between Beijing and Washington turned quiet. Although both sides were willing to upgrade the discussions between them to higher levels, neither the Chinese nor American leaders seemed to know exactly how to take the next step. One major obstacle was determining the issues that should be on the discussion agenda. The differences between Beijing and Washington were tremendous in this regard. For Beijing's leaders, the key issue was America's military intervention in Taiwan. They had argued for over two decades that in order to improve Sino-American relations, Washington had to stop meddling in China's internal affairs. For Washington, however, the key to resolving the Taiwan issue lay in Beijing recognizing that the Guomindang had effective control over Taiwan and agreeing that any resolution of the matter must be reached by peaceful means. The Chinese and Americans also differed significantly on other international issues, such as how to end the military conflict in Vietnam, how to deal with the division between North and South Korea, and how to evaluate Japan's reemergence as an economic giant. On none of these questions was it easy for the two sides to reach a compromise. In fact, during their initial contact in Warsaw early in 1970, they had already found that the gaps between them were as wide as ever.[88] In order to close the gaps, both sides believed it necessary to hold bilateral meetings at higher levels. Before such talks could begin, policymakers in Beijing and Washington spent the early months of 1971 assessing diplomatic options and formulating negotiation strategies.[89]

In the meantime, both the Chinese and Americans were waiting for the opportunity to take the next step. This was especially important for Beijing. In addition to weighing the pros and cons of reaching a rapprochement with Washington strategically and geopolitically, Beijing's leaders, and Mao in particular, needed to find a "triggering event" that would allow them to mobilize and gain the Chinese people's support for establishing a new relationship with the United States. It was against this background that in April 1971 an opportunity appeared almost suddenly in Nagoya, Japan, where the Chinese Ping-Pong team was participating in the Thirty-first World Table Tennis Championships.

In 1967 and 1969, because of the chaos of the Cultural Revolution, Chinese table tennis players—the best in the world—failed to show up at the world championships. Late in 1970, Chinese players began to reappear in international competitions. Early in 1971, Koji Goto, president of the Japanese Table Tennis Association, visited China to invite the Chinese to participate in the forthcoming world championships in Nagoya.[90] From the beginning, Beijing regarded whether to dispatch a team to Japan as a political issue, especially because this would be the first time since the height of the Cultural Revolution that a Chinese sports team would attend a major international event. The opinions among Chinese sports and foreign affairs officials were by no means unanimous. For several reasons, such as the fear that the Chinese players might have to play with players representing the "puppet regimes" in South Vietnam and Cambodia and that they might be attacked by the right-wing elements in Japan, the leaders of the Foreign Ministry and National Commission on Sports almost decided not to let the Chinese team go to Japan.[91] Zhou Enlai and Mao Zedong in particular, however, finally decided that "our team should go."[92]

In the early 1970s, table tennis was the most popular sport in China and the only one in which the Chinese players could defeat anyone in the world. Not surprisingly, Chinese participation in the Nagoya championships turned out to be a big national event, causing widespread "Ping-Pong fever" throughout China's cities and countryside. When the Chinese players won one gold medal after another (they eventually won four golds out of seven events), the fever rose higher and higher. Through the extensive media coverage of the championships—which was rare for this kind of event during the Cultural Revolution years—millions and millions of ordinary Chinese paid close attention to Nagoya.[93] In the meantime, the Chinese team leadership, who had been instructed to make two to four phone calls back to Beijing every day, kept top leaders in Beijing abreast of any new development in Nagoya.[94]

During the course of the championships, Chinese and American players had several unplanned encounters. On 27 March, the Chinese players talked to a few American players at the championships' opening reception. The next day, officials of the Chinese delegation telephoned Beijing, reporting that "some American players were very friendly to our players at yesterday's reception, and had talked a lot."[95] Three days later, Graham B. Steenhoven, manager of the American delegation, encountered Song Zhong, general secretary of the Chinese delegation, at an International Table Tennis Association meeting break. Reportedly, Steenhoven mentioned that only two weeks earlier the U.S. State Department had terminated all restrictions on the use of American passports for traveling to China and asked Song "if the American players could have the opportunity to visit China to learn from the Chinese players." Officials of the Chinese delegation met the same evening to discuss the "implications" of Steenhoven's comments, and they decided to report to Beijing that "the Americans want to visit China."[96] Officials at the Chinese Foreign Ministry and National Commission on Sports treated the report seriously. After carefully discussing the matter, they concluded in a report on 3 April that "the timing now is not yet mature for the Americans to visit China, and the Americans should be advised that there will be other opportunities in the future." The report was sent to Zhou Enlai for approval.[97] On 4 April, Zhou endorsed the report, remarking in the margin, "[We] might ask them [the American players] to leave their mailing addresses with us, and might tell their chief representative that we Chinese people firmly oppose the activities aimed at

Chinese Ping-Pong player Zhuang Zedong presents American player Glenn Cowen with an embroidered silk scarf at the Thirty-first World Table Tennis Championships, Nagoya, Japan, 4 April 1971. Xinhua News Agency.

making 'two Chinas' or 'one China and one Taiwan.' " The premier, however, was uncertain about his decision and sent the report to Mao for the chairman to make the final ruling.[98]

While Zhou was writing these remarks in Beijing, another incident occurred between Chinese and American players. On the afternoon of 4 April, Glenn Cowen, a nineteen-year-old American player from Santa Monica College in California, accidentally boarded a bus carrying Chinese players. The Chinese all smiled, but no one extended him a greeting. Suddenly, three-time world champion Zhuang Zedong approached him, presenting him with an embroidered scarf with a picture of scenic Yellow Mountain on it as a gift. Zhao Zhenghong, the head of the Chinese delegation, tried to stop Zhuang, but Zhuang told him: "Take it easy. As the head of the delegation you have many concerns, but I am just a player. It doesn't matter." [99] Five minutes later, Cowen and the Chinese players got off the bus in front of a crowd of journalists, who most likely had gathered because it was such a big matter for the Chinese and American players to be on the same bus and friendly to each other. The next day, Cowen returned the favor by offering Zhuang a T-shirt with the Beatles' popular slogan "Let It Be" on it as a gift.[100] Again, the exchange was caught by journalists and cameras.

In Beijing, Mao had been following the events in Nagoya from the start. According to the memoirs of Wu Xujun, the chairman's chief nurse, even before the competition started the chairman had instructed her to read to him all foreign news reports published in *Cankao ziliao* with references to activities of the Chinese team in Nagoya. Wu recollected that during the championships, the chairman was constantly excited, was losing sleep, and did not have much of an appetite. Wu noted that Mao's state was usually a sign that he was thinking about big decisions.[101] Zhou's report regarding the American players visiting China had been sitting on Mao's desk for more than two days when, on 6 April, the chairman finally approved it and returned it to the Foreign Ministry.[102] Yet the chairman's concerns were far from over. When Wu read to him foreign news reports about the encounters between Zhuang Zedong and Cowen, the chairman's eyes "suddenly turned bright." He asked Wu to read the reports again, commenting that "Zhuang Zedong not only plays good Ping-Pong but knows how to conduct diplomacy as well." That evening Mao went to bed at around eleven o'clock after taking several sleeping pills. But before he fell asleep, he suddenly called Wu to his bed, asking the chief nurse to call Wang Hairong at the Foreign Ministry immediately and to "invite the American team to visit China." [103] Wu did not at first trust her own ears because the chairman had reversed completely the decision he had endorsed when his mind had been clear. But the chairman, despite being under the strong influence of medicine, insisted Wu make the phone call. Only after confirming that the chief nurse indeed had made the call did the chairman allow himself to get to sleep.[104]

Mao's sudden change of mind caused a sleepless night for Zhou Enlai and many others at the Foreign Ministry and National Commission on Sports.[105] The next day, Chinese officials with the Ping-Pong team in Nagoya received the order from Beijing to extend an invitation to the American table tennis team to visit China.[106] Upon learning of the invitation, the White House immediately approved it.[107] The Americans' activities during their visit to China were widely covered by the Chinese media. Indeed, the matches between Chinese and American players received live television and radio coverage.[108] The highlight of the visit was a meeting held on 14 April between the American team, together with teams from four other countries, with Zhou Enlai at the Great Hall of the People, at which the premier announced, "[Y]our visit has opened a new chapter in the history of the relations between Chinese and American peoples." [109] A few hours after Zhou met with the American players, Washington announced five new measures concerning China, including the termination of the twenty-two-year-old trade embargo. In a few short days, Ping-Pong diplomacy had completely changed the political atmosphere between China and the United States, making the theme of improving relations between the two countries—as Kissinger put it—"an international sensation" that "captured the world's imagination."[110]

Although we have no way of knowing exactly what had changed Mao's mind on the evening of 6 April, we have reasons to believe that such a decision, again, was made not only for international concerns but also for domestic considerations. When the Americans were playing China's most popular and strongest sport in front of a huge Chinese audience (especially if radio and television audiences were included) it was almost as if a modern version of the ritual procedures related to the age-old Chinese "tribute system," wherein the foreign barbarians came to China to pay tribute to the superior Chinese emperor, was taking place. The Chinese players were very friendly toward the Americans, even allowing them to win quite a few matches. In the eyes of the Chinese audience, though, this was not just an indication of friendship but also, and more importantly, a revelation of superiority. Mao's efforts to guide popular opinion culminated in the Chinese media's widespread reporting of a conversation between Zhou Enlai and the American player Cowen: According to the media, when Cowen asked the premier about his opinion on American hippies, the premier provided him with some sophisticated advice, combining an understanding of the "desire on the part of youth to try new things" with profound philosophical observations on "the rules in the development of human history." Zhou then, reportedly, received a bunch of flowers from Cowen's mother, who wanted to thank the premier for "educating her son."[111] Nothing could produce more penetrating symbolic power than this story showing how a member of capitalist America's decadent "lost generation" found answers to questions about the truth of life in socialist China.

Mao moved quickly to fit this new Chinese popular mood toward America into the orbit of the relations he was planning to pursue with the United States. The chairman looked to Snow once again. In addition to permitting the American writer to publish his interview in the West, the chairman ordered that the complete transcript of the interview—in which he said that he was willing to meet Nixon in Beijing—be relayed to the entire party and the whole country.[112] Mao's maneuvers, as it turned out, further prepared the Chinese people politically and psychologically for the forthcoming transformation of Sino-American relations.

Kissinger's Secret Trip to Beijing

In the wake of the Ping-Pong diplomacy, Beijing and Washington immediately worked on plans for the high-level meeting that had been discussed since late 1970. The Pakistani channel continued to play a crucial role in facilitating communications between the two sides. On 21 April, Beijing sent a message to Washington that reiterated that Taiwan was "the principal and prerequisite problem, which had to be resolved before any relations could be restored." In the meantime, Beijing's leaders also made it clear that they were "now interested in direct discussions" as a means of reaching settlement and thus willing to "receive publicly in Beijing a special envoy of the president of the United States (for instance, Mr. Kissinger) or the U.S. secretary of state or even the president of the U.S. himself for a direct meeting and discussion." [113]

The White House received the message on 27 April. Although Nixon found that "in some important respects this message raised as many problems as it solved," he and Kissinger immediately began to work on formulating Washington's response. Because of domestic political considerations, Nixon thought it necessary for the contact with Beijing "to be kept totally secret until the final arrangement for the presidential visit had been agreed upon." In terms of who should be the person to go to China, he decided that Kissinger was the best choice.[114] On 10 May, Kissinger handed Washington's formal reply to Pakistani ambassador Hilaly to deliver to Beijing. The message stated that because of the importance Nixon had attached to normalizing relations with China, he was prepared to accept Zhou Enlai's invitation to visit Beijing "for direct conversations" with PRC leaders. It also proposed that Kissinger undertake a preparatory secret visit sometime after 15 June to begin a preliminary exchange of views and arrange an agenda for Nixon's visit. Beijing received the message on 17 May.[115] Three days later, when Washington and Moscow reached a procedural breakthrough in the Strategic Arms Limitation Talks, Kissinger asked the Pakistanis to convey an advance copy of the U.S.-Soviet agreement to Beijing, with an accompanying message stating that Washington would "conclude no agreement which would be directed against the People's Republic of China." [116]

After receiving these messages, Mao instructed Zhou Enlai to chair a politburo meeting to work out the Chinese responses.[117] On 25 May, Zhou called a meeting attended by leading members of the Foreign Ministry to discuss the technical issues involved in responding to Nixon's messages.[118] The next day, the politburo met to consider Beijing's specific strategies toward improving Sino-American relations. Zhou followed Mao's instructions to deliver a keynote speech at the meeting, pointing out that the United States had reached the peak of its power after the end of the Second World War and thus could willingly interfere with "anything anywhere in the world" at that time. However, U.S. power had declined in recent years. America's intervention in Vietnam had lost the people's support, forcing Washington to withdraw American troops gradually from Vietnam. In the meantime, America's economic position and, as a result, its political influence in the world had begun to decline. Under these circumstances, speculated Zhou, American leaders had to consider whether to continue their "going-all-out" policy or to reduce America's international involvement. As the first step toward the second choice Washington needed to get out of Vietnam, and the Americans thus found it necessary to establish contact with China. These developments, stressed the premier, had provided China with "an opportunity to improve Sino-American relations," which "will be beneficial for the struggle against imperialist expansionism and hegemonism, beneficial for maintaining peace in Asia as well as in the world, and beneficial for maintaining our country's security and pursuing the unification of the motherland in peaceful ways." [119]

The decisions reached by the politburo were summarized in a report drafted by Zhou Enlai after the meeting, which established eight "basic principles" regarding Kissinger's and Nixon's proposed visits to China:

1. All U.S. armed forces and military installations should be withdrawn from Taiwan and the Taiwan Strait area in a given period. This is the key to restoring relations between China and the United States. If no agreement can be reached on this principle in advance, it is possible that Nixon's visit would be deferred.

2. Taiwan is China's territory, and the liberation of Taiwan belongs to China's internal affairs. No foreign intervention should be allowed. Japanese militarism in Taiwan should be strictly prevented.

3. We will strive to liberate Taiwan in peaceful ways and will carefully work on the Taiwan issue.

4. The activities aimed at making "two Chinas" or "one China and one Taiwan" should be firmly opposed. If the United States is willing to establish diplomatic relations with China, it must recognize the People's Republic of China as the sole legal government representing China.

5. If the previous three conditions have not been met, it is not suitable for China and the United States to establish diplomatic relations, and a liaison office can be established in each other's capital.

6. We will not initiate the question concerning [China's seat in] the UN. If the Americans touch upon this question, we will make it clear that no arrangement involving "two Chinas" or "one China and one Taiwan" is acceptable to us.

7. We will not initiate the question concerning Sino-American trade. If the

Americans touch upon this question, we will discuss it with them after the principle of American troops withdrawing from Taiwan has been accepted. 8. The Chinese government stands for the withdrawal of U.S. armed forces from the three countries in Indochina, Korea, Japan, and Southeast Asia, so that peace in the Far East will be maintained.[120]

These basic principles clearly demonstrated that Beijing's leaders, though willing to improve relations with the United States, were not quite ready to make major compromises with Washington, especially on the Taiwan issue. Such an attitude was not surprising given the profound chasm that had existed between Beijing and Washington for over two decades. In addition, because the politburo fully understood the importance of justifying the decision to pursue a rapprochement with the United States, it knew too well that the decision should not leave any impression that it had softened the party's fighting attitude toward U.S. imperialism. The report thus specifically enumerated several possible outcomes of opening relations with the United States, arguing that a Sino-American rapprochement would impair the American people's struggle against the "monopoly capitalist ruling class" and would enhance Hanoi's position at the Paris talks, thus forcing American troops to withdraw from Indochina. In particular, the report argued that the opening of Sino-American communications represented the "victorious result of our struggles against imperialism, revisionism, and reactionary forces," as well as the "inevitable outcome of the internal and external crises facing the U.S. imperialists and the competition for world hegemony between the United States and the Soviet Union." If the opening succeeded, the "competition between the two super powers" would be more fierce; if the opening failed, the "reactionary face" of U.S. imperialism would be further exposed, and "our people's consciousness" would be further enhanced.[121]

On 29 May, Mao approved Zhou's report.[122] The same day, the premier, again via the Pakistani channel, sent Beijing's formal responses to Washington, informing the Americans that Mao was looking forward to "direct conversations" with Nixon "in which each side would be free to raise its principal issue of concern" and that Zhou welcomed Kissinger to China "for a preliminary secret meeting with high-level Chinese officials to prepare for and make necessary arrangements for President Nixon's visit to Beijing."[123] Nixon received the message four days later, commenting, "This is the most important communication that has come to an American president since the end of World War II."[124]

In order to prepare for Kissinger's visit, Beijing established a special task force headed by Zhou to deal with all kinds of technical and logistical issues.[125] In the meantime, Beijing's leaders paid special attention to further justifying to party cadres and members the decision to open Sino-American relations. Beginning at the end of May, the CCP leadership convened a series of meetings, including a working meeting attended by more than two hundred "responsible cadres" from Beijing and other parts of China, to relay to them the party's new policy toward the United States. Zhou stressed that it was Nixon and Kissinger who were coming to Beijing, thus "it is not we who need something from them, but they who need something from us."[126] This tone dominated Beijing's efforts to explain the Sino-American opening to ordinary party members and people throughout the following months.

After careful planning, Kissinger secretly visited Beijing from 9 to 11 July. During the forty-eight hours he stayed in Beijing, he met with Zhou and other high-ranking Chinese officials in six meetings lasting for a total of seventeen hours.[127] The two men quickly established respect for each other. While Zhou found Kissinger "very intelligent — indeed a Dr.," Kissinger found Zhou "one of the two or three most impressive men I have ever met."[128] Although Beijing had repeatedly emphasized that unless progress could be reached on the Taiwan issue no other question would be discussed, Zhou had a flexible attitude. The most important breakthrough was reached on the first day, when each leader tried to comprehend the other's basic stand. Kissinger spent much time explaining Washington's policies on a series of international issues, including the Taiwan question. He stated that Washington would withdraw two-thirds of U.S. armed forces from Taiwan after the end of the Vietnam War and would continue to withdraw more troops from Taiwan in concert with further improvements in Sino-American relations. Contrary to the statement made by the State Department only a few months earlier that Taiwan's status was "unsettled," Kissinger made it clear that the United States acknowledged Taiwan as part of China and would not support Taiwan's independence. Within this context, he emphasized that Washington firmly believed that the Taiwan issue should be solved in a peaceful manner. In explaining Washington's policy toward Indochina, Kissinger told the Chinese that the Nixon administration was committed to ending the Vietnam War through negotiations and thus was willing to establish a timetable to withdraw American troops from South Vietnam, if America's honor and self-esteem were protected. Zhou seemed satisfied with Kissinger's statement on Washington's recognition of Taiwan as part of China. Although he continued to emphasize that all American troops must withdraw from Taiwan and the U.S.-Taiwan treaty must be abolished, he also stated that the differences between Beijing and Washington should not prevent the two sides from living in peace and equality.[129]

Immediately after the meeting, Zhou briefed Mao. The chairman's reaction was interesting. When he learned that Washington would withdraw some but not all of American troops from Taiwan, he commented that it would take some time for a monkey to evolve into a human being, and that the Americans were now at the ape stage, "with a tail, though a much shorter one, in his back." More important, the chairman told the premier, was the Indochina issue. "We are not in a hurry on the Taiwan issue because there is no fighting there," stated the chairman. "But there is a war in Vietnam and people are being killed there. We should not invite Nixon to come just for our own interests." The chairman instructed the premier not to focus on specific issues the next day but to "brag to" (*chui* in Chinese) Kissinger about the big "strategic picture," that "although all under the heaven is in great chaos, the situation is wonderful." In particular, Mao instructed, Zhou should tell the Americans that China was prepared "to be divided by the United States, the Soviet Union, and Japan, with them all coming together to invade China." [130]

Mao's attitude determined that Kissinger's visit would not fail. Although Kissinger stated that the United States would neither withdraw all its troops from Taiwan nor abolish the U.S.-Taiwan treaty immediately, the chairman paid more attention to what Washington would do—withdrawing U.S. forces from Taiwan gradually, acknowledging Taiwan as part of China, and not supporting Taiwan's independence. For the chairman, Kissinger had *already* made the most important concessions—had begun the process of changing from "monkey" to "human being"—and Mao was willing to provide the Americans with the time needed to complete the change in policy. Since Beijing had always viewed the Taiwan issue as the single, most important obstacle for restoring relations with the United States, such an attitude on the chairman's part meant that the Taiwan issue no longer would block Zhou and Kissinger from reaching an agreement on the agenda for Nixon's visit. Within this context, the chairman, as he always did when dealing with a superpower (which used to be the Soviet Union, and, now, the United States), consciously or unconsciously attempted to demonstrate his superior vision and moral standard. By making Vietnam, rather than Taiwan, a priority, Mao intended to exhibit Beijing's altruism in handling important international issues. By the same token, through highlighting the hypothesis that China might face a simultaneous attack from the Soviet Union, Japan, and the United States at a time of "chaos all under the heaven," Mao meant not only to force Kissinger to define Washington's strategic purposes in East Asia but also, and more importantly, to remind the Americans not to ignore China's centrality in dealing with world affairs in general and in solving Asian/Pacific issues in particular.

Following the chairman's instructions, Zhou completely changed his approach the next day. Using ideologically aggressive language to draw a picture of "great chaos all under the heaven," the Chinese premier presented Beijing's "principal stands" on a series of international issues, including Vietnam, India, Japan, Korea, and Taiwan, challenging Washington's policy toward them. Zhou's "fierce litany" (in Kissinger's words), however, was not designed to block the negotiations but, in a sense, to complete a particular "ritual procedure" that was needed for socialist China to reach a compromise with imperialist America. Thus when Kissinger returned with a point-by-point rebuttal of Zhou's presentation, the premier's attitude changed again. Toward the end of the meeting, he proposed that the two sides discuss the date for Nixon to visit China, and, with little bargaining, an agreement was reached: Nixon would come in spring 1972.[131]

Because Zhou was to host a reception for a North Korean delegation visiting Beijing that evening,[132] Huang Hua, the Chinese ambassador to Canada, was assigned to draft with Kissinger a joint announcement of Nixon's visit to China. When Huang, who was late to the meeting, finally arrived,[133] he proposed a draft indicating that Nixon had solicited the invitation to China for the purpose of discussing the Taiwan issue as a prelude to normalizing Sino-American relations. When Kissinger made it clear that such a draft was absolutely unacceptable, Huang proposed a thirty-minute recess at 1:40 A.M. so that the Chinese could "rework on the language." At 3:00 A.M. the Americans were told that Huang would not come back until 9:00 A.M. Kissinger was puzzled by all of this. What he did not know was that Huang failed to return because he needed to get Mao's approval for a new draft to present to the Americans, but the chairman had already gone to bed.[134] When the meeting was resumed at 9:40 A.M., Huang presented a new draft, which Kissinger immediately found agreeable. It stated that Zhou Enlai extended the invitation "knowing of President Nixon's expressed desire to visit the People's Republic of China" and that the purpose of his visit "is to seek the normalization of relations between the two countries and also to exchange views on questions of concern to the two sides."[135] Thus Kissinger was able to send a one-word telegram to Washington, "Eureka," which, as agreed upon in advance, indicated that his Beijing trip was a success.[136] On 15 July, Beijing and Washington announced simultaneously that Nixon was to visit China "at an appropriate date before May 1972."

The Shock Wave of the "Lin Biao Affair"

Kissinger's trip to China shocked America's Asian allies; it also brought about suspicion, and even tension, between China and its allies and close friends. On 13–14 July, Zhou Enlai visited Hanoi to inform the Vietnamese Communist leaders of Beijing's contacts with the Americans. Within twenty-four hours, he held three meetings with Le Duan and Pham Van Dong. Zhou emphasized that it was Beijing's belief that, from a long-term perspective, Beijing's improved relations with Washington would help policymakers in Washington to better understand the reality that America's global strategic emphasis lay in Europe, rather than in Asia, and in turn would enhance Hanoi's bargaining power at the negotiation table.[137] Early on the morning of 14 July, Zhou flew to Pyongyang to brief the North Korean Communist leader Kim Il-sung, and, after having two meetings lasting for seven hours, flew back to Beijing in the evening.[138] Late the same evening, he met with and briefed Prince Sihanouk, who was then the leader of Cambodia's anti-American exile government in Beijing.[139] On 17 July, Zhou met with Xhorxihi Ropo, Albania's ambassador to China, and explained to him Beijing's new policy toward the United States.[140] Although Zhou must have tried his best to defend Beijing's new policy, it appears that he had barely convinced many of those who listened to him. The Vietnamese regarded Beijing's contact with Washington as China "throwing a life buoy to Nixon, who almost had been drowned."[141] Albania, which had been China's closest Communist ally during the Cultural Revolution, adopted an even harsher attitude, claiming that the Chinese had "betrayed" the cause of the world proletarian revolution.[142]

However, these international difficulties must have meant almost nothing to Mao in comparison with the huge domestic political storm that had been brewing during the same period. The potential for a battle between Mao and Lin Biao that might have distracted the chairman from taking action toward the United States in summer 1970 did not disappear after the Lushan conference. From late 1970 to mid-1971, Mao tried to uncover the "conspiracy activities" of several high-ranking party and military leaders within Lin Biao's inner circle, an endeavor that gradually exposed Lin himself.[143]

Kissinger's secret trip to Beijing occurred at the same time that the Mao-Lin contest had reached a crucial juncture. Late on the evening of 9 July, when Zhou Enlai and his assistants briefed Mao about the meetings with Kissinger, the chairman left the topic to spend more than one hour investigating whether or not several of Lin's close followers in the PLA's General Staff had made serious "self-criticism." When he learned that none of them had done so, he announced that "the struggle beginning at the Lushan conference has not finished yet" and that "behind them [Lin's followers] there is a big plot." [144] Late in August, the chairman began an inspection tour of south China, during which he repeatedly criticized Lin, revealing that he was preparing to have a political showdown with the man who, only two years earlier, had been designated as his "heir and successor." Reportedly, upon learning of Mao's activities, Lin's son, Lin Liguo, who had organized a squadron loyal to himself and his father, decided to stake everything on a desperate gamble—at his order, his squadron tried, but failed, to assassinate the chairman when he was returning to Beijing by train. Early on the morning of 13 September, Lin, his wife, and his son boarded a plane to flee from Beijing. A few hours later, the plane crashed in Mongolia. [145]

While much is still unknown about Lin Biao's exact motives for fleeing Beijing on 13 September 1971, the Lin Biao affair had influenced the development of the Sino-American rapprochement in two important respects. First, Lin Biao's downfall represented one of the biggest political crises in the PRC's history. Although Lin Liguo's alleged coup attempt was crushed and Lin Biao died, this was by no means Mao's victory. Since the early days of the Cultural Revolution, Lin had been known in China as Mao's "closest comrade-in-arms" and "best and most loyal student." He was handpicked by the chairman to be his "heir and successor." His reported betrayal not only completely buried the myth of Mao's "eternal correctness" but also, and more seriously, further withered Mao's fading continuous revolution. Under these circumstances, Mao was even more in need of a major breakthrough in China's international relations, one that could help boost the chairman's declining reputation and authority while enhancing the Chinese people's support for Mao's Communist state—if not necessarily for Mao's Communist revolution.

Second, Lin Biao's downfall might have removed a political obstacle as well as provided additional political justification for Beijing to improve relations with the United States. Although our knowledge about Lin Biao's exact attitude toward Sino-American rapprochement remains limited because of the lack of reliable sources, several official Chinese sources have pointed out that Lin opposed improving relations with the United States. [146] This claim appears to have the support of other available materials. For example, although Zhou Enlai almost always sent his reports on the United States to both Mao and Lin for approval, we almost never see any response from Lin. If silence implies objection, Lin's downfall certainly meant that a powerful opponent to Sino-American rapprochement had been eliminated. What is more certain is that Lin's ruin inevitably enhanced the position of Zhou Enlai, a strong advocate of opening China's relations with other parts of the world in general and the United States in particular. Therefore, we may safely conclude that although the Lin Biao affair began as a serious challenge to Mao, it turned out to be favorable to the Sino-American rapprochement.

Closing Moves

Not surprisingly, although the shock wave of the Lin Biao affair brought China's political situation into unprecedented chaos,[147] Mao, with Zhou's assistance, decided to continue the course toward rapprochement with the United States. The communications between Beijing and Washington became more direct after Kissinger's trip: in addition to the Pakistani channel, a new secret "Paris channel" was established. Vernon Walters and Huang Zhen, American and Chinese ambassadors to France, were assigned by Washington and Beijing to serve as messengers.[148]

In order to settle important details for Nixon's visit, Kissinger openly visited Beijing on 20–26 October. During his seven-day stay in Beijing, he and Zhou Enlai held ten meetings, which lasted a total of twenty-three hours and forty minutes.[149] In addition to exchanging opinions on a host of international issues and resolving specific items related to Nixon's visit (such as media coverage), the most difficult challenge facing the two leaders was to work out a draft summit communiqué. Before coming to China, Kissinger had prepared a draft in which he emphasized the common grounds shared by Beijing and Washington while using vague language to describe the issues on which the two had sharp differences. On the evening of 22 October, when Kissinger handed the draft to Zhou, the Chinese premier's first response was that although the draft was unsatisfactory, it could serve as the basis for discussion. When the two met again on the morning of 24 October, however, Zhou's attitude had changed dramatically. Declaring the American draft "totally unacceptable," the premier pointed out that the communiqué must reflect the fundamental differences between Beijing and Washington and not present an "untruthful appearance."[150]

Behind this dramatic change was Mao himself. As he was listening to Zhou's brief on his meetings with Kissinger on the evening of 23 October, the chairman told the premier, "I have said many times that all under the heaven is great chaos, so it is desirable to let each side speak out for itself." If the American side wanted to talk about "peace, security, and no pursuit of hegemony," the chairman continued, then the Chinese side should emphasize "revolution, the liberation of the oppressed peoples and nations in the world, and no rights for big powers to bully and humiliate small countries." The chairman acknowledged that stressing these goals was no more than "firing an empty cannon," yet he stressed at the same time that "all of these points must be highlighted; anything short of that is improper." [151]

Mao's sensitivity toward, as well as insistence upon, producing a summit communiqué that would "truthfully" reflect China's overall position revealed his determination not to allow Nixon's visit to jeopardize his revolution's image at home and abroad. More important, though, Mao aimed to demonstrate to the Americans his moral superiority in handling important international issues. What the Americans had proposed was a conventional agreement, one that would make the chairman's unprecedented acceptance of Nixon's visit look like no more than an ordinary diplomatic venture. The chairman wanted to emphasize the drama of the visit and thereby put the Chinese in an "equal" (as Mao defined the term), thus more superior, position vis-à-vis the Americans.

When, on the evening of 24 October, Kissinger received the Chinese draft communiqué that had been approved by Mao, his first reaction was disbelief. But when he had finished reading this document full of "empty cannons" and had time to reflect, he "began to see that the very novelty of the [Chinese] approach might resolve our perplexities." [152] The two sides then started working on a mutually acceptable draft that not only defined common grounds but also used clear yet moderate language to state each side's views on important issues. The most difficult in this regard was, of course, Taiwan. When Kissinger departed from Beijing on 26 October, the two sides had reached agreement on almost all points except for a few specific expressions concerning Washington's attitude toward Taiwan.[153]

When Kissinger was in Beijing, the United Nations General Assembly voted with the support of an overwhelming majority to let Beijing have China's seat at the UN and expel Taipei from it. This development was immediately propagated throughout China as a "great victory" of Chinese foreign policy as well as an indication of the "significant enhancement" of the PRC's international status and reputation.[154] In internal indoctrinations, the "victory" was also linked to Mao's "brilliant decision" to open relations with the United States. At a time when Mao and his revolution had suffered the loss of the Chinese people's inner support in the wake of the Lin Biao affair, the breakthrough in China's external relations, which allowed Beijing's leaders to proclaim that Mao's revolution had indeed transformed China from a weak country into a prestigious world power, played an increasingly important role in providing legitimacy to Mao's Communist regime.

Within this context, when Alexander Haig, Kissinger's deputy on the national security staff, visited China in early January 1972 to make the final technical preparations for Nixon's visit, he inadvertently offended his Chinese hosts. At a meeting with Zhou Enlai on 4 April, Haig delivered an assessment from Nixon and Kissinger about the recently concluded India-Pakistan crisis, which made clear that in managing the crisis the American leaders were concerned about China's viability and believed that maintaining it was in the fundamental interests of the United States. When Zhou reported the meeting to Mao, the chairman commented: "Why should our viability become America's concern? . . . If China's independence and viability should be protected by the Americans, it is very dangerous [for us]."[155] On 6 January, Zhou formally told Haig that he was "greatly surprised" by the American leaders' concern for "protecting China's independence and viability." It was Beijing's firm belief, the premier asserted, that "no country should depend upon a foreign power in maintaining its own independence and viability" because the dependent country "would become that [foreign] power's subordinate and colony."[156] Such emphasis—or overemphasis—on Beijing's determination to maintain China's independence and self-esteem reflected the CCP leaders' understanding of the importance of the viability issue in legitimizing the Communist regime in China.

On 21 February, Nixon arrived in Beijing. He had hardly settled down at the guest house when Zhou Enlai informed him that Mao was ready to meet him. The conversation between the Chinese chairman and the U.S. president lasted one hour and seems not to have had a central focus.[157] The chairman refused to get into details of any specific issues, announcing that he would only "discuss philosophical questions." It appears that the chairman was eager to demonstrate his broad vision, showing the Americans that not only was he in total control of matters concerning China, but he also occupied a privileged position to comprehend and deal with *anything* of significance in the known universe. In a sense, what was most meaningful for the chairman was not the specific issues he would discuss with the U.S. president but the simple fact that Nixon and Kissinger came to *his* study to listen to *his* teachings. The chairman probably was revealing some of his truest feelings when he said that he had "only changed a few places in the vicinity of Beijing." Yet, at the bottom of his heart, he also must have believed that he had indeed changed the world—had he not, the "head of international imperialism," would not have come to visit his country in the first place.

The Taiwan issue remained the key to finalizing the text of the joint communiqué, which Kissinger and Qiao Guanhua, China's vice foreign minister and one of Zhou's main associates, were responsible for composing. The main

Zhou Enlai greets Richard Nixon at the Beijing airport, 21 February 1972.
Xinhua News Agency.

challenge was finding a mutually acceptable expression of the United States'
stand toward the linkage between Washington's agreement to withdraw U.S.
troops from Taiwan and Beijing's commitment to a peaceful settlement of the
Taiwan issue. Although this was a sensitive issue for the Chinese because they
had to stick to the principle that anything concerning Taiwan "belonged to
China's internal affairs," they showed flexibility by allowing compromises to
be reached.[158]

On 28 February, the Sino-American joint communiqué was signed in

Mao Zedong and Richard Nixon shake hands at Zhongnanhai, Beijing, 21 February 1972. Xinhua News Agency.

Shanghai. This was an unconventional document in that in addition to emphasizing common grounds, it also highlighted differences between Beijing and Washington, with each side expressing in its own way its basic policies toward important international issues. From Beijing's perspective, such a format best served China's fundamental interests. In a geopolitical sense, Nixon's visit did establish the framework in which a strategic partnership could be constructed between China and the United States. The Shanghai communiqué announced that neither Beijing nor Washington "should seek hegemony in the Asia-Pacific region and each is opposed to efforts by any other country or group of countries to establish such hegemony"—a statement implicitly targeting the Soviet Union. More importantly, especially for Mao, the unique format of the communiqué allowed China not only to remain a revolutionary country but also to claim an equal footing with the United States in the world. Not just for propaganda purposes did Beijing claim that Mao had won a "great diplomatic victory."

Yet this was not a victory for international communism. As one of the most important events in the international history of the Cold War, the Sino-

American rapprochement, along with the deterioration of relations between Beijing and Moscow, caused the most profound shift in the international balance of power between the two contending superpowers. Whereas the great Sino-Soviet rivalry (first in the ideological field and then in military and strategic spheres) further diminished Moscow's capacity to wage a global battle with the United States, the Sino-American rapprochement enormously enhanced Washington's strategic position in its global competition with the Soviet Union. More importantly, the great Sino-Soviet split buried the shared consciousness among Communists and Communist sympathizers all over the world that communism was a solution to the problems created by the worldwide process of modernization. Nothing could be more effective in destroying the moral foundation of communism as an ideology and a revolutionary way of transforming the world than the self-denial of such possibility through the mutual criticism of the Communists themselves. Although the Cold War did not end until the late 1980s and early 1990s, when both the Soviet Union and the Communist bloc collapsed, one of the most crucial roots of that collapse certainly can be traced to the reconciliation between Beijing and Washington in 1969–72.

EPILOGUE
THE LEGACIES OF
CHINA'S COLD WAR
EXPERIENCE

Mao Zedong died on 9 September 1976. After a short period of leadership transition (1976–78), with Hua Guofeng serving as the nominal party and state head, Deng Xiaoping ascended in the late 1970s to become China's paramount leader.[1] China has since experienced a profound derevolutionization process, which has undermined Mao's revolution both as an ideal and as a reality, and has sunk the Communist state into an ever-deepening legitimacy crisis.

That Mao's revolutionary enterprise had lost people's inner support had become evident during the chairman's last years of life. Following the Lin Biao affair in 1971, a societywide "crisis of faith" began, causing millions and millions of everyday Chinese to question the ultimate benefits of the continuous revolution that prevailed in China for over two decades. When tens of thousands of ordinary men and women occupied Tiananmen Square early in April 1976 to mourn the late premier Zhou Enlai, who had died in January of that year, they meant to demonstrate the profound popular dismay over the economic stagnation and political cruelty conferred on the Chinese people by the chairman's revolution. Mao, who was then only a few months away from "the moment of departing to meet Karl Marx," ordered a dramatic crackdown of the masses at the square.[2] By reacting this way, the chairman virtually was admitting that his revolutionary enterprise aimed at placing a new social order in the hearts and minds of his own people had failed.

Deng Xiaoping was purged by Mao, for the second time in the Cultural Revolution, during the 1976 Tiananmen incident. The purge, though, allowed Deng to understand better than Mao the depth of the widespread moral crisis existing among ordinary Chinese. When he reemerged to become China's new ruler, he immediately abandoned Mao's class-struggle-centered discourse and his practice of continuous revolution, placing at the top of his agenda modernizing China's industry, agriculture, national defense, and science and technology. Following his pragmatic "cat theory" — "black cat or white cat, so long as it catches mice, it is a good cat" — Deng allowed economics to take precedence over politics, hoping that the improvement of people's standard of living would help bring legitimacy back to the Communist state.[3]

Along with implementing these domestic changes, the Chinese government under Deng's leadership dramatically reduced and, finally, stopped its support to revolutionary/radical nationalist states and movements in other parts of the world while adopting a new, open approach in China's external relations. Throughout the Maoist era, China maintained only minimal exchanges with other countries. Starting in the late 1970s and early 1980s, Deng took several important steps, including dispatching Chinese students to study abroad, promoting China's international trade, and welcoming foreign investments in China, to open China's door to the rest of the world.[4] As a result, the interconnections between China and the outside world have increased significantly, strengthening the interdependence between China and other parts of the world (especially the West). More than two decades before, Mao's China entered the Cold War as a revolutionary country, in its own terms defining many key aspects of the Cold War — and the Cold War in Asia in particular. With Mao's death and the end of his revolution as well as Deng's altering the basic courses of China's external policies, the Cold War in Asia — as far as some of its fundamental features are concerned — virtually came to an end in the late 1970s, almost one decade before the conclusion of the global Cold War.

But the legacies of China's Cold War experience will not fade away easily. A conspicuous example is the CCP's one-party reign, which has persisted during the post-Mao age. In addition, China's reform and opening policies, not surprisingly, have been highly unbalanced: Emphasis has been placed on the economic and technological fields, leaving politics and ideology a forbidden zone. Indeed, despite Beijing's general abandonment of revolutionary discourses during the post-Mao age, the CCP leadership has repeatedly called upon the party and the whole nation to fight against the influence of "bourgeoisie liberalization," warning ordinary Chinese people to boycott the "spiritual pollution" of Western influence as a side effect of China's opening to the outside world.[5] As has been identified by many China scholars, the huge gap between this political stagnation and the rapid social and economic changes brought about by the reform and opening process was one of the most important causes underlying the Tiananmen tragedy in 1989.[6]

In international affairs, the legacies of China's Cold War experience have been reflected in Beijing's frequent criticism and occasional challenge to the existing Western-dominated international economic and political order. Post-Mao Chinese leaders have consistently claimed that under no circumstances will the Chinese government allow foreign powers to impose their values on China's external behavior, or to use their norms to interfere with China's internal affairs. Since the Tiananmen bloodshed in 1989, the increasing criticism by other countries, especially those in the West, of Beijing's human rights abuses and hard-nosed policy toward Tibet and, more recently, Taiwan, have further offended Beijing's leaders. Beijing has persistently rebutted such criticism, claiming it to be a continuation of Western countries' interference with matters within the jurisdiction of Chinese sovereignty.[7] In these ways, a "Cold War" of another kind has continued between China and the West since the formal ending of the global Cold War in the late 1980s and early 1990s.

Behind China's behavior is the profound influence of the lingering Chinese "victim mentality." As has been pointed out throughout this volume, the Chinese have consistently regarded their nation as a victimized member of the Western-dominated international systems in modern history. During the Cold War period, this belief served as one of the most important reasons behind Mao's China's revolutionary behavior. The Chinese victim mentality persists today, as revealed in the Chinese responses toward NATO's mistaken bombing of the Chinese embassy in Belgrade in May 1999. Despite repeated U.S. explanations and apologies, the Chinese government, with the apparent support of a majority of the Chinese people, claimed the bombing to be an "American plot" designed to humiliate and intimidate China and the Chinese people. As a result, the government-controlled Chinese media resumed using Cold War language to denounce "Western imperialism" and "U.S. hegemonism."[8] A decade after the end of the global Cold War, China is no longer a revolutionary country, but it is not a real "insider" of the international community either.

Many Western analysts have been concerned about the orientation of China's future development, worrying that if China becomes stronger economically and militarily, it will pose a serious threat to world peace and stability in the twenty-first century. In a few extreme cases, the PRC is equated with Hitler's Germany, and the crisis scenario that could be created by the "China threat" is compared to "a Cold War as bad as the last."[9] They thus argue that in order to change China into a more "responsible" or, at least, less dangerous, member of the international community, it is necessary to "constrain" or to "contain" China, so that Beijing's leaders will be forced to behave less aggressively under pressure from without.

However, as is indicated in this volume, the reality is that China's external behavior has been primarily shaped by domestic concerns—both under Mao and continuously in the post-Mao era. Here is one of the biggest paradoxes facing both China and the rest of the world today: Although China is increasingly growing into a prominent world power, thus bearing considerable regional and global responsibilities, the orientation of China's external behavior is determined less by its connections with important regional or global issues than by an agenda overwhelmingly dominated by domestic dilemmas and challenges.

In this respect, Beijing's harsh attitude toward Taiwan—an issue created during the Cold War—is highly revealing. Despite facing great international pressures, Beijing's leaders have stubbornly refused to renounce military force as a possible means to resolve the Taiwan issue. Every time Beijing is criticized for maintaining such a coercive policy, its leaders have argued that the Taiwan issue is an internal Chinese problem and that their adoption of a Taiwan policy that does not exclude the use of force is necessary for maintaining China's sovereignty and territorial integrity.[10]

What should be emphasized is that, underlying Beijing's inflexible policy toward Taiwan is, again, the impact of the deepening legitimacy crisis facing the Chinese Communist state in the post–Cold War era. From a historical perspective, the CCP has justified its one-party reign by emphasizing two of the Chinese Communist revolution's fundamental missions: that the revolution would create in China a new, Communist society characterized by universal justice and equality; and that it would change China's status as a weak country and revive its central position on the world scene. Mao's revolution, although failing to end political privilege in Chinese society, succeeded in creating an egalitarian situation (though accompanied by poverty) in China's economic life. The post-Mao derevolutionization process, in challenging the economic poverty left over by Mao, has created sharp divisions between the rich and the poor within Chinese society, thus undermining Maoist egalitarianism both as an ideal and as a social reality. The Chinese Communist Party today, as the political scientist Thomas J. Christensen points out, "has all but obliterated the second of the two adjectives in its name."[11] As a consequence, the legitimacy of the Chinese *Communist* regime is seriously called into question.

Under these circumstances, the Chinese Communist state must attach more importance to the Chinese revolution's second mission in its effort to legitimize its existence. Appealing to the victim mentality among the Chinese people, the CCP has justified its one-party reign by promoting the view that without the CCP's successful revolution, China would have remained a weak, corrupt, and divided country with no status on the world scene. Consequently, maintaining China's unification and sovereignty becomes an issue of utmost importance for the CCP, and Taiwan represents a crucial test case in this regard.

In a deeper sense, this legitimacy crisis is not just one entangling the Chinese Communist state; it epitomizes a fundamental puzzle facing Chinese society in the post–Cold War era: If the ideology embodied in communism can no longer bind the nation together and direct the nation's path toward modernity, which "ism" (if any) could take over the mission? The lack of an answer to this basic question has caused a lingering moral crisis among the Chinese population (especially the younger generation). What is more, although this moral crisis has arisen from the failure of the Chinese Communist state, one of its direct political consequences is that it enhances the popular conviction that the Chinese Communist government must remain in power. The logic is simple: without the Chinese Communist regime—despite all of its deficiencies—things in China could get worse and, in the worst-case scenario, the Chinese nation and Chinese society could even suffer total disintegration.

The CCP's legitimacy crisis and the Chinese moral crisis not only reflect the uncertainty and extreme complexity of the course of China's political, economic, and social changes in the post–Cold War age but also increases the difficulty involved in predicting the role China will play in international affairs in the twenty-first century. Indeed, China's role in international affairs depends upon the outcome of China's political, economic, and social transformations.

China's hope of emerging from the shadow of the Cold War lies in the fate of the ongoing reform and opening (derevolutionization) process—only with its success will China become a genuine "insider" of the international community and consistently play the role as a coordinator and promoter of regional and global peace and stability. This process, indeed, involves the greatest transformation—political, economic, social, and cultural—China has ever experienced in its history. Two decades after its inauguration, the process presents tremendous challenges for the Chinese people, causing profound frustrations for China's intellectuals (especially in the face of the deepening moral crisis). The triumph of this transformation may lead China to economic prosperity, social stability, and political democratization. Indeed, these three goals of the process are closely interrelated—a China that is increasingly becoming an integral part of the regional and world economic system will have a larger stake in maintaining regional and global peace and stability; and a Chinese society that is dominated by a strong middle class will be more receptive to democratic political institutions characterized by checks and balances. At the same time, the triumph of the process will create an environment in which the Chinese "victim mentality" may gradually lose its appeal, enabling China to emerge as an equal member and a genuine "insider" of the international community. Such a China will play a highly positive role in security, economic, and environmental affairs in the Asia-Pacific region and the whole world.

By contrast, the failure of the process could lead to China's disintegration — this is particularly true since how to identify "China" remains a tough challenge for the Chinese people.[12] If the process fails, in a worst-case scenario, China's nuclear arsenal could get out of control; China's efforts to protect its environment could completely collapse; over a billion Chinese could make neighboring regions panic by creating huge migratory flows; and it would be impossible for China to play a key role in promoting regional and world stability and peace.

As far as the possible outcome of this process is concerned, the first fifteen to twenty years of the twenty-first century will be crucial. This is largely due to the anticipated result of two important developments. First, Chinese leaders, as well as a majority of Chinese scholars, have targeted the years 2015–20 as a deadline for achieving a series of goals in improving China's economy, polity, environment, and quality of life. Second, in fifteen to twenty years, the last generation of Chinese leaders who grew up in the Chinese revolutionary era will have disappeared completely from the central stage of Chinese politics. As a result, a new generation of Chinese leaders, who have gained their education and political experience in a more open environment, will find it much less difficult to commit themselves to transforming China into a true democracy and thus enabling China to become a true "insider" of the international community.

Although it is impossible for other countries (and those in the West in particular) to dictate the basic direction of China's derevolutionization process, there are things that can be done to help facilitate China's continuous integration into the international community and to help China rid itself of the last influences of the Cold War:

- Great and consistent efforts should be made to understand China's perspectives and problems; under no circumstances should a "second Cold War" be waged against China.
- Exchanges with China should be greatly strengthened in all areas, especially in economic and cultural fields, and the Chinese "victim mentality" should be handled with deep sensitivity.
- China's contributions to regional and global peace and stability should be adequately acknowledged and properly encouraged.
- Long-term perspectives should be adopted in formulating strategies and policies toward China. We should never be frustrated by China's

lack of sufficient change in the short run; we should never surrender an attitude of goodwill toward China.

- China should not be regarded as a passive reactor to outside influence; in order for China to play a stabilizing role in Asia-Pacific and global affairs, the international regimes should reform themselves by incorporating China's specific concerns and values.

The Cold War ended a decade ago, and now is the time finally to say farewell to its legacies. In looking into China's future, there is reason for optimism to prevail. In the final analysis, we must remember that China is one of the oldest and most continuous civilizations in the world. We should have confidence in the Chinese people's ability to make rational choices for their nation's future development, as well as to define the role their nation should play in regional and global affairs in the twenty-first century.

NOTES

Abbreviations

CCA	Chinese Central Archives, Beijing
CCFP	Zhang Shuguang and Chen Jian, eds., *Chinese Communist Foreign Policy and the Cold War in Asia: New Documentary Evidence, 1944–1950* (Chicago: Imprint Publication, 1996)
CWIHP*B*	Cold War International History Project *Bulletin*
DZJJG	Han Huaizhi et al., *Dangdai Zhongguo jundui de junshi gongzuo* (The Military Affairs of the Contemporary Chinese Army), 2 vols. (Beijing: Zhongguo shehui kexue, 1989)
FRUS	U.S. Department of State, *Foreign Relations of the United States* (Washington, D.C.: Government Printing Office, 1862–)
JMZW	*Jianguo yilai Mao Zedong wengao* (Mao Zedong's Manuscripts since the Founding of the People's Republic of China), 13 vols. (Beijing: Zhongyang wenxian, 1987–97)
LC	Library of Congress, Washington, D.C.
LSN	Liu Chongwen and Chen Shaoshou et al., comps., *Liu Shaoqi nianpu* (A Chronological Record of Liu Shaoqi), 2 vols. (Beijing: Zhongyang wenxian, 1996)
LSW	*Jianguo yilai Liu Shaoqi wengao* (Liu Shaiqi's Manuscripts since the Founding of the People's Republic of China), vol. 1 (Beijing: Zhongyang wenxian, 1999)
MZJW	*Mao Zedong junshi wenji* (A Collection of Mao Zedong's Military Papers), 6 vols. (Beijing: Junshi kexue, 1993)
MZN	*Mao Zedong nianpu* (A Chronological Record of Mao Zedong), 3 vols. (Beijing: Zhongyang wenxian and Renmin, 1993)
MZW	*Mao Zedong wenji* (A Collection of Mao Zedong's Works), 8 vols. (Beijing: Renmin, 1993–97)
MZWW	*Mao Zedong waijiao wenxuan* (Selected Diplomatic Papers of Mao Zedong) (Beijing: Shijie zhishi, 1994)
MZX	*Mao Zedong xuanji* (Selected Works of Mao Zedong), 5 vols. (Beijing: Renmin, 1965 and 1977)
NA	National Archives, College Park, Maryland
NSA	National Security Archive, Gelman Library, George Washington University, Washington, D.C.
PDN	*Peng Dehuai nianpu* (A Chronological Record of Peng Dehuai) (Beijing: Renmin, 1998)
RG	Record Group

Odd Arne Westad, Chen Jian, Stein Tønnesson, Nguyen Vu Tung, and James G. Hershberg, eds., *77 Conversations between Chinese and Foreign Leaders on the Wars in Indochina, 1964–1977*, CWIHP Working Paper no. 22 (Washington, D.C.: Woodrow Wilson International Center for Scholars, May 1998)

ZEJW   *Zhou Enlai junshi wenxuan* (Selected Military Papers of Zhou Enlai), 4 vols. (Beijing: Renmin, 1997)

ZENA   Jin Chongji et al., *Zhou Enlai nianpu, 1898–1949* (A Chronological Record of Zhou Enlai, 1898–1949) (Beijing: Zhongyang wenxian and Renmin, 1989)

ZENB   Jin Chongji et al., *Zhou Enlai nianpu, 1949–1976* (A Chronological Record of Zhou Enlai, 1949–1976), 3 vols. (Beijing: Zhongyang wenxian, 1998)

ZEWHDJ   The Diplomatic History Institute under the PRC Foreign Ministry, *Zhou Enlai waijiao huodong dashi ji, 1949–1975* (Important Events in Zhou Enlai's Diplomatic Activities, 1949–1975) (Beijing: Shijie zhishi, 1993)

ZEWW   *Zhou Enlai waijiao wenxian* (Selected Diplomatic Papers of Zhou Enlai) (Beijing: Zhongyang wenxian, 1990)

ZJG   The Editorial Group for the History of Chinese Military Advisers in Vietnam, ed., *Zhongguo junshi guwentuan yuanyue kangfa douzheng shishi* (A Factual Account of the Participation of the Chinese Military Advisory Group in the Struggle of Assisting Vietnam and Resisting France) (Beijing: Jiefangjun, 1990)

ZZWX   *Zhonggong zhongyang wenjian xuanji* (Selected Documents of the CCP Central Committee), 18 vols. (Beijing: Zhonggong zhongyang dangxiao, 1989–92)

Introduction

1. John Lewis Gaddis, *We Now Know: Rethinking Cold War History* (New York: Oxford University Press, 1997), 238. For a critical survey of the "new" Cold War history scholarship, see Melvyn P. Leffler, "The Cold War: What Do 'We Now Know'?" *American Historical Review* 104, no. 2 (April 1999): 501–24.

2. For a more detailed discussion, see Chen Jian, "Not Yet a Revolution: Reviewing China's 'New Cold War Documentation,'" a paper presented at a conference titled "The Power of Free Inquiry and Cold War International History," 25–26 September 1998, National Archives at College Park, Maryland. The paper is now available at http://www.nara.gov/research/coldwar/coldwar.html.

3. Andrew J. Nathan and Robert S. Ross, *The Great Wall and the Empty Fortress: China's Search for Security* (New York: W. W. Norton, 1997), 13.

4. John Lewis Gaddis, *Strategies of Containment: A Critical Appraisal of Postwar American National Security Policy* (New York: Oxford University Press, 1982), ch.

4; Ernest May, ed., *American Cold War Strategy: Interpreting NSC-68* (Boston: St. Martin's Press, 1993).

5. Vladislav Zubok and Constantine Pleshakov, *Inside the Kremlin's Cold War: From Stalin to Khrushchev* (Cambridge, Mass.: Harvard University Press, 1996), 54–62; Sergei Goncharov, John Lewis, and Xue Litai, *Uncertain Partners: Stalin, Mao, and the Korean War* (Stanford, Calif.: Stanford University Press, 1993), ch. 2, esp. 55–61.

6. Shi Zhe, "With Mao and Stalin: Liu Shaoqi in Moscow," *Chinese Historians* 6 (Spring 1993): 84–85; see also discussions in Chen Jian, *China's Road to the Korean War: The Making of the Sino-American Confrontation* (New York: Columbia University Press, 1994), 74–75.

7. Zhou Enlai, "The Enemy's Defeat and Our Victory," 11 December 1952, *ZEJW*, 4:292–305.

8. Vojtech Mastny, *The Cold War and Soviet Insecurity: The Stalin Years* (New York: Oxford University Press, 1996), 12.

9. Xue Mouhong et al., *Dangdai zhongguo waijiao* (Contemporary Chinese Diplomacy) (Beijing: Zhongguo shehui kexue, 1988), 4–5. For a more detailed discussion of Mao's China as a revolutionary country, see Chen Jian, *China's Road to the Korean War*, ch. 1.

10. This, of course, also meant that Mao's China would present challenges not only to the United States and other Western powers, but to the Soviet Union as a dominant world power as well.

11. In this regard, we only need to recall the "lost China" debate and, closely related to it, the emergence of the McCarthyism hysteria in the United States. The fear of Red China was at the core of the second "Red Scare."

12. For a more detailed discussion of Mao's "intermediate zone" theory, see Chen Jian, *China's Road to the Korean War*, 18–21; for the CCP's view of the connections between anti-imperialist/anticolonialist movements in non-Western countries and the "proletarian world revolution," see, for example, Mao Zedong, "Talks with the American Correspondent Anna Louise Strong," *MZX*, 4:1191–92; Liu Shaoqi, "On Internationalism and Nationalism," *Renmin ribao* (People's Daily), 7 November 1948; and Liu Shaoqi, "Speech at the Trade Union Meeting of Asian and Oceanic Countries," *Xinhua yuebao* (New China Monthly), 1 (1949): 440.

13. Gaddis, *We Now Know*, 283.

14. Here we see the predominant impact of Hans Morgenthau, author of the highly influential classic *Politics of Nations: The Struggle for Power and Peace* (New York: Knopf, 1948), and other influential "realist" theorists, such as George Kennan. For an informative review of the evolving scholarship in the field, see Douglas MacDonald, "Communist Bloc Expansion in the Early Cold War," *International Security* 20 (Winter 1995–96): 152–83; for a critical review emphasizing the failure of various schools of international relations theory to predict the development of the Cold War, see John Lewis Gaddis, "International Relations Theory and the End of the Cold War," *International Security* 17 (Winter 1992–93): 5–58.

15. Melvin Gurtov and Byong-Moo Hwang, *China under Threat: The Politics of*

Strategy and Diplomacy (Baltimore: Johns Hopkins University Press, 1980); see also essays by Nakajima Mineo, Thomas Robinson, and Jonathan Pollack in *The Cambridge History of China*, ed. Denis Twitchett and John K. Fairbank, vols. 14 and 15 (Cambridge, Eng.: Cambridge University Press, 1987 and 1991).

16. See, for example, telegram, Mao Zedong to Stalin, 2 October 1950, *JMZW*, 1:550–52; see also related discussions in Chapter 3.

17. See discussions in Chapter 6.

18. See discussions in Chapter 8.

19. See discussions in Chapters 4 and 7.

20. Mao Zedong, "Report to the Second Plenary Session of the CCP's Seventh Central Committee," *MZX*, 4:1439–40.

21. Edgar Snow, "A Conversation with Mao Tse-tung [Mao Zedong]," *Life* 70 (30 April 1971): 48.

22. Instruction, CCP Central Committee, "On Diplomatic Affairs," 18 August 1944, *CCFP*, 13–17.

23. Telegram, CCP Central Committee to CCP Northeast Bureau, 10 November 1948, quoted from Jin Chongji et al., *Zhou Enlai zhuan, 1898–1949* (A Biography of Zhou Enlai, 1898–1949) (Beijing: Zhongyang wenxian, 1998), 1:739; telegram, Mao Zedong to CCP Tianjin Municipal Committee, 20 January 1949; the original document is kept at the CCP Central Archives in Beijing.

24. For an insightful discussion, see Zhang Shuguang, "In the Shadow of Mao: Zhou Enlai and New China's Diplomacy," in *The Diplomats, 1939–1979*, ed. Gordon A. Craig and Francis L. Loewenheim (Princeton, N.J.: Princeton University Press, 1994), 337–70.

25. In 1958, when Marshal Chen Yi replaced Zhou Enlai as foreign minister, Zhou warned Chen that "you must remember that as foreign minister you have no decision-making power, you must report to the politburo and Chairman Mao, follow his instructions, and carry out his decisions" (author's interviews with Chen Xiaolu, June 1992); see also Chen Xiaolu, "Chen Yi and China's Diplomacy," in *Chinese Communist Foreign Relations, 1920s–1960s*, ed. Michael H. Hunt and Niu Jun (Washington, D.C.: Asian Program, Woodrow Wilson Center for International Scholars, 1994), 89–112.

26. For further discussion, see Xue Mouhong et al., *Dangdai zhongguo waijiao*, ch. 17.

27. According to Alastair Iain Johnston, of the major powers, the People's Republic of China during Mao's times was the most frequently involved in major military confrontations. See his *Cultural Realism: Strategic Culture and Grand Strategy in Chinese History* (Princeton, N.J.: Princeton University Press, 1996), 256–57.

28. This certainly was the case when Mao and his comrades made the decision to enter the Korean War. As I have argued elsewhere, in addition to defending the safety of the Chinese-Korean border, Mao made the decision to dispatch Chinese troops to Korea to promote revolutionary China's international prestige and reputation, to encourage an "Eastern Revolution" that would follow the Chinese model, and to further the domestic mobilization that would enhance the CCP's new regime at home. See Chen Jian, *China's Road to the Korean War.*

29. For these sources please refer to the Bibliographic Essay at the end of this volume.

30. William Stueck, *The Korean War: An International History* (Princeton, N.J.: Princeton University Press, 1995), 9.

31. My ongoing research project is tentatively titled "Revolution under the Heaven: Mao's China Encounters the World, 1949–1976." I intend to adopt a sociocultural approach to the study, using multi-archival/multisource research to pursue a broad and sophisticated understanding of the dynamics, conceptual resources, discourses, and, most important of all, human experiences involved in Mao's attempt to transform China's state, society, and international outlook.

Chapter One

1. For a summary of Jiang's reign in China from 1927 to 1939, usually known as the "Nanjing decade," see Lloyd Eastman, *The Abortive Revolution: China under Nationalist Rule, 1927–1937* (Cambridge, Mass.: Harvard University Press, 1974).

2. Recent Western and Chinese studies all agree that by 1936, the Communist forces in northern Shaanxi could hardly survive another of Jiang's all-out suppression campaigns. See, for example, Joseph Esherick, "Ten Theses on the Chinese Revolution," *Modern China* 21 (January 1995): 53; see also Yang Kuisong, *Zhonggong yu mosike de guanxi, 1920–1960* (The CCP's Relations with Moscow, 1920–1960) (Taipei: Dongda, 1997), 328–29.

3. The best study on the Xi'an incident in English literature remains Tienwei Wu, *Sian Incident: A Pivotal Point in Modern Chinese History* (Ann Arbor: Center for Chinese Studies, University of Michigan, 1976). Yang Kuisong's recent study, *Xi'an shibian xintan: Zhang Xueliang yu zhonggong guanxi zhi yanjiu* (A New Study of the Xi'an Incident: Exploring the Relations between Zhang Xueliang and the CCP) (Taipei: Dongda, 1995), uses previously unavailable CCP documents to shed much fresh light on this topic.

4. For an informative discussion of the history of Nationalist China during the war years, see Lloyd Eastman, *Seeds of Destruction: Nationalist China in War and Revolution* (Stanford, Calif.: Stanford University Press, 1984); for a discussion maintaining that Jiang's experiences during the war years both strengthened and weakened his position, and that "he won by failing, and failed by winning," see John Garver, "China's Wartime Diplomacy," in *China's Bitter Victory: The War with Japan, 1937–1945,* ed. James C. Hsiung and Steven Levine (Armonk, N.Y.: M. E. Sharpe, 1992), 3–32, esp. 27–28.

5. See Mao Zedong, "Problems in Strategy in the Guerrilla War against Japan," May 1938, *MZX,* 2:395–428.

6. See, for example, telegram, Mao Zedong to Peng Dehuai, 12 and 21 September 1937, *MZJW,* 2:44, 53–54.

7. For more detailed discussions of the CCP's military and political strategy during the war years, see Tienwei Wu, "The Chinese Communist Movement," in Hsiung and Levine, eds., *China's Bitter Victory,* 79–106, and Lyman P. Van Slyke, "The Chinese Communist Movement during the Sino-Japanese War, 1937–1945,"

in *The Cambridge History of China*, ed. Denis Twitchett and John K. Fairbank (Cambridge, Eng.: Cambridge University Press, 1986), 13:609–722; see also Chen Yungfa, *Zhongguo gongchan geming qishinian* (Seventy Years of the Chinese Communist Revolution) (Taipei: Lianjing, 1998), 315–32.

8. For discussions of the Wannan incident, see Tienwei Wu, "Chinese Communist Movement," 99–100; Van Slyke, "Chinese Communist Movement during the Sino-Japanese War," 665–71; for a documentary collection compiled by CCP historians, see Jin Zhi, ed., *Wannan shibian* (The Wannan Incident) (Beijing: Zhonggong dangshi, 1990).

9. Telegram, Mao Zedong to Zhou Enlai, Dong Biwu, and Ye Jianying, 23 January 1941, CCA; see also telegram, Mao Zedong, Zhu De, and Wang Jiaxiang to Peng Dehuai and Liu Shaoqi, 19 January 1941, and telegram, Mao Zedong to Zhou Enlai, Peng Dehuai, and Liu Shaoqi, 20 January 1941, *MZN*, 2:258–59, 260.

10. Circular by the Military Commission of the Nationalist Government on the Wannan Incident, 17 January 1941, Jin Zhi, ed., *Wannan shibian*, 124–26.

11. See *FRUS, 1941,* 4:81–86; see also the discussion in Michael Schaller, *The U.S. Crusade in China, 1937–1945* (New York: Columbia University Press, 1979), 48–49.

12. Telegram, Dimitrov to Mao Zedong, 25 January 1941, quoted from Yang Kuisong, *Zhonggong yu mosike de guanxi*, 462–63.

13. Jiang Jieshi, *Zhongguo zhi mingyun* (China's Destiny) (Chongqing: n.p., 1943).

14. See Mao Zedong, "Questioning the Guomindang," *MZX,* 3:905–12; see also the discussions in Wang Gongan et al., *Guogong liangdang guanxi tongshi* (A History of the Relations between the CCP and the GMD) (Wuhan: Wuhan daxue, 1991), 681–83.

15. For example, the inflation had made *fabi*, China's official currency, virtually wastepaper by 1944–45, although Jiang's government had received large amounts of financial aid from the United States since 1941. Compared with the standard of 1938, China's average price index at the end of 1944 had multiplied by 755. See Arthur N. Young, *China's Wartime Finance and Inflation, 1937–1945* (Cambridge, Mass.: Harvard University Press, 1965), 304.

16. In the spring and summer of 1944, the Japanese conducted a massive offensive on mainland China, known as the Ichi-go campaign, aimed at reestablishing the "imperial continental transportation line." The GMD troops collapsed under the Japanese offensive. For an informative account of the Ichi-go campaign, see Lloyd Eastman, "Nationalist China during the Sino-Japanese War," in Twitchett and Fairbank, eds., *Cambridge History of China*, 13:580–84.

17. Department of Military History under the Chinese Academy of Military Sciences, *Zhongguo renmin jiefangjun zhanshi* (A History of the Chinese People's Liberation Army) (Beijing: Junshi kexue, 1988), 2: appendix 4.

18. For a critical discussion of these aspects of the Chinese Communist movement during the war years, see Mark Selden, *China in Revolution: The Yenan Way Revisited* (Armonk, N.Y.: M. E. Sharpe, 1995); see also Chen Yungfa, *Zhongguo gongchan geming qishinian*, 332–85.

19. Quoted from Yang Kuisong, *Zhongjian didai de geming* (Revolution in the Intermediate Zone) (Beijing: Zhonggong zhongyang dangxiao, 1992), 391.

20. Instruction, CCP Central Committee, "On the Current Situation and the Party's Tasks," 25 December 1944, *ZZWX*, 14:431-34.

21. See, for example, telegram, Mao Zedong to Li Xiannian, 15 July 1944; telegram, Mao Zedong, Liu Shaoqi, and Chen Yi to CCP Central China Bureau, 3 August 1944; instruction, CCP Central Military Commission (CMC) to CCP Central China Bureau, 24 October 1944; and instruction, CCP Central Committee, "On the Current Situation and the Party's Tasks," 25 December 1944, *ZZWX*, 14:282-84, 302, 386-87, 431-34.

22. Report, CCP Southern Bureau, "Opinions on Diplomatic Affairs and Suggestions to the Central Committee," 16 August 1944, and instruction, CCP Central Committee, "On Diplomatic Affairs," 18 August 1944, *CCFP*, 5-17.

23. Instruction, CCP Central Committee, "On Establishing an Anti-Japanese United Front in the Asian-Pacific Area," 9 December 1941, in Chinese Central Archives, comp., *Zhonggong zhongyang kangri zhanzheng shiqi tongyi zhanxian wenjian huibian* (Selected United Front Documents of the CCP Central Committee during the War of Resistance against Japan) (Beijing: Dang'an, 1986), 3:587-89.

24. See *CCFP*, 10; see also telegram, CCP Central Committee to Lin Ping, 13 March 1945, *ZEJW*, 2:480-81.

25. CCP leaders widely used the term "democracy" in the 1940s, especially in denouncing Jiang Jieshi's "dictatorship." Scholars should not be confused by this phenomenon. As Mao made clear in "On New Democracy," the CCP defined "democracy" as "the other side of proletarian dictatorship," which had nothing to do with establishing political institutions with checks and balances. Before the CCP seized power, the party leadership's constant emphasis on "democracy" was a tactic designed to strengthen the party's position in its confrontation with the GMD government. For examples of how Mao emphasized democracy and nationalism in talks with Americans visiting Yan'an, see Joseph W. Esherick, ed., *Lost Chance in China: The World War II Dispatch of John S. Service* (New York: Random House, 1974). Particularly revealing are the records of Service's interview with Mao on 23 August 1944 (295-307).

26. For accounts of the Dixie mission's visit to Yan'an, see David D. Barrett, *Dixie Mission: The United States Army Observer Group in Yenan, 1944* (Berkeley: Center for China Studies, University of California-Berkeley, 1970); see also Carolle J. Carter, *Mission to Yenan: American Liaison with the Chinese Communists, 1944-1947* (Lexington: University Press of Kentucky, 1997). Yan'an celebrated warmly that year's 4th of July, praising President Roosevelt as "the great friend of the Chinese people." See *Jiefang ribao* (Liberation Daily), 4 and 5 July 1945.

27. On Wallace's visit to China and the tasks Roosevelt assigned to it, see Henry A. Wallace, *The Price of Vision: The Diary of Henry A. Wallace, 1942-1946*, ed. John Morton Blum (Boston: Houghton Mifflin, 1973), 332-33, 347-59.

28. For a brief yet informative discussion of the Jiang-Stilwell controversy, see Schaller, *U.S. Crusade in China*, ch. 8; for a Chinese account, see Wei Chuxiong,

"The Stilwell Affairs and Its Causes," in *Jindaishi yanjiu* (Modern History Studies, Beijing), no. 1 (1985).

29. For a recent general discussion of Hurley's mission, see Odd Arne Westad, *Cold War and Revolution: Soviet-American Rivalry and the Origins of the Chinese Civil War* (New York: Columbia University Press, 1993), ch. 1; for a critical Chinese account, see Niu Jun, *Cong heerli dao maxieer: Meiguo tiaoting guogong maodun shimo* (From Hurley to Marshall: American Mediation of the GMD-CCP Contradiction) (Fuzhou: Fujian renmin, 1988); for the text of the five-point agreement, see Lyman P. Van Slyke, ed., *The China White Paper, August 1949* (Stanford, Calif.: Stanford University Press, 1967), 74–75.

30. For the text of Jiang's three-point plan, see Van Slyke, ed., *China White Paper*, 75.

31. Telegram, Mao Zedong and Zhou Enlai to Wang Ruofei, 12 December 1944, and telegram, Mao Zedong to Zhou Enlai, 28 January 1945, *MZN*, 2:564–65, 574.

32. Instruction, CMC, "On Our Strategies toward the Reactionary U.S. China Policy," 7 July 1945, *CCFP*, 24–25.

33. Telegram, Mao Zedong to Zhou Enlai, 3 February 1945, ibid., 21.

34. Telegram, CCP Central Committee to Lin Ping, 26 October 1944 and 13 March 1945, *ZZWX*, 14:388–90, 15:59–60.

35. For a good discussion about the deal reached between Washington and Moscow on China at Yalta, see Westad, *Cold War and Revolution*, ch. 1.

36. *Zhonghua minguo zhongyao shiliao chubian* (A Preliminary Compilation of Important Historical Materials of the Republic of China) (Taipei: Guomindang dangshi weiyuanhui, 1981), Series III, 2:542–43, 546–47.

37. Instruction, CCP Jin-Cha-Ji Bureau, "On Actively Preparing for Cooperating with Soviet Military Operations," 18 April 1945. Mao Zedong ordered that the directive be conveyed to the whole party. See Niu Jun, *Cong yan'an zouxiang shijie: Zhongguo gongchandang duiwai guanxi de qiyuan* (From Yan'an Marching toward the World: The Origins of the CCP's Foreign Relations) (Fuzhou: Fujian renmin, 1992), 164.

38. Mao Zedong, "On Coalition Government," *MZX*, 3:1029–1100; see also discussions in Westad, *Cold War and Revolution*, ch. 3.

39. Mao Zedong, "Concluding Remarks at the CCP's Seventh Congress," 31 May 1945 (Yan'an mimeograph edition), from Yang Kuisong, *Zhonggong yu mosike de guanxi*, 519–20; see also *MZW*, 3:393, where Mao's joke is not included.

40. Quoted from Wang Gongan et al., *Guogong liangdang guanxi tongshi*, 752.

41. Rong Fengyuan, ed., *Zhongguo guomindang lici daibiao dahui ji zhongyang quanhui ziliao* (A Collection of Materials about Guomindang's National Congresses and Central Committee Plenary Sessions) (Beijing: Guangming ribao, 1985), 2:960.

42. Ibid., 921–22.

43. *Zhonghua minguo zhongyao shiliao chubian*, III, 2:573–615; for an excellent account of the Stalin-Soong meetings, see Westad, *Cold War and Revolution*, ch. 2.

44. Telegram, CCP Central Committee to CCP Guangdong Regional Committees, 16 June 1945, *CCFP*, 23–24.

45. Telegram, CCP Central Committee to Zheng Weisan, Li Xiannian, and Chen Shaomin, 4 August 1945, ibid., 26.

46. Mao Zedong, "The Last Battle against the Japanese Bandits," *MZX*, 3:1119.

47. For the text of a series of Zhu De's orders, see *Jiefang ribao*, 12 August 1945.

48. Telegram (drafted by Mao Zedong), CCP Central Committee to Zheng Weisan, Li Xiannian, and Chen Shaomin, 10 August 1945, and telegram (drafted by Mao Zedong), CCP Central Committee to Wang Zheng and Wang Shoudao, 11 August 1945, *MZN*, 3:1-2.

49. Report, Wang Ruofei to a party cadres' meeting at Yan'an, 13 August 1945, quoted from Niu Jun, *Cong yan'an zouxiang shijie*, 172-73. Wang was a member of the CCP politburo and CCP Central Secretariat.

50. See, for example, telegram, CCP Central Committee to the CCP Jin-sui and Jin-Cha-Ji Branches, 12 August 1945, *MZN*, 3:3.

51. See Mao Zedong, "The Situation after the End of the War and Our Policies," 13 August 1945, *MZX*, 4:1133-34.

52. Ibid., 1134.

53. Telegrams, Commander of the [CCP-led] 18th Army Corps to Jiang Jieshi, 13 and 16 August 1945, ibid., 1141-46.

54. Under Japan's military pressure, after 1938, Jiang and the GMD government moved to Chongqing, a city in the inland Sichuan province. During the war years, Sichuan and several neighboring provinces in southwestern China had since been called the "Great Rear" (*Da houfang*).

55. For a more detailed discussion, see Westad, *Cold War and Revolution*, 48-56.

56. *Zhongyang ribao* (Center Daily, Chongqing), 16 August 1945. Mao did not respond to the telegram. Jiang then sent two more telegrams on 20 and 23 August, to invite Mao to go to Chongqing. See *Zhongyang ribao*, 22 and 25 August 1945.

57. Cited from *MZN*, 3:13, and Shi Zhe, *Zai lishi juren shenbian: Shi Zhe huiyilu* (At the Side of Historical Giants: Shi Zhe's Memoirs), rev. ed. (Beijing: Zhonggong zhongyang dangxiao, 1998), 274-75. (Shi Zhe was Mao's Russian-language interpreter.) Although many Chinese sources have referred to these two telegrams, their originals have not been located in CCP Central Archives.

58. In fact, Mao and the other CCP leaders would never forget Stalin's betrayal of the Chinese revolution at this critical historical moment. Mao would repeatedly express his disappointment in, or even anger at, Stalin's betrayal in the years to come. See, for example, *Dangshi ziliao tongxun* (Party History Newsletter, Beijing), no. 22 (1982): 13.

59. Instruction, CMC, "On the Changes of Our Strategic Policy," 22 August 1945, *CCFP*, 29-30.

60. Minutes, Mao Zedong's speech to the CCP politburo meeting, 23 August 1945, ibid., 30-32.

61. Minutes, Mao Zedong's speech at a CCP politburo meeting, 26 August 1945, ibid., 32-33.

62. Inner Party Circular, CCP Central Committee, "On Conducting Peace Negotiations with the GMD," 26 August 1945, *MZN*, 3:15.

63. For a detailed account of the Jiang-Mao meetings in Chongqing, see Zhou Yonglin et al., *Chongqing tanpan jishi* (A Factual Record of the Chongqing Negotiations) (Chongqing: Chongqing, 1991).

64. On 26 August, the CCP leadership stated in an inner-party circular that since the Northeast had been covered by the Sino-Soviet treaty, and that the terms of the treaty granted the administrative power there to the GMD, it was uncertain whether it was still feasible for the party to send troops and cadres to the Northeast. See *MZN*, 3:15.

65. Yang Kuisong, *Zhonggong yu mosike de guanxi*, 529–30; see also instruction, CCP Central Committee to CCP Shandong Bureau Branch, 11 September 1945, *ZZWX*, 15:274–75. In this instruction, the CCP leadership observed that "our party and our army are now experiencing excellent conditions for development in the Northeast," and they thus directed the Shandong Bureau Branch to dispatch four divisions of troops to the Northeast.

66. Niu Jun, *Cong yan'an zouxiang shijie*, 185.

67. Instruction, CCP Central Committee, "Enter the Northeast and Control the Vast Rural Area," 29 August 1945, *CCFP*, 33–35.

68. Zeng Kelin, *Zeng Kelin jiangjun zishu* (General Zeng Kelin's Autobiography) (Shenyang: Liaoning renmin, 1997), 108–11 (General Zeng was one of the top commanders of CCP forces in the Northeast); see also Yang Kuisong, *Zhonggong yu mosike de guanxi*, 531–33; Niu Jun, *Cong yan'an zouxiang shijie*, 187.

69. Instruction, CCP Central Committee, "Maintaining a Defensive in the South and Waging an Offensive in the North," 19 September 1945, *CCFP*, 35–37. Since Mao was then in Chongqing, Liu Shaoqi drafted the decision, and Mao approved it.

70. On the landing operations of the U.S. Marines, see Henry I. Shaw Jr., *The United States Marines in North China* (Washington, D.C.: Historical Branch, G-3 Division, Headquarters, U.S. Marine Corps 1968), 1–5. For the CCP's assessment of the consequences of American marines landing in northern China, see instruction, CCP Central Committee, "On Our Policy after the Landing of American Troops," 29 September 1945, and Directive, CCP Central Committee, "Firmly Resist the Landing of American Troops," 6 October 1945, *CCFP*, 37, 40–41.

71. On the London conference, see Robert L. Messer, *The End of an Alliance: James F. Byrne, Roosevelt, Truman, and the Origins of the Cold War* (Chapel Hill: University of North Carolina Press, 1982), ch. 7, and Michael Schaller, *The American Occupation of Japan* (New York: Oxford University Press, 1985), 58–60; for analysis on Stalin's response to the London conference, see Westad, *Cold War and Revolution*, 119.

72. Yang Kuisong, *Zhonggong yu mosike de guanxi*, 542.

73. Telegram, Peng Zhen and Chen Yun to CCP Central Committee, 4 October 1945, CCA. In this telegram, Peng and Chen, two top CCP leaders in the Northeast, also reported that "the Soviet side has made the final determination to completely open the front door [in the Northeast] for us, putting us in charge of the affairs there."

74. Telegram, CCP Central Committee to CCP Northeast Bureau, 19 October 1945, *ZZWX*, 15:364.

75. Note, Chinese Foreign Ministry to Soviet Embassy in China, 15 November 1945, *Zhonghua minguo zhongyao shiliao chubian*, VII, 1:147.

76. Telegram, Jiang Jieshi to Harry Truman, 17 November 1945, ibid., 168–71.

77. Yang Kuisong, *Zhonggong yu mosike de guanxi*, 549.

78. *Zhonghua minguo zhongyao shiliao chubian*, VII, 1:154–56.

79. The CCP leadership made it clear that in order to "avoid complicating the Soviet Union's international obligations," the party had to agree to the Soviet request. See *CCFP*, 49.

80. Yang Kuisong, *Zhongjian didai de geming*, 415.

81. Telegram, CCP Central Committee to CCP Northeast Bureau, 20 November 1945, *CCFP*, 49–50.

82. *FRUS, 1945*, 7:603–5, 612–13, 627–28, 635–37.

83. Statement by President Truman on United States Policy toward China, 15 December 1945, in Van Slyke, ed., *China White Paper*, 607–9.

84. For discussions of the origins of the Marshall mission, see Westad, *Cold War and Revolution*, ch. 6; see also Steven Levine, "A New Look at American Mediation in the Chinese Civil War: The Marshall Mission in Manchuria," *Diplomatic History* (Fall 1979). For a recently published collection of studies on different aspects of the Marshall mission, see Larry I. Bland, ed., *George C. Marshall's Mediation Mission to China* (Lexington, Va.: George C. Marshall Foundation, 1998).

85. Mao Zedong, "On Coalition Government" and "The Situation Following the Victory of the War against Japan and Our Policy," *MZX*, 3:973, 1024–25; see also Zhou Enlai, "The GMD-CCP Negotiations," 5 December 1945, *Zhou Enlai 1946 nian tanpan wenxuan* (Zhou Enlai's Negotiation Papers, 1946) (Beijing: Zhongyang wenxian, 1996), 1–16.

86. Instructions, CCP Central Committee, "How to Deal with the Changing U.S. Policy toward China," 19 December 1945, *CCFP*, 57–58; instruction, CCP Central Committee to CCP Northeast Bureau, 21 December 1945, *Zhonggong zhongyang wenjian xuanji* (1987 internal edition), 13:251–52.

87. For an informative discussion, see Ramon H. Myers, "Frustration, Fortitude, and Friendship: Chiang Kai-shek's Reactions to Marshall's Mission," in Bland, ed., *George C. Marshall's Mediation Mission to China*, 149–71.

88. Zhang Zhizhong, *Zhang Zhizhong huiyilu* (Zhang Zhizhong's Memoirs) (Beijing: Zhongguo wenshi, 1985), 739–40. Zhang was a longtime close associate of Jiang but in 1949 abandoned Jiang to join the Communist side.

89. Instruction, CCP Central Committee, "On the Current Situation and Our Policies," 15 March 1946, *ZZWX*, 16:92–95.

90. *Zhonghua minguo zhongyao shiliao chubian*, VII, 1:453–54.

91. For a revealing discussion, see Yang Kuisong, "The Soviet Factor and the CCP's Policy toward the United States," *Chinese Historians* 5 (Spring 1992): 26.

92. Ibid., 27; see also Yang Kuisong, *Zhonggong yu mosike de guanxi*, 560–61.

93. Telegram, CCP Central Committee to Zhou Enlai, 13 March 1946, *ZZWX*,

16:89–90; telegram (drafted by Mao Zedong), CCP Central Committee to Zhou Enlai, 17 March 1946, *MZN*, 3:62.

94. Telegram (drafted by Mao Zedong), CCP Central Committee to CCP Northeast Bureau, 24 March 1946, *MZN*, 3:62–63.

95. Niu Jun, *Cong yan'an zouxiang shijie*, esp. ch. 11.

96. Westad, *Cold War and Revolution*, 176.

97. Michael M. Sheng, *Battling Western Imperialism: Mao, Stalin, and the United States* (Princeton, N.J.: Princeton University Press, 1997), 98.

Chapter Two

1. That the United states "lost a chance" with China was a prevailing argument among students of American policy toward China in the 1970s and 1980s. Since the early 1990s, however, this opinion has encountered increasing challenges from scholars both in China and in the United States. For a recent symposium focusing on reconsidering the "lost chance" issue, see John Garver, Michael M. Sheng, Odd Arne Westad, and Chen Jian, "Rethinking the Lost Chance in China," with an introduction by Warren I. Cohen, *Diplomatic History* 21 (Winter 1997): 71–115. The four participants of the symposium agreed that there existed little or no chance for the CCP and the United States to reach an accommodation in 1948–50. Cohen, though, was not fully convinced, pointing out that he "continue[s] to believe there was room for a modest level of diplomatic and economic contact, as the United States had with Hitler's Germany in the 1930s and with Stalin's Soviet Union in the 1940s" (ibid., 75). The debate on America's "lost chance" in China is far from over.

2. Ward and his staff remained in Shenyang both to protect American citizens living in the Northeast and to maintain a channel of contact with the new Chinese Communist authorities. For the U.S. State Department's discussion about whether Ward should stay in Shenyang after the Communist takeover, see *FRUS, 1948*, 7:809–25.

3. Ibid., 826–31.

4. After receiving a letter from Western diplomats asking for proper protection after the Communist troops occupied Shenyang, the Communist mayor of the city, Zhu Qiwen, summoned the British, American, and French consuls general to his office, promising that the Communists would protect the foreigners remaining in the city. He then visited the three Western consuls and had cordial talks with them (Ward to George C. Marshall, 5 and 9 November 1948, ibid., 829–31). See also Angus Ward, "The Mukden Affair," *American Foreign Service Journal* (February 1950): 15.

5. Telegram, CCP Central Committee to CCP Northeast Bureau, 10 November 1948. Part of the telegram is published in Jin Chongji et al., *ZENA*, 796. The unpublished part of the telegram, the part concerning "squeezing out" Western diplomats in Shenyang, can be found in Zhou Enlai files, CCA.

6. Angus Ward to George C. Marshall, 15 November 1948, *FRUS, 1948*, 7:834–

35; William Stokes, "The Future between America and China," *Foreign Service Journal* (January 1968): 15. See also telegram, CCP Northeast Bureau to CCP Central Committee, 15 November 1948, CCA.

7. See Bernard Gwertzman, "The Hostage Crisis: Three Decades Ago," *New York Times Magazine*, 4 May 1980, 42.

8. Telegram, Mao Zedong to Gao Gang, 17 November 1948, CCA. Mao emphasized in this telegram: "Several of Zhu Qiwen's actions are ridiculously naïve, such as notifying foreign consulates for the mayor's inauguration, returning visits of foreign consuls, allowing newspapers in Shenyang to publish the information that the U.S. consulate apologized for the enemy's bombardment, and promising without careful consideration to issue passes for American motor vehicles." Mao ordered Zhu and other leading members of the CCP Northeast Bureau to make "profound self-criticism" for having committed such "serious mistakes."

9. Telegram, Mao Zedong to Gao Gang, 18 November 1948, CCA. See also CCP Central Committee to Lin Biao, Luo Ronghuan, and Chen Yun and convey to CCP Northeast Bureau, 19 November 1948, CCA.

10. Telegram, CCP Northeast Bureau to CCP Central Committee, 12:00, 21 November 1948, CCA. See also John Leighton Stuart to George C. Marshall, 21 November 1948, and O. Edmund Clubb to Marshall, 26 November 1948, *FRUS, 1948*, 7:838–39, 840.

11. For a detailed and more comprehensive account of the Ward case, see Chen Jian, "The Ward Case and the Emergence of the Sino-American Confrontation, 1948–1949," *Australian Journal of Chinese Affairs*, no. 30 (July 1993): 149–70. The account provided here, though, includes some new information that was not available when I wrote that article in 1992–93.

12. In fact, CCP leaders in the Northeast already believed that American diplomats in Shenyang were "actively engaged in" collecting military intelligence information about "the Soviet Union, Outer Mongolia, and China's liberated zones." In a summary report to the CCP leadership on 24 November, the CCP Northeast Bureau concluded that a group of special spies existed at the U.S. consulate in Shenyang, who had conducted espionage activities on the GMD's behalf (telegram, CCP Northeast Bureau to CCP Central Committee, 24 November 1948, CCA).

13. For example, I. V. Kovalev, the Soviet general adviser who was then in Shenyang to help the Chinese Communists restore the railroad transportation system in the Northeast, had advised the CCP to "take control of the radio stations" in the Western consulates. See Sergei Goncharov, John Lewis, and Xue Litai, *Uncertain Partners: Stalin, Mao, and the Korean War* (Stanford, Calif.: Stanford University Press, 1993), 34. See also telegram, Gao Gang to the CCP Central Committee, 16 November 1948, CCA.

14. Telegram, Mao Zedong to Gao Gang, 17 November 1948, CCA.

15. CCP leaders established these three fundamental principles while formulating Communist China's foreign policy framework. For a plausible discussion of the three principles' creation see Zhang Baijia, "The Shaping of New China's

Diplomacy," trans. Chen Jian, *Chinese Historians* 7 (1994): 45–46. See also Xue Mouhong et al., *Dangdai zhongguo waijiao* (Contemporary Chinese Diplomacy) (Beijing: Zhongguo shehui kexue, 1988), ch. 2.

16. Telegram, CCP Central Committee to CCP Northeast Bureau, 23 November 1949, quoted in *ZENA*, 740.

17. Instruction, CCP Central Committee, "On Diplomatic Affairs," 19 January 1949, *CCFP*, 95–99; for Mao Zedong's remarks on the directive, see *Dangde wenxian* (Party History Documents, Beijing), no. 1 (1992): 27.

18. Mao Zedong, "Report to the Second Plenary Session of the Seventh Central Committee," *MZX*, 4:1436.

19. See, for example, Mao Zedong's conclusion at the Second Plenary Session of the Seventh Central Committee, 13 March 1949, CCA; Zhou Enlai, "Report on Problems Concerning the Peace Talks," *Zhou Enlai xuanji* (Selected Works of Zhou Enlai) (Beijing: Renmin, 1984), 1:323; and Zhou Enlai, "New China's Diplomacy," *ZEWW*, 4–5.

20. For details of the Stuart-Huang meetings, see *FRUS, 1949*, 8:741–67; for a recent Chinese account of the meetings, see Huang Hua, "My Contacts with Stuart after Nanjing's Liberation," trans. Li Xiaobing, *Chinese Historians* 5 (Spring 1992): 47–56.

21. See, for example, Mao Zedong, "Statement by the Spokesman of the General Headquarters of the Chinese People's Liberation Army," 30 April 1949, and "Address to the Preparatory Meeting of the New Political Consultative Conference," *MZX*, 4:1464, 1470.

22. Memorandum, "Mr. Chen Mingshu's Report on American Ambassador's Secret Visit to Shanghai," 26 March 1949, CCA. The secret meetings between Stuart and Chen Mingshu and the statements made by Stuart as reported in the memorandum were previously unknown. They cannot be confirmed by currently available American sources. This suggests that Stuart may have gone beyond the authorization of the State Department in an effort to provoke a CCP response that would help bring about a Sino-American accommodation.

23. Instruction (drafted by Mao), CCP Central Military Commission, "Our Policy toward British and American Citizens and Diplomats," 28 April 1949, *CCFP*, 109–11.

24. As far as the timing of Stuart's message is concerned, one should keep in mind that the PLA was preparing to cross the Yangzi River and "liberate" Nanjing and Shanghai, China's largest industrial and commercial center. The CCP leadership worried that this movement would result in America's military intervention, and was eager to find ways to reduce that possibility. For a more detailed analysis, see Chen Jian, *China's Road to the Korean War: The Making of the Sino-American Confrontation* (New York: Columbia University Press, 1994), 52–53.

25. Mao Zedong, "Statement by the Spokesman of the General Headquarters of the Chinese People's Liberation Army," 30 April 1949, *MZX*, 4:1464.

26. Telegram (drafted by Mao), CCP Central Committee to CCP Nanjing Municipal Committee, 10 May 1949, *CCFP*, 111–12.

27. Mao Zedong's conclusion at the Second Plenary Session of the Seventh Central Committee, 13 March 1949, CCA.

28. Huang Hua, "My Contacts with Stuart," 26–28.

29. *Renmin ribao* (People's Daily), 19 and 22 June 1949.

30. Telegram, Mao Zedong to the CCP Northeast Bureau, 22 June 1949, CCA.

31. Letter, Mao Zedong to Hu Qiaomu, 24 June 1949, *Mao Zedong shuxin xuanji* (Selected Correspondence of Mao Zedong) (Beijing: Renmin, 1983), 327–28. Hu Qiaomu was one of the CCP's propaganda heads.

32. See *MZX*, 4:1486–1520.

33. For a more detailed discussion, see Chen Jian, *China's Road to the Korean War*, 65–69; see also Niu Jun, "The Origins of the Sino-Soviet Alliance," in *Brothers in Arms: The Rise and Fall of the Sino-Soviet Alliance, 1945–1963*, ed. Odd Arne Westad (Washington, D.C., and Stanford, Calif.: Woodrow Wilson Center Press and Stanford University Press, 1998), 47–89, esp. 61–69.

34. Andrei Ledovsky, "Mikoyan's Secret Mission to China in January and February 1949," *Far Eastern Affairs*, no. 2 (1995): 72–94, esp. 75–77; Westad, *Brothers in Arms*, 298–300; Shi Zhe, *Zai lishi juren shenbian*, 326–27.

35. See Shi Zhe, "With Mao and Stalin: The Reminiscences of a Chinese Interpreter, Part I," trans. Chen Jian, *Chinese Historians* 5 (Spring 1992): 45–56. For a Russian account of the visit, see Ledovsky, "Mikoyan's Secret Mission to China," 72–94. It is important to note that the Chinese and Russian accounts of this visit are highly compatible.

36. For a detailed account of Liu's visit to Moscow, see Shi Zhe, "With Mao and Stalin: The Reminiscences of Mao's Interpreter, Part II: Liu Shaoqi in Moscow," trans. Chen Jian, *Chinese Historians* 6 (Spring 1993): 67–90; Zhu Yuanshi, "Liu Shaoqi's Secret Visit to the Soviet Union in 1949," *Dangde wenxian*, no. 3 (1991): 74–81; and Jin Chongji et al., *Liu Shaoqi zhuan* (A Biography of Liu Shaoqi) (Beijing: Zhongyang wenxian, 1998), 646–54; see also Goncharov, Lewis, and Xue Litai, *Uncertain Partners*, 61–75. During Liu's visit, he submitted to Stalin a comprehensive report summarizing China's situation and the CCP's domestic and international strategies, which Stalin read with care and consent. See *LSW*, 1:1–28.

37. For a more detailed analysis, see Chen Jian, *China's Road to the Korean War*, 69–78.

38. The Russian originals of these telegrams between Stalin and Mao were published in *Modern and Contemporary History* (in Russian), nos. 4–5 (1994): 133–39. For an English translation, see "Communications between Mao and Stalin, Seven Telegrams, January 1949," trans. Song Datu, *Chinese Historians* 7 (1994): 163–72.

39. Goncharov, Lewis, and Xue Litai, *Uncertain Partners*, 43.

40. For the Chinese version of the memorandum, see *LSW*, 1:1–28; see also *CCFP*, 118–22; for the Soviet version (with Stalin's comments), see Westad, *Brothers in Arms*, 301–13.

41. Yang Kuisong, "The Ward Case and the Shaping of New China's America Policy," *Lishi yanjiu* (Historical Studies), no. 5 (1994): 113.

42. S. Tikhvinsky, "The Zhou Enlai 'Demarche' and the CCP's Informal Ne-

gotiations with the Americans in June 1949," *Far Eastern Affairs* (in Russian), no. 3 (1994). I am grateful to Shen Zhihua for providing me with the Chinese translation of this important article.

43. Ibid.

44. I believe that "Central Kingdom" is a more accurate translation for "Zhong Guo" (China) than "Middle Kingdom." The term "Middle Kingdom" does not imply that China is superior to other peoples and nations around it—China just happens to be located in the middle geographically; the term "Central Kingdom," however, implies that China is superior to any other people and nation "under the heaven" and that it thus occupies a "central" position in the known universe.

45. For Mao's own statement on this issue, see Edgar Snow, *Red Star over China* (New York: Random House, 1938), 118-19; for a good discussion about how Mao adopted the restoration of China's historical glory as one of the top goals of the Chinese Communist revolution, see Mark Mancall, *China at the Center: 300 Years of Foreign Policy* (New York: Free Press, 1984), ch. 9.

46. See discussions in Chapter 3.

47. In actuality, after the People's Liberation Army occupied Shanghai, Qingdao, and China's other major coastal cities in the summer of 1949, Mao and the CCP leadership no longer regarded direct American military intervention as a real danger, although in open propaganda, the CCP would continue to call the Chinese people's attention to it. For a more detailed discussion, see Chen Jian, *China's Road to the Korean War*, 17.

48. Mao Zedong, "Report to the Second Plenary Session of the Seventh Central Committee," *MZX*, 4:1425-26, 1428; *MZN*, 3:410-11.

49. See discussions in Chapter 4.

Chapter Three

1. For recently available Chinese documents related to the 1969 Sino-Soviet border war, see Chen Jian and David L. Wilson, eds., "All Under the Heaven Is Great Chaos: Beijing, the Sino-Soviet Border Clashes and the Turn toward Sino-American Rapprochement, 1968-1969," *CWIHPB* 11 (Winter 1998-99): 155-75.

2. Mao Zedong, "On the People's Democratic Dictatorship," *MZX*, 4:1477.

3. See, for example, Lu Dingyi, "Explanations of Several Basic Problems Concerning the Postwar International Situation," *Jiefang ribao* (Liberation Daily), 4 January 1947; Liu Shaoqi, "On Internationalism and Nationalism," *Renmin ribao* (People's Daily), 7 November 1948; and Mao Zedong, "Concluding Remarks at the Second Plenary Session of the CCP's Seventh Central Committee," 13 March 1949, *MZW*, 5:261-62.

4. Mao Zedong, "The Current Situation and the Party's Tasks in 1949," January 8, 1949, and "Plans for Advancing on the Whole Country," 23 May 1949, *Mao Zedong junshi wenxuan* (Selected Military Papers of Mao Zedong) (Beijing: Zhanshi, 1981), 328, 338.

5. See, for example, Mao Zedong, "Casting Away Illusion, Preparing for Struggle" and "Friendship or Aggression," *MZX*, 4:1487-94, 1509-12.

6. Xue Mouhong et al., *Dangdai zhongguo waijiao* (Contemporary Chinese Diplomacy) (Beijing: Zhongguo shehui kexue, 1989), 4.

7. Mao Zedong, "The Bankruptcy of Historical Idealism," *MZX*, 4:1519-20; Mao Zedong, "The Chinese People Have Stood Up," *MZW*, 5:342-46.

8. In the 1940s, Mao Zedong divided the Chinese Communist revolution into two stages: the stage of new democratic revolution and the stage of socialist revolution. During the first stage, the revolution had to overthrow the rule of the bureaucratic-capitalist class, wipe out foreign influence, eliminate remnants of feudal tradition, and establish a Communist-led regime. The second stage of the revolution would transform China's state and society, laying the foundation of China's transition into a socialist and, later, Communist society. In 1949, he was thinking about leading the revolution into its higher, second stage. See Mao Zedong, "The Chinese Revolution and the Chinese Communist Party" and "On New Democracy," *MZX*, 2:626-47, 656-72, and Mao Zedong, "On People's Democratic Dictatorship," ibid., 4:1473-86.

9. See, for example, Mao Zedong, "Report to the Second Plenary Session of the Seventh Central Committee," *MZX*, 4:1439-40; see also Zhou Enlai, "Report on Problems Concerning Peace Talks," *Zhou Enlai xuanji* (Selected Works of Zhou Enlai) (Beijing: Renmin, 1984), 1:318.

10. Mao Zedong, "Report to the Second Plenary Session of the Seventh Central Committee," *MZX*, 4:1425-26; Mao Zedong, "The Chinese People Have Stood Up," *MZW*, 5:343.

11. Zhou Enlai, "Our Diplomatic Policies and Tasks," *ZEWW*, 48-51; see also Xue Mouhong et al., *Dangdai zhongguo waijiao*, 4-5; and Pei Jianzhang, *Zhonghua renmin gongheguo waijiao shi, 1949-1956* (A Diplomatic History of the People's Republic of China, 1949-1956) (Beijing: Shijie zhishi, 1994), 2-4.

12. Zhang Baijia, "The Shaping of New China's Diplomacy," *Chinese Historians* 7 (1994): 62.

13. Shi Zhe, *Zai lishi juren shenbian: Shi Zhe huiyilu* (At the Side of Historical Giants: Shi Zhe's Memoirs), rev. ed. (Beijing: Zhonggong zhongyang dangxiao, 1998), 389. In the Russian minutes of this conversation, this statement was not included (see "Conversation between Stalin and Mao, Moscow, December 16, 1949," CWIHP*B*, nos. 6-7 [Winter 1995-96], 5-7). I believe that a possible reason for this discrepancy lies in the cultural differences between Chinese and Soviet interpreters: While for Mao this was a statement with crucial importance, the Russians, without being able to catch the CCP chairman's underlying meanings, treated it only as a part of insignificant "greetings." For a discussion, see Chen Jian, "Comparing Russian and Chinese Sources: A New Point of Departure for Cold War History," CWIHP*B*, nos. 6-7 (Winter 1995-96): 21.

14. Telegram, Mao Zedong to Liu Shaoqi, 18 December 1949, *CCFP*, 128, and "Conversation between Stalin and Mao, Moscow, December 16, 1949," CWIHP*B*, nos. 6-7 (Winter 1995-96): 5-7.

15. Telegrams, Mao Zedong to the CCP Central Committee, 2, 3, and 5 January 1950, *CCFP*, 131-34. See also "More on Mao in Moscow," CWIHP*B*, nos. 8-9 (Winter 1996-97): 223-36.

16. Telegram, Zhou Enlai to Liu Shaoqi and the CCP politburo, 8 February 1950, in Jin Chongji, ed., *Zhou Enlai zhuan, 1949–1976* (A Biography of Zhou Enlai, 1949–1976) (Beijing: Zhongyang wenxian, 1998), 1:35–39. For plausible discussions of the signing of the Sino-Soviet alliance, see Sergei Goncharov, John Lewis, and Xue Litai, *Uncertain Partners: Stalin, Mao, and the Korean War* (Stanford, Calif.: Stanford University Press, 1993), ch. 4; see also Pei Jianzhang, *Zhonghua renmin gongheguo waijiao shi, 1949–1956*, 16–27.

17. During Mao's visit to the Soviet Union, China ordered 586 planes from the Soviet Union, including 280 fighters, 198 bombers, and 108 trainers. From 16 February to 5 March 1950, a mixed Soviet air-defense division, following the request of the PRC government, moved into Shanghai, Nanjing, and Xuzhou to take responsibility for the defense of these areas. From 13 March to 11 May, this Soviet division shot down five GMD planes in the Shanghai area, greatly strengthening Shanghai's air-defense system (*DZJJG*, 2:161; Wang Dinglie, *Dangdai zhongguo kongjun* (Contemporary Chinese Air Force) (Beijing: Jiefangjun, 1989), 78–79, 110.

18. Mao Zedong's address at the Sixth Session of the Central People's Government Council, 11 April 1950, *JMZW*, 1:291.

19. Mao later recalled that during his meetings with Stalin from December 1949 to February 1950, Stalin did not trust him and failed to treat him equally. See, for example, his statements to the Soviet ambassador in Beijing in 1956 and 1958, in CWIHP*B*, nos. 6–7 (Winter 1995–96), esp. 155–56, 165–66.

20. We now know that in 1949 and early 1950, Kim Il-sung, in order to get Stalin's support for his plans to unify Korea by military means, made extensive efforts to convince Stalin that a real revolutionary situation existed on the Korean peninsula. See Kathryn Weathersby, "Korea, 1949–1950: To Attack, or Not to Attack? Stalin, Kim Il-sung, and the Prelude to War," CWIHP*B*, no. 5 (Spring 1995): 1, 2–9.

21. For a more detailed discussion, see Goncharov, Lewis, and Xue Litai, *Uncertain Partners*, ch. 5.

22. For Stalin's discussions with Kim Il-sung, see Weathersby, "Korea, 1949–1950"; see also "New Russian Documents on the Korean War," trans. Kathryn Weathersby, CWIHP*B*, nos. 6–7 (Winter 1995–96): 36–39.

23. Mao Zedong, however, did not believe that the Americans would directly intervene in a revolutionary civil war in Korea. For a more detailed discussion, see Chen Jian, *China's Road to the Korean War: The Making of the Sino-American Confrontation* (New York: Columbia University Press, 1994), 88–90.

24. For a more detailed discussion of the relationship between Chinese and North Korean Communists prior to the Korean War, see ibid., 106–13.

25. For discussions, see Shen Zhihua, *Zhongsu tongmeng yu chaoxian zhanzheng yanjiu* (Studies on the Sino-Soviet Alliance and the Korean War) (Guilin: Guangxi shida, 1999), 238–42; see also Chen Jian, "Why and How China Entered the Korean War: In Light of New Evidence," a paper prepared for an international conference titled "The Korean War: An Assessment of the Historical Record," 24–25 July 1995, Georgetown University, Washington, D.C., 10–12.

26. For a more detailed discussion, see Chen Jian, *China's Road to the Korean War*, 87–88.

27. See ibid., 110–11; see also Bruce Cumings, *The Origins of the Korean War* (Princeton, N.J.: Princeton University Press, 1990), 2:363.

28. He Di, "The Last Campaign to Unify China: The CCP's Unmaterialized Plan to Liberate Taiwan, 1949–1950," *Chinese Historians* 5 (Spring 1992): 12–16; Xiao Jinguang, *Xiao Jinguang huiyilu* (Xiao Jinguang's Memoirs) (Beijing: Jiefangjun, 1990), 2:8, 26.

29. Letter, Mao Zedong to Nie Rongzhen, 7 July 1950, *JMZW*, 1:428; *DZJJG*, 1:449–50.

30. Telegram, Mao Zedong to Gao Gang, 18 August 1950, *JMZW*, 1:469; see also telegram, Mao Zedong to Gao Gang, 5 August 1950, ibid., 454.

31. Telegram, Stalin to Soviet ambassador in Beijing (N. V. Rochshin) with message for Zhou Enlai, 5 July 1950, *CWIHPB*, nos. 6–7 (Winter 1995–96): 43.

32. See Chen Jian, *China's Road to the Korea War*, 156; see also telegram, Filippov [Stalin] to Zhou Enlai, 27 August 1950, *CWIHPB*, nos. 6–7 (Winter 1995–96): 45.

33. Telegram, Stalin to Mao Zedong and Zhou Enlai, 1 October 1950, *CWIHPB*, nos. 6–7 (Winter 1995–96): 114. Stalin dispatched this telegram after UN forces crossed the 38th parallel and Kim Il-sung requested direct Soviet and Chinese intervention in the war.

34. Telegram, Mao Zedong to Stalin, 2 October 1950, *JMZW*, 1:539–40. The text of the telegram published in this volume is an abridged version. In a research trip to Beijing in November 1998, with the assistance of the CCP Central Archives, I obtained a xerox copy of the telegram's original text in Mao's own handwriting.

35. The quotations in this paragraph, which are not included in the telegram's published text in *JMZW*, are from Mao's original text.

36. Since the CCA has provided me with a xerox copy of the telegram's original text in Mao's own handwriting, there is no doubt that this is a genuine document, and that its contents reflected Mao's thinking. But the fact that this telegram is not found in Russian archives and that another version of Mao's message to Stalin does exist points to the possibility that although Mao had drafted the telegram, he may not have dispatched it. Also, most of Mao's telegrams carry Mao's office staff's signature indicating the time when the telegram was dispatched, but this telegram does not. For a discussion, see Shen Zhihua, "The Discrepancy between the Russian and Chinese Versions of Mao's 2 October 1950 Message to Stalin on Chinese Entry into the Korean War: A Chinese Scholar's Reply," trans. Chen Jian, *CWIHPB*, nos. 8–9 (Winter 1996–97): 237–42.

37. Telegram, Nikolai Rochshin in Beijing to Stalin, 3 October 1950, conveying 2 October 1950 message from Mao to Stalin, *CWIHPB*, nos. 6–7 (Winter 1995–96): 114–15.

38. Letter, Fyn Si [Stalin] to Kim Il-sung [via Shtykov], 8 [7] October 1950, *CWIHPB*, nos. 6–7 (Winter 1995–96): 116. Stalin cited the text of his message to Beijing in this telegram.

39. For a detailed discussion of these meetings, see Chen Jian, *China's Road to*

the Korean War, ch. 5; see also Zhang Xi, "Peng Dehuai and China's Entry into the Korean War," trans. Chen Jian, *Chinese Historians* 6 (Spring 1993): 8–16.

40. "Mao Zedong's Order to Establish the Chinese People's Volunteers," 8 October 1950, *JMZW*, 1:543–44.

41. Telegram, Mao Zedong to Kim Il-sung, 8 October 1950, ibid., 545; see also Chai Chengwen and Zhao Yongtian, *Banmendian tanpan* (The Panmunjom Negotiations) (Beijing: Jiefangjun, 1989), 84.

42. This is the phrase Shi Zhe, Mao Zedong's and Zhou Enlai's Russian-language interpreter, used in describing how Mao was dealing with Stalin in October 1950 (author's interviews with Shi Zhe, August 1992).

43. For a more detailed discussion based on Shi Zhe's recollections, the validity of which were checked against other Chinese sources, see Chen Jian, *China's Road to the Korean War*, 197–200.

44. Telegram, Mao Zedong to Peng Dehuai and others, 12 October 1950, *JMZW*, 1:552.

45. For a more detailed discussion, see Chen Jian, *China's Road to the Korean War*, 200–202.

46. Telegram, Mao Zedong to Zhou Enlai, 13 October 1950, *JMZW*, 1:556. The telegram published in *JMZW* is abridged. The citation here is based on the original of the telegram, kept at CCP Central Archives in Beijing. For a more comprehensive discussion of this key telegram, see Chen Jian, *China's Road to the Korean War*, 202–3.

47. Telegram, Mao Zedong to Peng Dehuai and Gao Gang, 17 October 1950, *JMZW*, 1:567; see also Chen Jian, *China's Road to the Korean War*, 206–7.

48. Telegram, Mao Zedong to Peng Dehuai, Gao Gang, and others, 17 October 1950, and telegram, Mao Zedong to Deng Hua, Hong Xuezhi, Han Xianchu, and Xie Fang, 18 October 1950, *JMZW*, 1:567–8; see also Chen Jian, *China's Road to the Korean War*, 207–8.

49. General Chinese Association of Resisting America and Assisting Korea, comp., *Weida de kangmei yuanchao yundong* (The Great Movement to Resist America and Assist Korea) (Beijing: Renmin, 1954), 7–8.

50. See State Council and Supreme People's Court, "Instructions on Suppressing Reactionary Activities," issued on July 23, 1950, in CCP Central Institute of Historical Documents, comp., *Jianguo yilai zhongyao wenxian xuanbian* (A Selection of Important Documents since the Founding of the People's Republic) (Beijing: Zhongyang wenxian, 1992–98), 1:358–60; and "Fifteen Telegrams and Documents on Suppressing Reactionary Activities during the Early Stage of the People's Republic," and Zhang Min, "A Survey of the Struggle to Suppress Reactionaries in the Early Years of the PRC," *Dangde wenxian* (Party History Documents, Beijing), no. 2 (1988): 31–41.

51. For documentary evidence on this issue, see "New Russian Documents on the Korean War," CWIHP*B*, nos. 6–7 (Winter 1995–96): 47–53.

52. Stalin approved Beijing's decision to come to the negotiation table at a meeting with Gao Gang and Kim Il-sung in June 1951. For a more detailed discussion, see Chapter 4; see also Shi Zhe, *Zai lishi juren shenbian*, 451–54; Nie Rongzhen, *Nie*

Rongzhen huiyilu (Nie Rongzhen's memoirs) (Beijing: Jiefangjun, 1984), 742–43; and "New Russian Documents on the Korean War," CWIHP*B*, nos. 6–7 (Winter 1995–96): 59–66.

53. Beijing maintained daily telegraphic communication with Moscow during the early stage of the armistice negotiations. Indeed, Beijing's leaders even forwarded to Stalin copies of correspondence between Chinese negotiators at Panmunjom and the leaders in Beijing to keep him abreast of the negotiations' development. Copies of these and other Russian documents on the Korean War obtained by the CWIHP are available for research at the National Security Archive at George Washington University in Washington, D.C. For examples of these communications, see "New Russian Documents on the Korean War," CWIHP*B*, nos. 6–7 (Winter 1995–96): 66–84.

54. When and how the Soviet air force entered operations in Korea have been confusing questions for scholars in recent years. While some scholars, basing their discussions on information provided by Russian recollections and documents, believe that the operations began as early as November 1950, others, following the insights gained from Chinese sources, argue that they began in January 1951. I believe that the key here is to make a distinction between operations for the purpose of defending China's Northeast and the transportation lines across the Chinese-Korean border, especially the bridge over the Yalu River, and operations designed for supporting Chinese–North Korean land forces fighting in Korean territory. While the former operations took place as early as November 1950 (as an inevitable extension of defending the airspace of China's Northeast), the latter did not occur until January 1951. See Tan Jinqiao et al., *Kangmei yuanchao zhanzheng* (The War to Resist America and Assist Korea) (Beijing: Zhongguo shehui kexue, 1990), 201.

55. Xue Mouhong et al., *Dangdai zhongguo waijiao*, 28–30; Pei Jianzhang, *Zhonghua renmin gongheguo waijiao shi*, 40–41.

56. Zhou Enlai, "The Enemy's Defeat and Our Victory," 11 December 1952, ZE*JW*, 4:297–98.

57. The Three Antis movement was designed to oppose corrupt Communist cadres; the Five Antis movement was aimed at the national bourgeoisie class "who should not be destroyed at this stage but who needed to be tightly controlled by the power of the people's state." For discussions of these movements, see Frederick C. Teiwes, "Establishment and Consolidation of the New Regime," in *The Cambridge History of China*, ed. Denis Twitchett and John K. Fairbank (Cambridge, Eng.: Cambridge University Press, 1987), 14:88–91.

58. See Mao Zedong, "The Great Victory of Resisting America and Assisting Korea," 12 September 1953, *MZX*, 5:101–6, esp. 103–4, and Zhou Enlai, "The Enemy's Defeat and Our Victory," 292–307.

59. During the war years, the Soviet Union provided China with military equipment for sixty-four army divisions and twenty-two air force divisions, which placed China 3 billion old rubles (about U.S. $650 million) in debt. China did not pay off this debt (plus interest) until 1965. See Xu Yan, *Diyici jiaoliang* (The First Test of Strength) (Beijing: Zhongguo guangbo dianshi, 1990), 31–32.

60. In March 1950 and July 1951, the Chinese and Soviet governments had signed four agreements, establishing a civil aviation company, an oil company, a nonferrous and rare metal company, and a shipbuilding company jointly owned by the two countries. In the last years of his life, Stalin refused to hand over to the Chinese full ownership of the companies, but Khrushchev agreed. See Xue Mouhong et al., *Dangdai zhongguo waijiao*, 26–27.

61. Ibid., 27–28.

62. Li Jue et al., *Dangdai zhongguo he gongyue* (Contemporary China's Nuclear Industry) (Beijing: Zhongguo shehui kexue, 1987), 20.

63. Even Mao himself later acknowledged that "the first time I met with Comrade Khrushchev, we had very pleasant conversations . . . and established mutual trust" (quoted from Li Danhui, "The Evolution of Sino-Soviet Relations in the Mid- and Late 1950s," *Dangshi yanjiu ziliao* [Party History Research Materials], no. 12 [1995]: 4). Still, Chinese sources report that when Khrushchev requested to visit historic sites in Lüshun dedicated to Russian generals who had participated in the Russo-Japanese War of 1904, the CCP leaders politely, yet firmly, turned him down. See Liu Guoxin, ed., *Zhonghua renmin gongheguo lishi changbian* (A Draft History of the People's Republic of China) (Nanning: Guangxi renmin, 1994), 1:117.

64. Pei Jianzhang, *Zhonghua renmin gongheguo waijiao shi*, 1:35–37.

65. For two detailed accounts about Zhou Enlai's visits to Moscow before the Geneva Conference, see Shi Zhe, *Zai lishi juren shenbian*, 482–86, and Li Lianqing, *Da waijiaojia Zhou Enlai: Shezhan rineiwa* (Great Diplomat Zhou Enlai: The Geneva Debate) (Hong Kong: Tiandi tushu, 1994), 13–33. See also discussions in Chapter 5.

66. For discussions of Sino-Soviet cooperation at the Geneva Conference, see Zhai Qiang, "China and the Geneva Conference of 1954," *China Quarterly*, no. 129 (March 1992), and Chen Jian, "China and the First Indochina War," ibid., no. 133 (March 1993): 106–10.

67. This was the view of the CCP leadership. See Li Yueran, *Waijiao wutai shang de xin Zhongguo lingxue* (New China's Leaders on the Diplomatic Scene) (Beijing: Jiefangjun, 1989), 52–53.

68. For more detailed discussions, see Chapter 7.

69. For discussions, see Xue Mouhong et al., *Dangdai zhongguo waijiao*, ch. 8.

70. See, for example, Mao's talks with the delegation of the Yugoslav Communist League, September 1956, in Zhang Shuguang and Chen Jian, trans. and eds., "The Emerging Disputes between Beijing and Moscow: Ten Newly Available Chinese Documents, 1956–1958," *CWIHPB*, nos. 6–7 (Winter 1995–96): 148–51.

71. I have argued elsewhere that Mao's definition of "equality" deeply reflected his perception of China's unequal exchanges with foreign countries in modern times. Behind Mao's pursuit of equality was his belief that revolutionary China was in a position to define the international standard of equality. In this sense, Mao's approach toward "equality" reflected a Chinese superiority mentality. See Chen Jian, *China's Road to the Korean War*, 42–43.

72. For more detailed accounts of the Gao Gang affair, see Frederick C. Teiwes,

Politics at Mao's Court: Gao Gang and Party Factionalism (Armonk: N.Y.: M. E. Sharpe, 1990), and Lin Yunhui et al., *Kaige xingjin de shiqi* (The Years of Triumphant Advance) (Zhengzhou: Henan renmin, 1989), 319–35.

73. Telegram, Mao Zedong to the CPSU Central Committee, September 1, 1954, *JMZW*, 4:537–38.

74. For Chinese accounts, see Shi Zhe, *Zai lishi juren shenbian*, 531–35; Wu Lengxi, *Shinian lunzhan, 1956–1966: Zhongsu guanxi huiyilu* (Ten-Year Polemic Debate, 1956–1966: A Memoir on Sino-Soviet Relations) (Beijing: Zhongyang wenxian, 1999), 3–5; Wu Lengxi, *Yi Mao zhuxi* (Recalling Chairman Mao) (Beijing: Xinhua, 1994), 2–3; and Liu Xiao, *Chushi sulian banian* (Eight Years as Ambassador to the Soviet Union) (Beijing: Zhonggong dangshi ziliao, 1986), 18. These Chinese sources differ on whether or not the Soviets provided the Chinese delegation with a copy of Khrushchev's speech after the secret session. While Shi Zhe recalls that the Soviets gave the transcripts to the Chinese the day after the speech, Wu Lengxi claims that the Chinese did not have knowledge of the contents of the speech until the Xinhua News Agency received the issue of the *New York Times* that published Khrushchev's speech. The *New York Times*, however, did not publish the speech until 4 June. According to the documentary sources now available, it seems that Shi Zhe's recollection is correct. Direct confirmation is that on 31 March 1956, in a meeting with Soviet ambassador to China P. F. Yudin, Mao Zedong mentioned that "the members of the Chinese delegation who had attended the 20th Congress . . . had brought back a copy of Comrade Khrushchev's speech regarding the cult of personality." See Mao's conversation with Yudin, 31 March 1956, CWIHP*B*, nos. 6–7 (Winter 1995–96): 164.

75. Mao Zedong and other CCP leaders later complained repeatedly that Khrushchev's secret speech came as a surprise to the CCP and other Communist parties. See, for example, Cong Jin, *Quzhe fazhan de suiyue* (The Years of Tortuous Development) (Zhengzhou: Henan renmin, 1989), 327.

76. *LSN*, 2:362; Wu Lengxi, *Shinian lunzhan*, 4–7.

77. See Wu Lengxi, *Shinian lunzhan*, 6. Wu Lengxi was then director of the New China News Agency and editor-in-chief of *Renmin ribao*, and he attended several Politburo Standing Committee meetings discussing the de-Stalinization issue. Mao would repeat the same claim in several later speeches.

78. Wu Lengxi, *Shinian lunzhan*, 6–7.

79. Ibid., 12–14. Mao would repeat the same narrative on many other occasions; see, for example, Mao Zedong, "Speech at the Tenth Plenum of the Eighth Central Committee," 24 September 1962, in *Chairman Mao Talks to the People: Talks and Letters: 1956–1971*, ed. Stuart Schram (New York: Pantheon Books, 1975), 191.

80. Quoted from Wu Lengxi, *Shinian lunzhan*, 15.

81. Ibid., 12–13.

82. *Renmin ribao*, 5 April 1956. The article's publication was intentionally timed to coincide with the arrival in Beijing on 6 April 1956 of a high-ranking Soviet delegation headed by Anastas Mikoyan. See Wu Lengxi, *Shinian lunzhan*, 22–23.

83. Mao's most famous deliberation in this regard was reflected in his article "On the Ten Great Relationships." A version of the article can be found in *MZX*,

5:267–88. For an English translation that is based on an earlier version of the article, see Schram, ed., *Chairman Mao Talks to the People*, 61–83.

84. In the winter of 1955–56, Mao wrote the preface and over 100 editor's notes for a volume titled *Zhongguo nongcun de shehui zhuyi gaochao* (The Socialist High Tide in China's Countryside), arguing that it was necessary and possible to accelerate the realization of a socialist society in China. See *JMZW*, 5:484–576.

85. Li Ping, *Kaiguo zongli Zhou Enlai* (The First Premier Zhou Enlai) (Beijing: Zhongyang dangxiao, 1994), 354–58.

86. According to Li Ping, at one politburo conference in late April 1956, Zhou Enlai had a face-to-face dispute with Mao: while Mao favored increasing a two-billion-yuan construction investment so that the speed of China's socialist construction would be accelerated, Zhou opposed it, arguing that this could cause tension in commodity supply as well as the overgrowth of the urban population. Zhou even told Mao that his conscience as China's premier would not allow him to yield to Mao's ideas. Mao was very offended and left Beijing soon after the conference. See ibid., 356.

87. Cong Jin, *Quzhe fazhan de suiyue*, 117.

88. Mao Zedong, "Speech Outlines at the Chengdu Conference," 10 March 1958, *JMZW*, 7:113.

89. Odd Arne Westad, intro., "Mao on Sino-Soviet Relations: Two Conversations with the Soviet Ambassador," CWIHP*B*, nos. 6–7 (Winter 1995–96): 164–69.

90. Zhou Wenqi and Zhu Liangru, eds., *Teshu er fuzha de keti: Gochan guoji, sulian he zhongguo gongchandang guanxi biannian shi, 1919–1991* (A Special and Complicated Subject: A Chronological History of the Relations between the Comintern, the Soviet Union, and the Chinese Communist Party) (Wuhan: Hubei renmin, 1993), 500.

91. Minutes, Mao Zedong's conversations with the Romanian ambassador to China, June 28, 1956, *MZWW*, 240–41.

92. Zhang Shuguang and Chen Jian, eds., "The Emerging Disputes between Beijing and Moscow: Ten Newly Available Chinese Documents," CWIHP*B*, nos. 6–7 (Winter 1995–96): 148–52.

93. In October 1956, following the suppression four months earlier of an uprising in Poznan, Polish Communists elected a new politburo of the Polish United Workers' Party, excluding pro-Soviet, Stalinist leaders. The Poles also requested that Moscow recall Marshal Konstantin Rokossovskii, a Russian who had been Poland's defense minister since 1949. In the meantime, beginning on 22–23 October, an anti-Communist revolt erupted in Hungary. Consequently, on 1 November, Imre Nagy, Hungary's new prime minister, announced that his country would withdraw unilaterally from the Warsaw Pact, maintain neutrality in bloc politics, and adopt a multiparty democracy. Three days later, the Soviets invaded to crush the revolution. For translations of important recently released Soviet-bloc materials on these events, see the articles and documents published in CWIHP*B*, no. 5 (Spring 1995): 22–57; CWIHP*B*, nos. 6–7 (Winter 1995–96): 153–54, 282; and CWIHP*B*, nos. 8–9 (Winter 1996–97): 355–410. See also discussions in Chapter 6.

94. Jin Chongji et al., *Liu Shaoqi zhuan* (A Biography of Liu Shaoqi) (Beijing: Zhongyang wenxian, 1998), 803–4; Wu Lengxi, *Shinian lunzhan*, 35–42; Shi Zhe, *Zai lishi juren shenbian*, 549–52.

95. Jin Chongji et al., *Liu Shaoqi zhuan*, 804–7; Wu Lengxi, *Shinian lunzhan*, 51–53.

96. See Shi Zhe, *Zai lishi juren shenbian*, 549–62; see also Chapter 6 for detailed discussions.

97. Zhou Wenqi and Zhu Liangru, eds., *Teshu er fuzha de keti*, 502–3; Wu Lengxi, *Shinian lunzhan*, 51–53.

98. Shi Zhe, *Zai lishi juren shenbian*, 560–62; Zhou Wenqi and Zhu Liangru, eds., *Teshu er fuzha de keti*, 503; Wu Lengxi, *Shinian lunzhan*, 53.

99. Mao Zedong, "Editor's Notes from *Socialist Upsurge in China's Country-side*," *MZX*, 5:225–26.

100. The best and most detailed account of the Anti-Rightist campaign is Zhu Zheng, *1957nian de xiaji: Cong baijia zhengming dao liangjia zhengming* (Summer 1957: From Competition among One Hundred Schools to Competition between Two Schools) (Zhengzhou: Henan renmin, 1998).

101. Zhou Enlai expressed his willingness to resign as premier, but because of the opposition of other members of the CCP leadership, his resignation did not materialize. See Li Ping, *Kaiguo zongli Zhou Enlai*, 362–63.

102. *ZEWHDJ*, 183–87.

103. Report, "My Observation on the Soviet Union," Zhou Enlai to Mao Zedong and the CCP Leadership, 24 January 1957, *CWIHPB*, nos. 6–7 (Winter 1995–96): 153–54.

104. Zhou Wenqi and Zhu Liangru, eds., *Teshu er fuzha de keti*, 504.

105. Mao Zedong, "Speeches at the Moscow Conference of Communist and Workers' Parties," 14, 16, and 18 November 1957, *JMZW*, 6:625–44.

106. Ibid., 635–36.

107. Li Ping, *Kaiguo zongli Zhou Enlai*, 360–61; Shi Zhongquan, *Zhou Enlai de zuoyue fengxian* (Zhou Enlai's Outstanding Contributions) (Beijing: Zhonggong zhongyang dangxiao, 1993), 329; Cong Jin, *Quzhe fazhan de suiyue*, 111–12.

108. For the main portion of the text of Zhou Enlai's self-criticism at the Nanning conference, see Xin Ziling, *Mao Zedong quanzhuan* (A Complete Biography of Mao Zedong) (Hong Kong: Liwen, 1993), 4:102–5.

109. Mao Zedong, "Sixty Articles on Work Methods (Draft)," January 1958, *JMZW*, 7:51.

110. Li Ping, *Kaiguo zongli Zhou Enlai*, 361–62.

111. For Zhou's self-criticism on foreign policy issues, see Jin Chongji, ed., *Zhou Enlai zhuan, 1949–1976*, 424–25; for a related discussion, see Chen Xiaolu, "Chen Yi and China's Diplomacy," in *Chinese Communist Foreign Relations, 1920s–1960s*, ed. Michael H. Hunt and Niu Jun (Washington, D.C.: Asian Program, Woodrow Wilson Center for International Scholars, 1994), 91–92.

112. For a detailed account of the Chengdu conference, see Roderick MacFarquhar, *The Origins of the Cultural Revolution*, vol. 2, *The Great Leap Forward, 1958–1960* (New York: Columbia University Press, 1983), 33–50; for a plausible Chinese

account, see Cong Jin, *Quzhe fazhan de suiyue*, 112–21. However, neither author touches upon Zhou's self-criticism of his "conservative mistakes" in handling the foreign relations of the People's Republic.

113. Liu Guoxin, ed., *Zhonghua renmin gongheguo lishi changbian*, 2:40.

114. Xue Mouhong et al., *Dangdai zhongguo waijiao*, 112–13.

115. Report, Peng Dehuai to Mao Zedong and the CCP Central Committee, 5 June 1958, *JMZW*, 7:634.

116. Xue Mouhong et al., *Dangdai zhongguo waijiao*, 113.

117. Wang Taiping et al., *Zhonghua renmin gongheguo waijiao shi, 1957–1969* (A Diplomatic History of the People's Republic of China, 1957–1969) (Beijing: Shijie zhishi, 1998), 224–25; Xue Mouhong et al., *Dangdai zhongguo waijiao*, 113.

118. Wang Taiping et al., *Zhonghua renmin gongheguo waijiao shi*, 225.

119. Zhou Wenqi and Zhu Liangru, eds., *Teshu er fuzha de keti*, 512–13; Xue Mouhong et al., *Dangdai zhongguo waijiao*, 113.

120. Zhou Wenqi and Zhu Liangru, eds., *Teshu er fuzha de keti*, 513; Xue Mouhong et al., *Dangdai zhongguo waijiao*, 113–14; Liu Guoxin, *Zhonghua renmin gongheguo lishi changbian*, 2:41.

121. Minutes, conversation between Mao Zedong and Ambassador Yudin, July 22, 1958, *MZWW*, 322–33; for an English translation, see CWIHP*B*, nos. 6–7 (Winter 1995–96): 155–59.

122. Minutes, "Conversation between N. S. Khrushchev and Mao Zedong," 31 July 1958, in Dimitry Volkoganov Collections, Manuscript Division, LC. See also Wang Taiping et al., *Zhonghua renmin gongheguo waijiao shi*, 226; Zhou Wenqi and Zhu Liangru, eds., *Teshu er fuzha de keti*, 513–14; and Xue Mouhong et al., *Dangdai zhongguo waijiao*, 114.

123. Wang Taiping et al., *Zhonghua renmin gongheguo waijiao shi*, 226–27; Xue Mouhong et al., *Dangdai zhongguo waijiao*, 114; Zhou Wenqi and Zhu Liangru, eds., *Teshu er fuzha de keti*, 514; Liu Guoxin, *Zhonghua renmin gongheguo lishi changbian*, 2:41; see also "Conversation between N. S. Khrushchev and Mao Zedong," 3 August 1958, in Dimitry Volkoganov Collections, Manuscript Division, LC.

124. Khrushchev was so upset that he said at one of the meetings: "Comrade Mao Zedong, the NATO countries have no problem in mutual cooperation and supply, and we cannot even reach agreement on such a matter!" See Liu Guoxin, *Zhonghua renmin gongheguo lishi changbian*, 2:41.

125. Quoted from Cong Jin, *Quzhe fazhan de suiyue*, 350.

126. Letter, Mao Zedong to Peng Dehuai and Huang Kecheng, July 27, 1958, in "Mao Zedong's Management of the Taiwan Crisis of 1958: Chinese Recollections and Documents," trans. and annot. Li Xiaobing, Chen Jian, and David L. Wilson, CWIHP*B*, nos. 6–7 (Winter 1995–96): 215–16.

127. Ibid., 208–18; see also more detailed discussions in Chapter 7.

128. Mao Zedong's Speech to the Supreme State Council, 5 September 1958, CWIHP*B*, nos. 6–7 (Winter 1995–96): 216–18.

129. During their meeting on the evening of 30 September 1959, Mao explained to the Soviet leader that "we did not discuss this issue [the Taiwan issue] at that time [during Khrushchev's visit to Beijing in July–August 1958] . . . because we only

were considering [the shelling], but had not made the final decision. We did not anticipate that the shelling would cause such a storm" (quoted from Shi Zhongquan, *Zhou Enlai de zuoyue fengxian*, 370). In November 1958, speaking at an inner-party meeting, Mao said that "at the Sino-Soviet talks [from July 31 to August 3, 1958] . . . nothing was mentioned about the Taiwan situation" (Mao Zedong, "Record of Talks with Directors of Various Cooperative Areas," 30 November 1958, *Mao Zedong sixiang wansui* [Long Live Mao Zedong Thought] [n.p., 1969], 255). See also "Memorandum of Conversation between Comrade N. S. Khrushchev and Chairman of the CCP Central Committee Mao Zedong," 2 October 1959, in Dimitry Volkoganov Collections, Manuscript Division, LC.

130. Wei Shiyan, "The Truth of Gromyko's Conversation with Chairman Mao Zedong on the Taiwan Issue," in Pei Jianzhang et al., *Xin zhongguo waijiao fengyun* (Experiences of New China's Diplomacy) (Beijing: Shijie zhishi, 1991–), 1:135–38; Xue Mouhong et al., *Dangdai zhongguo waijiao*, 115; Zhou Wenqi and Zhu Liangru, eds., *Teshu er fuzha de keti*, 515; Liu Guoxin, *Zhonghua renmin gongheguo lishi changbian*, 2:45; see also discussions in Chapter 7.

131. *Renmin ribao*, 9 September 1959; Zhou Wenqi and Zhu Liangru, eds., *Teshu er fuzha de keti*, 515.

132. Khrushchev later complained to Mao about their meetings: "[Y]ou do not let me say a word; what kind of equality can we talk about?" ("Memorandum of Conversation between Comrade N. S. Khrushchev and Chairman of the CCP Central Committee Mao Zedong," 2 October 1959, in Dimitry Volkoganov Collections, Manuscript Division, LC).

133. The State Economic Planning Commission, "Mobilizing the Whole Nation and Whole Party to Struggle for Realizing the Revised Plans for 1958," 6 May 1958, CCP Central Institute of Historical Documents, comp., *Jianguo yilai zhongyao wenxian xuanbian*, 11:326–33; see also Cong Jin, *Quzhe fazhan de suiyue*, 120–21, 132–33.

134. Allen Whiting, "The Sino-Soviet Split," in Twitchett and Fairbank, eds., *Cambridge History of China*, 14:500.

135. See, for example, Mao Zedong, "Speech Outlines on International Situation," December 1959, *JMZW*, 8:599–602, in which Mao angrily criticized Khrushchev's "unwitting" and "naïve" attitude toward the Great Leap Forward. In another letter, Mao wrote: "The Khrushchevs oppose, or are dubious about, these three things: letting a hundred flowers bloom, the people's communes, and the Great Leap Forward. I think they are in a passive position, whereas we are in an extremely active position" (Letter, Mao Zedong to Wang Jiaxiang, 1 August 1959, *JMZW*, 8:391).

136. Cong Jin, *Quzhe fazhan de suiyue*, 180–81.

137. "Materials on the Tibet Rebellion," *Zhonggong dangshi jiaoxue cankao ziliao* (Reference Materials on Teaching and Studying CCP History) (Beijing: Guofang daxue, n.d.), 23:23–40.

138. Cong Jin, *Quzhe fazhan de suiyue*, 352; Zhou Wenqi and Zhu Liangru, eds., *Teshu er fuzha de keti*, 516.

139. Liu Guoxin, *Zhonghua renmin gongheguo lishi changbian*, 2:71–72.

140. The best account of the Lushan conference is Li Rui, *Mao Zedong mishu shouji: Lushan huiyi shilu* (The Hand-Taken Notes of Mao Zedong's Secretary: A Factual Record of the Lushan Conference), rev. ed. (Zhengzhou: Henan renmin, 1994).

141. For the text of Peng Dehuai's letter to Mao, see *JMZW*, 8:358-61; for a plausible discussion, see Frederick C. Teiwes with Warren Sun, *China's Road to Disaster: Mao, Central Politicians, and Provincial Leaders in the Unfolding of the Great Leap Forward, 1955-1959* (Armonk, N.Y.: M. E. Sharpe, 1999), 206-8.

142. For discussions of Mao's criticism of Peng at the Lushan conference, see Li Rui, *Mao Zedong mishu shouji*, 128-40.

143. For the criticism of Peng Dehuai being a "Soviet agent" during and after the Lushan conference, see Cong Jin, *Quzhe fazhan de suiyue*, 305, and The Compilation Group of Peng Dehuai's Biography, ed., *Yige zhenzheng de ren: Peng Dehuai* (A True Man: Peng Dehuai) (Beijing: Renmin, 1994), 292-94.

144. Although the crisis emerging in Sino-Indian relations in 1959 was primarily a result of the disputes over the borders between the two countries, the Tibetan issue also played an important role. Beijing's leaders were extremely offended by New Delhi's covert support to the Dalai Lama. See Mao Zedong's remarks on an Indian news agency's reports on the Tibetan rebellion, 7 April 1959; Mao Zedong's remarks on Nerhu's speech on the Tibetan issue, 8 April 1959; and Mao Zedong's remarks on a Chinese Foreign Ministry memorandum to the Indian embassy, 25 April 1959, *JMZW*, 8:200-201, 202, 224-25.

145. Zhou Wenqi and Zhu Liangru, eds., *Teshu er fuzha de keti*, 517. Mao Zedong later complained that "in September 1959 during the Sino-Indian border dispute, Khrushchev supported Nehru in attacking us." See Mao Zedong, "Speech at the Tenth Plenum of the Eighth Central Committee," in Schram, ed., *Chairman Mao Talks to the People*, 190, and related findings in CWIHP*B*, nos. 8-9 (Winter 1996-97): 251-69, esp. 251-52, 259-62.

146. *Renmin ribao*, 1 October 1959.

147. Cong Jin, *Quzhe fazhan de suiyue*, 352; see also Mao Zedong, "Speech at the Tenth Plenum of the Eighth Central Committee," in Schram, ed., *Chairman Mao Talks to the People*, 190-91.

148. On the Soviet side, the participants include Khrushchev, Suslov, and Gromyko. On the Chinese side, the participants included Liu Shaoqi, Zhou Enlai, Zhu De, Lin Biao, Deng Xiaoping, Peng Zhen, Chen Yi, and Wang Jiaxiang. See Wang Taiping et al., *Zhonghua renmin gongheguo waijiao shi*, 229, and Cong Jin, *Quzhe fazhan de suiyue*, 352. For a Russian record of the meeting, see "Memorandum of Conversation between Comrade N. S. Khrushchev and Chairman of the CCP Central Committee Mao Zedong," 2 October 1959, in Dimitry Volkoganov Collections, Manuscript Division, LC.

149. Wang Taiping et al., *Zhonghua renmin gongheguo waijiao shi*, 229-30.

150. Ibid., 230; Liu Guoxin, *Zhonghua renmin gongheguo lishi changbian*, 2:64.

151. Cong Jin, *Quzhe fazhan de suiyue*, 353. At the meeting, the Chinese and Soviet leaders found that on only the Indochina issue were their policies identical; see Wang Taiping et al., *Zhonghua renmin gongheguo waijiao shi*, 230-31; see also

"Memorandum of Conversation between Comrade N. S. Khrushchev and Chairman of the CCP Central Committee Mao Zedong," 2 October 1959, in Dimitry Volkoganov Collections, Manuscript Division, LC.

152. "Memorandum of Conversation between Comrade N. S. Khrushchev and Chairman of the CCP Central Committee Mao Zedong," 2 October 1959, in Dimitry Volkoganov Collections, Manuscript Division, LC. The Chinese version of the meeting records is still inaccessible at Beijing's Central Archives but summaries of the meeting are provided in the following sources: Zhou Wenqi and Zhu Liangru, eds., *Teshu er fuzha de keti*, 517–18; Cong Jin, *Quzhe fazhan de suiyue*, 354; and Liu Guoxin, *Zhonghua renmin gongheguo lishi changbian*, 2:64–65.

153. Mao Zedong, "Speech Outlines on International Situation," December 1959, *JMZW*, 8:600.

154. Cong Jin, *Quzhe fazhan de suiyue*, 305–7.

155. The Chinese embassy in the Soviet Union submitted a detailed report about the speech to Beijing on 9 October 1959. See *JMZW*, 8:564–65.

156. Zhou Wenqi and Zhu Liangru, eds., *Teshu er fuzha de keti*, 518–19; Liu Guoxin, *Zhonghua renmin gongheguo lishi changbian*, 2:65.

157. For discussions about Mao's challenge-oriented character, see Chen Jian, *China's Road to the Korean War*, 27–28.

158. Xue Mouhong et al., *Dangdai zhongguo waijiao*, 116–19; Cong Jin, *Quzhe fazhan de suiyue*, 364; see also Chen Jian, "A Crucial Step toward the Breakdown of the Sino-Soviet Alliance: The Withdrawal of Soviet Experts from China in July 1960," CWIHP*B*, nos. 8–9 (Winter 1996–97): 246, 249–50.

159. In the wake of the Great Leap Forward, many top CCP leaders began to have serious doubts about Mao's radical plans to transform China's state and society, but they seldom questioned the wisdom of Mao's radical foreign policy.

160. Cong Jin, *Quzhe fazhan de suiyue*, 505–24; see also Roderick MacFarquhar, *The Origins of the Cultural Revolution*, vol. 3, *The Coming of the Cataclysm, 1961–1966* (New York: Columbia University Press, 1997), ch. 16.

161. Xu Dashen, ed., *Zhonghua renmin gongheguo shilu* (A Factorial History of the People's Republic of China) (Changchun: Jilin renmin, 1994), vol. 2, part B, 656–57.

162. Cong Jin, *Quzhe fazhan de suiyue*, 576–77, 579.

163. Minutes, "Mao Zedong's Conversations with Sasaki, Kuroda, and other Middle-Leftist members of the Japanese Socialist Party," 10 July 1964; "Mao Zedong's Conversations with the Director of French Technology Exhibition in Beijing and the French Ambassador to China," 10 September 1964; "Mao Zedong's Conversations with North Korean leader Choi Yong Kun," 7 October 1964, CCA.

164. See Wang Taiping et al., *Zhonghua renmin gongheguo waijiao shi*, 259–60; Jin Chongji, ed., *Zhou Enlai zhuan, 1949–1976*, 2:827–29.

Chapter Four

1. See Chen Jian, "China's Changing Aims during the Korean War, 1950–1951," *Journal of American–East Asian Relations* 1 (Spring 1992): 8–41, esp. 19–20.

2. The best studies on this issue include Rosemary Foot, *A Substitute for Victory: The Politics of Peacemaking at the Korean Armistice Talks* (Ithaca: Cornell University Press, 1990); and William Stueck, *The Korean War: An International History* (Princeton, N.J.: Princeton University Press, 1995).

3. A general discussion of this issue based on new Chinese sources can be found in Shu Guang Zhang, *Mao's Military Romanticism: China and the Korean War, 1950–1953* (Lawrence: University of Kansas Press, 1995), esp. ch. 9. However, the main attention of Zhang's book is given to the implications and significance of Chinese military experience in Korea. For a plausible study of China's negotiation style during the Korean War, see Alfred D. Wilhelm Jr., *The Chinese at the Negotiating Table: Style and Characteristics* (Washington, D.C.: National Defense University Press, 1994). For a more general study on China's negotiating behavior, see Richard H. Solomon, *Chinese Negotiating Behavior* (Washington, D.C.: United States Institute of Peace Press, 1999).

4. Although the North Korean Communists might not have informed the Beijing leadership of the exact date and specific details of their plans to invade the South, extensive exchanges existed between Beijing and Pyongyang before the outbreak of the Korean War. Beijing's leaders knew that the Korean Communists were determined to use military means to "liberate" the South. Beijing's leaders, and Mao in particular, did take into account the possibility of American intervention in the wake of such invasion, but the Chinese military planners did not believe that the Americans had the intention or capacity to engage in a major military intervention in Asia at that time. For more discussions, see Chen Jian, *China's Road to the Korean War: The Making of the Sino-American Confrontation* (New York: Columbia University Press, 1994), ch. 4.

5. For a revealing study of Beijing's changing strategies toward Taiwan in 1949–50 in general and after the outbreak of the Korean War in particular, see He Di, "The Last Campaign to Unify China: The CCP's Unmaterialized Plan to Liberate Taiwan, 1949-1950," *Chinese Historians* 5 (Spring 1992): 12–16.

6. For more on how the outbreak of the Korean War presented a variety of challenges to Beijing, see Chen Jian, *China's Road to the Korean War*, 126–30.

7. See, for example, instruction, PRC General Information Agency, "On the Propaganda against the U.S. Imperialists' Open Interference with China's Internal Affairs," 29 June 1950, in Xinhua News Agency, ed., *Xinhuashe wenjian ziliao huibian* (A Collection of Documentary Materials of the Xinhua News Agency) (Beijing, n.p., n.d.), 2:50.

8. Both Mao Zedong and Zhou Enlai emphasized this viewpoint at a CCP politburo meeting in early August 1950. See *Junshi lishi* (Military History), no. 6 (1996): 4; Bo Yibo, *Ruogan zhongda juece yu shijian de huigu* (Recollections of Several Important Decisions and Events) (Beijing: Zhonggong zhongyang dangxiao, 1992), 43; and *ZENB*, 1:62.

9. For a discussion of the intricate cooperation between Kim Il-sung's North Korean Communists and the CCP, see Bruce Cumings, *The Origins of the Korean War* (Princeton, N.J.: Princeton University Press, 1990), vol. 2, ch. 11; see also Chen Jian, *China's Road to the Korean War*, 106–13.

10. Report, Zhou Enlai at the Central Military Commission's Enlarged Meeting, 26 August 1950, in *CCFP*, 158–59; see also Shen Zonghong et al., *Zhongguo renmin zhiyuanjun kangmei yuanchao zhanshi* (A History of the Chinese People's Volunteers' War to Resist America and Assist Korea) (Beijing: Junshi kexue, 1988), 7.

11. Recollection, Xiao Jinguang, "The Taiwan Campaign Was Called Off," 30 June 1950, in *CCFP*, 155–56; see also Yang Guoyu et al., *Dangdai zhongguo haijun* (Contemporary Chinese Navy) (Beijing: Zhongguo shehui kexue, 1989), 41.

12. Letter, Mao Zedong to Nie Rongzhen, 7 July 1950, *JMZW*, 1:428; see also *DZJJG*, 1:449–50. Beijing's leaders consulted with Moscow while making the decision to establish the Northeast Border Defense Army. See ciphered telegram, Filippov [Stalin] to Zhou Enlai (via Soviet ambassador to China, N. V. Rochshin), 5 July 1950, CWIHP*B*, nos. 6–7 (Winter 1995–96): 43.

13. Telegram, Mao Zedong to Gao Gang, 18 August 1950, and telegram, Mao Zedong to Gao Gang, 5 August 1950, *JMZW*, 1:454, 469.

14. In Mao Zedong's management of the Korean crisis, he often referred to "beating American arrogance" as an important, even central, reason for China to intervene. See, for example, *JMZW*, 1:539, 556.

15. General Chinese Association of Resisting America and Assisting Korea, comp., *Weida de kangmei yuanchao yundong* (The Great Movement to Resist America and Assist Korea) (Beijing: Renmin, 1954), 7–8; "The Great Political Significance of the 'Special Week of Opposing the U.S. Invasion of Taiwan and Korea,'" *Shijie zhishi* (World Affairs), 22 (21 July 1950): 2.

16. See the State Council and Supreme People's Court, "Instructions on Suppressing Reactionary Activities," issued on 23 July 1950, in CCP Central Institute of Historical Documents, comp., *Jianguo yilai zhongyao wenxian xuanbian* (A Selection of Important Documents since the Founding of the People's Republic) (Beijing: Zhongyang wenxian, 1992–), 1:358–60; see also Zhang Min, "A Survey of the Struggle to Suppress Reactionaries in the Early Years of the PRC," *Dangde wenxian* (Party History Documents, Beijing), no. 2 (1988): 38–41.

17. Chai Chengwen and Zhao Yongtian, *Kangmei yuanchao jishi* (A Factual Record of the War to Resist America and Assist Korea) (Beijing: Jiefangjun, 1987), 47.

18. Speech, Zhou Enlai at the CCP Central Military Commission's Enlarged Meeting, 26 August 1950. In this speech, Zhou Enlai clearly pointed out that from Beijing's perspective, the settlement of the Korean issue should be related to Taiwan and China's seat at the UN. For a full transcript of the speech, see *ZEJW*, 4:42–49; for an English translation of part of the speech, see *CCFP*, 158–59. See also Zhou Enlai's talks with Indian ambassador to China K. M. Panikkar, 9 September 1950, *ZEWHDJ*, 21.

19. Except for a group of Chinese military-intelligence officers sent to Pyongyang in mid-July as diplomats, Beijing was unable to dispatch high-ranking military observers to Korea because Kim Il-sung did not want them. See Chai Chengwen and Zhao Yongtian, *Banmendian tanpan* (The Panmunjom Negotiations) (Beijing: Jiefangjun, 1989), 35–36, 77; and Hong Xuezhi, *Kangmei yuanchao zhanzheng huiyi* (Recollections of the War to Resist America and Assist Korea),

2d ed. (Beijing: Jiefangjun wenyi, 1992), 8–9. Indeed, during the early stage of the Korean War, the relationship between Beijing and Pyongyang was somewhat tense. In a telegram dated 8 July 1950, Stalin told Mao that "the Koreans are complaining that there is no representative of China in Korea." The Soviet leader urged the Chinese to send a representative to Korea, "if Mao Zedong considers it necessary to have communications with Korea." See ciphered telegram, 8 July 1950, Filippov [Stalin] to Soviet ambassador Rochshin, transmitting message to Mao Zedong, CWIHP*B*, nos. 6–7 (Winter 1995–96): 44.

20. For a comprehensive discussion, see Chen Jian, *China's Road to the Korean War*, chs. 6–7.

21. For a more detailed discussion about how the opinions of Beijing's leaders differed on whether or not China should enter the Korean War, see Chen Jian, *China's Road to the Korean War*, ch. 6, esp. 182–83.

22. Ciphered telegram, Filippov [Stalin] to Mao Zedong and Zhou Enlai, 1 October 1950, CWIHP*B*, nos. 6–7 (Winter 1995–96): 114.

23. For the top CCP leaders' discussion of the Korean crisis on 2 October 1950, see Zhang Xi, "Peng Dehuai and China's Entry into the Korean War," trans. Chen Jian, *Chinese Historians* 6 (Spring 1993): 6–8; see also Chen Jian, *China's Road to the Korean War*, 173–75.

24. Telegram, Mao Zedong to Stalin, 2 October 1950, *JMZW*, 1:539–40. See also discussions about the telegram's unpublished original text in Chapter 3.

25. For a more detailed discussion, see Shen Zhihua, "The Discrepancy between the Russian and Chinese Versions of Mao's 20 October 1950 Message to Stalin on Chinese Entry into the Korean War: A Chinese Scholar's Reply," trans. Chen Jian, CWIHP*B*, nos. 8–9 (Winter 1996–97): 237–42. See also discussions in Chapter 3.

26. Ciphered telegram, Rochshin to Stalin, 3 October 1950, CWIHP*B*, nos. 6–7 (Winter 1995–96): 114–16.

27. For a more detailed discussion, see Chen Jian, *China's Road to the Korean War*, 181–86.

28. "Mao Zedong's Order to Establish the Chinese People's Volunteers," 8 October 1950, *JMZW*, 1:543–44.

29. Telegram, Mao Zedong to Peng Dehuai and others, 12 October 1950, and telegram, Mao Zedong to Peng Dehuai, Gao Gang, and others, October 17, 1950, *JMZW*, 1:551, 567.

30. Zhou Enlai secretly visited the Soviet Union on 8–17 October and met with Stalin on the evening of 10 October. Stalin did agree to provide the Chinese with large amounts of military and other support, but on the key issue of how the Soviet air force would cover Chinese troops fighting in Korea, his attitude was ambiguous. See more detailed discussions in Chen Jian, *China's Road to the Korean War*, 196–208.

31. Michael H. Hunt, "Beijing and the Korean Crisis, June 1950–June 1951," *Political Science Quarterly* 107 (1992): 463.

32. Zhang Xi, "Peng Dehuai and China's Entry into the Korean War," 7–8; Chen Jian, *China's Road to the Korean War*, 173–75.

33. See Zhang Xi, "Peng Dehuai and China's Entry into the Korean War," 10–16, and Chen Jian, *China's Road to the Korean War*, 181–86.

34. For a more detailed discussion of this important episode in Beijing's decision to enter the Korean War, see Chen Jian, *China's Road to the Korean War*, ch. 7, and Li Taiwan, "How and When Did China Decide to Send Troops to Korea," trans. Chen Jian, *Korea and World Affairs* 18 (Spring 1994): 83–98.

35. Telegram, Mao Zedong to Stalin, 2 October 1950, and telegram, Mao Zedong to Zhou Enlai, 13 October 1950, *JMZW*, 1:539–41, 556.

36. Telegram, Stalin and Zhou Enlai to the CCP Central Committee, 11 October 1950, cited from Shi Zhe, *Zai lishi juren shenbian: Shi Zhe huiyilu* (At the Side of Historical Giants: Shi Zhe's Memoirs), rev. ed. (Beijing: Zhonggong zhongyang dangxiao, 1998), 442 n. 1; see also *CCFP*, 169 n. 33.

37. Telegram, Mao Zedong to Zhou Enlai, 13 October 1950, *JMZW*, 1:556; see also Zhang Xi, "Peng Dehuai and China's Entry into the Korean War," 23–24.

38. Peng Dehuai, *Peng Dehuai zishu* (The Autobiographical Notes of Peng Dehuai) (Beijing: Renmin, 1981), 259; Shen Zonghong et al., *Zhongguo renmin zhiyuanjun kangmei yuanchao zhanshi*, 37–38. According to Chinese statistics, about 15,000 South Korean soldiers were killed in this campaign.

39. Peng Dehuai, *Peng Dehuai zishu*, 259–60.

40. Stueck, *Korean War*, 139–40.

41. *FRUS, 1950*, 7, pt. 1, 1542.

42. Chai Chengwen and Zhao Yongtian, *Kangmei yuanchao jishi*, 70–71; see also Stueck, *Korean War*, 140–41.

43. For the exchanges between Beijing and Moscow concerning the Communist strategy toward the Korean conflict in December 1950, see VKP (b) CC Politburo decision with approved orders to Vyshinsky in New York and Rochshin in Beijing (with message for Zhou Enlai), 5 December 1950; ciphered telegram, Rochshin conveying message from Zhou Enlai to Soviet government, 7 December 1950; and ciphered telegram, Gromyko to Rochshin transmitting message from Filippov [Stalin] to Zhou Enlai, 7 December 1950, CWIHP*B*, nos. 6–7 (Winter 1995–96): 51–53.

44. K. M. Panikkar, *In Two Chinas* (London: Allen and Unwin, 1955), 118; Chai Chengwen and Zhao Yongtian, *Kangmei yuanchao jishi*, 69–70; Qi Dexue, *Chaoxian zhanzheng juece neimu* (The Inside Story of the Decision Making during the Korean War) (Shenyang: Liaoning daxue, 1991), 99.

45. Telegram, Peng Dehuai to Mao Zedong, 8 December 1950, *PDN*, 453–54. In this telegram, Peng told Mao that "even though we are able to cross the 38th parallel and occupy Seoul, unless we can give the enemy a decisive blow, we should not do it. Because if we march too deep into the south, pushing the enemy to the Taegu-Taejon line, the difficulties involved in our future operations will be dramatically increased. Therefore, we plan to stop dozens of kilometers north of the 38th parallel, and allow the enemy to occupy the parallel." In a 19 December 1950 telegram from Peng Dehuai to Mao Zedong, Peng further analyzed difficulties facing the Chinese troops. For a summary of the content of this telegram, see *CCFP*, 216–17 n. 81.

46. Quoted in Shen Zonghong et al., *Zhongguo renmin zhiyuanjun kangmei yuanchao zhanshi*, 56.

47. Telegram, Mao Zedong to Peng Dehuai, 13 December 1950, *CCFP*, 215.

48. Telegram, Mao Zedong to Peng Dehuai, 21 December 1950, ibid., 216–18.

49. Chai Chengwen and Zhao Yongtian, *Kangmei yuanchao jishi*, 71; *FRUS, 1950*, 7:1594–98.

50. Telegram, Peng Dehuai to CCP Central Committee and Gao Gang, 8 January 1951, *PDN*, 465; see also Shen Zonghong et al., *Zhongguo renmin zhiyuanjun kangmei yuanchao zhanshi*, 64.

51. For the text of the proposal, see *FRUS, 1951*, 7:64; for the background of the proposal, see Stueck, *Korean War,* 152–54; for a Chinese depiction of the proposal, see Chai Chengwen and Zhao Yongtian, *Kangmei yuanchao jishi*, 75.

52. Telegram, Peng Dehuai to Han Xianchu, Wu Ruilin, and Fang Hushan, 7 January 1951, *PDN*, 465; see also Hong Xuezhi, *Kangmei yuanchao zhanzheng huiyi*, 109–10, and Tan Jinqiao et al., *Kangmei yuanchao zhanzheng* (The War to Resist America and Assist Korea) (Beijing: Zhongguo shehui kexue, 1990), 100.

53. For a critical discussion of this issue, see Xu Yan, *Diyici jiaoliang* (The First Test of Strength) (Beijing: Zhongguo guangbo dianshi, 1990), 68–69.

54. Dean Acheson, *Present at the Creation: My Years in the State Department* (New York: North, 1969), 513; Stueck, *Korean War,* 153–54; Foot, *Substitute for Victory,* 31–32.

55. Chai Chengwen and Zhao Yongtian, *Kangmei yuanchao jishi*, 76; *FRUS, 1951*, 7:91–92.

56. Telegram, Mao Zedong to Peng Dehuai and Kim Il-sung, 14 January 1951, cited from Shen Zonghong et al., *Zhongguo renmin zhiyuanjun kangmei yuanchao zhanshi*, 67. Mao sent a copy of the telegram to Stalin; see ciphered telegram, Mao Zedong to Filippov [Stalin], 16 January 1951, CWIHP*B*, nos. 6–7 (Winter 1995–96): 55–56.

57. Telegram, Peng Dehuai to Mao Zedong and the CMC, 10 January 1951, *PDN*, 463. Peng reported in this telegram that the North Koreans were very unhappy with his decision to stop the offensive and they put forward their complaints through V. N. Razuvaev, Soviet ambassador in North Korea, who conveyed these complaints to the Chinese.

58. See Peng Dehuai, *Peng Dehuai zishu, neibu* (The Autobiographical Notes of Peng Dehuai, internal version) (Beijing: publisher unclear), 349–50. (The internal version of *Peng Dehuai zishu*, which differs significantly from the book's published edition, is based on Peng's personal accounts and papers.) See also Wang Yazhi, "General Nie Rongzhen's Two Talks during the War to Resist America and Assist Korea," *Dangshi yanjiu ziliao* (Party History Research Materials, Beijing), no. 11 (1992): 1–2.

59. Transcript, Peng Dehuai's conversation with Kim Il-sung and Pak Hong-yong, 11 January 1951, CCA; see also *PDN*, 466.

60. Chai Chengwen and Zhao Yongtian, *Kangmei yuanchao jishi*, 76; in an attached letter to Chinese chargé d'affaires Chai Chengwen, Zhou Enlai instructed

him to convey to Kim Il-sung that the memo had been "fully approved by the Soviet government" (*ZENB*, 1:117).

61. Telegram, Mao Zedong to Peng Dehuai, convey to Kim Il-sung, 14 January 1951, CCA. On 15 January, Mao sent a copy of the telegram to Stalin.

62. Chai Chengwen and Zhao Yongtian, *Kangmei yuanchao jishi*, 76. See also ciphered telegram, Mao Zedong to Filippov [Stalin], conveying 19 January 1951 telegram from Peng Dehuai to Mao re meetings with Kim Il-sung, 27 January 1951, CWIHP*B*, nos. 6-7 (Winter 1995-96): 56.

63. Mao Zedong's remarks, 19 January 1951, *MZJW*, 6:266.

64. Instruction, the CCP Central Committee, "On Further Promoting the Movement to Resist America and Assist Korea among All Walks in the Country," 2 February 1951, *Zhonggong dangshi jiaoxue cankao ziliao* (Reference Materials on Teaching and Studying CCP History) (Beijing: Guofang daxue, n.d.), 19:242-43.

65. "Main Points of the Resolutions Passed by the Enlarged Meeting of the CCP Politburo," 18 February 1951, *JMZW*, 2:126.

66. Telegram, Peng Dehuai to Mao Zedong, 27 January 1951, *PDN*, 469.

67. Telegram, Mao Zedong to Peng Dehuai, 28 January 1951, CCA. For a detailed discussion of the exchanges between Mao and Peng, see Chen Jian, "China's Changing Aims during the Korean War," 31-33. Mao Zedong also conveyed this telegram to Stalin, asking Stalin's opinion about whether this tactic was "advisable from the point of view of the international situation." Two days later, Stalin replied that "[f]rom the international point of view, it is undoubtedly advisable that the enemy not seize Chemulpo and Seoul, so that the Chinese-Korean troops can make a serious rebuff to attacking enemy troops." See ciphered telegram, Mao Zedong to Filippov [Stalin] conveying 28 January 1951 telegram from Mao Zedong to Peng Dehuai, 29 January 1951, and ciphered telegram, Filippov [Stalin] to Mao Zedong, 30 January 1951, CWIHP*B*, nos. 6-7 (Winter 1995-96): 57-58.

68. For Chinese accounts of this campaign, see Xu Yan, *Diyici jiaoliang*, 72-79, and Tan Jinqiao et al., *Kangmei yuanchao zhanzheng*, 112-21; for an American account, see Mattew B. Ridgway, *The Korean War* (Garden City, N.Y.: Doubleday, 1967), 106-8.

69. *PDN*, 480-81; Wang Yan et al., *Peng Dehuai zhuan* (A Biography of Peng Dehuai) (Beijing: Dangdai zhongguo, 1993), 451-53; Chai Chengwen and Zhao Yongtian, *Kangmei yuanchao jishi*, 15.

70. Telegram, Mao Zedong to Stalin, 1 March 1951, *JMZW*, 2:151-53. For a more detailed discussion of Mao's changing attitude toward Chinese victory in Korea, see Chen Jian, "China's Changing Aims during the Korean War," 34-36.

71. Shen Zonghong et al., *Zhongguo renmin zhiyuanjun kangmei yuanchao zhanshi*, 93.

72. While preparing for the fifth campaign, the Communist side fully understood that proper air cover would play a decisive role in determining the campaign's result. Early in March 1951, Stalin agreed to move the bases of two Soviet air divisions, which were then stationed in China's Northeast, into the territory of North Korea, so that they would better defend the Chinese–North Korean logisti-

cal lines. However, because of intensive American air bombardment, the Chinese and North Koreans were not able to complete the construction of the new airfields. For the exchanges between Chinese and Soviet leaders on this issue, see ciphered telegram, Filippov [Stalin] to Mao Zedong or Zhou Enlai (via Zakharov), 15 March 1951, CWIHPB, nos. 6–7 (Winter 1995-96): 59; ciphered telegram, Filippov to Mao Zedong, 3 March 1951; ciphered telegram, Mao Zedong to Filippov, 18 March 1951; ciphered telegram, Zhou Enlai to Filippov, 23 March 1951; and ciphered telegram, Zhou Enlai to Filippov, 1 April 1951, in Chinese Military Science Academy, ed., *Guanyu chaoxian zhanzheng de eguo wenjian* (Russian Archival Documents on the Korean War) (Beijing: Zhongguo junshi kexueyuan, 1996), 142, 143–44, 146.

73. For a Chinese account of the fifth campaign, see Shen Zonghong et al., *Zhongguo renmin zhiyuanjun kangmei yuanchao zhanshi*, 94–109; for a more extended discussion of the repercussions of China's failure to achieve its original goals in the fifth campaign, see Chen Jian, "China's Changing Aims during the Korean War," 37–38.

74. Telegram, Mao Zedong to Peng Dehuai, 26 May 1951, *JMZW*, 2:331–32. In this telegram, Mao acknowledged that it was impossible for the Chinese volunteers to annihilate an American division, or even an entire American regiment, in a single campaign, and that "the American troops at the present time still strongly desire to fight and are self-confident." Mao also conveyed the telegram to Stalin, asking for his opinions. Stalin replied that the Chinese/North Korean forces should be very cautious in planning a new campaign, and should fully understand that the U.S./UN forces were different from Jiang Jieshi's troops, who the PLA had defeated in China's civil war (ciphered telegram, Mao Zedong to Filippov [Stalin], 27 May 1951; and ciphered telegram, Filippov to Mao Zedong, 29 May 1951, in Chinese Military Science Academy, ed., *Guanyu chaoxian zhanzheng de eguo wenjian*, 151–52.

75. Nie Rongzhen, *Nie Rongzhen huiyilu* (Nie Rongzhen's Memoirs) (Beijing: Jiefangjun, 1986), 741–42.

76. See, for example, instruction, CCP Central Committee, "On the Propaganda of the Peace Negotiations in Korea," 3 July 1951, quoted in Qi Dexue, *Chaoxian zhanzheng juece neimu*, 188.

77. Xu Yan, *Diyici jiaoliang*, 268.

78. Letter, Kim Il-sung to Peng Dehuai, 30 May 1951, *PDN*, 500.

79. Telegram, Mao Zedong to Peng Dehuai, 2 June 1951, *JMZW*, 2:350.

80. Chai Chengwen and Zhao Yongtian, *Banmendian tanpan*, 115.

81. In reality, Kim Il-sung had lost much of his commanding power over North Korean troops after December 1950, when the Chinese and North Korean forces signed an agreement to establish a joint Chinese/North Korean headquarters. The contract put the commanding power of all Communist forces in Korea into the hands of Chinese commanders. For the agreement, see *ZEJW*, 4:122–24. See also telegram, Peng Dehuai to Mao Zedong, 7 December 1950, in which Peng reported that Kim Il-sung had agreed "not to intervene in military commanding affairs [in Korea] in the future" (*PDN*, 453).

82. Telegram, Mao Zedong to Peng Dehuai, 11 June 1951, *JMZW*, 2:355; Chai

Chengwen and Zhao Yongtian, *Banmendian tanpan*, 115-16; Tan Jinqiao at al., *Kangmei yuanchao zhanzheng*, 165.

83. Tan Jinqiao et al., *Kangmei yuanchao zhanzheng*, 165; Shen Zonghong et al. *Zhongguo renmin zhiyuanjun kangmei yuanchao zhanshi*, 118.

84. Handwritten letter, Mao Zedong to Gao Gang and Kim Il-sung, 13 June 1951, CWIHP*B*, nos. 6-7 (Winter 1995-96): 61-62.

85. After receiving Mao Zedong's 11 June 1951 telegram, Peng Dehuai commented that "it is good that Comrade Kim Il-sung has agree that [we] should not start another major offensive in the next two months, but the basic problem remains unresolved" (telegram, Peng Dehuai to Mao Zedong, 12 June 1951, *PDN*, 505-6). Peng did not specify what "basic problem" he meant here, but according to the context of the comment, it probably was Kim's attitude toward the new Chinese strategy.

86. Shi Zhe, *Zai lishi juren shenbian*, 451-54; author's interviews with Shi Zhe, August 1992.

87. Ciphered telegram, Filippov [Stalin] to Mao Zedong re meeting in Moscow with Gao Gang and Kim Il-sung, 13 June 1951, CWIHP*B*, nos. 6-7 (Winter 1995-96): 60-61. In this telegram, Stalin also agreed to send Soviet military advisers to Peng Dehuai's headquarters and help equip sixty Chinese divisions.

88. Stueck, *Korean War*, 208. The next day, Stalin wrote to Mao, "[Y]ou must already know from Malik's speech that our promise about raising the question of an armistice has already been fulfilled by us. It is possible that the matter of an armistice will move forward." See ciphered telegram, Filippov [Stalin] to Mao Zedong, 24 June 1951, CWIHP*B*, nos. 6-7 (Winter 1995-96): 62.

89. *Renmin ribao* (People's Daily), 25 June 1951; Chai Chengwen and Zhao Yongtian, *Banmendian tanpan*, 126.

90. *FRUS, 1951*, 7:547.

91. See discussions in Chapter 1.

92. Telegram, Mao Zedong to Peng Dehuai, Kim Il-sung, and Gao Gang, 2 July 1951, *JMZW*, 2:379-80. Mao conveyed this telegram to Stalin; see ciphered telegram, Mao Zedong to Stalin, 3 July 1951, CWIHP*B*, nos. 6-7 (Winter 1995-96): 67. See also Chai Chengwen and Zhao Yongtian, *Banmendian tanpan*, 118-19, and Du Ping, *Zai zhiyuanjun zongbu: Du Ping huiyilu* (My Days at the Headquarters of the Chinese People's Volunteers: Du Ping's Memoirs) (Beijing: Jiefangjun, 1989), 260-70.

93. Chai Chengwen and Zhao Yongtian, *Banmendian tanpan*, 119. Mao Zedong paid close attention to managing Chinese and North Korean negotiation strategies and tactics at Kaesong. He even dictated the texts of the Chinese delegation's news releases. See, for example, telegram, Mao Zedong to Peng Dehuai, Gao Gang, and Kim Il-sung, 3 July 1951, telegram, Mao Zedong to Li Kenong, 9 July 1950, telegram, Mao Zedong to Li Kenong, 11 July 1950, and telegram, Mao Zedong to Li Kenong, 14 July 1950, *JMZW*, 2:381-82, 390, 392, 415.

94. Chai Chengwen and Zhao Yongtian, *Banmendian tanpan*, 119-20, 124; Du Ping, *Zai zhiyuanjun zongbu*, 270.

95. Instruction, CCP Central Committee, "On the Propaganda Affairs Con-

cerning the Peace Negotiations in Korea," 3 July 1951, quoted in Qi Dexue, *Chaoxian zhanzheng juece neimu*, 188.

96. Telegram, Mao Zedong to Peng Dehuai, Gao Gang, and convey to Kim Il-sung, 2 July 1951, *JMZW*, 2:381. Mao also conveyed the telegram to Stalin; see ciphered telegram, Mao Zedong to Stalin, 7 July 1951, CWIHP*B*, nos. 6–7 (Winter 1995–96): 67.

97. Chai Chengwen and Zhao Yongtian, *Banmendian tanpan*, 150–51, 169–70.

98. Report, Peng Dehuai, "The Emphasis and Arrangement of Our Work in the Future," 26 June 1951, and telegram, Peng Dehuai to Mao Zedong, 1 July 1951, *PDN*, 506–8.

99. Chai Chengwen and Zhao Yongtian, *Banmendian tanpan*, 167–68; Nie Rongzhen, *Nie Rongzhen huiyilu*, 742.

100. Ciphered telegram, Mao Zedong to Filippov [Stalin], 3 July 1951, CWIHP*B*, nos. 6–7 (Winter 1995–96): 66.

101. Telegram, Peng Dehuai to CPV and KPA commanders, 2 July 1951, *PDN*, 509; see also Qi Dexue, *Chaoxian zhanzheng juece neimu*, 202, and Wang Yan et al., *Peng Dehuai zhuan*, 472–73.

102. Telegram, Mao Zedong to Peng Dehuai and Gao Gang, and convey to Kim Il-sung, 2 July 1951, *JMZW*, 2:381.

103. Qi Dexue, *Chaoxian zhanzheng juece neimu*, 203.

104. *FRUS, 1951*, 7:735.

105. Ibid., 739–45; Chai Chengwen and Zhao Yongtian, *Banmendian tanpan*, 167–70.

106. *FRUS, 1951*, 7:743; Chai Chengwen and Zhao Yongtian, *Banmendian tanpan*, 167.

107. Telegram, Mao Zedong to Li Kenong, and convey to Kim Il-sung and Peng Dehuai, 22:00 P.M., 17 July 1951; telegram, Mao Zedong to Li Kenong, and convey to Kim Il-sung and Peng Dehuai, 3:00 A.M., 23 July 1951; telegram, Mao Zedong to Li Kenong, and convey to Kim Il-sung and Peng Dehuai, 3:00 A.M., 28 July 1951; and telegram, Mao Zedong to Li Kenong, and convey to Kim Il-sung and Peng Dehuai, 1 August 1951, *ZEJW*, 4:200–201, 204–5, 207, 209–10.

108. Telegram, Peng Dehuai to Mao Zedong, 24 July 1951, *PDN*, 510; see also *JMZW*, 2:426 n. 2.

109. Telegram, Mao Zedong to Peng Dehuai, 26 July 1951, *JMZW*, 2:426.

110. Telegram, Mao Zedong to Peng Dehuai, 1 August 1951, ibid., 428.

111. Telegram, Deng Hua and Xie Fang to Peng Dehuai, 31 July 1951, quoted from Qi Dexue, *Chaoxian zhanzheng juece neimu*, 204.

112. Telegram, Peng Dehuai to Mao Zedong and Gao Gang, 8 August 1951, *PDN*, 512–13; see also Qi Dexue, *Chaoxian zhanzheng juece neimu*, 204–5.

113. *PDN*, 513; see also Qi Dexue, *Chaoxian zhanzheng juece neimu*, 204.

114. Du Ping, *Zai zhiyuanjun zongbu*, 278.

115. Telegram, Deng Hua to Peng Dehuai, 18 August 1951, quoted from Du Ping, *Zai zhiyuanjun zongbu*, 278; see also Deng Hua, *Lun kangmei yuanchao zhanzheng de zuozhan zhidao* (On the Operational Direction during the War to Resist America and Assist Korea) (Beijing: Junshi kexue, 1989), 25–34.

116. Telegram, Li Kenong to Mao Zedong, 12 August 1951, quoted from Qi Dexue, *Chaoxian zhanzheng juece neimu*, 217–18; see also ciphered telegram, Mao Zedong to Filippov [Stalin], 13 August 1951, conveying 12 August telegram from Li Kenong to Mao Zedong re armistice talks, CWIHP*B*, nos. 6–7 (Winter 1995–96): 67–68.

117. Letter, Zhou Enlai to Mao Zedong, 11 August 1951, *ZEJW*, 4:211–13. (In the letter, Zhou cited Mao's 10 August instructions to him.) The meeting attendees concluded that it would be difficult for the CPV/KPA forces to be ready to start another major offensive campaign in Korea in September.

118. Qi Dexue, *Chaoxian zhanzheng juece neimu*, 205.

119. Telegram (drafted by Zhou Enlai), CCP Central Military Commission to Peng Dehuai (and convey to Gao Gang), 19 August 1951, *ZEJW*, 4:217–19.

120. Foot, *Substitute for Victory*, 48; Chai Chengwen and Zhao Yongtian, *Banmendian tanpan*, 148–49.

121. Du Ping, *Zai zhiyuanjun zongbu*, 369; *PDN*, 515.

122. Ciphered telegram, Mao Zedong to Filippov [Stalin], 27 August 1951, CWIHP*B*, nos. 6–7 (Winter 1995–96): 68–69; see also Chai Chengwen and Zhao Yongtian, *Banmendian tanpan*, 148, and Du Ping, *Zai zhiyuanjun zongbu*, 369–70.

123. Ciphered telegram, Mao Zedong to Filippov [Stalin], 27 August 1951, CWIHP*B*, nos. 6–7 (Winter 1995–96): 68.

124. Report, "On the Korean Armistice Negotiation," Zhou Enlai at a Chinese Central People's Government meeting, 22 August 1951, and outline of report, "On the Korean Armistice Negotiation and the Peace Treaty with Japan," Zhou Enlai at Chinese Central Government Council meeting, 3 September 1951, *ZEJW*, 4:221–27, 234–37.

125. *ZEJW*, 4:235.

126. See, for example, telegram, Deng Hua to Peng Dehuai, 25 August 1951, quoted from *PDN*, 515; and Du Ping, *Zai Zhiyuanjun zongbu*, 375.

127. Zhou Enlai, "The Korean Armistice Talks and the Question of Signing a Peace Treaty with Japan," 3 September 1951, *ZEJW*, 4:235; Du Ping, *Zai zhiyuanjun zongbu*, 375–76.

128. Qi Dexue, *Chaoxian zhanzheng juece neimu*, 206.

129. Zhou Enlai, "The Korean Armistice Talks and the Question of Signing a Peace Treaty with Japan," 3 September 1951, *ZEJW*, 4:234–35; see also Chai Chengwen and Zhao Yongtian, *Kangmei yuanchao jishi*, 159–60; Du Ping, *Zai zhiyuanjun zongbu*, 387–88.

130. Telegram, Mao Zedong to Filippov [Stalin], 14 November 1951, *ZEJW*, 4:249–51; see also CWIHP*B*, nos. 6–7 (Winter 1995–96): 70–71.

131. Chai Chengwen and Zhao Yongtian, *Banmendian tanpan*, 179–83.

132. Stueck, *Korean War*, 241.

133. Foot, *Substitute for Victory*, 75–76; Chai Chengwen and Zhao Yongtian, *Banmendian tanpan*, 195.

134. Telegrams, Mao Zedong to Peng Dehuai, 18 and 14 November 1950, *JMZW*, 1:685.

135. Telegram, Mao Zedong to Peng Dehuai, 18 November 1950, *JMZW*, 1:672.

136. Telegram, Mao Zedong to Peng Dehuai and Gao Gang, 2 July 1951, *JMZW*, 2:381–82; see also telegram, Peng Dehuai to Li Kenong, Deng Hua, and Xie Fang, 16 July 1951, *Peng Dehuai junshi wenxuan* (Selected Military Papers of Peng Dehuai) (Beijing: Zhongyang wenxian, 1988), 413–14.

137. Telegram, Mao Zedong to Filippov [Stalin], 14 November 1951, *ZEJW*, 4:250.

138. Chai Chengwen and Zhao Yongtian, *Banmendian tanpan*, 183.

139. *FRUS, 1951*, 7:1421–23; Chai Chengwen and Zhao Yongtian, *Banmendian tanpan*, 201–2.

140. Xu Yan, *Diyici jiaoliang*, 281–82; Chai Chengwen and Zhao Yongtian, *Banmendian tanpan*, 204–5.

141. *FRUS, 1952–1954*, 15:6. See also Foot, *Substitute for Victory*, 96. Following Beijing's instructions, the Chinese/North Korean negotiators categorically rejected the U.S./UN nonforcible repatriation proposal on January 8. They argued that the proposal had violated the Geneva Convention, which called for the exchange of all POWs immediately after the end of hostilities, and that the proposal had politicized this military issue (Chai Chengwen and Zhao Yongtian, *Kangmei yuanchao jishi*, 116).

142. In a press release on May 7, for example, President Truman emphasized that forceful repatriation of Communist POWs under UN custody would be "repugnant to the fundamental moral and humanitarian principles which underlie our action in Korea." Quoted in Foot, *Substitute for Victory*, 108.

143. For a plausible discussion of the U.S./UN stand on the POW issue and the logic underlying it, see Foot, *Substitute for Victory*, ch. 5.

144. *FRUS, 1952*, 15:173–76, 179–80.

145. Du Ping, *Zai zhiyuanjun zongbu*, 465; Xu Yan, *Diyici jiaoliang*, 279–89.

146. Telegram (drafted by Zhou Enlai), Mao Zedong to Filippov [Stalin], 29 May 1952, *ZENB*, 1:239–40.

147. Telegram, Li Kenong to Mao Zedong, 13 July 1952, and telegram, Li Kenong to Mao Zedong, 14 July 1952, cited from Du Ping, *Zai zhiyuanjun zongbu*, 473; see also *ZEJW*, 4:290, and *ZENB*, 1:248.

148. Telegram (drafted by Zhou Enlai), Mao Zedong to Kim Il-sung and Li Kenong, 15 July 1952, *ZEJW*, 4:289–90. On 18 July 1952, Mao Zedong conveyed the text of the telegram to Stalin; see CWIHP*B*, nos. 6–7 (Winter 1995–96): 78–79.

149. Du Ping, *Zai zhiyuanjun zongbu*, 474–75.

150. Qi Dexue, *Chaoxian zhanzheng juece neimu*, 280; Tan Jinqiao et al., *Kangmei yuanchao zhanzheng*, 214–15; Shen Zonghong et al., *Zhongguo renmin zhiyuanjun kangmei yuanchao zhanshi*, 149–50.

151. *Renmin ribao*, 23 and 25 February 1952.

152. Zhou Enlai's talks with Panikkar, 5 April 1952, *ZENB*, 1:232; Shen Zonghong et al., *Zhongguo renmin zhiyuanjun kangmei yuanchao zhanshi*, 150; Tan Jinqiao et al., *Kangmei yuanchao zhanzheng*, 216–19.

153. Report, Nie Rongzhen to Zhou Enlai and Mao Zedong, 18 February 1952,

Nie Rongzhen junshi wenxuan (Selected Military Papers of Nie Rongzhen) (Beijing: Jiefangjun, 1992), 365–66.

154. Mao Zedong's remarks on Nie Rongzhen's report, 19 February 1952, *JMZW*, 3:239; see also *ZEJW*, 4:275–83, and *ZENB*, 1:243.

155. In a recent study, *The United States and Biological Warfare: Secrets from the Early Cold War and Korea* (Bloomington: Indiana University Press, 1998), Stephen Endicott and Edward Hagerman argue that Washington indeed was involved in experimental biological warfare in China's Northeast and North Korea in the winter of 1951–52. But their evidence is at most circumstantial. In a collection of recently available Russian documents titled "Deceiving the Deceivers: Moscow, Beijing, Pyongyang, and the Allegations of Bacteriological Weapons Use in Korea," Kathryn Weathersby and Milton Leitenberg point out that the Communist allegation of American use of biological weapons in Korea was fabricated and that it is time to conclude that the United States did not use biological weapons during the Korean War. See CWIHP*B*, no. 11 (Winter 1998): 176–85.

156. Telegram, Zhou Enlai to Li Kenong, 9 March 1952, and telegram, Zhou Enlai to CCP Northeast Bureau, 20 March 1952, *ZENB*, 1:224, 231–32.

157. Peng Dehuai's speech at the welcome ceremony of the "Investigation Delegation of U.S. Imperialist Crime of Biological War," 26 March 1952, *Peng Dehuai junshi wenxuan*, 435–36; see also Shen Zonghong et al., *Zhongguo renmin zhiyuanjun kangmei yuanchao zhanshi*, 149–52; Qi Dexue, *Chaoxian zhanzheng juece neimu*, 282.

158. Qi Dexue, *Chaoxian zhanzheng juece neimu*, 285; Tan Jinqiao et al., *Kangmei yuanchao zhanzheng*, 219.

159. Shi Zhe, *Zai lishi juren shenbian*, 455–58; *ZENB*, 1:256.

160. Qi Dexue, *Chaoxian zhanzheng juece neimu*, 316–17, 319; Xu Yan, *Diyici jiaoliang*, 139–41.

161. Shi Zhe, *Zai lishi juren shenbian*, 456; *ZENB*, 258–59.

162. Telegram (drafted by Zhou Enlai), Mao Zedong to Semenov [Stalin], 16 December 1952, *ZENB*, 4:308–11; Mao Zedong's remarks on Nie Rongzhen's report, 11 December 1952, *JMZW*, 3:640–41; see also Xu Yan, *Diyici jiaoliang*, 136–39, and Qi Dexue, *Chaoxian zhanzheng juece neimu*, 318.

163. Instructions (drafted by Mao), the CCP Central Committee, 20 December 1952, quoted from Qi Dexue, *Chaoxian zhanzheng juece neimu*, 314–15; for an informative discussion, see also Shu Guang Zhang, *Deterrence and Strategic Culture: Chinese-American Confrontations, 1949–1958* (Ithaca: Cornell University Press, 1992), 131–37.

164. Speech, Mao Zedong at the 38th session of the Chinese People's Political Consultative Conference, 4 August 1952, *MZJW*, 6:317–18; see also Zhou Enlai, "The Enemy's Defeat and Our Victory," 11 December 1952, *ZEJW*, 4:292–305.

165. Chai Chengwen and Zhao Yongtian, *Kangmei yuanchao jishi*, 138.

166. Zhou Enlai, "The Enemy's Defeat and Our Victory," 11 December 1952, *ZEJW*, 4:296–97; see also Qi Dexue, *Chaoxian zhanzheng juece neimu*, 314.

167. *FRUS, 1952–1954*, 15:554–57.

168. See, for example, Stueck, *Korean War,* 308–9; Kathryn Weathersby, "Stalin, Mao, and the End of the Korean War," in *Brothers in Arms: The Rise and Fall of the Sino-Soviet Alliance, 1949–1963,* ed. Odd Arne Westad (Washington, D.C., and Stanford, Calif.: Woodrow Wilson Center Press and Stanford University Press, 1999), 108.

169. *Renmin ribao,* 31 March 1953.

170. Weathersby, "Stalin, Mao, and the End of the Korean War," 108–10.

171. *ZEWHDJ,* 44.

172. See Staff of the Foreign Ministry of the Soviet Union, "Background Report on the Korean War, 9 August 1966," trans. Kathryn Weathersby, *Journal of American–East Asian Relations* 2 (Winter 1993): 445.

173. Telegram, Mao Zedong to Semenov [Stalin], 16 December 1952, *ZEJW,* 4:311.

174. Transcript, conversation between Stalin and Zhou Enlai, 20 August 1952, CWIHP*B,* nos. 6–7 (Winter 1995–96): 9–14; Shi Zhe, *Zai lishi juren shenbian,* 455–56.

175. Transcript, conversation between Stalin and Zhou Enlai, 20 August 1952, CWIHP*B,* nos. 6–7 (Winter 1995–96): 9–14; Shi Zhe, *Zai lishi juren shenbian,* 455–58.

176. Telegram, Zhou Enlai to Mao Zedong and CCP Central Committee, 23 August 1952, *ZENB,* 1:257; Shi Zhe, *Zai lishi juren shenbian,* 455–58.

177. *ZENB,* 1:257.

178. Ibid., 258; Shi Zhe, *Zai lishi juren shenbian,* 457–58.

179. Transcript, conversation between Stalin and Zhou Enlai, 19 September 1952, CWIHP*B,* nos. 6–7 (Winter 1995–96): 15–17; telegram, Mao Zedong to Zhou Enlai, 13 September 1952, *JMZW,* 3:544–45; Shi Zhe, *Zai lishi juren shenbian,* 468; Wang Yan et al., *Peng Dehuai zhuan,* 480.

180. Telegram, Mao Zedong to Semenov [Stalin], 16 December 1952, *ZEJW,* 4:308–12.

181. Chai Chengwen and Zhao Yongtian, *Banmendian tanpan,* 250.

182. Ibid.; Chai Chengwen and Zhao Yongtian, *Kangmei yuanchao jishi,* 147. On 23 March, four days before the Communists responded positively to the U.S./UN proposal regarding the exchange of sick and wounded prisoners, Mao Zedong argued that the reason that the Americans made the suggestion might be because Eisenhower intended to change the rigid American attitude at Panmunjom. See telegram, Mao Zedong to Ding Guoyu and convey to Kim Il-sung and Peng Dehuai, 23 March 1953, *JMZW,* 4:148–49.

183. *FRUS, 1952–1954,* 15:1151.

184. *ZENB,* 1:305–6; Chai Chengwen and Zhao Yongtian, *Banmendian tanpan,* 260.

185. Telegram, Peng Dehuai to Deng Hua (acting commander of CPV), 15 June 1953, *PDN,* 552–53; Qi Dexue, *Chaoxian zhanzheng juece neimu,* 340; Wang Yan et al., *Peng Dehuai zhuan,* 483–84.

186. Foot, *Substitute for Victory,* 183–84.

187. Telegram, Mao Zedong to CPV commanders and the Chinese negotiation

team, 19 June 1953, quoted from Qi Dexue, *Chaoxian zhanzheng juece neimu*, 344; see also Tan Jinqiao et al., *Kangmei yuanchao zhanzheng*, 307.

188. Telegram, Peng Dehuai to Mao Zedong, 20 June 1953, *PDN*, 553; see also Qi Dexue, *Chaoxian zhanzheng juece neimu*, 345; Wang Yan et al., *Peng Dehuai zhuan*, 484; and Tan Jinqiao et al., *Kangmei yuanchao zhanzheng*, 307–8.

189. Telegram, Mao Zedong to Peng Dehuai, 21 June 1953, *MZJW*, 6:350; *PDN*, 553.

190. See Peng Dehuai, *Peng Dehuai zishu, neibu*, 352. Kim Il-sung's reservation about launching the offensive was previously unknown to scholars. Kim most likely did not want to prolong the war further because he was then engaged in the purge of Pak Hon-yong and Pak Il-yu and other opposition leaders within the North Korean party.

191. Foot, *Substitute for Victory*, 186–87; Shen Zonghong et al., *Zhongguo renmin zhiyuanjun kangmei yuanchao zhanshi*, 205–13; Tan Jinqiao et al., *Kangmei yuanchao zhanzheng*, 305–25.

192. For a detailed analysis, see Chen Jian, *China's Road to the Korean War*, 220–22.

Chapter Five

1. King Chen, *Vietnam and China, 1938–1954* (Princeton, N.J.: Princeton University Press, 1969). Recently, the lacuna has been filled in by Zhai Qiang's *China and the Vietnam Wars, 1950–1975* (Chapel Hill: University of North Carolina Press, 2000).

2. Huang Zheng, *Hu Zhiming yu Zhongguo* (Ho Chi Minh and China) (Beijing: Jiefangjun, 1987), 6–11; Zhou Enlai would later recall that he had known Ho Chi Minh since the 1920s, and that they had respected each other and maintained a very close relationship. See Liang Feng, "Premier Zhou Enlai and the Sino-Vietnamese Friendship," in *Lao waijiaoguan huiyi Zhou Enlai* (Veteran Diplomats Remember Zhou Enlai), ed. Tian Zengpei and Wang Taiping (Beijing: Shijie zhishi, 1998), 147–48.

3. Huang Zheng, *Hu Zhiming yu Zhongguo*, 8–20; Ding Yanmo, *Bo Luoting yu zhongguo da geming* (Borodin and the Great Chinese Revolution) (Yinchuan: Ningxia renmin, 1993), 52–53.

4. Huang Zheng, *Ho Zhiming yu Zhongguo*, chs. 3–4; Hoang Van Hoan, *Canghai yisu: Huang Wenhuan geming huiyilu* (A Drop in the Ocean: Hoang Van Hoan's Revolutionary Reminiscences) (Beijing: Jiefangjun, 1987), chs. 3–4. For an account of Ho's early activities in China based on archival materials in Taiwan, see Jiang Yongjing, *Hu Zhiming zai zhongguo* (Ho Chi Minh in China) (Taipei: Zhuanji wenxue, 1972).

5. The Indochina Communist Party was established in 1930, after February 1951; its name was changed to Vietnamese Worker's Party (VWP or Dang Lao Dang Viet Nam).

6. Guo Ming et al., *Zhongyue guanxi yanbian sishinian* (Forty Years of Evolution of Sino-Vietnamese Relations) (Nanning: Guanxi renmin, 1992), 15–17. The Viet

Minh (League for Vietnamese Independence or Viet Nam Doc Lap Dong Minh) was a united-front organization controlled by the VWP.

7. Gao Hongdi, "The CCP's Financial and Economic Work in Hong Kong during the War of Liberation," *Zhonggong dangshi ziliao* (CCP History Materials), no. 54 (July 1995): 97.

8. The ICP and the CCP established telegraphic communication late in 1947, but, for technologic reasons, this channel of communication had never been stable. See Luo Guibo, "Remembering History: A Factual Account of Assisting Vietnam and Resisting France and the Relations between the Chinese and Vietnamese Parties and States," in *Kaiqi guomen: Waijiaoguan de fengcai* (Opening the Gate of the Country: The Glory of Diplomats), ed. Fu Hao and Li Tongchen (Beijing: Zhongguo huaqiao, 1995), 156–57; author's interview with Luo Guibo, August 1992.

9. Shi Zhe, "With Mao and Stalin: The Reminiscences of a Chinese Interpreter, Part II: Liu Shaoqi in Moscow," trans. Chen Jian, *Chinese Historians* 6 (Spring 1993): 1–24; author's interview with Shi Zhe, August 1992; Zhu Yuanshi, "Liu Shaoqi's Secret Visit to the Soviet Union in 1949," *Dangde wenxian* (Party History Documents, Beijing), no. 3 (1991): 76–77.

10. For a discussion of the meeting, see Pei Jianzhang, *Zhonghua renmin gongheguo waijiao shi, 1949–1956* (A Diplomatic History of the People's Republic of China, 1949–1956) (Beijing: Shijie zhishi, 1994), 18.

11. Luo Guibo, "Remembering History," 154–55.

12. Telegram, CCP Central Committee to Ho Chi Minh, 28 December 1949, *LSN*, 2:236; *LSW*, 1:196; Luo Guibo, "Remembering History," 153–54; author's interview with Luo Guibo, August 1992.

13. Telegram, CCP Central Committee to ICP Central Committee, 25 December 1949, and telegram, CCP Central Committee to Ho Chi Minh, 28 December 1949, *LSW*, 1:190, 196–97.

14. Hoang Van Hoan, *Canghai yisu*, 247–53; Luo Guibo, "The Inside Story of China's Support to Vietnam," *Shiji* (The Century), no. 2 (1993): 12.

15. Zhou Enlai's statement of recognizing the Democratic Republic of Vietnam, 18 January 1950, *Xinhua yuebao* (New China Monthly) (February 1950): 847. For exchanges between top CCP leaders concerning the decision, see telegrams, Mao Zedong to Liu Shaoqi, 17 and 18 January 1950, *JMZW*, 1:238–39. CCP leaders understood that recognizing Ho's government would inevitably make an early French recognition of the Chinese Communist regime unlikely. They still believed, however, that recognizing the DRV was in the fundamental interests of revolutionary China. Following the example of China, the Soviet Union and other Communist countries quickly recognized the DRV. The DRV government later named 18 January as the day of "diplomatic victory." See Hoang Van Hoan, *Canghai yisu*, 255–56, and *Renmin ribao* (People's Daily), 7 February 1951.

16. Luo Guibo, "Remembering History," 157–58; author's interview with Luo Guibo, 22 August 1992.

17. Due to the difficulties involved in maintaining reliable telegraphic communications with the CCP, the ICP did not inform the CCP of Ho Chi Minh's secret

trip to China in advance. See Luo Guibo, "Remembering History," 160; see also telegram, CCP Central Committee to CCP Southern-Central Bureau, 26 January 1950, *LSN*, 2:241; and *LSW*, 1:343.

18. Telegram, Liu Shaoqi to Mao Zedong, 30 January 1950, *LSN*, 2:241; *LSW*, 1:344-45; telegram, Mao Zedong and Zhou Enlai to Liu Shaoqi, 1 February 1950, *JMZW*, 1:254.

19. Luo Guibo, "Comrade Liu Shaoqi Sent Me to Vietnam," in He Jingxiu et al., *Mianhuai Liu Shaoqi* (In Commemoration of Liu Shaoqi) (Beijing: Zhongyang wenxian, 1988), 234-35; see also Hoang Van Hoan, *Canghai yisu*, 254-56; *ZJG*, 1-2; and Xue Mouhong et al., *Dangdai zhongguo waijiao* (Contemporary Chinese Diplomacy) (Beijing: Zhongguo shehui kexue, 1989), 55.

20. See *LSN*, 2:241; Hoang Van Hoan, *Canghai yisu*, 254-55.

21. Telegrams, Liu Shaoqi to Mao Zedong, 1, 2, 3 February 1950, *LSW*, 1:345-47; Luo Guibo, "Comrade Liu Shaoqi Sent Me to Vietnam," 235; Hoang Van Hoan, *Canghai yisu*, 254-55.

22. For Stalin's indifferent attitude toward Ho during Ho's visit to Moscow, see Nikita Khrushchev, *Khrushchev Remembers: The Glasnost Tapes* (Boston: Little, Brown, 1990), 154-56; Li Ke, "Chinese Military Advisers in the War to Assist Vietnam and Resist France," *Junshi lishi* (Military History, Beijing), no. 3 (1989): 27; and Wu Xiuquan, *Huiyi yu huainian* (Recollections and Commemorations) (Beijing: Zhonggong zhongyang dangxiao, 1991), 242-43; my interviews with Luo Guibo in August 1992 confirmed that during Ho's visit to Moscow, Stalin refused to offer direct military and financial support to the Viet Minh.

23. Huang Zheng, *Ho Chi Minh yu Zhongguo*, 125-26; Hoang Van Hoan, *Canghai yisu*, 254-55; *DZJJG*, 1:520, 576.

24. Liu Shaoqi, "Internationalism and Nationalism," *Renmin ribao*, 7 November 1948; Liu Shaoqi's address on the Conference of Union of the Asian-Pacific Region, *Xinhua yuebao*, no. 2 (1949): 440. See also Jin Zhonghua, "China's Liberation and the World Situation," *Shijie zhishi* (World Affairs) 20 (17 June 1949); Du Ruo, "China's Liberation and the Southeast Asia," *Shijie zhishi* 20 (8 July 1949); and "China's Revolution and the Struggle against Colonialism," *People's China* (16 February 1950): 4-5.

25. In the autumn and winter of 1949, Mao and other CCP leaders believed that China should prepare to confront the American threat in Vietnam, Korea, and the Taiwan Strait. They also believed, as later pointed out by Zhou Enlai, that a conflict between Communist China and the United States was inevitable. Accordingly, in the spring of 1950, CCP military planners decided to deploy their central reserves (three armies under the Fourth Field Army) along the railroad within easy reach of Shanghai, Tianjin, and Guangzhou, so they could move easily in any of these three directions. For a detailed analysis of the CCP's military preparations under the "three fronts" assumption, see Chen Jian, *China's Road to the Korean War: The Making of the Sino-American Confrontation* (New York: Columbia University Press, 1994), ch. 4.

26. From late 1949 to early 1951, Mao and Chinese military planners paid close attention to the annihilation of remnant Nationalist troops in areas adjacent to the

Vietnamese border. See, for example, telegram, CCP Central Military Commission to Lin Biao and others, 13 October 1949; telegram, Mao Zedong to Lin Biao, 17 October 1949; and telegram, Mao Zedong to Liu Shaoqi, 29 December 1949, *JMZW*, 1:56–57, 74, 198; see also discussions in Mo Yang and Yao Jie et al., *Zhongguo renmin jiefangjun zhanshi* (The War History of the Chinese People's Liberation Army) (Beijing: Junshi kexueyuan, 1987), 3:394–98.

27. Luo Guibo, "Remembering History," 157–58; Chen Geng, *Chen Geng riji* (Chen Geng's Diaries) (Beijing: Jiefangjun, 1984), 2:7; Yao Xu, *Cong yalujiang dao banmendian* (From the Yalu River to Panmunjom) (Beijing: Renmin, 1985), 21–22.

28. Telegram, Liu Shaoqi to Luo Guibo, 13 March 1950, *LSN*, 2:244.

29. *DZJJG*, 1:518–19.

30. Ibid., 519.

31. Ibid.; *ZJG*, 3.

32. *ZJG*, 3.

33. See Report, Zhou Enlai at the Central Military Commission's Enlarged Meeting, 26 August 1950, *CCFP*, 158–59; see also instruction, the PRC Information Bureau, 29 June 1950, Xinhua News Agency, ed., *Xinhuashe wenjian ziliao huibian* (A Collection of Documentary Materials of the Xinhua News Agency) (Beijing: n.p., n.d.), 2:50.

34. For a more detailed discussion of the overall change in the CCP's strategy vis-à-vis the United States after the outbreak of the Korean War, see Chen Jian, *China's Road to the Korean War*, 126–30.

35. *LSN*, 2:256; *DZJJG*, 1:519–20; *ZJG*, 5–6.

36. *DZJJG*, 1:520, *ZJG*, 4.

37. Telegram, CCP Central Committee to Chen Geng and CCP Southwestern Bureau, 23 May 1950, *LSN*, 2:252.

38. Xu Peilan and Zheng Pengfei, *Chen Geng jiangjun zhuan* (A Biography of General Chen Geng) (Beijing: Jiefangjun, 1988), 580–81; Mu Xin, *Chen Geng dajiang* (General Chen Geng) (Beijing: Jiefangjun, 1988), 581–99.

39. Telegram (drafted by Liu Shaoqi), CCP Central Committee to Chen Geng, 18 June 1950, *LSN*, 2:255.

40. Chen Geng, *Chen Geng riji*, 2:9, 11; *DZJJG*, 2:521–22; author's interview with Luo Guibo, 22 August 1992.

41. Telegram, Chen Geng to CCP Central Committee, 22 July 1950, *DZJJG*, 2:522–23.

42. Telegram, CMC to Chen Geng, 26 July 1950, ibid., 523; Chen Geng diary entry, 28 July 1950, *Chen Geng riji*, 2:13.

43. *DZJJG*, 2:524.

44. *ZJG*, 44.

45. Ibid., 44–46; Mu Xin, *Chen Geng dajiang*, 590–93.

46. Telegram (drafted by Liu Shaoqi), CCP Central Committee to Chen Geng and CCP Southwestern Bureau, 23 May 1950, *LSN*, 2:252. In this telegram, Liu particularly emphasized that the "training and rectification" of the Viet Minh troops should be aimed at getting them ready to participate in the forthcoming Border campaign.

47. Chen Geng diary entries, 18 and 19 September 1950, *Chen Geng riji*, 2:27.

48. Telegram, Mao Zedong to Chen Geng, 6 October 1950, *ZJG*, 22.

49. *DZJJG*, 2:524–27; Chen Geng diary entries, 12 and 13 October 1950, *Chen Geng riji*, 2:34.

50. Chen Geng diary entries, 1, 2, 3, 4, and 6 November 1950, *Chen Geng riji*, 2:39–41; *ZJG*, 25.

51. Giap even boasted that he would be able to put Ho Chi Minh back in Hanoi by the end of 1950. See William J. Duiker, *The Communist Road to Power in Vietnam* (Boulder, Colo.: Westview Press, 1996), 155–56. It is interesting to note that Chinese sources fail to provide as detailed coverage of the period in early 1951 when the Viet Minh forces suffered several setbacks as they do of the Border campaign, the Northwest campaign, and the Dien Bien Phu siege. In my interview with Luo Guibo in August 1992, however, he acknowledged that Chinese advisers also supported the "general counteroffensive" strategy.

52. *ZJG*, 27.

53. Phillip B. Davidson, *Vietnam at War: The History, 1946–1975* (Novato, Calif.: Presidio Press, 1988), 102, 113–14; Duiker, *Communist Road to Power in Vietnam*, 154–55.

54. Duiker, *Communist Road to Power in Vietnam*, 154–60; Davidson, *Vietnam at War*, 105–27.

55. *ZJG*, 29–30.

56. Davidson, *Vietnam at War*, 129–30.

57. *ZJG*, 31; Qian Jiang, "The Years of Being Chinese Advisers in Vietnam," *Shiji*, no. 14 (September–October 1995): 23.

58. *ZJG*, 31–32.

59. Ibid.; author's interview with Luo Guibo, August 1992.

60. The CCP Central Military Committee assigned Luo to head the CMAG in early 1952. In May 1952, Luo was formally appointed by the CMC as the head of the CMAG. See *ZJG*, 53.

61. Ibid.; author's interview with Luo Guibo, August 1992.

62. *DZJJG*, 2:527–28; *ZJG*, 55–56.

63. *ZJG*, 52.

64. Ibid., 56.

65. Ibid.

66. Ibid., 56–57; *DZJJG*, 2:528.

67. *ZJG*, 57.

68. Telegram, Luo Guibo and Mei Jiasheng to CMC, 11 July 1952, ibid., 57–58.

69. Telegram, CCP Central Committee to CMAG, 22 July 1952, ibid., 58; see also *DZJJG*, 2:528.

70. Ho Chi Minh, "Instructions on the Cadres' Meeting for Preparing the Northwest Campaign," 9 September 1952, *Selected Works of Ho Chi Minh* (Chinese-language edition, Hanoi: Foreign Language Press, 1962), 2:232–36; *ZJG*, 59.

71. *ZJG*, 58–59.

72. *DZJJG*, 2:529.

73. *ZJG*, 63.

74. Ibid., 64–65.

75. Davidson, *Vietnam at War,* 161–67.

76. Gary Hess, *Vietnam and the United States: Origins and Legacy of War* (Boston: Twayne, 1990), 43.

77. Telegram, VWP Central Committee to CCP Central Committee, 13 August 1953, *ZJG,* 87.

78. Ibid., 88; see also *DZJJG,* 2:529.

79. Telegrams, CCP Central Committee to CMAG and VWP Central Committee, 27 and 29 August 1953, *ZJG,* 88; see also Li Ke, "Chinese Military Advisers in the War to Assist Vietnam and Resist France," 28.

80. *DZJJG,* 2:529; *ZJG,* 88–89.

81. Pei Jianzhang, *Zhonghua renmin gongheguo waijiao shi,* 221.

82. Li Ke, "Chinese Military Advisers in the War to Assist Vietnam and Resist France," 28; *ZJG,* 89.

83. *ZJG,* 89–90.

84. *DZJJG,* 1:530; Guo Ming et al., *Zhongyue guanxi yanbian sishinian,* 34–35.

85. *DZJJG,* 1:530.

86. Pei Jianzhang, *Zhonghua renmin gongheguo waijiao shi,* 222.

87. For a Chinese account of the Communist "peace offensive," see Xue Mouhong et al., *Dangdai zhongguo waijiao,* 56–57.

88. *DZJJG,* 1:530; Guo Ming et al., *Zhongyue guanxi yanbian sishinian,* 35.

89. *DZJJG,* 1:530–31; *ZJG,* 90.

90. Telegram, CMC to Wei Guoqing and CMAG, 24 January 1954, *ZJG,* 98.

91. *DZJJG,* 1:532.

92. Ibid.; *ZJG,* 114. According to one Chinese source, China even sent an artillery division to participate in the Dien Bien Phu campaign; see Ye Fei, *Ye Fei huiyilu* (Ye Fei's Memoirs) (Beijing: Jiefangjun, 1988), 644–45. For understandable reasons, no Chinese source mentions that, as the standard Vietnamese account alleges, the Chinese high command or Chinese advisers to Vietnam urged "human wave" tactics on the Vietnamese during the initial stage of the Dien Bien Phu siege, causing heavy casualties for the Vietnamese—though no Chinese account rejects the Vietnamese allegation, either.

93. *ZENB,* 1:358; *ZJG,* 99.

94. Georges Bidault, *Resistance,* trans. Marianne Sinclair (London: Weidenfeld and Nicolson, 1965), 195.

95. Melanie Billings-Yun, *Decision against War: Eisenhower and Dien Bien Phu, 1954* (New York: Columbia University Press, 1988), ch. 2.

96. *DZJJG,* 1:532; *ZJG,* 101.

97. Letter, Mao Zedong to Peng Dehuai, 3 April 1954, *JMZW,* 4:474–75.

98. Telegrams, CMC to Wei Guoqing and CMAG, 9 April 1954, *ZJG,* 101.

99. Letter, Mao Zedong to Huang Kecheng and Su Yu, 17 April 1954, *JMZW,* 4:480.

100. *The Pentagon Papers: The Defense Department History of Decisionmaking on Vietnam* (Boston: Beacon Press, 1971), 1:98.

101. *Public Papers of the President of the United States: Dwight D. Eisenhower, 1954* (Washington, D.C.: Government Printing Office, 1958), 381–90.

102. John Newhouse, *War and Peace in the Nuclear Age* (New York: Knopf, 1988), 99–101.

103. For a brief yet informative analysis of America's stand toward the Dien Bien Phu crisis, see Hess, *Vietnam and the United States*, 46–48; for a more detailed analysis of the Eisenhower administration's attitude toward involving American forces in the Indochina War in 1954, see Billings-Yun, *Decision against War.*

104. *DZJJG*, 1:534; Guo Ming et al., *Zhongyue guanxi yanbian sishinian*, 38.

105. Guo Ming et al., *Zhongyue guanxi yanbian sishinian*, 38–39; Huang Zheng, *Hu Zhiming yu Zhongguo*, 136.

106. Quoted from *DZJJG*, 1:533–34.

107. Letter, Mao Zedong to Peng Dehuai and Huang Kecheng, 28 April 1954, *JMZW*, 5:91. (The editors mistakenly date this telegram 28 April 1955. This is probably because Mao wrote only the day and month on the letter and, for reasons unknown, the document was misplaced in Mao's 1955 files. As there was no real fighting happening around the Dien Bien Phu area in 1955 and as the content of this letter is compatible with the CMC's 30 April 1954 telegram and Su Yu's 3 May 1954 telegram, which I also cite here, I believe that 1954 is the correct date.)

108. *ZJG*, 103–4.

109. Chen Geng, *Chen Geng riji*, 2:22, 31.

110. The Foreign Ministry of the Socialist Republic of Vietnam, "The Truth about Vietnam-China Relations in the Last 30 Years," *Foreign Broadcast Information Service* (Asia and Pacific), Supplement, 19 October 1979.

111. See, for example, telegram, Mao Zedong to Wei Guoqing, 29 January 1951, *JMZW*, 2:90.

112. Telegram, Zhou Enlai to Ho Chi Minh and the VWP Central Committee, 11 March 1954, *ZENB*, 1:358. Zhou introduced in this telegram, which was dispatched on the eve of the PANV's general offensive at Dien Bien Phu, the idea of ending the war in Indochina by temporarily dividing Vietnam into two zones, probably along the 16th parallel.

113. For the Chinese assessment of America's intention at the Geneva Conference, see Xue Mouhong et al., *Dangdai zhongguo waijiao*, 65. See also Xu Yan, "The Outstanding Contribution to Extinguishing War Flames in Indo-China," *Dangde wenxian*, no. 5 (1992): 22–23.

114. Wang Bingnan, *Zhongmei huitan jiunian* huigu (Nine Years of Sino-American Ambassadorial Talks) (Beijing: Shijie zhishi, 1985), 5–6.

115. Shi Zhe, *Zai lishi juren shenbian: Shi Zhe huiyilu* (At the Side of Historical Giants: Shi Zhe's Memoirs), rev. ed. (Beijing: Zhonggong zhongyang dangxiao, 1998), 479–86. According to Khrushchev, Zhou Enlai told him in one of his visits to Moscow prior to the Geneva Conference: "We've already lost too many men in Korea—that war costs us dearly. We're in no condition to get involved in another war at this time" (Nikita S. Khrushchev, *Khrushchev Remembers* [Boston: Little, Brown, 1971], 481).

116. Li Lianqing, *Da waijiaojia Zhou Enlai: Shezhan rineiwa* (Great Diplomat Zhou Enlai: The Geneva Debate) (Hong Kong: Tiandi tushu, 1994), 85–86.

117. Li Haiwen, "The Role Zhou Enlai Played at the Geneva Conference for Restoring Peace in Indochina," unpublished paper (cited with author's permission), 1–2; Li Lianqing, *Da waijiaojia Zhou Enlai*, 86.

118. Guo Ming et al., *Zhongyue guanxi yanbian sishinian*, 100.

119. Qu Xing, "On Zhou Enlai's Diplomacy at the Geneva Conference of 1954," in Pei Jianzhang et al., *Yanjiu Zhou Enlai: Waijiao sixiang yu shijian* (Studying Zhou Enlai's Diplomatic Thought and Practices) (Beijing: Shijie zhishi, 1989), 255–56; Guo Ming et al., *Zhongyue guanxi yanbian sishinian*, 100–101.

120. Mao Zedong to the CCP Guangxi Province Committee, 20 June 1954, *JMZW*, 4:509.

121. For a plausible discussion, see Gary Hess, "Redefining the American Position in Southeast Asia: The United States and the Geneva and Manila Conferences," in *Dien Bien Phu and the Crisis of Franco-American Relations, 1954–1955*, ed. Lawrence S. Kaplan et al. (Wilmington, Del.: Scholarly Resources, 1990), 123–48.

122. *ZENB*, 1:383–84; Qu Xing, "On Zhou Enlai's Diplomacy at the Geneva Conference of 1954," 257; Li Lianqing, *Da waijiaojia Zhou Enlai*, 276.

123. *ZENB*, 1:385–87.

124. Chinese sources differ on the Vietnamese participants of the meeting. When I interviewed Luo Guibo in August 1992, he recalled that Truong Chinh also attended the meeting; but in *ZENB*, 1:394, a source based on archival materials, Chinh is not among the names of Vietnamese attendees.

125. *ZENB*, 1:394–95; Qu Xing, "On Zhou Enlai's Diplomacy at the Geneva Conference of 1954," 257–58; Wang Bingnan, *Zhongmei huitan jiunian*, 13.

126. Qu Xin, "On Zhou Enlai's Diplomacy at the Geneva Conference of 1954," 257.

127. Ho Chi Minh, "Report to the Sixth Meeting of the VWP Central Committee," 15 July 1954, *Selected Works of Ho Chi Minh*, 2:290–98.

128. *ZENB*, 1:395.

129. Li Lianqing, *Da waijiaojia Zhou Enlai*, 352–58; Qu Xing, "On Zhou Enlai's Diplomacy at the Geneva Conference of 1954," 258; *ZENB*, 1:397.

130. *ZENB*, 1:401.

131. The agreement was signed at 3:00 A.M. on 21 July but was dated 20 July so that Mendès-France could still allege that his deadline, which was set at the time that he became France's prime minister, had been met.

Chapter Six

1. See discussions in Chapter 3.

2. For an excellent discussion of the origins of the 1956 Polish crisis with the support of documents from Polish archives, see Leszek W. Gluchowski, "Poland, 1956: Khrushchev, Gomulka, and the 'Polish October,'" *CWIHPB*, no. 5 (Spring 1995): 1, 38–49, and Leszek W. Gluchowski, "The Soviet-Polish Confrontation

of October 1956: The Situation in the Polish Internal Security Corps," CWIHP Working Paper No. 17 (Washington, D.C.: Woodrow Wilson Center, April 1997).

3. For Mao Zedong's opinions on this issue, see *JMZW*, 6:320-21, 7:313.

4. Wu Lengxi, *Yi Mao zhuxi* (Recalling Chairman Mao) (Beijing: Xinhua, 1994), 12; Wu Lengxi, *Shinian lunzhan, 1956–1966: Zhongsu guanxi huiyilu* (Ten-Year Polemic Debate, 1956-1966: A Memoir on Sino-Soviet Relations) (Beijing: Zhongyang wenxian, 1999), 32–33.

5. Shi Zhe, *Zai lishi juren shenbian: Shi Zhe huiyilu* (At the Side of Historical Giants: Shi Zhe's Memoirs), rev. ed. (Beijing: Zhonggong zhongyang dangxiao, 1998), 550; Shi Zhe, "The Polish-Hungarian Incident and Liu Shaoqi's Visit to the Soviet Union," *Bainian chao* (Tide of the Century), no. 2 (1997): 11-12; Jin Chongji et al., *Liu Shaoqi zhuan* (A Biography of Liu Shaoqi) (Beijing: Zhongyang wenxian, 1998), 803. See also A. M. Oriekhov, E. D. Oriekhov, and V. T. Sereda, eds., "The Soviet Union and Poland in October 1956: CPSU Presidium Resolutions and Meeting Records," *Istorichekii Arkhiv* (Historical Archive), nos. 5-6 (1996): 178-91. I am grateful to Krzysztof Persak for directing me to this important Russian source.

6. Wu Lengxi, *Shinian lunzhan*, 35–36.

7. The CCP Politburo Standing Committee was the party's highest decision-making body, which in October 1956 was composed of Mao Zedong, Liu Shaoqi, Zhou Enlai, Zhu De, Chen Yun, and Deng Xiaoping.

8. Wu Lengxi, *Shinian lunzhan*, 35–36.

9. Ibid., 36; see also Shi Zhe, *Zai lishi juren shenbian*, 551, and Jin Chongji et al., *Liu Shaoqi zhuan*, 803-4.

10. Wu Lengxi, *Shinian lunzhan*, 39–40; Shi Zhe, *Zai lishi juren shenbian*, 551-52; *ZENB*, 1:631.

11. Shi Zhe, *Zai lishi juren shenbian*, 551; Wu Lengxi, *Shinian lunzhan*, 43–44; Jin Chongji et al., *Liu Shaoqi zhuan*, 803.

12. Wu Lengxi, *Shinian lunzhan*, 42–43; *ZENB*, 1:630; Jin Chongji et al., *Liu Shaoqi zhuan*, 803.

13. In a recent study, the Polish-Canadian historian Leszek W. Gluchowski points out that Dr. Samuel M. Flato (Fu La-to), a Polish Communist who had served as a member of an international Communist medical expedition in China during the Second World War and had since maintained close contacts with the CCP, might have been a source of information for Beijing's leaders during the Polish crisis in 1956. See Leszek Gluchowski, "The Mysterious Dr. Fu La-to," unpublished manuscript, quoted with the author's permission.

14. Wu Lengxi, *Shinian lunzhan*, 43-45; Jin Chongji et al., *Liu Shaoqi zhuan*, 803-4; *ZENB*, 1:630.

15. Shi Zhe, *Zai lishi juren shenbian*, 551-52; *ZENB*, 1:631.

16. Shi Zhe, *Zai lishi juren shenbian*, 552. In July 1963, during the great Sino-Soviet polemic debate, Deng Xiaoping, while leading a CCP delegation to hold a series of meetings with a CPSU delegation headed by CPSU presidium member Mikhail Suslov, quoted Mao's 23 October 1956 talk with Yudin. See CWIHP*B*, no. 10 (March 1998): 176.

17. Shi Zhe, *Zai lishi juren shenbian*, 552; Jin Chongji et al., *Liu Shaoqi zhuan*, 804.

18. *ZENB*, 1:631; *LSN*, 2:378; see also Wu Lengxi, *Shinian lunzhan*, 45.

19. Shi Zhe, *Zai lishi juren shenbian*, 552; *LSN*, 2:378; Jin Chongji et al., *Liu Shaoqi zhuan*, 804.

20. Jin Chongji et al., *Liu Shaoqi zhuan*, 804; Shi Zhe, *Zai lishi juren shenbian*, 552.

21. Shi Zhe, *Zai lishi juren shenbian*, 552–53; Shi Zhe, *Feng yu gu: Shi Zhe huiyilu* (High Peak and Low Ebb: Shi Zhe's Memoirs) (Beijing: Hongqi, 1992), 119.

22. Shi Zhe recalls that Khrushchev did not even leave any time for the Chinese, who had been traveling for the whole day, to sit down to have a comfortable dinner (Shi Zhe, *Zai lishi juren shenbian*, 553).

23. After returning to Beijing, Liu Shaoqi made a speech to the Second Plenary Session of the CCP's Eighth Central Committee on 10 November, in which he provided a detailed description of the Chinese delegation's visit to Moscow. This paragraph and the following paragraphs, unless otherwise noted, are all based upon Liu's speech, which is kept at CCA. See also Shi Zhe, *Zai lishi juren shenbian*, 553.

24. Shi Zhe, *Zai lishi juren shenbian*, 553–54; Shi Zhe's recollection here is compatible with Khrushchev's description of his phone conversation with Gero and talks with Zhukov on the evening of 23 October, although Khrushchev did not mention that he was with the Chinese delegation when he talked to Gero and Zhukov. According to Khrushchev, after he received a call from the Soviet embassy in Budapest, which reported that "the situation is extremely dangerous and that the intervention of Soviet troops is necessary," he informed Gero that if the Hungarian government made a formal written request, the Soviet Red Army would intervene. See "Hungary and Poland, 1956: Khrushchev's CPSU CC Presidium Meeting on East European Crises, 24 October 1956," trans. Mark Kramer, CWIHP*B*, no. 5 (Spring 1995): 54.

25. Shi Zhe, *Zai lishi juren shenbian*, 554.

26. According to the "Malin notes," a key document concerning Soviet decision making during the Hungarian crisis obtained from Russian archives, attending the meeting on the Soviet side were Nikolay Bulganin, Lazar Kaganovich, Alekei Kirichenko, Georgy Malenkov, Vyacheslav Molotov, Sbrurov, Khrushchev, Zhukov, Leonid Brezhnev, Dmitri Shepilov, Nikolay Shvernik, Yekaterina Furtseva, Pyotr Pospelov, and Soviet ambassador to China Yudin (TsKhSD, f. 3. op. 12. D. 1005. Fol. 52–52/v., quoted from Leszek W. Gluchowski, "Khrushchev, Mao Zedong, Gomulka, and Soviet 'Great-Power Chauvinism' in October 1956," unpublished paper, 9 [citation made with author's permission]). For a general discussion of the "Malin notes," see the translator's note, "The 'Malin Notes' on the Crises in Hungary and Poland, 1956," trans. and annot. Mark Kramer, CWIHP*B*, nos. 8–9 (Winter 1996–97): 385.

27. Shi Zhe, *Zai lishi juren shenbian*, 554–55.

28. Ibid., 555; Jin Chongji et al., *Liu Shaoqi zhuan*, 805.

29. Liu Shaoqi cited two examples here: In January 1950, *Pravda* published an article criticizing the Japanese Communist Party, which, according to Liu, proved

to be a mistake; on 20 October 1956, *Pravda* openly criticized the Polish Party's Eighth Plenum, which caused great resentment among the Polish comrades. See Shi Zhe, *Zai lishi juren shenbian*, 556.

30. Palmiro Togliatti was general secretary of the Italian Communist Party.

31. Shi Zhe, *Zai lishi juren shenbian*, 555–57; Jin Chongji et al., *Liu Shaoqi zhuan*, 805; Zhou Wenqi and Zhu Liangru, eds., *Teshu er fuzha de keti: Gochan guoji, sulian he zhongguo gongchandang guanxi biannian shi, 1919–1991* (A Special and Complicated Subject: A Chronological History of the Relations between the Comintern, the Soviet Union, and the Chinese Communist Party) (Wuhan: Hubei renmin, 1993), 502; Cong Jin, *Quzhe fazhan de suiyue* (The Years of Tortuous Development) (Zhengzhou: Henan renmin, 1989), 333. According to the "Malin notes," Khrushchev told the Chinese that "we agree with what was said by Comrade Liu Shaoqi" (TsKhSD, f. 3. op. 12. D. 1005. Fol. 52–52/v., quoted from Gluchowski, "Khrushchev, Mao Zedong, Gomulka, and Soviet 'Great-Power Chauvinism,'" 9).

32. It is interesting to note that the Soviet leaders probably failed to catch the subtext of Liu's statement. The "Malin notes," for example, recorded only that "Comrade Liu Shaoqi agrees with the decisions taken by the CC [CPSU] on Poland" and that the Chinese acknowledged "in principle" that "the Soviet Union is the center of the socialist camp." See TsKhSD, f. 3. op. 12. D. 1005. Fol. 52–52/v., quoted from Gluchowski, "Khrushchev, Mao Zedong, Gomulka, and Soviet 'Great-Power Chauvinism,'" 9. The question here is: Did the Soviet leaders really understand the meaning of the Chinese "principles"?

33. Shi Zhe, *Zai lishi juren shenbian*, 557.

34. Ibid., 557–58; Jin Chongji et al., *Liu Shaoqi zhuan*, 805–6. For Soviet record of the meeting, see "'Malin Notes,'" 389.

35. Shi Zhe, *Zai lishi juren shenbian*, 558–59.

36. The five principles of pancha shila include (1) mutual respect for sovereignty and territorial integrity, (2) nonaggression, (3) noninterference in another country's internal affairs, (4) equal and mutual benefit, and (5) peaceful coexistence. They were introduced in a joint statement by Indian prime minister Jawaharlal Nehru and Chinese premier Zhou Enlai in New Delhi in June 1954.

37. Shi Zhe, *Zai lishi juren shenbian*, 559–60; Zhou Wenqi and Zhu Liangru, eds., *Teshu er fuzha de keti*, 502; Cong Jin, *Quzhe fazhan de suiyue*, 33–334.

38. Shi Zhe, *Zai lishi juren shenbian*, 559; Cong Jin, *Quzhe fazhan de suiyue*, 334; for Soviet documentary sources reflecting the contents of the discussion at that day's meeting, see "'Malin Notes,'" 392–93.

39. Shi Zhe, *Zai lishi juren shenbian*, 559.

40. "'Malin Notes,'" 392.

41. *Renmin ribao* (People's Daily), 1 November 1956.

42. Shi Zhe, *Zai lishi juren shenbian*, 554; Cong Jin, *Quzhe fazhan de suiyue*, 335.

43. Li Jiao, "The Three Outstanding Female Members in the Foreign Ministry as I Know Them," *Zhuanji wenxue* (Biography Literature) (March 1996): 7–13. Hu Jibang was one of Zhou Enlai's top assistants before she transferred to *Renmin ribao*. When János Kádár, secretary of the Hungarian Communist Party, visited China and met with Mao Zedong in June 1957, it is reported that he expressed

gratitude to Beijing for dispatching Hu Jibang, "a very courageous and talented person," to Hungary. Mao replied: "It is through the reports she sent back home that we learned what was happening in your country." For Hu Jibang's impact upon top Beijing leaders, see CCP Central Committee Document, "The Reports by *Renmin ribao* Reporter Hu Jibang on the Association of Writers in Hungary," 3 February 1957, 101-5-982, Fujian Provincial Archives.

44. Zhou Wenqi and Zhu Liangru, eds., *Teshu er fuzha de keti*, 502–3; Wu Lengxi, *Shinian lunzhan*, 51–52.

45. For a plausible discussion, see Mark Kramer, "New Evidence on Soviet Decision-Making and the 1956 Polish and Hungarian Crises," CWIHP*B*, nos. 8–9 (Winter 1996–97): 367–69.

46. Shi Zhe, *Zai lishi juren shenbian*, 560; Wu Lengxi, *Shinian lunzhan*, 51; Zhou Wenqi and Zhu Liangru, eds., *Teshu er fuzha de keti*, 503.

47. Shi Zhe, *Zai lishi juren shenbian*, 560–61; Jin Chongji et al., *Liu Shaoqi zhuan*, 806. When in Hungary, Mikoyan and Suslov sent to Moscow a series of reports about the changing situation in Hungary; see Janos M. Rainer, "The Yeltsin Dossier: Soviet Documents on Hungary, 1956," CWIHP*B*, no. 5 (Spring 1995): 23, 29–32. Shi Zhe did not specifically identify which of Mikoyan's reports the CCP delegation received on the morning of 30 October, or if more than one report was involved here.

48. Shi Zhe, *Zai lishi juren shenbian*, 561.

49. *ZENB*, 1:632.

50. Wu Lengxi, *Shinian lunzhan*, 51–52; Jin Chongji et al., *Liu Shaoqi zhuan*, 806.

51. Shi Zhe, *Zai lishi juren shenbian*, 561.

52. Ibid., 561; Jin Chongji et al., *Liu Shaoqi zhuan*, 806; Cong Jin, *Quzhe fazhan de suiyue*, 335; Wu Lengxi, *Shinian lunzhan*, 52–53; the "Malin notes" on a CPSU presidium meeting on 30 October 1956 briefly record that "Cde. Liu Shaoqi indicates on behalf of the CCP CC that troops must remain in Hungary and in Budapest." See "'Malin Notes,'" 393.

53. Shi Zhe, *Zai lishi juren shenbian*, 561; Shi Zhe, *Feng yu gu*, 120.

54. Shi Zhe, *Zai lishi juren shenbian*, 561; Cong Jin, *Quzhe fazhan de suiyue*, 335; Wu Lengxi, *Shinian lunzhan*, 58.

55. Shi Zhe, *Zai lishi juren shenbian*, 561.

56. Ibid., 562; Wu Lengxi, *Shinian lunzhan*, 53.

57. Shi Zhe, *Zai lishi juren shenbian*, 561–62; Wu Lengxi, *Shinian lunzhan*, 53–54, 58; Zhou Wenqi and Zhu Liangru, eds., *Teshu er fuzha de keti*, 503.

58. How and why the CPSU leadership finally decided to use military force to suppress the Hungarian revolution have caught the attention of scholars in recent years. Harvard University–based scholar Mark Kramer argues that the Suez Canal crisis played a crucial role in pushing leaders in Moscow to reach the final decision to use military force in Hungary, while the role played by the Chinese delegation "did not have any discernible effect on the Soviet decision at this meeting [the 30 October presidium meeting] to eschew intervention" (Mark Kramer, "New Evidence on Soviet Decision-Making and the 1956 Polish and Hungarian

Crises," 369–70, 405 n. 94). Kramer's argument is questionable, since there is no direct evidence backing his claim that Beijing's support or objection had no effect on Khrushchev and his fellow CPSU leaders. At least, the fact that Khrushchev and his colleagues informed the Chinese delegation of the their decision to intervene in such a dramatic manner reveals that Beijing's attitude mattered. It is also important to note that no matter what role Beijing actually played in this process, Beijing's leaders believed that their role was decisive. This perception (or misperception) had a huge effect on the future development of Sino-Soviet relations.

59. *ZENB*, 1:634.

60. Wu Lengxi, *Shinian lunzhan*, 56; for the date of the meeting, see also *LSN*, 2:378.

61. Wu Lengxi, *Shinian lunzhan*, 57; see also Jin Chongji et al., *Liu Shaoqi zhuan*, 806.

62. Wu Lengxi, *Shinian lunzhan*, 57–58.

63. *LSN*, 2:379; *ZENB*, 1:636–37; Jin Chongji et al., *Liu Shaoqi zhuan*, 806.

64. *Renmin ribao*, 29 December 1956.

65. Wu Lengxi, *Yi Mao zhuxi*, 16.

66. Mao Zedong, "Speech at the Second Plenary Session of the CCP's Eighth Central Committee," 15 November 1956, *MZX*, 5:322.

67. Wu Lengxi, *Shinian lunzhan*, 59–69; Jin Chongji et al., *Liu Shaoqi zhuan*, 807; see also *JMZW*, 6:250.

68. Wu Lengxi, *Shinian lunzhan*, 58; Jin Chongji et al., *Liu Shaoqi zhuan*, 807.

69. In April 1956, *Renmin ribao* published a lengthy article, titled "On the Historical Lessons of the Proletarian Dictatorship," which reflected the CCP leadership's initial response to problems brought about by Khrushchev's de-Stalinization. See discussions in Chapter 3.

70. Wu Lengxi, *Shinian lunzhan*, 60–61; see also Mao Zedong, "Revisions Made on 'Another Discussion of the Historical Lessons of the Proletarian Dictatorship,'" December 1956, *JMZW*, 6:283–85.

71. Mao Zedong, "Editor's Notes from *Socialist Upsurge in China's Countryside*," *MZX*, 5:225–26. Here, the chairman argued that one of the basic lessons the Chinese Communist Party should draw from the Polish and Hungarian crises was that "neither socialist revolution nor socialist construction is smooth sailing, and we should be prepared to cope with the many great difficulties that may crop up at home and abroad."

72. The Hundred Flowers Campaign is a complicated historical event, and scholars differ regarding Mao's real intentions behind it. But they all agree that this event and the Anti-Rightist movement were related to the Hungarian crisis. For a plausible discussion of these two events, see Merle Goldman, "The Party and the Intellectuals," in *The Cambridge History of China*, ed. Denis Twitchett and John K. Fairbank (Cambridge, Eng.: Cambridge University Press, 1987), 14:242–58.

73. Instruction (drafted by Mao Zedong), CCP Central Committee, "Organize Our Strength to Oppose the Rampant Attack by the Anti-Communist Rightist Elements," 8 June 1957, *JMZW*, 6:497–98.

74. Jin Chongji et al., *Liu Shaoqi zhuan*, 807.

75. Report, "My Observation on the Soviet Union," Zhou Enlai to Mao Zedong and the CCP Leadership, January 24, 1957, CWIHP*B*, nos. 6–7 (Winter 1995–96): 153–54.

76. Zhou Wenqi and Zhu Liangru, eds., *Teshu er fuzha de keti*, 504.

Chapter Seven

1. Jinmen is an archipelago composed of twelve islands, including Big Jinmen (about forty-eight square miles in size) and Small Jinmen (about six square miles in size), situated about 2.5–6 miles off Xiamen, a coastal port city in Fujian province.

2. *DZJJG*, 1:5; Xu Yan, *Jinmen zhizhan* (The Jinmen Battle) (Beijing: Zhongguo guangbo dianshi, 1992), 229–30; for GMD accounts of the shelling, see *Jinmen guningtou zhoushan dengbudao zhizhan shiliao chubian* (A Preliminary Collection of Historical Materials about the Jinmen and Dengbu Battles) (Taipei: Guoshiguan, 1979), 561–63. Taiwan sources also reported that Yu Dawei, Taiwan's defense minister, who was then in Jinmen for an inspection tour, barely escaped being killed. The U.S. embassy in Taipei reported that "Reds are estimated to have fired a minimum of 35,000 rounds and caused over 500 casualties" (Everett F. Drumright [U.S. ambassador to the Republic of China] to the Department of State, 24 August 1958, *FRUS, 1958–1960*, 19:71).

3. See Dwight D. Eisenhower, *Waging Peace, 1956–1961* (Garden City, N.Y.: Doubleday, 1965), ch. 12; for discussions of U.S. policy toward Taiwan in the context of American-Soviet relations during the crisis, see Gordon H. Chang, *Friends and Enemies: The United States, China, and the Soviet Union, 1948–1972* (Stanford, Calif.: Stanford University Press, 1990), 182–99; Zhai Qiang, *The Dragon, the Lion, and the Eagle: Chinese-British-American Relations* (Kent, Ohio: Kent University Press, 1994), 183–89; and Shu Guang Zhang, *Deterrence and Strategic Culture: Chinese-American Confrontations, 1949–1958* (Ithaca: Cornell University Press, 1992), ch. 7.

4. For an insightful discussion of Soviet policy during the crisis, see Vladislav Zubok and Constantine Pleshakov, *Inside the Kremlin's Cold War: From Stalin to Khrushchev* (Cambridge, Mass.: Harvard University Press, 1996), 217–29; for two dated yet still useful accounts based on published contemporary materials, see Donald S. Zagoria, *The Sino-Soviet Conflict, 1956–1961* (Princeton, N.J.: Princeton University Press, 1962), ch. 7, and Morton H. Halperin and Tang Tsou, "The 1958 Quemoy Crisis," in *Sino-Soviet Relations and Arms Control*, ed. Morton H. Halperin (Cambridge, Mass.: MIT Press, 1967), 265–304. For details of Gromyko's visit, see discussions below.

5. *Renmin ribao* (People's Daily), 6 October 1958. The "Message" was drafted by Mao. See *JMZW*, 7:439–40. See also discussion later in this chapter.

6. Scholars have been debating these questions. Zhang Shu Guang argues that both Beijing and Washington entered the crisis under a "mutual deterrence" situation. (See Shu Guang Zhang, *Deterrence and Strategic Culture*, ch. 7). Thomas J. Christensen (*Useful Adversaries: Grand Strategy, Domestic Mobilization, and Sino-American Conflict, 1947–1958* [Princeton, N.J.: Princeton University Press, 1996],

ch. 6.), adopting a "two-level" analysis model, points out that Beijing's handling of the crisis was from the beginning dominated by Mao's desire to use it to promote domestic mobilization related to the Great Leap Forward.

7. Telegram, Mao Zedong to Su Yu, Zhang Zhen, Zhou Jingming, and the CCP East China Bureau, 14 June 1949, *CCFP*, 117.

8. Telegram, Mao Zedong to Su Yu, Zhang Zhen, Zhou Jingming, and the CCP East China Bureau, 21 June 1949, quoted from He Di, "The Last Campaign to Unify China: The CCP's Unmaterialized Plan to Liberate Taiwan, 1949-1950," *Chinese Historians* 5 (Spring 1992): 1-2.

9. Letter, Mao Zedong to Zhou Enlai, 10 July 1949, *CCFP*, 123. In this letter, Mao emphasized that in order to liberate Taiwan, "in addition to ground forces, we need to rely on internal cooperators and [establishing] an air force" with the assistance of the Soviet Union.

10. For discussions of Liu's meetings with Stalin on the air force issue, see Sergei Goncharov, John Lewis, and Xue Litai, *Uncertain Partners: Stalin, Mao, and the Korean War* (Stanford, Calif.: Stanford University Press, 1993), 69; see also Lü Liping, *Tongtian zhilu* (The Path Leading to the Sky) (Beijing: Jiefangjun, 1989), 132-69. Goncharov, Lewis, and Xue Litai, with the support of the recollections of Ivan Vladimirovich Kovalev, the Soviet general adviser to China in the late 1940s and early 1950s, claim that Liu Shaoqi requested that Stalin dispatch Soviet air force and submarines to support the PLA's Taiwan campaign. Shi Zhe, the Chinese interpreter who accompanied Liu Shaoqi to Moscow, claimed that Liu never made such a request. See Li Haiwen, "A Distortion of History: An Interview with Shi Zhe about Kovalev's Recollections," *Chinese Historians* 5 (Fall 1992): 59-64.

11. Letter, Mao Zedong to Zhou Enlai, 10 July 1949, *CCFP*, 123; see also *ZENA*, 833.

12. For discussions about the PLA's defeats in Jinmen and Dengbu in October and November 1949, see Chen Jian, *China's Road to the Korean War: The Making of the Sino-American Confrontation* (New York: Columbia University Press, 1994), 99-102; see also He Di, "Last Campaign to Unify China," 12.

13. He Di, "Last Campaign to Unify China," 12; Xu Yan, *Jinmen zhizhan*, 116-25, esp. 124-25; Lin Xiaoguang, "The Evolution of the CCP's Policy toward Taiwan," *Dangshi yanjiu ziliao* (Party History Research Materials, Beijing), no. 3 (1997): 2.

14. Early in June 1950, the Nationalist secret services succeeded in identifying General Wu Shi, deputy chief of staff of GMD military forces, as a hidden CCP spy. On 2 June, Wu was arrested, leading to the exposure of an underground CCP spy network in Taiwan. One week later, Wu and three of his top assistants were executed. This event, together with several other major breakthroughs on the part of GMD's secret services, led to the undermining of the CCP's underground spy network in Taiwan. See Xu Wenlong, *Zhonggong tegong: Dixia douzheng de yingxiong* (CCP Special Agents: Heroes in Underground Struggles) (Xining: Qinghai renmin, 1996), chs. 27-28, and Jiang Nan, *Jiang Jingguo zhuan* (A Biography of Jiang Jingguo) (Beijing: Zhongguo youyi, 1984), 227-28.

15. Recollection, Xiao Jinguang, "The Taiwan Campaign Was Called Off," 30 June 1950, *CCFP*, 155.

16. *DZJJG*, 1:384–85; Yang Guoyu et al., *Dangdai zhongguo haijun* (Contemporary Chinese Navy) (Beijing: Zhongguo shehui kexue, 1989), 41.

17. Telegram, CMC to Chen Yi, 11 August 1950, cited from He Di, "Last Campaign to Unify China," 15; see also Zhou Jun, "The Party Central Committee's Decision on the Strategic Transition from the War of Liberation to the War to Resist America and Assist Korea," *Dangshi yanjiu ziliao*, no. 4 (1992): 15.

18. He Di, "Last Campaign to Unify China," 15; *DZJJG*, 1:384–85.

19. For discussions of how the PLA maintained a defensive posture during the Korean War years, see Xu Yan, *Jinmen zhizhan*, 148–66; Ye Fei, *Ye Fei huiyilu* (Ye Fei's Memoirs) (Beijing: Jiefangjun, 1988): 616–26; and *DZJJG*, 1:322–34.

20. For discussion of Jiang's reforms in Taiwan, see Thomas Gold, *State and Society in the Taiwan Miracle* (Armonk, N.Y.: M. E. Sharpe, 1986), ch. 5.

21. Xu Yan, *Jinmen zhizhan*, 168.

22. Ibid., 168–69; Nie Fengzhi et al., *Sanjun heige zhan donghai* (The Three Services Fight at the East China Sea) (Beijing: Jiefangjun, 1985), 2.

23. Xu Yan, *Jinmen zhizhan*, 168.

24. *DZJJG*, 1:256; Xu Yan, *Jinmen zhizhan*, 171.

25. For discussions, see Nie Fengzhi et al., *Sanjun huige zhan donghai*, 11–12; Xu Yan, *Jinmen zhizhan*, 175.

26. Ye Fei, *Ye Fei huiyilu*, 627–39; Xu Yan, *Jinmen zhizhan*, 169–70.

27. Pei Jianzhang, *Zhonghua renmin gongheguo waijiao shi, 1949–1956* (A Diplomatic History of the People's Republic of China, 1949–1956) (Beijing: Shijie zhishi, 1994), 337; Wang Bingnan, *Zhongmei huitan jiunian* huigu (Recollections of the Nine Years of Sino-American Talks) (Beijing: Shijie zhishi, 1985), 41–42.

28. On 23 July 1954, *Renmin ribao* published an editorial essay titled "We Must Liberate Taiwan," initiating the propaganda campaign.

29. Ye Fei, *Ye Fei huiyilu*, 644.

30. See, for example, Pei Jianzhang, *Zhonghua renmin gongheguo waijiao shi*, 338. It is also interesting to note that another official history, *DZJJG* (1:254–71), while providing a detailed account of the Zhejiang campaign, completely omits the campaign's connection with the PLA's shelling of Jinmen in September 1954.

31. This is particularly true since it was risky for the PLA's artillery forces in Fujian to conduct massive and lasting shelling on Jinmen at that time. Because the PLA did not have an air force or effective air defense capacity (except for some antiaircraft artillery units), it would be easy for the GMD's bombers to destroy the PLA's artillery positions.

32. Telegram, CCP Central Committee to Zhou Enlai, 27 July 1954, *ZENB*, 1:405.

33. For plausible discussions supporting this line of reasoning, see Gordon H. Chang and He Di, "The Absence of War in the U.S.-China Confrontation over Quemoy and Matsu in 1954–1955: Contingency, Luck, Deterrence?" *American Historical Review* 98 (December 1993): 1500–1524, and Shu Guang Zhang, *Deter-*

rence and Strategic Culture, ch. 7. See also the discussion in Ye Fei, *Ye Fei huiyilu*, 644–45.

34. Telegram, CCP Central Committee to Zhou Enlai, 27 July 1954, *ZENB*, 1:405.

35. On 28 June 1954, Zhou Enlai and Indian prime minister Jawaharlal Nehru issued a joint statement in New Delhi, which endorsed the five principles of peaceful coexistence, also known as pancha shila. The PRC government then repeatedly announced that these principles would be the basis for their dealings with other countries. See Xue Mouhong et al., *Dangdai zhongguo waijiao* (Contemporary Chinese Diplomacy) (Beijing: Zhongguo shehui kexue, 1989), 79–89.

36. Because the PLA did not have air control, both shelling operations lasted for about one hour. Two American officers were killed in the first shelling. The GMD retaliated with a massive air bombardment of important targets on the mainland, including Fuzhou, the capital city of Fujian province. See Xu Yan, *Jinmen zhizhan*, 176–77.

37. For a detailed discussion on how the shelling helped Washington and Taipei overcome the obstacles in the way of signing the treaty of mutual defense, see Chang and He Di, "Absence of War in the U.S.-China Confrontation over Quemoy and Matsu"; for a more general discussion about the relationship between the crisis and the treaty's signing, see Robert Accinelli, *Crisis and Commitment: United States Policy toward Taiwan, 1950–1955* (Chapel Hill: University of North Carolina Press, 1996), chs. 8–9.

38. Accinelli, *Crisis and Commitment*, 178–80.

39. See Chang and He Di, "Absence of War in the U.S.-China Confrontation over Quemoy and Matsu," 1513–14.

40. Ibid., 1520–22; Xue Mouhong et al., *Dangdai zhongguo waijiao*, 77–78.

41. Zhou Enlai, "Statement on the Interference by the U.S. Government with Chinese People's Efforts to Liberate Taiwan," 24 January 1955, *Renmin ribao*, 25 January 1955.

42. The relationship between Mao and Zhou during the 1954–57 period was a complicated one. Although Mao supported the "peaceful coexistence" foreign policy, he regretted it in summer 1958, when the Great Leap Forward was emerging in China. The chairman said: "It seems to me my original policy is better, that is, to persist in a struggle against the United States, rather than to improve relations with the U.S. government. . . . This is an issue concerning whether or not the Chinese people indeed have stood up." Mao asked Chen Yi to convey this message to the staff of the Chinese Foreign Ministry. See Chen Yi, "Speech at the Foreign Ministry's Principle Discussion Meeting," 17 June 1958, CCA.

43. Liao Xinwen, "Zhou Enlai and the Policy to Settle the Taiwan Issue by Peaceful Means," *Dangde wenxian* (Party History Documents, Beijing), no. 5 (1994): 34.

44. Jin Chongji, ed., *Zhou Enlai zhuan, 1949–1976* (A Biography of Zhou Enlai, 1949–1976) (Beijing: Zhongyang wenxian, 1998), 1:477; *ZENB*, 1:542–43.

45. *Renmin ribao*, 29 June 1956.

46. Minutes, Zhou Enlai's conversation with Cao Juren, 7 October 1956, *ZENB*, 1:623–24.

47. *ZENB*, 1:624.

48. In its history, the CCP had twice entered the "united front" with the GMD, from 1924 to 1927 and from 1937 to 1945. For general discussions of the CCP's "united front" strategy, see Lyman Van Slyke, *Enemies and Friends: The United Front in Chinese Communist History* (Stanford, Calif.: Stanford University Press, 1967).

49. Report, Zhou Enlai to CCP Central Committee and Mao Zedong, 30 April 1955, *ZENB*, 1:474–75; Lin Xiaoguang, "Evolution of the CCP's Policy toward Taiwan," 3–4; Liao Xinwen, "Zhou Enlai and the Policy to Settle the Taiwan Issue by Peaceful Means," 32–33.

50. For Chinese accounts of the creation of the pancha shila and the "Bandung spirit," see Xue Mouhong et al., *Dangdai zhongguo waijiao*, 79–94; Pei Jianzhang, *Zhonghua renmin gongheguo waijiao shi*, 231–55.

51. For a plausible discussion of the CCP's Eighth Congress policy line and Mao's ambiguous attitude toward it, see Roderick MacFarquhar, *The Origins of the Cultural Revolution*, vol. 1, *Contradiction among the People, 1956–1957* (New York: Columbia University Press, 1974), 99–109; for an informative and critical Chinese account of the Eighth Congress, see Cong Jin, *Quzhe fazhan de suiyue* (The Years of Tortuous Development) (Zhengzhou: Henan renmin, 1989), 10–31.

52. Remarks by Mao Zedong, 18 December 1957, *PDN*, 667; *DZJJG*, 1:386–87. Beijing originally planned to let the air force occupy the airfields in Fujian in 1956. However, the plan was postponed so that the Chinese could coordinate the peace initiative. See Lin Xiaoguang, "Evolution of the CCP's Policy toward Taiwan," 6.

53. Report, Ye Fei to Peng Dehuai and convey to CMC, 17 January 1958, 101-12-221, Fujian Provincial Archives, 1–14.

54. Zheng Wenhan, *Mishu riji li de Peng laozong* (Marshal Peng as Recorded in His Secretary's Diary) (Beijing: Junshi kexue, 1998), 231–32, 239; *PDN*, 672.

55. Xu Yan, *Jinmen zhizhan*, 196; *DZJJG*, 1:387.

56. *PDN*, 676.

57. This interpretation prevails among Chinese scholars. See, for example, Lin Xiaoguang, "Evolution of the CCP's Policy toward Taiwan," 7; Chen Yunlin et al., *Zhongguo Taiwan wenti* (China's Taiwan Issue) (Beijing: Jiuzhou tushu, 1998), 100–101; *DZJJG*, 1:385; and Lei Yingfu, *Zai zhuigao tongshuaibu dang canmou: Lei Yingfu jiangjun huiyilu* (Being a Staff Member at the High Command: Lei Yinfu's Memoirs) (Nanchang: Baihuazhou wenyi, 1998): 174–75.

58. See, for example, Chen Yunlin et al., *Zhongguo Taiwan wenti*, 64–65; Liao Xinwen, "A Historical Examination of Mao Zedong's Decision to Shell Jinmen in 1958," *Dangde wenxian*, no. 1 (1994): 31–36; and Xiaobing Li, "Making of Mao's Cold War: The Taiwan Strait Crises Revised," in *China and the United States: A New Cold War History*, ed. Xiaobing Li and Hongshan Li (Lanham, Md.: University Press of America, 1998), 58–60.

59. For more in-depth accounts and discussions of Mao's activities, see Roder-

ick MacFarquhar, *The Origins of the Cultural Revolution*, vol. 2, *The Great Leap Forward, 1958–1960* (New York: Columbia University Press, 1983), 20–50, and Cong Jin, *Quzhe fazhan de suiyue*, 100–139.

60. For a more detailed discussion, see Chapter 3; see also Cong Jin, *Quzhe fazhan de suiyue*, 111–17, 123–28.

61. Mao Zedong, "Outline of Speech at the Second Plenary Session of the CCP's Eighth Congress," 8 May 1958, *JMZW*, 7:194.

62. For Zhou's self-criticism on foreign policy issues, see Jin Chongji, ed., *Zhou Enlai zhuan*, 424–25; for a related discussion, see Chen Xiaolu, "Chen Yi and China's Diplomacy," in *Chinese Communist Foreign Relations, 1920s–1960s*, ed. Michael H. Hunt and Niu Jun (Washington, D.C.: Asian Program, Woodrow Wilson Center for International Scholars, 1994), 91–92.

63. Scholars have long been willing to accept Beijing's official explanation for Zhou's resignation as foreign minister—that he resigned because he was too busy to be China's premier and foreign minister at the same time. However, recently available Chinese sources indicate that the situation was more complicated. Zhou resigned not because he was too busy but mainly because Mao was not happy with his management of China's external relations (author's interview with a senior Chinese diplomat, August 1994). See also Yang Kuisong, *Zhonggong yu mosike de guanxi, 1920–1960* (The CCP's Relations with Moscow, 1920–1960) (Taipei: Dongda, 1997), 655.

64. For discussions, see Chapter 3; see also Xue Mouhong et al., *Dangdai zhongguo waijiao*, 112–14; Wang Taiping et al., *Zhonghua renmin gongheguo waijiao shi, 1957–1969* (A Diplomatic History of the People's Republic of China, 1957–69) (Beijing: Shijie zhishi, 1998), 224–26; and Cong Jin, *Quzhe fazhan de suiyue*, 348–50.

65. Xue Mouhong et al., *Dangdai zhongguo waijiao*, 203–3; Wang Taiping et al., *Zhonghua renmin gongheguo waijiao shi*, 19–20.

66. See *JMZW*, 6:630–32, 650.

67. Remarks by Mao Zedong, 19 March 1958, *JMZW*, 7:139.

68. This unique Maoist "threat perception" dominated Chinese foreign policy and security strategy not only in 1958 but also in other periods. For a related discussion, see Chen Jian, *China's Road to the Korean War*, 24–27.

69. Mao Zedong's Speech to the Supreme State Council, 5 September 1958, *JMZW*, 7:386.

70. *DZJJG*, 1:385–86.

71. *Renmin ribao*, 17 July 1958; Xu Dashen, ed., *Zhonghua renmin gongheguo shilu* (A Factorial History of the People's Republic of China) (Changchun: Jilin renmin, 1994), 2, pt. 1, 215.

72. *DZJJG*, 1:386–87; *PDN*, 691.

73. According to one Chinese source, participants of this meeting included Marshals Peng Dehuai, He Long, Xu Xiangqian, Nie Rongzhen, Chen Yi, and Lin Biao, all vice chairmen of the CMC; Su Yu, deputy defense minister; Huang Kecheng, CMC general secretary and acting chief of staff; Chen Geng, deputy chief of staff; Xiao Jinguang, commander of the navy; Liu Yalou, commander of

the air force; Chen Xilian, commander of the artillery force; Chen Shiju, commander of the engineering force; Xiao Hua, deputy director of the PLA's General Political Department; and Hong Xuezhi, commander of the PLA's General Logistics Department. See Shen Weiping, *Paoji Jinmen* (Shelling Jinmen) (Beijing: Huayi, 1998), 51.

74. *DZJJG*, 1:387; *PDN*, 692.

75. Xu Yan, *Jinmen zhizhan*, 205-6; *DZJJG*, 1:386-87; *PDN*, 691.

76. *DZJJG*, 1:387-88; Ye Fei, *Ye Fei huiyilu*, 649-50.

77. *DZJJG*, 1:388.

78. Ibid.

79. Telegram, Ye Fei to Mao Zedong and CCP Central Military Commission, Shen Weiping, *Paoji Jinmen*, 75.

80. *PDN*, 694.

81. Letter, Mao Zedong to Peng Dehuai and Huang Kecheng, 10:00 A.M., 27 July 1958, *JMZW*, 7:326. Mao particularly mentioned these coastal cities because they had been attacked by the GMD air force in previous years.

82. In actuality, although the PLA's air force units had been preparing to move into those airfields since early 1958, after Mao issued the order to shell Jinmen on 18 July, their movement was hindered by bad weather. So, by 26 July it was clear to Mao that the earliest date that the PLA's air force could begin moving into airfields in Fujian would be 27 July. See *DZJJG*, 1:391.

83. Lei Yingfu, *Zai zhuigao tongshuaibu dang canmou*, 177-78; Liao Xinwen, "Historical Examination of Mao Zedong's Decision to Shell Jinmen in 1958," 32.

84. For the text of Mao's talks with Yudin, see *CWIHPB*, nos. 6-7 (Winter 1995-96): 155-59; see also discussion in Chapter 3.

85. Minutes, "Conversation between N. S. Khrushchev and Mao Zedong," 31 July and 3 August 1958, in Dimitry Volkoganov Collections, Manuscript Division, LC. For Chinese accounts of Khrushchev's meetings with Mao and other Chinese leaders on 31 July-3 August 1958, see Wang Taiping et al., *Zhonghua renmin gongheguo waijiao shi*, 226-27, and Li Yueran, *Waijiao wutai shang de xin Zhongguo lingxiu* (The Leaders of New China on the Diplomatic Scene) (Beijing: Jiefangjun, 1989), 167-78; see also Dr. Li Zhisui, *The Private Life of Chairman Mao* (New York: Random House, 1994), 261-67, and Zubok and Pleshakov, *Inside the Kremlin's Cold War*, 219-20.

86. Right after the PLA's air units occupied airfields in Fujian, the air war between the Communists and Nationalists began. The first major air battle occurred on 29 July, and Beijing claimed that the PLA's MiGs had shot down two GMD F-86 fighters and damaged one. See Wang Dinglie, *Dangdai zhongguo kongjun* (Contemporary Chinese Air Force) (Beijing: Jiefangjun, 1989), 338-40.

87. Ye Fei, *Ye Fei huiyilu*, 652-54; Shen Weiping, *Paoji Jinmen*, ch. 4.

88. Zheng Wenhan, *Mishu riji li de Peng laozong*, 330.

89. Liao Xinwen, "Historical Examination of Mao Zedong's Decision to Shell Jinmen in 1958," 32.

90. Mao Zedong, "Talks at the Beidaihe Conference," 17 August 1958, in *The Secret Speeches of Chairman Mao: From the Hundred Flowers to the Great Leap For-*

ward, ed. Roderick MacFarquhar et al. (Cambridge, Mass.: Council of East Asian Studies/Harvard University, 1989), 402–3.

91. Letter, Mao Zedong to Peng Dehuai, 1:00 A.M., 18 August 1958, *JMZW*, 7:348.

92. *DZJJG*, 1:394.

93. Before and during the shelling campaign, Mao consistently pointed out that the United States was not in a position to involve itself in a major war in East Asia, that U.S. allies would not support Washington's military venture in the Taiwan Strait, and that America's domestic situation precluded its involvement in a war on behalf of the GMD. See Liao Xinwen, "Historical Examination of Mao Zedong's Decision to Shell Jinmen in 1958," 32.

94. Ye Fei, *Ye Fei huiyilu*, 654.

95. Ibid., 654–55; see also *PDN*, 697. According to Ye Fei, after the first day's meeting, Lin Biao suggested to Mao that in order to avoid American casualties, China should inform the Americans of Beijing's intention to shell Jinmen through Wang Bingnan, the Chinese ambassador to Poland, who had been the Chinese representative at the ambassadorial talks between Beijing and Washington. Mao did not adopt Lin's suggestion.

96. Xu Yan, *Jinmen zhizhan*, 226–28; Shen Weiping, *Paoji Jinmen*, 224–28; Ye Fei, *Ye Fei huiyilu*, 656. In his memoir, Ye Fei recalled that the shelling began at noon, which, according to all other sources, is not correct.

97. Eisenhower, *Waging Peace*, 292–93.

98. Ibid., 297; see also Morton Halperin, "The 1958 Taiwan Straits Crisis," Rand Research Memorandum (Santa Monica, Calif.: Rand Corporation, 1966), 135–36, and Zhai Qiang, *Dragon, the Lion, and the Eagle*, 183–89.

99. Chang, *Friends and Enemies*, 185.

100. Wu Lengxi, *Yi Mao zhuxi* (Recalling Chairman Mao) (Beijing: Xinhua, 1994), 74.

101. Ibid.

102. Ibid., 74–75.

103. *DZJJG*, 1:397–98.

104. Beijing claimed that two GMD F-86 fighters were shot down, and only one of its own MiG-15 was downed, not by an F-86 but by the PLA's own antiaircraft artillery fire. See *DZJJG*, 1:398–99.

105. According to Wu Lengxi (*Yi Mao zhuxi*, 76), participants of the meeting included Mao Zedong, Liu Shaoqi, Zhou Enlai, Deng Xiaoping (all Politburo Standing Committee members), Peng Dehuai, Wang Shangrong (director of the Operation Department under the General Staff), Ye Fei, Hu Qiaomu (a Central Committee member in charge of propaganda affairs and one of Mao's political secretaries), and Wu Lengxi himself.

106. Ibid., 76–77.

107. *DZJJG*, 1:399; *PDN*, 698.

108. The U.S. State Department issued the text of this "surrender call" on 28 August (*New York Times*, 29 August 1958). See also Zheng Wenhan, *Mishu riji li de Peng laozong*, 336.

109. Department of State *Bulletin*, 10 September 1958; see also Eisenhower, *Waging Peace*, 298.

110. Christensen, *Useful Adversaries*, 219.

111. Zheng Wenhan, *Mishu riji li de Peng laozong*, 336–37.

112. Xu Yan, *Jinmen zhizhan*, 242–44; Shen Weiping, *Paoji Jinmen*, 1:362–64.

113. Shen Weiping, *Paoji Jinmen*, 364–67.

114. *Renmin ribao*, 5 September 1958; for a background discussion of the territorial water issue, see Xue Mouhong et al., *Dangdai zhongguo waijiao*, 105.

115. Jin Chongji, ed., *Zhou Enlai zhuan*, 2:467.

116. *DZJJG*, 1:400.

117. *FRUS, 1958–1960*, 19:134–36.

118. Jin Chongji, ed., *Zhou Enlai zhuan*, 2:467; Wu Lengxi, *Yi Mao zhuxi*, 78.

119. Jin Chongji, ed., *Zhou Enlai zhuan*, 2:467; Wu Lengxi, *Yi Mao zhuxi*, 78–79.

120. Speeches, Mao Zedong at the Fifteenth Meeting of the Supreme State Council, 5 and 8 September 1958, *JMZW*, 7:378–96. The quote is from 384.

121. *Renmin ribao*, 7 September 1958.

122. Xu Yan, *Jinmen zhizhan*, 208.

123. Zubok and Pleshakov, *Inside the Kremlin's Cold War*, 224–25.

124. Ibid., 225; *ZENB*, 2:166; *ZEWHDJ*, 242.

125. *ZENB*, 2:167; Wei Shiyan, "The Truth of Gromyko's Conversation with Chairman Mao Zedong on the Taiwan Issue," in Pei Jianzhang et al., *Xin Zhongguo waijiao fengyun* (Experiences of New China's Diplomacy) (Beijing: Shijie zhishi, 1991–), 1:137; Zubok and Pleshakov, *Inside the Kremlin's Cold War*, 225.

126. Wei Shiyan, "Truth of Gromyko's Conversation with Chairman Mao Zedong," 138; Wu Lengxi, *Yi Mao zhuxi*, 80–81.

127. Letter, Mao Zedong to Zhou Enlai, 7.00 A.M., 7 September 1958, *JMZW*, 7:494–95.

128. For the text of the letter, see the *New York Times*, 9 September 1958.

129. Zubok and Pleshakov, *Inside the Kremlin's Cold War*, 225. The account provided by Zubok and Pleshakov here is based on a report the Soviet embassy sent to Moscow on 10 September 1958.

130. *New York Times*, 22 February 1988, 1; Andrei A. Gromyko, *Memoirs* (New York: Doubleday, 1989), 251–52.

131. Wei Shiyan, "Truth of Gromyko's Conversation with Chairman Mao Zedong," 135.

132. Mao made this statement to the Finnish ambassador to China in January 1955; see *MZX*, 5:136–37.

133. According to M. S. Kapitsa, a China expert at the Soviet Foreign Ministry who accompanied Gromyko to Beijing, the Soviet foreign minister was "appalled" by what he experienced in Beijing. See A. Doak Barnett, "The 1958 Quemoy Crisis: The Sino-Soviet Dimension," *Problems of Communism* (July–August 1976): 38–39.

134. Ye Fei, *Ye Fei huiyilu*, 659.

135. Xu Yan, *Jinmen zhizhan*, 249; Eisenhower, *Waging Peace*, 302.

136. Order, CCP Central Military Commission to the Fujian Military Region,

the Frontal Headquarters, and convey to the Headquarters of the Air Force and the Navy, 24:00, 7 September 1958, quoted from Shen Weiping, *Paoji Jinmen*, 401-2.

137. Ye Fei, *Ye Fei huiyilu*, 659-60.

138. Ibid., 660; Eisenhower, *Waging Peace*, 302.

139. Xue Mouhong et al., *Dangdai zhongguo waijiao*, 10-104; Alfred D. Wilhelm Jr., *The Chinese at the Negotiation Table: Style and Characteristics* (Washington, D.C.: National Defense University Press, 1994), 185-98.

140. Xue Mouhong et al., *Dangdai zhongguo waijiao*, 104.

141. Wang Bingnan, *Zhongmei huitan jiunian huigu*, 70-71.

142. Xue Mouhong et al., *Dangdai zhongguo waijiao*, 107-8.

143. Letter, Zhou Enlai to Wang Bingnan, 9 September 1958, quoted from Shen Weiping, *Paoji Jinmen*, 752-53; see also Wang Bingnan, *Zhongmei huitan jiunian huigu*, 73-74.

144. How to "persuade" the Americans was the main topic in Mao's conversation with Wang Bingnan on the eve of Wang's departure for Warsaw. The chairman told Wang to tell the American negotiator: "America is a big country; China is a big country too. Why should you make yourselves the enemy of six hundred million Chinese simply for the sake of the Taiwan island with a population of less then ten million?" See Wang Bingnan, *Zhongmei huitan jiunian huigu*, 72-73.

145. *ZENB*, 2:168.

146. Letter, Mao Zedong to Zhou Enlai and Huang Kecheng, 13 September 1958, *JMZW*, 7, 416-17.

147. Letter, Zhou Enlai to Mao Zedong, 13 September 1958, quoted from *ZENB*, 2:470.

148. *ZENB*, 2:470; Xue Mouhong et al., *Dangdai zhongguo waijiao*, 107-8. See also telegrams, Beam to Department of State, 8 and 10 P.M., 15 September 1958, *FRUS, 1958-1960*, 19:191-96.

149. Information gained from author's interviews with a senior Chinese diplomat in August 1994, and confirmed by other author interviews. For a related discussion short of clearly mentioning Wang Bingnan's mistake and Mao's criticism of him, see *ZENB*, 2:470. In his memoirs, Wang did not mention that he had failed to follow Mao's instructions on the first day of the Sino-American ambassadorial talks, and that he was severely criticized by Mao. Indeed, reading Wang's memoirs, one gets the impression that he had never presented the five-point proposal and had been very tough toward the American negotiators (see Wang Bingnan, *Zhongmei huitan jiunian huigu*, 75-77). This discrepancy is another example of why scholars should take a critical approach to Chinese sources in general and memoirs in particular.

150. Author's interviews with a senior Chinese diplomat, August 1994; see also *ZENB*, 2:470.

151. *ZENB*, 2:471.

152. Letter, Zhou Enlai to Mao Zedong, 17 September 1958, quoted from *ZENB*, 2:170-71, see also Jin Chongji, ed., *Zhou Enlai zhuan*, 2:471.

153. Letter, Zhou Enlai to Mao Zedong, 18 September 1958, quoted from *ZENB*, 2:171.

154. Letter, Mao Zedong to Zhou Enlai, 19 September 1958, *MZWW*, 353.

155. In retrospect, U.S. officials may have missed a significant opportunity to resolve the Taiwan Strait situation in Warsaw in September 1958. If Washington had responded positively to Beijing's proposals and agreed to persuade the GMD troops to withdraw from Jinmen— this is what Washington did by the end of September, so it should not have been too difficult for Washington to do so in mid-September—not only would the tension in the Taiwan Strait have been greatly reduced, but also, and more important, a new and very different pattern of mainland China–Taiwan relations could have been established. With Beijing formally committing to not using force in "liberating" Taiwan, future developments concerning the "Taiwan issue" could have been dramatically different. At least, we probably would see a different attitude on Beijing's part regarding the use of force as a possible way to reunify China today.

156. Xue Mouhong et al., *Dangdai zhongguo waijiao*, 108; telegrams, Beam to Department of State, 3 P.M., 18 September 1958 and 22 September 1958, *FRUS, 1958–1960*, 19:209–16, 258–64.

157. *ZEWHDJ*, 242–43; *ZENB*, 2:171–72.

158. *ZENB*, 2:172–73.

159. *Renmin ribao*, 21 September 1958.

160. Jin Chongji, ed., *Zhou Enlai zhuan*, 2:471.

161. Letter, Zhou Enlai to Mao Zedong, 22 September 1958, *ZEJW*, 4:403; see also *JMZW*, 7:425.

162. Telegram, Mao Zedong to Zhou Enlai, 5:30 P.M., 22 September 1958, *JMZW*, 7:424.

163. Telegram, Peng Dehuai to PLA Fujian Frontal Headquarters, 24 September 1958, *PDN*, 703. In this telegram, Peng, following Mao's instructions, ordered the Frontal Headquarters to "concentrate on artillery shelling, and only under the condition that American ships and aircraft will not be hit and that victory can be guaranteed will the air force and navy be used in operations." See also Xu Yan, *Jinmen zhizhan*, 257–60.

164. *ZENB*, 2:175.

165. *FRUS, 1958–1960*, 19:301.

166. *ZENB*, 2:177; Wu Lengxi, *Yi Mao zhuxi*, 83.

167. Wu Lengxi, *Yi Mao zhuxi*, 84–85.

168. Letter, Mao Zedong to Peng Dehuai and Huang Kecheng, 8.00 A.M., 5 October 1958, *JMZW*, 7:437.

169. *ZENB*, 2:179.

170. Minutes, Zhou Enlai's conversation with S. F. Antonov, 5 October 1958, *ZEWW*, 262–67; see also *ZENB*, 2:179–80.

171. Letter, Mao Zedong to Peng Dehuai and Huang Kecheng, 2:00 A.M., 6 October 1958, *JMZW*, 7:437–38.

172. *Renmin ribao*, 6 October 1958; *JMZW*, 7:439–41; see also CCP Central Committee: "Notification on the Current Situation of the Anti-American Struggle," 17 October 1958, 101-12-160, Fujian Provincial Archives.

173. *Renmin ribao*, 13 October 1958; Mao had drafted "Another Message to the

Compatriots in Taiwan" to be read on 13 October, but, for whatever reason, he decided not to use it. See *JMZW*, 7:457–61.

174. Mao Zedong's remarks on the Defense Department's order to resume the shelling, 20 October 1958, *JMZW*, 7:466–67.

175. *Renmin ribao*, 25 October 1958; *JMZW*, 7:468–70.

176. Ironically, it was exactly because Beijing's leaders believed that, if the crisis was carefully managed, Washington would not retaliate against Beijing that they initiated the crisis. See Zhou Enlai, "Report on the Current Situation in the Taiwan Area and the Chinese People's Tasks in the Anti-Imperialist Struggle," 11 November 1958, 101-12-160, Fujian Provincial Archives.

Chapter Eight

1. For discussions of Hanoi's adoption of a "southern revolution" strategy in 1958–60, see William J. Duiker, *The Communist Road to Power in Vietnam* (Boulder, Colo.: Westview Press, 1996), 186–90; R. B. Smith, *An International History of the Vietnam War* (London: Macmillan, 1983–91), vol. 1, chs. 8 and 10; King C. Chen, "Hanoi's Three Decisions and the Escalation of the Vietnam War," *Political Science Quarterly* 90 (Summer 1975); Ang Cheng Guan, *Vietnamese Communists' Relations with China and the Second Indochina Conflict, 1956–1962* (Jefferson, N.C.: McFarland Publishers, 1997), esp. chs. 4–7; and Robert K. Brigham, *Guerrilla Diplomacy: The NLF's Foreign Relations and the Vietnam War* (Ithaca: Cornell University Press, 1998).

2. For an informative recent discussion, which is based on direct dialogue between former U.S. and Vietnamese policymakers, with active participation of scholars from Vietnam, America, and other countries, see Robert S. McNamara, James Blight, and Robert Brigham, *Argument without End: In Search of Answers to the Vietnam Tragedy* (New York: Public Affairs, 1999), ch. 4.

3. For a more extensive analysis, see discussions in Chapter 5; see also Zhai Qiang, "China and the Geneva Conference of 1954," *China Quarterly*, no. 129 (March 1992), and Zhai Qiang, *China and the Vietnam Wars, 1950–1975* (Chapel Hill: University of North Carolina Press, 2000), ch. 2.

4. For example, in meeting Ho Chi Minh and Pham Van Dong on 18–22 November 1956, Zhou Enlai repeatedly emphasized that "the unification should be regarded as a long-term struggle," and that "only when the North had been consolidated with extensive efforts, would it become possible to talk about how to win over the South and how to unify the country." See Shi Zhongquan, *Zhou Enlai de zhuoyue fengxian* (Zhou Enlai's Outstanding Contributions) (Beijing: Zhongyang zhongyang dangxiao, 1993), 286. See also Guo Ming et al., *Zhongyue guanxi yanbian sishinian* (Four Decades of Evolution of Sino-Vietnamese Relations) (Nanning: Guanxi renmin, 1992), 65–66.

5. *ZJG*, 142–43.

6. Guo Ming et al., *Zhongyue guanxi yanbian sishinian*, 66; for a Vietnamese version of this exchange, see The Foreign Ministry of the Socialist Republic of Vietnam, "The Truth about Vietnam-Chinese Relations over the Last 30 Years,"

Foreign Broadcast Information Service (Asia and Pacific), Supplement, 19 October 1979, 13–16.

7. Guo Ming et al., *Zhongyue guanxi yanbian sishinian*, 67; *ZEWHDJ*, 279–80.

8. We now know, from a Vietnamese perspective, that the "southern revolution" was primarily the initiative of revolutionary forces in South Vietnam. For an excellent discussion, see Brigham, *Guerrilla Diplomacy*, ch. 1.

9. See Huang Zheng, *Hu Zhiming yu Zhongguo* (Ho Chi Minh and China) (Beijing: Jiefangjun, 1987), ch. 6; see also Zhai Qiang, *China and the Vietnam Wars*, ch. 3.

10. During the 1958 Taiwan Strait crisis, Mao Zedong introduced his "noose strategy," arguing that overseas American military presence served as hangman's nooses for the United States, and that every military commitment abroad would add one more noose around the necks of the Americans. Mao therefore believed that the overextension of America's strength would lead to the final failure of U.S. foreign policy in general and its policy toward China in particular. See discussions in Chapter 7.

11. Li Ke and Hao Shengzhang, *Wenhua dageming zhong de renmin jiefangjun* (The People's Liberation Army during the Cultural Revolution) (Beijing: Zhonggong dangshi ziliao, 1989), 408–9. This work offers one of the best accounts of China's military development from the mid-1960s to the mid-1970s. Since the authors were alleged to have released confidential information without proper authorization, the book was withdrawn from circulation shortly after its publication.

12. Guo Ming et al., *Zhongyue guanxi yanbian sishinian*, 69; Qu Aiguo, Bao Mingrong, and Xiao Zhuyao, *Yuanyue kangmei: Zhongguo zhiyuan budui zai yuenan* (Assisting Vietnam, Resisting America: Chinese Supporting Units in Vietnam) (Beijing: Junshi kexue, 1995), 8.

13. Minutes, Mao Zedong's conversations with Vo Nguyen Giap and other Vietnamese guests, 5 October 1962, CCA.

14. Guo Ming et al., *Zhongyue guanxi yanbian sishinian*, 69; Qu Aiguo et al., *Yuanyue kangmei*, 8; Wang Xiangen, *Kangmei yuanyue shilu* (A Factual Account of Resisting America and Assisting Vietnam) (Beijing: Guoji wenhua chuban gongsi, 1990), 25–26; see also *Beijing Review*, 23 November 1979.

15. Qu Aiguo et al., *Yuanyue kangmei*, 9.

16. Qu Aiguo, "Chinese Supporters in the Operations to Assist Vietnam and Resist America," *Junshi shilin* (The Circle of Military History), no. 6 (1989): 40; *LSN*, 2:577.

17. Tong Xiaopeng, *Fenyu sishi nian* (Forty Years of Storms) (Beijing: Zhongyang wenxian, 1996), 2:219–20. Tong was one of Zhou Enlai's main assistants from the late 1930s until Zhou's death in 1976.

18. Hu Zhengqing, *Yige waijiaoguan de riji* (A Diplomat's Diary) (Jinan: Huanghe, 1991), 5; Quan Yanchi and Du Weidong, *Gongheguo mishi* (Secret Mission Dispatched by the Republic) (Beijing: Guanming ribao, 1990), 13–14.

19. Li Ke and Hao Shengzhang, *Wenhua dageming zhong de jiefangjun*, 418.

20. Minutes, Mao Zedong's conversations with Van Tien Dung, 18:30–19:45, 24 June 1964, CCA. See also Qu Aiguo et al., *Yuanyue kangmei*, 9–10.

21. Minutes, Mao Zedong's conversations with Tran Tu Binh and other Vietnamese guests, 27 July 1964, CCA. Tran Tu Bihn commented: "[I]t is not easy for the United States to send troops [to Vietnam]; the United States is located on the other side of the Pacific, and the Americans cannot reach [Vietnam] in one step."

22. Attending the meeting were Zhou Enlai, Chen Yi, Wu Xiuquan, Yang Chengwu, and Tong Xiaopeng from the Chinese Communist Party; Ho Chi Minh, Le Duan, Truong Chinh, Pham Van Dong, Vo Nguyen Giap, Nguyen Chi Thanh, Hoang Van Hoan, and Van Tien Dung from the Vietnamese Workers' Party; and Kaysone Phomvihane, Prince Souphanouvong, and Phoumi Vonvichit from the Laotian People's Revolutionary Party. See *ZEWHDJ*, 413.

23. Li Ke, "Chinese People's Support in Assisting Vietnam and Resisting America Will Be Remembered by History," *Junshi ziliao* (Military History Materials), no. 4 (1989): 30; Tong Xiaopeng, *Fenyu sishinian*, 2:220-21. Allen Whiting ("China's Role in the Vietnam War," in *The American War in Vietnam*, ed. Jayne Werner and David Hunt [Ithaca: Cornell University Southeast Asia Program, 1993], 73) reports that, according to information offered by Vietnamese scholars, Beijing promised Hanoi in 1964 that it would provide North Vietnam with air cover against American air attack but backed down from the promise in June 1965. Neither Chinese sources now available nor my interviews in Beijing can confirm this report. One Chinese military researcher points out that considering China's limited air combat capacity in the 1960s, it is doubtful that Beijing would have offered the Vietnamese any such promise in the first place.

24. Mao Zedong's remarks on and revisions of the communiqué of the Tenth Plenary Session of the CCP's Eighth Central Committee, 26 September 1962, *JMZW*, 10:195-98; for discussions, see Roderick MacFarquhar, *The Origins of the Cultural Revolution*, vol. 3, *The Coming of the Cataclysm, 1961-1966* (New York: Columbia University, 1997), ch. 12; see also Cong Jin, *Quzhe fazhan de suiyue* (The Years of Tortuous Development) (Zhengzhou: Henan renmin, 1989), 505-24.

25. MacFarquhar, *Origins of the Cultural Revolution*, vol. 3, ch. 15; Cong Jin, *Quzhe fazhan de suiyue*, 525-46.

26. See discussions in Chapters 3, 4, and 7.

27. Zheng Qian, "The Nationwide War Preparations before and after the CCP's Ninth Congress," *Zhonggong dangshi ziliao* (CCP History Materials), no. 41 (April 1992): 205; Cong Jin, *Quzhe fazhan de suiyue*, 502-4.

28. In one of these reports, Wang Jiaxiang argued that Beijing should learn from the lessons of the Korean War. During the initial stage of the Korean crisis, according to the report, Stalin encouraged China to enter the war by promising that the Soviet air force would cover Chinese ground troops in Korea; but when Beijing made the decision to enter the war, Stalin reneged on the promise. Wang warned that Khrushchev was repeating Stalin's trick by pushing China into another confrontation with the United States in Vietnam. See Wang Jiaxiang's report to the CCP Central Committee, 29 June 1962; the original document is kept at Chinese Central Archives. An abridged version of the report is published in *Wang Jiaxiang xuanji* (Selected Works of Wang Jiaxiang) (Beijing: Renmin, 1989), 446-60, but it omits the part on Chinese policy toward Vietnam.

29. *JMZW*, 10:188–89; Cong Jin, *Quzhe fazhan de suiyue*, 576–77, 579.

30. See discussions in Chapter 3; see also Cong Jin, *Quzhe fazhan de suiyue*, 322–71; MacFarquhar, *Origins of the Cultural Revolution*, vol. 3, ch. 16; and Allen S. Whiting, "The Sino-Soviet Split," in *The Cambridge History of China*, ed. Denis Twitchett and John K. Fairbank (Cambridge, Eng.: Cambridge University Press, 1987), 14:478–538.

31. For a more detailed discussion, see Chen Jian, *China's Road to the Korean War: The Making of the Sino-American Confrontation* (New York: Columbia University Press, 1994), ch. 1.

32. This idea was first openly suggested by D. N. Aidit, chairman of the Indonesian Communist Party and was soon widely adopted by Beijing.

33. In a meeting with former U.S. secretary of defense Robert McNamara on 5 December 1995, General Vo Nguyen Giap asserted that the 2 August attack "was ordered by a local commander, not by Hanoi," and that the 4 August attack "never occurred." See McNamara et al., *Argument without End*, 167.

34. Li Ke and Hao Shengzhang, *Wenhua dageming zhong de jiefangjun*, 408; Qu Aiguo, "Chinese Supporters," 40; *Beijing Review*, 30 November 1979, 14.

35. Wang Dinglie, *Dangdai zhongguo kongjun* (Contemporary Chinese Air Force) (Beijing: Jiefangjun, 1989), 384.

36. Transcript, Mao Zedong's conversations with Le Duan, 16:00–18:00, 13 August 1964, CCA. The Chinese participants at this meeting included Deng Xiaoping, Peng Zhen, Kang Sheng, and Wu Xiuquan.

37. Liu Yuti and Jiao Hongguang, "Operations against Invading American Planes in the Chinese-Vietnamese Border Area in Guangxi," in Wang Renshen et al., *Kongjun: Huiyi shiliao* (The Air Force: Memoirs and Reminiscences) (Beijing: Jiefangjun, 1992), 559–60. Liu was then the Seventh Army's deputy commander and Jiao was deputy political commissar.

38. Wang Dinglie, *Dangdai zhongguo kongjun*, 384. Right after the Gulf of Tonkin incident, American intelligence noted that China had moved thirty-six MiG fighters to the newly built airfield at Phuc-Yen in North Vietnam and had substantially strengthened its air strength in southern China. See Smith, *International History of the Vietnam War*, 2:300, and Allen Whiting, *The Chinese Calculus of Deterrence: India and Vietnam* (Ann Arbor: University of Michigan Press, 1975), 176.

39. Whiting, *Chinese Calculus of Deterrence*, 176–78.

40. Hanoi's leaders also believed it unlikely that the Americans would expand the war to North Vietnam. While meeting with Mao on 5 October 1964, Pham Van Dong said:

> The United States is facing many difficulties, and it is not easy for it to expand the war. Therefore, our consideration is that we should try to restrict the war in South Vietnam to the sphere of special war [a war that was restricted to South Vietnam], and should try to defeat the enemy within the sphere of special war. We should try our best not to let the U.S. imperialists turn the war in South Vietnam into a limited war, and try our best not to let the war be expanded to

North Vietnam. We must adopt a very skillful strategy, and should not provoke it [the United States]. Our politburo has made a decision on this matter, and today I am reporting it to Chairman Mao. We believe that this is workable. (*77 Conversations*, 75)

41. Transcript, Mao Zedong's conversations with Le Duan, 16:00–18:00, 13 August 1964, CCA.

42. *Renmin ribao* (People's Daily), 6 August 1965. Mao Zedong personally reviewed and approved the statement. See *JMZW*, 11:120.

43. "CCP Central Committee's Instructions on Organizing Demonstrations to Support the Vietnamese People and Oppose the U.S. Imperialist Military Aggression," 6 August 1964, 101-4-110, Fujian Provincial Archives; see also *Renmin ribao*, 7–13 August 1965.

44. For a personal recollection of widespread effects of this "Resisting America and Assisting Vietnam" movement in 1964–65, see Chen Jian, "Personal-Historical Puzzles about China and the Vietnam War," in *77 Conversations*, 21–22.

45. Cong Jin, *Quzhe fazhan de suiyue*, 465; Sun Dongsheng, "The Great Transformation of the Strategic Framework of Our Country's Economic Construction: The Making of the Third-Front Decision," *Dangde wenxian* (Party History Documents, Beijing), no. 3 (1995): 44–45.

46. As early 1964, Mao had begun to argue for the need to construct the Third Front, but it was not until after the Gulf of Tonkin incident that the CCP leadership decided to start the project. For discussions of the emergence and development of the Third Front phenomenon, see Barry Naughton, "The Third Front: Defense Industrialization in the Chinese Interior," *China Quarterly*, no. 115 (September 1988): 351–86; see also MacFarquhar, *Origins of the Cultural Revolution*, 3:369–70. For related documents, see "Selected Documents on the Decision-Making of Constructing the Third Front in the 1960s," *Dangde wenxian*, no. 3 (1995): 33–41.

47. Cong Jin, *Quzhe fazhan de suiyue*, 465.

48. Ibid., 465–66; Sun Dongsheng, "Great Transformation of the Strategic Framework," 45.

49. In January 1965, Zhou Enlai even exhorted a Vietnamese military delegation to attack the enemy's "main forces" and its "strategic hamlets" by the end of the year, optimistically predicting that such efforts would produce victory "even sooner than our original expectation." See *77 Conversations*, 75.

50. Minutes, Deng Xiaoping's speech at the politburo meeting, April 12, 1965, CCA.

51. Ibid.

52. Minutes, Liu Shaoqi, Deng Xiaoping, and Zhou Enlai's speeches at the politburo meeting, 12 April 1965, CCA; author interview with Beijing's military researchers, August 1992.

53. *Renmin ribao*, 25 March 1965.

54. Ibid., 30 March 1965.

55. Transcript, Zhou Enlai's conversation with Ayub Khan, 2 April 1965, 77

Conversations, 79–85. In this conversation, Zhou Enlai also mentioned that "if the United States expands the war to China, it will really suffer." But he did not, as Beijing did in delivering many later similar warnings, present this as a clearly defined fourth point.

56. Ironically, Washington's decision to postpone Ayub Khan's visit resulted from uneasiness with Pakistan's increasingly close relationship with China and, in particular, with the remarks about Vietnam that Ayub Khan made in Beijing early in March. See Robert McMahon, *The Cold War on the Periphery* (New York: Columbia University Press, 1996), 318–24.

57. *77 Conversations*, 88.

58. Peking (Mr. Hopson) to FO, No. 720, Priority/Confidential, 31 May 1965, FO 371/180996, Public Record Office, London. I am grateful to Jim Hershberg for providing me with a copy of this document.

59. Policymakers in Washington did heed these messages, and thus felt the pressure to act with extreme caution in attacking the North, lest a direct confrontation with China take place. See Editorial Note, *FRUS, 1964–1968*, 2:700–701; see also discussions in Whiting, *Chinese Calculus of Deterrence*, ch. 6.

60. Instruction, CCP Central Committee, "On Strengthening Preparations for War," 12 April 1965, in CCP Central Institute of Historical Documents, comp., *Jianguo yilai zhongyao wenxian xuanbian* (A Selection of Important Documents since the Founding of the People's Republic) (Beijing: Zhongyang wenxian, 1992–), 20:141–45.

61. Zheng Qian, "The Nationwide War Preparations before and after the CCP's Ninth Congress," 205; Qu Aiguo, "Chinese Supporters," 41; Yang Guoyu et al., *Dangdai zhongguo haijun* (Contemporary Chinese Navy) (Beijing: Zhongguo shehui kexue, 1989), 412.

62. It appears that the visit was divided into two parts. In early April, Le Duan and Vo Nguyen Giap arrived in Beijing secretly, and they met with Liu Shaoqi and other Chinese leaders on 8 April. The Vietnamese delegation then traveled to Moscow on 10 or 11 April and stayed there until 17 April to hold a series of talks with Soviet leaders. The Vietnamese then came back to Beijing on 18 April to continue their visit to China in an open manner. For a summary of the delegation's visit to the Soviet Union and the second half of its visit to China, see Smith, *International History of the Vietnam War*, 3:92–97.

63. Li Ke and Hao Shengzhang, *Wenhua dageming zhong de jiefangjun*, 415; Wang Xiangen, *Kangmei yuanyue shilu*, 44; *DZJJG*, 1:539–40.

64. In the spring and summer of 1965, Beijing ordered Chinese air units that had entered the Chinese-Vietnamese border area not to cross the border under any circumstances. See Liu Yuti and Jiao Hongguan, "Operations against Invading American Planes," 563.

65. Wang Xiangen, *Kangmei yuanyue shilu*, 39–44; Li Ke and Hao Shengzhang, *Wenhua dageming zhong de jiefangjun*, 422; see also *77 Conversations*, 86–87.

66. Andong is a border city on the Yalu. During the Korean War, Chinese and Soviet air forces used bases on the China side of the Sino-Korean border to fight

the American air force over northern Korea. This strategy was known as the "An-dong model."

67. Li Ke and Hao Shengzhang, *Wenhua dageming zhong de jiefangjun*, 417. According to Whiting ("China's Role in the Vietnam War," 73), Vietnamese scholars claim that Beijing informed Hanoi in June 1965 that "it would be unable to defend the North against U.S. air attack." The Chinese sources cited here clearly contradict the Vietnamese claim.

68. For a discussion of Luo Ruiqing's purge and its possible connections with Beijing's strategies toward the Vietnam War, see Harry Harding and Gurtov Melvin, *The Purge of Lo Jui-ch'ing: The Politics of Chinese Strategic Planning* (Santa Monica: Rand Corp., R-548-PR, February 1971), and MacFarquhar, *Origins of the Cultural Revolution*, 3:448–50.

69. After Luo Ruiqing's purge, Li Xiannian became the real head of the group. During the years of the Cultural Revolution, both Bo Yibo and Liu Xiao were also purged. Some members, such as Ji Dengkui, a Cultural Revolution star, would be added to the group. Zhou Enlai would frequently take charge of the group's activities himself. See Wang Xiangen, *Kangmei yuanyue shilu*, 48; Li Ke and Hao Shengzhang, *Wenhua dageming zhong de jiefangjun*, 413; and author interviews with Beijing's military researchers, August 1992.

70. Wang Xiangen, *Kangmei yuanyue shilu*, 48.

71. Li Ke and Hao Shengzhang, *Wenhua dageming zhong de jiefangjun*, 415.

72. Ibid., 418.

73. Mao Zedong ordered in 1965 that only the best Chinese engineering and antiaircraft artillery troops be sent to Vietnam. See ibid., 409–10.

74. Qu Aiguo, "Chinese Supporters," 41; Wang, *Kangmei yuanyue shilu*, 45; Li Ke and Hao Shengzhang, *Wenhua dageming zhong de jiefangjun*, 418.

75. Wang Xiangen, *Kangmei yuanyue shilu*, 45.

76. *DZJJG*, 1:545; Li Ke and Hao Shengzhang, *Wenhua dageming zhong de jiefangjun*, 421; Wang Xiangen, *Kangmei yuanyue shilu*, 100–101.

77. Wang Xiangen, *Kangmei yuanyue shilu*, 46; Li Ke and Hao Shengzhang, *Wenhua dageming zhong de jiefangjun*, 422.

78. Wang Xiangen, *Kangmei yuanyue shilu*, 39–42.

79. *DZJJG*, 1:548.

80. Qu Aiguo, "Chinese Supporters," 41.

81. *DZJJG*, 1:545–47; Qu Aiguo, "Chinese Supporters," 41–42.

82. Li Ke and Hao Shengzhang, *Wenhua dageming zhong de jiefangjun*, 418–19; *DZJJG*, 1:540–41.

83. Li Ke and Hao Shengzhang, *Wenhua dageming zhong de jiefangjun*, 420; *DZJJG*, 1:543; for discussions of American knowledge of Chinese involvement in the construction of the air base, see Whiting, *Chinese Calculus of Deterrence*, 188, and "China's Role in the Vietnam War," 75.

84. *DZJJG*, 1:548; Qu Aiguo, "Chinese Supporters," 41–42.

85. *DZJJG*, 1:550.

86. Ibid., 540–41. Qu Aiguo, "Chinese Supporters," 42.

87. Li Ke and Hao Shengzhang, *Wenhua dageming zhong de jiefangjun*, 420; Qu Aiguo, "Chinese Supporters," 41–42.

88. Li Ke and Hao Shengzhang, *Wenhua dageming zhong de jiefangjun*, 423.

89. *DZJJG*, 1:550; Li Ke and Hao Shengzhang, *Wenhua dageming zhong de jiefangjun*, 423.

90. *DZJJG*, 1:551; Wang Dinglie, *Dangdai zhongguo kongjun*, 397.

91. This summary of the operations of Chinese antiaircraft artillery forces in Vietnam is based on the following sources: *DZJJG*, 1:550–53; Qu Aiguo, "Chinese Supporters," 43; and Wang Dinglie, *Dangdai zhongguo kongjun*, ch. 17.

92. Li Ke and Hao Shengzhang, *Wenhua dageming zhong de jiefangjun*, 341.

93. Yang Chengwu's report to Zhou Enlai and the CCP Central Committee, 9 April 1965, and Mao Zedong's remarks on Yang Chengwu's report, 9 April 1965, *MZJW*, 6:403.

94. Li Ke and Hao Shengzhang, *Wenhua dageming zhong de jiefangjun*, 341–42.

95. Ibid., 344; Wang Dinglie, *Dangdai zhongguo kongjun*, 392; for a comparison of American and Chinese records, see Whiting, *Chinese Calculus of Deterrence*, 179.

96. *JMZW*, 11:376–77, 381–82.

97. Cong Jin, *Quzhe fazhan de suiyue*, 467.

98. Li Ke and Hao Shengzhang, *Wenhua dageming zhong de jiefangjun*, 410–11.

99. For a detailed discussion, see Zhai Qiang, *China and the Vietnam Wars*, ch. 9; see also John W. Garver, "Sino-Vietnamese Conflict and the Sino-American Rapprochement," *Political Science Quarterly* 96 (Fall 1981): 445–64.

100. In his study, Whiting points out that a total of 50,000 Chinese troops were sent to Vietnam, but Vietnamese sources claim that there had been only 20,000. See Whiting, "China's Role in the Vietnam War," 74.

101. Whiting, *Chinese Calculus of Deterrence*, 194–95; Garver, "Sino-Vietnamese Conflict," 447–48.

102. Wang Xiangen, *Kangmei yuanyue shilu*, 61–72.

103. Ibid., 74; see also transcript, conversation between Zhou Enlai, Deng Xiaoping, and Kang Sheng and Le Duan and Nguyen Duy Trinh, 13 April 1966, in *77 Conversations*, 94–98. Much of the conversation was about problems related to Chinese troops in Vietnam. Deng Xiaoping mentioned in particular that Mao had told Le Duan that the Chinese should not exhibit "too much enthusiasm" in their support of Vietnam.

104. Wang Xiangen, *Kangmei yuanyue shilu*, 255.

105. For a more in-depth discussion, see Smith, *International History of the Vietnam War*, vol. 2, ch. 12, and vol. 3, ch. 9; and King C. Chen, "North Vietnam in the Sino-Soviet Dispute, 1962–1964," *Asian Survey* 4 (September 1964): 1023–36.

106. Recent Russian scholarship confirms that after 1965, Soviet military and economic support to Vietnam increased steadily. See Ilya V. Gaiduk, *The Soviet Union and the Vietnam War* (Chicago: Ivan R. Dee, 1996), chs. 2–3.

107. For a more detailed description of Mao's conversation with Kosygin, see Cong Jin, *Quzhe fazhan de suiyue*, 607–8.

108. Beijing's leaders were extremely unhappy with Hanoi's attitude toward

Moscow. For example, in a conversation with Le Duan in April 1966, Deng Xiaoping asked of the Vietnamese: "Why are you afraid of displeasing the Soviets?" (77 *Conversation*, 94).

109. For a detailed record of Miyamoto's visit to China and Vietnam in spring 1966, see Masaru Kojima, ed., *The Record of the Talks between the Japanese Communist Party and the Communist Party of China: How Mao Zedong Scrapped the Joint Communiqué* (Tokyo: Central Committee of the Japanese Communist Party, 1980).

110. In meetings with Le Duan in April 1966 and Pham Van Dong in August 1966, Zhou Enlai mentioned the propaganda and warned that it had violated the fundamental interests of the Vietnamese and Chinese people in their common struggle against the U.S. imperialists. See Guo Ming et al., *Zhongyue guanxi yanbian sishinian*, 102, and 77 *Conversations*, 98–99.

111. See Wang Xiangen, *Kangmei yuanyue shilu*, 225.

112. Ibid., 255–56; see also 77 *Conversations*, 95–96.

113. Zhou Enlai made it clear in his meeting with Le Duan in April 1966 that since China's own railway system was overloaded, the Chinese were not in a position to establish a united transportation system with the Soviets to handle Soviet materials going through Chinese territory (Wang Xiangen, *Kangmei yuanyue shilu*, 226).

114. According to official Chinese sources, during the entire Vietnam War, China "helped transfer 5,750 train trucks of materials in aid from other socialist countries to Vietnam, including materials from the Soviet Union" (ibid., 226). See also Chinese Foreign Ministry, "Outlines for Rebutting 'China Has Hindered Soviet Aid to Vietnam,'" 1 April 1965, 77-11-7, Jilin Provincial Archives, 36–39.

115. In April 1968, a Chinese unit stationed in the Dien Bien Phu area had an altercation with a group of Soviet officers there. Chinese soldiers temporarily detained the Soviets and, following the practice established as part of the Cultural Revolution, held a denunciation meeting criticizing the "Soviet revisionists." The local Vietnamese authorities were greatly offended and protested vehemently. The Chinese denied this allegation immediately. See Wang Xiangen, *Kangmei yuan yue shilu*, 229–35.

116. Quan Yanchi and Du Weidong, *Gongheguo mishi*, 249–51; Hu Zhengqing, *Yige waijiaoguan de riji*, 161–66.

117. Quan Yanchi and Du Weidong, *Gongheguo mishi*, 250–51.

118. For a good discussion of Mao's changing domestic agenda in 1968 and 1969, see Wang Nianyi, *Dadongluan de niandai* (The Years of Great Chaos) (Zhengzhou: Henan renmin, 1989), chs. 8–9; see also discussions in Chapter 9.

119. In 1969, with Mao's approval and under Zhou's direct supervision, Beijing officially started to reassess its relations with the United States. For a more detailed discussion, see Xiong Xianghui, "The Prelude to the Opening of Sino-American Relations," *Zhonggong dangshi ziliao*, no. 42 (June 1992): 56–96. See also discussions in Chapter 9.

120. As early as 19 December 1965, on the eve of Washington's "Christmas bombing pause," Zhou Enlai told Nguyen Duy Trinh, North Vietnam's foreign

minister: "[W]e are not against the idea that when the war reaches a certain point negotiations will be needed, but the problems is, the time is not right." See *77 Conversations*, 92.

121. Guo Ming et al., *Zhongyue guanxi yanbian sishinian*, 68; see also Garver, "Sino-Vietnamese Conflict," 448–50.

122. *ZEWHDJ*, 524; see also transcripts, Zhou Enlai's conversations with Pham Van Dong, 13 and 19 April 1968, *77 Conversations*, 123–29.

123. *77 Conversations*, 134–35.

124. Ibid., 139–40.

125. See discussions in Chapter 3.

126. Qu Aiguo, "Chinese Supporters," 43.

127. Ibid.; Yang Guoyu et al., *Dangdai zhongguo haijun*, 421–29; Ma Faxiang, "Zhou Enlai Directs the Operations of Helping Vietnam Sweep Mines," *Junshi lishi* (Military History, Beijing), no. 5 (1989): 35–27.

Chapter Nine

1. *Renmin ribao* (People's Daily), 28 January 1969. For the English text of the essay, see *Peking Review*, 31 January 1969, 7–10.

2. When the editors of *Renmin ribao* and *Hongqi* sent the commentator's essay to Mao for approval for publication, the chairman instructed: "Publish the essay as it is. Nixon's address should also be published." See Chen Jian and David L. Wilson, eds., "All Under the Heaven Is Great Chaos: Beijing, the Sino-Soviet Border Clashes, and the Turn toward Sino-American Rapprochement, 1968–1969," *CWIHPB*, no. 11 (Winter 1998): 161.

3. Nixon stated: "Let all nations know that during this administration our lines of communication will be open. We seek an open world—open to ideas, open to the exchange of goods and people—a world in which no people, great or small, will live in angry isolation." For Nixon's address, see *Public Papers of the Presidents of the United States: Richard Nixon, 1969* (Washington, D.C.: Government Printing Office, 1971), 1–4.

4. When Mao met with Nixon in February 1971, he told the president that he had observed the presidential election of 1968 and had wanted Nixon to win. See "Memcon of Nixon and Mao, 21 February 1972," in *The Kissinger Transcript: The Top-Secret Talks with Beijing and Moscow*, ed. William Burr (New York: New Press, 1999), 61.

5. Policymakers in Washington, however, failed to notice such a subtle sign. Henry Kissinger quoted *Renmin ribao*'s editorial essay in his memoirs but completely left out that Nixon's address had been published in its entirety. He thus commented: "Nixon's Inaugural address may have been more statesmanlike but the Chinese had more pungent writers." See Henry Kissinger, *White House Years* (New York: Little, Brown, 1979), 167–68.

6. The strategic/geopolitical interpretation has prevailed among scholars and policy practitioners both in China and in the United States. See, for example, Gong Li, *Mao Zedong waijiao fengyunlu* (A Record of Mao Zedong's Diplomacy)

(Zhengzhou: Zhongyuan nongmin, 1996), 196–206; Qian Jiang, *Ping Pong wai-jiao mahou* (Behind the Ping-Pong Diplomacy) (Beijing: Dongfang, 1997), ch. 8; Henry Kissinger, *Diplomacy* (New York: Simon and Schuster, 1994), ch. 28; Robert Ross, *Negotiating Cooperation: The United States and China, 1969–1989* (Stanford, Calif.: Stanford University Press, 1995), ch. 1; and John W. Garver, *Foreign Relations of the People's Republic of China* (Englewood Cliffs, N.J.: Prentice-Hall, 1993), 74–81.

7. See discussions in Chapter 8.

8. Li Ke and Hao Shengzhang, *Wenhua dageming zhong de renmin jiefangjun* (The People's Liberation Army during the Cultural Revolution) (Beijing: Zhong-gong dangshi ziliao, 1989), 249–51.

9. Wang Hongwei, *Ximalaya shan qingjie: Zhongyin guanxi yanjiu* (The Hima-layas Sentiment: A Study on Sino-Indian Relations) (Beijing: Zhongguo zangxue, 1998), 271–73.

10. See discussions in Chapter 3.

11. Yang Kuisong, "From the Zhenbao Island Incident to Sino-American Rap-prochement," *Dangshi yanjiu ziliao* (Party History Research Materials, Beijing), no. 12 (1997): 7–8; Xu Yan, "The Sino-Soviet Border Clashes of 1969," ibid., no. 6 (1994): 6–10.

12. Kissinger recorded in his memoir (*White House Years*, 183) that in August 1969, a Soviet diplomat in Washington inquired about "what the U.S. reaction would be to a Soviet attack on Chinese nuclear facilities." See also discussions in Yang Kuisong, "From the Zhenbao Island Incident to Sino-American Rapproche-ment," 12.

13. See discussions in previous chapters, especially Chapters 4, 7, and 8.

14. See, for example, Sergei Goncharov, John Lewis, and Xue Litai, *Uncertain Partners: Stalin, Mao, and the Korean War* (Stanford, Calif.: Stanford University Press, 1993), 219–20; Andrew J. Nathan and Robert S. Ross, *The Great Wall and the Empty Fortress: China's Search for Security* (New York: W. W. Norton, 1997), chs. 3–4; and Jonathan D. Pollack, "The Opening to America," in *The Cambridge History of China*, ed. Denis Twitchett and John K. Fairbank (Cambridge, Eng.: Cambridge University Press, 1991), 15:402–74.

15. See, for example, editorial essay, "March Forward along the Path of the October Revolution," *Renmin ribao*, 6 November 1967, and Lin Biao speech at the rally celebrating the fiftieth anniversary of the October Revolution, *Renmin ribao*, 8 November 1967.

16. See, for example, editorial essay, "Leninism or Social-Imperialism," *Renmin ribao*, 22 April 1970.

17. See, for example, "The Notice by the CCP Central Committee" (revised by Mao Zedong), 16 May 1966, *Renmin ribao*, 17 May 1967.

18. A well-known example in this regard was that during China's War of Resis-tance against Japan, the CCP formed a "united front" with the Guomindang.

19. This idea was explicitly revealed in Mao's attitude toward personality cults. The chairman had consistently favored a "correct" personality cult, which he saw as an important condition for the Chinese revolution to advance along the correct

lines. See Cong Jin, *Quzhe fazhan de suiyue* (The Years of Tortuous Development) (Zhengzhou: Henan renmin, 1989), 117; see also *JMZW*, 7:113.

20. This reveals a fundamental paradox that faced Mao's continuous revolution: it had to find the means to destroy the "old" world from nowhere but the "old" world itself.

21. Remarks by Mao Zedong, 5 August 1968, *JMZW*, 12:516–17; see also transcript, "Mao Zedong's Talks with the Red Guard Leaders from Five Universities in Beijing," 28 July 1968, CCA.

22. Mao Zedong, "A Series of Remarks on External Propaganda and Diplomatic Affairs," March 1967–March 1971, *JMZW*, 12:275–76, 283–84.

23. See, for example, Mao Zedong's speech at the opening session of the Enlarged Twelfth Plenary Session of the CCP's Eighth Central Committee, 13 October 1968, in Xu Dashen, ed., *Zhonghua renmin gongheguo shilu* (A Factorial History of the People's Republic of China) (Changchun: Jilin Renmin, 1994), 3:431–32, and Mao Zedong's speech at the First Plenary Session of the CCP's Ninth Central Committee, 28 April 1969, *JMZW*, 13:35–41.

24. First in a pioneering case study on the changing behavior of Mao's China as a revolutionary state, then in a comprehensive study on the relationship between revolutionary states and world order, David Armstrong has developed a sophisticated concept useful for understanding how and why revolutionary states, such as Mao's China, become "socialized" during the process of encountering the existing world order. According to Armstrong, "Socialization denotes the process 'where men consciously or unconsciously conform to the conventions of the society in which they live in order to function more effectively within it (and) whereby an increasing entanglement within an existing structure of relationships brings about an increasing degree of adaptation to the normal behavior patterns of that structure.'" See David Armstrong, *Revolution and World Order: The Revolutionary State in International Society* (New York: Oxford University Press, 1993), 7–8; see also Armstrong, *Revolutionary Diplomacy: Chinese Foreign Policy and the United Front Doctrine* (Berkeley and Los Angeles: University of California Press, 1977).

25. *Cankao ziliao* (Reference Materials) was a journal published two or three times daily that carried translations of foreign news reports and other important information for CCP leaders.

26. Richard Nixon, "Asia after Viet Nam," *Foreign Affairs* 46 (October 1967): 121.

27. Gong Li, *Mao Zedong waijiao fengyunlu*, 206–7.

28. Even the Sino-American ambassadorial talks in Warsaw were suspended virtually indefinitely after January 1968. See Luo Yisu, "My Years in Poland," in Wang Taiping, ed., *Zhongguo shijie waijiao shengya* (Chinese Diplomats' Diplomatic Careers) (Beijing: Shijie zhishi, 1995–), 4:177–78.

29. See John H. Holdridge, *Crossing the Divide: An Insider's Account of Normalization of U.S.-China Relations* (Lanham, Md.: Rowman and Littlefield, 1997), 25. Reportedly, Beijing's quick and positive response was approved by Mao himself. See Gong Li, *Mao Zedong waijiao fengyunlu*, 207.

30. *Renmin ribao*, 20 February 1969.

31. See, for example, conversation between Mao Zedong and Beqir Balluku, 1 October 1968, and conversation between Mao Zedong and E. F. Hill, 28 November 1968, CWIHP*B*, no. 11 (Winter 1998): 156–61. Balluku was Albania's defense minister, and Hill was chairman of the Australian Communist Party (Marxism-Leninism).

32. Hu Shiwei et al., *Chen Yi zhuan* (A Biography of Chen Yi) (Beijing: Dangdai zhonguo, 1991), 614; Du Yi, *Daxue ya qingsong: wenge zhong de Chen Yi* (An Unyielding Green Pine in Big Snow: Chen Yi in the Cultural Revolution) (Beijing: Shijie zhishi, 1997), 208.

33. The account in this paragraph about the four meetings and the main contents of the two reports is based on the following sources: Fan Shuo et al., *Ye Jianying zhuan* (A Biography of Ye Jianying) (Beijing: Dangdai zhongguo, 1995), 598–99; Wei Wei et al., *Nie Rongzhen zhuan* (A Biography of Nie Rongzhen) (Beijing: Dangdai zhongguo, 1994), 676–77; Hu Shiwie et al., *Chen Yi zhuan*, 614; Liu Zhi et al., *Xu Xiangqian zhuan* (A Biography of Xu Xiangqian) (Beijing: Dangdai zhongguo, 1995), 541–42; and Zheng Qian, "The Nationwide War Preparations before and after the CCP's Ninth Congress," *Zhonggong dangshi ziliao* (CCP History Materials), no. 41 (April 1992): 211.

34. *Renmin ribao*, 25 April 1969.

35. Xiong Xianghui, "The Prelude to the Opening of Sino-American Relations," *Zhonggong dangshi ziliao*, no. 42 (June 1992): 61.

36. Ibid., 61–62.

37. Ibid., 62–63. Xiong Xianghui, a longtime assistant to Zhou Enlai, had held such important positions as Chinese chargé d'affaires in London. Yao Guang was head of the European and American sections under the Foreign Ministry.

38. Report by Four Chinese Marshals to the Central Committee, "A Preliminary Evaluation of the War Situation," 11 July 1969, CWIHP*B*, no. 11 (Winter 1998): 166–68.

39. Xiong Xianghui, "Prelude to the Opening of Sino-American Relations," 76–77.

40. Ibid., 78–79.

41. Xu Yan, "Sino-Soviet Border Clashes of 1969," 10; Yang Kuisong, "From the Zhenbao Island Incident to Sino-American Rapprochement," 11–23.

42. See "The CCP Central Committee's Order for General Mobilization in Border Provinces and Regions," 28 August 1969, CWIHP*B*, no. 11 (Winter 1998): 168–69.

43. Report by Four Chinese Marshals, "Our Views about the Current Situation," 17 September 1969, CWIHP*B*, no. 11 (Winter 1998): 170.

44. "Further Thoughts by Marshal Chen Yi on Sino-American Relations," ibid., 170–71.

45. Dr. Li Zhisui, *The Private Life of Chairman Mao* (New York: Random House, 1994), 514.

46. Kissinger, *White House Years*, 180.

47. Ibid., 180–81.

48. Jin Chongji, ed., *Zhou Enlai zhuan, 1949–1976* (A Biography of Zhou Enlai, 1949–1976) (Beijing: Zhongyang wenxian, 1998), 1088; *ZENB*, 3:334.

49. Xue Mouhong et al., *Dangdai zhongguo waijiao* (Contemporary Chinese Diplomacy) (Beijing: Zhongguo shehui kexue, 1989), 218; see also telegram, Stoessel to Secretary of State, 3 December 1969, RG 59, Department of State Records, Subject-Numeric Files, 1967–69, POL 23-8 US, NA. Stoessel mentioned in the telegram that the Chinese diplomat he tried to approach was Lei Yang, Chinese chargé d'affaires to Poland, but actually, it was Li Juqing, the Chinese embassy's second secretary. See Luo Yisu, "My Years in Poland," 179–80. Luo was the chief Chinese interpreter at the embassy in Warsaw; in the 1980s he became Chinese consul general to the Polish city Gdansk.

50. Jin Chongji, ed., *Zhou Enlai zhuan*, 1087.

51. *ZENB*, 3:336; Jin Chongji, ed., *Zhou Enlai zhuan*, 1088. See also Kissinger, *White House Years*, 188.

52. Gong Li, *Kuayue honggou: 1969–1979nian zhongmei guanxi de yanbian* (Bridging the Chasm: The Evolution of Sino-American Relations, 1969–1979) (Zhengzhou: Henan renmin, 1992), 49; Luo Yisu, "My Years in Poland," 180–81; see also Kissinger, *White House Years*, 188–89. Kissinger particularly emphasizes that Stoessel's visit to the Chinese embassy was "the first such invitation in *any* Sino-American contact since the Communists had taken power in China."

53. *ZENB*, 3:338; *ZEWHDJ*, 546.

54. Kissinger, *White House Years*, 191.

55. Luo Yisu, "My Years in Poland," 181; telegram, Stoessel to the Secretary of State, 8 January 1970, RG 59, Department of State Records, Subject-Numeric Files, 1967–69, CHICOM-US, NA. Two points should be noted here. First, in the past, the ambassadorial talks had been held in a meeting place arranged by the Polish government; this time, the Americans, obviously for the purpose of maintaining secrecy, proposed to move the meetings to the two embassies, to which the Chinese agreed immediately. Second, since China did not have an ambassador in Poland at that time, the Americans agreed to hold the meeting between Chinese chargé d'affaires Lei Yang and American ambassador Stoessel.

56. Luo Yisu, "My Years in Poland," 181; report, Stoessel-Lei talks, 20 January 1970, RG 59, Department of State Records, Subject-Numeric Files, 1970–73, POL CHICOM-US, NA. Zhou Enlai personally reviewed and revised the Chinese Foreign Ministry's instructions to Lei Yang, adding the paragraph emphasizing that Beijing was willing to consider "holding meetings at higher levels or through other channels." See *ZENB*, 3:344, and Jin Chongji, ed., *Zhou Enlai zhuan*, 1089.

57. *ZENB*, 3:348; Jin Chongji, ed., *Zhou Enlai zhuan*, 1089. Zhou Enlai made a key change in the statement's wording. In the original text prepared by the foreign ministry, it read that the Chinese government "will *consider receiving*" the American official. Zhou changed "will consider receiving" to "will receive." Next to the change, the premier added: "Considering that at the 135th meeting [the meeting held on 20 January], our side had already mentioned that we are willing to consider [receiving the American official] or [making the contact] through other channels,

and the American side also mentioned at the last meeting that [they will send an envoy] to Beijing for direct discussion, if we still use 'will consider,' it is too light a statement, therefore I changed it to 'will receive.' This is still lighter than 'will welcome,' but it is more substantial than 'will consider.'"

58. Gong Li, *Kuaiyue honggou*, 50–51; see also report, Stoessel-Lei talks, 21 February 1970, RG 59, Policy Planning Staff (Director's) Files, 1969–77, POL CHICOM-US, NA.

59. *ZENB*, 3:356; Jin Chongji, ed., *Zhou Enlai zhuan*, 1089–90.

60. *ZENB*, 3:357.

61. Kissinger, *White House Years*, 692.

62. *ZENB*, 3:367.

63. *Renmin ribao*, 19 and 20 May 1970; see also Gong Li, *Kuayue honggou*, 55–57.

64. Kissinger, *White House Years*, 695.

65. Ibid., 696; Gong Li, *Kuayue honggou*, 59.

66. *ZENB*, 3:372.

67. *Renmin ribao*, 11 July 1970. At the same time, Beijing announced that another American, Hugh Redmond, who had been imprisoned since 1954, had committed suicide three months earlier.

68. In 1959, Mao resigned the position as chairman of the PRC and Liu Shaoqi took his place. During the Cultural Revolution, Liu was purged and the chairmanship of the PRC was virtually vacated. In 1970, in discussing drafting a new constitution, Mao wanted the state chairmanship to be abolished. See remarks by Mao Zedong, *JMZW*, 13:94.

69. For a detailed study of the Lushan conference of 1970, see Wang Nianyi, *Dadongluan de niandai* (The Years of Great Chaos) (Zhengzhou: Henan renmin, 1989), 394–406.

70. Remarks on Wu Faxian's letter of self-criticism, 14 October 1970, *JMZW*, 13:139. Wu was then commander of China's air force and a main follower and supporter of Lin Biao.

71. *ZENB*, 3:406; see also Richard Nixon, *Memoirs of Richard Nixon* (New York: Grosset & Dunlap, 1978), 546–47.

72. Jin Chongji, ed., *Zhou Enlai zhuan*, 1091; *ZENB*, 3:410–11; Yang Mingwei and Chen Yangyong, *Zhou Enlai waijiao fengyun* (Zhou Enlai's Diplomatic Career) (Beijing: Jiefangjun wenyi, 1995), 244; see also Nixon, *Memoirs*, 546–47.

73. *ZENB*, 3:417; Yang Mingwei and Chen Yangyong, *Zhou Enlai waijiao fengyun*, 244.

74. Kissinger, *White House Years*, 700–703; Nixon, *Memoirs*, 546–47.

75. Edgar Snow, *The Long Revolution* (New York: Random House, 1972). In this book, Snow published the full text of his 1965 interviews with Mao (191–223).

76. Yin Jiamin, *Jiangjun buru shiming* (The General Has Succeeded in Carrying Out the Mission) (Beijing: Jiefangjun wenyi, 1992), 211–14.

77. All of this was carefully directed by Zhou Enlai. The premier even intervened over the size of the photo that was to be published in *Renmin ribao*, which served as an example for all other major Chinese papers to follow. See Yang Mingwei and Chen Yangyong, *Zhou Enlai waijiao fengyun*, 243.

78. Kissinger, *White House Years*, 698.

79. As an eighteen-year-old "educated youth" in Shanghai, I, as well as many of my friends, noticed the photo with Mao and Snow standing together at the Gate of Heavenly Peace. We all sensed that it meant something, although we did not know exactly what that "something" was.

80. Since early October, Snow had been waiting to interview the chairman. On 5 November, he had a lengthy interview with Zhou Enlai, which focused on international issues. Then, a few times he thought he was to meet the chairman soon, but the meeting date was postponed repeatedly. A possible reason for the delay was that, given the importance the chairman attached to the interview, he had to carefully consider what he was going to say.

81. Minutes, interview with Edgar Snow, 18 December 1970, *JMZW*, 13:166–68.

82. Edgar Snow, "A Conversation with Mao Tse-tung [Mao Zedong]," *Life* 70 (30 April 1971): 46–48; see also Mao's comments on not publishing the interview records, *JMZW*, 13:164.

83. Nixon, *Memoirs*, 547.

84. Kissinger, *White House Years*, 702–3.

85. One reason that Mao asked Snow that he not immediately publish the interview might have been that he wanted to have the time to relay it to his party and people.

86. Lin Biao introduced the four titles for Mao.

87. For the full text of the interview transcript, see *JMZW*, 13:163–87; for Snow's account, see his "Conversation with Mao Tse-tung [Mao Zedong]," 46–48.

88. Gong Li, *Kuayue honggou*, 50–51.

89. Kissinger mentioned (*White House Years*, 704–5) that in the early months of 1971, he "used the interval to try to educate myself on China" by meeting academic China experts for policy suggestions.

90. *Peking Review*, 5 February 1971, 4; see also Qian Jiang, *Ping Pong waijiao muhou*, 21–40.

91. Jin Chongji, ed., *Zhou Enlai zhuan*, 1093; Zhao Zhenghong, "The Ping-Pong Diplomacy as I Knew," *Zhonggong dangshi ziliao*, no. 39 (1991): 133–36. Zhao was the head of the Chinese delegation to the Nagoya Championships.

92. In mid-March 1971, when Zhou Enlai made the decision that the Chinese Table Tennis Team would participate in the world championship in Japan and reported the matter to Mao, the chairman wrote on Zhou's report: "Our team should go. [Our players] should be prepared not only for enduring hardship but also for encountering death. We should be prepared to lose a few [players], although it is better not to lose any." See *JMZW*, 12:284–85.

93. I still remember vividly the many hours I and my friends spent in front of a radio waiting to hear the most recent development at the championships.

94. Zhao Zhenghong, "Ping-Pong Diplomacy as I Knew," 144.

95. Qian Jiang, *Ping Pong waijiao muhou*, 159–60; Gong Li, *Kuayue honggou*, 78.

96. Qian Jiang, *Ping Pong waijiao muhou*, 170–72.

97. Ibid., 195.

98. Gong Li, *Kuayue honggou*, 79; Qian Jiang, *Ping Pong waijiao muhou*, 211.

99. Zhao Zhenghong, "Ping-Pong Diplomacy as I Knew," 143–44; Qian Jiang, *Ping Pong waijiao muhou*, 197–98.

100. Qian Jiang, *Ping Pong waijiao muhou*, 199–200.

101. Wu Xujun, "Mao Zedong's Five Superior Moves in Opening Sino-American Relations," in Li Ke, Xu Tao, and Wu Xujun, *Lishi de zhenshi* (The Truth of History) (Hong Kong: Liwen, 1995), 302–3.

102. Ibid., 306.

103. Wang Hairong was the granddaughter of Mao's cousin Wang Jifan. In the early 1970s, she was a close assistant to Mao and, in 1971, head of the Protocol Department of the Foreign Ministry. Beginning in the early 1970s, many of Mao's decisions on Chinese foreign policy were conveyed through Wang Hairong to Zhou Enlai and the Foreign Ministry.

104. Wu Xujun, "Mao Zedong's Five Superior Moves," 306–9.

105. Jin Chongji, ed., *Zhou Enlai zhuan*, 1094; *ZENB*, 3:449.

106. The text of the invitation dictated by Beijing to the Chinese delegation read: "Considering that the American team has requested several times to visit China, and that they have expressed warm and friendly feelings, we have decided to invite the team, including the officials with the team, to visit our country. Entry visas will be issued in Hong Kong, and, if they are short of travel funds, we will subsidize them." See Zhao Zhenghong, "Ping-Pong Diplomacy as I Knew," 144–45.

107. Nixon, *Memoirs*, 548.

108. The Chinese television commentator's opening remarks at the matches, which emphasized that "for a long time, friendship has existed between the Chinese and American peoples" and that "the visit by the American table tennis team will enhance such friendship," were carefully examined and revised by Zhou Enlai himself. See Qian Jiang, *Ping Pong waijiao muhou*, 268–71.

109. Minutes, Zhou Enlai, "Conversations with the American Table Tennis Delegation," 14 April 1971, *ZEWW*, 469–75. The Chinese media widely reported the meeting. See, for example, *Renmin ribao*, 15 April 1971, front page, where the quote can be found.

110. Kissinger, *White House Years*, 710.

111. Qian Jiang, *Ping Pong waijiao muhou*, 280.

112. On 31 May 1971, the CCP Central Committee, with Mao's approval, ordered the "distribut[ion of] the printed text [of the interview] to the party's bottom branches" and that it be "verbally relay[ed] to every party member." The Central Committee also ordered that "study of the interview should be carefully organized, so that the spirit of the chairman's talks will be correctly comprehended." See *JMZW*, 13:182.

113. *ZENB*, 3:452–53; Gong Li, *Kuayue honggou*, 97; Kissinger, *White House Years*, 714. It was Mao who believed that America's special envoy should come to Beijing publicly. The chairman, in reviewing the message, commented: "If they want to come, they should come in the open light. Why should they hide the[ir]

head and pull in the[ir] tail?" See Wei Shiyan, "The Inside Story of Kissinger's Secret Visit to China," in Pei Jianzhang et al., *Xin Zhongguo waijiao fengyun* (Experiences of New China's Diplomacy) (Beijing: Shijie zhishi, 1991-), 2:36.

114. Nixon, *Memoirs*, 549-50; Kissinger, *White House Years*, 715-18.

115. Kissinger, *White House Years*, 723-24; see also Jin Chongji, ed., *Zhou Enlai zhuan, 1949-1976*, 1095-95; Gong Li, *Kuayue honggou*, 97-98.

116. Kissinger, *White House Years*, 725-26; Gong Li, *Kuayue honggou*, 98.

117. *ZENB*, 3:458.

118. Ibid.; Jin Chongji, ed., *Zhou Enlai zhuan*, 1096.

119. Yang Mingwei and Chen Yangyong, *Zhou Enlai waijiao fengyun*, 247-48.

120. "The Central Committee Politburo's Report on the Sino-American Meetings" (drafted by Zhou Enlai), 26 May 1971, quoted from Gong Li, *Kuayue honggou*, 103-4; see also Jin Chongji, ed., *Zhou Enlai zhuan*, 1096-97, and *ZENB*, 3:458-59.

121. Gong Li, *Kuayue honggou*, 105-6.

122. Jin Chongji, ed., *Zhou Enlai zhuan*, 1096; *ZENB*, 3:458-59.

123. Gong Li, *Kuayue honggou*, 107; Kissinger, *White House Years*, 726-27.

124. Nixon, *Memoirs*, 552.

125. Gong Li, *Kuayue honggou*, 108.

126. Jin Chongji, ed., *Zhou Enlai zhuan*, 1097; *ZENB*, 3:461.

127. Transcripts of these meetings are now available in RG 59, Policy Planning Staff (Director's) Files, 1969-77, NA.

128. Speech, Zhou Enlai, "Explaining the Sino-American Communiqué," 3 March 1972, CCA (an excerpt of the speech is published in *ZENB*, 3:515); Kissinger, *White House Years*, 745.

129. Alexander Haig to Theodore Eliot, 28 January 1972, enclosing Kissinger to the president, "My Talks with Chou Enlai [Zhou Enlai]," 17 July 1971, RG 59, Top Secret Subject-Numeric Files, 1970-72, POL 7 Kissinger, NA; see also Wei Shiyan, "Inside Story of Kissinger's Secret Visit to China," 40-41.

130. Wei Shiyan, "Inside Story of Kissinger's Secret Visit to China," 41-42.

131. Kissinger, *White House Years*, 750; see also Wei Shiyan, "Inside Story of Kissinger's Secret Visit to China," 42-43.

132. In his memoirs, Kissinger mentioned that Zhou was hosting the reception for the North Korean leader Kim Il-sung. Actually, the guest was Kim Jung-rin, a politburo member and secretary of the Korean Workers' Party. See *ZEWHDJ*, 596, and Wei Shiyan, "Inside Story of Kissinger's Secret Visit to China," 43.

133. Wei Shiyan, "Inside Story of Kissinger's Secret Visit to China," 43-44. Kissinger, not knowing why Huang did not show up on time, mentioned in his memoirs: "We never found out whether it was a deliberate tactic to unsettle us, whether there was a Politburo meeting, whether Mao insisted on reviewing the talks, or whether, as was most likely, we faced a combination of all these" (*White House Years*, 751). In actuality, Huang was at Mao's home waiting for the chairman's instructions.

134. The chairman did get up early the next morning and approve the new draft, which Huang later presented to Kissinger.

135. Wei Shiyan, "Inside Story of Kissinger's Secret Visit to China," 44–45; Kissinger, *White House Years,* 752–53.

136. Nixon, *Memoirs,* 553.

137. *ZEWHDJ,* 596–97; *ZENB,* 3:469.

138. *ZEWHDJ,* 597.

139. Ibid.; *ZENB,* 3:469.

140. *ZENB,* 3:469.

141. Guo Ming et al., *Zhongyue guanxi yanbian sishinian* (Four Decades of Evolution of Sino-Vietnamese Relations) (Nanning: Guanxi renmin, 1992), 102–3.

142. On 12 August 1971, the Albanian Party of Labour Central Committee sent a letter to Mao and the CCP Central Committee, attacking Beijing's rapprochement with the United States. See *ZENB,* 3:474, and Fan Chengzuo, "The Spring, Summer, Autumn, and Winter in Chinese-Albanian Relations," in Wang Taiping, *Zhongguo shijie waijiao shengya,* 4:245–46.

143. Wang Nianyi, *Da dongluan de niandai,* 392–94; see also Jin Qiu, *The Culture of Power: The Lin Biao Incident in the Cultural Revolution* (Stanford, Calif.: Stanford University Press, 1999), esp. ch. 4.

144. Xiong Xianghui, *Lishi de zhujiao: Huiyi Mao Zedong, Zhou Enlai ji si laoshuai* (Historical Notes: Remembering Mao Zedong, Zhou Enlai, and the Four Marshals) (Beijing: Zhongyang dangxiao, 1995), 30–33.

145. Wang Nianyi, *Da dongluan de niandai,* 415–33. In her recently published study, Jin Qiu, who is the daughter of General Wu Faxian, former commander of the Chinese air force and one of Lin Biao's close associates, challenges Beijing's official account of the Lin Biao affair. She points out that Lin Liguo had never executed his unsophisticated plan to assassinate Mao and that Lin Biao himself was never prepared to challenge Mao's authority, let alone to kill him. Jin Qiu argues that Lin Biao's flight from Beijing on 13 September 1971 was "accidental," primarily resulting from his fear of Mao's purge. See Jin Qiu, *Culture of Power,* esp. ch. 7 and conclusion.

146. See, for example, Zhou Enlai (?), "Several Issues Concerning the Current International Situation," 22 March 1972, 244-1-77, Fujian Provincial Archives, which claims, "Lin Biao was the one who opposed Chairman Mao's decision of relaxing relations with the United States."

147. On 20 September, Beijing decided to cancel the annual National Day celebration parade at Tiananmen Square. The reason for the cancellation lay in the need to cover up Lin Biao's sudden disappearance from China's political scene — Lin's death would remain a top state secret until mid-October. The symbolism of the cancellation was significant since, from the day the PRC was established, the celebration parade had been a crucial component of the rituals of Mao's revolutionary China, making Tiananmen Square, at least once every year, the center stage of the grand drama of Mao's continuous revolution. The celebration has not taken place since October 1971.

148. Cao Guisheng, "Recalling the Secret 'Paris Channel' between China and the United States," in Pei Jianzhang, et al., *Xin Zhongguo waijiao fengyun,* 2:46–56.

149. *ZEWHDJ*, 608–9. For Kissinger's report on the trip, as transmitted to the State Department, see Alexander Haig to Theodore Eliot, 28 January 1972, RG 59, Top Secret Subject-Numeric Files, 1970–73, POL 7 Kissinger, NA.

150. Wei Shiyan, "Kissinger's Second Visit to Beijing," in Pei Jianzhang et al., *Xin Zhongguo waijiao fengyun*, 3:66–67; Kissinger, *White House Years*, 781.

151. Wei Shiyan, "Kissinger's Second Visit to Beijing," 67.

152. Kissinger, *White House Years*, 782.

153. Wei Shiyan, "Kissinger's Second Visit to Beijing," 69–70; Kissinger, *White House Years*, 787. An important breakthrough during the negotiation on the Taiwan issue occurred after Kissinger diplomatically expressed the U.S. attitude toward Taiwan's status: "The United States acknowledges that all Chinese on either side of the Taiwan Strait maintain there is but one China and that Taiwan is part of China. The United States Government does not challenge that position." Zhou Enlai later mentioned that this paragraph in the communiqué was "Kissinger's contribution, because none of us could figure out the proper expression," commenting that "after all, a Dr. is indeed useful as a Dr." See Jin Chongji, ed., *Zhou Enlai zhuan*, 1108.

154. See, for example, editorial essay, "The Tide of History Cannot Be Stopped," *Renmin ribao*, 28 October 1971.

155. Wei Shiyan, "The Haig Advance Group's Experience for Arranging Nixon's Visit," in Pei Jianzhang, et al., *Xin Zhongguo waijiao fengyun*, 3:76–79.

156. Minutes, Zhou Enlai's conversations with Alexander Haig, 6 January 1971, quoted from Jin Chongji, ed., *Zhou Enlai zhuan*, 1104–5.

157. Memcon of Nixon and Mao, 21 February 1972, in Burr, ed., *Kissinger Transcripts*, 59–65.

158. The text on the issue reads: "It [the United States] reaffirms its interest in a peaceful settlement of the Taiwan question by the Chinese themselves. With this prospect in mind, it affirms the ultimate objective of the withdrawal of U.S. forces and military installations from Taiwan. In the meantime, it will progressively reduce its forces and military installations on Taiwan as the tension in the area diminishes." For an account of how this language was worked out, see Kissinger, *White House Years*, 1076–80.

Epilogue

1. Deng Xiaoping never held top party and government positions such as chairman of the CCP Central Committee, president of the People's Republic, or premier of the Chinese State Council, but throughout the 1980s and early 1990s, he was China's paramount leader. Even after his formal retirement in 1992, his influence could still be felt in Beijing's decision making until his death in 1997.

2. The Tiananmen incident of 1976, though less known in other parts of the world than the bloodshed of 1989, is one of the most important events in China's modern history. Qingming, an annual festival dedicated to remembering the departed spirits of loved ones, was to be held that year on 5 April. Beginning in late March, thousands and thousands of ordinary Chinese citizens began to gather at

the Tiananmen Square. Mao, shocked by the fact that such mass "counterrevolutionary" activities could take place in the heart of Beijing, ordered a crackdown of the masses on 5 April. For an account of the incident, see Richard Baum, *Burying Mao: Chinese Politics in the Age of Deng Xiaoping* (Princeton, N.J.: Princeton University Press, 1994), 32–37.

3. For a critical survey of Deng Xiaoping's "reform and opening" policies in China, see Maurice Meisner, *The Deng Xiaoping Era: An Inquiry into the Fate of Chinese Socialism, 1978–1994* (New York: Hill and Wang, 1996); see also Harry Harding, *China's Second Revolution: Reform after Mao* (Washington, D.C.: Brookings Institution, 1987), and Merle Goldman, *Sowing the Seeds of Democracy in China: Political Reform in the Deng Xiaoping Era* (Cambridge, Mass.: Harvard University Press, 1994).

4. For more detailed discussions on Deng's foreign policy changes, see Harding, *China's Second Revolution*, ch. 6; Bruce Cumings, "The Political Economy of China's Turn Outward," and William R. Feeney, "Chinese Policy toward Multilateral Economic Institutions," in *China and the World: New Directions in Chinese Foreign Policy*, ed. Samuel Kim (Boulder, Colo.: Westview Press, 1989), chs. 9–10; and Madelyn C. Ross, "China's International Economic Behavior," in *Chinese Foreign Policy: Theory and Practice*, ed. Thomas W. Robinson and David Shambaugh (Oxford: Clarendon Press, 1994), esp. 442–50.

5. For the CCP leadership's arguments against "bourgeoisie liberalization," see, for example, Deng Xiaoping, "Take a Clear-Cut Stand to Oppose 'Bourgeoisie Liberalization,'" in *Deng Xiaoping wenxuan* (Selected Works of Deng Xiaoping) (Beijing: Renmin, 1994), 3:194–97; for scholarly discussions, see Goldman, *Sowing the Seeds of Democracy in China*, esp. ch. 7, and Richard Baum, "The Road to Tiananmen: Chinese Politics in the 1980s," in *The Politics of China, 1949–1989*, ed. Roderick MacFarquhar (Cambridge: Cambridge University Press, 1997), 355–63, 373–75.

6. An extensive literature exists on the origins of the Tiananmen tragedy. For a good comprehensive analysis, see Goldman, *Sowing the Seeds of Democracy in China*; see also Baum, "Road to Tiananmen," esp. 381–86; for a discussion focusing on Tiananmen's connections with Chinese political culture, see Lucian W. Pye, "Tiananmen and Chinese Political Culture: The Escalation of Confrontation from Moralizing to Revenge," *Asian Survey* 30 (April 1990): 331–47.

7. It should be pointed out that from Beijing's perspective, Tibet and Taiwan are both part of China's territory, and therefore the problems concerning them are part of China's internal affairs.

8. An extreme example in this regard can be found in a lengthy editorial essay in *Renmin ribao* (People's Daily), which systematically compares the behavior of "the U.S. hegemonists" with Hitler's Germany, denouncing the American ambition of "conquering the world and dominating the world." See "Advise the Hegemonists Today to Look at Themselves in the Mirror of History," *Renmin ribao*, 22 June 1999.

9. A statement made by former assistant secretary of defense Richard Perle, quoted in the *Washington Post*, 19 May 1997.

10. For a more detailed discussion, see Chen Jian, "Understanding the Logic of Beijing's Taiwan Policy," *Security Dialogue* 27 (December 1996): 459–63.

11. Thomas J. Christensen, "Chinese Realpolitik," *Foreign Affairs* (September–October 1996): 46.

12. For a more detailed discussion about the challenge facing the Chinese people on how to identify China and its position in the world, see Chen Jian, "The China Challenge in the 21st Century," Peacework 21 (Washington, D.C.: United States of Peace, 1998), 11–13.

BIBLIOGRAPHIC ESSAY

The following is a general overview of the historical literature on China and the Cold War during the Maoist era. It introduces and evaluates primary and secondary sources as well as directs interested readers to a selection of scholarship in both English and Chinese.

Primary Sources

As far as high-politics-centered Cold War documents are concerned, Chinese archives, especially the Chinese Communist Party Central Archives (*Zhongyang dang'an guan*) in Beijing, are still generally closed to scholars. But in recent years, scholars have gained access to original documents at various provincial and regional archives, especially for the period between 1949 and 1966. Most useful among these materials are CCP Central Committee papers that were relayed to provincial and regional party committees and therefore have been kept at related provincial and regional archives. However, the level of access to these archives differs from place to place and from time to time, often depending upon the specific archival authorities' attitudes toward how documents should be declassified—sometimes even depending upon the concerned researchers' luck or lack thereof. In addition, frequently there are more restrictions on foreign scholars than Chinese scholars in terms of getting access to the documents.

Since the collapse of the former Soviet Union, scholars have gained some access to archives in Russia and former Communist bloc countries in Eastern Europe, which contain large numbers of valuable documents concerning or related to China. The National Security Archive, a nonprofit research library located at George Washington University, and the Cold War International History Project (CWIHP), at the Woodrow Wilson International Center for Scholars in Washington, D.C., have made consistent efforts in the past decade to collect these materials. Many documents have been translated into English and are available in the CWIHP *Bulletin*. For an example of how newly released Russian sources challenge the information scholars have obtained from Chinese sources and force them to ask new questions and pursue new answers, see Shen Zhihua, "The Discrepancy between the Russian and Chinese Versions of Mao's 2 October 1950 Message to Stalin on Chinese Entry into the Korean War: A Chinese Scholar's Reply," CWIHP *Bulletin*, nos. 8–9 (Winter 1996–97): 237–42.

Since the mid-1980s, Chinese archival authorities, especially the CCP Central Archives and the CCP Central Institute of Historical Documents (*Zhongyang wenxian yanjiushi*), have published large numbers of party documents and CCP leaders' works concerning or related to China's Cold War experience on a selective basis. Many of these publications, though, are for "internal circulation only" (*neibu faxing*), and thus sometimes difficult to obtain from outside of China.

Among collections of party documents covering the pre-1949 period, the most important is *Zhonggong zhongyang wenjian xuanji* (Selected Documents of the CCP Central Committee), 18 vols. (Beijing: Zhonggong zhongyang dangxiao, 1989–92). In the early 1980s, this collection first appeared in a fourteen-volume edition for "internal circulation only," and then, in the late 1980s and early 1990s, an eighteen-volume edition was openly published. Although the latter edition contains almost 15–20 percent more documents than the earlier one, it does not include a few politically "sensitive" documents. Many of the key documents in the collection have been translated into English and published in Tony Saich, ed., *The Rise to Power of the Chinese Communist Party: Documents and Analysis* (Armonk, N.Y.: M. E. Sharpe, 1996).

Other important pre-1949 documentary collections include *Zhonggong zhongyang kangri zhanzheng shiqi tongyi zhanxian wenjian xuanbian* (Selected United Front Documents of the CCP Central Committee during the War of Resistance against Japan), 3 vols. (Beijing: Dang'an, 1986); *Zhonggong zhongyang jiefang zhanzheng shiqi tongyi zhanxian wenjian xuanbian* (Selected United Front Documents of the CCP Central Committee during the War of Liberation) (Beijing: Dang'an, 1988); and *Zhonggong zhongyang zai Xibaipo* (The CCP Central Committee at Xibaipo) (Beijing: Haitian, 1998). Many of the documents published in these volumes have been translated into English in Zhang Shuguang and Chen Jian, eds., *Chinese Communist Foreign Policy and the Cold War in Asia: New Documentary Evidence, 1944–1950* (Chicago: Imprint Publications, 1996).

For the post-1949 period, a twenty-volume collection, CCP Central Institute of Historical Documents, comp., *Jianguo yilai zhongyao wenxian xuanbian* (A Selection of Important Documents since the Founding of the People's Republic) (Beijing: Zhongyang wenxian, 1992–98), provides some of the key documents on China's domestic and foreign policies. Several other documentary collections include materials concerning or related to China's Cold War experience: *Zhonggong dangshi jiaoxue cankao ziliao* (Reference Materials on Teaching and Studying CCP History), 27 vols. (Beijing: Guofang daxue, n.d.), the last nine volumes of which cover the 1945–76 period; *Gongheguo zouguo de lu* (The Path That the Republic Had Gone Through), 2 vols. (Beijing: Zhongyang wenxian, 1988); and *Dang de xuanchuan gongzuo wenjian xuanbian* (Selected Propaganda Affairs Documents of the Party), vol. 4 (Beijing: Zhongyang dangxiao, 1994). In addition, *Dangde wenxian* (Party Historical Documents), a bimonthly issued by the CCP Central Institute of Historical Documents, frequently publishes valuable original documents.

Chinese archival authorities have published "selected works" of almost all top CCP leaders. The most valuable in this category is surely *Jianguo yilai Mao Zedong wengao* (Mao Zedong's Manuscripts since the Founding of the People's Republic of China), 13 vols. (Beijing: Zhongyang wenxian, 1987–97). Other useful works published in the past decade include *Mao Zedong wenji* (A Collection of Mao Zedong's Works), 8 vols. (Beijing: Renmin, 1993–97); *Mao Zedong waijiao wenxuan* (Selected Diplomatic Papers of Mao Zedong) (Beijing: Shijie zhishi, 1994); *Mao Zedong junshi wenxuan* (Selected Military Papers of Mao Zedong) (Beijing: Zhanshi, 1981); *Mao Zedong junshi wenji* (A Collection of Mao Zedong's Military Papers), 6 vols. (Beijing: Junshi kexue, 1993);

Jianguo yilai Liu Shaoqi wengao (Liu Shaoqi's Manuscripts since the Founding of the People's Republic), vol. 1 (Beijing: Zhongyang wenxian, 1999); *Zhou Enlai junshi wenxuan* (Selected Military Papers of Zhou Enlai), 4 vols. (Beijing: Renmin, 1997); and *Zhou Enlai waijiao wenxuan* (Selected Diplomatic Papers of Zhou Enlai) (Beijing: Zhongyang wenxian, 1990). The officially sanctioned *Mao Zedong xuanji* (Selected Works of Mao Zedong), 5 vols. (Beijing: Renmin, 1965 and 1977), remains a useful source. Outside mainland China, Japanese scholar Takeuchi Minoru supervised a major project to collect Mao's works, resulting in the publication of *Mao Zedong ji* (A Collection of Mao Zedong's Writings), 10 vols. (Tokyo: Hokubosha, 1971–72), and *Mao Zedong ji bujuan* (A Supplementary Collection of Mao Zedong's Writings), 9 vols. (Tokyo: Sososha, 1983–85). Part of Mao's post-1949 writings are available in English translation in Roderick MacFarquhar et al., ed., *The Secret Speeches of Chairman Mao: From the Hundred Flowers to the Great Leap Forward* (Cambridge: Council on East Asian Studies/Harvard University, 1989); Stuart Schram, ed., *Chairman Mao Talks to the People: Talks and Letters, 1956–1971* (New York: Pantheon, 1975); and Michael Y. M. Kau and John K. Leung, eds., *The Writings of Mao Zedong, 1949–1976*, 2 vols. (Armonk, N.Y.: M. E. Sharpe, 1986–).

Since the late 1980s, Chinese archival authorities have compiled and published many "chronological records" (*nianpu*) of top CCP leaders, which often contain revelations of valuable documents. In terms of China's Cold War history, the most important ones in this category are *Mao Zedong nianpu* (A Chronological Record of Mao Zedong), 3 vols. (Beijing: Zhongyang wenxian and Renmin, 1993); Jin Chongji et al., *Zhou Enlai nianpu, 1898–1949* (A Chronological Record of Zhou Enlai, 1898–1949) (Beijing: Zhongyang wenxian and Renmin, 1989); Jin Chongji et al., *Zhou Enlai nianpu, 1949–1976* (A Chronological Record of Zhou Enlai, 1949–1976), 3 vols. (Beijing: Zhongyang wenxian, 1997); *Liu Shaoqi nianpu* (A Chronological Record of Liu Shaoqi), 2 vols. (Beijing: Zhongyang wenxian, 1996); and *Peng Dehuai nianpu* (A Chronological Record of Peng Dehuai) (Beijing: Renmin, 1998).

For a general introduction to Chinese sources published in the early 1990s, see Michael H. Hunt and Odd Arne Westad, "The Chinese Communist Party and International Affairs: A Field Report of the New Historical Sources and Old Research Problems," *China Quarterly*, no. 122 (Summer 1990): 258–72; see also Michael H. Hunt, "CCP Foreign Relations: A Guide to the Literature," CWIHP *Bulletin*, nos. 6–7 (Winter 1995–96): 129, 136–43. Steven M. Goldstein and He Di provide a brief overview in "New Chinese Sources on the History of the Cold War," CWIHP *Bulletin*, no. 1 (Spring 1992): 4–6. Chen Jian offers a critical review of the "selected documents" in "Not Yet a Revolution: Reviewing China's 'New Cold War Documentation,' " a conference paper now accessible at http://www.nara.gov/research/coldwar/coldwar.html.

General Treatment of China's Cold War Experience

John Lewis Gaddis, *We Now Know: Rethinking Cold War History* (New York: Oxford University Press, 1997), offers a highly thoughtful account of the "new Cold War history" scholarship, of which study of China's Cold War experience has been an important part. Melvyn P. Leffler provides a critical review of recent publications in Cold War studies, including scholarship on China, in "The Cold War: What Do 'We Now Know'?" *American Historical Review* 104, no. 2 (April 1999): 501–24.

For overviews of twentieth-century Chinese history, see Jonathan Spence, *The Search for Modern China* (New York: Norton, 1999), and Denis Twitchett and John K. Fairbank, eds., *The Cambridge History of China*, vols. 12–15 (Cambridge, Eng.: Cambridge University Press, 1978–83). The best general account about the origins and development of the CCP's foreign policy is Michael H. Hunt, *The Genesis of Chinese Communist Foreign Policy* (New York: Columbia University Press, 1996). John W. Garver offers a general survey of the PRC's foreign relations in *Foreign Relations of the People's Republic of China* (Englewood Cliffs, N.J.: Prentice-Hall, 1993). Also useful are Thomas W. Robinson and David Shambaugh, eds., *Chinese Foreign Policy: Theory and Practice* (Oxford: Clarendon Press, 1994), and Quansheng Zhao, *Interpreting Chinese Foreign Policy* (Hong Kong: Oxford University Press, 1996).

The best and most courageous accounts about PRC history during the Maoist era recently published in China can be found in the first three volumes of the four-volume series titled "1949–1980nian de Zhongguo" (China from 1949 to 1989) (Zhengzhou: Henan renmin, 1989): Lin Yunhui et al., *Kaige xingjin de shiqi* (The Years of Triumphant Advance); Cong Jin, *Quzhe fazhan de suiyue* (The Years of Tortuous Development); and Wang Nianyi, *Dadongluan de niandai* (The Years of Great Turmoil). Xu Dashen, ed., *Zhonghua renmin gongheguo shilu* (A Factorial History of the People's Republic of China), 10 vols. (Changchun: Jilin renmin, 1994), serves as a good reference book for PRC history. For a general survey of PRC foreign relations, see Xue Mouhong et al., *Dangdai zhongguo waijiao* (Contemporary Chinese Diplomacy) (Beijing: Zhongguo shehui kexue, 1988); Pei Jianzhang, *Zhonghua renmin gongheguo waijiao shi, 1949–1956* (A Diplomatic History of the People's Republic of China, 1949–1956) (Beijing: Shijie zhishi, 1994); and Wang Taiping et al., *Zhonghua renmin gongheguo waijiao shi, 1957–1969* (A Diplomatic History of the People's Republic of China, 1957–69) (Beijing: Shijie zhishi, 1998). A helpful overview of the early development of Chinese Communist foreign policy is provided in Niu Jun, *Cong Yan'an zouxiang shijie: zhongguo gongchandang duiwai guanxi de qiyuan* (From Yan'an Marching toward the World: The Origins of the CCP's Foreign Relations) (Fuzhou: Fujian renmin, 1992). Han Huaizhi et al., *Dangdai zhongguo jundui de junshi gongzuo* (The Military Affairs of the Contemporary Chinese Army), 2 vols. (Beijing: Zhongguo shehui kexue, 1989), offers an informative survey of PRC strategic and military history.

Sources on Mao Zedong and Zhou Enlai

The best Mao biographies now available in English are Philip Short, *Mao: A Life* (New York: Henry Holt, 2000), and Ross Terrill, *Mao Zedong: A Biography*, rev. ed. (Stanford, Calif.: Stanford University Press, 2000), both of which were written with the support of recently available Chinese-language sources. Jonathan Spence, *Mao Zedong* (New York: Viking, 1999), offers a highly readable yet brief account of Mao's life. Jung Chang and Jon Halliday's forthcoming Mao biography, based on extensive documentary research and interviews, is believed to be a pathbreaking contribution to Mao studies. Useful revelations about Mao's life can also be found in Dr. Li Zhisui, *The Private Life of Chairman Mao* (New York: Random House, 1994). The best English-language studies on Mao thought and Mao's revolution remain Stuart Schram, *The Thought of Mao Zedong* (Cambridge, Eng.: Cambridge University Press, 1989); Brantly Womack, *The Foundation of Mao Zedong's Political Thought* (Honolulu: University of Hawai'i Press, 1982); Frederic Wakeman Jr., *History and Will: Philosophical Perspectives of Mao Tse-tung's Thought* (Berkeley: University California Press, 1973); and Richard Solomn, *Mao's Revolution and the Chinese Political Culture* (Berkeley: University of California Press, 1971). Among recent Chinese publications about Mao, the most notable are Jin Chongji et al., *Mao Zedong zhuan, 1893–1949* (A Biography of Mao Zedong, 1893–1949) (Beijing: Zhongyang wenxian, 1993), and Xin Ziling, *Mao Zedong quanzhuan* (A Complete Biography of Mao Zedong), 4 vols. (Hong Kong: Liwen, 1993).

On the career of Zhou Enlai, Mao's chief lieutenant, see Han Suyin, *Eldest Son: Zhou Enlai and the Making of Modern China, 1898–1976* (New York: Kodansha International, 1994), which offers a comprehensive account with the support of Han's extensive interviews in China. Chae-Jin Lee's *Zhou Enlai: The Early Years* (Stanford, Calif.: Stanford University Press, 1994), traces Zhou's childhood and youth. Basic information about Zhou's diplomatic activities is provided in Ronald C. Keith, *The Diplomacy of Zhou Enlai* (New York: St. Martin's, 1989). The most important PRC publication on Zhou Enlai is Jin Chongji et al., *Zhou Enlai zhuan* (A Biography of Zhou Enlai, 1898–1949), 2 vols. (Beijing: Zhongyang wenxian, 1998). *Zhou Enlai waijiao huodong dashi ji, 1949–1975* (Important Events in Zhou Enlai's Diplomatic Activities) (Beijing: Shijie zhishi, 1993), compiled by the Diplomatic History Institute under the PRC's Foreign Ministry, chronicles Zhou's management of PRC foreign affairs. Also informative is Li Lianqing, *Da waijiaojia Zhou Enlai* (Great Diplomat Zhou Enlai), 4 vols. (Hong Kong: Tiandi, 1992–), which was written with the support of the author's privileged access to Chinese archival sources.

Sources on the Chinese Civil War and the Emergence of the Cold War in Asia

Using Chinese Communist, Nationalist, Soviet, and American sources, Odd Arne Westad reconstructs the origins of the Chinese civil war in the context of the emerging Soviet-American confrontation in *Cold War and Revolution: Soviet-American Rivalry and the Origins of the Chinese Civil War* (New York: Columbia University Press, 1993). Westad's forthcoming study on the Chinese civil war sheds new light on the social and political, as well as cultural, aspects of the war. Steven Levine vividly portrays the CCP's political and social revolutions in the Northeast and America's responses to them in *Anvil of Victory: The Communist Revolution in Manchuria, 1945–1949* (New York: Columbia University Press, 1987). Marc S. Galliccio, *The Cold War Begins in Asia* (New York: Columbia University Press, 1988), discusses how the Cold War emerged between the United States and the Soviet Union shortly after the end of World War II. Michael M. Sheng, by emphasizing the decisive role ideology played, provides a provocative account of the CCP's cooperation with the Soviet Union and its confrontation with the United States in *Battling Western Imperialism: Mao, Stalin, and the United States* (Princeton, N.J.: Princeton University Press, 1997).

In addition to the relevant materials contained in *Mao Zedong nianpu, Zhou Enlai nianpu, Zhou Enlai zhuan,* and other aforementioned Chinese documentary sources, see especially Huang Youlan et al., *Zhengqu heping minzhu, 1945–1946* (Pursuing Peace and Democracy, 1945-1946) (Shanghai: Shanghai renmin, 1995), which discusses the political, social, and military processes leading to the outbreak of the civil war; The Military History Research Institute under the Chinese Academy of Military Science, comp., *Zhongguo renmin jiefangjun quanguo jiefang zhanzheng shi* (A History of People's Liberation Army in the War of Liberation in the Whole Country), 5 vols. (Beijing: Junshi kexue, 1993), which offers the most comprehensive account of the military history of the civil war; and Yang Kuisong, *Zhongjian didai de geming* (Revolution in the Intermediate Zone) (Beijing: Zhonggong zhongyang dangxiao, 1992), which, in its closing chapters, depicts the CCP's changing international strategies during the civil war.

Sources on the "Lost Chance" Debate and the Making of the Sino-American Confrontation

The debate over whether or not the United States had "lost a chance" in China in the late 1940s first emerged in the early 1970s. Joseph W. Esherick, ed., *Lost Chance in China: The World War II Dispatches of John S. Service* (New York: Random House, 1974), points out that U.S. policy toward China was responsible for throwing away a real opportunity to befriend the CCP as an emerging dominant political force in China. Scholars of Chinese-American relations continued to debate the issue into the late 1970s and 1980s, with the majority favoring the "lost chance" thesis. See, for example, Dorothy Borg and Waldo Heinrichs, eds., *Uncertain Years: Chinese-American Relations, 1947–1950* (New York: Columbia University Press, 1980). The lost-chance thesis was challenged in the early 1990s, when newly available Chinese sources indicated that the CCP had firmly adopted an anti-American stand by 1949. For a recent symposium focusing on reconsidering the "lost chance" issue, see Warren I. Cohen, Chen Jian, Michael Sheng, John Garver, and Odd Arne Westad, "Rethinking the Lost Chance in China," *Diplomatic History* 21 (Winter 1997): 71-115. For an argument emphasizing that in spite of U.S. policy toward China it was still possible for the CCP and the United States to establish a "working relationship" in 1949, see Thomas J. Christensen, "A Lost Chance for What? Rethinking the Origins of U.S.-PRC Confrontation," *Journal of American–East Asian Relations* 4 (Fall 1995): 249-78.

The best survey of changing American perceptions of, as well as attitudes toward, China remains Warren I. Cohen, *America's Response to China,* 4th ed. (New York: Columbia University Press, 2000). The complicated domestic and international environments in which the Truman administration made China policy are carefully studied in Nancy Berncopf Tucker, *Patterns in the Dust: Chinese-American Relations and the Recognition Controversy, 1949–1950* (New York: Columbia University Press, 1983). Harry Harding and Yuan Ming, eds., *Sino-American Relations, 1945–1955: A Joint Assessment of a Critical Decade* (Wilmington, Del.: Scholarly Resources, 1989), collects analyses of the development of the Sino-American confrontation by a group of leading Chinese and American scholars. Among the new Chinese sources available in English, Huang Hua, "My Contacts with Stuart after Nanjing's Liberation" (trans. Li Xiaobing), *Chinese Historians 5* (Spring 1992): 47–56, provides valuable firsthand information about the CCP's handling of relations with the United States in 1949. The most important Chinese study on the topic is Zi Zhongyun, *Meiguo duihua zhengce de yuanqi he fazhan, 1945–1950* (The Origins and Development of American Policy toward China, 1945–1950) (Chongqing: Chongqing, 1987).

Sources on the Rise and Demise of the Sino-Soviet Alliance

The single most important new study on this subject is Odd Arne Westad, ed., *Brothers in Arms: The Rise and Fall of the Sino-Soviet Alliance, 1945–1963* (Washington, D.C., and Stanford, Calif.: Woodrow Wilson Center Press and Stanford University Press, 1998), a collection of nine essays, all written with the support of new documentation, by Chinese, Russian, American, and Norwegian scholars. John W. Garver, *Chinese-Soviet Relations, 1937–1945: The Diplomacy of Chinese Nationalism* (New York: Oxford University Press, 1988), argues that Chinese nationalism played a decisive role in determining both the Chinese Communist and Nationalist policies toward the Soviet Union. In comparison, Michael M. Sheng, in *Battling Western Imperialism* (cited above), emphasizes that ideology played a central role in the creation of the CCP/PRC-Soviet alliance. Gordon H. Chang, *Friends and Enemies: The United States, China, and the Soviet Union* (Stanford, Calif.: Stanford University Press, 1990), studies the triangular relations between Washington, Beijing, and Moscow. Vladislav Zubok and Constantine Pleshakov, *Inside the Kremlin's Cold War: From Stalin to Khrushchev* (Cambridge, Mass.: Harvard University Press, 1996), uses recently available Russian sources to create a vivid narrative of the exchanges between top Soviet and Chinese leaders, especially between Nikita Khrushchev and Mao Zedong.

The best recent Chinese studies on the subject are two books by Yang Kuisong: *Zhonggong yu mosike de guanxi, 1920–1960* (The CCP's Relations with Moscow, 1920–1960) (Taipei: Dongda, 1997) and *Mao Zedong he mosike de enen yuanyuan* (Mao's Gratitude and Grievance with Moscow) (Nanchang: Jiangxi renmin, 1999). Also very useful are the chronological records in Zhou Wenqi and Zhu Liangru, eds., *Teshu er fuzha de keti: gochan guoji, sulian he zhongguo gongchandang guanxi biannian shi, 1919–1991* (A Special and Complicated Subject: A Chronological History of the Relations between the Comintern, the Soviet Union, and the Chinese Communist Party) (Wuhan: Hubei renmin, 1993).

Several Chinese memoirs by individuals involved in Sino-Soviet policymaking that have been published in the past decade provide valuable information on Sino-Soviet relations, the most important of which is that by Shi Zhe (Mao Zedong's Russian-language interpreter from 1941 to 1957), *Zai lishi juren shenbian: Shi Zhe huiyilu* (At the Side of Historical Giants: Shi Zhe's Memoirs), rev. ed. (Beijing: Zhonggong zhongyang dangxiao, 1998). See also Wu Lengxi (Mao's political secretary and director of Xinhua News Agency), *Shinian lunzhan, 1956–1966: zhongsu guanxi huiyilu* (Ten-Year

Polemic Debate, 1956–1966: A Memoir on Sino-Soviet Relations) (Beijing: Zhong-yang wenxian, 1999); and Liu Xiao (Chinese ambassador to Moscow from 1954 to 1962), *Chushi sulian banian* (Eight Years as Ambassador to the Soviet Union) (Beijing: Zhong-gong dangshi ziliao, 1986).

Sources on China and the Korean War

The literature on the Korean War is extensive. Bruce Cumings, in *The Origins of the Korean War*, 2 vols. (Princeton, N.J.: Princeton University Press, 1981, 1990), presents the most comprehensive and provocative analysis of the origins of the war. Burton I. Kaufman, *The Korean War: Challenge in Crisis, Credibility, and Command* (Philadelphia: Temple University Press, 1986), provides a comprehensive account of the war's history. Rosemary Foot's *The Wrong War: American Policy and the Dimensions of the Korean Conflict* (Ithaca: Cornell University Press, 1985) and *A Substitute for Victory: The Politics of Peacemaking at the Korean Armistice Talks* (Ithaca: Cornell University Press, 1990) offer critical analyses of American strategies toward the war. The international dimension of the war is extensively discussed by William Stueck in *The Korean War: An International History* (Princeton, N.J.: Princeton University Press, 1995).

Allen S. Whiting's *China Crosses the Yalu: The Decisions to Enter the Korean War* (New York: Macmillan, 1960) has become the classic for anyone who is interested in the topic. Two recent studies relying upon newly available Chinese sources are Chen Jian, *China's Road to the Korean War: The Making of the Sino-American Confrontation* (New York: Columbia University Press, 1994), and Shu Guang Zhang, *Mao's Military Romanticism: China and the Korean War, 1950–1953* (Lawrence: University of Kentucky Press, 1995). Sergei Goncharov, John Lewis, and Xue Litai, *Uncertain Partners: Stalin, Mao, and the Korean War* (Stanford, Calif.: Stanford University Press, 1993), examines the Sino-Soviet alliance and the outbreak of the Korean War. Stalin's policies toward the Korean War are reevaluated by Kathryn Weathersby in her various articles (see, for example, "Soviet Aims in Korea and the Origins of the Korean War," CWIHP working paper no. 8, Woodrow Wilson International Center for Scholars, Washington, D.C., November 1993).

Official Chinese perspectives about the war are presented in Tan Jingqiao et al., *Kangmei yuanchao zhanzheng* (The War to Resist America and Assist Korea) (Beijing: Zhongguo shehui kexue, 1990), and Shen Zonghong et al., *Zhongguo renmin zhiyuan-jun kangmei yuanchao zhanshi* (A History of the Chinese People's Volunteers' War to Resist America and Assist Korea) (Beijing: Junshi kexue, 1988). Other important recent Chinese studies include Shen Zhihua, *Zhongsu tongmeng yu chaoxian zhanzheng yanjiu* (Studies on the Sino-Soviet Alliance and the Korean War) (Guilin: Guangxi shida, 1999); Shen Zhihua, *Mao Zedong, sidalin yu hanzhan* (Mao Zedong, Stalin, and the Korean War) (Hong Kong: Tiandi, 1998); Xu Yan, *Diyici jiaoliang: kangmei yuan-chao zhanzheng de lishi huigu yu fansi* (The First Test of Strength: A Historical Review and Evaluation of the War to Resist America and Assist Korea) (Beijing: Zhongguo guangbo dianshi, 1990); and Qi Dexue, *Chaoxian zhanzheng juece neimu* (The Inside Story of the Decision-Making during the Korean War) (Shenyang: Liaoning daxue, 1991). Recent Chinese scholarship on the Korean War is reviewed by Chen Jian in

"China and the Korean War: A Critical Historiographical Review," *Korea and World Affairs* 19 (Summer 1995): 314–36.

Among the abundant Chinese memoirs about the Korean War published in the past decade, the most important ones include Chai Chengwen and Zhao Yongtian, *Banmendian tanpan* (The Panmunjom Negotiations) (Beijing: Jiefangjun, 1989); Du Ping, *Zai zhiyuanjun zongbu: Du Ping huiyilu* (My Days at the Headquarters of the Chinese People's Volunteers: Du Ping's Memoirs) (Beijing: Jiefangjun, 1989); Hong Xuezhi, *Kangmei yuanchao zhanzheng huiyi* (Recollections of the War to Resist America and Assist Korea), 2d ed. (Beijing: Jiefangjun wenyi, 1992); Nie Rongzhen, *Nie Rongzhen huiyilu* (Nie Rongzhen's Memoirs) (Beijing: Jiefangjun, 1984); Peng Dehuai, *Peng Dehuai zishu* (The Autobiographical Notes of Peng Dehuai) (Beijing: Renmin, 1982); and the aforementioned Shi Zhe's memoirs.

Sources on China and the First Indochina War

Standard treatments of the First Indochina War can be found in Marilyn B. Young, *The Vietnam Wars, 1945–1990* (New York: Harper Collins, 1990); Jacques Dalloz, *The War in Indo-China, 1945–1954* (Savage, Md.: Barnes and Noble, 1990); R. E. M. Irving, *The First Indo-China War* (London: Croom Helm, 1975); and Ellen Hammer, *The Struggle for Indo-China, 1946–1955* (Stanford, Calif.: Stanford University Press, 1966). King Chen, *Vietnam and China, 1938–1954* (Princeton, N.J.: Princeton University Press, 1969), which was written with the support of contemporary newspaper and radio information, remains a useful source. Zhai Qiang's comprehensive study, *China and the Vietnam Wars, 1950–1975* (Chapel Hill: University of North Carolina Press, 2000), will be the new standard treatment on China and the First Indochina War and the Vietnam War.

In terms of newly available Chinese sources, in addition to the aforementioned *Jianguo yilai Mao Zedong wengao*, *Jianguo yilai Liu Shaoqi wengao*, and *Liu Shaoqi nianpu*, the most valuable is The Editorial Group for the History of Chinese Military Advisers in Vietnam, ed., *Zhongguo junshi guwentuan yuanyue kangfa douzheng shishi* (A Factual Account of the Participation of the Chinese Military Advisory Group in the Struggle of Assisting Vietnam and Resisting France) (Beijing: Jiefangjun, 1990), which provides a detailed account of the activities of Chinese advisers in Vietnam based on archival sources. Firsthand information can be found in Luo Guibo (Chinese general adviser to Vietnam), "Remembering History: A Factual Account of Assisting Vietnam and Resisting France and the Relations between the Chinese and Vietnamese Parties and States," in *Kaiqi guomen: Waijiaoguan de fengcai* (Opening the Gate of the Country: The Glory of Diplomats), ed. Fu Hao and Li Tongchen (Beijing: Zhongguo huaqiao, 1995); and Chen Geng (chief Chinese military adviser to Vietnam in 1950), *Chen Geng riji* (Chen Geng's Diaries), vol. 2 (Beijing: Jiefangjun, 1984).

Sources on Beijing and the Polish and Hungarian Crises

Our knowledge about the Polish and Hungarian crises of 1956 has improved greatly with access to new information from the former Communist bloc. For Moscow's handling of the crises, see Mark Kramer, trans. and ed., "The 'Malin Notes' on the Crises in Hungary and Poland, 1956," CWIHP *Bulletin*, nos. 8–9 (Winter 1996–97): 385–410. New Polish evidence is presented by L. W. Gluchowski in "Poland, 1956: Khrushchev, Gomulka, and the 'Polish October,'" CWIHP *Bulletin*, 5 (Spring 1995): 1, 38–49. Among new Chinese-language sources the most important is Shi Zhe, "The Polish and Hungarian Incident and Liu Shaoqi's Visit to the Soviet Union," in *Zai lishi juren shenbian: Shi Zhe huiyilu* (At the Side of Historical Giants: Shi Zhe's Memoirs), rev. ed. (Beijing: Zhonggong zhongyang dangxiao, 1998), 549–63. Wu Lengxi, in *Shinian lunzhan, 1956–1966: zhongsu guanxi huiyilu* (Ten-Year Polemic Debate, 1956–1966: A Memoir on Sino-Soviet Relations) (Beijing: Zhongyang wenxian, 1999): 1–91, presents a detailed, though not always accurate, account of top CCP leaders' handling of the Polish and Hungarian crises.

Sources on the Taiwan Strait Crisis

U.S. policy toward Taiwan in the first half of the 1950s is carefully studied in Robert Accinelli, *Crisis and Commitment: United States Policy toward Taiwan, 1950–1955* (Chapel Hill: University of North Carolina Press, 1996). He Di, "The Last Campaign to Unify China: The CCP's Unmaterialized Plan to Liberate Taiwan, 1949–1950," *Chinese Historians* 5 (Spring 1992): 1–16, examines the CCP's Taiwan strategy up to the outbreak of the Korean War. Gordon H. Chang and He Di, "The Absence of War in the U.S.-China Confrontation over Quemoy and Matsu in 1954–1955: Contingency, Luck, Deterrence?" *American Historical Review* 98 (December 1993): 1500–1524, offers provocative interpretations about why the PRC and the United States did not go to war during the Taiwan Strait crisis of 1954–55. Shu Guang Zhang, *Deterrence and Strategic Culture: Chinese-American Confrontations, 1949–1958* (Ithaca: Cornell University Press, 1992), chs. 7–8, argues that both Beijing and Washington entered the crisis under a "mutual deterrence" situation. Thomas Christensen, *Useful Adversaries: Grand Strategy, Domestic Mobilization, and Sino-American Conflict, 1947–1958* (Princeton, N.J.: Princeton University Press, 1996), emphasizes domestic mobilization as the decisive reason for bringing Beijing into the crisis. Also useful is Thomas E. Stolper, *China, Taiwan, and the Offshore Islands* (Armonk, N.Y.: M. E. Sharpe, 1985). Key documents concerning Washington's handling of the 1958 crisis are available in U.S. Department of State, *Foreign Relations of the United States, 1958–1960*, vol. 19 (Washington, D.C.: Government Printing Office, 1996).

New Chinese documentary sources have been released in *Jianguo yilai Mao Zedong wengao, Mao Zedong waijiao wenxuan, Mao Zedong junshi wenji, Zhou Enlai waijiao wenxuan, Zhou Enlai junshi wenxuan*, and *Zhou Enlai nianpu* (all cited above). Some of the documents have been translated into English in Li Xiaobing et al., "Mao Zedong's Handling of the Taiwan Strait Crisis of 1958," CWIHP *Bulletin*, nos. 6–7 (Winter 1995–96): 208–18. Informative memoirs by Chinese participants include Ye Fei, *Ye Fei huiyilu* (Ye Fei's Memoirs) (Beijing: Jiefangjun, 1988); Lei Yingfu, *Zai zhuigao tongshuaibu dang canmou: Lei Yingfu jiangjun huiyilu* (Being a Staff Member at the High Command: General Lei Yinfu's Memoirs) (Nanchang: Baihuazhou wenyi, 1998); Wang Bingnan, *Zhongmei huitan jiunian huigu* (Nine Years of Sino-American Ambassadorial Talks) (Beijing: Shijie zhishi, 1985); Wu Lengxi, *Yi Mao zhuxi* (Recalling Chairman Mao) (Beijing: Xinhua, 1994); and Zheng Wenhan, *Mishu riji li de Peng laozong* (Marshall Peng as Recorded in His Secretary's Diaries) (Beijing: Junshi kexue, 1998).

Two important Chinese studies on the 1958 crisis are Xu Yan, *Jinmen zhizhan* (The Jinmen Battle) (Beijing: Zhongguo guangbo dianshi, 1992), and Shen Liping, *Paoji jinmen* (Shelling Jinmen) (Beijing: Huayi, 1998). For a Nationalist account of the crisis, see *Jinmen guningtou zhoushan dengbudao zhizhan shiliao chubian* (A Preliminary Collection of Historical Materials about the Jinmen and Dengbu Battles) (Taipei: Guoshiguan, 1979).

Sources on China and the Vietnam War

English-language literature on the Vietnam War is huge. George C. Herring, *America's Longest War: The United States and Vietnam, 1950–1975*, 3d ed. (New York: McGraw-Hill, 1996), has been widely recognized as the standard treatment on the subject. Robert S. McNamara, James Blight, and Robert Brigham, *Argument without End: In Search of Answers to the Vietnam Tragedy* (New York: Public Affairs, 1999), reevaluates the lessons of the Vietnam tragedy on the basis of direct dialogues between several key decision makers in Washington and Hanoi. Fredrik Logevall, *Choosing War: The Lost Chance for Peace and the Escalation of War in Vietnam* (Berkeley: University of California Press, 1999), examines a crucial episode in the escalation of the Vietnam War — the 1964–65 period — to explore why peace failed to prevail. R. B. Smith's comprehensive study, *An International History of the Vietnam War*, 3 vols. (London: Macmillan, 1983–91), offers an excellent treatment of the international dimension of the war. Ilya V. Gaiduk, *The Soviet Union and the Vietnam War* (Chicago: Ivan R. Dee, 1996), depicts the Soviet connection to the war with the support of newly available Russian sources. A North Vietnamese perspective is provided by Bui Tin, *Following Ho Chi Minh: The Memoir of a North Vietnamese Colonel* (Honolulu: University of Hawai'i Press, 1995). The NLF's policies are examined in Robert Brigham, *Guerrilla Diplomacy: The NLF's Foreign Relations and the Vietnam War* (Ithaca: Cornell University Press, 1998).

Despite the difficulties involved in accessing Chinese sources, plausible studies on China and the Vietnam War do exist in English-language literature. With privileged access to "information available to the author" drawing on "hard intelligence," Allen S. Whiting, in *The Chinese Calculus of Deterrence: India and Vietnam* (Ann Arbor: University of Michigan Press, 1975), ch. 6, draws an impressively accurate picture — judged by new Chinese sources — of the scope and nature of China's involvement with the Vietnam War from 1965 to 1968. In an early 1990s article, "China's Role in the Vietnam War," in *The American War in Vietnam*, ed. Jayne Werner and David Hunt (Ithaca: Cornell University Southeast Asia Program, 1993), 71–76, Whiting further proves the accuracy of his study's conclusions in light of the opinion of Vietnamese scholars. Roderick MacFarquhar, in the third and last volume of his monumental study on the origins of the Chinese Cultural Revolution, devotes a whole chapter, "The Sino-Soviet Rupture and the Vietnam War," to the discussion of the interconnections between the Vietnam War and the start of the Cultural Revolution (MacFarquhar, *The Origins of the Cultural Revolution*, vol. 3, *The Coming of the Cataclysm, 1961–1966* [New York: Oxford University Press and Columbia University Press, 1997], 349–77). Zhai Qiang depicts Beijing's attitude toward the peace negotiation in 1965–68 in "Opposing Negotiations: China and the Vietnam Peace Talks," *Pacific Historical Review* 68, no. 1 (February 1999): 21–49. Useful information and analyses can also be found in William J. Duiker, *China and Vietnam: The Roots of Conflict* (Berkeley, Calif.: Institute of East Asian Studies, 1986); Robert S. Ross, *The Indochina Tangle: China's Vietnam Policy, 1975–1979* (New York: Columbia University Press, 1988); and Anne Gilks, *The Breakdown of the Sino-Vietnamese Alliance, 1970–1979* (Berkeley: Center for Chinese Studies, 1992).

Odd Arne Westad et al., eds., "77 Conversations between Chinese and Foreign Leaders on the Wars in Indochina, 1964–1977," CWIHP working paper, no. 22, Woodrow Wilson International Center for Scholars, Washington, D.C., 1998, collects minutes from top level meetings among Chinese, Vietnamese, Cambodian, and Laotian leaders, although the authenticity and accuracy of the documents included are yet to be fully verified. In addition to *Pentagon Papers* (Boston: Beacon Press, 1971), key American documents concerning U.S. policy toward China during the war years are now available in *Foreign Relations of the United States, 1964–1968*, vol. 30 (Washington, D.C.: Government Printing Office, 1998).

For a review of newly accessible Chinese archival sources on the Vietnam War, see Zhai Qiang, "Local Chinese Sources on the Vietnam War" (a paper presented to a CWIHP workshop titled "Recasting the International History of the Vietnam War," 26 March 1998, Washington, D.C.). Important Chinese studies that have appeared in the past decade include Guo Ming et al., *Zhongyue guanxi yanbian sishinian* (Four Decades of Evolution of Sino-Vietnamese Relations) (Nanning: Guanxi renmin, 1992); Wang Xiangen, *Kangmei yuanyue shilu* (A Factual Account of Resisting America and Assisting Vietnam) (Beijing: Guoji wenhua chuban gongsi, 1990); Li Ke and Hao Shengzhang, *Wenhua dageming zhong de renmin jiefangjun* (The People's Liberation Army during the Cultural Revolution) (Beijing: Zhonggong dangshi ziliao, 1989); Qu Aiguo, Bao Mingrong, and Xiao Zhuyao, *Yuanyue kangmei: Zhongguo zhiyuan budui zai yuenan* (Assisting Vietnam, Resisting America: Chinese Supporting Units in Vietnam) (Beijing: Junshi kexue, 1995); and Shi Yingfu, *Mimi chubing yare conglin* (Sending Troops Secretly to the Subtropical Jungles) (Beijing: Jiefangjun wenyi, 1990). Useful information is also contained in the aforementioned *Zhou Enlai waijiao huodong dashiji*, *Zhou Enlai nianpu*, and *Dangdai zhongguo jundui de junshi gongzuo*.

Sources on the Sino-American Rapprochement

While the accounts provided in Richard Nixon, *Memoirs of Richard Nixon* (New York: Grosset & Dunlap, 1978), and Henry Kissinger, *White House Years* (New York: Little, Brown, 1979), remain useful in understanding how and why Washington reached the decision to improve relations with Beijing, they must be supplemented by William Burr, ed., *The Kissinger Transcripts: The Top-Secret Talks with Beijing and Moscow* (New York: New Press, 1999), which contains newly declassified Kissinger papers, especially meeting records between Nixon, Kissinger, Mao Zedong, and Zhou Enlai. Additional newly declassified U.S. documents are now available at Record Group 59 at the National Archives at College Park, Md., and the National Security Archive at George

Washington University, and are scheduled to be published in *Foreign Relations of the United States* in 2000–2001.

Rosemary Foot, *The Practice of Power: U.S. Relations with China since 1949* (Oxford, Eng.: Oxford University Press, 1997), examines different aspects of Sino-American relations crucial for understanding the background of the Sino-American rapprochement. Jim Mann, *About Face: A History of America's Curious Relationship with China, from Nixon to Clinton* (New York: Knopf, 1999), and Robert Ross, *Negotiating Cooperation: The United States and China, 1969–1989* (Stanford, Calif.: Stanford University Press, 1995), put the Sino-American rapprochement into a broad context of changing Sino-American relations in the last decades of the twentieth century. John W. Garver, *China's Decision for Rapprochement with the United States, 1968–1972* (Boulder, Colo.: Westview, 1982), offers an interesting analysis of Beijing's motives to improve relations with Washington. Chinese documents helpful for understanding Beijing's decision making are translated in Chen Jian and David L. Wilson, eds., "All Under the Heaven Is Great Chaos: Beijing, the Sino-Soviet Border Clashes, and the Turn toward Sino-American Rapprochement, 1968–1969," CWIHP *Bulletin*, no. 11 (Winter 1998–99): 155–75.

The most informative Chinese account on the subject is offered by Xiong Xianghui in "The Prelude to the Opening of Sino-American Relations," *Zhonggong dangshi yanjiu*, no. 42 (1992). Other useful information can be found in *Jianguo yilai Mao Zedong wengao*, vol. 13, *Zhou Enlai nianpu*, and *Zhou Enlai waijiao wenxuan* (all cited above). Important Chinese studies that have appeared in recent years include Gong Li, *Kuaiyue honggou: 1969–1979nian zhongmei guanxi de yanbian* (Bridging the Chasm: The Evolution of Sino-American Relations, 1969–1979) (Zhengzhou: Henan Renmin, 1992); Qian Jiang, *Ping Pong waijiao muhou* (Behind the Ping Pong Diplomacy) (Beijing: Dongfang, 1997); and Yang Kuisong, "The Sino-Soviet Border Clash of 1969: From Zhenbao Island to Sino-American Rapprochement," *Cold War History* 1 (2000): 21–52.

INDEX

39–41, 42; Commissions of Economic Affairs, State Economic Planning and Foreign Economic Affairs of, 220; confrontation with the United States, 241–42, 329 (n. 25), 351 (n. 176); Defense Ministry of, 206; emergence as a revolutionary power, 2–4, 35; Foreign Ministry of, 12–13, 173, 185, 190, 194, 206, 220, 250, 258–59, 261, 263; Foreign Trade Ministry of, 220; and Geneva Conference (1954), 139–40; "Headquarters for National Economic and National Defense," 215; and India, 240, 312 (n. 144); and Japan, 174, 240; and Korean War, 53–61, 85–117, 139, 314 (n. 4), 315 (n. 19); legitimacy crisis, 280–81; Material Supply Ministry of, 220; National Commission on Sports of, 258–59, 261; patterns of use of force, 14; perception of confronting America in Korea, Indochina, and Taiwan, 122–23; and Polish and Hungarian crises, 145–62; Postal Service Ministry of, 220; Railway Ministry of, 220; rapprochement with the United States, 2, 9, 10, 238–76; and Soviet Union, 7, 9, 63–64, 240, 242–43, 302 (n. 17), 305 (nn. 53, 59); State Council of, 220; State Planning Council of, 220, 227; territorial water of, 185; Transport Ministry of, 220; UN and, 89, 93, 239, 272; and Vietnam, 7, 14, 121–22, 124, 126, 132–35, 137, 206–12, 215–17, 221–37, 240, 328 (n. 15), 359 (nn. 114, 115)

"China under threat" approach, 6

China White Paper, 43, 48

Chinese Changchun Railroad, 27, 32, 34

Chinese civil war: 1927–36, 20; 1945–49, 17, 20, 26–34

Chinese Communist Party (CCP), 17, 20–22, 25, 33, 36, 40, 290 (n. 25); Central Committee of, 12, 26, 39, 130, 132, 168, 214, 217, 220, 248, 367 (n. 112); centralized decision-making structure,

12; Central Military Commission of (CMC), 104, 123, 125–26, 134, 136–37, 166–67, 172, 176, 213, 226–27, 345 (n. 73); Central Secretariat of, 12, 90, 214; diplomatic initiative (1944–45), 22–24; "Directive on Diplomatic Affairs," 40; Eighth Congress of, 68, 171; Hong Kong Bureau Branch of, 119; Kim Il-sung and, 88, 94; and Marshall mission, 34; Nanjing Municipal Committee of, 42; Ninth Congress of, 246–47, 253; Northeast and, 29–32, 294 (n. 64); Northeast Bureau of, 31, 34, 39, 40, 43, 45, 297 (nn. 12, 13); politburo of, 12, 28, 143, 216, 251–52, 263–65; politburo Standing Committee of, 146–49, 182–83, 185–86, 199, 335 (n. 7); Seventh Congress of, 25; Soviet Union and, 24, 29–32, 44–46, 50, 306 (n. 60); Stalin and, 25–29, 293 (n. 58); and Taiwan, 165–66, 168–69, 172, 190–91, 279–80; and United States, 23–24, 27, 47–48, 99; and Vietnamese Communists, 118–20, 138–39, 142, 328 (nn. 8, 17); and War of Resistance against Japan, 21

Chinese Communist revolution, 47, 51; Mao's vision of, 11, 301 (n. 8). *See also* Continuous revolution

Chinese ethnocentrism, 5, 237

Chinese Military Advisory Group (CMAG), 123–24, 129, 206

Chinese Nationalist Party. *See* Guomindang

Chinese People's Volunteer Engineering Force (CPVEF), 221, 223–25, 230, 232

Chinese People's Volunteers (CPV), 56, 58, 110–11, 116

Chinese Political Consultative Conference (1946), 33

Chinese "tribute system," 262

Chinese universalism, 237

Chinese victim mentality, 12, 13, 42, 75, 203, 279, 281

Chongchun River, 91

Hoang Van Hoan, 121, 142, 353 (n. 22)

Hong Hoa Tham campaign, 128

Hong Kong, 1, 250, 367 (n. 106)

Hong Xuezhi, 346 (n. 73)

Hongqi (Red Flag, journal), 238, 360 (n. 2)

Hongqi (Red Flag, ship), 232

Hopson, Donald Charles, 217

Hu Jibang, 155, 337-38 (n. 43)

Hu Qiaomu, 150, 347 (n. 105)

Hua Guofeng, 277

Huang Hua, 41-43, 268, 368 (nn. 133, 134)

Huang Kecheng, 136-37, 177, 193, 200, 345 (n. 73)

Huang Zhen, 255, 271

Huang-Stuart meetings, 41-43, 46

Humphrey, Hubert, 78

Hundred Flowers Campaign, 161, 173, 339 (n. 72)

Hungary, 7, 68-69

Hungarian crisis (1956), 145-46, 155-62, 308 (n. 93)

Hunt, Michael, 90

Hurley, Patrick, 23-24

Ichi-go campaign, 22, 290 (n. 16)

Ideology, 6-10; and China's Cold War experience, 7; "ideology versus national security interest" dichotomy, 8-9, 242; and "lean-to-one-side," 50-51; and legitimacy issue, 9-10; and "power," 6; and religious belief, 8; and Sino-Soviet split, 9

Inchon landing, 55, 89

India, 78, 79-80, 197, 240, 249, 312 (n. 144)

India-Pakistan crisis (1971), 273

Indochina Communist Party (ICP), 118, 123, 233, 328 (nn. 8, 17). *See also* Vietnamese Workers' Party

Indonesia, 200, 208, 217

"Intermediate zone" theory, 5

International Communist movement, 7, 9, 64-65, 67, 68, 70, 71, 153, 162

International tension: Mao's view about, 163, 175, 179-80, 202

Iraq, 175, 181-82

Japan, 17, 20, 26, 31, 89, 174, 186, 240, 249, 258

Japanese Communist Party, 231, 336 (n. 29)

Ji Chaozhu, 255

Ji Dengkui, 357 (n. 69)

Jiang Jieshi, 17, 20-26, 33-34, 36, 45, 115, 167-69, 171, 180, 188, 193, 198-99, 291 (n. 25); *China's Destiny*, 22; dispute with Joseph Stilwell, 23; and Mao, 17, 27-29, 293 (n. 56); and Sino-Soviet treaty of 1945, 27; Stalin and, 25-26; Truman and, 31-32; and Xi'an incident, 20

Jiang Jingguo, 252

Jiangxi province, 20

Jilin, 15

Jin Qiu, 369 (n. 145)

Jinmen (Quemoy) islands, 10, 14, 77, 163-69, 175-88, 190-94, 197-203, 340 (n. 1), 342 (nn. 30, 31), 346 (n. 82)

Jinping, 130

Jinxi, 224

Johnson, Lyndon, 208, 212, 215, 217

Johnson, U. Alexis, 191

Johnston, Alastair Iain, 288 (n. 27)

Jordan, 175-76, 181-82

Joy, Charles Turner, 102

Kádár, János, 160, 337 (n. 43)

Kaesong, 85, 99, 101, 104, 321 (n. 93)

Kaganovich, Lazar, 146, 336 (n. 26)

Kaiser, K. M., 251

Kang Sheng, 354 (n. 36)

Kapitsa, M. S., 348 (n. 133)

Karachi, Pakistan, 217

Karim, Abdel Karim, 175

Ke Qingshi, 67, 70

Kennan, George, 287 (n. 14)

Kep, 222

Qingdao, 300 (n. 47)
Qinghua University, 244
Qiu Huizuo, 235
Quang Trung campaign, 128
Quemoy. *See* Jinmen islands

Radulescu, Gheorghe, 254
"Rash advance," 72; Mao Zedong and,
   70, 72–73, 173; Zhou Enlai and, 66, 72,
   173
Razuvaev, V. N., 318 (n. 57)
Rectification campaign, 22
Red Army. *See* Soviet Red Army
Red Army (Chinese), 20, 21
Red Guards, 244
Red River delta, 128, 130, 132, 224. *See
   also* Tonkin Delta
Redmond, Hugh, 365 (n. 67)
"Reform and opening" era, 1
Renmin ribao (People's Daily), 65, 159,
   200, 216, 238, 339 (n. 69), 342 (n. 28),
   360 (nn. 2, 5), 365 (n. 77), 371 (n. 8)
"Resist America and Assist Vietnam"
   movement, 214
Rhee, Syngman, 55, 56, 108, 115–16
Rochshin, Nikolai V., 56, 90
Rokossovskii, Konstantin, 146, 153, 308
   (n. 93)
Romania, 154, 249, 254
Roosevelt, Franklin D., 21, 23–25, 291
   (n. 26)
Ropo, Xhorxhi, 269
Ross, Robert S., 2
Route Colonial Four, 126
Route Colonial Nine, 142
Russian Bolshevik revolution, 35, 70
Russo-Japanese War (1904), 24, 306
   (n. 63)

Saigon, 127, 132
Salan, Raoul, 131
San Francisco, 104
Second World War, 7
Seoul, 92, 317 (n. 45), 319 (n. 67)
Seventh Fleet (U.S.), 55, 124, 163, 166

Shaanxi province, 20, 254, 289 (n. 2)
Shandong province, 29
Shanghai, 15, 20, 41, 56, 167, 175, 298
   (n. 24), 300 (n. 47), 302 (n. 17), 329
   (n. 25), 366 (n. 79)
Shanghai communiqué, 239, 274–75
Shanhaiguan Pass, 32
Shantou, 178
Shanxi province, 29
Sheng, Michael M., 37, 296 (n. 1)
Shenyang, 34, 39–40, 43, 45, 56, 296
   (nn. 1, 4), 297 (nn. 8, 12)
Shenyang Municipal Military Control
   Commission, 39
Shepilov, Dmitri, 336 (n. 26)
Shi Zhe, 45, 53, 58, 98, 139–40, 150–52,
   293 (n. 57), 304 (n. 42), 307 (n. 74),
   336 (nn. 22, 24), 338 (n. 47), 341 (n. 10)
Shvernik, Nikolay, 336 (n. 26)
Sichuan province, 293 (n. 54)
Sichuan-Guizhou Railway, 215
Sidewinder missile, 182
Sihanouk, Prince Norodom, 247, 252,
   269
Sino-American ambassadorial talks, 172,
   186, 191–96, 199, 249–52, (n. 28), 362
   (n. 28), 364 (n. 55); Mao Zedong and,
   192–96, 349 (n. 144); Zhou Enlai and,
   192–95, 233
Sino-American rapprochement, 9, 10,
   238–76, 370 (nn. 153, 158)
Sino-Indian border war, 14, 240
Sino-Japanese War. *See* War of Resis-
   tance against Japan
Sino-Soviet alliance, 1, 9, 49–50; agreements, 62, 75; and air force support in
   Korea, 57–58, 305 (n. 54); breakdown
   of, 82–84; and Cold War, 49; and the
   Korean War, 53–61; and Mao's continuous revolution, 63; Sino-Soviet
   treaty (1950), 52; and United States
   threat, 50
Sino-Soviet alliance treaty (1945), 27,
   29–32, 52, 294 (n. 64)
Sino-Soviet relations: and construction